Located throughout REVEL, **quizzing** affords students opportunities to check their understanding at regular intervals before moving on.

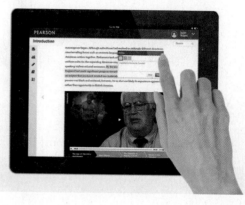

REVEL enables students to read and interact with course material on the devices they use, **anywhere** and **anytime**. Responsive design allows students to access REVEL on their tablet devices, with content displayed clearly in both portrait and landscape view.

Highlighting, **note taking**, and a **glossary** personalize the learning experience. Educators can add **notes** for students, too, including reminders or study tips.

REVEL's variety of **writing** activities and assignments develop and assess concept **mastery** and **critical thinking**.

Superior assignability and tracking

REVEL's assignability and tracking tools help educators make sure students are completing their reading and understanding core concepts.

REVEL allows educators to indicate precisely which readings must be completed on which dates. This clear, detailed schedule helps students stay on task and keeps them motivated throughout the course.

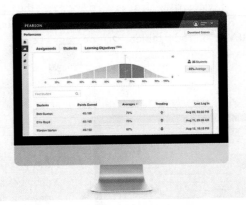

REVEL lets educators monitor class assignment completion and individual student achievement. It offers actionable information that helps educators intersect with their students in meaningful ways, such as points earned on quizzes and time on task.

Personality Psychology

Understanding Yourself and Others

Jean M. Twenge
San Diego State University

W. Keith Campbell
University of Georgia

Boston Columbus Indianapolis New York City San Francisco
Amsterdam Cape Town Dubai London Madrid Milan Paris Montréal Toronto
Delhi Mexico City São Paulo Sydney Hong Kong Seoul Singapore Taipei Tokyo

VP, Product Development: *Dickson Musslewhite*
Senior Acquisitions Editor: *Amber Chow*
Editorial Assistant: *Stephany Harrington*
Director, Content Strategy and Development:
  Brita Nordin
Senior Development Editor: *Thomas Finn*
Director, Program and Project Management
  Services: *Lisa Iarkowski*
Project Management Team Lead: *Denise Forlow*
Project Manager: *Barbara Mack*
Program Management Team Lead: *Amber Mackey*
Program Manager: *Cecilia Turner*
Director of Field Marketing: *Jonathan Cottrell*
Vice President of Product Marketing: *Maggie*
  Moylan
Senior Product Marketing Manager: *Lindsey*
  Prudhomme Gill

Executive Field Marketing Manager: *Kate Stewart*
Marketing Assistant, Field Marketing: *Amy Pfund*
Operations Manager: *Mary Fischer*
Operations Specialist: *Carol Melville*
Associate Director of Design: *Blair Brown*
Interior Design: *Kathryn Foot*
Cover Art Director: *Janet Slowik*
Cover Design: *QT Design*
Cover Photo: *Jon Hicks/Corbis*
Digital Studio Product Manager: *Christopher Fegan*
Digital Studio Project Manager: *Pamela Weldin*
Revel Production Manager: *Peggy Bliss*
Full-Service Project Management and
  Composition: *SPi Global*
Printer/Binder: *RR Donnelley/Crawfordsville*
Cover Printer: *Phoenix Color/Hagerstown*

Acknowledgments of third party content appear on page 476, which constitutes an extension of this copyright page.

10 9 8 7 6 5 4 3 2 1

Instructor's Review Copy
ISBN-10: 0-13-388405-8
ISBN-13: 978-0-13-388405-0

Contents

Preface   x
About the Authors   xv

Part I: Defining Personality and Methods of Assessment   1

1   Understanding Yourself and Others   2

What Is Personality?   4
Where Can We See Personality?   8
Person and Situation   11
Where Will We Go Next?: What You Will Learn in This Book   16
Concluding Thoughts   19

2   Assessment and Methods   21

Self-Report Questionnaires: The Most Common Way to Measure Personality   22
  The Example of the Cat Person Scale   23
  Correlations: What You Need to Know to Understand the Research   26
Reliability and Validity: Evaluating Personality Scales   28
  Reliability   28
  Validity   30
  The Example of Horoscopes   32
The Statistical Side of Questionnaires   34
  How to Use Statistics to Understand Your Personality   34
  What Your Score on the Marlowe–Crowne Says About You   36
Alternatives to Self-Report Questionnaires   38
  Informant Reports   38
  Clinical Interviews   39
  Measuring Behavior   39
  Archival or Life Outcomes Data   40
  Projective Tests   40

  Physiological Measures   40
  The Importance of Triangulation   42
Correlational Versus Experimental Studies   43
Best Practices for Scientific Research   45
Concluding Thoughts   47

Part II: Approaches to Understanding Personality   51

3   The Big Five Personality Traits   52

What Traits Make up the Big Five?   54
  The Facets of the Big Five   57
  Distinct Categories or a Continuum?   58
What Do the Big Five Traits Really Mean?   59
  Extraversion   60
  Agreeableness   63
  Conscientiousness   66
  Neuroticism   69
  Openness to Experience   72
The Development of the Big Five and Its Usefulness   75
  What Does the Big Five Tell Us About Our Survival Ability?   76
  How Does the Big Five Translate to Other Personality Research?   77
  Does the Big Five Translate Across Other Cultures?   79
Concluding Thoughts   80

4   Biological Underpinnings of Personality   82

The Heritability of Personality: Twin Studies   85
  Why Siblings Can Be So Different   88
  The Limitations of Twin Studies   90
Gene–Environment Interactions and Epigenetics   91

The Biology of Personality   93
  The Big Five and the Brain   95
  Neurotransmitters   98
  Are You a Morning Person or a Night
  Person?: Understanding Your
  Circadian Rhythm   98
Evolution and Personality   101
  Survival and Reproduction   102
  The Need to Belong   104
  If Evolution Is Universal, Why Do People
  Still Differ in Their Traits?   105
  Challenges to Evolutionary Psychology   107
Hormones and Behavior   107
Concluding Thoughts   111

**5 Self-Concept and
Self-Processes**   **114**

The Self-Concept   118
  The I and the Me   118
  The Material Self   119
  The Social Self   120
  The Spiritual Self   123
  The True Self   123
Evaluating the Self: Self-Esteem   125
  Is Self-Esteem Good or Bad?   125
  Explicit Versus Implicit Self-Esteem   128
  Maintaining Self-Esteem   128
Self-Compassion, Self-Efficacy, and Narcissism:
Three More Variations on Self-Evaluation   130
  Self-Compassion   130
  Self-Efficacy   131
  Narcissism   132
Self-Regulation   136
  Possible Selves   136
  Self-Control as a Mental Muscle   137
Concluding Thoughts   140

**6 Psychodynamic
Approaches**   **142**

An Overview of Psychodynamic Theories   143
Freud's Topographical and Structural Model   146
  The Topographical Model   146
  The Structural Model   147

Freudian Theory
of Psychosexual Development   150
  Libido: Sexual Energy   150
  Developmental Stages   150
Dreams: How We Access the Unconscious   153
Mechanisms of Defense   156
  Denial   157
  Reaction Formation   157
  Projection   158
  Repression   159
  Displacement   159
  Sublimation   160
  Humor   161
  Defensive Pessimism   162
Testing Freud's Theories   163
  Empirical Evidence
  for the Defense Mechanisms   163
  Challenges to Freudian Theories and
  Applications to Modern Psychology   164
Carl Jung   165
  The Archetypes   165
  The Ego, Its Attitudes, and Its Functions   169
  The Process of Individuation   171
Adler, Horney, and Object Relations Theory   172
  Alfred Adler   172
  Karen Horney   174
  Object Relations Theory   175
Concluding Thoughts   176

7 Motivation   **179**

Approach and Avoidance   182
Maslow's Hierarchy of Needs   187
  The Major Needs   187
  Self-Actualization
  and Humanistic Psychology   189
Implicit Motives   191
  Three Major Implicit Motives   192
  How Do Implicit and Explicit Motives
  Affect Behavior?   194
  The Implicit Motives of Presidents
  and Eras   196
Self-Determination Theory   197
Extrinsic Versus Intrinsic Goals   200

Which Goals Are More Likely to Make
You Happy?   201

How Are Goals the Same and Different
Across Cultures?   201

How Do Goals Affect the Way You Think?   202

What Works Better: Extrinsic
or Intrinsic Motivation?   203

Mindfulness, Flow, and Meaning   205

   Mindfulness   206

   Peak Experiences and Flow   207

   Meaning and Purpose in Life   208

Concluding Thoughts   209

**8 How Learning Shapes
Behavior**   212

Operant Conditioning: How to Get People
(and Pets) to Do What You Want   214

   Four Ways of Modifying Behavior   214

   Reinforcement Schedules   219

   Socialization   222

Behavior Modification: Using Operant
Conditioning in the Real World   223

   How Behavior Modification Works   223

   Using Behavior Modification on Yourself 225

   How Far Can Behavior Modification Go?   226

Expectancies and Locus of Control   227

Classical Conditioning: How to Get
People (and Pets) to Drool   229

   Classical Conditioning and Fear   230

   Habituation   233

   Sleep Conditioning: How Did You
Sleep Last Night?   234

   Phobias and Their Cure   235

Concluding Thoughts   237

**Part III: Applying Personality
Psychology in the Real
World**   239

**9 Personality Across
the Lifespan**   240

Methods for Measuring Personality
over Time   242

Personality During Childhood
and Adolescence   243

   Child Temperament   243

   Changes in the Big Five Personality
Traits During Childhood and
Adolescence   247

   Changes in Self-Esteem During Childhood
and Adolescence   248

Personality from Young Adulthood
to Old Age   250

   Changes in the Big Five Personality Traits
from Young Adulthood to Old Age   250

   Changes in Self-Esteem and Narcissism
from Young Adulthood to Old Age   253

Significant Life Experiences and Social
Investment Theory   254

   Entering the Full-time Workforce 255

   Being in a Serious Relationship
or Getting Married   257

   Becoming a Parent   259

   Experiencing Negative or Positive
Life Events   260

Birth Order   261

Life Outcomes   263

Concluding Thoughts   266

10 Gender and Personality   268

Biology, Culture, and Their Interaction:
Origins of Sex Differences   273

   The Origins of Gender Roles   274

   The Roles of Evolution and Culture 275

   Cultural Change and Cross-Cultural
Variations in Sex Differences   277

Comparing Men and Women   278

   Big Five Personality Traits   279

   Leadership   282

   "Masculinity" and "Femininity"   283

   Jobs and Hobbies   286

   Nonverbal Behaviors and Appearance 288

   Self-Esteem   290

   Sexual Behaviors and Attitudes   291

   Cognitive Abilities   293

Concluding Thoughts   295

11 Culture and Personality   297

How Cultures Shape People   300

Cultural Differences in Individualism
and Collectivism   302

Cultural Differences in Attributions   304

Cultural Differences in Views of the Self   306

Cultural Differences in the Big Five
Personality Traits   312

Cross-Cultural Research Methods   312

Cultural Differences in Extraversion   314

Cultural Differences in Agreeableness   316

Cultural Differences in Conscientiousness   317

Cultural Differences in Neuroticism   319

Cultural Differences in Openness
to Experience   320

Concluding Thoughts   321

**12 Personality in
the Workplace**   324

Vocational Fit   325

The Role of Personality in Getting the
Job Done   330

Job Satisfaction: What Traits Make
You Happy at Work?   331

Job Performance: What Traits Make
for a Good Worker?   332

Compensation: What Traits Predict
High Pay?   334

Leadership: What Personality
Traits Make for a Good Leader?   334

How Employers Use Personality
for Job Selection   338

What Traits Do Employers Look For?   338

The Use of Personality Tests   339

What About People Who Lie on
Personality Tests?   340

Finding Passion at Work   341

Concluding Thoughts   343

**13 Personality and
Relationships**   345

Attachment: The Building Blocks
of Relationships   347

Childhood Attachment   347

Attachment in Adult Relationships   350

The Dimensional Approach to Attachment   352

The Big Five: Basic Personality Traits
and Relationships   353

The Relationship Outcomes of Each
of the Big Five Traits   353

Do Opposites Really Attract (and
Stay Together)?   355

Empathy, Compassion, and Self-Control:
Three Positive Forces in Relationships   356

The Dark Triad: Three Negative Forces
in Relationships   358

Online Relationships: The Next Frontier   362

Online Dating   363

Personality and Social
Networking Websites   365

Concluding Thoughts   366

**14 Personality and
Mental Health**   369

Personality Disorders   371

Diagnosing Personality Disorders   373

Personality Disorders and the Big Five   375

Developing Personality Disorders   377

The PID-5 Diagnostic Model   379

Other Mental Disorders Associated
with Personality   380

Major Depressive Disorder   381

Anxiety Disorders   383

Bipolar Disorder   384

Schizophrenia   387

Eating Disorders   388

Addictive Disorders   390

Types of Therapy   392

Concluding Thoughts   395

**15 Personality and
Physical Health**   397

The Big Five and Physical Health   398

Conscientiousness   399

Neuroticism   402

Extraversion (and Type T)   408

Agreeableness   409

Openness to Experience   409

Motives and Explanatory Style   411

Psychological Motives   411

Pessimistic Versus Optimistic
Explanatory Style   413

Concluding Thoughts   416

References   418

Glossary   467

Credits   476

Name Index   481

Subject Index   487

Preface

Why do people do what they do? Most people jump at the opportunity to learn about their personality and the personality of their romantic partners, friends, family, coworkers, and even enemies. More than any other subfield in psychology, personality tells us what makes people tick. Our passion for understanding personality—and sharing that knowledge with students—compelled us to write this book. We've dedicated our lives to the study of people and their personalities, and we're excited to share what we've learned.

A Modern, Empirical Approach

Research in personality psychology is enjoying a renaissance, exploring topics such as the Big Five traits, neuroimaging and brain chemistry, and the influence of personality on everything from workplace relationships to mental disorders. Although such research is the basis for advancing our understanding of personality, it doesn't need to be dry, boring, or difficult to understand. Personality should be the most interesting and relevant subfield in psychology for undergraduate students, who often want to learn as much as they can about themselves and their life paths.

- *How can I get ahead in my studies and in my career?*
- *How am I perceived on social media?*
- *How can I live a longer, happier life?*
- *Which job is the best fit for my personality?*
- *Why do I keep falling in love with jerks?*

Questions such as these are front and center in students' lives—and these are the topics students are motivated to address and understand. To us, this is what personality psychology is all about.

In this book, we strive to deliver not only what students *need* to know but also what they *want* to know—and to do it a way that is engaging and accessible to undergraduates today. This approach is essential because today's college students are different: They are enmeshed in online networks, fascinated by their own personalities, more comfortable with short passages of text, and crave an interactive—not passive—experience with a textbook.

Personality Psychology: Understanding Yourself and Others satisfies the needs of today's students with a concise, conversational style; vivid, relatable examples; and an abundance of research-based personality questionnaires to help students learn about themselves. We also include interactive features allowing students to express and share their opinions, and self-assessments so they can gauge how well they're learning the material as they go.

We used our simple, two-part rule—what students *need* to know and what they *want* to know—to organize this text, which breaks from the standard conventions of our predecessors. Most personality textbooks adhere to a theories-based approach, covering all approaches to personality equally. While there's certainly still a need to understand the foundational theories of personality psychology, there's also a need to move beyond them to focus on modern personality psychology and its applications to the lives of students. We let the research of today dictate what receives the most coverage, conveying these findings in the real-world contexts that will shape our students' lives long after they finish the course.

The text is divided into three parts. Part I introduces the basic concepts of personality psychology and the methods for studying it. Part II presents the foundational approaches to personality. Finally, Part III explores personality in applied contexts, such as choosing a career, developing personal relationships, and physical health. With an emphasis on the Big Five and the very latest research, we are able to address the most pressing questions in students' lives: How different are women and men? Can people *really* change? Is it possible to get away with lying on my job application?

We address questions such as these and many more throughout this text: How can I become a better friend? What are the warning signs of a bad relationship? How can I finally stick to my diet? . . .

Remembering Our Roots

Some personality textbooks focus exclusively on theories, leaving out the modern empirical research. Others include both classic thought and recent research. We take this latter approach, but with a twist: We focus primarily on modern empirical research, but include classic theories if they (1) inform modern research, (2) continue to echo through the culture and our lives, and/or (3) attempt to explain phenomena difficult to capture with empirical methods. For example, a personality textbook would not be complete without the ideas of Freud, Jung, Adler, and the object relations theorists, whose theories fully satisfy the last two conditions. Research on learning and behaviorism continues to shape behavior modification programs. And classic models of motivation, like those of Maslow and Murray, still resonate in society and are included in the text along with current models such as self-determination theory, intrinsic and extrinsic motives, and approach versus avoidance.

We also feature the history of certain areas of research in timelines, giving students a concise overview of classic theories and theorists. Likewise, most chapters spotlight a critical moment in the history of personality psychology in the feature *Personality's Past*. For example, in Chapter 2 there's a feature discussing the genesis of personality questionnaires; in Chapter 3, we cover the development of the lexical method of discovering personality traits; the Chapter 7 feature presents the classic study of tracing achievement motivation in children's books; and Chapter 10 recalls the groundbreaking work of Maccoby and Jacklin in *The Psychology of Sex Differences*.

A Truly Interactive Text

Personality Psychology: Understanding Yourself and Others doesn't just lecture students; it engages them. In the REVEL version, students can take more than 25 personality questionnaires, all valid and reliable measures from the research literature. These questionnaires provide a welcome opportunity for students to immediately begin to understand themselves better, as well as to better understand how they relate to others. The questionnaires also help students understand how personality scientists measure constructs in the field and how researchers compare an individual's responses to others'.

Each chapter also contains journal and shared writing prompts. The journal writing prompts allow students to take concepts from the text and apply them to their own lives, thus helping them not only better learn the material but also better learn about their lives. The shared writing prompts conclude each section of the chapter and are meant to foster a dialogue among students in the class. Such meaningful exchanges of perspectives and ideas will help students gain a greater appreciation for others' lived experiences as well as to apply the concepts from the chapter to real-world contexts and situations. These are a natural fit for a generation of students who grew up with texting and social media.

We are also dedicated to helping students not only learn about themselves, but also learn about the science of personality. To that end, most chapters include a feature titled *The Science of Personality*, which details how research is conducted, data are analyzed, and conclusions are reached in the scientific community. These mini-simulations walk students through the research process one step at a time to help them better see and relate to the scientific process.

As we mentioned earlier, many chapters include timelines as well as a history feature focused on spotlighting the roots of personality psychology. In addition, each chapter includes embedded videos as well as interactive figures for students to better visualize and digest the data we present.

Finally, every chapter has brief multiple-choice quizzes at the end of every section and a longer multiple-choice test at the conclusion of the chapter. These assessments provide students with immediate feedback on how well they're learning the concepts.

All of these elements are dedicated to enriching students' learning experience and helping them engage with and understand the material. In sum, we hope all of our efforts have worked to achieve our primary goals in writing this book: to teach students about personality psychology, but also to teach them about life.

We welcome your reactions to *Personality Psychology: Understanding Yourself and Others*. Please send comments to Jean M. Twenge at jtwenge@mail.sdsu.edu or to W. Keith Campbell at wkc@uga.edu. We look forward to hearing from you.

Acknowledgments

Many, many people have helped make this book better. The editors and managers at Pearson played a crucial role in shepherding this book into existence, including Jeff Marshall, Erin Mitchell, Susan Hartman, Carly Czech, Amber Chow, and Thomas Finn.

My (J. M. T.) PSY 351: Psychology of Personality students at San Diego State University provided extensive, thoughtful, and refreshing feedback on the book. Thanks for both your enthusiastic praise and your constructive criticism. It was immensely helpful to hear what you liked and didn't like. Hearing so many of you say that the book was easy to read and made you laugh, or that the material helped you in your own life, made it all worthwhile.

The faculty reviewers of this book provided many useful suggestions as well. We thank all of them for their help: Sarah Angulo, Texas State University; John Bickford, University of Massachusetts, Amherst; Claudia Brumbaugh, Queens College; Bernardo Carducci, Indiana University, Southeast; Dana Dunn, Moravian College; Michael Faber, Woodbury University; William Fry, Youngstown State University; Jennifer Gibson, Tarleton State University; Susan Goldstein, California; Rachael Grazioplene, University of Minnesota; James Hall, Montgomery College; Chelsea Hansen, Upper Iowa University; Robert Harvey, Virginia Tech; Selena Kohel, Cottey College; Peter Lifton, Northeastern University; Eric Lindsey, Pennsylvania State University, Berks; Martha Low, Winston Salem State University; Steven Ludeke, University of Minnesota; David Nelson, Sam Houston State University; Randall Osbourne, Texas State University; Bernardo Carducci, Indiana University, Southeast; Peg Racek, Minnesota State University; Stephanie Sogg, Harvard Extension School; Lyra Stein, Rutgers University; Suzan Tessier, Rochester Institute of Technology; Sandra Tobin, Clackamas Community College; and Jennifer Wartella, Virginia Commonwealth University.

We owe a special thanks to Joshua Miller (University of Georgia), who played a role in writing Chapter 3 on the Big Five. Another special thanks to David G. Myers (Hope College), my (J. M. T.) mentor and hero in textbook writing, for the encouragement and for several specific suggestions.

Other colleagues also provided suggestions, encouragement, materials, ideas, and support, including (but not limited to) Roy Baumeister, Florida State University; Christopher Bryan,

University of Chicago; Bryan Caplan, George Mason University; Nathan Carter, University of Georgia; Jody Davis, Virginia Commonwealth University; Mark Davis, Eckerd College; Nathan DeWall, University of Kentucky; Alice Eagly, Northwestern University; Andrew Elliot, University of Rochester; Julie Exline, Case Western Reserve University; Eli Finkel, Northwestern University; Craig Foster, U.S. Air Force Academy; R. Chris Fraley, University of Illinois; Brittany Gentile, ICON; Jeff Green, Virginia Commonwealth University; Patricia Greenfield, University of California, Los Angeles; Chris Harris, University of California, San Diego; Martie Haselton, University of California, Los Angeles; Brian Hoffman, University of Georgia; Rick Hoyle, Duke University; Janet Hyde, University of Wisconsin; Oliver John, University of California at Berkeley; Tim Kasser, Knox College; Heejung Kim, University of California, Santa Barbara; Laura King, University of Missouri; Sonja Lyubomirsky, University of California, Riverside; Roy P. Martin, University of Georgia; Jessica McCain, University of Georgia; Beth Morling, University of Delaware; Julie Norem, Wellesley College; Stephen Nowicki, Emory University; Constantine Sedikides, University of Southampton; Ken Sheldon, University of Missouri; Judith Siegel, University of California, Los Angeles; Mark Snyder, University of Minnesota; Harry Triandis, University of Illinois; Michelle vanDellen, University of Georgia; Kathleen Vohs, University of Minnesota; and David G. Winter, University of Michigan.

We would also like to thank our families and friends. For J. M. T.: My endless gratitude to Brandelyn Jarrett, who not only kept my children occupied as I wrote this book but was my sounding board for the mind of an undergraduate. My friends Amy and Paul Tobia listened to many a textbook story. Thanks to my husband, Craig, for his support and encouragement. Thanks to my daughters, Kate, Elizabeth, and Julia, for their love and fascinating personalities—I hope you like your starring role here!

For W. K. C: I am lucky to be able to hang out with so many fun and interesting people. In particular, Josh Miller has played a major role in shaping how I think about personality. Love and thanks to my wife, Stacy, for both supporting me through another long book project and for providing some great feedback on the project when wearing her Dr. Stacy Campbell hat. And finally thanks to my daughters, McKinley and Charlotte—when you are old enough to read this text, you will realize why Daddy drank so much coffee when you were young.

Teaching and Learning Aids
Revel™

Educational Technology for the Way Today's Students Read, Think, and Learn

When students are engaged deeply, they learn more effectively and perform better in their courses. This simple fact inspired the creation of REVEL, an immersive learning experience designed for the way today's students read, think, and learn. Built in collaboration with educators and students nationwide, REVEL is the newest, fully digital way to deliver respected Pearson content.

REVEL enlivens course content with media interactives and assessments—integrated directly within the authors' narrative—that provide opportunities for students to read about and practice course material in tandem. This immersive experience boosts student engagement, which leads to better understanding of concepts and improved performance throughout the course.

Learn More about REVEL

www.pearsonhighered.com/revel/.

For Instructors

Pearson Education is pleased to offer the following supplements to adopters:

Instructor's Resource Manual (ISBN: 0133884023)
Designed to make your lectures more effective and

save you preparation time, this resource gathers together the most effective activities and strategies for teaching your course. Materials are broken up by chapter and include chapter outlines, key terms, lecture suggestions and discussion topics, and classroom activities. It is available for download on the Instructor's Resource Center at www.pearsonhighered.com/irc.

Test Bank (ISBN: 013388404X) Each chapter contains multiple choice, true–false, short-answer, and essay questions. It is available for download on the Instructor's Resource Center at www.pearsonhighered.com/irc.

MyTest Test Bank (ISBN: 0133884031) A powerful assessment-generation program that helps instructors easily create and print quizzes and exams. Questions and tests can be authored online, allowing instructors ultimate flexibility and the ability to efficiently manage assessments any time, anywhere! Instructors can easily access existing questions and edit, create, and store them using simple drag-and-drop techniques and Microsoft Word–like controls. Data on each question provide information on difficulty level and page number of corresponding text discussion. In addition, each question maps to the text's major section and learning objective. For more information, go to www.PearsonMyTest.com.

Enhanced Lecture PowerPoint Slides with Embedded Videos (ISBN: 0134474848): The enhanced lecture PowerPoints offer detailed outlines of key points for each chapter supported by selected visuals from the textbook, and include videos featured in the text. Standard Lecture PowerPoints without embedded videos (ISBN: 0133884082) are also available. A separate *Art and Figure* version (ISBN: 0134474856) of these presentations contains all art from the textbook for which Pearson has been granted electronic permissions. It is available for download on the Instructor's Resource Center at www.pearsonhighered.com/irc.

Accessing All Resources: For access to all instructor supplements for *Personality Psychology: Understanding Yourself and Others*, go to www.pearsonhighered.com/irc and follow the directions to register (or log in if you already have a Pearson user name and password). Once you have registered and your status as an instructor is verified, you will be e-mailed a log-in name and password. Use your log-in name and password to access the catalog.

About the Authors

Jean M. Twenge, Ph.D., Professor of Psychology at San Diego State University, is the author of more than 100 scientific publications and the books *Generation Me: Why Today's Young Americans Are More Confident, Assertive, Entitled—and More Miserable Than Ever Before* and *The Narcissism Epidemic: Living in the Age of Entitlement* (with W. Keith Campbell). She frequently gives talks and seminars on teaching and working with today's young generation based on a dataset of 11 million young people. Her research has been covered in *Time, Newsweek, The New York Times, USA Today, U.S. News and World Report,* and *The Washington Post,* and she has been featured on *Today, Good Morning America, CBS This Morning, Fox and Friends, NBC Nightly News, Dateline NBC,* and National Public Radio.

W. Keith Campbell, Ph.D., Professor of Psychology at the University of Georgia, is the author of more than 100 scientific publications and the books, *When You Love a Man Who Loves Himself: How to Deal with a One-Way Relationship; The Narcissism Epidemic: Living in the Age of Entitlement* (with Jean Twenge); and *The Handbook of Narcissism and Narcissistic Personality Disorder: Theoretical Approaches, Empirical Findings, and Treatments* (with Josh Miller). His work on narcissism has appeared in *USA Today, Time,* and *The New York Times,* and he has made numerous radio and television appearances, including *The Today Show,* NPR's *All Things Considered,* and *The Glenn Beck Show.* Dr. Campbell speaks to organizations around the globe on the topics of narcissism, generations, and cultural change.

Part I
Defining Personality and Methods of Assessment

Who are you? You might answer with your name, or where you're from, or with your gender or ethnicity. But when you really think about who you are as a person, you'll probably focus on your personality: Are you outgoing or shy? Relaxed or tense? Neat or messy? Forceful or laid-back?

This book—and the personality questionnaires that come with it—will give you the chance to find out. In Chapter 1, you learn how psychologists define that elusive thing known as personality. What is it, and where can we observe it? How can we understand others better by identifying their personality traits? We also consider the interplay between people and their environments—after all, even people with consistent personalities don't act the same in class as they would at a party (at least we hope they don't!).

Chapter 2 covers how personality can be measured. How is it possible to describe someone's personality—such a large and unwieldy thing—with a series of numbers? And how do we know that a personality measure is any good? You might have already taken a personality questionnaire or two online, and wondered if it was accurate. Did it really capture who you are? That's an important question, and you learn how researchers make personality measures as valid and reliable as possible. You also peek behind the scenes to see how personality studies are actually done.

Welcome to personality psychology! It's going to be a fun ride.

Chapter 1
Understanding Yourself and Others

Learning Objectives

LO 1.1 Define personality.

LO 1.2 List various contexts in which personality might appear.

LO 1.3 Describe the two sides of the person–situation debate, how the debate was resolved, and the conditions under which personality can best predict behavior.

LO 1.4 Know the major topics in personality psychology.

Steve Jobs was about to get fired. In the years after cofounding Apple, Jobs had alienated many people with his argumentative, emotional personality. Before one meeting in the mid-1980s, Apple CEO John Sculley begged Jobs to be nice. But as soon as everyone sat down, Jobs said, "You guys don't have any clue what you're doing." And that was the end of the meeting. "I'm sorry—I just couldn't help myself," Jobs explained.

That, it turned out, *was* Jobs being nice—many other days, he screamed at employees or began crying when things went wrong. In May 1985, Jobs was forced to leave the company he had founded.

By 1997, Apple was struggling to survive, and Jobs returned as CEO. He was still blunt, argumentative, and stubbornly opinionated, but he had mellowed somewhat—or at least learned from failure. A self-described "humanities person," fascinated with new experiences and ideas, he believed that technology had to consider the experience of the person using it. That philosophy led to incredible success: During Jobs's second stint as CEO, Apple introduced the iMac, the iPod, the iPhone, and the iPad and debuted the Apple Stores. When Jobs died of cancer at age 56 in October 2011, the world mourned him as a lost genius.

Yet much of the fascination with Jobs centers on his odd personality. He experimented with drugs and extreme vegan diets, often walked around barefoot, and sometimes refused to shower. If he didn't like something, he would tell people it sucked. He was confident in himself and dismissive of others. "People don't know what they want until you show it to them," he famously said. He had such a loose relationship with the truth that friends joked he had a "reality distortion field." The central question in Walter Issacson's bestselling biography *Steve Jobs* (2011) is whether Jobs succeeded because of his personality—or in spite of it.

Are all computer magnates like Jobs—emotional, perfectionistic, outgoing, and open to new ideas? Not really. Bill Gates, the cofounder of Microsoft, is also known for being somewhat odd—but in a very different way from Jobs. He rocks back and forth as he speaks and continually multitasks. A programmer by training, he shows little curiosity about other people or their personal lives and rarely displays much emotion. His father recalls that Gates lacked confidence in social situations as a teen—he worried for two weeks about asking a girl to the prom and then got turned down. While heading Microsoft in the 1990s, Gates rarely called anyone, instead preferring to send more than 100 emails a day (Isaacson, 1997). After scaling back his role at Microsoft in 2006, Gates and his wife, Melinda, turned their attention to philanthropy, much of it toward promoting the health and well-being of poor children.

On the surface, Steve Jobs and Bill Gates have a lot in common. Both founded computer companies. Both were born in 1955. Both became multibillionaires. Both were extraordinarily brilliant and driven, and both were famously blunt: Gates's version of "You guys don't have any clue what you're doing" is "That's the stupidest thing I've ever heard."

Steve Jobs was known for having a more extraverted personality. Bill Gates is precise and introverted.

Yet their personalities are strikingly different—and so are the companies they founded. Gates is detail oriented and mathematical, and his company focused on businesses that needed dependable software. Jobs favored creativity, and Apple emphasized uniqueness and marketed their products first to artistic types. Gates had little concern for the whole person, perhaps the reason why Microsoft software runs on many different types of computers, often with little thought to design. Jobs favored the totality of experience, so he sought to control every aspect of a product, from the store to the design to the software. "The personality of Bill Gates determines the culture of Microsoft," said Gates's friend Nathan Myhrvold (Isaacson, 1997). The same was true of Jobs, perhaps even more so: His intense, perfectionistic vision was so central to Apple that many worried the company would lose its way after he died. Even without Jobs and Gates at their helms, Apple and Microsoft—two companies that changed the world—are the products of the complex personalities of these two men.

What Is Personality?

LO 1.1   Define personality.

Personality shapes our lives in many ways: It determines whether you think skydiving or reading a book is more fun and predicts whether you usually arrive 5 minutes early or 15 minutes late. Personality can forecast who—at least on average—lives a long life and who doesn't, who is successful at work and who isn't, and who has a happy marriage and who doesn't (Ozer & Benet-Martinez, 2006; Roberts et al., 2007). It can suggest that certain careers might be a good fit, or that certain romantic partners might not be.

So what exactly is personality—that elusive and ineffable entity that is nevertheless so important? **Personality** describes someone's usual pattern of

personality
someone's usual pattern of behavior, feelings, and thoughts

behavior, feelings, and thoughts. By *usual*, we mean how someone acts across time or across situations. For example, how would you react to skydiving? Most people will have some fear of jumping out of an airplane, but some people are exhilarated by the jump while others are terrified. The same situation elicits different reactions in different people because people have different personalities. To be indicative of personality, this reaction must be fairly consistent: Someone who is terrified of skydiving on Tuesday should also be terrified on Friday. If they're not, their reaction might not be due to their personality but to a difference in the situation (maybe the plane on Tuesday was in great condition and flown by an experienced pilot, but the plane on Friday was a rusty claptrap flown by a high school student who just got his pilot's license).

If risk taking is part of your personality, this tendency should also be similar across different situations. If you are inclined to jump out of airplanes, you also are probably more willing to go cage diving with great white sharks or drive a race car than your more cautious friends.

Personality includes human tendencies we all share, but also considers how we differ from each other. Everyone takes some risks, but some take more and some take less. In other words, understanding your own comfort with risk taking will also help you understand other people.

Some individual differences in personality are relatively easy to quantify. For example, we can describe someone as "neurotic" (someone who worries about flying in a plane, much less skydiving) or "calm" (someone who doesn't worry much about anything). Using a personality questionnaire, for example, we can determine how neurotic or calm someone is compared to others (more about this in Chapter 2). But how many personality characteristics should we consider? As you learn in Chapter 3, personality psychologists have identified five personality factors that explain much of the individual variation in personality. Although this "Big Five" system is incredibly useful, it can't possibly include every personality trait. There are other ways of identifying personality, from unconscious defense mechanisms to views of the self to motivations.

And of course no personality system can truly capture all of the unique differences among people and their life experiences. As Malcolm X wrote: "Why am I as I am? To understand that of any person, his whole life from birth must be reviewed. All of our experiences fuse into our personality. Everything that ever happened to us is an ingredient." In other words, each person's psychology is incredibly complex. Personality psychology aims to define and measure what it can, while acknowledging that will not be everything. So although definable personality might be the tip of the iceberg, it's a fascinating and increasingly well-understood slice of ice.

Then there's the question of where personality comes from—what makes people who they are? For example, Steve Jobs was adopted. Was his personality more likely to resemble his biological parents, whom he did not meet until he was in his 30s, or his adoptive but not genetically related parents, who raised him?

Personality is complex and shaped by many factors, including genetics, parenting, and relationships with peers.

Personality is shaped by many factors, including genetics, parents, peers, birth order, and culture. We explore which of these influences is the strongest—and which are weaker than you might think.

Personality psychology deals with a lot of fundamental questions about who we are and how we got that way. It touches on topics important across many different areas of psychology, including developmental psychology (How does personality change as we get older?), neuroscience (How can we see personality in the brain?), clinical psychology (What is the relationship between personality traits and mental health issues?), and industrial-organizational psychology (Do good workers have certain personality traits?). Personality is a "hub" topic, at the center of the web of subareas within psychology (see Figure 1.1).

Differences in personality are one of the main reasons people are so endlessly fascinating—sometimes maddening and sometimes delightful, but often fascinating. Why did he do that? How does she really feel? Will he ever change? Psychology is the study of what makes people tick, and why they behave the way they do. Of all the subareas of psychology, personality psychology takes the most direct approach to answering these questions. If you're looking to better understand yourself and others, you've come to the right place.

Figure 1.1 The Personality Hub

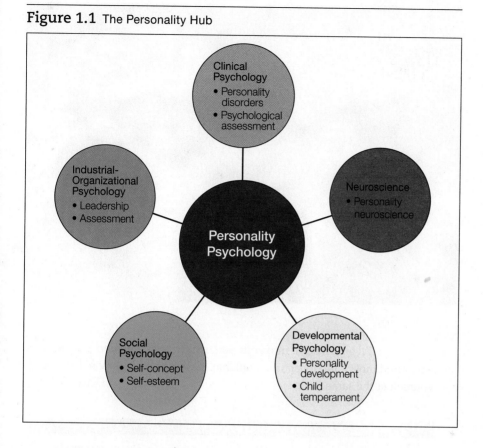

In this book, you learn about the exciting modern research emerging from the labs of innovative personality researchers as well as classic theories and ideas that continue to resonate throughout our language and culture. We want to give you the information you crave the most: understanding your own personality and those of your friends and family. You'll also learn about how you got that way, whether you are likely to change, and how to improve your personality and habits.

One of the best ways to meet these goals is for you to complete personality questionnaires—the same cutting-edge, scientifically validated questionnaires used by researchers in the field. Through these questionnaires, you'll see how personality scientists measure the traits you're learning about. You'll also discover how your scores compare to a previous group of students in a personality psychology class. You might wonder, for example, if you're above or below average (and by how much) in how neat and organized, outgoing and talkative, or nice and pleasant you are. You'll also see how your personality has changed since you were a child, what your relationship style is, and which type of career might be

Who are you? The study of personality, perhaps more than any other area of psychology, can help you understand yourself and others.

best for you. You'll gain insight into your personality and preferences using some of the best and most valid measures available, learning about personality science and yourself at the same time.

JOURNAL PROMPT: UNDERSTANDING YOURSELF

Before you get too far into the study of personality, how would you at this moment define your own personality? Describe your personality as best you can.

Where Can We See Personality?

LO 1.2 List various contexts in which personality might appear.

Personality is everywhere, whether we're interacting with others in person or online, in virtual reality or through text messages. One well-known personality trait is **extraversion**, or how outgoing, assertive, and talkative you are (versus its opposite, **introversion**, or how shy and reserved you are; we explore this trait more in Chapter 3). For example, Steve Jobs was probably an extravert, and Bill Gates—with his penchant for emailing instead of calling—is probably an introvert.

But how do we guess the personality of someone we've just met, or someone we just can't figure out, if he's not a well-known public figure? You could give him a personality questionnaire, but that's sometimes difficult to pull off

extraversion

how outgoing, assertive, and talkative someone is

introversion

how shy and reserved someone is; the opposite of extraversion

(You: "Hey, will you fill out this survey for me?" Him: "Why?" You: "Oh, no reason—I just want to see if you're worth dating.") As an alternative, you can gather clues about his personality without him even realizing you're doing it. In one study, college students allowed researchers to look at their Facebook pages, read their transcripts, peek into their student conduct records, and note how long it had been since they received or sent a text message. The extraverts had more friends on Facebook and were more likely to have violated campus conduct rules (for example, getting caught with alcohol). Extraverts also texted more frequently; one extraverted student even sent a text while the researcher was asking how long it had been since her last text message (Thalmayer et al., 2011).

So does personality predict whether you use a Mac or a PC? Surprisingly, it doesn't—perhaps because many other factors determine which computer you choose. But personality does predict preferences for features associated with each brand (Nevid & Pastva, 2014). For example, anxious people prefer a computer that is easy to use, and those who are very open to new ideas prefer a stylish design—both of which might incline them to use a Mac if the decision were up to them. So there's at least a little truth to the idea that Mac users, like Steve Jobs, are more likely to be broad thinkers interested in ideas—and maybe a little more anxious, too.

Several studies show that observers can guess your personality based on your Facebook page, especially your level of extraversion. People could also tell who was an organized person and who was not (Back et al., 2010; Ivcevic & Ambady, 2012). Observers can even guess your personality fairly accurately by seeing how you build your city in a virtual reality game such as CityVille (Wohn & Wash, 2013). Somewhat surprisingly, Facebook profiles and other personal Web pages are usually consistent with people's true personalities, not the personalities they think they "should" have (Back et al., 2010; Vazire & Gosling, 2004).

What do extraverts and introverts post about online? A study of nearly 70,000 Facebook users lets us see. As the word clouds in Figure 1.2 demonstrate, extraverts are focused on going out, relationships, and positive emotions. Words such as *tonight, party, love,* and *amazing* distinguish them most from introverts. Introverts discuss more solitary pursuits; their posts use words such as *computer, internet,* and *read* more than extraverts' do (Park et al., 2015). The word *clouds* bring to mind the starkest of personality stereotypes: the party girl extravert and the computer geek introvert.

Observers were also able to accurately guess people's personalities by seeing their offices or their bedrooms. As John Steinbeck wrote, "[A] human occupying a room for one night [im]prints his character, his biography, his recent history, and sometimes his future plans and hopes. . . . Personality seeps into walls and is slowly released." Extraverts' bedrooms, for example, are noisier and more likely to have disorganized piles of papers. Perhaps because they want people to drop by and chat, extraverts' offices are more likely to have

Figure 1.2 Word Clouds for Low and High Extraversion

Words used more frequently in Facebook posts by introverts (left) and extraverts (right).

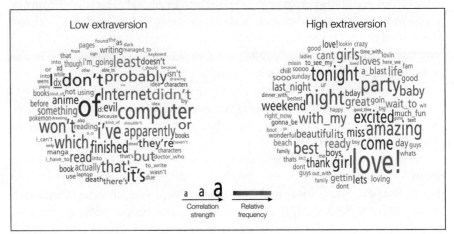

SOURCE: Park et al. (2015).

a comfortable guest chair or a candy dish on the desk (Gosling et al., 2002). Introverts' offices are less welcoming—they'd rather be alone. And perhaps you should oblige. As personality psychologist Sam Gosling advises, "After a few minutes perched on a hard chair surrounded by gloomy, sparse walls, make your excuses and run for it—everyone will be happier that way" (2008, p. 181).

Your physical appearance and mannerisms also give off whiffs of personality. Vain, self-centered people are more likely to wear stylish, expensive clothes and cultivate a carefully groomed appearance (Vazire et al., 2008). Extraverts smile more, speak in louder voices, and swing their arms more when they walk. One finding even confirmed a suspicion I (J. M. T.) have had since high school: People who are more anxious and depressed really do wear dark clothes more often (Borkenau & Liebler, 1992, 1995).

JOURNAL PROMPT: UNDERSTANDING YOURSELF

What does your bedroom or office say about your personality? What about the bedroom or office of someone close to you?

Not only can other people guess our personality, but personality can predict what we might do next, even online. For example, extraverts leave more comments on Facebook, view their own and others' pages more often, and are more

What would you guess about the personality of this room's occupant?

likely to post pictures of themselves with other people (Amichai-Hamburger & Vinitzky, 2010; Gosling et al., 2011). Anxious people are more likely to post status updates on Facebook, especially negative ones (Locatelli et al., 2012), and to post about their feelings (Seidman, 2013).

So whether you're posting on Facebook, making your bed, sneaking beer into a dorm party, wearing black jeans and a black t-shirt, or sending text messages, watch out—your personality is showing.

Person and Situation

LO 1.3 **Describe the two sides of the person–situation debate, how the debate was resolved, and the conditions under which personality can best predict behavior.**

Students taking a personality course often have two big questions right from the start: "How can you possibly measure something as elusive and complicated as personality?" and—especially if they just took social psychology—"Isn't behavior determined more by the situation someone is in, and not their personality?"

We answer the first question about personality measurement in Chapter 2. For now, know that personality—at least some of it—can be measured, and well enough to predict behavior, work success, and even how long you live (Judge et al., 2009; Martin et al., 2007; Roberts et al., 2007). But what about the second question—how much does the situation matter? Or, as one psychologist put it, "How can we talk about the way a person typically acts if that way is always changing? The same person acts very differently on different occasions" (Fleeson, 2004, p. 83).

Back in the 1960s, this question caused a crisis in the field of personality. Social psychologists were finding that the **situation**—the other people and the physical environment surrounding a person—had powerful effects on behavior. For example, social psychologist Stanley Milgram found that most men would obey an experimenter's orders to administer a high level of electric shock—so high it's marked with an ominous "XXX" on the shock generator. Left to choose a level of shock on their own, virtually no one went this high (Milgram, 1963, 1974). A later reanalysis found that personality did predict behavior in Milgram's study, but that result isn't as well known (Blass, 1991).

situation

the other people and the physical environment surrounding a person

Watch PERSON–SITUATION

WATCH
the video in
REVEL →

In 1968, psychology researcher Walter Mischel argued that the effect of personality on behavior was too small to matter. Personality traits, he maintained, did not do a very good job of predicting how people acted. The field entered a long period of dormancy and self-doubt, even though Mischel (1990) later said he was misinterpreted and that he had not meant to attack the field of personality as a whole. A debate ensued between those who defended the idea that stable personality traits could predict behavior and those who argued that personality didn't really exist and that the situation was much more important. This became known as the **person–situation debate**. At issue was the question, Do people have consistent behavioral tendencies across situations (in other words, personality)? Yes, said those on the "person" side; "no," said those on the "situation" side. (Note that the person–situation debate is distinct from the

person–situation debate

the view that stable personality traits predict behavior versus the view personality doesn't really exist and the situation is much more important

nature–nurture debate, which instead asks what *causes* personality traits—genetics or environment. The person–situation debate instead asks whether personality traits exist at all).

During one of the years when this debate was raging, psychology researchers gathered for a small conference held in the woods of the Pacific Northwest. One attendee was a researcher we'll call Dr. Context, who insistently argued that behavior was due to the situation and not to stable personality traits. One night, the attendees heard some alarming news: A famous serial killer had escaped from a nearby prison. Dr. Context quickly sprang into action, making plans to nail the windows shut and post guards in rotating shifts. A professor on the other side of the debate—let's call him Dr.

Is this person's behavior determined by personality or by the situation?

Personality—patted Dr. Context on the back and told him not to worry. "Relax, Dr. Context," he said sarcastically. "If the killer does show up, what he does next will depend on the situation!" (Funder, 2008, p. 568).

As this story suggests, even those who believe in the power of the situation understand that people vary systematically in their usual behavior—in other words, people's personalities differ. Dr. Context felt no need to protect himself from his fellow researchers but was terrified of the escaped serial killer. He knew that a serial killer is much more likely to kill someone than the average person. But that doesn't mean the situation is unimportant: As social psychology experiments have shown, ordinary people will harm others in certain situations (such as in Milgram's experiments, when they obeyed the experimenter's authority). In other words, both personality and situations influence behavior.

Eventually, researchers came to recognize this. For example, several analyses found that situations and personality traits predict behavior about equally well (Funder & Ozer, 1983; Richard et al., 2003). In addition, most situations in everyday life are weaker than those explored in the famous social psychology experiments. For example, personality influences behavior during everyday life much more than it influences behavior during a riot.

Of course, people's behavior is not completely consistent, which is why personality measures ask people to report their *usual* traits and behaviors. What happens if we instead try to predict one particular behavior, instead of the average of many? For example, let's say you decide to see if a measure of extraversion predicts how social your friends are. Instead of measuring their behavior over a long

nature–nurture debate

the view that genetics cause personality traits versus the view that the environment causes personality traits period of time and across several situations, you decide to record their behavior on a particular Thursday night in the middle of the semester. Your friend Emily, an extravert, had a big test the next day, so she spent the whole evening studying alone. Your friend Isaac, an introvert, didn't have any tests until next week, so he went out for dinner with some friends.

JOURNAL PROMPT: UNDERSTANDING YOURSELF

When has your behavior been determined more by the situation than by your personality? And when has your personality been a stronger predictor of your behavior?

If extraversion means someone is more social, what went wrong here? The problem was you measured behavior on only one evening. In most cases, personality traits will predict behavior more accurately across many situations, not just at one isolated time (Epstein, 1979; Fishbein & Ajzen, 1974). As you saw, testing schedules influenced Emily's and Isaac's behavior. If you instead measured Emily's and Isaac's social behavior for 2 weeks—or, better yet, 2 months—the chances are good that Emily would go out more than Isaac did. Averaging their behavior across several situations would increase the predictive power of personality (Buss & Craik, 1983).

conscientiousness

being neat, organized, and achievement oriented

As another example, consider the personality trait called **conscientiousness**, which includes being neat, organized, and achievement oriented. A good measure of conscientiousness should predict, for example, whether a student arrives on time for class or not: Those high in conscientiousness should be more likely to arrive early, and those low in conscientiousness should be more likely to arrive late.

But Conscientious Courtney's score might not predict whether she will arrive to class on time on one specific day (for example, Personality Psychology; Thursday, October 15). If she's late, it might be because her bus showed up late, she couldn't find a parking space, her roommate took too long in the shower, or her alarm didn't go off because the electricity went out during the night. All sorts of situations could have interfered. So, while conscientiousness might not do a good job predicting whether Courtney arrives on time for that one class on that one specific day, it will most likely be correlated with her average arrival time for the class across the entire semester. Even stability in behavior from one week to another is reasonably high (Fleeson, 2001). This is one of the core features of personality: It's about someone's behavior most of the time, not in one isolated moment. You might think about that the next time a friend of yours does or says something inconsiderate—that's probably not who he really is. If he's usually inconsiderate, though, that might be his personality—and you might not want to be his friend anymore.

Here is the take-home message: It is tough for anyone—even with the best personality measures—to predict perfectly what a person will do at any random time. Introverts can sing out loud, sloppy people can dress nicely, and unhappy

Table 1.1 How the Person and the Situation Can Work Together to Influence Behavior

Factor	Example
Personality can be impacted by experiences	You and your friends go to different colleges. Over time, you notice that your friends seem different than when you were in high school.
People respond differently to the same situation	Some of your friends thrive at parties, whereas others shrink into the background.
People choose their situations	You choose to read a book on a Saturday afternoon. Your friend chooses to take a cooking class, while another friend chooses to go rock-wall climbing. In each case, you are each choosing the situation you're most comfortable with.
People change the situations they enter	You are having a serious private conversation with a friend when someone else unexpectedly walks in. Do you put the conversation on hold? Include the other person? Whatever you choose, the previous situation is changed by the presence of the third person.

people can laugh. We are not prisoners of our personalities. Instead, because personality is someone's *usual* tendency—not just their behavior in one minute or during one day—measuring behavior over a longer time span and across situations is a better way to show how personality can predict behavior. This is another answer to Mischel's criticism that behavior and personality are only weakly linked. That might be true for one behavior in one situation, but the link is much stronger when many behaviors are averaged.

Rather than competing to see who has the biggest role in shaping behavior, the person and situation actually work together in many different ways, called **person–situation interaction** (see Table 1.1). First, personality can be impacted by experiences—situations that last a long time, such as going to a certain school or moving in with someone. Let's say you and your friend Rose were very close in high school and had very similar personalities. But you decided to go to college, and she decided to join the military. Four years later, your personalities will probably be different based on these experiences. Second, people respond differently

person–situation interaction
when the person and situation work together to determine behavior

Lots of fun or lots of crazy? Personality influences the situations people enter.

to the same situation. For example, extraverts get energized at parties with large numbers of people, and introverts find such situations tiring. Third, people choose their situations—an extravert is more likely to choose to go to that party than the introvert. Some people pay to go skydiving; other people would pay to never have to go skydiving. Fourth, people change the situations they enter. If three people are calmly debating free will versus determinism in the dining hall and they are then joined by an argumentative hall mate, the discussion will suddenly become louder and more heated (Buss, 1979; Funder, 2008).

You'll want to keep these ideas about situations in mind when you fill out the personality questionnaires in the online Test Bank—yes, your behavior probably changes from one situation to the next, but how do you behave *most* of the time? And how do you behave when you have a choice? The rules of society require that you do things like wear clothes, stop at stoplights, and raise your hand before you ask a question in class. Virtually everyone does those things. But are you the type who asks questions in class in the first place? That's a pretty good indicator of personality—specifically, of extraversion.

Where Will We Go Next?: What You Will Learn in This Book

LO 1.4 Know the major topics in personality psychology.

In Chapter 2, we explore how researchers measure personality and the methods they use in their research. Throughout the book, you will complete questionnaires that will give you fascinating information about your personality and how you compare to others. However, a personality score by itself isn't a scientific study. Instead, a personality research study will ask a question and provide an answer that tells us something about people. For example, they'll take a group of people's personality scores and see how they predict certain behaviors or outcomes.

As you read this chapter, you may have noticed the parentheses with last names and years. These are references to research studies, almost all of which are published in academic journals. You can read them yourself—the full references are listed at the end of the book, and you can use that information to find the article's listing in a database such as PsycInfo. From there, you can read the full text of the article by downloading a PDF from your university's library website.

So what have these studies found? As you might have guessed, that's the focus of the rest of the book. Personality research tries to answer questions such as:

- How can we describe personality in the fewest number of dimensions possible but still have meaningful detail? (Chapter 3)

- Is your personality primarily determined by your genes or your environment, and how do the two interact? How do hormones influence behavior? (Chapter 4)

- How does the way we see ourselves—for example, self-esteem or narcissism—affect our school and work success and our relationships? (Chapter 5)

- How do your unconscious thoughts influence your behavior? (Chapter 6)

- How do people differ in what motivates them the most? (Chapter 7)

- How can you change someone else's behavior—or your own bad habits? (Chapter 8)

- How much does personality change as you get older? And how does birth order—being an only child or the oldest, middle, or youngest sibling—influence personality? (Chapter 9)

- How do the average man and woman differ in their personality traits? (Chapter 10)

- How do people from different cultures and generations differ in their personality traits? (Chapter 11)

- What personality traits make someone a good leader or a successful boss? Are certain personality types better suited to certain professions? (Chapter 12)

- What personality traits are linked to successful relationships? And is it better to have personality traits that are similar to or different from those of your romantic partner? (Chapter 13)

- How is personality related to mental health disorders such as depression or borderline personality disorder? (Chapter 14)

- Are people with certain personality traits healthier, and do they live longer? (Chapter 15)

In the Revel edition of this text, features called "The Science of Personality" also provide further insight into how personality researchers explore the many factors that shape who we are. These brief features walk you through the scientific methods and statistical calculations researchers use to conduct studies and analyze data on personality, so you'll understand not just the research findings but how personality scientists actually conduct their studies and interpret the results. The Revel version also provides full text scientific journal articles that allow you to see firsthand how studies are conducted and findings derived.

JOURNAL PROMPT: UNDERSTANDING YOURSELF

Which of the major topics in personality psychology are you most interested in learning about, and why?

Although exploring the cutting edge of personality science is the primary focus of this text, it's also important to understand how we got here. To meet that goal, we provide several historical timelines featuring a brief overview of important figures and events important to each chapter's topic. In addition, the feature "Personality's Past" provides a glimpse into the genesis of many theories and scientific methods that have proven influential to the science of personality psychology.

Of course, personality psychology isn't just about the science—it's also about you! Throughout the text, you will find personality questionnaires that help you understand yourself better. At times you might find that the questionnaire confirms what you believed about yourself; other times, you may be quite surprised by the results. Both outcomes help you figure out who you are, who you are not, and who you want to be. In the Revel edition of this text, you will also find many opportunities to explore ideas about yourself and others through writing prompts. The "Understanding Yourself" journal prompts pose questions asking you to reflect on your life and beliefs that help you better understand not only yourself and others, but also the personality psychology concepts you're reading about.

Finally, each chapter concludes with a summary of the chapter's learning objectives, as well as definitions of all the boldface key terms. In the Revel edition, there's also a flashcard function that allows you to test your comprehension of the key concepts from the chapter, as well as a multiple-choice quiz that will help you assess your understanding. All of the chapters end with essay questions asking you to summarize and synthesize what you've learned. The goal is to help you learn the concepts by engaging in deeper processing than just memorization. This reflection should also help you peel back the layers of personality and motivation and guide you to understand yourself and others a little better.

Concluding Thoughts

Learning about personality can be an exciting adventure, especially when you gain insight into your own personality and those of others. Studying personality gives you a view into both the deep recesses of your mind and an explanation for the sometimes confusing behavior of others. If you understand personality traits, you can suddenly access a whole wealth of information about how someone is likely to act, whether he'll be a good friend or romantic partner, and whether he's likely to be a good student or business colleague. You'll also learn more about how we know these things—how we define and measure personality and how personality relates to behavior—both in general and in specific situations such as in relationships or in the workplace.

Perhaps even more important, knowledge of personality psychology can help you make positive changes—for example, to become a better romantic partner, be more successful at work or in school, and even live a longer, healthier life. Although you are born with certain tendencies, personality is not, as some once believed, "set like plaster, and will never soften again" (James, 1890/1950, p. 121). You can bolster your self-control, fight anxiety and depression, become less self-centered, and redirect negative thoughts (Butler et al., 2006; Lyubomirsky et al., 2011; Nelis et al., 2011; Oaten & Cheng, 2006). These techniques are by no means a cure-all, but research has shown that they work. We tell you how you can practice these strategies in the later chapters, focusing on what you can do—right now—to become who you'd like to be.

Sound good? Then let's get started.

Learning Objective Summaries

LO 1.1   Define personality.

Personality describes someone's usual pattern of behavior, feelings, and thoughts.

LO 1.2   List various contexts in which personality might appear.

Personality can appear in people's behaviors, their social networking profiles, their physical appearance and clothing, and their offices and bedrooms.

LO 1.3   Describe the two sides of the person–situation debate, how the debate was resolved, and the conditions under which personality can best predict behavior.

Psychologists have debated whether the person (relatively set characteristics such as personality) or the situation (the specific environment you're in) better determines behavior. This is different from the nature-versus-nurture debate, which instead debates the origin of differences within the person. In recent years, most agree that the effects of the person versus the situation on behavior are about equal. Characteristics of the person explain behavior better when behavior is measured more than once and in several situations.

traits, biological influences on personality, the self, motivational learning, psychodynamic approaches to personality, how personality changes over the lifespan, how gender and culture affect personality, and how personality affects relationships, careers, and mental and physical health.

LO 1.4 Know the major topics in personality psychology.

The chapters to come explore topics such as how personality is measured, the Big Five personality

Key Terms

personality, p. 4
extraversion, p. 8
introversion, p. 8

situation, p. 12
person–situation debate, p. 12
nature–nurture debate, p. 13

conscientiousness, p. 14
person–situation
 interaction, p. 15

Essay Questions

1. Define personality and explain the factors that influence one's personality.

2. How can personality be considered a hub topic in the social sciences? Explain what fields of study go into trying to understand personality.

3. Dissect the person–situation dynamic. How does each contribute to our understanding of behavior, and what are the four factors that we need to consider as we negotiate the interaction between the two?

Chapter 2
Assessment and Methods

⌄ Learning Objectives

LO 2.1 Explain how personality is assessed using self-report questionnaires.

LO 2.2 Understand how to determine if a scale is reliable and valid.

LO 2.3 Learn how to apply statistics to personality measurement, and define social desirability bias.

LO 2.4 Describe alternative ways of measuring personality and the importance of triangulation.

LO 2.5 Explain the correlational and experimental methods, including the advantages and disadvantages of each.

LO 2.6 Provide examples of the best practices for scientific research.

Think for a moment about your personality. How would you describe yourself?

To answer this question, most people will generate a list of adjectives and maybe a few nouns—nice, outgoing, laid-back, determined, opinionated, loving, a planner, a worrier.

Of course, this isn't the sum total of who you are. You grew up in a certain culture, at a certain time, and within a certain family. You might be a student, an athlete, a pizza delivery person—or all three. You have physical attributes such as height, hair color, and gender. You have a lifetime of experiences, impressions, and relationships complicated enough to fill several books (or even a whole library!) if you wrote them all down. Somewhere in this is your personality, and **personality assessment**—the way we measure and capture personality—tries to find it. This chapter focuses on the scientific methods personality psychologists use to measure personality and conduct personality research.

personality assessment
the way we measure and capture personality, using a variety of methods

self-report measure
questionnaires asking people to report on their own personalities, usually through rating themselves on a list of adjectives or statements

socially desirable responding
the tendency of people to make themselves look better than they actually are

Self-Report Questionnaires: The Most Common Way to Measure Personality

Self-report questionnaires are the most common way to measure personality.

LO 2.1 Explain how personality is assessed using self-report questionnaires.

Personality psychologists use many different measures and techniques to capture this most elusive of ideas—who we are as people and how we differ from one another. These days, questionnaires are the most common way to measure personality. Most questionnaires are a more structured version of the adjectives or phrases people might use to answer the question, How would you describe yourself? Questionnaires provide the list of adjectives or statements, and people answer as true/false or an incremental scale from agree to disagree. This is usually called a **self-report measure**. It's a simple and effective way to quantify personality, which at first glance seems unquantifiable.

Self-report measures aren't perfect—for one thing, how do we know people are telling the truth? The most common way for people to lie on questionnaires is to make themselves look better than they actually are, which is called **socially desirable responding**.

Even when people know their responses are anonymous, they might exaggerate their good qualities and downplay their bad ones. Fortunately, researchers make sure right from the start that the personality questionnaires used in research aren't affected too much by social desirability bias (we tell you how a little later). Nevertheless, self-report measures are limited to the person's own self-assessment. For example, if someone is unaware of their motivations, they won't be able to report them. That's why there are many other ways of measuring personality, and we cover several later in the chapter. However, self-report measures have many advantages, including being easy, convenient, and simple to administer, so we start there.

You'll be taking many self-report measures of personality throughout this text, learning about yourself using the same scientific tools researchers use. You'll also be able to see how your scores compare to a norm group of other undergraduates—for example, what percentage of them score lower than you do on each personality trait. Through the science features, you'll learn how researchers see how the traits measured by these questionnaires are related to each other or how they determine if men's responses are significantly different from women's on a particular trait.

JOURNAL PROMPT: UNDERSTANDING YOURSELF

Why do you think people tend to respond in ways that are "socially desirable"? In what contexts do you see it occurring in your own life? How often do you find yourself responding in such a way?

The Example of the Cat Person Scale

For now, we'll make up a simple scale (see Table 2.1) so you can see how personality questionnaires work. Let's call it the Cat Person Scale (if we wanted to be optimistic, we could call it the Very Scientific Cat Person Scale).

Complete this scale with your own responses:

Table 2.1 The Cat Person Scale

For each question, circle only one response.

1. I like cats.				
1	2	3	4	5
Strongly disagree	Disagree	Not sure	Agree	Strongly agree
2. Cats freak me out.				
1	2	3	4	5
Strongly disagree	Disagree	Not sure	Agree	Strongly agree

Table 2.1 (Continued)

3. I love petting cats.				
1	2	3	4	5
Strongly disagree	Disagree	Not sure	Agree	Strongly agree

4. The idea of petting a cat freaks me out.				
1	2	3	4	5
Strongly disagree	Disagree	Not sure	Agree	Strongly agree

5. I consider myself a "cat person."				
1	2	3	4	5
Strongly disagree	Disagree	Not sure	Agree	Strongly agree

6. If it were my choice, I wouldn't own a cat.				
1	2	3	4	5
Strongly disagree	Disagree	Not sure	Agree	Strongly agree

reverse-scored items

items scored in the opposite direction from the responses

acquiescence response set

the tendency of some respondents to agree with many items on a questionnaire

Likert scale

a range of numbers that correspond to how much someone agrees or disagrees with an item

First, we'll score the Cat Person Scale. We'll accomplish the weird but useful goal of all personality scales: to capture a characteristic of a person as a number. Questions 1, 3, and 5 are easy to score—high numbers mean you are more of a cat person. But questions 2, 4, and 6 go the opposite direction, with high numbers meaning you are *not* a cat person. Many personality scales include such **reverse-scored items**, or items worded in the opposite direction from the measured trait. That's because some people have a tendency to agree with everything, known as the **acquiescence response set**. With half of the items scored in the opposite direction, we can be more certain that the high scorers really are cat people and not just those who agree with everything.

To score the scale, the first thing we have to do is reverse the scores of the reverse-scored items (makes sense, right?). For the questionnaires in this text, the program will do this for you, but it's good to know how it's done. The Cat Person Scale uses a **Likert scale**—a range of numbers that correspond to how much someone agrees or disagrees with an item. (Just so you know, Likert is usually pronounced as "Lickert" rather than "Like-ert.") This one is a 5-point Likert scale. Remember that items 1, 3, and 5 are already in the right direction, so you leave them alone. For items 2, 4, and 6, though, change any 5s to 1s, 4s to 2s, 2s to 4s, and 1s to 5s. 3s stay the same.

Then add these numbers together with your responses to items 1, 3, and 5 and you have your score on the Cat Person Scale. The higher your score, the more of a cat person you are. The lower your score, the less of a cat person you are. The highest score anyone can get on this scale is 30 (for a real cat lover), and the lowest score is 6 (a real cat hater). For the personality scales in this text, you'll also be able to compare your score to others in the class. There's one later in the chapter, so we cover comparing scores there. (See Personality's Past feature for a brief discussion of the first attempts at creating personality questionnaires.)

Fill out the Cat Person Scale to see if you are worthy of holding me—well, *after* you give me my food.

Personality's Past

The Birth of Personality Scales

"Do you usually feel well and strong?" Yes/No
"Have you *ever* fainted away?" Yes/No
"Did you have a happy childhood?" Yes/No
"Are you ever bothered by the feeling that people are reading your thoughts?" Yes/No
"Do you get rattled easily?" Yes/No

These are just a small sample of items from the first known personality test, the Woodworth Personal Data Sheet (Woodworth, 1920).

Personality scales arrived on the scene almost a century ago. Robert S. Woodworth developed the first during World War I. His scale was designed to measure symptoms linked to shell-shock, which we now know as *posttraumatic stress disorder (PTSD)*. It examined childhood experience, substance use, anxiety, and mind–body problems (like fainting). It was a very simple scale: answers were "yes" or "no" to 116 items and the results were added—the more times a person answered yes, the more likely he or she was to have problems (Garrett & Schneck, 1928).

This scale brought about a wave of similar efforts. During the early years, personality scales were designed for specific applications. Some were designed for assessing military fitness, others for workplace performance. The goal was often to screen out people who were constitutionally unfit for service or work (Gibby & Zickar, 2008). The Woodworth test was originally used by the military and was adapted to measure neurotic symptoms in psychiatric practice (Papurt, 1930).

Another breakthrough happened about a decade later when the first multifactor personality scale was developed (Bernreuter, 1931). This scale was a combination of four subscales that measured neuroticism, extraversion, dominance, and self-sufficiency, allowing psychologists to learn about multiple aspects of personality from a single personality test.

All the self-report scales we have today owe their existence to these early efforts.

Correlations: What You Need to Know to Understand the Research

Just because we optimistically called the Cat Person Scale very scientific doesn't mean it actually is. To evaluate a personality scale, you first need to understand correlations. You might have already learned about correlations in a statistics class. But if you haven't had statistics (or you wish you hadn't!), a **correlation** measures the relationship between two things. More precisely, a correlation is the statistical relationship between two variables. Correlations also come up in many personality studies. For example, you learned in Chapter 1 that extraverts send more text messages, which means extraversion was correlated with the number of text messages. Correlations range between –1 and 1 and are often reported using the letter r—for example, $r = .35$. There are **positive correlations** and **negative correlations**.

For positive correlations, when one thing is high, the other tends to be high as well (see Figure 2.1A)—for example, height and weight, number of kids at a birthday party and noise level, or being female and owning lots of shoes. (This last one isn't just a stereotype—for my [J. M. T.] undergraduate honors thesis, I asked male and female college students how many pairs of shoes they owned. Men averaged four, and women 12.) None of these examples produce a "perfect" correlation of 1, so that's why it's more correct to say that when one is high, the other *tends* to be high as well. Not everyone who's tall weighs more than everyone who is short. A large group of kids at a birthday party could be unusually quiet. Women own more shoes on average, but some men own a lot of shoes and some women own few. The strength of the relationship between two things is reflected in the size of the correlation. The higher the correlation, the stronger the relationship. It's common for correlations in psychology to hover between .20 and .40—Cohen (1988) labeled correlations this size "moderate"; around .10 he called "small" and over .40 "large." Cohen did not see these as absolute cutoffs, but they give you some idea of the size of correlations in psychology.

correlation
the statistical relationship between two variables

positive correlations
when one variable is high, the other variable tends to be high as well

negative correlations
when one variable is high, the other variable tends to be low

When two things are negatively correlated with each other, there's also a relationship, but it goes in the opposite direction: When one is high, the other tends to be low, for example, temperature and the amount of clothing worn, hours of sleep and tiredness, or amount of exercise and weight gained (see Figure 2.1B). When the temperature is high, people wear less clothing; when you sleep fewer hours, you feel more tired; and when you exercise for longer, you will gain less weight and might even lose some.

The third possibility is no correlation, sometimes called a **null correlation** (see Figure 2.1C). This means there is no relationship between two things. That can be a correlation of 0 or a negative or positive correlation that is not large enough to be **statistically significant**, or having a probability of less than 5% that the results are due to random chance. A less than 5% probability means that if a study were repeated 100 times, five studies or less would find such a result purely from random chance, and 95 would be finding a "true" result. As you might remember from statistics class, statistical significance depends both on the size of the

null correlation
when two variables are not related to each other

statistically significant
having a probability of less than 5% that the results are due to random chance.

Figure 2.1 Scatterplots of Positive (A), Negative (B), and Null Correlations (C), with Regression Lines

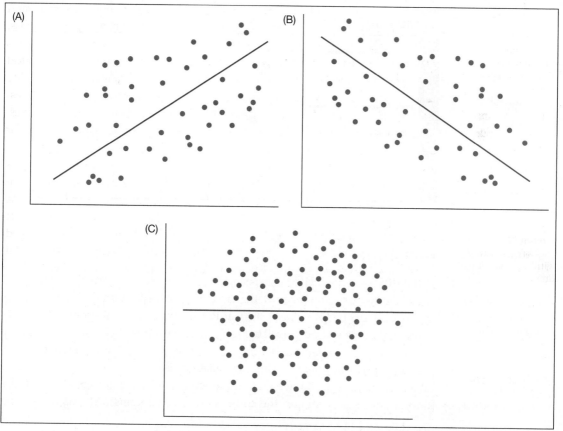

correlation and on the number of people in the study. For example, a correlation of $r = .08$ is statistically significant in a sample of 5,000 people, but not in a sample of 50 people. That's because a larger sample of people makes it less likely that the result is due to the chance selection of a few people who show a certain result. A correlation that is not statistically significant is considered null because we cannot be sure the correlation actually is any higher (or lower) than zero.

Reliability and Validity: Evaluating Personality Scales

LO 2.2 Understand how to determine if a scale is reliable and valid.

Now let's get back to evaluating personality questionnaires. How do we decide if a personality scale is any good or not? Researchers use two main criteria to evaluate scales: reliability and validity. A good personality questionnaire is both reliable and valid. Before reading on, take your first personality questionnaire below.

TAKE the Questionnaire in **REVEL** →

Questionnaire 2.1 MARLOWE–CROWNE SOCIAL DESIRABILITY SCALE

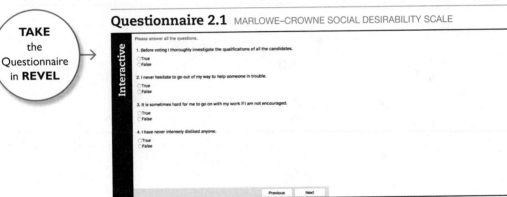

reliability
consistency, either within a scale or over time

internal reliability
when all of the items on a questionnaire measure the same thing

Cronbach's alpha
a statistical measure of internal reliability

Reliability

Reliability means a scale is consistent. First, it should be internally reliable—all of the questions should measure the same thing, called **internal reliability**. Let's say we had 100 people fill out the Cat Person Scale. Their responses to the six individual items should correlate highly with each other. People who say they like cats should also tend to say they like petting cats and disagree that cats (or petting them) freaks them out. Internal reliability is often reported using a statistic called **Cronbach's alpha**, which looks much like a correlation (and, in fact, the formula for alpha averages the correlations among items). Alphas need to be higher than ordinary correlations: Most personality questionnaires have an alpha of at least .70, though alphas of around .60 are acceptable. Lower than that and the items may not measure the same thing.

For example, say we added a seventh question to our cat person questionnaire: "I like disco." Some cat people like disco and some don't, so this item would probably not correlate highly with the others. That would bring down the internal reliability of the scale. If we got that result, the best solution would be to remove that item from the scale. Items that few people endorse can also bring down internal reliability. Let's say we added "I like to eat cat food" to the Cat Person Scale. Even cat lovers don't usually heat up a tin of cat food for an afternoon snack (at least we hope not), so that item likely wouldn't correlate with the others. If we were silly enough to include it, we'd take it out after getting that result.

Another type of reliability is **test–retest reliability**. If the Cat Person Scale has acceptable test–retest reliability, your score should be about the same if you took it again 2 weeks from now. It would be even better to get 100 people to fill it out now and in 2 weeks and measure the correlation between the two sets of responses. This correlation should be high enough (around .70 or .80) to show that the scale produces about the same result over time. Because being a cat person shouldn't change much in 2 weeks, the responses to the Cat Person Scale should be fairly consistent over time. If we instead wanted to measure something more changeable, such as current stress level, we would not expect test–retest reliability to be very high.

test–retest reliability
taking the test at two different times produces roughly the same result

Santa likes disco. But is he a cat person? The two probably aren't related.

Validity

Let's say we get the happy result that the Cat Person Scale is reliable, both internally consistent and stable over time. Is that enough to use it for scientific research? No, because being reliable is not enough. A broken clock is very reliable—it consistently gives the same answer—even though it's correct only twice a day. To be considered scientifically correct, a scale also needs to be valid. The usual definition of **validity** is that a scale measures what it's supposed to measure. Admittedly, that's a vague definition. But it means something very important: Does the scale do what it's supposed to do?

In one personality class, I (J. M. T.) asked students to find a personality scale—most found one online—and write a brief paper on how they knew it was a valid scale. Many students wrote things like "I believe this is a valid scale of anxiety because the items look like they measure anxiety." That's sometimes called **face validity**—a fancy way of saying the items look like they measure the thing they are supposed to measure. However, face validity is not the best way to show that a scale actually works. Just because an item looks good doesn't mean it predicts real outcomes or measures what it's supposed to measure.

What is a better way to show that our Very Scientific Cat Person Scale is valid? One way is **predictive validity**—that the measure is related to a concrete outcome or behavior. We could have a group of people fill out the Cat Person Scale and observe how they behave when they encounter a friendly cat in a lab waiting room. If people who score high on the Cat Person Scale pay more attention to the cat and are more likely to pet her, pick her up, and play with her (and those who score low

> If people who score high on the Cat Person Scale spend more time looking at LOLcats, that may be a sign of the scale's predictive validity.

show the opposite behavior), the scale would demonstrate predictive validity. We could also test whether the scores on the Cat Person Scale predicted cat ownership or looking at websites devoted to cats (such as the many LOLcat sites).

To see predictive validity in action with a real research scale, we'll use the example of a scale measuring psychological entitlement—the tendency to think one is special and deserves more than others. (The scale includes items such as "If I were on the *Titanic*, I would deserve to be on the *first* lifeboat!") One study was specifically designed to test the scale's predictive validity. After participants completed the entitlement scale, the experimenter mentioned she had a bucket of candy intended for children in the developmental lab, and that participants could take "as much candy as you think you deserve." Sure enough, the participants with higher entitlement scores took more candy—essentially taking candy from children (Campbell et al., 2004).

Another type of validity is **convergent validity**, which occurs when the scale correlates with similar scales. To determine the convergent validity of the Cat Person Scale, we'd have to find another scale that measures being a cat person. If the two scales correlate highly with each other, that would demonstrate convergent validity. The entitlement scale, for example, correlated with a measure of narcissism, a related trait (Campbell et al., 2004). If we write a new measure of shyness, it should correlate with previous measures of shyness. You might be thinking that convergent validity sounds kind of circular—how do we know the other scale is valid? This is a limitation of convergent validity, and that's why it's best to establish validity in other ways as well.

The flip side of convergent validity is **discriminant validity**—the scale shouldn't correlate with measures of something different. If our Cat Person Scale correlated very highly with a measure of IQ, that would suggest that it's measuring IQ instead of being a cat person. A small correlation would be OK—just not a correlation big enough that it might be measuring the same thing. (Right now, all the cat people are sure that the correlation with IQ would be positive, and all of the dog people think it would be negative.) To demonstrate discriminant validity, we'd want to show that our scale does *not* correlate with unrelated things like IQ.

discriminant validity
when a scale does not correlate with unrelated scales

Researchers also want their scales to show divergent validity with measures of socially desirable responding—people's tendency to make themselves look better than they actually are. These measures are sometimes known as "lie scales." If the Cat Person Scale was strongly correlated with a measure of socially desirable responding, that would challenge the validity of the scale, as it would suggest a high score means someone is trying to look good, not that they really like cats. (Remember that the definition of validity is "it measures what it is supposed to measure.")

So how do measures of socially desirable responding work? They ask questions about things we know we should do but usually don't (like always being nice to disagreeable people) and things we usually do but know we shouldn't (like gossiping). The Marlowe–Crowne scale you took in this chapter is a measure of socially desirable responding. If you didn't want to admit to ever playing sick, hating someone, or having sloppy table manners, you probably scored high on the scale. If you were more brutally honest about yourself, you probably scored lower. (And what does your score say about you? More on that later. *Hint:* It's not necessarily bad to score high.)

The Science of Personality HOW TO MAKE A PERSONALITY SCALE

Interactive

Step 1: Define your construct of interest.
Let's say we are interested in measuring entitlement, often defined as "a pervasive sense that one is more deserving or entitled than others" (Campbell et al., 2004). We'll go through the steps that Campbell et al. did to construct a scale measuring entitlement.

1 of 9   Previous   Next

EXPLORE in REVEL

Knowing about reliability and validity helps determine which personality scales to trust. When students search for personality scales online, they usually find plenty—but few websites provide much information about the reliability or validity of the scales. Instead, sites often mention how popular the scale is, or the famous person who developed it. Neither of these says anything about a scale's reliability or validity. Understanding more about reliability and validity will help you be a smarter user of these tests and evaluate whether your scores on them mean anything.

The Example of Horoscopes

Many people know their Zodiac sign based on their birthday—say, Virgo if you were born between August 23 and September 22. ("What's your sign?" is the old-school pickup line in a bar, right after "Do you come here often?") You've probably seen the daily or monthly horoscope for each sign in a magazine or online. They often make vague but intriguing predictions and advice, such as "You may find yourself a bit overworked, perhaps going too far out of your way to give someone assistance. Line up people to help so you don't have to do everything." They are usually vague enough that they'll come true for some people, giving them the illusion of validity even though they are accurate by chance (Fichten & Sunerton, 1988).

But, you might be thinking, zodiac signs are supposed to be linked to personality traits. If you're a Scorpio, you're deeply emotional and always causing trouble. If you're a Taurus, you're stubborn and unyielding. If you're a Gemini, you're always changing. Although it seems unlikely that the stars influence personality, the theory is not completely implausible—perhaps babies born in different seasons are exposed to different influences *in utero* and right after birth. Many people believe deeply in star sign personalities, reading books and using online tools to understand more about themselves. Some people decide whether or not to date or marry someone based on whether their signs are compatible.

The good news about horoscopes as personality measures is that they are pretty reliable. They are based on your birthday, which is stable, so every measure of horoscopes will give you the same star sign. For example, if you are born on December 10, every horoscope you check will describe you as a Sagittarius. If you check again in 2 weeks, you will still be a Sagittarius, showing test–retest reliability. However, not every book and website will have exactly the same description of the personality traits associated with each sign, which creates some problems with reliability.

So how would we determine if zodiac signs are a valid measure of personality? Here, a key consideration is convergent validity—if the scale correlates with similar measures. With star signs, the measures are the personality traits associated with your sign. The best similar measures are personality questionnaires that measure these traits. For example, Tauruses should score high on a measure of stubbornness, and Virgos high on a measure of neatness.

Watch ASSESSING WHAT MAKES A VALID PERSONALITY QUESTIONNAIRE

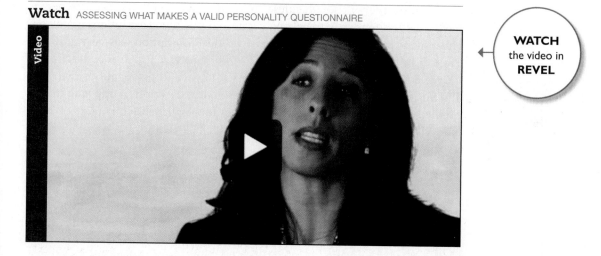

Video

WATCH
the video in
REVEL

A few studies have done just this—asked people their birth dates, had them complete a battery of personality tests, and seen whether there was any correlation. Most of these studies show no relationship between star signs and personality (Kelly, 1979; Saklofske et al., 1982). Thus, making dating and life decisions based on star signs might not be the best idea. Another reason to doubt: Apparently the alignment of the stars has changed since the signs were first identified centuries ago, changing the signs by about a month (so, for example, Virgo is now September 16 to October 30; Friedman, 2011). So what you thought was a personality description that fit you well might have actually belonged to people born the month after you instead.

People who are sure their horoscopes describe them might be influenced by the **Barnum effect,** or the tendency to believe vague, positive statements about themselves. The name "Barnum effect" comes from early-20th-century circus founder P. T. Barnum's famous observation that "there's a sucker born every minute." For example, imagine this is the description given for your star sign:

Horoscopes: reliable but not valid.

You have a strong need for other people to like and to admire you. You have a tendency to be critical of yourself. At times you are extraverted, mild-mannered, and social; at other times you are introverted, wary, and reserved. You worry about things more than you let on, even to your best friends. You are adaptable to social situations and your interests are wide ranging.

Barnum effect
the tendency for people to believe vague, positive statements about themselves

Most people will say this description fits them very well because people have a natural tendency to believe vague and positive descriptions of personality. In one study, 87% of people believed this description was very accurate. They didn't find out until later that everyone received the same description (Boyce & Geller, 2002; Forer, 1949). Fortunately, valid personality scales usually fare better. If you give people a personality description opposite to that predicted by personality questionnaires, few will believe it (Andersen & Nordvik, 2002).

The Statistical Side of Questionnaires

LO 2.3   Learn how to apply statistics to personality measurement, and define social desirability bias.

Earlier in the chapter, you took the Marlowe-Crowne Social Desirability Scale. Scales like the Marlowe–Crowne measure socially desirable responding, sometimes called "need for social approval" (Crowne & Marlowe, 1960, 1964). Because it's the first personality questionnaire you've taken in this book, we use it as an example to illustrate how to interpret your scores on personality measures.

How to Use Statistics to Understand Your Personality

descriptive statistics
numbers such as the mean, median, and mode

mean
the average score on a scale, calculated by adding everyone's scores and dividing by the number of scores

median
the score that falls in the middle of all the scores on the test (also called the 50th percentile)

mode
the most frequent score

How high or low was your score on the Marlowe–Crowne scale? You can compare your score to others' using **descriptive statistics**. Several numbers were displayed. The first was your raw score on the scale. But what does that number mean? For it to mean something, it needs to be compared to other scores. Our comparison group—called a *norm sample*—is a class that took personality psychology a few semesters ago. The first step to comparing scores is to calculate the **mean**, or average, score on the scale for the norm sample. The mean is calculated by adding everyone's scores and dividing by the number of scores. Another important value is the **median**, the score that falls in the middle of all the scores on the test (also called the *50th percentile*). Finally, the **mode** is the most frequent score. For example, if scores on the Marlowe–Crowne are 11, 14, 25, 15, 8, 18, 10, 21, 9, and 15 in a class of 10 students, the mean is 14.60, the median is 14, and the mode is 15. The mean is typically the score we're most interested in, but the

Figure 2.2 Normal Distribution Bell Curve with SDs and Percentiles

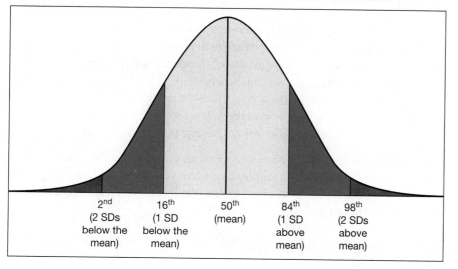

2nd	16th	50th	84th	98th
(2 SDs below the mean)	(1 SD below the mean)	(mean)	(1 SD above mean)	(2 SDs above mean)

median or mode is useful if some scores are really high or really low, which can skew the mean.

The next question of interest is how much people's scores may differ; we want to understand the range of scores. Much of the time, scores fall into a **normal distribution**, often called a "bell curve" (Figure 2.2). That means most people score in the middle and fewer score at the extremes (here, very high in the need for social approval, or very low). Scores don't always make a perfect bell curve, but they usually follow this basic pattern. You might have taken a class where the professor graded "on a curve," with only a few students getting A's and F's, a few more getting B's and D's, and most in the middle getting C's.

The normal distribution uses a **standard deviation (SD)**, a measure of how far a score is from the average. In the normal distribution, two-thirds of people score within one standard deviation of the average (either higher or lower), and 95% score within two SDs of the average. The survey showed you your SD score, or how many standard deviations above or below the mean you scored. Your SD score can be converted into a **percentile score**, which represents the percent of students in the norm sample who scored lower than you. A high percentile score on the Marlowe–Crowne means you are higher in the need for social approval than most of the norm sample; around 50% means you score near the average; and a low percentile score means you are lower in need for social approval than your peers. These percentiles work just like those for standardized tests such as the SAT. If your math SAT percentile was 80%, for example, you scored higher than 80% of the other people taking the test.

normal distribution
a distribution of scores in which most people score in the middle and fewer score at the extremes; also known as a "bell curve"

standard deviation (SD)
a measure of spread around the mean. In a normal distribution, two-thirds of the data will lie within one standard deviation of the mean

percentile score
the percentage of people someone scores higher than on a scale or test; a score at the 90th percentile means someone scores higher than 90% of the people who took the scale

Here are a few rough guidelines for understanding percentile scores and standard deviations:

98–99% = 2 SDs or more above average (a very high score)
84% or higher = 1 SD above average (a high score)
71% or higher = ½ SD above average (a moderately high score)
about 50% = average (an average score)
29% or lower = ½ SD below average (a moderately low score)
16% or lower = 1 SD below average (a low score)
2% or lower = 2 SDs or more below average (a very low score)

If you scored high on the Marlowe–Crowne, you have a strong need for other people to approve of you, and you try to present yourself in the best light. If you scored low, you are willing to admit to your faults and feel less need to change your behavior to suit others.

What Your Score on the Marlowe–Crowne Says About You

The Marlowe–Crowne measures socially desirable responding. The original authors of the scale said it measured "need for social approval." Similar scales are sometimes called "lie scales." It sounds odd to think of someone high in the need for social approval as "lying," but that's because people often tell little white lies to please others. It's like what you say to the friend with the terrible haircut who asks, "What do you think of my haircut?"—you say, "I like it!"

Look back at the items on the Marlowe–Crowne scale. One is "I have never been irked when people expressed ideas very different from my own." If we were

Do people try to make themselves look good on questionnaires just as they try to look good on a date?

all being 100% truthful with ourselves, hardly anyone would answer "true" to this item. Similarly, someone who answers "false" to "I like to gossip at times" probably isn't being completely honest. But we all know we shouldn't get irked at others and gossip about them, so people concerned with social approval will try to portray themselves as virtuous.

The Marlowe–Crowne and other measures of social desirability (such as Paulhus's Balanced Inventory of Desirable Responding [Paulhus, 1991] or the Lie scale from the Eysenck Personality Questionnaire [Eysenck & Eysenck, 1975]) are used in a variety of ways. Sometimes these scales are used to screen out people who may not be telling the truth on other questionnaires. Researchers also use these scales when they are developing a new measure of a personality trait—a new scale should show divergent validity with socially desirable responding. If it doesn't, it's just measuring the tendency to make a good impression, instead of what it's supposed to be measuring.

Social desirability scales are also personality measures themselves (Paulhus, 1991). In this view, people who score high on the social desirability measures aren't really "lying"; they are doing what they usually do in real life, which is following social rules and trying to get along with other people. So these measures capture both a response bias and a real personality trait.

Scores on these measures have also changed over generations. Compared to Americans born in the 1940s and 1950s, those born in the 1970s and later score lower on the Marlowe–Crowne and on the socially desirable responding scales of another personality measure (Twenge & Im, 2007; Twenge et al., 2010). That means your

Hard to believe, but men really did wear suits and hats to baseball games (here, in 1951 New York).

grandparents are probably more concerned with how people present themselves in public than you and your parents are. Ask your grandparents some time about how people dressed in the 1950s and early 1960s, when women wore gloves and men wore suits, even to baseball games—a far cry from today's casual and comfortable t-shirts and jeans. The good news for personality psychologists is that fewer people filling out self-report questionnaires now are high in social desirability bias. These days, we're more willing to be honest about ourselves—with the trade-off that we might not always be as respectful toward others (just ask your grandmother!).

JOURNAL PROMPT: UNDERSTANDING YOURSELF

You've already taken the Marlowe–Crowne scale to assess your level of socially desirable responding, but how would you view your inclination to be viewed positively by others? Do you feel you have a strong desire to be accepted? Why or why not?

Alternatives to Self-Report Questionnaires

LO 2.4 Describe alternative ways of measuring personality and the importance of triangulation.

As we discussed before, self-report measures have some disadvantages—for example, the risk of socially desirable responding and people not having an accurate view of themselves. So it's important to have other ways of measuring personality outside of self-report that are still reliable and valid. So how else can we measure someone's personality?

Informant Reports

One alternative is to use the same questionnaires, but ask someone who knows the person to fill it out—for example, his or her roommate or partner. This will tell you how someone else sees the person, at least as the informant has experienced his or her personality. ("Informant" makes them sound like a spy, and in a way they are!) For example, if we did a study on shyness, we might want to ask people to report on themselves and also ask a roommate to report on them. This way we have two assessments of personality. **Informant reports** work especially well for undesirable traits—for example, who wants to admit that they are a grumpy or disagreeable person?

informant reports
when the people close to someone (roommates, family, friends) report on his or her personality

Reports from others are also commonly used in research on children, as children often don't yet have enough insight into their own personalities or enough reading ability to fill out a personality questionnaire themselves. So parents and teachers will report on children's behavior, such as how easily they make friends or how aggressive they are.

Clinical Interviews

Another way to gather personality data is by doing an interview. Interviews are rarely used for measuring normal personality but can be useful for assessing abnormal levels of personality traits such as personality disorders—when a personality trait is so high that it causes problems in someone's life. These interviews can be unstructured (which means the interviewer has a lot of latitude in the choice and sequence of questions to ask), semi-structured (with set questions that must be asked but follow-up questions allowed), or fully structured (with only certain questions asked). For example, to assess borderline personality disorder, which is characterized by intense mood swings and erratic behavior, a semi-structured interview might ask questions such as "Do you tend to experience frequent and intense changes in your moods?" or "Do you tend to behave impulsively such that you act without considering the consequences of your behavior?"

Measuring Behavior

Personality can also be assessed by observing behavior. Some researchers have participants report what they are doing at random times throughout the day (through cell phones or tablets; Richards & Larson, 1993; Weinstein et al., 2007). Behavior can also be measured in a controlled lab setting. If you're interested in measuring antisocial and aggressive tendencies, you can tell people they're playing a game and give them the opportunity to blast their opponent with loud noise (Bushman, 2002; Taylor, 1967). As you read in Chapter 1, personality studies have looked at how traits correlate with behaviors like sending more text messages (Thalmayer et al., 2011) or using certain words on Facebook (Park et al., 2015).

How often do you text, and what do you write? Personality can be seen through behaviors.

Archival or Life Outcomes Data

Researchers can also examine real-life aggressive behavior by finding school records of fights or police records of violent crimes. Other researchers study archival records to get a view of other aspects of personality "from a distance"—for example, studying a U.S. president's major speeches to determine his personality (Winter, 1987; we explore this research more in Chapter 7). Personality researchers have used personal websites, Facebook pages, and even bedrooms to discern personality (Buffardi & Campbell, 2008; Gosling et al., 2002). Other researchers tracked down students' campus conduct records, and found that extraverted students were more likely to have been disciplined for violations such as underage drinking (Thalmayer et al., 2011).

Projective Tests

projective tests
measures designed to elicit personality characteristics without directly asking

Projective tests of personality are sometimes used to elicit personality characteristics without directly asking. You might have heard of one such measure: Rorschach inkblots. Participants are shown inkblots (which make abstract images) and are asked, "What might this be?" (not "What is this?"—because the answer to that, especially to a literal-minded person, is "an inkblot"). In theory, the answers someone gives reveal their personality—presumably because they are "projecting" their personality onto the inkblots. Most studies find that the Rorschach is valid for measuring nonpersonality variables such as cognitive impairment, but is valid for only some of the aspects of personality it aims to measure. For example, focusing on color in the inkblots is a fairly valid measure of being highly emotional, but seeing body parts in the inkblots does not seem to be a valid measure of body preoccupation (Wood et al., 2015).

intercoder reliability
occurs when people coding stories or written material agree, using a set of rules, that it meets certain criteria

The Thematic Apperception Test (TAT), which asks participants to tell or write stories based on pictures, measures motives such as achievement that in turn predict certain life outcomes (Winter, 2010). Researchers code the stories for motives using a set of guidelines. More than one person codes each story to make sure the coding is reliable; this is called **intercoder reliability**. A high intercoder reliability means that the coders are in good agreement about which motives appear in the participant's story. This type of coding can also be used for any type of written material, such as a politician's speech or a children's book. Although the TAT's validity has been questioned (Spangler, 1992), recent studies suggest it does predict behaviors (Schultheiss & Brunstein, 2002). We learn more about the TAT and psychological motives in Chapter 7.

Physiological Measures

physiological measures
measurements assessing physical reactions such as heart rate or sweating

Physiological measures assess physical reactions such as heart rate or sweating—the same measurements used in lie detector tests. Physiological measures are expensive and inconvenient to use but can reveal reactions untapped by self-report measures. For example, people who score high on the Marlowe–Crowne Social Desirability Scale often score low on self-report measures of anxiety. But when put in a stressful situation—say, told they are going to give a speech—physiological measures such as blood pressure and heart rate show they react more strongly than most people, a sign of underlying anxiety (King et al., 1990). These people are called **repressive copers**—they're the type who deny their anxiety even when they're feeling very worried. The label is based on Sigmund Freud's idea of repression, in which people push their true feelings into their unconscious. In this case, the physiological measure is tapping their true underlying anxiety.

A new way to measure personality is through brain scans, often using a machine that conducts **fMRI** (short for functional magnetic resonance imaging; see Figure 2.3). An fMRI shows which areas of the brain are receiving more blood flow and are thus more active during certain tasks, such as thinking about a romantic partner or doing a math problem. One study found that anxious people's brains reacted more strongly to seeing unusual information than nonanxious people's brains did. This brain reaction was a better predictor of anxious behavior than a self-report measure of anxiety (Eisenberger et al., 2005). Many brain scan studies, though, still begin with self-report questionnaires. One study found that extraverts' brains react differently to stimuli than introverts' brains—but to identify extraverts versus introverts in the first place, the researchers used a self-report questionnaire (Brück et al., 2011). Just as with physiological measures, brain scans are very

repressive copers
people who deny their anxiety even when they're feeling very worried; they score high on social desirability and low on self-report measures of anxiety

fMRI
functional magnetic resonance imaging, a type of brain scanning

Figure 2.3 Brain Scans and Personality

fMRI studies have identified differences in the brains of people with different personality traits.

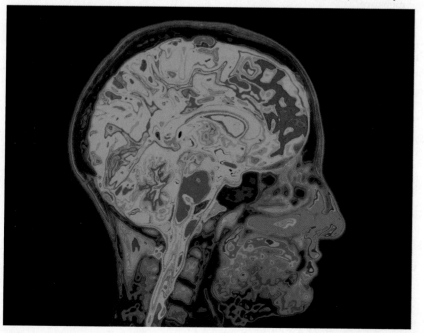

expensive. An fMRI machine costs more than $2 million, and each scan costs hundreds of dollars. As a result, research studies using this technology typically have small sample sizes, so it's sometimes hard to say if their results apply broadly.

JOURNAL PROMPT: UNDERSTANDING YOURSELF

Of the various methods for measuring personality discussed in this chapter, which would you choose if you were conducting a personality study? Why would you choose this method over the others?

The Importance of Triangulation

There is no one best way to assess an individual's personality. Self-report data are usually—but not always—the easiest, and they work well most of the time. However, the best and most careful personality research uses multiple and converging methods to triangulate personality. The term **triangulation** comes from navigation—it means using known points to determine an unknown location. In personality psychology, triangulation means using data from several different sources to hone in on that ultimate unknown: someone's personality (Figure 2.4).

triangulation
using different research methods to answer the same question, in order to be more certain of the answer

For example, if you wanted to assess someone's anxiety level, you might give her a self-report questionnaire, ask her roommate about her anxiety level (informant report), and give her a lab assessment of anxiety (physiological measure). Together, these will give you a more complete picture of her personality than any one measure.

Figure 2.4 Triangulation

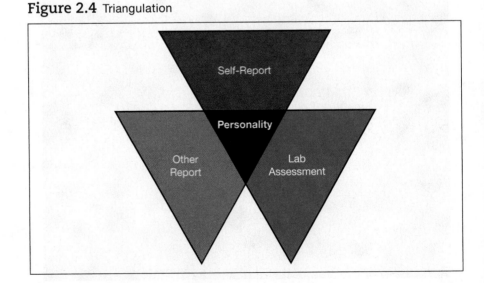

Correlational Versus Experimental Studies

LO 2.5 **Explain the correlational and experimental methods, including the advantages and disadvantages of each.**

Most personality research studies are **correlational**—they examine the relationship between two or more characteristics of people. We might see if people who live in apartments versus houses score higher on average on the Cat Person Scale or if people who score high on socially desirable responding are less likely to swear in everyday life. If you've taken a research methods class, you might remember that correlational studies have a downside: They can't prove that one thing causes another. If people who live in apartments are more likely to be cat people, maybe they are cat people because they live in an apartment and that's the only pet allowed; maybe they live in an apartment because they own a cat (if they had a dog, they'd need a house); or maybe some outside variable causes both.

As another example, consider the small positive correlation for children between having high self-esteem and getting good grades (Figure 2.5). This creates three possibilities that are not mutually exclusive (meaning one, two, or all three can be true at the same time):

> High self-esteem causes good grades.
> Good grades cause high self-esteem.
> Some third variable (say, having good parents) causes both high self-esteem and good grades.

correlational
studies that examine the relationship between two or more characteristics of people

---

Figure 2.5 Correlation Is Not (Necessarily) Causation

The three possibilities when variables are correlated: Variable A causes Variable B, Variable B causes Variable A, or Variable C causes both. In this example, high self-esteem could cause good grades, good grades could cause high self-esteem, or a third variable (like having good parents) could cause both.

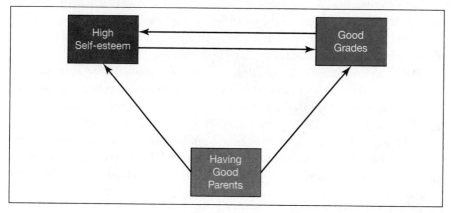

confounding variables

in a correlational study, an outside variable related to the primary variables; also known as *third variables*

Third variables are sometimes called **confounding variables**—factors that impact both of the original variables and make it look like the two are causing each other. As it turns out, third variables such as good parenting and a stable family background explain most of the correlation between high self-esteem and good grades. The rest is explained by good grades causing high self-esteem (Baumeister et al., 2003). Yet most people, when hearing about a correlation between high self-esteem and good grades, assume that high self-esteem must help kids succeed.

Here's another example: One researcher found that women who use condoms were more likely to be depressed (and thus those who didn't use condoms were less depressed; Gallup et al., 2002). The researcher concluded that semen acts as an antidepressant. But what are some possible confounding variables? Perhaps women with certain personality traits are more likely to use condoms and more likely to be depressed. Even more likely, women in committed, trusting relationships are less likely to use condoms and less likely to be depressed. The study did measure whether the women were in a relationship and its duration, but didn't examine commitment or trust. It also didn't measure the women's personality or attitudes. Unless the study can rule out these possible third variables, many people will remain skeptical that semen is a natural antidepressant. So, guys, it's a little premature to use this study as an excuse not to wear a condom—or as a pickup line ("Hey babe, you look a little depressed. Want to have unprotected sex?").

Does this mean that correlational studies are bad? No—it just means it's important to remember that reverse causation or confounding variables are always possible. Sometimes this isn't as relevant—for example, studies finding racial or gender differences in personality generally don't have to worry about the personality trait causing someone's race or gender. But confounding variables could still play a role—for example, race is correlated with family income, which might be causing the differences instead of race. Many studies also try to take confounding variables into account by statistically controlling for them. For example, studies looking at racial differences often control for family income.

Let's say we find a correlation between anxiety and overeating. We should then try to rule out confounding variables such as amount of exercise, gender, sleep, and free time. If the correlation between anxiety and eating is still there, it's more likely that anxiety is actually causing overeating.

longitudinal study

a study that collects data on the same people at more than one time

But could overeating be causing anxiety? We could try to rule out this possibility by doing a **longitudinal study** (a study that collects data on the same people at more than one time). For example, we could measure anxiety, overeating, and all of the other variables once (called Time 1) and then repeat the measures 3 months later (Time 2). If anxiety at Time 1 predicted eating at Time 2 (and, even better, the increase in eating between Time 1 and Time 2), we would feel even more confident that anxiety was causing overeating instead of the other way around.

The only way to prove causation is to do an **experiment**, considered the gold standard in research. Participants in an experiment are randomly assigned to an experimental or control condition. These two conditions are the **independent variable**, or the variable that the researcher manipulates in the experiment. Participants might receive a drug (experimental condition) or not receive a drug (control condition), or edit their Facebook page (experimental) versus tracing their route to campus on Google Maps (control). Researchers use random number tables and other techniques to ensure that respondents are equally likely to be assigned to each condition—thus the label **random assignment**. The researcher would then measure the **dependent variable**, or the outcome: whether the drug made people better, or whether editing their Facebook page increased their self-esteem. Because random chance puts participants in the experimental or control groups, confounding variables are generally ruled out. And because the independent variable is manipulated before the dependent variable is measured, we know that the cause goes from the independent variable to the dependent variable.

Here's the catch: In personality research you can't randomly assign people to have certain personalities, to grow up in certain cultures, or to be male or female. That's why so many personality studies—compared to those in other subfields of psychology—use correlational designs. However, clever researchers often will find ways to try to create an independent variable in the lab that looks a lot like personality. For example, we can't make someone have an anxious personality in an experiment (and even if we could, it wouldn't be ethical). We can, however, make people feel a little anxious and sad. For example, they can watch a sad scene from a movie and see how this temporary change in mood affects some dependent variable. If we're looking at anxiety and overeating, we might randomly assign people to watch a sad movie or a neutral movie. The dependent variable might be how many cookies people eat in a fake taste test after they watch the movie.

experiment
a study in which people are randomly assigned to conditions

independent variable
the experimental or control conditions in an experiment

random assignment
participants are equally likely to experience the experimental or control condition

dependent variable
the outcome the researcher is interested in measuring

JOURNAL PROMPT: UNDERSTANDING YOURSELF

Think of a personality-related issue you'd like to study. Would it be better to study it using the correlational or experimental method? Why?

Best Practices for Scientific Research

LO 2.6   Provide examples of the best practices for scientific research.

How do we know scientific results are accurate? Not every study is well conducted, and single studies aren't always definitive. Some studies are wrong or at least misleading (Ioannidis, 2005). To use an example from health research, this is why you hear bran muffins are the secret to health and then a year later find out that gluten (found, of course, in bran muffins) is actually bad for you. In addition, academic journals like to publish studies that find significant results, not those that show no effect. (How many times do you read a headline that says, "Scientists really don't know what food to eat"?) The one study that finds an effect is more likely to get published, while 10 other studies that don't find anything never leave the researcher's files, giving a false picture of results in the area.

As consumers of science, how do we know what to believe and what not to believe? To be convinced about a finding, there are a few things we want to see scientists do. First, research should use **sufficiently large samples**, or enough observations or people in the study to reliably detect an effect. This is what we were referring to earlier with regard to being statistically significant. When scientists only study 20 or 30 people, one extreme data point can change the results. Analyses suggest that most studies in psychology should have samples that are at least 150 or 200 people. This is good news for personality psychology because most personality studies are this large (Funder et al., 2014). Large samples aren't always available—for example, it is difficult to get 200 people with certain medical or psychological disorders into a study—but they are ideal.

Second, we shouldn't completely trust any one study. Results should **replicate**, meaning that when the same or very similar study is conducted again, the results are similar. Let's say a study found extraversion is positively correlated with having more friends on Facebook. If another study of different people found the same thing, the effect replicated. Once several replications have been done, these results can then be examined with a **meta-analysis**, or a study of studies that statistically analyzes all of the results together. Meta-analyses also provide a more precise estimate of how big an effect or correlation is, so you will know if extraversion is strongly or only weakly correlated with having more Facebook friends (Cumming, 2014).

Third, solid findings often emerge from the **many labs approach**, when different groups of researchers do the exact same study at the same time (Klein et al., 2014). When a dozen labs do the same study and come to the same conclusion, you can be pretty certain it is correct (Ioannidis et al., 2104). This method is newer to personality psychology, but will likely grow in use.

Fourth, researchers can use **open practices**, scientific practices that result in a high level of transparency (Blohowiak et al., 2014). Open practices include making research materials and data public so other scientists can check the work. If researchers are willing to be transparent, you can be more confident in their research. Some scientific journals are now labeling research with open practice badges, similar to the "green" labels found on some consumer products.

Personality scientists are on the forefront of many of these practices. Most personality studies use large samples and replicate many results (Fraley & Vazire,

sufficiently large samples
having enough observations or people in a study to reliably detect an effect

replicate
when the same or a very similar study is conducted again, the results are similar

meta-analysis
a study that statistically analyzes the results of many studies on the same topic

many labs approach
when different groups of researchers do the exact same study at the same time

open practices
scientific practices that result in a high level of transparency, such as making data or research materials available to other researchers

2014). Many studies mentioned in this book are from meta-analyses or large national samples. In other cases, though, the results are from single studies. These are often the best results available—perhaps it's the only study so far looking at a particular topic—but the findings are

necessarily not as robust. New and better data might find something different. That is what makes doing science both exciting and frustrating—and why in a few years you shouldn't be surprised if gluten-free has turned out to be just another diet fad and the new thing is low-carb.

Some academic journals use badges like these to show that the research in the article meets certain requirements for open research practices.

JOURNAL PROMPT: UNDERSTANDING YOURSELF

You just read a news article that claims narcissists spend five times longer each day looking at themselves in the mirror than the average person. As a smart consumer of science, what are three questions you would ask to better understand this research finding?

Concluding Thoughts

Our knowledge of personality improves when research studies use valid and reliable measures, employ different methods, and adopt the best practices for scientific research. If researchers find similar results when using both correlational studies and experimental studies, control for confounds, use several different measures of personality, use longitudinal methods, have large samples, and replicate results, we can gain confidence in the findings. Our knowledge of personality—what it is, how to measure it, what causes it—grows stronger as each study adds a piece of the puzzle. As you learned in this chapter, one of the most important pieces of that puzzle is using personality measures that are reliable and valid. If a measure isn't consistent (low reliability) or doesn't measure what it should (low validity), the pursuit of knowledge is over before it began. In contrast, a reliable and valid measure can be used repeatedly to identify how those with certain personality traits behave and react. That's the power of a good personality assessment: It helps us understand ourselves and others.

Learning Objective Summaries

LO 2.1 Explain how personality is assessed using self-report questionnaires.

Self-report measures often use Likert scales with reverse-scored items to minimize the effect of the acquiescence response set. Socially desirable responding is a concern in self-report measures. Correlations help us understand the relationship between two variables, either positive or negative.

LO 2.2 Understand how to determine if a scale is reliable and valid.

Personality scales must be reliable (giving a consistent answer) and valid (measuring what they are supposed to measure; e.g., predicting relevant behavior or correlating with related measures).

LO 2.3 Learn how to apply statistics to personality measurement, and define social desirability bias.

To understand how your score compares to others', we compare your score to the mean score of the norm sample. A percentile score tells you what percent of the norm sample scores lower than you. The first scale you took measures the personality trait of social desirability, or the tendency to want to look good in the eyes of others.

LO 2.4 Describe alternative ways of measuring personality and the importance of triangulation.

Alternatives to self-report personality questionnaires include informant reports (others reporting on someone's personality), structured clinical interviews, direct measurements of behavior, archival or life outcomes data, projective tests (where someone responds to a picture or inkblot), and physiological measures such as blood pressure measurements. Obtaining data using more than one of these methods is known as triangulation.

LO 2.5 Explain the correlational and experimental methods, including the advantages and disadvantages of each.

Correlational studies examine how two variables relate to each other; they can measure naturally occurring variables but cannot determine causation. Experimental studies can determine causation but cannot always be used because not all variables can be artificially manipulated.

LO 2.6 Provide examples of the best practices for scientific research.

To get as close as possible to scientific truth, it is best to collect sufficiently large samples, to replicate findings, to combine the results from many researchers, and to make data and methods publicly available through open practices.

Key Terms

personality assessment, p. 22
self-report measure, p. 22
socially desirable
    responding, p. 22
reverse-scored items, p. 24
acquiescence response set, p. 24

Likert scale, p. 24
correlation, p. 26
positive correlations, p. 26
negative correlations, p. 26
null correlation, p. 27
statistically significant, p. 27

reliability, p. 28
internal reliability, p. 28
Cronbach's alpha, p. 28
test–retest reliability, p. 29
validity, p. 30
face validity, p. 30

predictive validity, p. 30
convergent validity, p. 30
discriminant validity, p. 31
Barnum effect, p. 33
descriptive statistics, p. 34
mean, p. 34
median, p. 34
mode, p. 34
normal distribution, p. 35
standard deviation (SD), p. 35

percentile score, p. 35
informant reports, p. 38
projective tests, p. 40
intercoder reliability, p. 40
physiological measures, p. 40
repressive copers, p. 41
fMRI, p. 41
triangulation, p. 42
correlational, p. 43
confounding variables, p. 44

longitudinal study, p. 44
experiment, p. 45
independent variable, p. 45
random assignment, p. 45
dependent variable, p. 45
sufficiently large samples, p. 46
replicate, p. 46
meta-analysis, p. 46
many labs approach, p. 46
open practices, p. 46

Essay Questions

1. What parts of your personality would be difficult to capture with a self-report questionnaire? Would any of the alternative methods do a better job?

2. Why is it important for personality scales to be reliable and valid? What would happen if researchers, individuals, and businesses relied on scales that were not reliable and valid?

3. A researcher finds a correlation between going to religious services and better health. What are the three possibilities for causation in that study? What are some possible third or confounding variables?

Part II
Approaches to Understanding Personality

Personality is big—deep, complex, multifaceted. It's not just one thing, but many. More than any area of psychology, personality seeks to explain the whole person, and how she or he got that way.

To do that, we draw from many theories and areas of study, both classic and modern. We begin in Chapter 3 with the Big Five personality traits, the system used in the vast majority of recent research papers in personality. The Big Five allows researchers to capture a broad but focused array of traits about someone, and they can also help you understand yourself and others in a deeper, more informed way. Chapter 4 explores the genetic and biological underpinnings of personality, from twin studies to hormones. Chapter 5 poses the fascinating question of how we understand ourselves. Do you like yourself? How much do you change your behavior from one situation to the next?

Chapter 6 covers classic theories on the deeper recesses of the mind, such as Freud's idea of the unconscious, how people use defense mechanisms to deal with uncomfortable thoughts, and how certain themes echo throughout classic stories. Chapter 7 asks why we get out of bed in the morning—what motivates us, and how much does that differ across people? Chapter 8 explores the role of outside influences on our behavior, how we do what we're rewarded for and avoid what we're punished for, and how we learn to associate otherwise unrelated things.

At the end of these chapters, you'll have a solid understanding of all the ways personality affects us—and why.

Chapter 3
The Big Five Personality Traits

 ## Learning Objectives

LO 3.1 Name and define the Big Five personality traits.

LO 3.2 Describe the behaviors, attitudes, and characteristics of people high and low in each of the Big Five traits.

LO 3.3 Explain how the Big Five traits were developed and how they are used to help us better understand ourselves.

The tornado spun just a few hundred yards away. "Back up! Back up!" yelled Reed Timmer, taking video of the giant twister as the car sped away in reverse. A meteorology student and veteran storm chaser, Reed knew that he and his friends Jim and Stefan were too close to the tornado, but he was thrilled with the footage and the experience. "It was about feeling that tornado's energy, that hyperfocused, tornadic might that I could totally relate to," he wrote later.

Stefan reacted differently. Sitting in the back of the car, he began dry heaving and shaking uncontrollably. In the midst of a panic attack, he was breathing rapidly, sweat dripping down his face. "Go, go, go!" he pleaded. Jim backed the car away in reverse, eventually turning around to drive away from the tornado. Even after they were safely out of the tornado's path, Stefan was terrified, his face ghost-white.

"Escaping a tornado," Reed wrote. "What kind of person thinks of doing that? Stefan's breakdown reminded me that I lived in a parallel universe to most people. A very foreign parallel universe" (Timmer, 2010). That parallel universe Reed refers to is, in a word, his personality. It's why Reed gets energized chasing tornadoes and Stefan freaks out.

You can probably think of many other differences among people that involve personality. Some people worry a lot; others don't. Some people thrive on conflict and love to argue, but others would rather avoid conflict and lose the argument. Some people make their beds in the morning and organize their to-do list with five different highlight colors, and some can barely find a pair of clean underwear under the mountain of empty pizza boxes in their apartment.

These aspects of personality are called **traits**—relatively stable tendencies of individuals. But which traits are the most important? How can we possibly describe someone's personality in just a few words, or with just a few concepts?

traits
relatively stable tendencies of individuals

Reed Timmer's unflappable, sensation-seeking personality is well suited to chasing tornadoes.

Personality psychologists have struggled with these issues for more than a century. Many questionnaires have tried to be a comprehensive measure of personality traits, such as the 16PF, the Multidimensional Personality Questionnaire, and the Eysenck Personality Questionnaire (Cattell et al., 1970; Eysenck & Eysenck, 1975; Tellegen & Waller, 2008). Within the past two decades, researchers have begun to agree on five comprehensive personality domains that incorporate many of the traits measured by earlier questionnaires. These are called the **Big Five** (or the *Five-Factor Model*; John et al., 2008). The Big Five and the Five-Factor Model are slightly different theoretically, but here we refer to both with the one label *Big Five*. We explore more on the origins of the Big Five later in the chapter; for now, we focus on how the Big Five captures personality. First, you'll take a Big Five measure to see how you score.

Big Five

Five comprehensive personality domains: extraversion, agreeableness, conscientiousness, neuroticism, and openness to experience

TAKE the Questionnaire in **REVEL**

Questionnaire 3.1 IPIP

Interactive

Please answer all the questions.

1. Worry about things.

○ Strongly Agree
○ Moderately Agree
○ Neither Agree nor Disagree
○ Moderately Disagree
○ Strongly Disagree

2. Get angry easily.

○ Strongly Agree
○ Moderately Agree
○ Neither Agree nor Disagree
○ Moderately Disagree
○ Strongly Disagree

Previous   Next

What Traits Make up the Big Five?

LO 3.1 Name and define the Big Five personality traits.

If you've ever seen online dating profiles, you've probably noticed that people describe their personalities using adjectives—*friendly, caring, hardworking, curious, confident, kind, thoughtful, fearless,* or *ambitious*. Notice these are all positive adjectives—after all, it's online dating, where everyone has a great personality!

Instead of having people choose words to describe themselves, personality measures instead ask people to rate themselves on a list of selected items. Try it below (see Table 3.1): Rate yourself on a scale of 1 (*not at all like me*) to 5 (*very much like me*) on each adjective, considering how you typically behave, think, or feel.

If everyone you knew filled out this questionnaire, you'd notice that people would differ. Some people would rate themselves high on "assertive" (say, a 5), and others would use a lower rating (a 2). And people who scored high on "organized" would likely score high on similar adjectives ("detail oriented"). In

Table 3.1 Personality Trait Self-Ratings

	Stressed	Talkative	Creative	Sympathetic	Hardworking
Rating:					
	Energetic	Happy	Manipulative	Organized	Traditional
Rating:					
	Modest	Impulsive	Curious	Anxious	Assertive
Rating:					
	Detail oriented	Trusting	Attention seeking	Open-minded	Angry
Rating:					
	Preferring routine	Responsible	Calm	Shy	Honest
Rating:					

the chart in Table 3.2, items with the same color go together—in large samples of people, responses to these items are highly correlated with each other. If you rated yourself high on "open minded" in blue, you're more likely to rate yourself high on "creative."

Some of the adjectives are reverse scored (marked with an *r*), which means they are negatively correlated with the other traits with the same color: A high score on one usually corresponds to a low score on the other. For example, if you rate yourself high on "anxious," you'll probably rate yourself low on "calm." If you rate yourself high on "talkative," you'll probably rate yourself low on "shy." These items are negatively correlated.

The five colors in Table 3.2 correspond to the Big Five: extraversion (E), agreeableness (A), conscientiousness (C), neuroticism (N), and openness to experience (O). Rearranged, they spell OCEAN or CANOE. The items of the same color correlate highly with each other (either positively or negatively),

Table 3.2 What Your Personality Trait Self-Ratings Mean

Rating:	Stressed	Talkative	Creative	Sympathetic	Hardworking
Rating:	Energetic	Fearless (r)	Manipulative (r)	Organized	Traditional (r)
Rating:	Modest	Impulsive (r)	Curious	Anxious	Assertive
Rating:	Detail oriented	Trusting	Attention seeking	Open-minded	Angry
Rating:	Preferring routine (r)	Responsible	Calm (r)	Shy (r)	Honest

Extraversion

being outgoing and experiencing positive emotions; opposite: introversion or shyness

Agreeableness

caring for others and getting along with other people; opposite: being argumentative, combative, and self-centered

Conscientiousness

organized, ambitious, and self-controlled; opposite: being messy, unmotivated, and impulsive

Neuroticism

negative emotions such as worry and anger; opposite: calmness and emotional stability

Openness to experience

being interested in trying new activities and playing with new ideas, beliefs, and value systems; opposite: being conventional and less comfortable with change

and the items that are different colors do not. They cluster into five factors: the Big Five.

So what do these actually mean? **Extraversion** (yellow in Figure 3.1) means being outgoing and experiencing positive emotions; its opposite is introversion or shyness. **Agreeableness** (green) means caring for others and getting along with other people; its opposite is argumentative, combative, and self-centered. **Conscientiousness** (red) means organized, ambitious, and self-controlled; its opposite is messy, unmotivated, and impulsive. **Neuroticism** (blue) covers negative emotions such as worry and anger; its opposite is calmness and emotional stability. **Openness to experience** (orange) means being interested in trying new activities and playing with new ideas, beliefs, and value systems; its opposite is being conventional and less comfortable with change.

These five traits don't capture everything about human personality, of course. In later chapters, we'll tell you about other important ways that people differ from each other, such as self-esteem, achievement motivation, needs and goals, and attachment style. Nevertheless, much of the modern research on personality focuses on the Big Five, so it makes sense to start with these traits (see Figure 3.1).

Figure 3.1 The Big Five Personality Traits

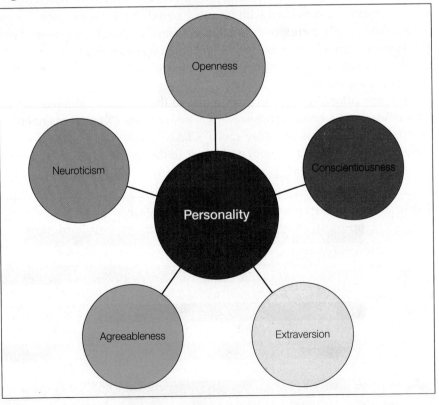

Watch THE BASICS: PERSONALITY THEORIES: TRAIT

WATCH
the video in
REVEL

The Facets of the Big Five

Another way to understand the Big Five is to break them down into more specific components, often called **facets** (Costa & McCrae, 1992; Maples et al., 2014). Because the Big Five are, well, big, they include several subcategories of traits. Although almost all researchers acknowledge that facets are important, the specific facets vary. Here is one system:

facets
more specific components of the Big Five, subcategories of Big Five traits

1. *Extraversion*: friendliness, gregariousness, assertiveness, activity level, excitement seeking, cheerfulness
2. *Agreeableness*: trust, morality, altruism, cooperation, modesty, sympathy
3. *Conscientiousness*: self-efficacy, orderliness, dutifulness, achievement-striving, self-discipline, cautiousness
4. *Neuroticism*: anxiety, anger, depression, self-consciousness, immoderation, vulnerability
5. *Openness to experience*: imagination, artistic interests, emotionality, adventurousness, intellect, liberalism

Knowing the facets of each broader personality domain helps you see the diversity of characteristics within each larger grouping. For example, people usually think of extraversion as being outgoing and talkative. But that's only one component—extraverted people also tend to be assertive, happy risk takers.

JOURNAL PROMPT: UNDERSTANDING YOURSELF

Describe a friend, family member, or public figure who you think is particularly high or low in one of the Big Five traits. How is he or she a prototypical example of someone with this personality trait?

Remembering the facets can also help you avoid common misunderstandings about the traits. Students often mistakenly think that conscientiousness means consideration for others—but as you can see here, it instead refers to someone who is organized and hardworking. Consideration for others is agreeableness, which is just what it sounds like—someone who would rather agree than argue.

How did you score on the Big Five? Your percentile score will tell you how your score compares to the norm sample on each of the five traits. This is your personality profile according to the most prominent and well-researched model of personality available today. (For more on how these scores are calculated, see the Science of Personality feature.)

EXPLORE
in
REVEL

The Science of Personality UNDERSTANDING HOW PEOPLE DIFFER: THE EXAMPLE OF EXTRAVERSION

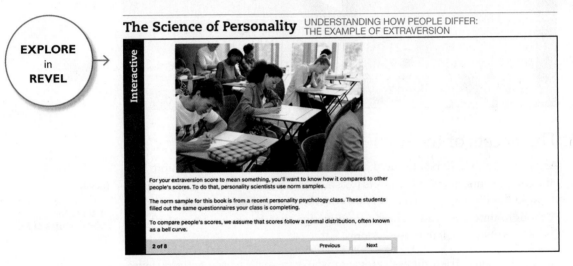

For your extraversion score to mean something, you'll want to know how it compares to other people's scores. To do that, personality scientists use norm samples.

The norm sample for this book is from a recent personality psychology class. These students filled out the same questionnaires your class is completing.

To compare people's scores, we assume that scores follow a normal distribution, often known as a bell curve.

2 of 8   Previous   Next

Distinct Categories or a Continuum?

Most people don't score at the extremes of traits—only a few people are 100% extra-verted or 100% introverted—so most score somewhere in the middle (Figure 3.2). For that reason, it's better to think of traits as a continuum instead of two categories. Although labels such as *extravert* and *introvert* can be useful, they leave behind a lot of important information. Someone who scores at the 40th percentile on Extraversion, for example, is technically an introvert, but not as much as someone who scores at the 5th percentile. In research, the whole score is usually used, similar to the percentile you got for each of the Big Five when you got your own results. We use labels such as *extravert* in this book for the sake of simplicity, but keep in mind that the label captures a wide range of above-average extraversion scores from the 51st to the 99th percentile. In general, research results about extraverts will apply even more strongly to someone with a very high score (the 99th percentile) than to someone with a merely above-average score (the 51st percentile).

Students often wonder if scoring high on one Big Five trait makes it more or less likely they will score high (or low) on another. For example, are introverts also more neurotic, on average? Yes, they are: Neurotic people are less extraverted, less agreeable, and less conscientious. Extraverts are higher in agreeableness, conscientiousness, and openness to experience. However, this is not always the case—these correlations are fairly weak, so it's definitely possible to be a neurotic extravert or a conscientious introvert (Costa & McCrae, 1992).

Figure 3.2 A Normal Distribution

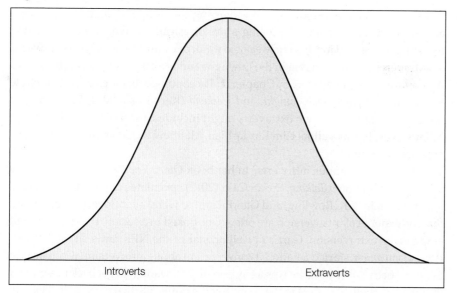

Introverts   Extraverts

What Do the Big Five Traits Really Mean?

LO 3.2 **Describe the behaviors, attitudes, and characteristics of people high and low in each of the Big Five traits.**

It's fun to know if you're an extravert or an introvert, neurotic or not, but what does that really mean? How do people with each trait behave, and how does it impact their lives? These are important questions, and this section explores each of the Big Five traits in more detail.

As you read, remember that there's no "right" or "wrong" personality—each trait has upsides and downsides. Traits have trade-offs. The agreeable person might be a better coworker, but might be paid less because he is too nice to ask for a raise. The neurotic person might be anxious a lot, but this might protect her from being a knucklehead who chases tornadoes. This trade-off is sometimes tough to remember, as some of the Big Five trait labels aren't exactly neutral (e.g., neuroticism, openness to experience).

A couple of other things to keep in mind. First, research studies are based on averages. Not everyone with each trait will behave exactly like the average. For example, not every introvert will stay in the corner at a party, but on average introverts are more likely to stay in the corner than extraverts. Second, scales with the same name can still have some small differences. For example, three different measures of extraversion should correlate, but they will not be exactly the same. With that in mind, let's explore more about each trait in the Big Five.

Extraversion

Extraversion includes enjoying and preferring the company of others (vs. being alone), wanting to be a leader, being more physically active, and experiencing more happiness and joy. It's fairly easy to think of examples of famous extraverts, as extraverts are comfortable in the limelight and are often "the life of the party." As you might remember from Chapter 1, Facebook posts by extraverts include words such as *party, love, tonight,* and *weekend* (Kern et al., 2014; Park et al., in press). A list of well-known extraverts might include Russell Brand, Bill Clinton, Miley Cyrus, Jimmy Fallon, Kim Kardashian, Matthew McConaughey, Katy Perry, and Donald Trump.

What about famous introverts? In her book *Quiet: The Power of Introverts in a World That Can't Stop Talking,* Susan Cain (2012) speculates that Charles Darwin, Albert Einstein, J. K. Rowling, and Gandhi are (or were) all introverts. Cain argues that the benefits of introversion are often overlooked in a society that rewards and emphasizes extraversion. Garrison Keillor, star of the NPR radio show *A Prairie Home Companion,* started a national conversation about introversion when he quit his show because, he said, he was a shy person and wanted to get back to a quieter life. He eventually returned to the show, but the public life that came with it clearly made him uncomfortable. Dave Chappelle, who skyrocketed to fame with his sketch comedy show in the early 2000s, abruptly quit because the fame and pressure was too much. Taking a trip to South Africa at the height of his success in the U.S., Chapelle said, "Coming here, I don't have the distractions of fame. It quiets the ego down. I'm interested in the kind of person I've got to become. I want to be well rounded and the industry is a place of extremes. I want to be well balanced."

Like Jimmy Fallon, many extraverts would love to get paid to talk all day. *Harry Potter* series author J. K. Rowling, an introvert, created a magical world for her readers.

Most introverts are not hermits who isolate themselves. Instead, they prefer the company of close friends and family to the (over)stimulation of large gatherings. Personality psychologist Hans Eysenck (Eysenck & Eysenck, 1967) theorized that introverts are highly sensitive to stimuli, which causes them to prefer quiet and solitude. In contrast, extraverts seek stimulation and excitement, similar to Reed Timmer, the tornado chaser. This might be linked to extraverts' higher levels of dopamine, a brain chemical we explore more in the next chapter (Depue & Collins, 1999; Wacker et al., 2006). Extraverts are also more sensitive to rewards and experience more positive feelings when they have the chance to earn rewards (Smillie et al., 2012).

You might wonder exactly how we know these things. Smillie et al.'s (2012) study, and others you read about in this chapter, are based on large numbers of people—at least 100 and sometimes more than 10,000—who completed a Big Five personality questionnaire and provided data on another characteristic (say, a measure of positive emotion or the language on their Facebook page). The researchers then analyze the data to see if Extraversion is correlated with these other variables. For example, in the Smillie et al. study, extraversion was positively correlated with positive emotion among 252 U.S. university students. Remember that correlations aren't perfect: this correlation means that *more* extraverts (not all) will experience more positive emotions. There are exceptions to the general rule.

Extraversion is linked to better mental health. Extraverts are less likely to suffer from mood and anxiety disorders (Kotov et al., 2010) and most personality disorders (Samuel & Widiger, 2008). They are more likely to experience happiness, well-being, and positive moods (Argyle & Lu, 1990; Lucas et al., 2008; Pavot et al., 1990). Most of these benefits occur not from extraversion itself but because extraverts are better at creating and maintaining the good social relationships linked to physical and mental health (Roberts et al., 2007).

Other people usually rate extraverts as more likable and popular (e.g., van der Linden et al., 2010). Extraverts are also more likely to emerge as leaders (Judge et al., 2002), especially as transformational leaders who inspire, challenge, and motivate others (Bono & Judge, 2004). This makes sense given that assertiveness (sometimes called *dominance*) is one of the facets of extraversion.

JOURNAL PROMPT: UNDERSTANDING YOURSELF

Think about your scores on each of the Big Five. Do your scores line up with the correlates discussed in this chapter? For example, if you are high in Openness to Experience, are you also a political liberal on social issues? Do you think your level of conscientiousness predicts your work performance?

In the workplace, extraversion is associated with better performance in jobs such as sales that require interacting with many different people (Barrick & Mount, 1991). For professions that require quiet and solitary work much of the time, such as computer programming or plumbing, extraversion isn't necessarily an advantage and might even be a disadvantage. For example, extraverts have more financial problems such as credit card debt, perhaps because they are more focused on financing their social lives than reining in their spending (Brown & Taylor, 2014).

Many jobs require both extraversion and introversion. Trial lawyers draw on their extraversion when speaking in the courtroom and their introversion when writing a brief or an opening argument. Professors switch between the extraverted task of teaching large classes to the more introverted task of writing a textbook or a scientific journal article. You probably do the same as a student, behaving as an introvert when you're reading and as an extravert when you're giving a class presentation. Class presentations may be difficult for many introverts, but extraverts often find them energizing. Of course, most introverts can be extraverted when they need to (say, a job interview), just as most extraverts can be introverted when necessary (say, when reading).

Extraversion may affect how you study. If you're highly extraverted, sitting and reading quietly might not be stimulating enough for you—you probably play music and check in on Facebook frequently. An introvert is less likely to multitask—or at least multitask as much. Extraverts perform better with a high level of background noise; introverts do better with a lower level (Geen, 1984). So your extraversion score might predict how you prefer to study, whether that's at home with as little noise as possible (low extraversion) or in a busy coffee shop while listening to music (high extraversion).

Do some places have more extraverts than others? Americans have a reputation around the world for being very outgoing and optimistic, and sure enough, Americans score above average in extraversion (Allik & McCrae, 2004; Terracciano et al., 2005). To explore differences among regions within the U.S., researchers analyzed the responses of 619,397 Americans who completed the Big Five

Extraverts are more likely to study while listening to music.

Figure 3.3 Extraversion in the United States

Residents of the Midwest and South score higher in extraversion.

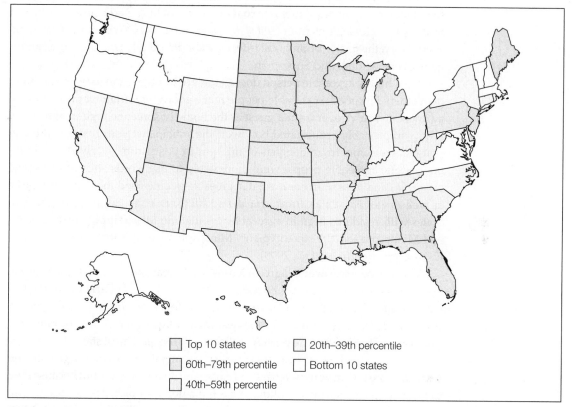

☐ Top 10 states   ☐ 20th–39th percentile

☐ 60th–79th percentile   ☐ Bottom 10 states

☐ 40th–59th percentile

SOURCE: Rentfrow et al. (2008)

online. The residents of North Dakota, Wisconsin, and the District of Columbia scored the highest in extraversion, while residents of Maryland, New Hampshire, and Alaska scored the lowest. The residents of states higher in extraversion were more likely to go to bars and to club meetings—which makes sense, as these are activities extraverts enjoy (Rentfrow et al., 2008; see Figure 3.3).

Agreeableness

Agreeable people trust others and are sympathetic to others' needs and feelings. They prefer cooperation to competition and tend to be honest, forthright, humble, self-effacing, and compliant. The opposite of agreeableness, which has been labeled *antagonism* or *disagreeableness*, includes skepticism, cynicism, dishonesty, manipulativeness, grandiosity, aggressiveness, egocentricism, and callousness.

Can you think of some public figures high in agreeableness? Princess Diana was known for her empathy for the sick and suffering and for being a warm and loving mother. In the *Divergent* series of books and movies, the factions Amity and Abnegation would both score high in Agreeableness: Amity specializes in smoothing over any possible conflicts, and Abnegation members devote themselves to helping others. Other fictional examples include Ned Flanders from *The Simpsons*, Frodo Baggins from *Lord of the Rings*, Luke Skywalker, Santa Claus, the Tooth Fairy, the Easter Bunny (the trifecta of childhood gift-, money-, and candy-giving benefactors), and Superman.

But a highly agreeable person doesn't have to be Superman (or give candy) to help others feel good. Agreeable people make good friends and caring romantic partners. If you've ever been a guest at the home of someone high in agreeableness, you probably appreciated how well she anticipated your needs and made you feel welcome. In an analysis of millions of posts from nearly 70,000 Facebook users, agreeable people were more likely to use words such as *thank you*, *wonderful*, and *blessed*. In contrast, disagreeable people used more swear words, as well as words such as *drunk*, *stupid*, and *kill* (Kern et al., 2014; see Figure 3.4). States with residents high in agreeableness include Mississippi, North Dakota, and Minnesota—so the stereotype of "Minnesota nice" is apparently more than just a myth (Rentfrow et al., 2008).

Famous people lower in agreeableness—both real and fictional—include Sue Sylvester on *Glee*, Frank Underwood on *House of Cards*, Vee Parker on *Orange is the New Black*, Jay Pritchett on *Modern Family*, the Joker in *Batman*, Lord Voldemort from the *Harry Potter* books and movies, Osama Bin Laden, Tony Soprano, Mr. Burns from *The Simpsons*, ex-president Richard Nixon, and most stars of reality TV shows, especially the *Real Housewives* series. The members of the *Divergent* faction of Candor are low in agreeableness—not necessarily out of spite, but because they say exactly what they are thinking, even if it's not very nice. That example also shows one of the upsides of low agreeableness: If you *really* want to know if your new outfit looks good on you, ask a friend low in agreeableness.

Figure 3.4 Word Clouds for Agreeableness

Words used more often on Facebook by people low (left) and high (right) in agreeableness.

SOURCE: Kern et al. (2014)

Unfortunately, low agreeableness is also correlated with antisocial behavior. Disagreeable people are more likely to involve themselves in crime (Miller & Lynam, 2001), acts of aggression (Jones et al., 2011), risky sex (Hoyle et al., 2000), drug abuse (Kotov et al., 2010), and gambling (MacLaren et al., 2011). Low agreeableness is also linked to psychological disorders involving a lack of caring for others, such as psychopathy, often defined as not having a conscience (Miller et al., 2001). Of course, not everyone who scores low in agreeableness is antisocial—the correlations between agreeableness and antisocial behavior are statistically significant but not enormous (around .25–.40, typical for most personality traits predicting behavior).

U.S. states whose residents are lower in agreeableness (such as Alaska, the District of Columbia, Nevada, and Wyoming) have significantly higher murder and robbery rates and lower life expectancies (Rentfrow et al., 2008; see Figure 3.5). The conclusion: Grumpy people aren't nice to their neighbors, but at least they will die sooner.

Why are disagreeable people prone to crime and other risky behaviors? They may have a **hostile attribution bias**—basically, they see the worst in people (Jensen-Campbell & Graziano, 2001; Miller et al., 2008). Imagine you're driving on the highway and someone cuts you off. Did she do that because she didn't see you, or because she's a jerk? Someone with a hostile attribution bias would assume that the other driver was a jerk. A really antagonistic person might think the other driver was purposely trying to upset him—he would assume that the other person was hostile and antagonistic, much like himself (Srivastava et al., 2010).

This negative view of the world doesn't come out of nowhere; sadly, it is sometimes the result of childhood abuse, neglect, and bullying (Jensen-Campbell et al., 2002; Miller et al., 2010). Someone treated badly in the past expects to be treated badly in the future. Perhaps as a defense, antagonistic people are more likely to respond to ambiguous situations with aggression (Jensen-Campbell & Graziano, 2001). Disagreeable people also have more difficulty managing their anger and continue to focus on their angry and aggressive feelings and behaviors (Meier et al., 2006; Ode & Robinson, 2009). They are also less likely to forgive others for perceived transgressions (Strelan, 2007) and are more interested in seeking revenge (Lee & Ashton, 2012).

However, being a little disagreeable isn't all bad. Disagreeable men earn more money (and so do disagreeable women, but not by as much; Judge et al., 2012). American presidents tend to be less agreeable than the average American. When historians rated American presidents, those perceived as the greatest—including Franklin D. Roosevelt and Theodore Roosevelt—were also rated as lower in agreeable traits (Rubenzer et al., 2000).

Coach Sylvester from *Glee*: not an agreeable person.

hostile attribution bias

the tendency to see others as hostile and aggressive

Figure 3.5 Agreeableness in the United States

Residents of the U.S. Midwest and South score higher in agreeableness on average.

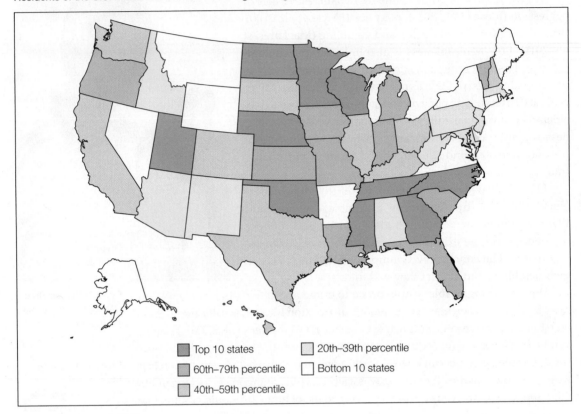

■ Top 10 states	☐ 20th–39th percentile
■ 60th–79th percentile	☐ Bottom 10 states
■ 40th–59th percentile	

SOURCE: Rentfrow et al. (2008)

Disagreeableness can also motivate people, especially when it's spiked with humor. Robb Wolf, author of the diet and lifestyle book *The Paleo Solution* (2011), is a good example. Wolf has no tolerance for whiners and repeatedly addresses readers as "Buttercup." In one blog post he wrote, "Are you getting 8–9 hrs of sleep per night in a pitch dark room? I do not give two squirts about your excuse here! DO IT. Inadequate sleep [prevents] fat loss. And give me a break! I'm asking you to SLEEP! How much easier can I make this?" More than likely, his advice wouldn't be as helpful, or as funny, if he were nicer about it.

Conscientiousness

Conscientiousness involves willpower: being able to delay gratification, consider potential consequences before acting, and work hard toward goals. Conscientious people are organized and diligent and can usually get work done despite

Figure 3.6 Word Clouds for Conscientiousness

Words used more often on Facebook by people low (left) and high (right) in conscientiousness.

Low conscientiousness   High conscientiousness

SOURCE: Kern et al. (2014)

"If you're my lab partner, you'd better practice your spells before class. Or I will turn you into a frog." *Harry Potter* character Hermione Granger is highly conscientious.

distractions, frustration, or boredom. People low in conscientiousness are impulsive, easily distracted, less ambitious, unorganized, and more likely to give up easily. In the study of 70,000 Facebook users, conscientious people were more likely to use words such as *ready*, *work*, and *thankful*. Less conscientous people used more swear words, as well as words such as *Youtube*, *Pokemon*, and *bored* (Kern et al., 2014; see Figure 3.6).

Jerry Seinfeld—or at least his character on *Seinfeld*—is high on conscientiousness: He is very fastidious and keeps his apartment clean and organized. In contrast, his low-conscientiousness neighbor Kramer constructs a hot tub in his apartment, never seems to have a job, and apparently rarely combs his hair. Other examples of high-conscientiousness characters include Sheldon on *Big Bang Theory* (who chooses a place to sit very carefully) and Hermione Granger from the *Harry Potter* books and movies (known for following the rules and always doing the assigned reading). Low-conscientiousness characters include Lena Dunham's character Hannah on *Girls*, who rarely notices that her clothes don't fit, Homer Simpson from *The Simpsons* (unmotivated at work and continually covered in donut crumbs), and PigPen from *Peanuts* (perpetually followed by a cloud of dirt).

Like those low in agreeableness, people low in conscientiousness are more likely to abuse drugs and alcohol and engage in crime, risky sex, and

Figure 3.7 Conscientiousness in the United States

States in the middle of the country score higher on conscientiousness.

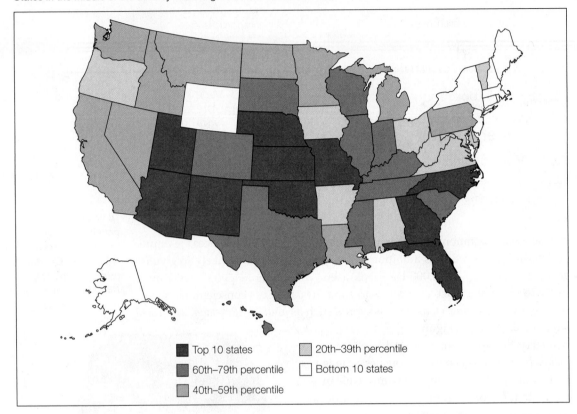

Top 10 states

60th–79th percentile

40th–59th percentile

20th–39th percentile

Bottom 10 states

SOURCE: Rentfrow et al. (2008)

gambling (Hoyle et al., 2000; Kotov et al., 2010; MacLaren et al., 2011; Miller & Lynam, 2001). These correlations are not perfect—not everyone who, for example, abuses drugs is low in conscientiousness. The correlation between these two variables is .43. Using a statistical conversion, that means that 72% of people who abuse drugs are low in conscientiousness (and 28% are not). However, because only a small percentage of people abuse drugs, most people low in conscientiousness do *not* abuse drugs. Low conscientiousness is also linked to mental disorders involving a lack of caring for others, such as psychopathy (Decuyper et al., 2009; Samuel & Widiger, 2008).

Highly conscientious people enjoy better mental health (Kotov et al., 2010) and physical health, including living longer (Bogg & Roberts, 2004; Kern & Friedman, 2008; Roberts et al., 2005). Greater willpower motivates these individuals to exercise, follow an appropriate diet, avoid drug abuse, and work hard to avoid stressful financial problems (Atherton et al., 2014; Lodi-Smith et al., 2010). For example, conscientious people are more likely to eat vegetable salads and are less likely to be overweight (Keller & Siegrist, 2015). Conscientiousness may also benefit health because it helps people manage negative emotions (Javaris et al., 2012). Perhaps as a result, conscientious people are more likely to have stable marriages (Claxton et al., 2012; Tucker et al., 1998).

Of the Big Five, conscientiousness is the strongest predictor of academic and professional success. Conscientious people are organized, ambitious, and motivated. Highly conscientious people earn better grades in college (McAbee & Oswald, 2013; Vedel, 2014) and perform better at work (Barrick et al., 2001). Although one trait cannot capture all aspects of workplace success, conscientiousness may be the most important quality to seek in employees.

U.S. states high in conscientiousness include New Mexico, North Carolina, and Georgia; low-conscientiousness states are Alaska, Maine, and Hawaii (see Figure 3.7). The residents of high-conscientiousness states are more religious and are less likely to make their living in the arts and entertainment industry (Rentfrow et al., 2008).

Neuroticism

Neuroticism is the tendency to experience negative emotions such as anger, depression, anxiety, shame, and self-consciousness. Highly neurotic people may experience negative emotions both more frequently and more intensely. Stefan, who had a panic attack during the tornado chase, was clearly higher in neuroticism than Reed, who thrived on the excitement. (Though given how close the tornado was, Reed probably had the more abnormal reaction!) In the study of Facebook users, neurotic people used words such as *depressed*, *lonely*, and *sick of*, whereas those low in neuroticism used words such as *workout*, *success*, and *basketball* (Kern et al., 2014; see Figure 3.8).

Most of the characters on the TV show *Girls* are high in neuroticism, as they are usually worried about something—especially Hannah, who worries when she has a job and when she doesn't, and worries about her relationship with her boyfriend even when it's going well. On *NCIS*, forensic scientist Abby neurotically worries any time one of the agents gets in the least bit of trouble, and tackles each with a hug when they return safely. Mothers often get the rap for being neurotic, a perception parodied in the *Simpsons* episode featuring Marge's favorite magazine, *Fretful Mother* (sample story: "Why Baby Can't Read"). Rex, the Tyrannosaurus toy from the *Toy Story* movies, seems quite neurotic. When his owner Andy is opening birthday presents, Rex says, "What if Andy gets another dinosaur? A mean one? I just don't think I can take that kind of rejection!" When Rex practices his roar, he says, "I'm going for fearsome here but I just don't feel it. I think I'm coming off as annoying."

Figure 3.8 Word Clouds for Neuroticism

Words used more often on Facebook by people low (left) and high (right) in neuroticism.

Low neuroticism

High neuroticism

SOURCE: Kern et al. (2014)

"What if I'm not a real dinosaur? And why does my butt say, 'Made in China'?" Rex seems high in neuroticism.

James Bond would probably score particularly low on neuroticism; even in the most dangerous of situations, he seems to experience little fear or anxiety. Even when his life is in danger, he can shoot a gun accurately, play high-stakes poker, drive at high speeds, and seduce the most attractive women. Sure enough, studies find that people low in neuroticism perform better under pressure than those high in neuroticism; neurotic people tend to choke under pressure (Byrne et al., 2015). Science fiction, such as the *Star Trek* series, imagines a world without neurotics—everyone goes about their business fairly calmly even when the ship is about to break apart. Maybe all of the worriers are left back on Earth.

Neurotic people are more prone to mental health issues (Lahey, 2009), including depression, anxiety disorders such as generalized anxiety disorder, posttraumatic stress disorder, obsessive–compulsive disorder, substance abuse disorder, eating disorders, and personality disorders such as borderline, avoidant, dependent, or paranoid disorder (Kotov et al., 2010; Samuel & Widiger, 2008). Someone who scores above average in neuroticism will not necessarily develop one of these disorders, but he is more likely to do so than someone low in neuroticism.

Neurotic people are more likely to have physical health problems such as heart issues (Terracciano et al., 2008), obesity (Sutin et al., 2011), and irritable bowel syndrome (Hazlett-Stevens et al., 2003). Perhaps as a result, neurotic people do not live as long as calmer people (Shipley et al., 2007). People can even suffer from others' neuroticism. One study found that heart surgery patients had more depressive symptoms 18 months later if they had a neurotic spouse (Ruiz et al., 2006). The costs of neuroticism (e.g., in health care and lost productivity at work) far exceed the costs of psychiatric disorders, partially because neuroticism is more common (Cuijpers et al., 2010).

West Virginia, Rhode Island, and New York are the U.S. states highest in neuroticism; Utah, Colorado, and South Dakota are the lowest (Figure 3.9). Maybe the jokes about all of the psychiatrists practicing in New York aren't far off. The states with higher neuroticism also had more heart disease and cancer and lower life expectancies (Rentfrow et al., 2008).

Figure 3.9 Neuroticism in the United States

A "neuroticism belt" runs through the Northeastern U.S., with neuroticism also higher in some Southern states.

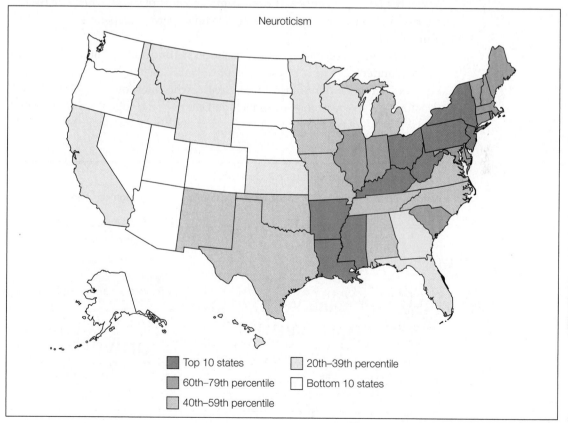

SOURCE: Rentfrow et al. (2008)

Openness to Experience

Openness to Experience is the most difficult of the Big Five to define. McCrae (1996) described it as "vivid fantasy, artistic sensitivity, depth of feeling, behavioral flexibility, intellectual curiosity, and unconventional attitudes" (p. 323). High-openness people enjoy trying new things (e.g., eating unusual foods, traveling to exotic locations, taking on new challenges at work), playing with complex ideas (e.g., "What happens when you die?"), and considering alternative perspectives and value systems (e.g., "Is it better to be part of a collectivist or individualistic society?"). High-openness people are more likely to name travel as an important personal goal (Reisz et al., 2013). Low-openness people, in contrast, prefer routine, value the status quo, and favor traditional and conventional activities, including identifying with a religion (Sibley & Bulbulia, 2014). In the study of Facebook users, those high in openness used words such as *universe*, *writing*, and *music*, whereas those low in openness were more likely to use phrases such as "can't wait" and text-speak words such as *wat* and *ur* (Kern et al., 2014; see Figure 3.10).

Your friend who says she won't rest until she's visited every continent is probably high on openness. Andrew Zimmer—host of the show *Bizarre Foods*—must be high on openness; after all, he eats tuna sperm, bull penis soup, and cow urine. Yum!

People high in openness include celebrity chef and author Anthony Bourdain, Apple founder Steve Jobs, physicist Stephen Hawking, the *Harry Potter* character Luna Lovegood, and Tris Prior in *Divergent*, who questions her society's very structure. Those low in openness include Dolores Umbridge from *Harry Potter*, who wants students to follow the rules and read from the book. My (J. M. T.)

Figure 3.10 Word Clouds for Openness

Words used more often on Facebook by people low (left) and high (right) in openness to experience.

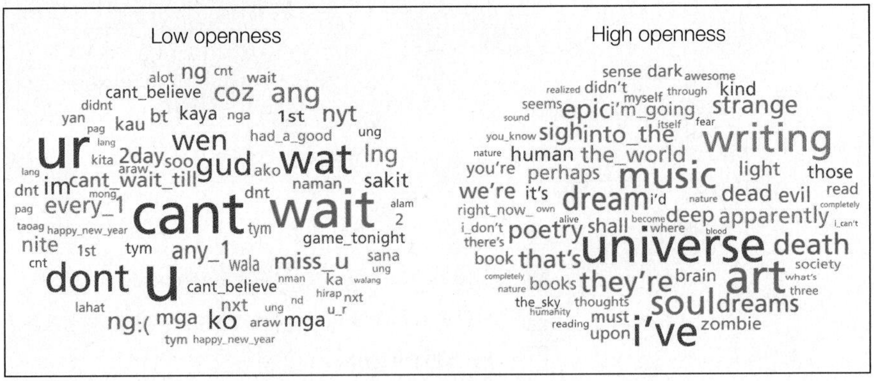

SOURCE: Kern et al. (2014)

father is low on openness. He always orders the same thing at restaurants and did the same job in the same place for 30 years. He likes routine and finds change difficult. He shows how low openness can have its advantages: He doesn't have to spend much time making decisions.

People high in openness also tend to be creative (Feist, 1998). This creativity apparently pays off: U.S. states with the highest average openness scores receive more patents for new inventions (Rentfrow et al., 2008).

High openness is correlated with more liberal political views and low openness to more conservative political views (McCrae, 1996), although the correlation is relatively small (Sibley et al., 2012). U.S. states high in openness include New York, the District of Columbia, and Oregon; low-openness states are North Dakota, Wyoming, and Alaska. If you follow politics, you probably noticed right away that the high-openness states are all "blue" states that tend to vote for Democrats, and the low-openness states are "red" states that vote for Republicans. Sure enough, the

People high in openness are more willing to try new things.

residents in high-openness states are more likely to hold liberal social views, such as supporting gay marriage and advocating the legalization of marijuana. They are also less religious (Rentfrow et al., 2008; see Figure 3.11).

High-openness people are more likely to experience political and social events as personally meaningful and are more interested in social activism (Curtin et al., 2010). Openness is also correlated with political success among U.S. presidents. Using ratings of presidents' personality traits made by historians, Rubenzer and colleagues (2000) found that openness was the best predictor of presidential greatness among the Big Five. Presidents rated high on openness included Thomas Jefferson and Abraham Lincoln.

Openness is the least intuitive of the Big Five. You can probably think of many synonyms for the other Big Five traits—for example, that extraverted people are outgoing, talkative, social, and so on. But it's harder to immediately think of words to describe openness. It's also the trait least likely to appear in other cultures and languages (DeRaad et al., 2010). Openness has gone by many different labels in different personality questionnaires, including *intellect*, *culture*, and *imagination*.

Openness has only small links to psychiatric disorders, although those high in openness are a little less likely to suffer from anxiety disorders or depression (Kotov et al., 2010). There is debate about whether openness can be *too* high—for example, whether having too vivid an imagination overlaps with psychotic symptoms such as hallucinations or unusual beliefs (Watson et al., 2008; Widiger, 2011).

Figure 3.11 Openness in the United States

The residents of socially liberal states score higher on openness, with a few exceptions.

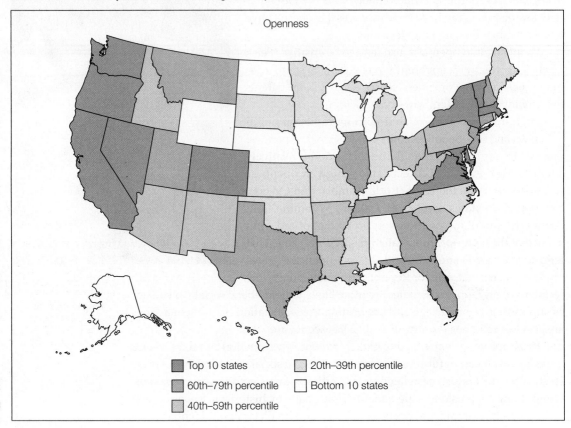

Openness

Legend:
- Top 10 states
- 60th–79th percentile
- 40th–59th percentile
- 20th–39th percentile
- Bottom 10 states

SOURCE: Rentfrow et al. (2008)

Openness is the only Big Five dimension linked to intelligence; those high in openness tend to score higher on intelligence (IQ) tests, although the correlation is small (Ackerman & Heggestad, 1997; DeYoung et al., 2005). Openness apparently keeps the brain flexible as people age, minimizing any decline in cognitive abilities (Curtis et al., 2015; Hogan et al., 2012). High-openness people also live longer (Turiano et al., 2012).

Situational factors can alter openness. People who took psilocybin (the active component in psychedelic mushrooms) under carefully supervised medical conditions increased in openness (MacLean et al., 2011). Older adults who challenged their minds with crossword puzzles or Sudoku also increased in openness (Jackson et al., 2012).

With these findings and the rest we've covered, it pays to repeat the caveat: These results are based on averages, and will not necessarily apply to everyone. That's true of every scientific study comparing people. Ultimately, in our view, it's important to see these findings for what they are: Intriguing clues about the behavior, characteristics, and future lives of people with certain personality traits. Learning about personality is like being a detective: Some of the clues will be red herrings that lead nowhere, but others will help you understand people better.

The Development of the Big Five and Its Usefulness

LO 3.3 **Explain how the Big Five traits were developed and how they are used to help us better understand ourselves.**

Some of you—maybe those lower in agreeableness and/or higher in openness— might be wondering: "Wait a minute—where did the Big Five come from in the first place? How do we know there are just five? Why not 20? Did somebody just make this up?"

They didn't. The development of the Big Five was guided by the **lexical hypothesis**—the idea that traits important for survival and reproduction became embedded in our language as single words (also see the feature "The Dawn of the Lexical Hypothesis"). The more of these trait words, the more important the trait should be. Starting with this idea, researchers recorded all of the adjectives in an English-language dictionary that could be used to describe people. They screened out words referring to temporary states (e.g., *rushed*) or social evaluations (*rotten*) and those of questionable use (*round-headed*), leaving only the stable, psychological attributes of people—in other words, personality traits such as outgoing, nervous, and neat (Allport & Odbert, 1936; Cattell, 1943).

In the next step of the development of the Big Five, many people rated themselves on these adjectives. The researchers then did a **factor analysis** on the responses—basically, they analyzed which words correlated with each other and formed clusters of adjectives (e.g., Norman, 1963; Tupes & Christal, 1961). They found that five clusters had the most adjectives. In order of size, they are Extraversion, Agreeableness, Conscientiousness, Neuroticism, and Openness to experience (the same order in which we presented them earlier). That means there are the most words in English that describe traits in the extraversion cluster, and the fewest in the openness to experience cluster. For more on the history of trait models leading up to the Big Five, see the history timeline (Figure 3.12).

The idea that more words correspond to greater importance makes theoretical sense as well. If a trait is important for humans to survive and reproduce, people probably came up with lots of different words for it (Ellis et al., 2002). For example, it was (and is) useful to know if someone is cooperative versus aggressive. So people used a lot of different words to describe the continuum from nonaggressive to aggressive behavior—from compliant, collaborative, and collegial to defiant, adversarial, quarrelsome, argumentative, vexatious, or combative. (Pop quiz: Which of the Big Five is this?)

lexical hypothesis
that traits important for survival and reproduction became embedded in our language, with the most important traits represented by the largest number of words

factor analysis
analyzing correlations among items to see which form related clusters

Personality's Past

The Dawn of the Lexical Hypothesis

The lexical hypothesis—the idea that personality traits can be found in language—stretches all the way back to the late 1800s. Francis Galton, known for his work on the heritability of intelligence, wrote of personality science at the time:

> New processes of inquiry are yearly invented, and it seems as though there was a general lightening up of the sky in front of the path of the anthropometric experimenter, which betokens the approaching dawn of a new and interesting science. (1884, p. 179)

Galton began to realize that a person's individual character, or personality, was highly important, and more powerful than free will. He came to believe this for three reasons. First, Galton realized from his own research that much of a person's character is heritable. Genes were not known at the time, but it was understood that traits passed from parent to offspring. Second, and relatedly, Galton realized that identical twins were often remarkably alike in their personalities. Third and finally, he looked at his own behavior and saw that what he thought was free will was, under closer inspection, just his character at work. Thus, it seemed important to understand personality.

Galton reasoned that language would be a good place to look for personality. In his case, he consulted a thesaurus and found 1,000 words describing personality traits.

> I tried to gain an idea of the number of the more conspicuous aspects of the character by counting in an appropriate dictionary the words used to express them. Roget's *Thesaurus* was selected for that purpose, and I examined many pages of its index here and there as samples of the whole, and estimated that it contained fully one thousand words expressive of character, each of which has a separate shade of meaning, while each shares a large part of its meaning with some of the rest. (1884, p. 183)

The rest, as they say, is history. Other researchers built on this lexical approach and a major branch of personality science grew (Goldberg, 1993).

What Does the Big Five Tell Us About Our Survival Ability?

Imagine you are a competitor in a life-or-death contest like that portrayed in the *Hunger Games*. You've just been dropped in an environment where everyone is out to kill you. You might be able to form an alliance with one or two other competitors who could help you survive, even if just temporarily. What traits would be most important in choosing your allies? Being able to trust the person comes to mind immediately. Sure enough, many words in the English language convey information about trustworthiness (e.g., *sincere, genuine, reliable, authentic, believable, truthful, honest*) or its opposite (e.g., *insincere, dishonest, deceptive, disingenuous, sneaky, devious, unreliable*).

Overall, the Big Five includes important information about people's ability to survive and reproduce (Nettle, 2006). Extraversion helps people connect with others, useful for both survival (hunting in a group) and reproduction (gregariousness, one of the facets of extraversion, is linked to more sexual activity;

Cliff dwellings at Mesa Verde National Park in Colorado. If you lived in rooms this small, you'd probably learn to be agreeable too.

Miller et al., 2004). The downside of extraversion is its connection to risk taking, which can lead to accidents. Agreeableness is useful for getting along with others, which was even more necessary in our evolutionary past when people lived very close to each other in caves, mud huts, and other small dwellings. However, other people might also take advantage of high-agreeableness individuals, so they might not receive as many resources as they deserve.

Conscientiousness helps people survive through careful planning and hard work, although too much conscientiousness could be a disadvantage if it leads to too much rigidity. Neuroticism may help people survive by making them wary of danger. In the past, that might have meant being scared of the bear 100 yards away. In the present, it means being scared of the creepy-looking guy walking toward you on the street. However, too much neuroticism may lead people to be too wary and miss out on important opportunities. High neuroticism can also drive other people away; it's difficult to be around someone who is constantly fretting over something. Finally, openness is linked to creativity, which can have benefits both for survival in new circumstances and for attracting mates and reproducing. Too much openness, though, might lead to delusional beliefs or ostracism by others for being too different or not following the rules.

How Does the Big Five Translate to Other Personality Research?

The Big Five is also useful because it can incorporate traits used in other models of personality. For example, many previous models and questionnaires included traits similar to neuroticism, such as Hans Eysenck's neuroticism measure (Eysenck & Eysenck, 1975) or the State–Trait Anxiety Inventory (Spielberger,

Figure 3.12 A Brief and Selected History of Personality Trait Models

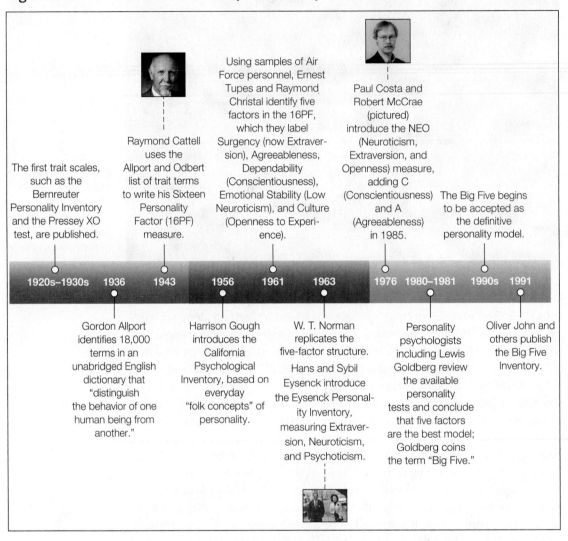

The first trait scales, such as the Bernreuter Personality Inventory and the Pressey XO test, are published.

Raymond Cattell uses the Allport and Odbert list of trait terms to write his Sixteen Personality Factor (16PF) measure.

Using samples of Air Force personnel, Ernest Tupes and Raymond Christal identify five factors in the 16PF, which they label Surgency (now Extraversion), Agreeableness, Dependability (Conscientiousness), Emotional Stability (Low Neuroticism), and Culture (Openness to Experience).

Paul Costa and Robert McCrae (pictured) introduce the NEO (Neuroticism, Extraversion, and Openness) measure, adding C (Conscientiousness) and A (Agreeableness) in 1985.

The Big Five begins to be accepted as the definitive personality model.

| 1920s–1930s | 1936 | 1943 | 1956 | 1961 | 1963 | 1976 | 1980–1981 | 1990s | 1991 |

Gordon Allport identifies 18,000 terms in an unabridged English dictionary that "distinguish the behavior of one human being from another."

Harrison Gough introduces the California Psychological Inventory, based on everyday "folk concepts" of personality.

W. T. Norman replicates the five-factor structure.

Hans and Sybil Eysenck introduce the Eysenck Personality Inventory, measuring Extraversion, Neuroticism, and Psychoticism.

Personality psychologists including Lewis Goldberg review the available personality tests and conclude that five factors are the best model; Goldberg coins the term "Big Five."

Oliver John and others publish the Big Five Inventory.

1983). So if a researcher wants to find studies on neuroticism, he or she can include these other measures of anxiety and neuroticism in addition to the Big Five measures. Even though these other measures were developed before the Big Five, they measure the same basic trait. This is what makes the Big Five so versatile; it can incorporate scales developed using different models and theories and at different times.

In other cases, a trait from another questionnaire might be a mix of Big Five factors, or it might be a piece of a Big Five factor. For example, Eysenck's three-factor model of personality included neuroticism, extraversion, and psychoticism (Eysenck & Eysenck, 1975). His extraversion and neuroticism were very similar to the Big Five concepts, and psychoticism appears to be a combination of low agreeableness and low conscientiousness (Aluja et al., 2002; McCrae & Costa, 1985). The California Psychological Inventory dominance scale (Gough, 1956) is similar to the assertiveness facet of extraversion. Overall, the Big Five is a useful way of translating many different personality models into a common language—it's like a Rosetta Stone for personality.

There are two other points that are important to make. First, even though the lexical hypothesis focused on trait adjectives, not all modern Big Five measures use adjectives. Most, including the one you took, use statements instead. The original researchers focused on adjectives as a way to zero in on the most important traits, but these are often not the best tools for making scales. Second, the decision to use five factors as opposed to four or six is not carved in stone. A "Big Six" model adds a factor measuring honesty (Lee & Ashton, 2004). Some even argue for a "Big One" personality scale composed of high extraversion, high agreeableness, high conscientiousness, low neuroticism, and high openness (Musek, 2007).

Does the Big Five Translate Across Other Cultures?

You might remember that the Big Five was developed using words in English. Does the Big Five "work" in other languages and cultures? It seems to work pretty well. Schmitt and his colleagues (2007) translated the Big Five Inventory into 28 languages and administered it to individuals from 56 nations, finding the same five personality domains. Researchers have also used the lexical method to identify adjectives in other languages that describe personality and cluster together just as the Big Five does. For example, Spanish has a "Big Seven" with two factors more unique to Spanish (positive valence and negative valence) and the last five similar to the Big Five (Benet & Waller, 1995). In Chinese, the first four of the Big Five stay the same, but openness to experience is replaced by a different trait called interpersonal relatedness (Cheung et al., 2001).

Overall, most languages have domains for extraversion, agreeableness, and conscientiousness, with more variation in whether neuroticism or openness is included and whether a domain capturing traits related to honesty and humility is added (Ashton & Lee, 2010; DeRaad et al., 2010). Research using Big Five measures has been conducted in countries on every continent except Antarctica. (Although researchers *have* used the Big Five to predict who is best suited to work in Antarctica! As you might expect, it's those high in openness to experience; Grant et al., 2007.)

JOURNAL PROMPT: UNDERSTANDING YOURSELF

Think of people you know or have met from other countries. Are you able to describe their personality using Big Five traits alone? Try it.

Do animals have the Big Five personality traits, too? The answer appears to be yes (Gosling & John, 1999). For example, cats show differences in emotional reactivity (similar to neuroticism), affection (similar to agreeableness), energy (similar to extraversion), and competence (similar to conscientiousness; Gosling & John, 1998). Pigs differ in their level of aggression (similar to agreeableness), sociability (similar to extraversion), and exploration-curiosity (similar to openness to experience; Forkman et al., 1995). Pet owners also differ in their personality traits—dog owners are more extraverted, agreeable, and conscientious and less neurotic and open-minded than cat owners (Gosling et al., 2010). You can even test this yourself—in the online test bank, see if your class's scores on the Cat Person Scale correlate with the Big Five. Do they confirm the results of Gosling's study?

Concluding Thoughts

The Big Five is an incredibly useful model of personality; it captures many of the ways we talk about other people, and it works across different theories, cultures, and even species. Extraversion, agreeableness, conscientiousness, neuroticism, and openness to experience do the best job of capturing the most personality in the fewest factors. Because they come from the language people use to describe others, it's no surprise that they easily lend themselves to predicting behavior and identifying the traits of well-known people—either real or fictional.

We use the Big Five often throughout the remainder of the book—so as you read the chapters that follow, feel free to come back here to refresh your memory about the Big Five and what they mean. You will enjoy understanding your friends, family, coworkers, fellow students, and yourself through the lens of the most comprehensive and empirically based personality model ever developed.

Learning Objective Summaries

LO 3.1 Name and define the Big Five personality traits.

The Big Five traits are extraversion (outgoing, assertive, happy); agreeableness (nice, giving); conscientiousness (neat, achievement-oriented); neuroticism (worried, angry); and openness to experience (interested in big ideas, open to new experiences).

LO 3.2 Describe the behaviors, attitudes, and characteristics of people high and low in each of the Big Five traits.

Extraversion is linked to enjoying being with people and to better health; agreeableness to getting along with others and less criminal behavior; conscientiousness is linked to better self-control, better health, and better work performance; neuroticism is linked to mental and physical health issues; and openness to experience is linked to liberal views on social issues and to being creative.

LO 3.3 **Explain how the Big Five traits were developed and how they are used to help us better understand ourselves.**

The Big Five was developed under the lexical hypothesis, gathering personality words from a dictionary, having respondents rate themselves, and then seeing which words correlated with each other. The Big Five captures traits important for survival and reproduction, can be used to understand other personality systems, and can be used in other cultures and even with other species.

Key Terms

traits, p. 53
Big Five, p. 54
Extraversion, p. 56
Agreeableness, p. 56

Conscientiousness, p. 56
Neuroticism, p. 56
Openness to experience, p. 56
facets, p. 57

hostile attribution bias, p. 65
lexical hypothesis, p. 75
factor analysis, p. 75

Essay Questions

1. Name and describe each of the Big Five traits.

2. For each of the Big Five traits, provide an example of how someone high in that trait would behave.

3. Explain what facets are and how they are important to understanding the Big Five.

4. Provide a brief explanation of how the Big Five traits were derived by researchers.

Chapter 4
Biological Underpinnings of Personality

Learning Objectives

LO 4.1 Describe the usefulness and findings of twin studies, and note their limitations.

LO 4.2 Understand how genes and the environment can interact to shape personality traits.

LO 4.3 Describe how personality traits appear in the brain, and explain how people differ on morningness–eveningness.

LO 4.4 Describe how evolutionary psychology explains human tendencies, and describe some of the challenges to this approach.

LO 4.5 Explain how hormones can influence behavior among women and men.

While watching their son, Wade, play at a birthday party, Robin and her partner, Cindy, began chatting with another mother, Maren, who was with her baby daughter, Lila. The women soon discovered that both Wade and Lila had been conceived with donor sperm from the Fertility Center of California. "What donor number did you use?" Maren asked casually. "48QAH," answered Cindy. The number sounded familiar to Maren, and then it dawned on her. "Yeah," said Maren, "the doctor who likes Sarah McLachlan." They had used the same donor, making their children biological half-siblings. The two families soon became close, and subsequently decided to try to find the donor's identity—a difficult prospect, as most remain anonymous. However, they were delighted to find that the donor was willing to be contacted.

48QAH was Matthew Niedner, a pediatrician practicing in Michigan; the clinic's label of QAH stood for "Quite a Hunk." When Robin and Cindy saw a video clip of Dr. Niedner as part of a *60 Minutes* story, they immediately saw familiar traits. "He's animated, like my Wade," said Cindy. "And look at the eyebrows," said Robin. "There is my boy's eyebrows," Cindy agreed (Schindehette, 2006; Schorn, 2006).

We all know that physical traits such as eyebrows, eye color, and skin color are genetic—primarily determined by the merging of our biological mother's and biological father's DNA. But is Wade an animated child because Dr. Niedner—whom Wade has never met—is his genetic father or because his mothers have encouraged him to have a lively personality?

Research on the biological underpinnings of personality aims to answer difficult questions such as: What makes you who you are? How much of your personality is caused by your genes ("nature") and how much by your environment ("nurture")? Research on the intersection of personality and biology also explores how personality appears in the human brain, how our desires (sexual and otherwise) are rooted in our evolutionary past, why some people are more energetic in the morning and others in the evening, and how hormones influence our behavior.

First, let's define some terms: **Genetics** refers to the DNA you've had since the moment of conception—the genetic legacy you inherit from your biological mother and biological father. *Environment* means everything else. Anything that has happened to you since you were born has the potential to influence who you are and how you behave. In an attempt to better understand the effects of genetics and environment, scientists often make a distinction between siblings' shared and nonshared environments. **Shared environment** is the family environment that

genetics
the DNA from one's biological mother and biological father

shared environment
the effects of growing up with the same parents; also known as *family environment*

These three siblings are experiencing the shared environment of growing up with the same parents.

nonshared environment

experiences not shared by siblings, such as certain friends, personal injuries, or participating in different activities

siblings share; it attempts to account for the effects of growing up with the same parents and in the same home. **Nonshared environment** means experiences not shared by siblings, such as certain friends, personal injuries, participation in different activities, or individual experiences (Plomin & Daniels, 1987).

Genetics, shared environment, and nonshared environment are the three main influences considered by those who have researched the origins of personality. That is, they are the three most-studied causes of differences in personality among individuals. At least one influence is missing from this list: culture. Most studies that try to separate the effects of genetics and environment compare people within the same culture (in the same country and during the same time period). So cultural and generational variation aren't included in those studies' calculations of how much of personality is due to genetics and how much to environment (we come back to cultural influences on personality in Chapter 11).

biology

everything that appears in the body and brain, whatever its origin

It's also important to understand that genetics and **biology** are not the same thing. Biology is the broader term, including everything that appears in the body and brain, whatever its origin (genetic or environmental or a combination of both). For example, your brain is shaped by genetics, but your experiences can also change your brain. For example, a taxi driver's brain has a larger posterior hippocampus—the brain region responsible for navigational skills (Maguire et al., 2000).

Now that we have some basic definitions down, we can start looking more closely at how scientists are attempting to understand the origins of personality traits. For example, if you're high in neuroticism, is that mostly due to genetics, or mostly due to environment? And how do those influences interact?

The Heritability of Personality: Twin Studies

LO 4.1   Describe the usefulness and findings of twin studies, and note their limitations.

The most common method for answering this "nature-versus-nurture" question about genetics and environment is the **twin study**, which examines twins raised apart and together (see the Personality's Past feature for how these studies began). The most straightforward twin studies examine identical twins adopted and raised apart by two different families (for example, Bergeman et al., 1993). Also called **monozygotic twins**, identical twins share the same genetic profile. They make, at least in theory, the perfect test case for examining how much of personality is caused by genetics and how much by environment. If personality variation is due more to genetics, identical twins raised apart should be similar in their personalities. If more personality variation is due to family environment, identical twins raised apart should be very different from each other.

twin study
a study examining twins raised apart and together, usually to explore whether characteristics are caused by genetics or environment

monozygotic twins
identical twins sharing the same genetic profile

Personality's Past

The Beginning of Twin Research

But twins have a special claim upon our attention; it is, that their history affords means of distinguishing between the effects of tendencies received at birth, and of those that were imposed by the special circumstances of their after lives. (Galton, 1883, p. 216)

So begins Sir Francis Galton's chapter "History of Twins" in his 1883 book. In other words, twins provide a special window into what is nature and what is nurture. Galton was a scientist, so he set about to collect data on twins—something nobody outside medicine had done.

This kind of research is challenging today, and was even more difficult in Galton's day. He started out sending a list of 13 groups of questions to all the twins he could find. The final question on the list asked for the name of additional twins whom could be contacted for the research. As Galton wrote, "This happily led to a continually widening circle of correspondence, which I pursued until enough material was accumulated for a general reconnaissance of the subject" (p. 218). Today, we call this way of collecting research participants

snowball sampling. At the end of the process he had data on 35 pairs of likely identical twins.

Unlike modern twin research, the results of this study were largely descriptive. Some findings included: Twins often wore different color ribbons as children so their parents could tell them apart; twins often used their similarity in appearance to pull pranks and then escape punishment by blaming each other; twins' interests were generally similar; and twins seemed to get ill at the same time but not catch the illness from each other, suggesting that they had very similar constitutions. He also found that twins typically spoke similarly, but often sang in different keys. The twins were not completely similar, however: Galton found that their handwriting was usually distinct.

And what about personality? Galton found that 16 of the 35 pairs of twins had very similar personalities. For the remainder, the personalities were largely similar, but differed in assertiveness or dominance. So, for example, one twin was bold and energetic but the other was more fearful. Or one was driven and the other calm.

Since Galton's time, twin research has become much more sophisticated, but he was the scientist who started it all.

Identical (monozygotic) twins share the same genetic profile.

percentage of variance

explained by genetics or environment; this number refers to the variation among a group of people and not within one individual

Most studies report their results as the **percentage of variance** explained by genetics or environment. This number refers to the variation among a group of people, and not within one individual. For example, about 90% of the variance in human height is determined by genetics and 10% by environment. So genetics are a much stronger influence on height than environment is. But that does not mean that 90% of any one individual's height is due to genetics and 10% to environment. It means that among a group of people, 90% of their differences in height are due to genetics and 10% to where and how they grew up. (For more on how to conduct a twin study, see the Science of Personality feature.)

So is personality primarily genetic or environmental? What percentage of the variance is explained by each? Twin studies have found that 50% of the variation among people in personality traits is due to genetics (Bergeman et al., 1993; Bouchard & McGue, 2003; Jang et al., 1996; Johnson & Krueger, 2004; Loehlin, 1992; Loehlin et al., 1998; Scarr et al., 1981; Tellegen et al., 1988). The remaining 50% is primarily caused by nonshared environmental factors, such as friends, individual experiences, and random variance due to imprecise measurement. Shared environment—growing up with the same parents—hardly influences personality at all. So, outside of the DNA you may have inherited from them, your parents may well have less impact on your personality than your friends do (Harris, 2009).

This is a somewhat shocking conclusion, so let's explore it further using the thought experiment that economist Bryan Caplan (2011, p. 43) calls "Switched at Birth":

Imagine you have an identical twin, but there's a mix-up at the hospital:
A nurse accidentally switches your twin with another family's baby. You

and the strangers' baby grow up with your biological parents. Your twin grows up with the strangers. Decades later, the hospital discovers its mistake and arranges a meeting between you, your identical twin, and your accidentally adopted sibling.

Based on the twin studies, you and your accidentally adopted sibling would be only slightly more similar in personality than randomly selected strangers. If you score high in extraversion, your genetically unrelated sibling raised by the same parents is no more likely to also score above average in extraversion (she would have the same 50/50 chance as anyone). In other words, growing up in the same house, with the same parents, has virtually no influence on extraversion. If you score high in agreeableness, your genetically unrelated sibling is only a little more likely to also score above average in agreeableness (about a 57% chance, compared to 50% for anyone). Apparently parents have a little more influence on how agreeable their children are. But this effect is still smaller than that of genetics. Your identical twin—even if you have never met him or her—has about a 67% chance of also scoring above average in extraversion and agreeableness, which must be due to genetics since you never inhabited the same shared environment (Johnson & Krueger, 2004).

The Science of Personality   HOW TO DO A TWIN STUDY

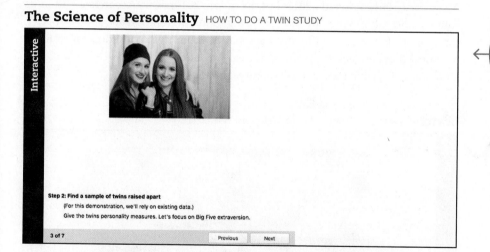

Interactive

Step 2: Find a sample of twins raised apart
(For this demonstration, we'll rely on existing data.)
Give the twins personality measures. Let's focus on Big Five extraversion.

3 of 7   Previous   Next

EXPLORE
in
REVEL

Some studies have found that shared environment does have a bigger effect on personality. One (Borkenau et al., 2001) videotaped 300 pairs of adult twins doing various tasks and asked people to rate them on personality traits. These reports from others are a different way of measuring personality than the self-reports used in most of the other studies. Using this method, the effect of shared environment was much bigger (26% versus the zero or near-zero often found), and the effect of genetics was a little smaller (41% of the variance, compared to 50% or more). This suggests that family environment is more important for how others judge your personality than how you judge it yourself.

Other personality traits, behaviors, and attitudes also have strong genetic components. **Impulsivity**—the tendency to take risks, not plan, and seek high levels of

impulsivity
the tendency to take risks, not plan, and be high in sensation-seeking, roughly equivalent to low conscientiousness

stimulation, roughly equivalent to low conscientiousness—is also about 50% genetic (Bezdjian et al., 2010). Sense of well-being, traditionalism, and aggression are more than 50% determined by genetics (Bouchard & McGue, 2003). Even political opinions may begin with genetically determined leanings; one study found a significant genetic influence on socially conservative attitudes such as supporting the death penalty and opposing gay rights. Genetic effects are somewhat weaker for traits such as achievement orientation and social closeness (Abrahamson et al., 2002).

Some identical twins separated at birth eventually meet in adulthood. In one of the most famous cases, identical twin boys were adopted by different families in Ohio in 1940. Both were named Jim, both liked math and carpentry—but not spelling—in school, and both worked in law enforcement. Both bit their fingernails, chain-smoked, and built circular benches around trees in their yards. In the strangest coincidence, each married women named Linda and then got remarried to women named Betty (Rawson, 1979).

Studies have begun to explore which specific genes may influence certain personality traits. It is unlikely that just one gene causes all of these traits, but several may influence certain tendencies. For example, some studies have linked extraversion, neuroticism, sensation-seeking, and depression to specific genes (De Moor et al., 2012; Li et al., 2011; Luciano et al., 2010). This research is still in its infancy, and future years are likely to bring more information about how specific genes work together to influence personality. From twin and adoption studies, we know that genetics matters a great deal for personality, but we are a long way from knowing which specific genes are responsible.

Watch GENETIC MECHANISMS AND BEHAVIORAL GENETICS

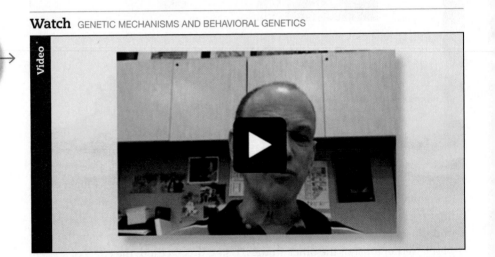

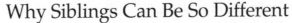

Why Siblings Can Be So Different

The family is a different experience for every child, which is one reason why nonshared environmental effects—effects other than growing up with the same parents—are fairly large (Plomin & Daniels, 1987). First, siblings often try to differentiate themselves from each other, known as a **contrast effect**. Girls with brothers report more feminine occupational interests than girls with sisters—presumably because a girl with brothers can stand out more by being feminine (Grotevant, 1978). Siblings close in age seem to make a special effort to differentiate themselves (Feinberg & Heatherington, 2000). My (J. M. T.) brother and I are just 2½ years apart, and while I played the viola in the orchestra, my brother chose to play the trumpet in the band instead—I've always assumed because he didn't want to do the same thing I did. (Though it may have been a carefully considered calculation of whether orchestra or band was less nerdy.)

contrast effect
when one sibling consciously tries to be different from the other

---

JOURNAL PROMPT: UNDERSTANDING YOURSELF

If you have a brother or a sister, how are you similar and how are you different? What do you think caused your differences and similarities? If you are an only child, what qualities do you think you inherited from your biological parents, and which were more influenced by your environment?

Second, birth order—being the oldest, middle, youngest, or only child—may shape personality in different ways. Each child experiences his parents a little differently. The oldest child in the family gets the advantage of having his parents to himself at first, but perhaps the disadvantage of an inexperienced mom and dad—there's the old joke that first kids are the "practice child." Youngest children may receive less attention when young but more when they are older, and middle children presumably never get to be the center of attention. (We cover birth order and personality in more depth in Chapter 9.)

Siblings share 50% of their genetics and may experience different influences in their nonshared environments.

Third, siblings are different from each other due to genetics: Full siblings share only 50% of their genetics on average (identical twins share 100%). That's one reason why one sibling could be shy and another very outgoing, one a worrier and another happy-go-lucky. It's been said that with your first child you believe in the power of parenting, but with your second child you believe in the power of genetics.

I (J. M. T.) see this every day in my own house: My daughter Kate's reaction to the trash trucks driving onto our street is to run full-tilt to the window, yelling, "Trash trucks! Trash trucks!" and then to wave enthusiastically to the driver. Kate's sister Elizabeth hangs back, often with her fingers in her mouth. She doesn't like the loud noises of the trash trucks and says they are scary (which comes out "sckawy"). In terms of the Big Five, Kate is extraverted, and Elizabeth is more introverted. When they're teenagers, Kate will probably like loud parties, and Elizabeth won't. Even though they are full siblings raised in the same house, they are—and will be—different in their fundamental personalities.

The Limitations of Twin Studies

Twin studies are not perfect, and their limitations may mean that genetics do not explain as much variance in personality as first appears. First, due to adoption agencies screening parents, twins were usually adopted into similar homes. Virtually all grew up in stable, middle-class homes with married parents (Joseph, 2001; Stoolmiller, 1999). This is sometimes called the "restriction of range" problem—the family environments of the twins did not differ very much. Twin studies also leave out culture because they are usually done within one country and are always done within one generation (also called *birth cohort*), as twins are always born at the same time. This is yet another range restriction. It is also rare to find separated identical twins who have had no previous contact with each other, and talking to each other could potentially create some similarity (Joseph, 2001).

Overall, then, twin studies don't answer the question, How much is personality determined by genetics? They instead answer the question, Within one culture and one time, and assuming a relatively stable, at least middle-class, upbringing, how much is personality determined by genetics? This is arguably just as important a question, but is not the same.

It's also important to keep in mind that nonshared environmental factors—things unique to each individual—seem to have just as much influence on personality as genetics. The problem is that researchers have not been able to identify exactly what these nonshared factors are. One meta-analysis found that nonshared environmental effects—including friends, different treatment by parents, birth order, and teachers—accounted for, at most, 13% of the 50% left after accounting for genetics (and thus only about 7% overall). Most specific effects, such as different treatment by parents, explained 2% or less of the variance (Turkheimer & Waldron, 2000).

Twin studies also can't rule out confounding variables—other things that twins share that might influence personality. For example, identical twins look alike. If they are both treated the same by others due to their appearance, this is an environmental influence that twin studies will mistakenly attribute to genetics (Joseph, 2001). For example, perhaps identical twins Ella and Emma are very cute children, and thus get more positive attention from other children and adults—an environmental influence both will experience as they look exactly alike. Identical twins also experienced the same prenatal environment in their mother's womb, such as her diet and drug exposure while pregnant—both environmental influences. New research suggests that prenatal environment has a surprisingly strong influence on health (Paul, 2010) and perhaps even on personality (de Rooij et al., 2012).

Gene–Environment Interactions and Epigenetics

LO 4.2 Understand how genes and the environment can interact to shape personality traits.

Although the influences of genetics and environment are often posed as "nature *versus* nurture," nature and nurture actually work together to shape personality, often called a **gene–environment interaction**. For this reason, many twin and adoption studies are incomplete because they assume genetics and environment are independent influences and don't take into account the way someone's genetic predispositions can influence his or her environment. For example, people seek out environments that suit them. Shy, introverted people seek quiet places and activities, and outgoing, extraverted people seek excitement and social interaction, further increasing their extraversion and perhaps shaping other traits as well. A highly agreeable, cheerful child makes friends easily, while a disagreeable, anxious child has trouble making friends. These experiences deepen the existing personality traits, making the agreeable child even more friendly and the disagreeable one even more distrusting (Caspi et al., 2005).

gene–environment interaction
when genetics and environment work together to shape personality

---

JOURNAL PROMPT: UNDERSTANDING YOURSELF

Do you tend to seek out environments that suit your personality? How so?

The dynamic between parents and children also creates a gene–environment interaction; your genetically influenced personality probably affected how your parents treated you. If you were a high-energy, aggressive child from birth, your parents probably got frustrated with you more often and punished you more (Jaffee et al., 2004). Your parents might not have felt as close to you, but you would have gotten a fair amount of parental attention. If you were instead a laid-back rule-follower, your parents might have felt more positively about you, but you might also have been ignored occasionally (especially if you had a sibling who was higher-energy and hogged all of the attention).

Environments can also influence whether a genetic predisposition is expressed or not. For example, in families who fight a lot, pretty much everybody is worried and anxious. But when families are fairly calm, the genetic variation in neuroticism is greater—only those more genetically prone to worrying end up worrying (Jang et al., 2005). This is similar to a distinction you may have learned in biology between a **genotype** (the genetic predisposition) and a **phenotype** (how it actually appears in the organism). Here, the phenotype is a personality trait or behavior rather than the organism's physical appearance, but the idea is the same.

Beliefs can also impact whether behavior reflects genetic influences. Among teenagers who are not religious, genetic influences on smoking are strong; however, among those who are highly religious, genetics have less of an influence (Timberlake et al., 2006). In other words, teens who are genetically predisposed to smoke are less likely to express that trait when raised in an environment that is highly religious and are more likely to express that trait in the absence of religion.

Scientists are also beginning to learn more about **epigenetics**, or differences in **gene expression** that may be passed down to future generations. The genes themselves don't change, but the way they are transcribed by the cells does. For example, children raised in Russian orphanages (vs. those raised by their biological parents) showed chemical alterations that affected the expression of genes responsible for brain development and function (Naumova et al., 2012).

genotype
an organism's genetic predisposition

phenotype
observable characteristics of an organism resulting from the interaction of the genotype and the environment

epigenetics
the idea that some environments can influence how much genetics will matter

gene expression
how much a gene influences traits or outcomes

Genetic variation in neuroticism is lessened in families who fight a lot.

Some animal studies have shown that these changes can even be passed down to the next generation. In one study, mice experienced a stressful environment as newborns, including being separated from their mothers. The mice then became socially anxious, choosing not to interact with another mouse—the mouse equivalent of not playing with the other kids on the playground, and similar to neuroticism and introversion. Not only that, but their children and grandchildren were socially anxious, too. Their DNA was not altered by their ancestors' experiences, but the way certain genes were expressed was, causing heritable changes in behavior (Franklin et al., 2011).

Genetics and the environment are not two forces working independently; instead, they are like two partners at a dance, creating something new as they dip and waltz together.

Watch EPIGENETICS

WATCH
the video in
REVEL

The Biology of Personality

LO 4.3 Describe how personality traits appear in the brain, and explain how people differ on morningness–eveningness.

You've taken several personality questionnaires so far. Here's a new one: Tie a thread around the center of a cotton swab. Swallow three times and put one end of the cotton swab on the end of your tongue for 20 seconds. Then put four drops of lemon juice under your tongue, and put the other end of the cotton swab on your tongue for 20 seconds. Take the cotton swab out and hold it by the thread. Does it tip toward the end that was on your tongue after the lemon juice, indicating it has more saliva on it? If so, you are likely an introvert. If it instead stays horizontal, you are likely an extrovert.

This might sound like you just went to a psychic reader, but there is a reason this "lemon juice test" works (Eysenck & Eysenck, 1967). Introverts are more sensitive to stimuli than extraverts, so they salivate more in response to the lemon juice, so the end of the cotton swab is heavier. (See if this lines up with your introversion–extraversion score from Chapter 3.) Introverts do not have a higher baseline level of arousal; introverts and extraverts share a similar baseline with no stimulation or only mild stimulation. But introverts are more reactive to stimuli (Bullock & Gilliland, 1993). For example, introverts are more sensitive to noise (Geen, 1984)—just like my (J. M. T.) introverted daughter Elizabeth reacting negatively to the loud clangs of the trash trucks. In one study, introverts (vs. extraverts) performed equally well on a test when things were quiet, but introverts performed more poorly when music was played in the background (Furnham & Bradley, 1997).

The link between introversion and reactivity is displayed in a choice many students make every day: Where are you going to study? Extraverts are more likely to study in an open area with lots of people and activity, and introverts are more likely to choose a quiet cubicle (Campbell, 1983). Do your study habits line up with your extraversion score?

These studies suggest that personality affects how our brains respond to stimuli, which implies that personality is physically manifested in the brain. If that's true, changes to the physical brain should alter personality traits. A story from the early days of neurology provides some insight. One September day in 1848, railroad worker Phineas Gage was leaning over a rock, putting blasting powder into a hole using an iron rod. When the powder unexpectedly exploded, it shot the iron rod through Phineas's cheek, behind his eye, into the front part of his brain, and out through the top of his skull, landing 75 feet away. Surprisingly, Phineas survived the accident and even retained most of his cognitive abilities. However, his personality was never the same again. Instead of the reliable, agreeable man

Introverts often react more strongly to stimuli such as loud noise, and that may affect their ability to perform at optimal levels.

he had been before, Phineas became undependable and unable to follow through on his plans (Macmillan, 2000). He also started cursing a lot and, as his doctor wrote, "manifesting but little deference for his fellows . . . [and becoming] pertinaciously obstinate" (Harlow, 1868, quoted in Valenstein, 1986, p. 90). In other words, Phineas became a real jerk.

The Big Five and the Brain

The likely reason for Phineas's personality transformation was the damage to the front part of his brain, known as the **frontal lobe**, which makes plans, considers decisions, and helps regulate emotions and behavior. When the frontal lobe is damaged, self-control is impaired, which leads to disagreeableness and low conscientiousness (Beer & Lombardo, 2007; Lowenstein, 2002).

frontal lobe
the front part of the brain, which makes plans and considers decisions

Studies using brain scans (usually functional magnetic resonance imaging [fMRI], as we discussed in Chapter 2) have begun to identify areas of the brain associated with certain personality traits. People high in agreeableness show more activation in their frontal lobe (Haas et al., 2007), most likely because they excel at regulating their emotions. After all, getting along with people often depends on not getting angry or sad too easily (Tobin et al., 2000). This is probably why Phineas Gage became difficult to get along with after his injury. Other types of injuries can also affect personality traits and psychological symptoms related to them. For example, brain scans often show damage to the brains of NFL football players who suffered concussions, and the amount of damage is correlated with the former players' levels of depression (Strain et al., 2013).

Long before brain scanning technology was available, Gray (1982) theorized that the brains of people high in neuroticism are more sensitive to surprising and novel information. Sure enough, brain scan studies now show that people high in neuroticism have stronger responses in the **amygdala**, the part of the brain responsible for processing reactions to fear (Canli et al., 2001; Sehlmeyer et al., 2011). After being exposed to frightening things, the brains of highly neurotic people took a longer time to return to normal. Overall, neurotic people show more activation in brain areas associated with self-evaluation and fear (Adelstein et al., 2011; see Figure 4.1).

amygdala
the part of the brain responsible for processing reactions to fear

The brains of people high in neuroticism also show stronger responses in an area associated with **discrepancy detection**, or noticing things that are unusual or surprising (Eisenberger et al., 2005). This makes sense—people who worry a lot are on the lookout for things to worry about, and in most environments that means unusual things. In the human past, that might have been a saber-tooth tiger heading in your direction; now, it might mean a car barreling toward you. Either way, neurotic people are attuned to the possibility that such imminent disasters might occur at any moment. In the Midwest, where tornadoes are frequent, neurotic mothers often herd their children into interior hallways when the sky darkens. This is good in the rare chance a tornado hits the house but not particularly beneficial when thunderstorms gather every summer afternoon and you have better things to do.

discrepancy detection
noticing something that is different in the environment

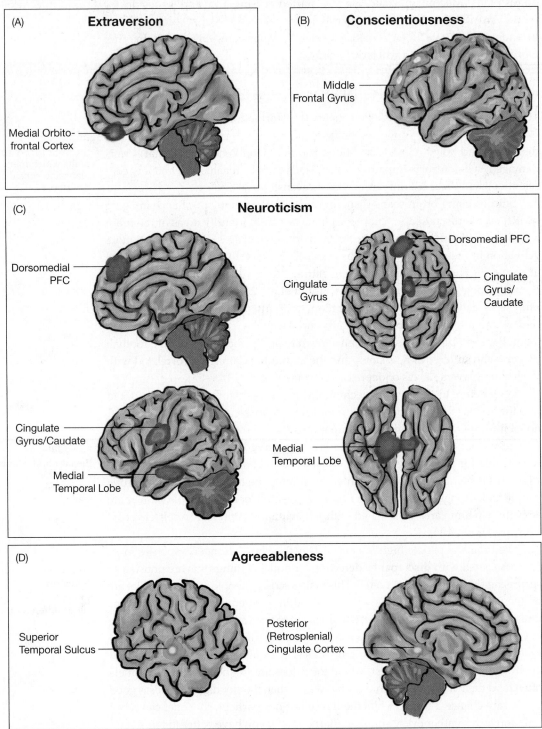

Figure 4.1 Personality in the Brain

A brain scan study showed the regions of the brain most active for those high in extraversion, conscientiousness, neuroticism, and agreeableness.

(A) **Extraversion**

Medial Orbito-frontal Cortex

(B) **Conscientiousness**

Middle Frontal Gyrus

(C) **Neuroticism**

Dorsomedial PFC

Cingulate Gyrus/Caudate

Medial Temporal Lobe

Dorsomedial PFC

Cingulate Gyrus

Cingulate Gyrus/Caudate

Medial Temporal Lobe

(D) **Agreeableness**

Superior Temporal Sulcus

Posterior (Retrosplenial) Cingulate Cortex

People who are shy (often those who are introverted as well as moderately high in neuroticism) also show increased activation in their brains after, for example, seeing pictures of people displaying various emotions (Beaton et al., 2010). These tendencies toward brain reactivity may be one of the genetic bases for personality. One study traces a path from a specific genetic marker to higher reactivity in the right amygdala to anxiety, similar to high neuroticism (Fakra et al., 2009).

The personality trait of extraversion is linked to increased activation of the amygdala and other brain regions as well, but extraverts are more sensitive to positive emotions in contrast to the negative emotion sensitivity of neurotics (Amin et al., 2004; Canli et al., 2001, 2003). Only the warmth, gregariousness, excitement-seeking, and positive emotion facets of extraversion showed this link; the facets of assertiveness and activity did not (Haas et al., 2006). Brain scan findings support the data from self-report questionnaires, which consistently find that extraversion is linked to positive emotions and neuroticism to negative emotions (Costa & McCrae, 1980).

Low conscientiousness (also known as *high impulsivity*) appears in the brain as greater activity in the ventral striatum (Hariri et al., 2006), the brain region that responds to rewards such as food and money (see Figure 4.2 to see

Figure 4.2 The Frontal Lobe, Amygdala, and Ventral Striatum Portions of the Human Brain

Three brain regions associated with personality traits: The frontal lobe, amygdala, and ventral striatum.

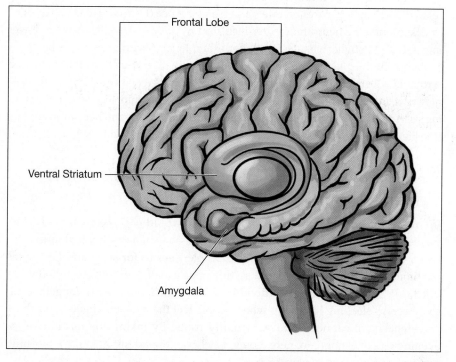

where this region is in the brain). This is also the same region that responds too strongly in drug addicts (Kalivas & Volkow, 2005). The brains of highly impulsive people also take longer to recover from negative emotional experiences and have less gray matter overall, suggesting less higher-order thinking (Antonucci et al., 2006).

Openness to experience—the most abstract and difficult to define of the Big Five traits—also manifests itself in the brain. Those who score high in the ideas facet of openness have better short-term memories, suggesting they are more skilled at thinking through complex ideas (DeYoung et al., 2009). The values facet of openness, however, shows more mixed results, with some studies finding it predicts memory and others finding only limited correlations (Amodio et al., 2007; DeYoung et al., 2009).

Neurotransmitters

neurotransmitters
chemicals that carry signals over the gap between synapses in the brain

Emerging research goes further to suggest links between specific **neurotransmitters**—the chemicals that carry signals over the gap between synapses in the brain—and personality. For example, low conscientiousness has been linked to higher levels of the neurotransmitter dopamine. Patients with Parkinson's disease are often treated with dopamine replacements, and some begin to act impulsively—gambling to excess, binge eating, or becoming overly sexual (O'Sullivan et al., 2009). However, lab studies attempting to link dopamine to low conscientousness have produced mixed results (Burke et al., 2011; Dalley & Roiser, 2012). Another study found that genes related to higher dopamine levels are correlated with higher scores on openness to experience (DeYoung et al., 2011).

Serotonin, the neurotransmitter increased by antidepressants, seems to lower impulsivity (Dougherty et al., 2007). For example, men with a history of behavior problems showed less impulsivity when treated with medications that increased serotonin (Cherek & Lane, 2001). Thus, highly controlled and conscientious people may have low levels of dopamine and high levels of serotonin. Research in the coming years will likely provide more clarity on personality traits and neurotransmitters (see Figure 4.3 for a history of research on biology and personality).

Are You a Morning Person or a Night Person?: Understanding Your Circadian Rhythm

circadian rhythm
physical, mental, and behavioral changes following a daily, 24-hour cycle

If you could choose your own schedule, when would you go to bed and when would you wake up? Humans have a biological **circadian rhythm** that influences when we sleep and eat; darkness, for example, cues us for sleep and fasting (as the time between going to bed and getting up is usually our longest period without food). However, there are individual differences in preferences for getting up early versus sleeping in, and in when people feel the most energetic—and these preferences are connected to personality traits. By taking the morningness–eveningness questionnaire here, you get a chance to find out if you're a morning person or an evening person, or neither one.

Questionnaire 4.1   MORNINGNESS–EVENINGNESS SCALE

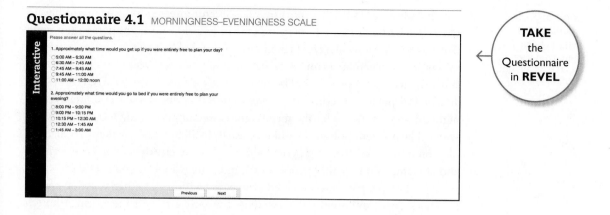

TAKE the Questionnaire in REVEL

Figure 4.3 A Brief and Selected History of Biological Models of Personality

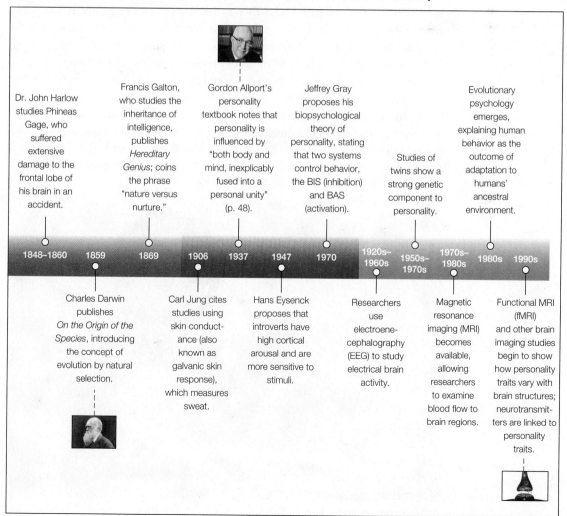

**morningness–
eveningness**
whether you are
a morning person
(a lark) or a night
person (an owl)

Even before taking the **morningness–eveningness** quiz, you might have a sense of whether you are a morning person (a lark) or a night person (an owl). Being a lark or an owl isn't just about when you go to bed and wake up—so many things influence that, from work schedules to early classes to children. I'm (J. M. T.) an evening person, but because I have kids who are up early, I can't keep an evening-person schedule anymore. I often describe myself as a "recovering night person." That's why the morningness–eveningness quiz focuses on when you feel best. Even though I'm often up early, I still have more energy in the evening on most days. Evening people also think more clearly in the late afternoon and evening, and morning people in the morning (Monk & Leng, 1986).

Morning people tend to be higher in conscientiousness than evening people (Tsaousis, 2010); apparently it's true that "the early bird gets the worm" (though a lot of night people would respond that the early bird has less fun). But this does make sense: Conscientious people are good at keeping to schedules, and the world runs on a morning schedule. There's a story about an artist who normally slept very late but had to get up early one day to report for jury duty. His assistant went to much effort to get the artist out of bed by 7:00 A.M. When they left the building, the artist was astonished to see so many people and cars busily going their way on the street. "Are all of these people on the jury?" he asked.

Morning people are also higher in agreeableness and lower in extraversion, neuroticism, and openness to experience. So the morning person is, on average, neater and more achievement oriented, more introverted, less anxious, more caring, and more conventional (Tsaousis, 2010). The evening person is messier, more outgoing, more anxious, and more freewheeling and open to new ideas. It makes sense that the late-rising jury member was an artist, given the field's link to openness.

"Sure, I'll try to be a
morning person. I just
need four more cups
of coffee. Yes, this big."

Circadian rhythms change with age. Teenagers and young adults are often evening people (Randler, 2008), apparently due to hormonal shifts. Most people tend toward morningness as they grow older, especially over age 50 (Cavallera & Giudici, 2008; Sverko & Fabulic, 1985). The crowd of senior citizens for the early-bird special at Denny's is not just a myth.

Mismatches on morningness–eveningness can cause conflicts among people. When a morning person and an evening person are roommates, they tend to be less satisfied with each other (Watts, 1982). This makes sense—there's nothing worse than a roommate who keeps you from sleeping when you want to. Even if you keep similar schedules, evening people often find morning people's early cheeriness annoying, and morning people can't understand why evening people are so energetic when they're trying to relax before bed. This applies at home, too: If you are an evening person as so many young college students are, you've probably had at least one run-in with your earlier-rising parents, who don't understand why you sleep all morning.

JOURNAL PROMPT: UNDERSTANDING YOURSELF

Do you know someone who scores the opposite from you on morningness–eveningness? Has this caused conflict in your relationship?

Evolution and Personality

LO 4.4 **Describe how evolutionary psychology explains human tendencies, and describe some of the challenges to this approach.**

For the vast majority of human history, people hunted and gathered their food, living in small groups. Agriculture did not exist, and animals we now associate with farms, such as cows and chickens, were wild aurochs and jungle fowl. There was no birth control, children were breastfed until they were at least 2 (and often 3) years old, and shelter meant a cave, a simple structure made of leaves, or perhaps a mud hut.

The theory of evolution observes that living beings evolve in response to their environments. Animals that live in cold places are selected based on their ability to grow fur. Birds whose beaks can break the seeds and shells of the land they inhabit survive, and those whose beaks are the wrong shape die and do not reproduce. The theory of **evolutionary psychology** suggests that evolution shaped human psychology just as it shaped animal and human bodies. Because we humans spent most of our history as hunter–gatherers with no technology, many of our desires and preferences are "stuck" in that time (Buss, 2003; Confer et al., 2010). Evolutionary psychology aims to discover the universal preferences and needs of people, and thus the personality traits we have in common, though we also discuss how evolution explains individual differences in personality traits as well.

evolutionary psychology
the field of research exploring how evolution shaped human psychology

Survival and Reproduction

Evolutionary psychology suggests that people will act in ways that maximize both their survival and their reproduction. For example, people almost universally love having a view of the water—houses, apartments, and hotel rooms with water views cost more money. Why? The prosaic answer is that oceans and lakes are beautiful. But that's a circular argument—*why* are they beautiful?

One reason might be because humans need a lot of water to survive—even the undrinkable ocean often has freshwater flowing into it (not to mention nutritious fish). For the vast majority of our history, water did not come out of a faucet. We can now just turn on the tap and get water whenever we want, or buy fish at the grocery store, but our love of seeing water remains (Ulrich, 1993). On the more negative side, people have an inherent fear of snakes and spiders. Although in our modern environment cars and guns are more dangerous, the human fear of snakes and spiders appears to be innate (Mineka & Öhman, 2002).

We're not only motivated by our own survival, but by reproduction and the survival of others close to us. Imagine you startle awake in the middle of the night and smell smoke. To your horror, you realize that the house is burning down. You see an escape route, but you will have time to save only one other person—and because you have guests, your house is full of friends and relatives. Who will you save—your brother, your cousin, or your friend?

When researchers posed this scenario to participants, more people said they would save a close relative (a brother or sister) than a more distant one (a cousin). They were least likely to save someone unrelated to them (a friend). Age also makes a difference: people were most likely to say they would help the

Would you like to have this view from your window? Why?

youngest victims and least likely to say they would help the oldest in a life-and-death situation (Burnstein et al., 1994).

Why are people most willing to rescue those most closely related to them and the youngest? Evolutionary psychology posits that this is due to the "selfish gene" (Dawkins, 1976). That is, our genes try to save themselves. We share 50% of our genes with a brother, 12.5% with our first cousins, and only a small percentage with friends. And people are more likely to save younger individuals in the life-and-death scenario because younger people are more likely to go on to reproduce.

What qualities are you looking for in a mate?

Reproduction and sex are also influenced by evolutionary pressures. Because birth control is a fairly recent invention, our brains still inherently link sex with reproduction. For example, evolutionary psychology argues that men usually find younger women more attractive than older women because younger women are more fertile (Buss & Schmitt, 1993). Physical appearance may also be an indicator of female fertility, which is why heterosexual men value appearance in a mate more than women do. Women, on the other hand, are more likely to value "good earning capacity," presumably because such men are more likely to be able to support children (Buss & Barnes, 1986).

Evolutionary psychology predicts that men will be more interested in sex and in having many sexual partners, and women less interested, because women must invest more in children through pregnancy and breastfeeding (Buss, 1991; Trivers, 1972). Take the following questionnaire to get a better sense of your own views about sex.

Questionnaire 4.2 SOCIOSEXUAL ORIENTATION SCALE

Interactive

Please answer all the questions.

1. With how many different partners have you had sex within the past 12 months?
○ zero
○ one
○ two
○ three
○ four
○ five or six
○ seven to nine
○ 10-19
○ 20 or more

2. With how many different partners have you had sexual intercourse on one and only one occasion?
○ zero
○ one
○ two
○ three
○ four
○ five or six
○ seven to nine
○ 10-19
○ 20 or more

Previous   Next

TAKE the Questionnaire in **REVEL**

sociosexuality
individual differences in attitudes toward sex without commitment

Sociosexuality describes attitudes toward sex without commitment (Gangstead & Simpson, 1990). As the sociosexuality scale you took shows, some people are more comfortable with uncommitted sex than others. As evolutionary theory would predict, men report more desire for uncommitted sex than women do. However, actually *having* uncommitted sex does not differ between men and women on average, perhaps because heterosexual men must find willing female partners (Penke & Asendorpf, 2008).

People with different levels of sociosexuality pursue what evolutionary psychologists call different "mating strategies." One mating strategy is to form a committed, monogamous relationship (a "long-term mating strategy") and another is to have many brief sexual encounters (a "short-term mating strategy"; see, for example, Greiling & Buss, 2000). Although sociosexuality indicates that some people will prefer long-term and other people short-term strategies, their preferences can change over time. Many younger people pursue a short-term strategy and later use a long-term one. Sociosexuality may even influence specific aspects of attraction. One study found that men with a short-term strategy preferred women with larger breasts (Zelaniewicz & Pawlowski, 2011). Try discussing this study at the next fraternity party you attend.

WATCH the video in **REVEL** →

Watch EVOLUTIONARY PSYCHOLOGY: WHY WE DO THE THINGS WE DO

The Need to Belong

People also have a nearly universal need to belong (Baumeister & Leary, 1995). You've probably seen this on your campus, with students joining fraternities or sororities or school clubs to feel a sense of belonging. When people are excluded from groups, they often behave badly. Even rejection by a group of strangers or a vague prediction that they might be lonely later in life is enough to cause people to become hostile and aggressive (DeWall et al., 2009; Twenge et al., 2001) and to act shortsightedly by eating junk food or procrastinating (Twenge et al., 2002).

One study found that being ostracized by others caused activation in the same brain region associated with physical pain, leading the researchers to describe social rejection as "social pain" (Eisenberger et al., 2003). Taking a painkiller such as acetaminophen (the active ingredient in Tylenol) reduces feelings of social rejection, again suggesting a link between the psychological pain of rejection and physical pain (DeWall et al., 2010). Rejection by others might be so impactful because in our evolutionary past, groups worked together to hunt and gather food. Early humans who were left out of the group often starved to death—and even if they got enough to eat, they couldn't reproduce by themselves. This universal need to belong could be considered a personality trait common to all humans, though of course we differ in how much social interaction we like (with extraverts liking more, and introverts less).

JOURNAL PROMPT: UNDERSTANDING YOURSELF

Do you feel you have an intrinsic need to belong? Evaluate the groups you've belonged to over your life. Were you joining simply because you found each one interesting, or was there something more going on?

Evolutionary psychologists also argue that humans are fascinated by personality differences for a reason: Understanding individual differences in personality helped humans survive and reproduce in their hunter–gatherer groups. After all, the Big Five was developed from the enormous number of words people use to describe differences among themselves. Extraversion tells us who is most likely to take on a leadership role, agreeableness who will cooperate and be a good friend or caretaker of children, and conscientiousness who will work hard and not flake out on us. Neuroticism tells us whom not to ask to run toward the large animal the tribe wants to kill and eat for dinner, and openness shows us who we can rely on for good advice and another perspective (Buss, 1991; Ellis et al., 2002).

If Evolution Is Universal, Why Do People Still Differ in Their Traits?

Much of evolutionary psychology concerns itself with universal mechanisms— preferences and behaviors common to all humans who survived and reproduced. It's tempting to think that extraversion, low neuroticism, high agreeableness, high conscientiousness, and high openness would always be beneficial. But environments are not constant over time, and evolution rewards species with enough variation to adapt to different environments.

The classic example is the "peppered" moth, which ranges in color from white to brown. White moths survived when trees had white fungus on them (making them less visible to predators such as birds), and brown moths survived

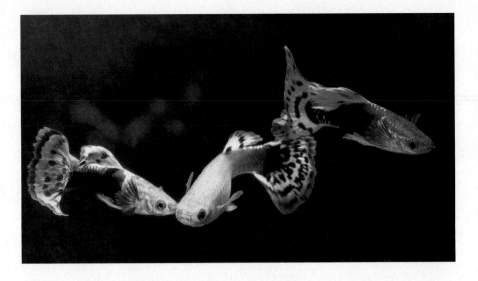

"Don't kiss me. I'm a wary guppy." Neuroticism has probably survived because neurotic people and animals took fewer risks.

when the fungus died off and they could blend into the brown of the tree trunk (Grant, 2004). The same principle occurs with personality traits. For example, guppies (the colorful, prolifically breeding fish popular in children's fish bowls) vary in how wary they are of predators—a trait analogous to neuroticism in humans. In environments with many predators, wary/neurotic guppies are more likely to survive, but in predator-free environments, wary/neurotic guppies are less likely to survive, perhaps because they are too cautious and thus don't eat enough or mate with other guppies enough (Dugatkin, 1992; O'Steen et al., 2002).

Individual differences in extraversion may also be caused by adapting to different environments. For example, birds that travel farther to explore their environment are similar to human extraverts. Extraverted birds are more likely to survive than introverted birds when the seeds they need to survive are scarce because they can gather more over a larger area and are more aggressive in competing with other birds. When seeds are abundant, the less adventurous, introverted birds are more likely to survive and reproduce, perhaps because the extraverted birds were eaten by predators during their explorations, or were too aggressive and got injured or killed (Dingemanse et al., 2002).

This suggests that people have different personalities because environments have sometimes favored one type of personality and sometimes another. If species are to survive over many years, they need individuals with different levels of traits. At least in terms of evolution, different strokes for different folks help the species survive changing times. That's at least one reason for the wide variety in human personality.

On the other hand, if the environment never favored a trait, it would die out. If it always favored a trait, it would become very common. That leads to the second interest of evolutionary psychology: explaining universal human tendencies in survival, sex, and reproduction.

Challenges to Evolutionary Psychology

Evolutionary psychology has inspired both much research and much criticism. Isn't it possible that cultural expectations drive men to value appearance and women to value resources in a mate? Evolutionary psychologists respond that this pattern of sex differences appears across 37 cultures (Buss, 1989). Critics counter that most cultures are patriarchal—meaning men are in charge—so this is not necessarily proof that the differences are due to biological drives (Wood & Eagly, 2002), though less patriarchal societies don't always show fewer sex differences (Lippa, 2010).

The sex differences in mate preferences fit evolutionary theory well, but some have argued that an evolutionary argument could be made no matter what mate preferences men and women express (Schlinger, 1996). If men preferred intelligent women, for example, that would make evolutionary sense, as smart women would be more likely to have intelligent children, and their intelligence should make it more likely that those children will survive. Yet, on average, men rank physical appearance higher than intelligence in their mate preferences. Evolutionary psychologists respond that physical appearance must have conferred a greater reproductive advantage. Overall, critics argue that it is impossible to prove that evolution caused these preferences.

Some people worry that evolutionary psychology justifies bad behavior—that a man who abandons his family and runs off with his young secretary can say, "I can't help it—it's in my genes!" Evolutionary psychologists respond that their work attempts to explain why people have certain urges but does not justify such behavior (Buss, 2003).

Hormones and Behavior

LO 4.5   Explain how hormones can influence behavior among women and men.

Geoffrey Miller, a psychology professor at the University of New Mexico, wanted to test the idea that men were more attracted to women during the more fertile days of their menstrual cycles. He relied on a sample most researchers might not have considered: professional lap dancers. On high-fertility days, lap dancers collected $335 in tips from men during their shifts, compared to $260 on low-fertility days (not including days when they had their periods, when tips were even lower). The women who were taking birth control pills (and thus were not fertile) showed no change in their tips across their cycles (Miller et al., 2007). "I have heard, anecdotally, that some lap dancers have scheduled shifts based on this research," he said after receiving an "Ig Nobel Prize" from a journal called the *Annals of Improbable Research* (Associated Press, 2008).

The dancers' greater earnings on high-fertility days might have occurred because the women acted differently or because they smelled differently; subsequent research has found that men prefer women's body scents on high-fertility days to those on low-fertility days (Gildersleeve et al., 2012). Women's voices are also higher-pitched and judged as more attractive by men on high-fertility days (Bryant & Haselton, 2009; Pipitone & Gallup, 2008).

Another study asked women to rate how attracted they were to different men. Some men were described as having stereotypically masculine interests such as rugby and weightlifting and others as having more feminine interests such as designing clothes or playing the flute. Women were more attracted to the stereotypically masculine men on high-fertility days (Flowe et al., 2012). When asked to show what they would wear to an evening social event (say, going to a club), women chose more sexually provocative clothing on more fertile days of their cycles (Durante et al., 2008). Women also tend to avoid their fathers on fertile days—presumably an outcome of the incest taboo (Liebermann et al., 2011). So even if women (and the men around them) aren't consciously aware of how their fluctuating fertility affects their behavior and preferences, the influences still occur—a modern-day expression of the ancient urge to reproduce.

testosterone

a hormone much higher in men than in women

You might have heard that **testosterone**—a hormone much higher in men than in women—causes people to be aggressive. For example, steroids raise testosterone and can cause so-called "roid rage." Animal studies support this idea, especially among males. Male monkeys with higher levels of testosterone act more dominantly and aggressively (Rose et al., 1971). Two meta-analyses found a weak but positive relationship between testosterone and aggression in humans (Archer, 1991; Book et al., 2001). Violent criminals are higher in testosterone than those convicted of nonviolent crimes, and women who were injected with testosterone reacted more strongly to seeing angry faces (Dabbs et al., 1987; Van Honk et al., 2001).

How much is our attraction to others influenced by the fluctuation in our hormones?

This suggests that testosterone can cause aggression. However, the causation can go the opposite way as well: Experiences can cause rises and falls in testosterone rather than testosterone causing people to behave in a certain way. Men's testosterone levels rise when they expect to compete with another man, rise further if they win, and decline if they lose (Mazur & Booth, 1998). Men experience a rise in testosterone when their favored sports team or even political candidate wins (Bernhardt et al., 1998; Stanton et al., 2009). This might be why victory parties sometimes get out of hand—the city with the winning Super Bowl team often sees young men with a little too much testosterone (and a little too much alcohol) smashing car windows and participating in other types of mayhem.

In men high in power motive—who desire to control others (more on this in Chapter 7)—testosterone rises after success and falls after a loss in a one-on-one contest (Schultheiss et al., 2005). The testosterone of women high in power motive increases after such a contest whether they win or lose, and their estrogen levels rise if they win (Stanton & Schultheiss, 2007). When power-motivated men and women lose a contest, levels of the stress hormone cortisol increase (Wirth et al., 2006). The hormones of those low in power motive, however, don't react as much to competition. In other words, personality can influence hormonal reactions— some people (those high in power motive) really care about competition, and their bodies react accordingly; other people (those low in power motive) don't really care, so their hormones don't either.

Insults can also affect testosterone levels. In one experiment, a confederate who squeezed by participants in a hallway muttered "assholes" under his breath as he passed. The insulted men's testosterone levels rose—but only if they were

Testosterone can cause aggression, but experiences can also cause a rise in testosterone. Even watching your favorite team winning or losing a game can cause levels to rise or fall. (These guys have no idea just how much is at stake.)

angered by the encounter (Cohen et al., 1996). Among those who found it funny, testosterone levels did not change.

Whether you have a sexual partner or not can also influence hormone levels. Men and women who are single tend to have higher testosterone levels than those who have partners (Kuzawa et al., 2010; Van Anders & Siciliano, 2010), perhaps because testosterone helps people initiate sexual relationships (Ellison, 2001). Apparently the guy on the prowl in the bar needs some hormonal inspiration to hit on women (or the woman on the guys—testosterone levels are more consistently correlated with sexual initiation among men, but some evidence suggests they influence women's sexual behavior as well). Another study found that men's testosterone levels increase prior to a divorce and then decrease when they remarry (Mazur & Michalek, 1998). Among single people, testosterone levels do not correlate with sociosexuality—so testosterone is about the same whether you're single and looking for one-night stands or single and looking for a committed partner. Among men and women with partners, however, those higher in sociosexuality had higher testosterone levels. Thus, even while partnered, people who retain an interest in uncommitted sex also retain the testosterone levels they need to go on the prowl (Edelstein et al., 2011).

People also vary in how much testosterone they were exposed to in the womb, and thus how much their brains were exposed to. This "baseline" measure of testosterone is linked to personality and behavior. Believe it or not, you can get a rough measure of your prenatal testosterone exposure using just a ruler and your hand. Measure the length of your index (first) finger and your ring (third) finger on your right hand (from the crease at your palm to the tip), and divide your index finger length by your ring finger length (the research literature calls this the **2D:4D ratio**, as these are technically your second and fourth digits when you start counting fingers starting with the thumb; see Figure 4.4). On average, people higher in testosterone have longer ring fingers, and thus lower 2D:4D ratios (Manning et al., 1998). These are subtle differences: In one large U.S. sample, the average 2D:4D ratio was .985 for men and .998 for women (Manning & Fink, 2011).

2D:4D ratio
the length of someone's index finger divided by the length of their ring (third) finger; a low ratio is linked to high testosterone

JOURNAL PROMPT: UNDERSTANDING YOURSELF

Based on your finger ratio and your tendencies, do you think you are high or low on testosterone for your gender? How does that affect your life?

Women with a low 2D:4D ratio—which means high testosterone exposure—are more likely to be assertive and high in sensation-seeking (Austin et al., 2002), and men exposed to more testosterone are more likely to take risks such as going skydiving, investing money in risky stocks, or expressing an unpopular opinion at a social occasion (Stenstrom et al., 2011). They also score lower in neuroticism and lower in agreeableness (Luxen & Buunk, 2005; Manning & Fink, 2011). So Terry, who's high in testosterone, might go to his investment banking job on Friday, jump

Figure 4.4 The 2D:4D Ratio

The 2D:4D ratio is the length of the index finger divided by the length of the ring finger. Low 2D:4D ratios are linked to higher testosterone.

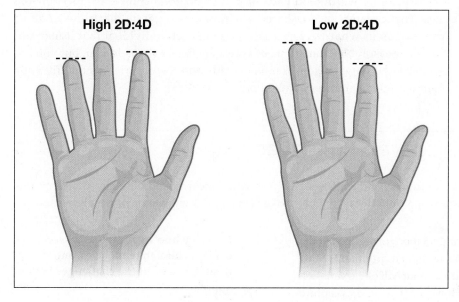

out of a plane on Saturday morning, and then loudly argue his political views at a dinner party that night. Larry, who is lower in testosterone, might invest his money in a savings account, think skydiving is crazy, and keep his opinions to himself.

A meta-analysis found that 2D:4D ratio is not consistently connected to aggression (Honekopp & Watson, 2011), although some studies have found effects. One study found that low 2D:4D (and thus high testosterone) women making unsuccessful "cold calls" hung up their phones with more force and were more hostile in follow-up letters (Benderlioglu & Nelson, 2004).

Some research also links 2D:4D ratio and thus testosterone with better mathematical reasoning (Luxen & Buunk, 2005), musical ability (Sluming & Manning, 2000), and athletic performance (Honekopp & Schuster, 2010). So the next time you lose at intramural Frisbee golf, you can hold up your hand and yell, "It's not my fault! It was my relative lack of prenatal testosterone exposure!" Or maybe not.

Concluding Thoughts

Our genetics, the structure of our brains, our evolutionary history, and sometimes our hormones exert a strong influence on our personality traits and behavior, and many personality differences are correlated with specific reactions in the brain. Obviously, though, biology and genetics are not the whole story. We are also shaped by our environments and unique experiences, and our genes interact with environments in complex ways that research is just beginning to understand.

These findings do not mean the end of free will; we most definitely still have the ability to control our own actions. Everyone has certain tendencies and vulnerabilities, and everyone has certain early experiences, but these can be channeled toward good ends or bad ones, good choices or questionable ones. The research on nonshared environment suggests that almost half of what makes us what we are is so unique to each individual that it may not even be measurable. You are what your genetics have made you, but you are also the sum of the choices you have made and the experiences that fill your brain with the memories of a lifetime.

Learning Objective Summaries

LO 4.1 Describe the usefulness and findings of twin studies, and note their limitations.

Twin studies are a useful method for separating the effects of genetics and family environment. Most find that genetics explains about half of the variation in personality traits. However, twin studies capture variance within one culture and time period.

LO 4.2 Understand how genes and the environment can interact to shape personality traits.

Environments can influence genetic expression; the phenotype (actual behavior and appearance) is determined only partially by the genotype (the genes). Gene–environment interactions include epigenetic influences that can be passed down to future generations.

LO 4.3 Describe how personality traits appear in the brain, and explain how people differ on morningness–eveningness.

Personality influences physiological reactions, including the reactivity to stimuli (which is more pronounced among introverts) and the reactivity of brain regions such as the amygdala (which reacts more strongly among those high in neuroticism).

Personality is correlated with circadian rhythms like being a morning person or a night person.

LO 4.4 Describe how evolutionary psychology explains human tendencies, and describe some of the challenges to this approach.

Evolutionary psychology argues that humans' psychological mechanisms evolved to promote survival and reproduction. For example, humans seem to have an inherent need to belong. Individual differences such as those in personality may have evolved to adapt to different environments. Some argue that it is difficult to prove that preferences are caused by evolution.

LO 4.5 Explain how hormones can influence behavior among women and men.

Men respond differently to women depending on whether they are in the fertile phase of their cycle, and women express different mate preferences based on hormonal variations. Testosterone is linked to aggressive behavior, and men's and women's experiences can change their testosterone levels. The ratio of the length of the second and fourth fingers may indicate the amount of testosterone someone was exposed to *in utero*.

Key Terms

genetics, p. 83
shared environment, p. 83
nonshared environment, p. 84
biology, p. 84
twin study, p. 85
monozygotic twins, p. 85
percentage of variance, p. 86
impulsivity, p. 87
contrast effect, p. 89

gene–environment
   interaction, p. 91
genotype, p. 92
phenotype, p. 92
epigenetics, p. 92
gene expression, p. 92
frontal lobe, p. 95
amygdala, p. 95
discrepancy detection, p. 95

neurotransmitters, p. 98
circadian rhythm, p. 98
morningness–eveningness,
   p. 100
evolutionary psychology, p. 101
sociosexuality, p. 104
testosterone, p. 108
2D:4D ratio, p. 110

Essay Questions

1. Explain why twin studies are so important to the study of genetic and environmental influences on personality.

2. How do genes and the environment interact to shape personality traits?

3. Explain what areas of the brain appear to be associated with personality and what role neurotransmitters play in how we feel and behave.

4. How does evolutionary psychology help explain human tendencies, and what are some of the limitations to this theory?

5. Discuss how hormones can affect our moods and behavior.

Chapter 5
Self-Concept and Self-Processes

 Learning Objectives

LO 5.1 Define self-concept and its parts; explain how the self as "I" differs from the self as "me," and discuss the modern view of the self as a knowledge structure or schema.

LO 5.2 Define self-esteem and explain its benefits and costs.

LO 5.3 Describe self-compassion, self-efficacy, and narcissism.

LO 5.4 Understand how self-regulation and self-control operate.

The *Harry Potter* novels and movies start with the premise that an orphaned boy has no real idea of who he is. Sure, he knows what he looks like, and he knows a bit about his personality, his attitudes, and his tastes, but he doesn't know a great deal about himself. Who are his parents? What is he capable of doing? Who was he in the past? There is a massive hole in Harry's understanding of himself that is slowly filled throughout seven novels and eight movies.

Most of us have a much better understanding of ourselves than the fictional Harry Potter, but we are still trying to gain a better understanding of ourselves. Even though we spend every hour of every day with ourselves—and we are not secret orphan wizards living under stairs—we still don't have a great grasp on ourselves. When you think about it, this is a strange set of affairs. As children and teens, we took classes in math, English, history, social studies, and art but had little formal instruction on our own selves.

Not surprisingly, psychologists have thought a lot about the self (see Figure 5.1). William James (1891) dedicated a full chapter to the self in his classic

Figure 5.1 A Brief and Selected History of Research on the Self

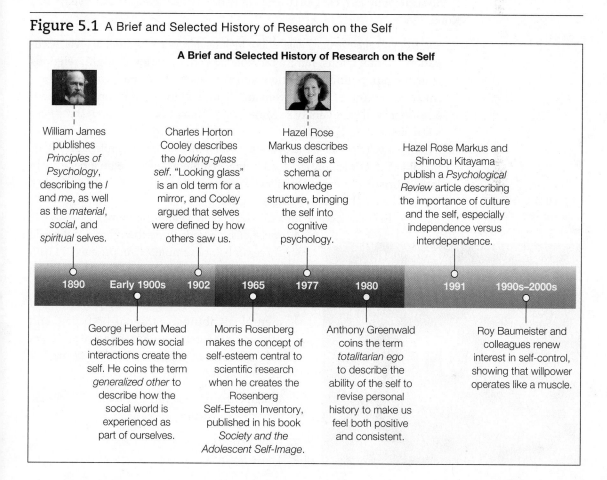

book *The Principles of Psychology*. Sigmund Freud used the German concept of "selbst" (or "self") in his writings, which was translated to "ego" in English. And Carl Rogers, the great humanistic psychologist, thought changing the self in a more honest and ideal direction was at the heart of psychotherapy (Rogers, 1961). Modern personality science has drawn from many of these original ideas.

There is one question at the center of understanding the self: Who am I? The easiest way to find an answer is to ask people (or even ask yourself) to complete the statement "I am . . . " in 20 different ways. Not surprisingly, this is called the Twenty Statements Test (TST; Kuhn & McPartland, 1954). One of the most deceptively simple tests in psychology, the TST gives 20 lines on a sheet of paper, each beginning with "I am . . . ". All you have to do is fill in the blanks. It can be tough to start the process, but once you get going, it's easy to write down 20 self-statements fairly quickly. Try it.

Unlike the other questionnaires you've completed so far, you score the TST yourself. It doesn't yield one numerical answer like most personality questionnaires—though we describe one way it can be quantified below.

To score your TST, categorize each of your responses into one of five groups (Kuhn, 1960):

1. *Social groups and classifications*: These include age, sex, educational level, occupation, marital status, family relationships, race, national origin, religious membership, political affiliation, and formal and informal group memberships. For example, "I am a woman," "I am Latino," "I am a brother," "I am a student at the University of Minnesota," "I am Chinese American," "I am a Muslim."

2. *Ideological beliefs*: These include statements of a religious, philosophical, or moral belief. For example, "I am living a righteous life," "I am a believer in Jesus Christ." ("I am a Christian," however, might go in the first category instead, as it's about belonging to a group).

3. *Interests*: For example, "I am a Cowboys fan," "I am a swimmer."

4. *Ambitions*: These include thoughts about being successful. For example, "I am pre-med," "I am going to own my own business," "I am going to be a winner."

5. *Self-evaluations*: These include physical and mental attributes, personality traits, and other characteristics. For example, "I am tall," "I am a nice person," "I am smart," "I am energetic."

Imagine that Jessica fills out the TST. Here are her first seven answers:

1. I am a student.
2. I am a woman.

Finish this sentence 20 different ways to learn about yourself.

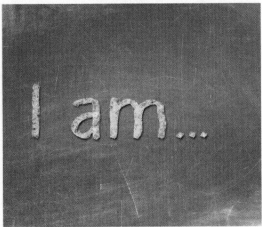

3. I am nice.
4. I am an environmentalist.
5. I am a cyclist.
6. I am good-looking.
7. I am successful.

Can you classify these into the five categories above? Use these as practice before you classify your own TST statements. Some statements are not going to fit clearly into any of these categories. When my (J. M. T.) class does this exercise, someone almost always volunteers, "I am tired" or "I am hungry." (To the first, I often reply that I hope that's not a reflection on my teaching; to the second, I usually offer the student an energy bar.) You can label these as self-evaluations. If others come up that don't seem to fit anywhere, you can just put them in an "other" category.

Research on the TST has uncovered a number of interesting trends. First, people often name what makes them stand out. In a classroom full of U.S. citizens, students from other nations are more likely to see their nationality as part of their identity (McGuire et al., 1978). Likewise, in a classroom full of 18- to 21-year-old college students, a 40-year-old student is more likely to see her age as part of her identity. Your self is often linked to what makes you unique.

Your responses to the TST may also say something about how individualistic versus collectivistic you are, perhaps as a function of the culture you experienced growing up. Count how many of your TST answers fell into "social groups and classifications" and enter that number online to compare it to the average for your class or the nation. If your number is higher, you are more collectivistic than the average student; if it is lower, you are less collectivistic (see, for example, Cousins, 1989).

What exactly do these terms mean? **Individualism** is a cultural system that values the needs of the self more than those of the group; **collectivism** values the group ahead of the self. Collectivistic cultures are sometimes described as "traditional" or "family-oriented." Individualism also emphasizes standing out and being unique, whereas collectivism emphasizes fitting in. The United States is an example of an individualistic culture; an American proverb claims that "the squeaky wheel gets the grease." In Japan, a collectivistic culture, a proverb warns that "the nail that stands out gets pounded down" (Markus & Kitayama, 1991). At first it might seem strange that culture has so much influence on something so personal like how we see ourselves. But culture is not just TV shows and different foods—we learn cultural values as we grow up, and eventually these values become deeply intertwined with how we see ourselves and what we value. We discuss this in detail in Chapter 11.

In this chapter, we examine several answers to the question, Who am I? First, we look at the topic of self-concept—how we see ourselves. We then examine self-esteem, how we feel about ourselves. Finally, we look at self-regulation, how we control and direct ourselves.

individualism
a cultural system that values the needs of the individual self more than those of the group

collectivism
a cultural system that values the needs of the group more than those of the individual self

The Self-Concept

LO 5.1   **Define self-concept and its parts; explain how the self as "I" differs from the self as "me"; and discuss the modern view of the self as a knowledge structure or schema.**

self-concept
a person's image of him- or herself

Your **self-concept** is the image you have of yourself—which is not necessarily the same as how others see you or how you actually are. This is why it's called a *concept*. The TST does a good job in giving an overview of the self-concept, but it doesn't give the entire picture. We provide that in this section discussing four main aspects of the self-concept: the material self, the social self, the spiritual self, and the true self. But first, let's wade into some more challenging philosophical waters and try to separate the self-concept from the self as observer.

JOURNAL PROMPT: UNDERSTANDING YOURSELF

What aspects of your self-concept are most important to you? For example, do your social roles matter more to you than your physical qualities? Why?

The I and the Me

William James, the great American psychologist and philosopher (and brother of writer Henry James), wrote the 1891 classic analysis of the self that has driven research on the topic ever since. James started with a seemingly simple question: When you think about yourself, who does the thinking and who are you thinking about? James realized that a part of ourselves is observing and a part of ourselves is observed. He called the observing part the "I." The part of the self we see he called the "me." This is easy to remember because the "I" sees the "me."

When Jessica took the TST, for example, her "I" looked at her "me." What she wrote is really a description of that "me." Another way to see this is to think about who you are. Part of you, the "I," will feel like an observer. What you are thinking about—your traits or relationships, for example—is the "me."

Of course, the nature of the "I" is very tricky—the very notion of exactly what in our brains is looking at the "me" is, at essence, what psychologists, philosophers, and neuroscientists debate when they consider what consciousness really is. James concluded that, as a psychologist, all he knew for sure was the "thought is itself the thinker" (1891, p. 401). In other words, he was sure about the "me" but not about the "I." We're not going to jump into the fray on that one—it will just make your brain hurt.

The "me," however, is somewhat easier to understand because it is, at base, the self-concept. Again, James divided the "me" into three main parts: the material self, the social self, and the spiritual self. These are accompanied by an overarching fourth, the true self—the person you really are.

The Material Self

James's first great insight was that the self extends beyond the mind into the body and even into what we wear: "The body is the innermost part of the **material self** in each of us; and certain parts of the body seem more intimately ours than the rest. The clothes come next" (1891, p. 292).

Our clothing has a major impact on how we see ourselves (and, of course, on how others see us). When you put on a business suit, for example, you might feel professional and respectable. In contrast, when you put on old sweats, you might feel relaxed or even lazy (Hannover & Kühnen, 2002). You can even strategically change how you feel by putting on a certain set of clothes—this is part of the allure of "retail therapy" (Pratt, 2004).

The material self extends even further into the world. Your physical possessions can become part of your sense of self. You can see this clearly with certain possessions such as cars. For many people, a car is part of the self. When you're driving down the highway and press the accelerator, it almost feels like the car is part of you. It might also express something about your identity. Jessica, for example, might drive a hybrid Prius as part of her identity as an environmentalist. Jack might drive a BMW to show that he is sporty or sophisticated.

The extension of the self into possessions becomes most apparent when possessions become damaged or threatened. People whose cars have been broken into often say that they felt personally violated. The car is closely tied to the self.

Now imagine you were fighting with your ex-romantic partner—maybe he or she cheated on you. What do you do? Well, you would handle it in a mature and dignified way, of course. But imagine someone else in your place—maybe

material self
the extension of the self into the body, clothes, and possessions

A gentleman with a classy material self.

someone lower in agreeableness and conscientiousness. That someone spray-paints the ex's car with a nasty phrase or scratches the side of the car with a key. Why attack the cheating partner's car? It's a very emotional way of hurting someone, because the car is a part of the self. As James (1891) put it, "[a]n equally instinctive impulse drives us to collect property; and the collections thus made become, with different degrees of intimacy, parts of our empirical selves" (p. 307). Carrie Underwood is more direct in her song "Before He Cheats," singing about smashing the headlights of her cheating boyfriend's car with a baseball bat.

The Social Self

social self

the part of the self related to group membership

The second part of James's "me" is the **social self**. James's second great insight was that the self was not just a single unified entity. Instead, our individual self is tied directly to our social relationships. James's famous statement on the issue was, "Properly speaking, *a man has as many social selves as there are individuals who recognize him* and carry an image of him in their mind" (1891, p. 294). So different aspects of your self will be active when you interact with different people (see the Personality's Past feature for more historical perspective on the social self).

Personality's Past

Historical View
of the Social Self

'What am I? companion, say.'
And the friend not hesitates
To assign just place and mates;
Answers not in word or letter,
Yet is understood the better;
Each to each a looking-glass,
Reflects his figure that doth pass.
　　　—Ralph Waldo Emerson, *Astræa*

This poem by Emerson inspired one of psychology's great insights: We learn about ourselves by seeing others' reactions to us. "Each to each a looking-glass," Emerson writes, meaning that each person is a mirror to another. If people smile at us we know we are liked; if they frown we know we are disliked. If people show fear we know we are scary; and if people laugh we know we are funny. And if you have ever spoken to someone who made no reaction, you know how uncomfortable it can be not knowing if your message is getting across.

Charles Horton Cooley (1902) used Emerson's verse to coin the phrase *looking-glass self.* Cooley's insight was that the self evolved through the process of seeing others' reactions. This was of particular importance in childhood when people learn about themselves from watching the reaction of parents, other caregivers, and siblings.

Several great thinkers followed Cooley's path for examining the social self. James Mark Baldwin (1930) took the step of adding a new social unit, the *socius.* The socius is the social self—the outcome of the exchange between the self and the other (or "alter"). Baldwin then went further by claiming that all of society is really one "protoplasm" with individuals emerging from this protoplasm, but not causing it:

Society, genetically considered, is not a composition of separate individuals; on the contrary, the individuals are differentiations of a common social protoplasm. The conclusion is drawn that the individual is a "social outcome not a social unit." We are members one of another.

George Herbert Mead (1913) went in another direction. He wanted to make sense of the inner voices in our head that tell us how we are doing and constantly judge our own actions. He called this voice the *generalized other*. Imagine lying in bed thinking about how you did on an exam. Part of you might be criticizing yourself for not studying hard enough or congratulating yourself for doing so well. This judging is the generalized other at work. As Mead wrote:

> The self which consciously stands over against other selves thus becomes an object, an other to himself, through the very fact that he hears himself talk, and replies. The mechanism of introspection is therefore given in the social attitude which man necessarily assumes toward himself, and the mechanism of thought, in so far as thought uses symbols which are used in social intercourse, is but an inner conversation.

These ideas about the social self have an important place in the history of the self. Along with the work of William James, they led researchers to consider the individual not only as a unit, but as a piece of a greater network of relationships.

For example, our friend Jessica waits tables at a restaurant to help pay for her tuition. While there, she will be pleasant, polite, and focused—and will see herself that way. Later that night, though, Jessica goes out to a club with some of her friends from school. She might see herself as (and be) extraverted, edgy, and risk taking. She is a very different Jessica when she is with a different group of people. As James (1891, p. 294) put it, "[m]any a youth who is demure enough before his parents and teachers, swears and swaggers like a pirate among his 'tough' young friends."

Then Jessica goes home over the weekend to see her parents. She might start feeling like a young teenager or a little kid again. She might want her parents to take care of her (instead of her usual independence at school), or she might start fighting with her mom about clothes just like a 12-year-old. She might not like this adolescent self, but the social relationship with her mom activates it. Seeing your siblings—say, being in the same house again after holiday break—can have the same effect, bringing you back to your earlier immature self.

Social media can make these multiple selves more difficult to negotiate. Sites such as Facebook force people to present one self to many different social groups. So, instead of presenting different sides of yourself to different social groups—such as college friends, high school friends, coworkers, and your family—you have one giant social network that includes your mom and your best friend as well as people you hardly know. This leads to all sorts of problems as the different selves and social groups collide. Do you become one generic self that works for all groups? Do you create multiple online identities? Do you defriend your mom or your boss?

A watermelon hat suggests low self-monitoring.

self-monitoring
the tendency to adapt behavior to fit the demands of the situation

Say Jessica posts a picture of her new tattoo. Her cool friends love it, but her mom sees it and flies off the handle. Edgy Jessica and Daughter Jessica collide. Politicians once gave different speeches to, say, a blue-collar crowd or a white-collar crowd. Now either speech might be picked up and put online, so they have to give more generic speeches everywhere they go. This makes politicians in some ways more honest, but can make for bland speeches.

Some people are more comfortable navigating these various social situations than others. Imagine Jessica attends a luncheon held at a fancy country club by a women's charity in her town. Because Jessica is naturally attuned to social situations, she will observe how the other women are acting: They are keeping their voices at a moderate volume, using formal language, and smiling a lot. Jessica wants to blend in to this social situation, so she carries herself in the same way as the other women at the luncheon. In personality terms, Jessica has a high level of the trait **self-monitoring**, meaning she easily adapts her behavior to fit the situation (Snyder, 1974).

Jessica's friend Ashley then arrives at the party. Unlike Jessica, she is a low self-monitor. Ashley does not pay much attention to the social situation and instead acts the way she would with a group of friends her age. She uses a lot of slang, curses occasionally, and tells dirty jokes. The rest of the women at the luncheon are surprised by her behavior—it just does not fit the social context.

High self-monitors try to fit into different social situations. Low self-monitors do not. Take the self-monitoring questionnaire below to see how you score—and see if you can tell which items indicate high self-monitoring and which indicate low self-monitoring.

TAKE
the
Questionnaire
in **REVEL**

Questionnaire 5.1 THE SELF-MONITORING SCALE

Please answer all the questions.

1. I find it hard to imitate the behavior of other people.
 ○ True
 ○ False

2. At parties and social gatherings, I do not attempt to do or say things that others will like.
 ○ True
 ○ False

3. I can only argue for ideas that I already believe.
 ○ True
 ○ False

4. I can make impromptu speeches even on topics about which I have almost no information.
 ○ True
 ○ False

Previous   Next

When my (J. M. T.) class takes this test, we always discuss the advantages and disadvantages of each personality type. High self-monitoring is useful for adapting to different social situations. The downside is you're always changing and might sometimes wonder who you really are or what you really want. Then we usually get into a discussion about swearing and self-monitoring. The low self-monitors admit that editing their swearing is difficult, and even the high self-monitors often say it can be hard. If you've ever let one slip in front of a small child or your grandmother, you have experienced the downside of low self-monitoring.

The Spiritual Self

The final component of William James's self is the most closely related to personality traits. James believed that the **spiritual self** is a person's moral center and also includes a person's "inner or subjective being [and] psychic faculties or dispositions" (1891, p. 296). This includes classic personality traits such as extraversion or agreeableness as well as cognitive abilities such as intelligence and creativity. For Jessica, her *nice* personality would be part of her spiritual self. The spiritual self also includes moral beliefs, so Jessica's environmentalism would be here as well.

spiritual self
a person's moral center

The True Self

Who are you really? What is the truest, most core aspect of the person you are? These are the questions of the **true self**, or the most real, authentic self (James, 1891). Some people go on a quest to "find themselves"—a pilgrimage to Spain, a trip to Tibet, or just a summer spent working in Colorado. Others do not think about their true self at all.

true self
the person you really are

The true self can take very different forms in different people (Turner & Schutte, 1981). For some, the true self reflects social relationships and roles. Jessica might feel closest to her true self when she is spending the holiday with her family; this experience just seems to capture who she really is. Jessica's friend Luis, in contrast, might feel closest to his true self when he is working on projects with the debate team. Something about being in that role taps into his deepest nature. Kayla, however, is her truest self when she loses herself in the moment. When she is dancing at a club late in the evening and focusing completely and totally on what she is doing and experiencing, she feels real, true, and authentic. Jaden feels his truest self when he is surfing, especially when alone in the ocean before dawn (Turner & Schutte, 1981).

Modern personality psychologists have measured how close or far away someone is from her true self. This is called **authenticity**, or how much people feel they are living their true self (Kernis & Goldman, 2006). Some people feel more authentic than do others (this does not mean they are more *real* than other people; they just *feel* that way). Authenticity of the self has four related components. The first is **awareness**: Are you aware of your motives, strengths, and weaknesses? Authentic individuals

authenticity
the extent to which a person feels aligned to his or her true self

awareness (as part of authenticity)
awareness of your motives, strengths, and weaknesses

Follow the signs
to authenticity.

are aware of their strengths but also understand what they need to improve. They also understand why they do things like eating too much after a stressful day at work or feeling ashamed after getting negative feedback. The second is **unbiased processing**: Are you able to take in information from the world in an unbiased, direct, and realistic way? Authentic people can see the good and the bad in the world and make decisions based on this information.

The third aspect is **behavior**: Do your actions reflect your true emotions, values, and beliefs? As much as possible, authentic people act in a way that matches their true selves. The fourth and last aspect is **authentic relationships**: Are you able to express your true, authentic self in your relationships with others? Authentic people will strive to have relationships in which they can be themselves rather than pretending to be the person they think their partner wants. Singer/satirist Christine Lavin captured inauthenticity in relationships perfectly, cycling through a litany of things she doesn't like (skiing, going to the opera, eating sushi) but does anyway because her boyfriend likes them. The song is titled, appropriately, "Good Thing He Can't Read My Mind."

One form of not feeling like your true self is the **imposter phenomenon** (Fried-Buchalter, 1992; Ross et al., 2001), or feeling like a phony, a fraud, or a fake. Imagine Jessica graduates from college and enters medical school. As part of her training, she works in the emergency room at a big hospital. Jessica feels a bit like a phony. She doesn't know exactly what she is doing and assumes that people can see her lack of skills, or that she doesn't belong in the position at all. This is a classic example of the impostor phenomenon.

When are people most likely to feel like imposters? It is usually when they shift from one social role to the next, especially when they are doing something just beyond their skills or training. When I (W. K. C.) first became the head of our psychology department, one of my friends from graduate school also became a department head at a major research university. He sent me an email that contained nothing but a link to the song "The Lunatics Have Taken Over the Asylum." Clearly, we both felt a bit of the imposter phenomenon. Similarly, many college seniors find it strange to put on business clothes and go on a job interview, especially at a large, traditional company where workers dress and act formally. After all, the day before they were wearing shorts and a t-shirt at a party. So, when you first enter college, go to graduate school, start a new job, get married, become a parent, or go through any other life transition, you might feel like an imposter at first. Some people have this experience more than others, and it is certainly not a bad thing in moderation. It's just part of growing as a person (for example, Brown & Olshansky, 1997; Legassie et al., 2008).

unbiased processing (as part of authenticity)
ability to see the good and the bad in the world and make decisions based on this information

behavior (as part of authenticity)
acting in a way that reflects the true self

authentic relationships (as part of authenticity)
a relationship in which someone can be who they really are

imposter phenomenon
the experience of feeling like a phony, a fraud, or a fake

Evaluating the Self: Self-Esteem

LO 5.2 Define self-esteem and explain its benefits and costs.

Do you feel good about yourself? Do you like yourself? Are you a person of worth
or value? All of these questions measure **self-esteem**. Self-esteem is a person's
attitude toward him- or herself. Like all attitudes, it is an evaluation: "I like
myself" or "I don't like myself." Take the questionnaire to better understand the
level of your self-esteem.

self-esteem
a person's attitude
toward him- or
herself

Questionnaire 5.2 ROSENBERG SELF-ESTEEM SCALE

Please answer all the questions.

1. I feel that I am a person of worth, at least on an equal basis with others.
○ Strongly Agree
○ Agree
○ Disagree
○ Strongly Disagree

2. I feel that I have a number of good qualities.
○ Strongly Agree
○ Agree
○ Disagree
○ Strongly Disagree

3. All in all, I am inclined to feel that I am a failure.
○ Strongly Agree
○ Agree
○ Disagree
○ Strongly Disagree

4. I am able to do things as well as most people.
○ Strongly Agree
○ Agree
○ Disagree

Previous   Next

TAKE the Questionnaire in **REVEL**

The most commonly used measure for assessing general self-esteem is the
one you just completed: the Rosenberg Self-Esteem Scale (Rosenberg, 1989), a
10-item scale that asks about self-esteem in a very straightforward, face-valid way.
The highest score on the Rosenberg is 40, and the lowest 10, with a midpoint of
25. During recent years, the average score for college students has been around
35 (Gentile et al., 2010). In other words, college students, on average, have pretty high self-esteem. They like themselves quite a bit.
In fact, what we think of as "low" self-esteem is actually a score
somewhere in the middle of the self-esteem scale (Baumeister et
al., 2003). Did you score low or high on self-esteem? Even if your
score was below average, the average score is so high that your
self-esteem is likely still pretty solid.

Self-liking is one
aspect of self-esteem.

Is Self-Esteem Good or Bad?

The answer to this question might seem obvious: Of course, high
self-esteem is good and low self-esteem is bad. But things are more
complex than that. A few generations ago, self-esteem was often

seen as a dubious blessing. Too much self-esteem was suspect because cockiness and pride interfere with social relationships.

That began to change in the 1980s when self-esteem became seen as a more uniformly positive trait. In fact, your school might have had a program designed to boost self-esteem (Sykes, 1995). You have probably heard self-esteem-focused advice such as "Believe in yourself and anything is possible" or "You have to love yourself first before you can love someone else."

So, what does the research say? In an extensive research review, self-esteem had two primary outcomes: It feels good and it leads people to initiate action (Baumeister et al., 2003). And feeling good it not a trivial thing—low self-esteem is both a component of depression and predicts depression over time (Orth & Robins, 2013).

Getting a trophy for participating is based on the idea of self-esteem boosting. But does it work?

Self-esteem, however, does not appear to *cause* a range of other positive outcomes such as high academic performance, better behavior, choosing better relationship partners, or performing better at work. This can be a little confusing because self-esteem often correlates with these positive outcomes. So, for example, people in healthy relationships also tend to have higher self-esteem. Why, then, can't we assume self-esteem is *causing* these positive outcomes? As you learned in Chapter 2, correlation does not necessarily mean causation. First, the causal path could go from the positive outcome to self-esteem. If you perform well in school or make friends, your self-esteem might increase. Also, there could be something else at work (a confounding variable) that leads to both high self-esteem and positive outcomes. For example, coming from certain family backgrounds might lead to both low self-esteem and poor performance at school. Some studies have found correlations between low self-esteem and crime or mental health problems, but when third variables such as family background are taken into account, the link all but disappears (Boden et al., 2007, 2008). Here's one example that illustrates how self-esteem doesn't cause success: In the United States, the ethnic group with the lowest self-esteem is Asian Americans (Twenge & Crocker, 2002), who also have the best academic performance. As you learn in Chapter 11, this might be due to Asian cultures focusing less on the self.

If self-esteem does not necessarily cause good outcomes beyond those mentioned, are self-esteem-boosting programs a good idea? Surprisingly, no research investigated this question before these programs were widely implemented. Recently, however, one experiment examined the effects of self-esteem enhancement on exam grades among low-performing students in an introductory psychology course—in theory, the students who should need self-esteem boosting the most. Students who were making Cs, Ds, or Fs received study questions each week during the semester, some of which included messages at the end. One-third of the students (the *self-responsibility* group) received messages such as this one:

> Past research suggests that when students get back their tests, they tend to blame poor scores on external factors: they say things like "the test was too hard," "the prof didn't explain that," or "the questions are too picky." Other studies suggest, though, that students who take responsibility for their grades not only get better grades, but they also learn that they, personally, can control the grades they get . . . . Bottom line: Take personal control of your performance.

Another third of students (the *self-esteem boost* group) read this:

> Past research suggests that when students get back their tests, they tend to lose confidence: they say things like "I can't do this," "I'm worthless," or "I'm not as good as other people in college." Other studies suggest, though, that students who have high self-esteem not only get better grades, but they remain self-confident and assured. . . . Bottom line: Hold your head—and your self-esteem—high.

The final third (the *control* group) did not get a message.

So what happened? The self-esteem boost backfired (see Figure 5.2). Students with Ds and Fs who received the self-esteem message performed much worse on the final. Those with Cs performed about the same on the final no matter what message (or none) they received.

Figure 5.2 Exam Scores of D and F Students by Self-Esteem-Boosting Group

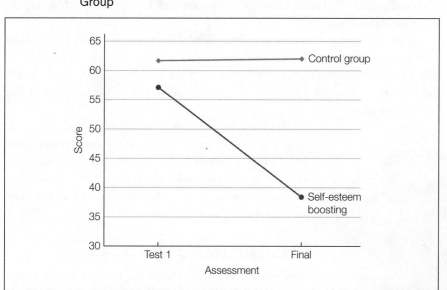

SOURCE: Based on Forsyth et al., (2007)

There was another wrinkle to this story. The students who got the self-esteem-boosting messages did in fact get their self-esteem boosted. When self-esteem was assessed at the end of the study, these students' self-esteem was higher than those who received messages about personal responsibility—even though the self-esteem-boosting group's performance was worse.

Overall, then, the self-esteem boost was a reasonably good strategy for raising self-esteem but a bad strategy for improving performance (Forsyth et al., 2007).

Explicit Versus Implicit Self-Esteem

Like most personality traits, self-esteem is usually measured with a self-report questionnaire such as the Rosenberg scale that you took. But perhaps some people are insecure only deep down inside, and won't—or can't—admit that on a questionnaire. These "deep down inside" feelings are called **implicit self-esteem**—the self-esteem you are not necessarily aware of having. It's in contrast to **explicit self-esteem**, the self-esteem you are aware of having.

implicit self-esteem
self-esteem you are not necessarily aware of having

explicit self-esteem
self-esteem you are aware of having

So how can implicit self-esteem possibly be measured? Most implicit measures are based on the idea that we make unconscious links between ourselves and positive and negative things. If you think of yourself and that brings to mind positive things, you have high implicit self-esteem. If, however, you think of yourself and that brings to mind negative things, you have low implicit self-esteem.

These links can be measured using clever computer programs such as the Implicit Association Test (IAT; Greenwald & Farnham, 2000; Greenwald et al., 1998). Imagine you are seated at a computer, and you are shown the word *joy* and then quickly had to hit a key for *me* (vs. another key for *not me*). Now do the same for the word *vomit*.

High explicit self-esteem and low implicit self-esteem suggests a donut personality. The outside looks tasty, but there's a hole in the middle.

If you are faster to say *joy* is related to *me* than to *not me*—and the opposite pattern occurs for *vomit*—you will have higher implicit self-esteem on the IAT. Most people who have high explicit self-esteem also have high implicit self-esteem, but exceptions definitely occur when self-esteem is low on one test and high on the other.

High explicit self-esteem and low implicit self-esteem suggest a "donut personality"—someone who feels good about him- or herself on the outside but feels bad about him- or herself or "hollow" on the inside. Research is still exploring implicit self-esteem, as its measurement remains somewhat controversial (Bosson et al., 2000).

Maintaining Self-Esteem

How much does self-esteem matter to us? In a recent study, college students rated getting self-esteem boosts as more important than eating sweets, getting paid, drinking alcohol, and having sex. When college students like something more than sex and beer, it clearly matters a lot (Bushman et al., 2011).

Because self-esteem feels good to us, most people do things to maintain it. These include **self-enhancement**, the desire to maintain and increase a positive self-concept, and **self-esteem regulation**, the actions involved in maintaining high self-esteem.

self-enhancement
the desire to maintain and increase the positivity of the self-concept

Many strategies for keeping self-esteem high are straightforward. One of the most important is forming close relationships. People who have secure relationships tend to have higher self-esteem (Brennan & Morns, 1997). People also maintain self-esteem by belonging to social groups. Apparently self-esteem works like a meter for social belonging, similar to the gas meter in your car—feeling you belong is like fuel in your tank (Leary et al., 1995). According to **sociometer theory**, when belongingness is low, self-esteem drops. This is a warning—like the low-fuel light going on in a car—that you need to seek relationships. When you have a strong sense of belonging, though, your self-esteem will stay high and you'll be like an electric car that rarely needs to stop for gas. Another way of thinking about this involves **loneliness**, or the experience of having fewer relationships than are desired (Peplau & Perlman, 1979). People who are lonely often report lower self-esteem (Leary, 1990; Russell, 1996).

self-esteem regulation
the actions involved in maintaining high self-esteem

sociometer theory
a theory linking level of self-esteem with level of belongingness

loneliness
the experience of having fewer relationships than are desired

JOURNAL PROMPT: UNDERSTANDING YOURSELF

How do you maintain your self-esteem? Are your attempts successful, or not?

Another way to maintain self-esteem is to succeed at something. When you do well in school, or in athletics, or at work, your self-esteem will stay high or increase. Like relationships, this is pretty basic. When we do well, we feel good.

Other ways we protect our self-esteem are not as clearly in our best interests. The best known of these is the **self-serving bias** (Heider, 1958)—the tendency to take credit for success but deny responsibility for failure. Imagine that you get an A on your psychology test. If you take credit for this, attributing it to your intelligence and work ethic, you will feel good about yourself. In contrast, if you get an F on a psychology test, the best way to protect your self-esteem is to blame something outside yourself for your failure. So you might say the test was unfair or it was "bad luck" that you didn't pass (Campbell & Sedikides, 1999).

self-serving bias
the tendency to take credit for success but deny responsibility for failure

Here's the problem: When someone takes credit for successes but blames bad luck or other people for failures, he will feel good but will not learn from his failures. It's often better to figure out what happened when you failed—maybe you didn't study hard enough or didn't study the right material, or maybe psychology is not a strength of yours. Even though taking responsibility for failure will feel bad, you can learn from it and do better on the next test—and thus will feel good in the future.

Self-Compassion, Self-Efficacy, and Narcissism: Three More Variations on Self-Evaluation

LO 5.3   Describe self-compassion, self-efficacy, and narcissism.

In this section we explore three traits also related to self-evaluation that receive a good amount of attention in the scientific literature. They are self-compassion, self-efficacy, and narcissism.

Self-Compassion

self-compassion

being kind to yourself; treating yourself with the same sense of compassion that you would treat others

self-kindness

being kind to yourself

common humanity

the awareness that all humans make mistakes

mindfulness

being aware of your thoughts and feelings without becoming attached to them

While self-esteem is about liking yourself, **self-compassion** is about being kind to yourself, treating yourself with the same sense of compassion that you would treat others (Neff, 2003; Neff et al., 2007). Self-compassion has three specific components: self-kindness, common humanity, and mindfulness.

Self-kindness is being kind to yourself, especially when you make mistakes. Imagine you did something stupid or embarrassing such as shouting out a dumb answer in class. Self-kindness would mean treating yourself like a good friend; you might say to yourself, "Hey, you messed up, but at least you tried. Don't worry about it." This allows you to bounce back from mistakes much better than you would if you experienced shame or some other negative emotion.

Second, self-compassion involves a sense of **common humanity**—the awareness that all humans mess up sometimes. Many, many other people have made dumb mistakes or felt afraid. Suffering and imperfection are part of the nature of being human. So when you shout out a stupid answer, tell yourself that this

The traditional practice of meditation can increase mindfulness.

experience, as unpleasant as it is, is common. Having this bad experience can even bring you closer to others because you have now experienced a common form of embarrassment. And when experiences are even more negative—not getting the job you wanted, losing a loved one, getting in an accident—living through it can create empathy for others' suffering.

Third and finally, self-compassion includes **mindfulness**. Mindfulness means being aware of your thoughts and feelings without becoming attached to them, and living in the present moment without dwelling on the past (Brown & Ryan, 2003). When you shout out a stupid answer, you might feel a burst of shame, but rather than let that shame overtake you and think about it for the rest of the day, you can simply be mindfully aware of it.

By doing so, you will experience the shame without getting emotionally attached to it. You will watch it arise and then float away. As a result, you will not have to spend the day thinking about it (or trying not to think about it). The practice of mindfulness is rooted in Buddhist philosophy and can be learned through *mindfulness meditation*, a structured practice that involves becoming aware of your thoughts and bodily sensations as they occur (Kabat-Zinn, 1990).

People high in self-compassion are able to experience negative events and set-backs in life without becoming reactive, defensive, or depressed. Instead, they learn from their misfortunes and even use them to feel closer to others (Terry et al., 2012).

Self-Efficacy

Another trait often confused with self-esteem is **self-efficacy**, the belief that one will be effective and successfully work toward goals (Bandura, 1977). For example, imagine that you have to give a class presentation next month. If you have high self-efficacy, you will believe that you will be able to get it done; if you have low self-efficacy, you will doubt you can. This is the difference between self-esteem and self-efficacy: Someone with high self-esteem thinks, "I'm great, so I will give a great presentation"; someone high in self-efficacy thinks, "I can give a great presentation if I work hard at it."

self-efficacy
the belief that one will be effective and successfully work toward goals

---

Watch WHAT'S IN IT FOR ME?

Video

WATCH
the video in
REVEL

Given its links with goal setting, it seems logical that self-efficacy should predict performance at school and at work. But what does the research show?

In the classroom, self-efficacy does indeed predict performance (Multon et al, 1991). However, this correlation is highest for low-achieving students and for basic skills. Self-efficacy is four times more important for predicting performance on basic tasks than performance on challenging standardized tests (Multon et al., 1991). Similarly, self-efficacy does predict performance at work, but again especially on simple tasks. Self-efficacy does still predict performance on more complex tasks, but the correlation is smaller (Stajkovic & Luthans, 1998).

How does self-efficacy compare to self-esteem in predicting job performance? Remember, self-efficacy is about feeling that you can effectively master challenges and self-esteem is about liking yourself. As you might have guessed, self-efficacy predicts job performance about twice as well as self-esteem (Judge & Bono, 2001).

The second question, though, is more complicated: Does self-efficacy *cause* better performance on tasks? That is, if I can make Michael feel a greater sense of self-efficacy, will he do better in school? Self-efficacy is a mixed bag. When the task is something simple such as squeezing a handgrip, high self-efficacy seems to help (Hutchinson et al., 2008). In contrast, on complex tasks, high self-efficacy can let you down. In one study, for example, people played a complex analytical game. Those with high self-efficacy actually did worse, probably because they were overconfident in their abilities and therefore didn't focus enough (Vancouver, et al., 2002).

Overall, then, people with high self-efficacy seem to be high performers—and higher performers than those with high self-esteem. The catch is that self-efficacy might not *cause* this high performance, especially on complex and challenging tasks. Instead, self-efficacy is more likely to be an outcome of success.

Narcissism

Before we begin this section, take the questionnaire. You can then apply your results to the discussion that follows.

TAKE
the
Questionnaire
in **REVEL**

Questionnaire 5.3 NARCISSISTIC PERSONALITY INVENTORY

Interactive

1. I have a natural talent for influencing people.
   ○ True
   ○ False

2. Modesty doesn't become me.
   ○ True
   ○ False

3. I would do almost anything on a dare.
   ○ True
   ○ False

4. When people compliment me I get embarrassed.
   ○ True
   ○ False

Previous   Next

Imagine you meet someone who initially appears very confident, charming, and likable. She is well groomed and seems very successful. You might be romantically attracted to her, and if she were running for political office, you would be likely to vote for her.

But then you hear some negative things about this person. She doesn't have a lot of emotionally close relationships (although she is socially popular). She's been unfaithful in past relationships. Her ethics are suspect—she puts selfish needs in front of the needs of others. She shows flashes of anger when these negative things are mentioned. What explains behavior like this? In short, she might be a narcissist (Campbell & Campbell, 2009; Morf & Rhodewalt, 2001).

Narcissism is a personality trait that includes a very positive—even grandiose—view of the self. Narcissism comes in two major forms: grandiose and vulnerable. Of the two, grandiose narcissism is more studied and is more in line with what most people think of as narcissism (as in the example above). **Grandiose narcissism** is associated with a more extraverted, socially bold, self-centered, egotistical, vain, and cocky personality. Grandiose narcissists focus on being better, smarter, or more attractive than others.

In contrast, **vulnerable narcissism** is linked to lower extraversion and assertiveness and more neuroticism, anxiety, and depression. Imagine someone living in his mom's basement at age 30. He won't take a job because he is too smart for all the jobs out there and nobody understands his brilliance. He spends a lot of time online mocking people. He has no girlfriend because in the real world he is shy and awkward. Despite seeing himself as special, he has low self-esteem. This more vulnerable form of narcissism (Cain et al., 2008; Miller et al., 2011) is more often seen in psychiatric settings (Pincus et al., 2009).

narcissism
a personality trait that includes a very positive, grandiose view of the self

grandiose narcissism
narcissism including high extraversion and dominance but low neuroticism

vulnerable narcissism
narcissism including low extraversion and dominance but high neuroticism

---

JOURNAL PROMPT: UNDERSTANDING YOURSELF

Do you think most people are honest about their level of narcissism? That is, do you think most people who have narcissistic tendencies would identify themselves as narcissistic? Would you identify yourself as narcissistic? Why or why not?

In this section, our focus is on grandiose narcissism, so when we say narcissism, we are referring to the grandiose form. Grandiose narcissistic personality traits are often measured with the Narcissistic Personality Inventory (NPI; Raskin & Terry, 1988), which you completed. It consists of 40 pairs of statements—one narcissistic and one not. NPI scores are the total of narcissistic statements chosen, so they vary from 0 to 40. The NPI is a measure of narcissistic personality traits and is not the same as a diagnosis of the clinical disorder called *narcissistic personality disorder* (NPD), although NPD individuals do tend to score high on the NPI (Miller & Campbell, 2010). However, plenty of narcissists—meaning people who score high on the NPI—do not fit the diagnostic criteria for NPD, which is by definition more severe and includes serious deficits in life functioning (more on this in Chapter 14). There is no set cutoff for a "high" score on the NPI—instead, each point higher is correlated with more narcissistic behavior (Foster & Campbell, 2007).

Narcissists with the more grandiose form usually score high on extraversion and low on agreeableness on the Big Five (Paulhus, 2001). They have a positive self-concept—most also score high on explicit self-esteem measures such as the Rosenberg scale (Bosson et al., 2008). But are narcissists just saying they feel good about themselves? Could they actually have low self-esteem and be using their grandiosity as a cover for insecurity? When narcissists complete an implicit self-esteem measure with general items such as *good* and *bad*, they score high on self-esteem (Campbell et al., 2007). So deep down inside, narcissists think that they're awesome! Narcissism cannot be easily explained away as a cover for insecurity. (For more on the correlation between self-esteem and narcissism, see "The Science of Personality" feature.)

EXPLORE in REVEL →

The Science of Personality UNDERSTANDING CORRELATION: SELF-ESTEEM AND NARCISSISM

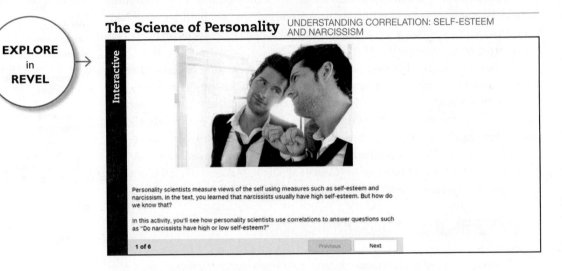

Personality scientists measure views of the self using measures such as self-esteem and narcissism. In the text, you learned that narcissists usually have high self-esteem. But how do we know that?

In this activity, you'll see how personality scientists use correlations to answer questions such as "Do narcissists have high or low self-esteem?"

1 of 6   Previous   Next

Narcissists differ from others with high self-esteem in at least one major way, however: They do not describe themselves as caring. They freely admit that deep, emotionally close relationships are not particularly interesting to them (Campbell et al., 2002; Foster et al., 2006). They can be charming, likable, and social, but the basic sense of warmth and reciprocity is not there. Narcissists are grandiose, socially confident, see themselves as unique, and feel entitled to special treatment (Miller et al., 2011; Paulhus, 2001). Basically, narcissists think that they are better than they are and better than other people (John & Robins, 1994).

So, narcissistic individuals are in a bind. They think they are better than they actually are; they are legends in their own minds. Thus, they need to constantly get positive, self-enhancing feedback. A narcissistic person might brag and show off, value flashy material possessions, have plastic surgery to become more attractive, jump at chances to be on film or to see him- or herself in a mirror (Robins & John, 1997), and continually turn the conversation back to him- or herself. It's important to note that doing just one of these things does not make you a narcissist; being a narcissist is a whole package of these tendencies along with an inflated sense of self. A narcissist will also show a pronounced self-serving bias and will be willing to steal credit from his or her friends (Campbell et al., 2000). She will even use her relationships to get self-esteem and social status by, for example, getting "trophy" partners or "playing games" in her relationships (more on this in Chapter 14).

I love me.

When narcissists do all this effectively, they feel good about themselves—their self-esteem will stay high and they will not be depressed. When they fail in these areas, however, they are at risk for depression and anxiety (Miller et al., 2007). The problem is that narcissists are not more beautiful, successful, or smarter than anyone else. Narcissists may appear to be more successful, but their actual performance is sometimes even worse than non-narcissists (Robins & Beer, 2001). As for beauty, narcissism has a small link to appearance, but it is likely a result of caring about appearance rather than basic good looks (Holtzman & Strube, 2010). Another study found that narcissists believed they were more attractive than others, but others did not actually rate them as more attractive. The study's title summed it up well: "Narcissists think they are so hot, but they are not" (Bleske-Rechek et al., 2008).

So, is narcissism good or bad? It is, in short, a trade-off between good and bad (Campbell & Campbell, 2009). On the negative side, narcissism is linked to poor decision making, such as taking risks and not learning from mistakes (Campbell et al., 2004), and to relationships lacking commitment and emotional intimacy (Campbell & Foster, 2002). On the positive side (at least positive for the individual), narcissism is good for starting relationships. After one meeting of a group, the narcissists were liked more than others. However, after several meetings, the narcissistic individuals were liked less (Paulhus, 1998). Narcissistic individuals are more likely to emerge as leaders in groups of strangers (Brunell et al., 2008). Narcissistic individuals have more friends on

Figure 5.3 Narcissism Among Celebrities

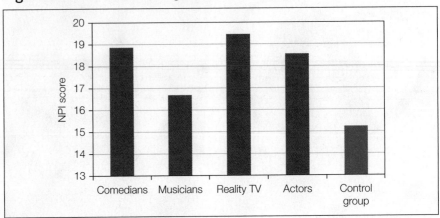

SOURCE: Based on Young & Pinsky (2006).

Facebook; they are very good at establishing shallow relationships (Buffardi & Campbell, 2008) like those often seen online (there's more on this topic in Chapter 13).

Finally, narcissism may be useful for becoming a celebrity (see Figure 5.3). Mark Young and Drew Pinsky (also known as "Dr. Drew") gave the NPI to celebrities on Dr. Drew's show *Loveline*. It turns out that celebrities are more narcissistic than the average person, and this was especially true for reality television stars (Young & Pinsky, 2006). So, when you are watching reality television, you are seeing more narcissistic individuals. (Surprised? We'd bet not.)

Self-Regulation

LO 5.4 Understand how self-regulation and self-control operate.

Your life, like everyone's, involves setting and trying to achieve goals. You might want to graduate from college with honors, meet an ideal romantic partner, and/or become financially well off. In other words, you want the person you are now to become the person you want to be. This process—guiding and directing yourself to a desired state—is called **self-regulation**. We discuss two aspects of self-regulation—possible selves and self-control as a mental muscle—using the example of losing weight to illustrate each.

self-regulation
the process of guiding and directing yourself to a desired state

Possible Selves

We not only know who we are, but also who we could be. These *could-be* selves are called **possible selves**, a term that goes back to William James and that has reemerged in modern psychology (Markus & Nurius, 1986).

possible selves
the selves you imagine you could be, whether ideal or feared

What are your possible selves? They could be desired or hoped-for selves, such as "a physically fit student." They could also be feared selves, such as "an overweight student." Many people have a feared self of being lonely that is especially acute right before or after a breakup—in our despair, we wonder if we will ever date again. Feared selves can be very motivating, but they can sometimes also trap us in bad patterns (such as staying with a romantic partner we know is bad for us).

Possible selves link the self to both emotion and motivation. When you think of a desired self, like "being physically fit," this can motivate you to work toward a goal and feel good while doing so, perhaps by exercising and eating right. In contrast, when you think of a feared self, like "being obese," this makes you feel bad and motivates you to avoid this feared self by, for example, staying away from junk food and getting some exercise.

Two of the most studied forms of possible selves are **ought selves** and **ideal selves**, part of **self-discrepancy theory** (Higgins, 1987). Ought selves are the person we think we *should* be; ideal selves are the people who we *want* to be. If your mother is always nagging you to lose weight, this would create an ought self of someone who is thin. If your mother doesn't care about your weight, but you yourself really want to be thin, you would have an ideal self of being thin. The difference between our ideal or ought selves and our actual self is the **discrepancy** in self-discrepancy theory.

Ought and ideal selves can have the same goal, in this case being thin, but feel very different. When you fail to live up to your ought self, you are likely to feel anxious and worried—imagine seeing your mom again after you gained 20 pounds. In contrast, when you fail to live up to your ideal self, you are likely to feel depressed—how people often feel when they look in the mirror after having gained weight.

Living up to the standard of an ought self versus an ideal self is also different. When you live up to your ought self, you are likely to feel relaxed and at peace—imagine your mom coming to see you when you are thin. You will feel calm about seeing her. In contrast, when you live up to your ideal self, you are likely to feel happy and excited. Imagine looking in the mirror and seeing your new, thin shape. You feel good and might go celebrate by buying some new clothes.

ought self
the person you think you should be

ideal self
the person you want to be

self-discrepancy theory
a model linking the distance between the actual self and the ought and ideal selves to emotion

discrepancy
the difference between where you are (your actual self) and where you want to be (for example, your ideal or ought self)

Self-Control as a Mental Muscle

Controlling your baser impulses—eating, yelling, lust, all that good stuff—is usually a good idea (Tangney et al., 2004). Imagine you are sitting in your apartment. You are trying to lose those 20 pounds, and you are staring at a large slice of chocolate cake that your roommate brought back from a birthday party. You want to take a bite (or two or three) of that cake with almost every fiber of your being, but you remember your diet and a part of you—think of it as your will—holds you back and you successfully resist. In this case, you see your willpower,

The total loss of self-control.

or **self-control**, in action, and you can feel the effort it exerts to control your behavior.

Self-control, it turns out, works a lot like a muscle. Imagine lifting a heavy weight and resisting chocolate cake. First, both self-control and muscles involve exerting effort. Second, both self-control and muscles are limited. You can't simply lift as much weight as you want. If you decide to do a 300-pound bench press without training, in most cases you will fail. You have to work at building your muscle strength incrementally, with a lot of practice, over time. The same is true for self-control. If you've been on a diet for only a few days, you might be able to resist a single slice of chocolate cake one night, but imagine your roommate brings home a week's worth of the finest chocolate pastries from around the globe: eclairs, petite fours, chocolate mousse, and hand-dipped chocolate truffles. Without having had enough time to practice sufficient self-control over time, you likely wouldn't stand a chance of resisting all those delicious confections for such an extended period.

Third, both self-control and muscles get tired. If you do 50 push-ups and then immediately lift weights, your muscles will be tired and you will not be able to lift as much. The same process occurs with self-control. If you exert a great deal of self-control during the day—say, smiling at rude customers while waiting on tables or taking a really demanding exam—you will have less self-control available when that chocolate cake is put in front of you. Even though you would normally resist, you may not have the willpower left to control your eating.

self-control
willpower; the ability to control one's own behavior

ego depletion
a state of exhausted self-control

Researchers call this loss of self-control **ego depletion** and have demonstrated it in several clever experiments. In one study, students were asked not to eat for several hours before coming to the lab for a "taste test." When they showed up to the lab, freshly baked chocolate chip cookies were waiting on the table and the scent of the cookies wafted through the room. A plate of radishes sat next to the cookies. In the low-depletion condition, the students were told to taste the cookies and not the radishes. That was easy to do and took little self-control. In the high-depletion condition, the students were told to taste the radishes and not the cookies. This took self-control.

JOURNAL PROMPT: UNDERSTANDING YOURSELF

Describe a time when you weren't able to maintain your self-control. What factors that are discussed in this section might have contributed to that inability?

Both groups were then asked to work on geometry problems that were, unknown to them, impossible to solve. Working on a difficult and frustrating task like this takes a lot of self-control. As predicted, the students who had to resist eating the cookies—thus depleting their self-control—gave up more easily at trying to solve the problems (see Figure 5.4) (Baumeister et al., 1998).

Both self-control and muscles get stronger if you exercise them regularly. If you do 50 push-ups every day, you will strengthen your muscles. The same process occurs with self-control. If you exert significant self-control every day, your self-control will become stronger over time. In one study, individuals built up their self-control by starting and maintaining an exercise program for 2 months. Compared to a control group, the exercise group improved their self-control in other areas of their lives, such as studying, spending money, and being healthy. So by practicing self-control in one area, they improved their self-control in another area (Oaten & Cheng, 2006).

So, if self-control works like a muscle, how can you use that information to your advantage? First, if you want to resist temptation, try to avoid the forbidden thing. It is very difficult to avoid a chocolate cake that is sitting right in front of you; it is much easier to keep the chocolate cake out of your apartment in the first place. This is why dieting programs and books suggest not buying dessert at the grocery store—out of sight, out of mind, or at least easier to resist if the ice cream isn't right there in your freezer. Second, be especially careful with self-control when you are tired or frustrated. If you have been working all day, you are going to be especially vulnerable to temptation. Third, make a habit of exercising your self-control. William James talked about doing something every day that you did not want to do. Not something horrible, but something that takes self-control,

Figure 5.4 Time Spent on Unsolvable Problems by Self-Control Condition

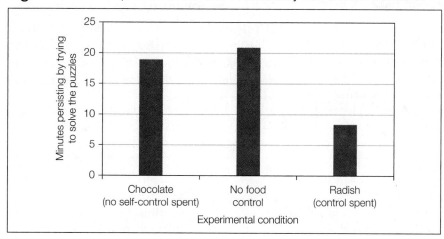

SOURCE: Based on Baumeister et al. (1998).

such as using good table manners even when you are eating alone. This will build your self-control just as hitting the gym will build your muscles. Then, when you really need your self-control to avoid a chocolate cake or solve math problems for a test, it will be there for you (Baumeister et al., 1994).

Concluding Thoughts

So, who are you? Reading this chapter probably didn't give you a straightforward answer to this question, but it should have helped you to figure out how to break it into some smaller, more manageable concepts that gave you more insight than you had when you started reading.

Understanding yourself is the work of a lifetime, and the answers will change as your self continues to grow and change. By using what you learned in this chapter, you can make some meaningful progress toward self-knowledge.

Learning Objective Summaries

LO 5.1   Define self-concept and its parts; explain how the self as "I" differs from the self as "me"; and discuss the modern view of the self as a knowledge structure or schema.

The "I" is the perceiver and the "me" is the object of perception. More recent views consider the self a complex cognitive knowledge structure.

LO 5.2   Define self-esteem and explain its benefits and costs.

Self-esteem is the positive or negative evaluation of one's self. High self-esteem is associated with many positive outcomes, but that does not necessarily mean self-esteem caused those outcomes.

LO 5.3   Describe self-compassion, self-efficacy, and narcissism.

Self-compassion is a feeling of kindness and compassion for the self; self-efficacy is the confidence that one can effectively meet challenges; narcissism is an inflated view of oneself.

LO 5.4   Understand how self-regulation and self-control operate.

Self-regulation is a broad construct involving directing one's thoughts, feelings, or behaviors in a desired direction. Self-control is more limited, involving overcoming impulsive thoughts, feelings, or behaviors.

Key Terms

individualism, p. 117
collectivism, p. 117
self-concept, p. 118

material self, p. 119
social self, p. 120
self-monitoring, p. 122

spiritual self, p. 123
true self, p. 123
authenticity, p. 123

awareness (as part of authenticity), p. 123
unbiased processing (as part of authenticity), p. 124
behavior (as part of authenticity), p. 124
authentic relationships (as part of authenticity), p. 124
imposter phenomenon, p. 124
self-esteem, p. 125
implicit self-esteem, p. 128

explicit self-esteem, p. 128
self-enhancement, p. 129
self-esteem regulation, p. 129
sociometer theory, p. 129
loneliness, p. 129
self-serving bias, p. 129
self-compassion, p. 130
self-kindness, p. 130
common humanity, p. 130
mindfulness, p. 130
self-efficacy, p. 131

narcissism, p. 133
grandiose narcissism, p. 133
vulnerable narcissism, p. 133
self-regulation, p. 136
possible selves, p. 136
ought self, p. 137
ideal self, p. 137
self-discrepancy theory, p. 137
discrepancy, p. 137
self-control, p. 138
ego depletion, p. 138

Essay Questions

1. Describe the difference between the "I" and the "me," and explain the various types of selves that comprise the self-concept.

2. Discuss the positives and negatives of self-esteem, and the difference between explicit and implicit self-esteem.

3. Explain self-discrepancy theory, making sure to detail how our possible selves factor into our emotional state.

Chapter 6
Psychodynamic Approaches

Learning Objectives

LO 6.1 Discuss some of the basic concepts common to the various psychodynamic approaches.

LO 6.2 Explain Freud's topographical and structural model of personality.

LO 6.3 Describe the stages of psychosexual development.

LO 6.4 Discuss the relevance of dream interpretation in psychodynamic theory.

LO 6.5 Evaluate the defense mechanisms and explain criticisms of Freudian theories.

LO 6.6 Appraise the empirical evidence that appears to support Freud's theories, as well as the criticism.

LO 6.7 Describe the theories of Carl Jung and where Jungian ideas appear in modern psychology.

LO 6.8 Discuss the importance of Alfred Adler, Karen Horney, and the object relations theorists in the history and development of personality theory.

When you first started learning about psychology, many of your questions were probably about the deeper, darker, and stranger recesses of the mind. Why did you dream about riding a roller coaster while holding an umbrella? Why did you have a nightmare about violently killing your brother? Why did your friend who was abused as a child decide to start a relationship with a violent man when that's so obviously a bad idea? Why do you spend so much time fantasizing about sex or food or being famous? And why do you sometimes wish that the woman who's now dating your ex-boyfriend would be hit by a car (not killed, because wishing for that would be wrong) and need to spend the next 4 years in a Norwegian hospital?

In this chapter, we focus on history's most influential psychodynamic thinkers. The most important is Sigmund Freud, who developed **psychoanalysis**. Freud was in many ways the trunk of a tree that sent out branches in many new and interesting directions. As a group, the thinkers who branched out, challenged, and built on the ideas of Freud can be called **neo-analytic theorists**. In contrast to Freud, neo-analytic theorists downplayed the central role of sex in psychological conflict. They also placed more emphasis than Freud did on interpersonal relationships and social context. The neo-analytic thinkers are a complex group who developed many different theories about the human psyche generally and personality in particular. We focus primarily on Carl Jung, who developed **analytical psychology**, then explore the ideas of Alfred Adler and Karen Horney, and finally discuss object relations theory. But we begin with an overview of psychodynamic ideas and how they relate to personality.

psychoanalysis
the study of the dynamics of the mind developed by Freud

neo-analytic theorists
the psychodynamic theorists who came after Freud and took his ideas in new and interesting directions

analytical psychology
the study of the personal and collective unconscious developed by Jung

An Overview of Psychodynamic Theories

LO 6.1 **Discuss some of the basic concepts common to the various psychodynamic approaches.**

Questions about the stranger and darker aspects of the mind are traditionally the province of psychodynamic approaches to personality. Psychodynamic approaches share several features in common. They involve the **unconscious**

unconscious
the part of the mind outside of conscious awareness

conscious

the part of the mind within our usual awareness

mind—the part outside of our usual awareness—as well as the **conscious** mind—the part we are aware of. Because much of personality is not available to conscious inspection, you need to dig deeper. If you ask your friend, "Can you tell me about your unconscious?" his answer will be "No." You would have to discover his unconscious thoughts in more indirect ways. This might involve examining dreams or free associations (saying whatever comes into your head), using projective personality tests such as Rorschach inkblots, measuring reaction time to words or images, creating art, or examining **transference** (the way the client perceives the therapist).

transference

the way the client perceives the therapist

Psychodynamic approaches focus on the interaction and conflict between the conscious and the unconscious—thus the *dynamic* in psychodynamic. For example, your unconscious mind may want one thing but your conscious mind may want another. If this conflict is bad enough—say, unconsciously wanting approval for who you are, but consciously choosing partners who aren't likely to appreciate you—you might end up in therapy. Most of the time, though, such conflicts are not so extreme, just part of the human condition.

Most psychodynamic and neo-analytic thinkers did not conduct personality science the way we do today. Psychodynamic theory used a "big-picture" approach to understand personality, relying far less on empirical data than modern personality researchers. Instead, the goal was to develop large theoretical models that could explain a wide range of clinical observations. Furthermore, many concepts in psychodynamic theory are difficult to measure empirically, you can't just ask people to report on thoughts that they are not conscious of having. And so, unlike most of this book, our focus in this chapter is more on theory and thought than on research and data.

So why, you might be asking, do you need to know this stuff as a modern psychology student? Psychodynamic ideas have not only influenced personality psychology but also completely permeated Western culture. When asked to name a famous psychologist, most people would say Sigmund Freud. Many of Freud's ideas may be dated (he published his first book in 1895 and died in 1939); he was not technically a psychologist, but a medical doctor; and few personality researchers today use his ideas as a starting point for their work. However, Freud's ideas and those of the neo-analytic theorists are very important for several reasons:

1. The psychodynamic school included many "big-picture" theorists (see Figure 6.1). There is something to admire and perhaps emulate in this intellectual boldness, although of course it's better if research can eventually ground these theories in hard data.

2. Many of the ideas described by Freud and others are pervasive in popular culture. Many cultural touchpoints—from movies such as *Star Wars, Star Trek, Harry Potter,* and *The Hunger Games* to great books such as Hesse's *Siddhartha*—have direct links to psychodynamic and neo-analytic ideas. It is more challenging to understand art and entertainment without some knowledge of psychodynamic and neo-analytic theory.

Figure 6.1 A Brief and Selected List of Important Psychodynamic Thinkers

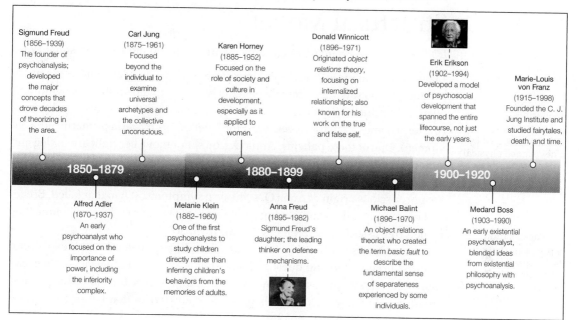

3. Freud's work was generative, meaning it led to a lot of research. Some of this research confirmed Freud's ideas, and some of it didn't. Scientists don't just want answers, they want questions—and great ideas lead to many, many questions. In fact, many of Freud's own students disagreed with him on several issues, but without Freud's foundational theories they likely wouldn't have developed their own ideas.

4. Similarly, many modern research topics, from self-control to narcissism to attachment theory, have deep roots in psychodynamic thought. Freud's work has had an enormous impact on the field: It has been referenced by scholars over 350,000 times. Just for comparison, we have both published many articles and books, but combined we've been cited only 25,000 times. So when a researcher says "Freud doesn't matter," go to Google Scholar and compare the research citation impact of the person saying this to Freud's impact.

5. Psychodynamic and neo-analytic thinkers explore ideas that are difficult to measure empirically with today's technology. This does not mean, however, that some of these ideas will not be testable as we improve neuroimaging or cognitive technologies that look beyond conscious self-reports. For example, there is a fascinating new field of psychodynamic neuroscience that attempts to find evidence for psychodynamic processes through brain scans (e.g., Carhart-Harris, 2007). And who knows what the next decade will bring?

Freud's Topographical and Structural Model

LO 6.2 Explain Freud's topographical and structural model of personality.

Like many great ideas, Freud's theories started with a puzzle. Freud was a medical doctor who saw many female patients with unexplained physical symptoms such as blindness, fainting, or paralysis—a condition then known as **hysteria** (the term comes from the Greek word for "uterus," as hysteria primarily afflicted women). One of these patients, Anna O., could not move her right arm or leg and suffered terrifying hallucinations, such as an enormous black snake attacking her sick father. Freud and another doctor, Josef Breuer, first tried hypnosis to discover the unconscious origin of Anna O.'s physical symptoms. When that failed, Breuer had her simply talk to him, saying whatever came to her mind—a technique they named **free association** (Breuer & Freud, 1895/2000).

Anna O. was not cured by Breuer and Freud's treatments, but this experience inspired Freud's lifelong quest to understand how psychological conflicts can cause neurotic symptoms and how these symptoms can be treated. In the process, Freud developed several models of the human psyche that became powerful forces in personality psychology.

hysteria

a psychological disorder characterized by unexplained physical symptoms such as blindness, fainting, or paralysis

free association

a psychoanalytic technique involving saying whatever comes into your head

The Topographical Model

One Saturday, you plan to drive home to see your parents. You wanted to wake up at 7:00 A.M. but forgot to set your alarm, so you wake up at 10:00 A.M. instead. Then you start driving to your parents' house as usual, but you get distracted and end up going the wrong direction, so you decide to give up and go back to campus. That night, you go out with your friends. As you sleep, you dream that you are eating cookies with some childhood friends in a house while two clumsy bears paw at the window.

The next day, you talk to one of your friends who is taking personality psychology. She suggests that maybe, on some unconscious level, you didn't really want to visit your parents. Instead, you wanted to have fun with your friends. Your unconscious desire to avoid your parents caused you to forget to set your alarm and to get lost. In your dream, you're enjoying time with your friends while your parents—represented by the two clumsy bears—are shut outside. You tell your friend she is wrong, and that you love your parents, but later you think that maybe

Freud with a cigar.

some deep, dark part of you did want to spend the evening with your friends instead of your parents.

This is the potential conflict captured in Freud's **topographical model** of the psyche. Think of the mind as having three main parts. The conscious mind is what we are aware of or can easily be aware of. This is the basic reality we live in. The unconscious mind is the part of our minds that we are not aware of; this includes wishes, drives, and fantasies that are often sexual and aggressive. Between the two extremes is the **preconscious mind**, the barely conscious part of our minds that engages in **censorship**—keeping the unconscious out of conscious awareness (Freud, 1900/1913).

The unconscious mind is generally governed by the **pleasure principle**: It wants whatever brings pleasure. This could be food or sex or whacking someone on the head. The conscious mind, in contrast, is generally governed by the **reality principle**: It wants what it knows works in reality. Food or sex or whacking your boss is not always the right choice.

Our unconscious and conscious minds are often in conflict. We wish for pleasure, but that pleasure often conflicts with reality. So, in the example above, your unconscious wish to hang out with your friends and your conscious desire to see your parents conflicted. Your preconscious kept this unconscious wish out of your conscious mind, but the wish still came out in your dreams and actions (like sleeping in and getting lost). The pleasure-versus-reality conflict commonly appears around sex—one reason Freud focused so much on sexuality. We cannot act upon every sexual impulse we have, so we try to find other ways of managing our desires.

JOURNAL PROMPT: UNDERSTANDING YOURSELF

Can you apply these concepts of the pleasure and reality principles to explain a conflict you experienced in your own life?

The Structural Model

Freud found that the topographical model was not sufficient to explain all psychic conflicts—not everything is reality versus pleasure. Another part of our minds— Freud called it the *super-ego*—is strict and demanding, like a parent sitting in the back of your mind telling you how to behave. When you do something that brings you pleasure—for example, indulging in sexual activity or eating chocolate—you might feel guilt or shame. Sometimes this guilt is literally painful (as in the popular expression "a pang of guilt"), which makes it difficult to enjoy things even if you want to. Sometimes we won't let ourselves feel good.

Freud's **structural model** of the mind has three parts: the **id** (or "it"), the **ego** (or "I"), and the **super-ego** (or "above I"). The id operates on the pleasure principle, driving you toward sex, food, and aggression. The id is the more deeply rooted, animalistic part of yourself—thus the label "it." When you have an

---

topographical model
Freud's model of the mind that highlights the conflict between the pleasure principle and the reality principle

preconscious mind
the barely conscious part of our minds that keeps the unconscious out of conscious awareness

censorship
the process of keeping the unconscious from entering consciousness

pleasure principle
the driving force of the unconscious that wants whatever brings pleasure

reality principle
the goals of the conscious mind, which finds what works in reality

structural model
Freud's model of the mind with three parts: the id (or "it"), the ego (or "I"), and the super-ego (or "above I")

id
the unconscious mind, motivated for pleasure and wish fulfillment

ego
the conscious part of the mind that navigates between the ego and the super-ego

super-ego
the strict and demanding part of the mind

impulsive urge to eat raw cookie batter, throw something at your roommate, or hook up with the attractive specimen working the front desk at the gym, your id is at work.

The ego operates under the reality principle, navigating the world in a rational way. Freud compared the ego to a chariot driver trying to control the unwieldy, running horses of the id (Freud, 1923/1962). Someone with a strong ego—for example, someone high in conscientiousness—can control his id impulses and navigate through life reasonably well. Someone with a weak ego will be overrun by unconscious impulses and may watch his life spin out of control. Other times, the ego shows just a temporary weakness. When what you really think deep down comes out as a slip of the tongue, that's your id talking, known as a **Freudian slip**. If Kayla is unconsciously still in love with her ex-boyfriend, she might accidentally say his name at an inopportune moment with her current boyfriend. It's an embarrassing Freudian slip, and a sign her ego has momentarily failed to keep her id from leaking to the surface.

Freudian slip
when what you really think deep down comes out as a slip of the tongue.

Watch YOUR TURN: FREUDIAN SLIPS

WATCH
the video in
REVEL

The super-ego is the seat of the conscience. It's the voice in your head that tells you that hooking up with the guy you met at the bar or throwing a party at your parents' house is wrong. In contrast to the ego, the super-ego often acts by administering pain. Your ego might point out that you'll regret the hookup or the donut tomorrow, but your super-ego will instead make you feel guilty, ashamed, or anxious. Even when your ego has decided that the donut is worth the carbs, your super-ego might make you feel so much guilt and anxiety that you can't enjoy it. The super-ego is the buzzkill of the psyche.

Where does the super-ego come from? Babies are clearly born with an id but without a super-ego. Children must learn what is right and wrong—and what's right and wrong differs from one place to another and one time to another. The super-ego consists of the rules of the culture in which you

Figure 6.2 The Classic Iceberg Illustration of Freud's Structural Model

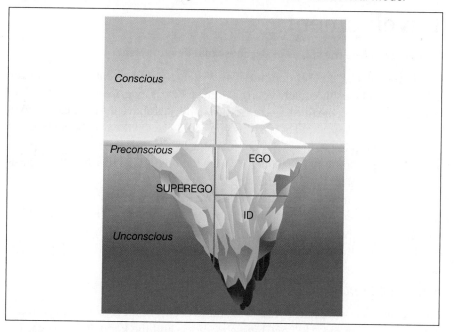

were raised (Freud, 1930/1989). Modern personality science has focused on children's development of impulse control and socialization to answer these questions(see Chapter 9).

How much are you aware of these three components of your mind? In Freud's early diagram (see Figure 6.2) of the structural model, the id, ego, and super-ego spanned across levels of the conscious and unconscious. The id is primarily unconscious, but the ego and super-ego exist at both the conscious and unconscious levels.

Watch FREUD'S THEORY OF PERSONALITY

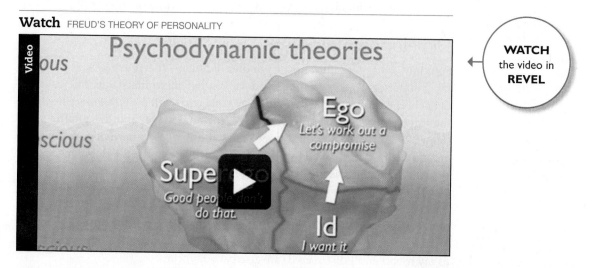

WATCH
the video in
REVEL

Freudian Theory of Psychosexual Development

LO 6.3 Describe the stages of psychosexual development.

When my (W. K. C.) older daughter was very young, we went to the local zoo with my friend and his equally young daughter. Before long, my friend's daughter started chewing on the filthy, germ-riddled handrails above the otter cage. I commented that this was about as nasty as you could get. On the way home from the zoo, my friend pointed to my daughter. Sitting in her stroller with her leg up, she was licking the bottom of her shoe. My friend and I decided the shoe-licking was actually nastier than handrail chewing.

Why do infants and toddlers get such pleasure from chewing, biting, and sucking on things? And why do sources of pleasure change as children get older? In other words, how do the desires of the id change over the life course? Freud tried to answer these questions with his theory of psychosexual development.

libido
Freud's term for sexual psychic energy

cathexis
the attachment of libido to thoughts, objects, or parts of the body

developmental stages
the stages children go through as the libido moves through the body

oral stage
the attachment of libido to the mouth

anal stage
the attachment of libido to the anus

phallic stage
the attachment of libido to the genitals

latent stage
the quieting of the libido from age 6 until puberty

genital stage
when the child begins adult sexual development in puberty

Libido: Sexual Energy

Several religions and philosophies focus on an energy or life force moving through the body, such as the "chi" of Chinese medicine and the kundalini of yoga. The *Star Wars* movies called it "the force"; in blues music, it's "mojo."

Freud's version of a life force is the **libido**, a Latin term meaning "lust or desire." Freud believed that the libido begins its influence in childhood and shapes the adult personality. The libido can become attached to an object—in other words, obsessed with it—through a process called **cathexis**. Imagine a shoe salesman who seems almost sexually excited when he describes the latest Gucci pumps. You start to wonder if he has a closet full of women's shoes at home and spends many evenings with them. In this case, the shoe is the object to which the shoe salesman's libido has cathected. The result is a foot or shoe fetish.

Developmental Stages

Freud thought of infants as little bundles of libido—they have lots of id but not much super-ego or ego. As the child develops, her libido attaches to different parts of her body during certain **developmental stages** (see Table 6.1). Freud identified the three early stages as the **oral stage**, the **anal stage**, and the **phallic stage** (Freud, 1905/1962). After these three stages, the libido is somewhat dormant (after around age 6). Freud called this the **latent stage**. Finally, the development of adult sexuality in puberty is the **genital stage**.

The oral stage is associated with breastfeeding/suckling and thus lasts through the first year of life. During this time, infants get a great deal of satisfaction from putting items in their mouths. The main object is the breast (or bottle), but pacifiers, fingers, thumbs, feet, rattles, and keys (or even handrails and shoes, as my friend and I discovered) are also baby favorites.

Table 6.1 Freud's Developmental Stages

Age	Developmental stage	Issue
Infancy (0–12 months)	Oral	Everything goes in the mouth
Toddlers (1–3 years)	Anal	Potty training
Preschool and kindergarten (4–6 years)	Phallic	Oedipal and Electra complexes
School age (7–11 years)	Latent	Libido dormant
Adolescence (12+ years)	Genital	Emerging adult sexuality

Most of the time, the libido eventually moves on from the oral stage, but sometimes the libido gets stuck on oral behaviors, known as **oral fixation** (Freud, 1905/1962). For example, many parents worry when a 3-year-old is still using a pacifier. In our [J. M. T.] house, this necessitated the arrival of the Binky Fairy, who took the pacifiers to the babies who needed them and left big-girl gifts in return (the look on my daughter Kate's face perfectly blended fear and pride). In an adult or older child, an oral fixation might appear in gum chewing, binge eating, and

oral fixation
having libido attached to the mouth

The oral stage

The anal stage

The phallic stage

chewing tobacco. Eric Cartman from *South Park* seems to have an oral fixation, as—in the words of one student—he is "preoccupied with keeping his mouth full of desired foods such as KFC, Cheesypoofs, and chicken pot pies" (Cassidy, 2012).

During their second and third years, children move on to the anal stage as they focus on potty training. Ideally, the child works through this challenge appropriately and moves forward in development. Sometimes, though, the process goes awry, usually in one of two ways. Some children get a sense of pleasure from holding their bowels—when a parent asks them if they need to "go potty," they refuse. This early experience of power and self-control stays with them into adulthood, creating an **anal-retentive** personality focused on neatness and order (Freud, 1905/1962). This is similar to high conscientiousness combined with power motivation (more on power motive in Chapter 7). If you've ever complained about a boss or a coworker being "anal," you were probably saying he was overly controlled. It's no coincidence that these complaints often include the mention of him having something "up his butt" or, if minds are even further into the gutter, that he "just needs to get laid." Freud would agree with this interpretation, as it would involve the libido finding expression in adult sexuality where it belongs. (Of course, actually saying something like this to your boss is a very efficient way to get yourself fired.)

Other people have the opposite problem—they gain pleasure from releasing the bowels, called the **anal-expulsive** type (we know: gross). This might start with a child who won't use the toilet when it is available but then relieves herself when she is playing and then keeps on playing. As adults, anal expulsives are the opposite of anal retentives—they are sloppy and disorganized like someone low in conscientiousness (Freud, 1905/1962). Two of my (J. M. T.) daughters show signs of these two types. When Kate was 2, she liked the idea that the trash trucks took away her stinky diapers—she would gleefully say, "Bye-bye, poop!" But when I informed Elizabeth of the ultimate destination of her diapers, she looked at me with wide eyes. The next time the trash trucks came, she solemnly announced, "They're taking my poop." If Freud is right, Kate may grow up to be disorganized (anal expulsive) and Elizabeth to be more controlled (anal retentive).

The final stage of early childhood is the phallic stage, which occurs around 4–6 years of age, when, according to Freud, the libido migrates to the genitals. At this age, children might start masturbating and becoming curious about the differences in the genitals of boys and girls. The phallic stage is crucial to Freudian theory because it contains the **Oedipus complex** (Freud, 1905/1962), named after the ancient Greek play *Oedipus Rex*. In the play, Oedipus—who was adopted and did not know his biological parents—ends up as a young man unknowingly falling in love with and marrying his biological mother and killing his biological father in the process. When Oedipus realizes what he has done, he blinds himself in grief.

anal retentive
gaining pleasure from retaining the bowels

anal expulsive
gaining pleasure from releasing the bowels

Oedipus complex
the male child's love for the mother and wish for the father's death during the phallic stage

JOURNAL PROMPT: UNDERSTANDING YOURSELF

In what ways do Freud's developmental stages reflect your own experiences growing up? In what ways do they seem off?

So what does this Greek play have to do with a 5-year-old boy's psychosexual development? According to Freud, young boys become sexually attracted to their mothers and see their fathers as rivals for their mothers' love. Thus, the boy wants to kill his father and possess his mother. Because the boy is small and his father is large and powerful, this creates anxiety in the boy. He wonders if his father will castrate him if he finds out about his desires (the boy has noticed girls don't have penises, so he believes they can be removed). This fear of castration becomes **castration anxiety**.

Ideally, the Oedipus complex is resolved in a psychologically healthy way. The boy eventually identifies with his father and wants to become a strong male just like him. Then the boy resolves to find a woman like his mother to marry. When the Oedipus conflict is not resolved, however, the boy becomes a man overly attached to his mother who can't form healthy relationships with women (Freud, 1905/1962).

We know this sounds crazy, but the Oedipal drama appears in everything from classic Western literature to American popular culture. In Shakespeare's *Hamlet*, Hamlet's inability to confront the man who killed his father leads to psychological suffering and death. In *Star Wars*, Luke's father, Darth Vader, cuts off Luke's hand, which could be seen as a symbolic castration. If you have a hipster friend who collects vinyl records—or you can check YouTube—listen to a live recording of "The End" by The Doors.

What about girls? Freud's student Carl Jung theorized that girls want to marry their fathers, which he named the **Electra complex**, also the title of a classic Greek play (Jung, 1915). However, Freud was said to disagree with the idea of an Electra complex (Erwin, 2002).

Freud's main theory about girls was that they wanted to have a penis (known as **penis envy**), which implies that females long to be males (Freud, 1905/1962). As we will see, others have suggested that Freud did not understand women and that some of his ideas were profoundly sexist (Friedan, 1963).

castration anxiety
the male child's fear of being castrated by the father

Electra complex
the daughter's love for the father and wish for the mother's death (attributed to Jung)

penis envy
the idea that girls desire to have penises

Dreams: How We Access the Unconscious

LO 6.4 Discuss the relevance of dream interpretation in psychodynamic theory.

One of the biggest challenges in psychodynamic approaches is accessing the unconscious. How do you understand something that, by definition, you can't consciously access? Let's say you are unconsciously sexually attracted to one of your friends. How would you make this knowledge conscious?

Freud believed that dreams were the "royal road" to understanding the unconscious, a place where unconscious wishes express themselves in disguised form (Freud, 1900/1913). Interpreting what dreams mean is the key, hence the title of Freud's masterwork, *The Interpretation of Dreams* (1900/1913). According to Freud, dreams cannot be understood from the content on the surface, or **manifest content**. That makes it necessary to look beneath the surface to find the real meaning, or **latent content**.

manifest content
the outward content of a dream

latent content
the unconscious meaning of a dream

wish fulfillment
the unconscious desire to have one's fantasies realized

day residue
experiences from the day incorporated into a dream's manifest content

Freud believed that all dreams were **wish fulfillments** based on unconscious wishes. Some wishes, such as drinking water when you're thirsty, are innocuous; others, such as having sex with your platonic friend, are more highly charged. If the unconscious wish becomes conscious while you are asleep, you will wake up (in the first case, to get a drink of water and, in the second, because the thought of sex with your friend freaks you out). To protect your sleep, the wish becomes disguised, mixing images from the previous day, or **day residue**, with dream symbols. The disguised dream does not have the power of the initial wish, so you are often able to sleep through it (although even if your wish is disguised, you may wake up from a powerful dream). Then, when you eventually wake up, you will often have trouble remembering the details of the dream or even forget the dream altogether, which is a second form of disguise.

Freud described one of his own dreams:

> There is, for example, a dream which I can cause as often as I like, as it were experimentally. If in the evening I eat anchovies, olives, or other strongly salted foods, I become thirsty at night whereupon I waken. The awakening, however, is preceded by a dream, which each time has the same content, namely, that I am drinking. I quaff water in long draughts, it tastes as sweet as only a cool drink can taste when one's throat is parched, and then I awake and have an actual desire to drink. The occasion for this dream is thirst, which I perceive when I awake. The wish to drink originates from this sensation, and the dream shows me this wish as fulfilled. It thereby serves a function the nature of which I soon guess. I sleep well, and am not accustomed to be awakened by a bodily need. If I succeed in assuaging my thirst by means of the dream that I am drinking, I need not wake up in order to satisfy it. It is thus a dream of convenience. The dream substitutes itself for action, as elsewhere in life. (1900/1913, p. 104)

So, in this case, Freud is thirsty in his sleep. He wants to quench his thirst, but to protect his sleep, he dreams of drinking. Sometimes these dreams allow him to sleep through the night; at other times, the thirst is so powerful that he wakes up and has to drink water.

Freud maintained that many symbols in dreams are nearly universal. Although he did not have any scientific data to support his observations, they are still interesting to contemplate:

> Emperor and Empress (King and Queen) in most cases really represent the parents of the dreamer; the dreamer himself or herself is the prince or princess.
>
> All elongated objects, sticks, tree trunks, and umbrellas (on account of the stretching-up which might be compared to an erection), all elongated and sharp weapons, knives, daggers, and pikes are intended to represent the male member. A frequent, not very intelligible symbol for the same is a nail-file.
>
> Little cases, boxes, caskets, closets, and stoves correspond to the female part.

The symbolism of lock and key has been very gracefully employed by Uhland in his song about the "Grafen Eberstein" to make a common smutty joke.

The dream of walking through a row of rooms is a brothel or harem dream. Staircases, ladders, and flights of stairs, or climbing on these, either upwards or downwards, are symbolic representations of the sexual act.

Of articles of dress the woman's hat may frequently be definitely interpreted as the male genital. In dreams of men one often finds the cravat as a symbol for the penis; this indeed is not only because cravats hang down long, and are characteristic of the man, but also because one can select them at pleasure a freedom, which is prohibited by nature in the original of the symbol. Persons who make use of this symbol in the dream are very extravagant with cravats and possess regular collections of them.

All complicated machines and apparatus in dream are very probably genitals, in the description of which dream symbolism shows itself to be as tireless as the activity of wit. Likewise many landscapes in dreams, especially with bridges or with wooded mountains, can be readily recognised as descriptions of the genitals. (1900/1913, pp. 247–248)

A MAN'S WORLD

What sexual imagery would Freud see?

No wonder people say Freud saw sex everywhere!

However, many dream symbols are more individual. For example, you might dream you are wearing a fancy hat—which Freud thought represented a penis—but in your case the hat might express a wish for social status. Freud suggested free association as the best way of uncovering the meaning of dreams.

Imagine you had a dream where you saw a good friend wearing a fancy hat. Freud might ask, "What thoughts does that bring to your mind?" You respond, "I don't know. When I was a child, I had a friend at school who always wore fancy hats to the derby. I was jealous of her. I think I always wanted to be as popular as she was." Through this process of free association, the meaning of the dream was revealed: The core wish was for status and popularity.

Simply discussing what is on your mind in a rambling, unrestricted way can uncover important unconscious processes even beyond **dream interpretation**. When Freud settled on the method of free association as part of the **talking cure**, he asked therapy clients to lie on a couch looking away from him. This was designed to create a situation where their minds could wander, free from external constraints.

dream interpretation
the therapeutic technique of uncovering the hidden meaning of dreams

talking cure
Freud's term for the treatment of hysteria by talking in therapy sessions

JOURNAL PROMPT: UNDERSTANDING YOURSELF

Think of a particularly interesting dream of yours. How would you interpret it from a Freudian perspective?

Freud's couch.

So, was Freud right about dream content as a window to the unconscious? The answer seems to be pretty mixed. There is no good evidence for Freud's wish fulfillment model of dreams. However, Freud was correct that dreams are not just meaningless nonsense; they do tell us about out personality. For example, people high in neuroticism have more nightmares (Schredl, 2003). In contrast, people low in neuroticism and high on openness to experience tend to have more dreams about flying (Schredl, 2007). Highly agreeable people see more people in their dreams, and those high in openness to experience see more strange and different people (Bernstein & Roberts, 1995). People high in openness to experience are also more likely to remember their dreams (Schredl et al., 2003).

Mechanisms of Defense

LO 6.5 **Evaluate the defense mechanisms and explain criticisms of Freudian theories.**

defense mechanisms
strategies used to keep unconscious thoughts from the conscious mind

Defense mechanisms are psychological processes that keep us from consciously experiencing things that could cause us suffering (A. Freud, 1936/1992). The concept of psychological defense was central to Freud's work, but the specific defense mechanisms were best described in the writings of Freud's daughter, Anna Freud.

You're probably familiar with some common defense mechanisms even if you don't know their names. Maybe you tried to talk to a friend about a problem and he wouldn't even acknowledge it. Or maybe he said the problem wasn't his, but it was really your problem. These are examples of psychological defenses in action.

Psychologists have described a long list of defense mechanisms, but here we highlight only the best known. We also highlight the modern research that supports these defense mechanisms. Throughout this section, we often use the example of homosexual impulses. Modern culture has fewer taboos against expressing sexual and aggressive impulses, so people do not need to defend against these impulses as much as they did in Freud's time. In contrast, negative attitudes toward homosexuality are still prevalent (though they are decreasing; The Pew Center, 2012).

Denial

Imagine someone who is homophobic but also has unconscious homosexual impulses. This would be a problem because recognizing her forbidden homosexual desires would make her very upset.

One straightforward defense is to simply deny the impulses. A homophobic man, for example, may simply think, "I am not attracted to men." This is a classic example of **denial**. Denial is very common, thus the popular saying, "Denial is not a river in Egypt."

denial
not acknowledging unconscious content

People can be in denial about all sorts of things, from their lack of talent (witness the early rounds on talent shows like *American Idol* or *America's Got Talent*) to their true feelings about someone (whether they are denying loving someone or hating someone). Many people prefer to live in a state of denial about their own death—in fact, an entire subfield of social psychology called "terror management" explores the results of our mostly unconscious fear of death (Greenberg et al., 1997).

Reaction Formation

Imagine you have a friend (let's call him Ray) with unconscious homosexual impulses. Many people assume Ray is gay, but he is openly homophobic. During college football games he stands in a corner with a bullhorn, denouncing homosexuality. A few years later, Ray surprises everyone by coming out of the closet. He came to terms with his homosexual drives and now publicly admits to being gay.

Freud might say that Ray was using the defense mechanism of **reaction formation**; that is, he consciously experienced the opposite of his unconscious feelings. So, instead of loving gay men, he hated them. This defense protected him from the distressing feeling of coming to grips with his own homosexual desires (A. Freud, 1936/1992). Reaction formation goes beyond denial—it involves not just denying your feelings, but acting as if you feel the opposite. As another example, if Sophia dislikes her mother-in-law but is always extremely nice, even fawning, toward her, she might be using reaction formation.

reaction formation
disguising unconscious content by turning it into its opposite

In one study (Adams et al., 1996), men completed a scale measuring homophobia. They then watched one of three types of porn—male–female heterosexual, female–female homosexual, or male–male homosexual—while wearing a device

Figure 6.3 Men's Sexual Arousal in Response to (A) A Heterosexual Video, (B) A Lesbian Video, and (C) A Gay Male Video, Depending on Their Level of Homophobia

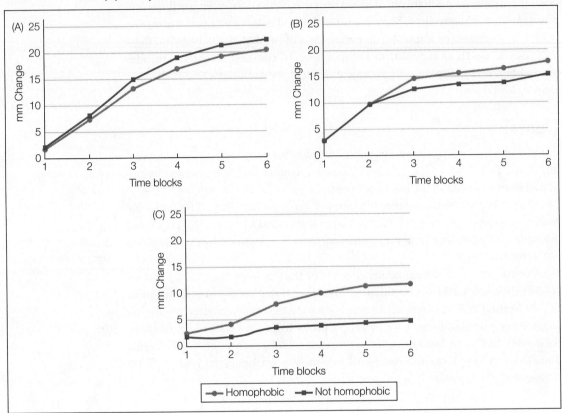

SOURCE: Adams et al. (1996).

that measures erections (officially, this device is called penile plethysmography; colloquially, it's called the "peter meter"; see Figure 6.3).

Both homophobic and nonhomophobic men were equally aroused by heterosexual and female–female porn. But homophobic men were more aroused than nonhomophobic men when watching male–male porn. So the men who consciously endorsed items such as "I would feel nervous being in a group of homosexuals" were more sexually turned on by watching homosexuals engage in sex. These men were apparently using homophobia as a defense against their unconscious homosexual desires.

Projection

Let's get back to secretly gay Ray. Instead of acknowledging his own homosexual impulses, he believes someone else has them instead. He might, for example, feel an unconscious attraction to another man. As a defense, he projects that attraction onto the other man. The unconscious "I love him" becomes the conscious "he loves me." For example, Ray might think guys are checking him out. He might tell them, "Stop looking at my butt." The psychoanalytic interpretation might be that he actually wished people were looking at his butt (A. Freud, 1936/1992).

Basically, **projection** involves projecting your feelings onto someone else, much like a movie projector onto a screen (you're the movie projector, and the other person is the screen). Imagine being in an argument with someone who angrily yells, "Why are you so angry with me?" as you just look at her. She's probably projecting her anger onto you—*she's* angry, but she thinks *you're* angry.

projection
seeing one's own unconscious content in others rather than oneself

Repression

The defense mechanism of **repression** involves keeping unconscious impulses or wishes completely out of consciousness (A. Freud, 1936/1992). This is different from denial because in denial someone acknowledges the possibility of the impulses and then discards them; in repression, people are not aware of the impulses. Instead, the unconscious impulses simply spill out in other ways. In a sense, repression is key to all defense mechanisms. In our previous example of reaction formation, the homosexual impulse is first repressed and then taken a step further when it is reversed and turned into homophobia.

repression
keeping the unconscious from consciousness by pushing it away

Empirical research finds that people differ in a trait called **repressive coping**—not allowing your anxiety to become fully conscious (Weinberger et al., 1979). Repressive coping is usually defined as a high score on the Marlowe–Crowne Social Desirability Scale and a low score on neuroticism. Do you know someone who says he doesn't become anxious or upset easily but seems to do things that suggests he is actually anxious? So, for example, he swears he isn't scared watching the horror movie *Paranormal Activity 10*, but keeps grabbing his seat and fidgeting. This could be evidence of repressive coping.

repressive coping
not allowing your anxiety to become fully conscious

Reaction times to potentially disturbing sexual and aggressive phrases can reveal repressive coping tendencies. Participants heard phrases such as "the prostitute slept with the student" or "his roommate kicked him in the stomach" and were then asked to respond verbally with whatever came into their mind as soon as the phrase was over. The repressive copers took the longest to respond to the disturbing phrases, compared to calm people and those who admitted to their anxiety (Weinberger et al., 1979; see Figure 6.4). The anxious people and the repressors also showed elevated heart rates when they heard the phrases. This suggests repressive copers were experiencing anxiety even though they claim they are not prone to anxiety (Weinberger et al., 1979).

Displacement

Displacement involves moving a troubling impulse onto a different, less-threatening object. Displaced anger is common. If Hayley has a bad day at work

displacement
moving a troubling impulse onto a different, less threatening object

Figure 6.4 Reaction Time to Neutral, Aggressive, and Sexual Phrases Among Repressive Copers, High-Anxiety People, and Low-Anxiety People

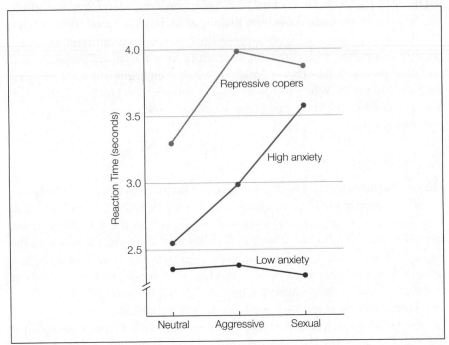

SOURCE: Weinberger et al. (1979).

because her boss was unfair, she might get angry more easily at her kids or her pets. She really wants to kick her boss, but she kicks her poor dog instead. She displaces her anger onto the less-threatening object of her dog—after all, her dog can't fire her. In the classroom where I (J. M. T.) taught personality psychology one semester, there was a hole in one of the walls. When we covered displacement, the students and I mused about who was angry enough, and at whom or what, to have displaced his anger onto the wall.

Sublimation

sublimation

channeling unconscious impulses into work

According to Freud, channeling unconscious impulses into your work is a relatively healthy defense mechanism (Freud, 1947). **Sublimation** involves turning unacceptable desires into acceptable, laudatory ones. For example, someone who has an unconscious desire to cut people might become a surgeon. Someone who has the urge to smear things around might become an artist. Freud argued that Leonardo da Vinci's childhood relationship with his mother and his latent homosexuality led to great art such as the *Mona Lisa* (Freud, 1947).

Anthropologist Alan Dundes (1978) took a Freudian approach when he wondered what made American football so popular. He observed that it involves only men; the men wear tights, cups, and pads that make them look hypermasculine; they bend over at the start of every play; it is socially appropriate for men to slap each other on the butt while on the field (don't try that at the office!) Then there is the big one: "The object of the game, simply stated, is to get into the opponent's endzone while preventing the opponent from getting into one's own endzone" (p. 81).

In other words, Dundes argued that football is a sublimated homosexual dominance contest, with the goal to sexually penetrate the opponent's turf while protecting your own. Not surprisingly—especially since it was the 1970s—many people were not amused by Dundes's thesis. Dundes even received death threats, which he interpreted as lending support to his theory because it suggested he'd hit a nerve. Or at least this is the story he told when I (W. K. C.) was an undergraduate in his class at UC Berkeley.

The *Mona Lisa*

Humor

Humor is another somewhat healthy defense mechanism—at least most of the time. Humor is not harmless—one person's joke can be another person's cruel attack. Many jokes have a scapegoat (for example, different ethnicities, blondes, celebrities, fat people, "yo' mama," and so on). But humor can also diffuse an uncomfortable situation or help people cope with otherwise negative experiences. Take the questionnaire here to get a sense of your style of humor.

Questionnaire 6.1 HUMOR STYLES SCALE

Interactive

Please answer all the questions.

1. I usually don't laugh or joke around much with other people.

○ Strongly Agree
○ Moderately Agree
○ Somewhat Agree
○ Neither Agree nor Disagree
○ Somewhat Disagree
○ Moderately Disagree
○ Strongly Disagree

2. I don't have to work very hard at making other people laugh—I seem to be a naturally humorous person.

○ Strongly Agree
○ Moderately Agree
○ Somewhat Agree
○ Neither Agree nor Disagree
○ Somewhat Disagree
○ Moderately Disagree
○ Strongly Disagree

Previous   Next

TAKE the Questionnaire in **REVEL**

Freud argued that humor can be used to release the tension between the unconscious and the conscious (Freud, 1905/1989). Secretly gay Ray, for example, loves making penis jokes. Every object he sees that is long and cylindrical—or has any of the multitude of names for a penis—is a source of humor for him.

Do you use any defense mechanisms? How would you know if you are being defensive? Can you see defenses in your friends even if you can't see them in yourself?

The rocket scene from the 1999 movie *Austin Powers: The Spy Who Shagged Me* is a good example of this form of humor. When you first see the rocket launched by Dr. Evil, you realize it looks exactly like a flying penis and testicles. You've just had time to think, "That looks just like . . ." when an army sergeant onscreen says, "Privates! We have reports of an Unidentified Flying Object. It has a long, smooth shaft, complete with—" (cut to a baseball diamond with an umpire). "Two balls! No strikes," he says and, looking up, adds, "What is that? It looks just like an enormous—" (cut to radar room with two men). "Johnson!" one barks. "Yes, sir?" says the other.

Why is this funny? Well, more mature readers don't think it's funny. It's juvenile and immature. The rest find it humorous because of the tension that occurs between talking about male genitals and the desire to keep those thoughts unconscious. You're never quite sure if the characters are directly commenting on the rocket's genital appearance or not. Are you the only one who immediately thought that?

Humor can be used for many different purposes. The Humor Styles Questionnaire that you took identifies four main types of humor. People who have an **affiliative humor style** like to use humor that makes others laugh and brings people together. Those with a **self-enhancing humor style** use humor to cheer themselves up. In contrast, individuals with an **aggressive humor style** use humor to mock or tease others, and those with a **self-defeating humor style** put themselves down (Martin et al., 2003). Which scale did you score the highest on?

Defensive Pessimism

One modern area of research has used the idea of defense mechanisms as a springboard to identify a relatively new personality trait: **defensive pessimism**, or

---

affiliative humor style
humor that makes others laugh and brings people together

self-enhancing humor style
humor used to help someone look and feel better

aggressive humor style
humor used to mock or tease others

self-defeating humor style
humor used to mock oneself

defensive pessimism
thinking negative thoughts to prepare for negative outcomes

TAKE the Questionnaire in **REVEL** →

Questionnaire 6.2 DEFENSIVE PESSIMISM SCALE

Interactive

1. I often start out expecting the worst, even though I will probably do OK.
○ Strongly Agree
○ Moderately Agree
○ Somewhat Agree
○ Neither Agree nor Disagree
○ Somewhat Disagree
○ Moderately Disagree
○ Strongly Disagree

2. I worry about how things will turn out.
○ Strongly Agree
○ Moderately Agree
○ Somewhat Agree
○ Neither Agree nor Disagree
○ Somewhat Disagree
○ Moderately Disagree
○ Strongly Disagree

Previous   Next

preparing for the worst (Norem, 2002). Take the questionnaire here before reading any further.

Defensive pessimism is not one of Freud's ideas, but an extension of his ideas. Imagine the day is marked on your calendar: In a week, you have an important job interview. You really want the job but know you might not get it. If you are a defensive pessimist, you're likely to set your expectations low, telling yourself you probably won't get the job. That way, you won't be as crushed if you don't and can only be pleasantly surprised if you do.

But that doesn't mean you won't prepare for the interview—in fact, if you're a defensive pessimist, you might prepare even more and will also process the feelings you think you'll have if you don't get the job. Defensive pessimists feel bad or worried now to avoid feeling even more anxious or worried later—they think negative thoughts to prepare for negative outcomes. Researcher Julie Norem (2002) refers to this as the "positive power of negative thinking." The preparation is a key part of the strategy—without it, it's just plain pessimism and leads to certain failure. With it, defensive pessimism can lead to greater academic success in the face of anxiety (Norem & Cantor, 1986). Your score on the defensive pessimism scale should tell you whether you use this strategy more or less than your peers.

Testing Freud's Theories

LO 6.6   Appraise the empirical evidence that appears to support Freud's theories, as well as the criticism.

Freud has always been a controversial figure, in large part because his theories have often proven difficult to test. In this section, we briefly review what aspects of Freudian theory have and have not received empirical support.

Empirical Evidence for the Defense Mechanisms

Empirical research has found evidence for some of the defense mechanisms, but these often appear under different names and work in somewhat different ways than Freud hypothesized. In particular, there is considerable evidence for reaction formation and denial, and some for projection, but little for displacement or sublimation (Baumeister et al., 1998).

Overall, Baumeister and his colleagues (1998) concluded that defense mechanisms were more likely to protect self-esteem than to defend against unconscious drives. In other words, people become defensive in order to feel good (or at least not feel so bad) about themselves. For example, the **false consensus effect**, in which someone overestimates how many people agree with her in part to feel good about her opinions, is somewhat similar to the defense of denial (Ross et al., 1977). This self-esteem-driven defensiveness is easy to see in children (and

false consensus effect
the belief that others share your opinions

unfortunately also in adults). My (W. K. C.) kids occasionally get into taunting matches, with one saying "You smell like a monkey" and the other retorting with "Well, you smell like a super monkey" or "You smell like a skunk ape." Each sister protects her own self-esteem until the match devolves into "You are! *No, you are!* You! *You!* . . . "

Challenges to Freudian Theories and Applications to Modern Psychology

Freud's theories have been endlessly dissected and critiqued over the years—Freudian theories have many detractors (Szasz, 1990). For one thing, Freud's theories are difficult to prove or disprove. Seeming counterexamples can be explained away through new applications of the ideas. For example, Freud told his patients that all dreams were wish fulfillments. One patient later told him she'd dreamed she went on vacation with her mother-in-law, whom she disliked. The dream was clearly not a wish fulfillment. So, she challenged Freud, didn't this mean not all dreams are wish fulfillments? No, Freud replied, because the patient's wish was that he was wrong, "and her dream showed that wish fulfilled" (1900/1913, p. 185). It seems Freud had an answer for everything.

> **JOURNAL PROMPT: UNDERSTANDING YOURSELF**
>
> What do you see as Freud's greatest contribution to personality psychology? What do you see as his most problematic contribution?

Another major problem with Freud's ideas is that they are not parsimonious (meaning simple or straightforward). For example, a Freudian psychoanalyst might say that cigarette smoking makes up for a lack of breastfeeding in childhood (not parsimonious), when it might just be that nicotine is addictive (parsimonious). A general rule in psychology—and science in general—is to prefer the simpler explanation over the complex one (sometimes referred to as *Ockham's razor*). If you have a headache, you don't get an MRI to check for a brain tumor. The most obvious cause is noise—say, the screaming next-door neighbors. If the noise goes away and the headache stays, maybe you're tired or stressed. Freud has also been rightly criticized for not empirically testing his theories. On the other hand, as we noted previously, Freud's ideas provided the inspiration for several areas of modern research. For example, the idea of a super-ego is at the heart of modern work on self-control (Chapter 5). Freud's ideas on narcissism inspired modern research on narcissism (also Chapter 5). Freud's thoughts on childhood relationships influencing adult romantic relationships led directly to modern work on attachment theory (Chapter 9). So, like all good ideas, Freud's were generative.

Carl Jung

LO 6.7   Describe the theories of Carl Jung and where Jungian ideas appear in modern psychology.

The neo-analytic theorists who followed Freud challenged and expanded his ideas. We could write an entire book on these different schools of thought. To simplify things, however, we are going to focus on four major neo-analytic theories. We spend the most time on the ideas of Carl Jung, as he had the greatest impact on modern thinking, not just in personality psychology, but in religion, storytelling, and the arts. We also focus on the ideas of Alfred Adler, who gave us concepts such as the inferiority complex; Karen Horney, who brought a more feminist eye to psychoanalytic ideas and developed an important model of personality; and finally the object relations school that focused on relationships, especially those in early childhood. Let's start with Jung.

The Archetypes

Jung went deeper in the unconscious and created a much larger and more complex view of the human psyche than Freud. Jung believed that Freud's id and super-ego were the **personal unconscious**, which accompanied a larger human unconscious that he called the **collective unconscious**. The collective unconscious was filled with psychological structures universal across cultures and times, called **archetypes**. Under Jung's theory, for example, archetypes appearing in Indonesian tribal myth, art, and religion would also appear in modern U.S. movies. Jung's best known archetypes include the shadow, the anima/us, and the self.

personal unconscious
Jung's term for the unconscious of the individual

collective unconscious
Jung's term for the unconscious archetypes shared by all humans

archetypes
unconscious psychic structures shared by all people

Personality's Past

Jung's "House Dream"

One of the most important events in the history of psychoanalysis was the split between Sigmund Freud and Carl Jung. Jung looked up to Freud and saw him as a mentor and father figure; however, Jung's very different view of the unconscious led him away from Freud.

Fittingly for a psychodynamic story, this intellectual split was revealed largely in a series of dreams. The most famous of these was Jung's "house dream" that he describes in his autobiography *Memories, Dreams, Reflections* (Jung, 1965).

Jung dreamt that he was in a two-story house. The top floor was an ornate, rococo-style that Jung found pleasant. But he was curious to see the rest of the house. He ventured downstairs and realized it was from a much older time.

> Descending again, I found myself in a beautifully vaulted room which looked exceedingly ancient. Examining the walls, I discovered layers of brick among the ordinary stone blocks, and chips of brick in the mortar. As soon as I saw this I knew that the walls dated from Roman times.

Jung then looked at the floor and saw a ring. Pulling on it he realized there was a deeper, hidden layer to the house. He walked down the stairs:

> I . . . entered a low cave cut into the rock. Thick dust lay on the floor, and in the dust were scattered

bones and broken pottery, like remains of a primitive culture. I discovered two human skulls, obviously very old and half disintegrated. Then I awoke.

Jung told this dream to Freud. Freud pushed Jung to interpret the dream as a death wish. He asked Jung which two people he wanted to die—clearly, the two skulls were two individuals. Jung replied that the skulls represented his wife and sister-in-law.

Freud liked this answer because it fit his theory of dreams as disguised wishes. But Jung thought the dream had a much deeper meaning. Instead of being a disguised wish, Jung thought the dream was communicating to him on a more primitive level:

> To me dreams are a part of nature, which harbors no intention to deceive, but expresses something as best it can, just as a plant grows or an animal seeks its food as best it can.

And what the dream expressed was that there was an even deeper layer to the unconscious than Jung and Freud had already explored. The subbasement of the house was the representation of the collective unconscious, Jung's idea that there was a symbolic unconscious that all people shared. As Jung wrote:

> My dream was giving me the answer. It obviously pointed to the foundations of cultural history—a history of successive layers of consciousness. My dream thus constituted a kind of structural diagram of the human psyche; it postulated something of an altogether impersonal nature underlying that psyche.

This dream sparked Jung's reading of history, anthropology, and mythology, and the result was his theory of the collective unconscious.

---

shadow
the archetype of the same sex as the individual

THE SHADOW The **shadow** archetype is the personification of the "dark side" of the ego (Jung, 1959) and has some overlap with the Freudian id: a dark, sexual, and aggressive place. Your "dark side" can also be the opposite of your usual self—say, an introvert when you are usually an extravert.

Many cultures have stories featuring a relatively normal protagonist (the ego) paired with a shadowy version of him- or herself (the shadow). The shadow leads the person to do all sorts of frightening, negative, or scary things. This can lead to great harm, but if the shadow can be faced and the challenges met, the protagonist is left stronger.

The classic *The Strange Case of Dr. Jekyll and Mr. Hyde* is an example of the shadow overcoming the protagonist. Dr. Jekyll takes a potion that turns him into a primitive, murderous, simian creature, Mr. Hyde. In this story, the ego (Dr. Jekyll) and the shadow (Mr. Hyde) are not combined into a unified personality. Instead, Dr. Jekyll disappears, a final triumph for the shadow Mr. Hyde.

A much more positive outcome of a meeting with the shadow occurs in *The Hangover* movies. Stu is a clean-cut dentist—perhaps the most boring person in the world. Through the effects of intoxication and poor choices of company, a dark side of Stu emerges. He extracts his own tooth, gets a facial tattoo, and has sex with a male transvestite prostitute. In the end, Stu embraces his shadow, giving him the strength to confront his future father-in-law and earn his respect.

Or see the movie *21 & Over*, where a young man named Jeff Chang is drawn into an intoxicated adventure by two old friends. Through the process, Jeff is transformed from a boy scared of his father to a man capable of having a relationship with a woman and finding his own way in the world. Rather than a lost tooth

Dr. Jekyll and Mr. Hyde;
The Hangover Part II.

or tattoo, Jeff ends up essentially going through another painful rite of manhood: circumcision.

ANIMA/ANIMUS   The **anima/animus** is Jung's term for the archetype of the soul. For Jung, the anima/us was an image of the other sex inside of ourselves. Thus, a man will have a feminine soul (anima) and a woman will have a masculine soul (animus).

For a man, coming into contact with the anima is the Jungian version of "getting in touch with your feminine side"; for a woman, the animus leads to more masculine attributes. The anima (the female archetype for men) appears in religious images of feminine compassion such as the Virgin Mary or Kwan Yin.

The animus (the male archetype for women) is often represented by a heroic image. In human form, he can be a stereotypically masculine guy, such as Ryan Gosling's character in the movie *Drive*. Or could be an identity, such as in the *Divergent* series. The heroine, Beatrice, is raised as a caring group member of Abnegation, but finds herself drawn to the bold, fearless group called Dauntless.

However, the anima and animus are not always positive images. The dark side of the anima, for example, can be seen in deity figures such as the Hindu goddess Kali, who wore a chain of human skulls around her neck and demanded

anima/animus
the soul; the archetype of the opposite sex of the individual

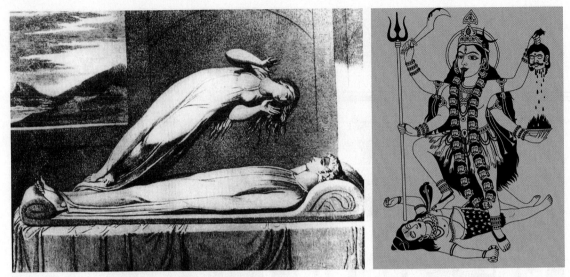

William Blake's painting *The Soul*; the Hindu goddess Kali.

Figure 6.5 The Ego and the Self

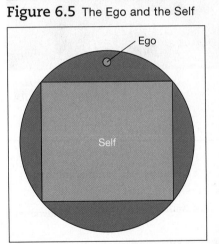

Self
the archetype at the center of the collective unconscious

mandala
a squared circle; a classic representation of the Self in Jungian theory

ego functions
the ways the individual interprets the world

sacrifices. A dark anima also appears in "femme fatale" characters who use their sexuality to ensnare and harm men—an extremely common plot in movies from the past 20 years (for example, Irene Adler in the BBC *Sherlock* series, Malkina in *The Counselor*, or Amy Elliot Dunne in *Gone Girl*). In the *Twilight* series book *Breaking Dawn*, three of the evil vampires are sisters who seduce men and then kill them by drinking their blood.

THE SELF   Freud saw the ego as the center of the psyche. Jung, however, believed that the **Self** was at the core, with the ego orbiting around it (see Figure 6.5). It's similar to the difference between the old model of the universe, with the Sun rotating around Earth, and the modern, correct version with Earth rotating around the Sun. This is the way Jung thought about the ego—sure, it was important, like Earth, but the Self, like the Sun, was at the center.

This image from *Man and His Symbols* (Jung, 1968) illustrates the relationship between the Self and the ego. As you can see, the Self is at the center of collective unconscious, and the ego is on the outside.

The Self appears in religion, myth, and fictions in both human and nonhuman forms. One popular image of the Self is the wise old man, a revered figure who knows all and aids a younger character while allowing the youth to learn for himself. Yoda and Obi-Wan from the *Star Wars* movies and Professor Dumbledore from *Harry Potter* are all wise old men. Romantic comedies sometimes feature a wise old woman who gives a younger woman comfort and advice. In many stories, the younger character struggles when her mentor—supposedly a wise old man—isn't much of a help, such as the perpetually drunk Haymitch in *The Hunger Games*.

A notable nonhuman image of the Self is the squared circle, or **mandala**, often used in Tibetan Buddhism. The mandala is a powerful image of the Self because it represents the union of opposites (the square and circle together). The Chinese symbol of yin and yang, representing the union of opposites and the dynamics of change, is another nonhuman self-image.

The Ego, Its Attitudes, and Its Functions

Jung's idea of the ego was similar to Freud's. However, Jung believed that the ego could be divided into different attitudes and **ego functions**—ways people perceive and engage with the world. All of these are pairs of opposites. The two attitudes are **extraversion versus introversion**. The four functions are **thinking versus feeling**, and **intuition versus sensation** (Jung, 1962).

A Tibetan mandala

extraversion versus introversion
getting energy from social situations versus being alone, in Jungian theory

thinking versus feeling
the rational functions in Jungian theory

intuition versus sensation
the irrational functions in Jungian theory

Many people take a personality questionnaire modeled on Jung's ideas called the Myers–Briggs Type Indicator (Briggs et al., 2009) or modifications of it such as the Keirsey Temperament Sorter (Keirsey, 1998). These scales are often used in business to help people understand how they see the world compared to others (for example, Barr & Barr, 1989). They are based on Jung's work, but also include another independent function, **judging versus perceiving**. If you've heard statements such as "Engineers are always INTJ," (or Introverted, iNtuitive, Thinking and Judging) you've been exposed to Jung's personality ideas. Take the Jung Type Indicator Questionnaire, a variation of the Myers–Briggs. It will tell you your four-letter personality type under this system. So, what do those letters actually mean?

Questionnaire 6.3 JUNG TYPE INDICATOR

Interactive

1. I make friends easily.
- Strongly Agree
- Moderately Agree
- Neither Agree nor Disagree
- Moderately Disagree
- Strongly Disagree

2. I require lots of time alone to recharge.
- Strongly Agree
- Moderately Agree
- Neither Agree nor Disagree
- Moderately Disagree
- Strongly Disagree

Previous   Next

TAKE the Questionnaire in **REVEL**

judging versus perceiving
functions added to Jung's types by Myers and Briggs; being planful versus more spontaneous

EXTRAVERSION VERSUS INTROVERSION In Jung's (1962) model, extraverts are energized from contact with others and introverts are drained or depleted by interactions with others. This is a somewhat different definition from Big Five extraversion, which also includes positive emotion and assertiveness. However, if you're a Big Five extravert, you are probably also an extravert under Jung's definition.

Let's say you're going to a big party tonight. You will know a few people there, but most will be strangers. How does that make you feel? If you are extraverted, you will get excited and energized thinking about the party. After the party you might head out to the after-party. If you are introverted, though, you might get exhausted just thinking about the party. When you get home you will want to turn into a vegetable in front of the TV or just go to sleep. You will be mentally wiped out from the social interaction even though it might have been a fun evening.

THINKING VERSUS FEELING As you'd expect from the labels, the thinking type likes to think through issues, and the feeling type relies on feelings. Imagine that your friends Tiffany and Faith are trying to help you decide whether to break up with your boyfriend, Michael. Tiffany, a thinking type, says, "Just t-bar him." "What?" you ask. "Draw a T on a piece of paper," she suggests, "and list Michael's positive qualities on the left and his negative qualities on the right. Then add them up. If the right column is longer than the left column, dump him."

Faith, a feeling type, is shocked by this approach. She asks you how you feel about Michael deep down. "Look into your heart," she says. "If you love him, then stay with him."

Both approaches are perfectly legitimate, even rational, according to Jung. But they are very different ways of approaching the same problem.

INTUITION VERSUS SENSATION The intuitive type likes to see the patterns in issues, even if that involves big leaps in logic. The sensation type, however, relies on concrete connections.

Let's say your friends Isabella and Sanjay also offer you advice about whether or not to break up with Michael. Isabella, the intuitive type, listens to your description and asks a few questions. Then her face lights up and she says, "Dump him." You ask why, and she says simply that dumping him is the call. Isabella has made an intuitive leap of thought about the relationship and has come to a conclusion but can't exactly say where it came from. Sanjay, the sensing type, tells you to get together with Michael, discuss the issues in your relationship one by one, and then make a decision.

Again, both of these approaches are legitimate, though very different. The intuitive approach gets you to the end, but you are not sure how; the sensing approach gives you very concrete action steps but doesn't supply an answer.

JUDGING VERSUS PERCEIVING Katharine Briggs added another pair of functions to Jung's original model: judging versus perceiving (Briggs et al.,

2009). Jamal, who is the judging type, prefers to have things planned and settled. Paul, the perceiving type, is more spontaneous and likes to do things on the fly. So Jamal might tell you to quickly make a definite decision about Michael, and Paul might tell you to see him again and just see how it goes. As you might have guessed, judging has some overlap with high conscientiousness (Furnham, 1996).

JOURNAL PROMPT: UNDERSTANDING YOURSELF

Think of a movie you saw recently and analyze it using Jung's ego functions. How do the characters line up with Jung's four functions of thinking, feeling, sensing, and intuition?

EGO FUNCTIONS IN ACTION Prototypical examples of Jung's original four functions of thinking, feeling, intuition, and sensation have appeared in many TV shows and movies throughout the years. In *Star Trek*, four of the main characters represent the four Jungian personality types: thinking (Spock), feeling (McCoy), intuition (Kirk), and sensation (Scotty). The show's plot often involved Spock coming up with a perfectly logical plan, Kirk going with his gut, McCoy yelling passionately about something, and Scotty trying to get the ship to work. The characters in the *Harry Potter* series also cover some of the functions. Hermione is clearly thinking, Harry is intuitive, and Ron is feeling, though no one is clearly sensing (although Hagrid is a good candidate for that).

Jung believed that each of these functions can also exist within one person. For example, many people are thinking at some times and feeling at others. Jung (1962) also argued that you can have both a primary function and a secondary function. For example, a thinking type might also be comfortable being intuitive. She might first think through problems step by step but also search for patterns and make some leaps of logic. This is a good thing: Jung believed that expanding our abilities in our weak function areas was one of the best ways to grow as a person.

The Process of Individuation

Jung wrote a great deal about the process of **individuation**, or becoming an individual. In Freud's world, individuation occurred primarily during childhood (for example, though the Oedipus conflict). Jung believed that individuation was more complex and took much longer because it involved archetypes and the collective unconscious.

individuation
Jung's term for the process of psychological development

In the simplest terms, individuation involves changing the center of your psychological universe from your ego to the Self. Using the earlier metaphor of astronomy, it resembles the shift from seeing Earth as the center of the universe to seeing the Sun as the center.

Jungian individuation often appears in stories called a **hero's journey** (Campbell, 1949). The protagonist leaves home, goes on an adventure, descends

hero's journey
Joseph Campbell's model of individuation, including a descent and a return

into a literal or figurative underworld, and returns with a gift for society. The first *Harry Potter* book is a heroic journey: A boy is pulled from a normal world into an adventure of mythical proportions, including a battle with an evil figure in the dungeon of the school. In Britain, the first *Harry Potter* book was called *Harry Potter and the Philosopher's Stone*, which echoes Jung's idea that a philosopher's stone—which turns lead into gold—resembles the process of personal transformation. The hero's journey is seen in many epic stories, from the *Lord of the Rings* to *Star Wars* to *The Hunger Games*.

What does this mean for you? Jung thought that growing as a person meant embarking, at least in some way, on a hero's journey. Like Freud, he felt that the path involved dreams, art, and myths. He also thought that when someone was experiencing the collective unconscious, strange things could happen. For example, meaningful coincidences occur in most people's lives, which Jung termed **synchronicity** (Jung, 1952/1993). Many people ascribe deeper meaning to running into the same person more than once, concluding they were "meant to be together."

synchronicity
an acausal connecting principle in which things go together but are not causally linked

I (W. K. C.) had a strange synchronous experience when I was planning to create a new seminar room in the psychology building. I asked our department historian to identify a female psychologist we could name the room after. He suggested Celeste Parrish, who started the first experimental psychology laboratory in the South. Later I went into the room with two of the departmental secretaries to see what needed to be moved before construction. One of them opened a closet in the room and saw a wooden object tucked back on the top shelf. She pulled it out, and it was the famous lost portrait of Celeste Parrish. We all had chills run up our spines. I showed it to our historian, who confirmed it was the portrait shown in a 1916 newspaper story. The painting now hangs in the new seminar room—synchronicity in action.

Adler, Horney, and Object Relations Theory

LO 6.8 Discuss the importance of Alfred Adler, Karen Horney, and the object relations theorists in the history and development of personality theory.

We now turn our attention from Carl Jung to other neo-analytic theorists. This is only a selection of thinkers in this tradition. We want to give you a good taste of these ideas but not leave you stuffed with information.

Alfred Adler

Alfred Adler was an early colleague of Freud's, but Freud focused more on sexual impulses and Adler on the drive for power. Here we examine two of Adler's better-known theories in relation to this drive.

Have you heard the expressions "little man's syndrome," "short man's disease," or "Napoleon complex"? Maybe you've had a friend who was short or physically weak but took any opportunity to prove how tough he or she was by getting into conflicts with others. A good but extreme example of this is Joffrey Baratheon in *Game of Thrones*. He was basically a loser—small, weak, and cowardly. However, he compensated dramatically by becoming a power-hungry despot.

From Adler's perspective, everyone has a drive for power, but that everyone also has challenges expressing that power—and in some cases this can lead to significant issues. Imagine you are a young child and have a deformed arm or terrible asthma. All the other kids can play rough-and-tumble sports but you have to stay indoors. Some children with this experience will become somewhat more shy and cautious. They might even develop an **inferiority complex**, or a belief that they are of lower status or weaker than others (Adler, 1917).

Some people, however, will psychologically **compensate** for, or react against, this perceived inferiority by behaving as if they were strong and power-ful. For example, an inferior child could become exceptionally bold and fearless in his or her later life. Theodore Roosevelt was famous for being sickly as a child but strong and adventurous as an adult (Lilienfeld et al., 2012). He even has a river in South America named after him because he was one of the first to explore it.

There is not a lot of modern research on this topic, unfortunately. However, in the field of aggression there is a strong pattern of research showing that people who are insecure in their positive views of themselves do become violent when they are challenged (Baumeister et al., 1996).

inferiority complex
the belief that one is of lower status or weaker than others

compensate
to react against per-ceived inferiority by asserting power

Joffrey Baratheon in
Game of Thrones

birth order
the order in which siblings are born, an important concept in Adler's psychology

Adler was also interested in **birth order**, or how being an oldest, middle, or youngest child influenced people. Adler believed that siblings' experiences were wrapped up in power struggles with each other and their parents. For example, oldest children might become domineering due to the power they have over their siblings, and youngest children might be especially competitive because of their struggles with the oldest child (Adler, 1928). We discuss the modern scientific findings on birth order in Chapter 9.

Karen Horney

Freud's ideas were often rooted in a male-centric view of the world. This is not surprising, as Freud was a man in Victorian-era Europe, a culture that viewed women as the weaker sex. Psychoanalysis welcomed female theorists sooner than most professions did, but was still very male-dominated. Neo-analytic thinker Karen Horney questioned both the male-centric ideas of psychoanalysis and its emphasis on childhood as the primary source of neurosis.

One of Horney's (1924, 1967) most notable critiques was of Freud's idea of penis envy, which she thought was significantly exaggerated. In contrast, she argued that men actually had a strong desire for an ability possessed solely by women: the ability to give birth. By making arguments like this, she was able to balance out some of the psychodynamic gender bias.

Horney (2013) also developed a model of personality that focuses on coping with anxiety using one of three techniques:

moving toward
connecting with others as a way of dealing with anxiety

moving against
gaining control in a competitive world through exploitativeness and aggressiveness

moving away
trying to find peace by avoiding others and escaping conflict

- **Moving toward**, or connecting with others as a way of reducing anxiety. For example, Mark goes to social and community groups to keep his anxiety at bay.

- **Moving against**, or exploitativeness and aggressiveness to gain control in a competitive world. Molly doesn't trust the world and sees it as a dangerous place. She tries to overcome and control her world by starting a company and putting her competitors out of business.

- **Moving away**, or trying to find peace by avoiding others and escaping conflict. Malik doesn't have a lot of trust in the world, so he does his best to stay out of it. He spends a lot of time alone meditating and making art.

Horney saw these personality styles as somewhat adaptive, as long as they didn't become too extreme:

> . . . each of the basic attitudes towards others has its positive value. In moving toward people the person tries to create for himself a friendly relation to his world. In moving against people he equips himself for survival

in a competitive society. In moving away from people he hopes to attain a certain integrity and serenity. (2013, p. 89)

Horney's ideas have spread into modern personality science. Her focus on gender balance has led researchers to consider different perspectives, especially in clinical psychology. Her work in personality styles has also appeared in discussions of different personality processes. For example, Horney's model has been useful for understanding how business leaders and employees work under stress (Hogan & Hogan, 2001; there's more on personality at work in Chapter 12).

Object Relations Theory

Unlike other neo-analytic theories, object relations theory is not associated with one main theorist but several, including Ronald Fairbairn, Melanie Klein, Donald Winnicott, and Michael Balint. Although they developed somewhat different theories, they all emphasize how early relationships impact our personalities into adulthood. **Object relations theory** understands individuals by examining how they think about other people. This school of thought led to an emphasis on understanding relationships with other people as central to psychology and personality.

object relations theory
a model for understanding individuals by examining how they think about other people

In this theory, an object is an internal or psychological representation of another person. For example, if you think about your mother right now, your mental image of her is an object. An object relations theorist would believe that understanding your relationship with your mother would provide insight into your personality.

For example, Bill is a 35-year-old man who has trouble forming adult romantic relationships. He starts to get close to women, but when the relationship gets serious he pulls away. Freud might have focused on understanding Bill's sexual and aggressive impulses during his childhood. Was he sexually attracted to his mother? Was he scared of being castrated by his father? Did he want to hurt or even kill his father at some unconscious level?

An object relations theorist would look at this issue differently. She would focus on Bill's relationship with his mother. She might ask him: How close were you to your mother? Did you feel secure in your relationship? Do your current relationships with women resemble the relationship you had with your mother?

Object relations theorists also focused on **object integration**, or whether they can see other people as complex and multidimensional. Someone with well-integrated object relations realizes that although her loved ones are generally caring and moral, they can also make mistakes and do hurtful things.

object integration
the level of unification of an internalized relationship

In contrast, other people have an overly simplistic view of their friends and family. Ana loves her mother, but then her mother forgets to return a text message and Ana decides her mother is self-centered and wicked. A few days later, she sees her mother as a saint because her mother bought her dinner. This overly

split-object image
thinking about a single person in extreme positive and negative ways

basic fault
a lack of connection between the child and mother that can later impact adult relationships

black-and-white thinking about an object is called a **split-object image** (Klein & Mitchell, 1986). Learning to integrate these split images is a major challenge in psychotherapy and in becoming an adult.

Overall, object relations theory emphasizes that very early relationships can have a long-term influence on adult individual psychology. Michael Balint (1991) theorized that when a child feels unloved or unconnected to his mother, the **basic fault** occurs. The child with this fault grows up feeling something is missing inside and becomes an adult who has a difficult time forming close relationships. In other words, our early relationships with our parents impact our later adult relationships.

Object relations theory has had a major impact on modern personality science. In more social-cognitive work, objects have been examined as cognitive structures or schemas, and these turn out to have important psychological effects (e.g., Baldwin, 1992; Pierce & Lydon, 1998). This approach also led to a massive interest in research on attachment theory in relationships. We discuss this important area in Chapter 13. The theory has also informed the treatment of personality disorders that involve split object relations, such as borderline personality disorder, which we discuss in Chapter 14.

Concluding Thoughts

Like all models of personality, psychodynamic and neo-analytic models have some issues, and their direct contribution to scientific psychology will likely continue to diminish. But it is important not to dismiss these ideas out of hand. The psychodynamic and neo-analytic approaches give us a big, complex view of our own experience and the human condition. They help us see that our early relationships impact how our relationships go as adults. They show us that the conscious ego is not the center of the universe—or even the center of our own psychology. They make us realize that much of what we do is not the result of well-reasoned or conscious intentions. They also show us that being conflicted is extremely common. Life is complex, and we often want things that are not the best for us in the long term. We have to learn to balance these demands and have compassion for ourselves—and for others—when we do unwise things from time to time. And we have to understand that our current relationships are linked, for better or worse, to our relationships in the past. The psychodynamic approach can also teach us to appreciate our unconscious desires and hidden relationships and bring them out into the open. Denial ain't just a river in Egypt, but we can learn to overcome it.

Learning Objective Summaries

LO 6.1 **Discuss some of the basic concepts common to the various psychodynamic approaches.**

They focus on the role of the unconscious as well and the conscious mind. They are interested in the dynamic conflicts between these different aspects of the mind and how these conflicts can be resolved. Finally, psychodynamic thinkers tended to have "grand theories" or comprehensive models of the person.

LO 6.2 **Explain Freud's topographical and structural model of personality.**

The topographical model includes the conscious, preconscious, and unconscious. The structural model includes the id, ego, and superego.

LO 6.3 **Describe the stages of psychosexual development.**

Psychosexual development describes the movement of libido throughout the child's mind and body. Stages include oral, anal, phallic, and genital.

LO 6.4 **Discuss the relevance of dream interpretation in psychodynamic theory.**

Dreams are a pathway to understanding the unconscious mind. This process is called dream interpretation.

LO 6.5 **Evaluate the defense mechanisms and explain criticisms of Freudian theories.**

Defense mechanisms are processes that keep unconscious content out of conscious awareness.

Examples are denial, reaction formation, and projection.

LO 6.6 **Appraise the empirical evidence that appears to support Freud's theories, as well as the criticism.**

Freud's theories are difficult to operationalize and test empirically. Many of his central ideas are inconsistent with modern psychology. Yet several of his ideas, often in a modified form, have been tested successfully.

LO 6.7 **Describe the theories of Carl Jung and where Jungian ideas appear in modern psychology.**

Jung's main contributions were archetypes, the collective unconscious, and his model of personality including extraversion and introversion and the four functions of thinking, feeling, intuition, and sensation.

LO 6.8 **Discuss the importance of Alfred Adler, Karen Horney, and the object relations theorists in the history and development of personality theory.**

The neo-analytic theorists that included Adler, Horney, and the object relations group examined different drives, such as power, and focused more directly on the importance of childhood relationships.

Key Terms

psychoanalysis, p. 143
neo-analytic theorists, p. 143

analytical psychology, p. 143
unconscious, p. 143

conscious, p. 144
transference, p. 144

hysteria, p. 146
free association, p. 146
topographical model, p. 147
preconscious mind, p. 147
censorship, p. 147
pleasure principle, p. 147
reality principle, p. 147
structural model, p. 147
id, p. 147
ego, p. 147
super-ego, p. 147
Freudian slip, p. 148
libido, p. 150
cathexis, p. 150
developmental stages, p. 150
oral stage, p. 150
anal stage, p. 150
phallic stage, p. 150
latent stage, p. 150
genital stage, p. 150
oral fixation, p. 151
anal retentive, p. 152
anal expulsive, p. 152
Oedipus complex, p. 152
castration anxiety, p. 153
Electra complex, p. 153

penis envy, p. 153
manifest content, p. 153
latent content, p. 153
wish fulfillment, p. 154
day residue, p. 154
dream interpretation, p. 155
talking cure, p. 155
defense mechanisms, p. 156
denial, p. 157
reaction formation, p. 157
projection, p. 159
repression, p. 159
repressive coping, p. 159
displacement, p. 159
sublimation, p. 160
affiliative humor style, p. 162
self-enhancing humor style,
    p. 162
aggressive humor style, p. 162
self-defeating humor style, p. 162
defensive pessimism, p. 162
false consensus effect, p. 163
personal unconscious, p. 165
collective unconscious, p. 165
archetypes, p. 165
shadow, p. 166

anima/animus, p. 167
Self, p. 168
mandala, p. 168
ego functions, p. 168
extraversion versus
    introversion, p. 169
thinking versus feeling, p. 169
intuition versus sensation,
    p. 169
judging versus perceiving,
    p. 170
individuation, p. 171
hero's journey, p. 171
synchronicity, p. 172
inferiority complex, p. 173
compensate, p. 173
birth order, p. 174
moving toward, p. 174
moving against, p. 174
moving away, p. 174
object relations theory, p. 175
object integration, p. 175
split-object image, p. 176
basic fault, p. 176

Essay Questions

1. Explain Freud's topographical model of personality.

2. In what ways are Freudian and Jungian theory similar? In what ways are they different?

3. Describe Jung's ego functions as later applied to the Myers-Briggs Type Indicator.

4. Name and explain one theoretical contribution each from Adler, Horney, and the object relations theorists.

Chapter 7
Motivation

∨ Learning Objectives

LO 7.1 Distinguish approach and avoidance motivation.

LO 7.2 Name the needs in Maslow's hierarchy and describe the contributions of humanistic psychology.

LO 7.3 Describe the three major implicit motives, how they are measured, and how they affect behavior.

LO 7.4 Name and describe self-determination theory's three universal human needs.

LO 7.5   Describe intrinsic and extrinsic goals and intrinsic and extrinsic motivation.

LO 7.6   Explain the benefits of mindfulness, flow, and meaning in life.

When 30-year-old Elise Stefanik walked up the steps of the U.S. Capitol building early in 2015, the police stopped her. Only members of Congress could come this way, they said. So Stefanik took out her ID: She *was* a member of Congress—the youngest woman ever elected to the U.S. House of Representatives.

Stefanik focused on achievement at a young age, running for student council in the sixth grade. She then went to Harvard and ran her family's lumber business in upstate New York. After helping write the 2012 Republican Party platform, Stefanik decided to run for Congress, driving 100,000 miles around her district while campaigning. She won the election by a substantial 22 percentage points (Naugle, 2015).

goals
specific outcomes people desire

motives
the psychological entities that drive us to behave in ways that will help us meet our goals

Stefanik is obviously highly motivated: She knew what she wanted and went after it. Not all motives are related to career, as in this example; people are also motivated to form relationships, to develop skills, and to gain control over others. The study of psychological motives explores the differences in our goals and how we think about reaching them. Motives seek to answer an essential question of personality research: What do you want the most? In other words, what gets you out of bed in the morning? Motives are more fluid and changeable than personality traits such as the Big Five, but they capture something just as important: *why* people do what they do. To gain the full view of someone's personality, it really helps to figure out what "makes them tick"—and that means understanding their motivations.

Elise Stefanik is highly motivated to achieve her political goals.

Research on motivation has a long history (see Figure 7.1), and psychologists have used many different labels to describe what motivates people. Let's start with a term you already know: goal. A **goal** is a specific outcome someone desires. You have the goal of earning your college degree. Elise Stefanik had the goal of winning election to the U.S. Congress. Harry has the goal of getting married within the next 2 years, and Destiny has the goal of completing her first marathon. **Motives** are the psychological entities that drive us to behave in ways that will help us meet our goals. You have a motive to get an education, which drives you toward your goal of earning a college degree. Elise Stefanik was

Figure 7.1 A Brief and Selected History of Theory and Research on Motivation

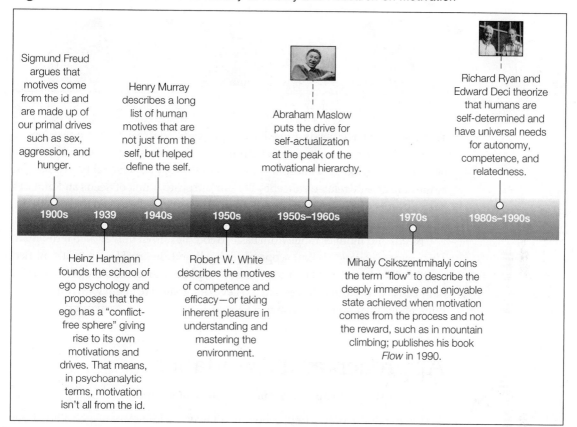

Sigmund Freud argues that motives come from the id and are made up of our primal drives such as sex, aggression, and hunger.

Henry Murray describes a long list of human motives that are not just from the self, but helped define the self.

Abraham Maslow puts the drive for self-actualization at the peak of the motivational hierarchy.

Richard Ryan and Edward Deci theorize that humans are self-determined and have universal needs for autonomy, competence, and relatedness.

1900s   1939   1940s   1950s   1950s–1960s   1970s   1980s–1990s

Heinz Hartmann founds the school of ego psychology and proposes that the ego has a "conflict-free sphere" giving rise to its own motivations and drives. That means, in psychoanalytic terms, motivation isn't all from the id.

Robert W. White describes the motives of competence and efficacy—or taking inherent pleasure in understanding and mastering the environment.

Mihaly Csikszentmihalyi coins the term "flow" to describe the deeply immersive and enjoyable state achieved when motivation comes from the process and not the reward, such as in mountain climbing; publishes his book *Flow* in 1990.

motivated to campaign to meet her goal of winning the election. Harry is motivated to meet a woman and form a serious relationship to meet his goal of getting married, and Destiny is motivated to train for the marathon to meet hers. As these examples show, the strength of certain motives can vary from one person to another. Some people are more interested in getting an education than others, and some people are more interested in career success or marriage or sports than others. This variation among people is one of the reasons why motives are an important topic in personality psychology. Other motives are more universal to all humans and don't vary as much. For example, the motivation to eat leads people to meet the goal of having a meal.

Motives are based in **needs**—something that is necessary to survive or thrive (Sheldon & Gunz, 2009). In other words, motives follow from needs (see Figure 7.2). Elise Stefanik has a need for high achievement, so she was motivated to run for Congress, reaching her goal of getting elected. Harry has a need for committed companionship, motivating him to date and eventually marry, reaching his goal. Destiny has a need to feel a sense of personal power, which motivates her to train for the marathon, reaching her goal of finishing a marathon.

needs
something that is
necessary to survive
or thrive

Figure 7.2 Needs, Motives, and Goals

This applies to basic needs as well: Angela has a need to eat, so when she doesn't have food, she is motivated to get more food. The terms *needs* and *motives* have been used interchangably at some points in the history of personality psychology, as they are closely related concepts. For our purposes, think of needs and motives as two events that occur in quick sucession: You experience a need for something, and that creates the motive to seek it out.

Needs and motives range from basic to complex, from universal to individual. This chapter covers a broad scope of research and theory. However, it's all tied together by one theme: the myriad reasons we haul ourselves out of bed to fulfill our needs, satisfy our motives, and achieve our goals. We begin with how people think about their goals: Do you work toward success, or try to avoid failure?

Approach and Avoidance

LO 7.1 Distinguish approach and avoidance motivation.

Avery attended a public high school in a lower-middle-class neighborhood but was accepted to a prestigious college. Surrounded by students from more advantaged backgrounds, he is terrified of failing his classes. April, who also attended a less-than-stellar high school, lives down the hall from Avery. Instead of fearing failure, however, she anticipates success, thinking of how proud she and her parents will be if she makes the Dean's List despite her background.

How do you react to a challenge? There are two types: people like April who anticipate rewards for success, called **approach motivation**, or those like Avery who worry about the negative consequences of failure, called **avoidance motivation** (Elliot & Thrash, 2002). The approach-oriented person focuses on rewards, just as April thinks about making the Dean's List. The avoidance-oriented person focuses on punishments and negative feedback, just as Avery worries about failing. Approach versus avoidance is one of the most basic concepts in psychology and behavior. Even one-celled organisms move toward food and away from a predator. For human psychology, the key question is: What motivates you more—moving toward the goal (approach), or moving away from danger or failure (avoidance)? Take the questionnaire on approach/avoidance motivation to find out what motivates you.

approach motivation
anticipating rewards for success

avoidance motivation
worrying about the negative consequences of failure

Questionnaire 7.1 APPROACH VERSUS AVOIDANCE TEMPERAMENT SCALE

Interactive

1. Thinking about the things I want really energizes me.
- Strongly Agree
- Moderately Agree
- Somewhat Agree
- Neither Agree nor Disagree
- Somewhat Disagree
- Moderately Disagree
- Strongly Disagree

2. When I see an opportunity for something I like, I immediately get excited.
- Strongly Agree
- Moderately Agree
- Somewhat Agree
- Neither Agree nor Disagree
- Somewhat Disagree
- Moderately Disagree
- Strongly Disagree

Previous   Next

TAKE the Questionnaire in REVEL

Another way to measure these personality types is by listing personal goals that appear in your daily life (Elliot & Sheldon, 1998). If you wrote "do the best I can in my classes" or "seek new and exciting experiences," you're likely approach oriented. If you wrote "avoid procrastination" or "try to keep from being lonely," you're likely avoidance oriented.

JOURNAL PROMPT: UNDERSTANDING YOURSELF

Are you oriented more toward approach or avoidance? What are the advantages and disadvantages of that orientation?

Approach and avoidance have some overlap with the Big Five. Approach-oriented people tend to be high in extraversion (as extraversion focuses on positive emotion), and avoidance-oriented people tend to be high in neuroticism (as neuroticism focuses on negative emotion) (Costa & McCrae, 1992; Elliot & Thrash, 2002, 2010). However, approach and avoidance motivation focus more on internal psychological processes (say, being more sensitive to rewards), whereas traits such as extraversion predict behaviors (talking to people at a party).

Approach and avoidance are also related to basic tendencies that may be rooted in evolution—the "fight-or-flight" choice (Cloninger, 1987; Gray, 1982). Imagine two male deer during mating season, their antlers a majestic tangle as they challenge each other over a female deer. Each male has a choice: He can fight the other male and get the chance to mate with the female, or he can run away and avoid being killed. Approach-oriented people are more likely to "fight" in search of positive rewards, and avoidance-oriented people are more likely to take "flight" away from negative consequences (Carver & White, 1994). Some experiments asked people to trace mazes to put them in an approach versus an avoidant mindset. The approach maze helps a mouse find its way to a slice of cheese, and the avoidance maze helps the mouse run to its hole to avoid a hovering predatory bird (Forester et al., 2006; see Figure 7.3).

Reed, the tornado chaser from Chapter 3, is approach oriented—he focuses on the rewards of seeing a destructive tornado, including the adrenaline rush and getting great video. His panicked friend Stefan is avoidance oriented, as he focuses on getting the heck out of there so he's not injured or killed by the tornado. Consider an approach-oriented pep talk from a coach: "Play hard. This is your day. Score. Win!" You'd head out for the game feeling pumped up. If she instead said, "Don't be soft out there. Don't let them score. Don't lose!" you'd probably feel anxious instead.

Knowing whether you are approach or avoidance oriented might also predict your philosophy about class work, just as it did for April and Avery. Approach-oriented students agree "[i]t is important for me to understand the content of this course as thoroughly as possible" and "[i]t is important for me to do well compared to others in this class." Avoidance-oriented students say, "I just want to avoid doing poorly in this class." Not surprisingly, students who just wanted to avoid failing performed more poorly on class exams (Elliot & Thrash, 2010; MacKinnon et al., 2002). Overall, avoidance-oriented people are lower in self-esteem and express lower life satisfaction (Elliot et al., 2011). However, they may be well suited for professions that focus on detecting errors, such as accounting and air-traffic control.

Figure 7.3 Approach–Avoidance

The mouse finding her way to the cheese has approach motivation, but the mouse scurrying toward his hole away from the hawk has avoidance motivation.

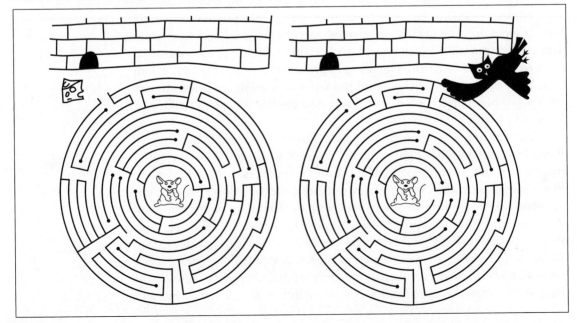

Thus, avoidance motivation is useful in some situations, but thinking about failure tends to hinder performance on difficult tasks. For example, an approach-oriented set of directions might say: Follow the yellow brick road, wind through the forest, don't stop, and then arrive at the Emerald City. The avoidance set says: Find the yellow brick road, watch out for flying monkeys, keep an eye out for strange creatures, don't get killed, and if you are very careful the Emerald City is at the end. In this example, the approach goal will probably get you to the city faster, but the avoidance goal will probably help you see the flying monkeys sooner. It is a trade-off. Given that most of modern life doesn't involve high degrees of danger, though, approach generally works better. It you live in a dangerous neighborhood, are clearing IEDs in a war zone, or have actually seen a flying monkey, avoidance motivation is better. But if you're studying for an exam, writing a brief for a court case, or preparing a presentation about a new product, approach orientation helps you focus on success. Some tasks might require both approach and avoidance orientation, such as a surgeon who needs to watch carefully for dangerous complications (avoidance) but also needs to focus on doing the surgery as well and as quickly as possible (approach).

Approach–avoidance motivation can also shift based on subtle changes in the situation. In one experiment, people asked to bend their arms toward themselves—what we usually do when receiving an object—became more approach oriented and focused on the positive aspects of good things, such as rating chocolate as more delicious. People asked instead to push their arms away from themselves—as we usually do when rejecting something—rated such strange foods as kidney meat (ugh) as more unappetizing (Friedman & Forester, 2010).

Even subtle differences in situations can influence performance. In one study, students took a cognitive performance test with their subject number written in ink on the first page. The experiment randomly varied the color of the ink: red, green, or black. This subtle difference produced surprising results: Those who saw red ink performed worse on the test than those who saw green or black ink. Why? Red primed avoidance motivation, due to its association with red pens and negative feedback and with red stop signs. At least in Western cultures, red is strongly associated with avoidance (Elliot et al., 2007). Even hearing they were in the "red group" or reading the word *red* on the test reduced students' cognitive performance (Lichtenfeld et al., 2009).

Seeing someone else—like your opponent in a wrestling match—wearing red may also affect performance. In combat sports such as boxing, tae kwon do, and

"No thank you, I don't want any kidney meat." In an experiment, those who pushed their arms away from themselves were more likely to rate foods as unappetizing.

wrestling, Olympic competitors who wore red were more likely to win, possibly because their opponents had to look at red, priming their avoidance motivation and harming their performance (Hill & Barton, 2005). The same was true of British soccer teams: Those who wore red were more likely to win championships (Attrill et al., 2008). Of course, it could also be that wearing red led to better performance by increasing dominance. Either way, it's an intriguing look at how color can influence performance.

Red is not negative in every context. Men who saw a picture of a woman wearing a red shirt (vs. the same woman wearing a blue shirt) described her as more attractive, were more likely to ask her out, and were more likely to want to have sex with her. The authors suggest that red has been explicitly linked to sexuality across time and cultures—for example, red-light districts, red hearts on Valentine's Day, red body paint as a symbol of female fertility, and red as a symbol of adultery (as in *The Scarlet Letter*; Elliot & Niesta, 2008). Even in an isolated tribe in Africa, men were more attracted to women in red (Elliot et al., 2013). Women also view men wearing red as more attractive, apparently because red indicates male status (Elliot et al., 2010).

Life experiences can also shift avoidance motivation. In January 2009, southern Israel was hit by a series of deadly missile attacks. Hundreds of missiles landed on streets and buildings, and loud sirens warning of attacks went off several times daily. Those exposed to the attacks were higher in avoidance motivation than those who were not exposed to the missile attacks. Approach motivation, however, did not differ between the two groups. This is a real-life demonstration of how situations can affect approach–avoidance motivation: Under threat, people

Seeing red, whether on an opponent's jersey or on a test, seems to cause performance to suffer by activating avoidance motivation.

become more focused on avoiding negative outcomes (Van Dijk et al., 2013). It also demonstrates how motives are more changeable than personality traits, shifting more with the situation.

Maslow's Hierarchy of Needs

LO 7.2 **Name the needs in Maslow's hierarchy and describe the contributions of humanistic psychology.**

Think about the goals you have for your life and what you do every day to achieve them. Now consider: Would any of these goals matter to you if you didn't have enough to eat, or were completely isolated from other people? Probably not, and that's the focus of Abraham Maslow's (1970) hierarchy of needs (Figure 7.4). Maslow was a proponent of **humanistic psychology**, a movement that focused on free will, creativity, and seeing the "whole person" to understand human psychology. Maslow theorized that humans must fulfill their needs in a certain order. The hierarchy is usually illustrated as a pyramid, with the most fundamental needs at the base and each higher need built upon them.

humanistic psychology
A branch of psychology focused on the "whole person," including free will, creativity, and human potential.

The Major Needs

The needs Maslow (1970) identified are as follows:

- *Physiological needs*, such as breathing, food, water, shelter, clothing, and sleep. If you don't get these things, it's tough to think about anything else. Many movies and real-life stories focus on what happens when people are

Figure 7.4 Maslow's Hierarchy of Needs

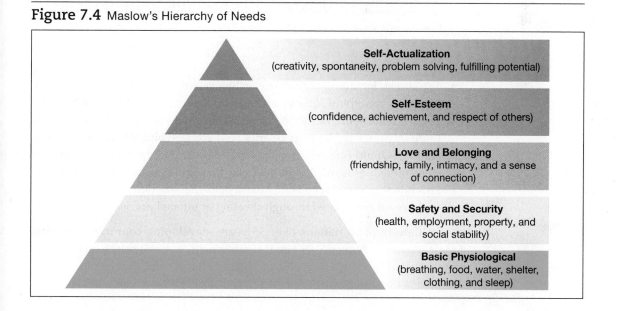

suddenly put in a situation where they struggle to fulfill physiological needs they once took for granted. For example, physiological needs come to the forefront when people survive a plane crash, get lost in the wilderness, or face starvation.

- *Safety and security*, such as health, employment, property, and social stability. If your needs for safety and security are met, that means you are reasonably healthy, have a job that pays the rent, and live in a place without (much) violence or war. These are again fairly basic needs—if you are sick or in danger, it's difficult to focus on anything other than getting better, getting safe, and just breathing, eating, and drinking (Wicker & others, 1993).

- *Love and belonging*, including friendship, family, intimacy, and a sense of connection. Once physical needs are (more or less) satisfied, humans need to have relationships with other people and feel that they belong. An influential review concluded that the need to belong is a fundamental human motivation (Baumeister & Leary, 1995). For example, people with many social connections are physically healthier (Cohen & Wills, 1985). In contrast, people rejected and ostracized by others, even briefly, feel alienated and sad (Van Beest & Williams, 2006) and are more likely to hurt and less likely to help others (Twenge et al., 2001, 2007). Even people who are dismissive about relationships feel happy when they are accepted by others (Carvallo & Gabriel, 2006). This is similar to the need for affiliation in self-determination theory. The need to belong creates the motive to affiliate with others.

JOURNAL PROMPT: UNDERSTANDING YOURSELF

Does it make sense to you that Maslow saw love and belonging as a more fundamental need than self-esteem?

- *Self-esteem*, including confidence, achievement, and the respect of others. Maslow's concept of self-esteem is somewhat broader than the self-esteem you learned about in Chapter 5. For Maslow, self-esteem means a feeling of pride in your work (not necessarily paid work—volunteer work or raising children would certainly qualify). It also includes admiration and respect from others. Maslow (1970) believed that self-esteem is best when it is grounded in actual achievement and behavior, or "deserved," rather than undeserved and gained through cheating or inflated praise.

In a study of 88 nations over 35 years, developing countries tended to follow Maslow's sequence of needs, with growth in basic needs such as food (physiological needs) coming first, then safety and security, then belonging, then self-esteem through political democracy, and so on. However, growth in one area

Watch MASLOW'S HIERARCHY OF NEEDS

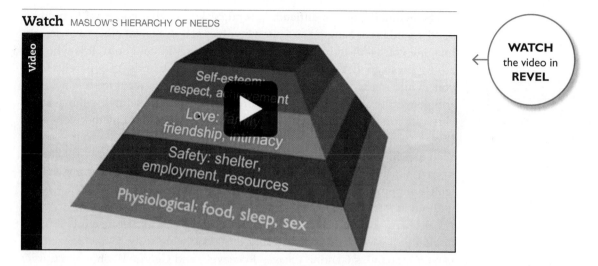

WATCH
the video in
REVEL

did not stop once another area began to progress—for example, progress in food and safety continues in China even as the country inches closer to democracy (Hagerty, 1999).

Self-Actualization and Humanistic Psychology

At the top of Maslow's pyramid is **self-actualization**, the need to actualize or "make actual" your unique talents and abilities. As Maslow famously wrote, "What humans *can* be, they *must* be. They must be true to their own nature. This need we may call self-actualization" (Maslow, 1970, p. 22, original emphasis). Take the questionnaire here to get a general idea of how self-actualized you are.

self-actualization
the need to actualize or "make actual" your unique talents and abilities

Questionnaire 7.2 SELF-ACTUALIZATION SCALE

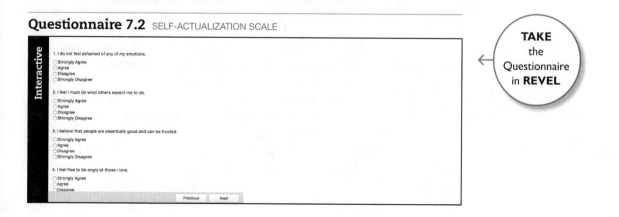

TAKE
the
Questionnaire
in **REVEL**

Self-actualization is difficult. You might know what you want to become, but the road is challenging and often involves acting against others and society. Imagine you want to be a musician. You feel this in your soul. It is who you are. So far, so good. But then you run into societal demands. Your parents think you should study accounting so you can get a job. You want to have a family, and you know a musician's life (staying out late and traveling) will make that very difficult. Plus, the words "poor" and "musician" go together very well. I (W. K. C.) live in Athens, Georgia, known for its great music scene—bands such as REM, the B-52s, and Widespread Panic launched successful careers from Athens. Most of the current crop of great musicians, however, are waiting tables, slinging coffee, or doing construction. Actualizing music ability is not without its sacrifices.

Self-actualization is at the small top of the pyramid because it is difficult to attain. Maslow believed that very few people are fully self-actualized. He named Mohandas Gandhi, Eleanor Roosevelt, and George Washington Carver as examples of self-actualized individuals, although it is not necessary to be well known to be self-actualized (Maslow, 1970).

Watch HUMANISTIC PERSONALITY THEORY

WATCH
the video in
REVEL

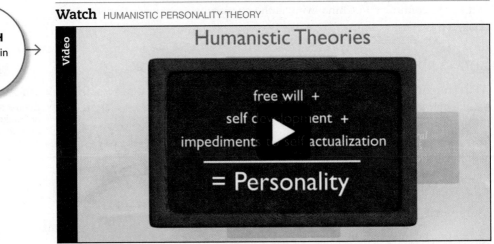

Another humanistic psychologist, Carl Rogers, believed that self-actualization was not just the province of a few selected individuals. He believed that people can get closer to self-actualization when they experience **unconditional positive regard**—acceptance and love of their whole selves without conditions attached. For example, parents should not say, "I love you when you pick up your room," "You're a good girl for getting such good grades," or "You are a bad boy." Instead, they should say that they like or dislike the child's actions, but they love the child no matter what she does. Similarly, therapists should express unconditional positive regard for their clients, never disapproving of them as people. Rogers believed that therapy best leads to clients' successful personality change and growth when the therapist experienced positive self-regard and empathy toward the client, and

unconditional positive regard
acceptance and love of someone's whole self without conditions attached

when the client could tell the therapist felt this way. In other words, if a person who is open to change (the client) comes into contact with someone who is empathetic and has unconditional positive regard for him or her (the therapist), there is a possibility for change and growth (Rogers, 1959).

One self-actualization questionnaire includes items measuring time competence (living in the present moment), self-acceptance (including of weaknesses), capacity for intimate contact, spontaneity, and inner-directedness (for example, "I feel free to not do what others expect of me"; Jones & Crandall, 1986; Shostrom, 1964). This disregard for external standards is not due to narcissistic self-centeredness but an acceptance of higher moral standards. Self-actualized people are described as enthusiastic, adaptable, giving, and modest. Those who are not self-actualized are instead rigid, fearful, inhibited, and confused (Shostrom, 1964). In short, self-actualized people are intrinsically motivated. So here's a challenge to consider: How could you become more self-actualized as a person?

Implicit Motives

LO 7.3 Describe the three major implicit motives, how they are measured, and how they affect behavior.

Near the top of Maslow's pyramid, just below self-actualization, are the needs for belonging and self-esteem. Once basic physical needs are accounted for, people start to focus on these motives. But which is more important to you: self-esteem or belonging? And are you fully aware of your own motives?

Spencer Grant/PhotoEdit, Inc.

The Thematic Apperception Test (TAT) asks people to write stories in response to pictures such as these.

implicit motives
unconscious motivations, usually measured with projective tests

projective measures
indirect measures; in theory, people project their motives onto the characters in a picture

power motive
wanting to have an impact on others

achievement motive
wanting to accomplish things—usually on one's own and without help

affiliation motive
being motivated by one's relationships with others

Building on the psychodynamic tradition (see Chapter 6), Henry Murray (1937) theorized that people are driven by mostly unconscious motivations, called **implicit motives**. According to this theory, you might not know the underlying motives for your own behavior. Because people don't have access to their unconscious motives, implicit motives are often measured by having people tell stories in response to pictures. This measure was originally called the Thematic Apperception Test (TAT; Murray, 1937), and has been updated more recently as the Picture Story Exercise (PSE; Schultheiss et al., 2008). Both are **projective measures** (which you first learned about in Chapter 2)—presumably, you project your motives onto the characters in the story. The PSE is usually a series of six pictures (Schultheiss et al., 2008; Smith, 1992). To use people's stories in research, psychologists developed standard scoring systems organized around common motives. Two or more coders read the stories and note the motives expressed in each sentence or paragraph. What are the motives? Read on.

Three Major Implicit Motives

Murray came up with a list of 27 implicit motives, but by far the most research has centered on three: **power motive**, **achievement motive**, and **affiliation motive**. When the motives were first named, they were called needs (as in "need for achievement") and were abbreviated nAch, nAff, and nPow (McClelland, 1951). Power and achievement overlap with Maslow's need for self-esteem, and affiliation is similar to Maslow's need for belonging.

Someone high in achievement motivation wants to accomplish things—usually on her own and without help (Spangler, 1992). She will prefer moderately challenging tasks—not so hard that they cannot be accomplished and not so easy that she doesn't gain a feeling of accomplishment (Koestner & McClelland, 1990; McClelland, 1987). For example, she might be more interested than others in starting her own business (Sagie & Elizur, 1999). Detectives on police shows, such as Olivia Benson on *Law & Order: SVU*, are high in achievement motive. When Detective Benson solves a challenging case, she has a strong feeling of accomplishment.

Someone high in affiliation motive values relationships with others (Atkinson et al., 1958). He wants to be around people, especially when he will be accepted and happy (Schultheiss, et al., 2005a, b). In negotiations or conflicts with others, he is better able to make concessions and end the conflict (Langner & Winter, 2001). He is more likely to have a satisfying job and family life and to cope well with stress (McAdams & Vaillant, 1982). He won't necessarily be high in extraversion (be outgoing and assertive), as affiliation focuses more on just a few close relationships and that can be important to both extraverts and introverts. The characters of Edward and Bella from the *Twilight* series are high in affiliation, as they are intensely focused on the tight bond of their relationship. On *Glee*, Mr. Schuster is high in affiliation because he wants everyone to feel that they belong.

People high in affiliation motive focus on warm relationships with others.

Someone high in power motive wants to have an impact on others and does not like others having an impact on her (Schultheiss, et al., 2005a, b; Winter, 1973). She is not necessarily more assertive or less likeable, but she seeks to influence others' beliefs in more subtle ways, such as appearing more competent and persuasive (Schultheiss & Brunstein, 2002). Someone who puts her name on her dorm door, frequently argues with others, or runs for student government is likely to be high in power motivation. Men high in power motivation prefer mates who are dependent on them and favor friends who are lower in status than they are (Winter, 1973). When power-motivated people do not gain the status and control they crave, they show signs of stress such as muscle tension and high blood pressure (Fodor, 1985; McClelland, 1979). Dwight from *The Office* is high in power motivation—he has a deep and abiding desire to be in charge. In *Despicable Me*, Gru wants to steal the moon, which sounds like power motive.

JOURNAL PROMPT: UNDERSTANDING YOURSELF

Which of the three implicit motivations do you think you're highest in? What examples in your life help to illustrate your choice?

Now that you know the three major motives, read these sample stories written in response to a picture showing two people on a bench near a frozen river (Table 7.1). Each story is a prototypical example of one of the three motives (Winter, 1996). Can you guess which is which?

Table 7.1 Understanding Motives

Story #1
They were young and in love. Time seemed to stop. Hours would pass as they sit together, taking in the shining beauty of the snow and ice, talking softly. Anyone could tell they were totally in love by the contentment that shone from their faces. They smiled secret smiles, exchanged understanding glances, and planned for a future together. Yet their future was not the security they would have wished. The air was full of the tensions of war. They didn't know if they would even see the beginning of another winter. So they retreated into their world, where no one could come, where they could dream and plan, feel safe and protected, and hope.

Story #2
The woman is a brilliant scientist at a well-known university. The man next to her is a colleague. They have done excellent work, slowly advancing toward their goal of curing cancer. Today they are in the middle of a crucial experiment. Within a few hours they will have the results. Some apparatus broke unexpectedly, making them impatient. So they have taken a lunch break by the river to figure out how to fix things. In fact, both are excited, anticipating a great discovery yet trying to keep some composure. Each is worried about making a mistake at this point.

Story #3
The man is an agent of the notorious secret police, pretending to be a potential member of a revolutionary group. The woman is an active member of the group. She originally joined in anger, after her mother (a famous leader) was framed by the government and imprisoned. Now she wants to carry on the campaign. The police have been checking up on her. The agent is pretending to be a man who wants to join the group. Actually he is eagerly waiting for the chance to plant a listening device on her.

Answers

Story #1: affiliation motive
Story #2: achievement motive
Story #3: power motive

How Do Implicit and Explicit Motives Affect Behavior?

explicit motives

conscious motivations, usually measured by self-report

Implicit motives are, by definition, mostly unconscious. They differ from **explicit motives**—motives people are aware of that can be measured by responses to direct questions. For example, a questionnaire might ask about how much someone wants to affiliate with others, and this can be compared to their affiliation motive in the stories they told in the PSE. Surprisingly, a person's explicit and implicit motives are often quite different (McClelland et al., 1989; Pang & Schultheiss, 2005; Spangler, 1992). Someone who writes stories high in affiliation motive (an implicit measure) is no more or less likely to endorse affiliation goals on a questionnaire (an explicit measure) (King, 1995). However, some people have more consistent implicit and explicit motives. For example, people low in self-monitoring, who don't change their self-presentation much from one situation to another, are more likely to score about the same on an implicit measure and explicit measure of motives (Thrash et al., 2007). Also, those who have similar implicit and explicit motives are higher in self-determination—they know what they want (Thrash & Elliot, 2002). In contrast, explicit and implicit measures are less consistent for other types of people, such as those who readily adopt the values of others (Hofer et al., 2006).

Implicit and explicit measures of motives also predict different types of behavior. Someone high in implicit achievement motive performs better than others on cognitive tasks but is no more likely than others to volunteer to lead a group. Those high in explicit achievement show the opposite pattern: no differences in cognitive performance but a greater likelihood of wanting to be a leader (Biernat, 1989). If you have high implicit, but not explicit, power motive, you'll perform better in a video game where your high scores obliterate previous players' entries. But if you are instead high only in explicit power, you will *say* you want to get a high score, but your performance will be no better (Schultheiss & Brunstein, 1999). Overall, implicit motives are more likely to predict performance (which is influenced by both conscious and unconscious factors), and explicit motives to predict choices and judgments (which are primarily conscious).

Where do implicit motives come from? Most research has focused on family environment, especially the parent–child relationship. Achievement-motivated people were more likely to have parents who encouraged independence—for example, through earlier and stricter potty training (McClelland & Pilon, 1983). Stronger affiliation motives may come from having parents who didn't respond as quickly to your needs as an infant. And parents who allow more aggressive or sexual behavior tend to have children higher in power motive (Schultheiss, 2008).

Personality's Past

Achievement Motivation in Children's Books

The study of personality deals with individual motivations. For example, in this chapter you responded to TAT cards and estimated your motivation from the narrative.

But what if you tried to measure the motivation of society by coding the society's stories? Could the motivations in stories predict its economic outcomes? That is just what psychologist David McClelland tried to do in many of his historical studies such as those described in his book *The Achieving Society* (1961).

McClelland decided to collect children's school readers from every industrialized country from 1925 (before the Great Depression) to 1950 (after World War II). It was a very challenging task; McClelland had to write to education ministries around the world. In the end, he was able to locate books from 23 countries between 1920 and 1929 and sets of books from 40 countries between 1946 and 1950. He then selected 21

stories from each country and had them translated into English, changing the names to typical American names (e.g., Mary, Bob) so it wasn't clear which country the stories were from.

McClelland then had coders rate the need for achievement expressed in each story. So, for example, a story that dealt with the desire for success would be rated high in need for achievement.

Then came the fun part—McClelland saw whether the achievement scores predicted economic progress—specifically, electricity production. With all countries combined, the need for achievement expressed in the children's stories in 1925 positively predicted economic growth between 1925 and 1950 ($r = .25$). But the same was not true backward: need for achievement in 1950 did not predict economic growth between 1925 and 1950 ($r = -.10$). That's exciting because that means achievement motives in books predicted future growth, but that economic growth did not predict achievement motives. This suggests that achievement motivation may have driven economic growth.

The Implicit Motives of Presidents and Eras

Implicit motives can, in theory, be coded from any example of someone's language, not just stories written in response to pictures. Psychologist David Winter (1987, 1991, 2005, 2009) has coded implicit motives in every U.S. president's inaugural speech. He used the same scoring system used for motives in TAT or PSE pictures, noting the presence of achievement, power, and affiliation motive in each sentence of the speech. Thus he was able to gain insight at a distance into the presidents' personalities, discerning their implicit motives.

President George H. W. Bush (in office 1989–1993), scored very high on affiliation motive, as did John F. Kennedy (1961–1963), Richard Nixon (1969–1974), and George W. Bush (2001–2009). High-affiliation presidents' terms are more likely to be touched by scandal and staff resignations, most likely because they are influenced by the suggestions of close friends (Winter, 2005). That proved to be true for Nixon: The Watergate scandal led to his resignation. Of course, similar to the other personality research you've read about, these are correlations and not absolute predictions, some high-affiliation presidents did not have these issues, but on average more do.

Jimmy Carter (1977–1981) and Bill Clinton (1993–2001) both scored very high in achievement motive. Presidents high in achievement motive are more likely to be idealistic, with terms characterized by a flurry of activity but few lasting accomplishments (Winter, 2005). The high-achievement-motive presidents' independence and reluctance to compromise seem to make politics—and management positions in general—a frustrating undertaking.

High-power-motive presidents include Kennedy, Harry Truman (1945–1951), George W. Bush, and Barack Obama (2009–). High-power-motive presidents are more likely to be ranked as "great" by historians and are more likely to start wars (Winter, 2005, 2009). That was true for Truman (Korea), Kennedy (Vietnam), and George W. Bush (Iraq and Afghanistan).

Do these motives coded from speeches accurately reflect presidents' personalities or are they simply the views of speechwriters? Winter (2002) argues that speechwriters adapt to presidents' styles and goals, and at the very least represent the viewpoint of the president's administration.

Motives can also be coded from media sources such as songs and books, capturing the implicit motives of a particular time and place. Thus, researchers can connect a society's motives to events over time. For example, when popular children's books in a culture showed more achievement motive, the society experienced greater economic growth and more new inventions about 20 years later (deCharms & Moeller, 1962; McClelland, 1961).

Motives may even predict war and peace. Speeches and communications immediately before a war are saturated with

Personality psychologist David Winter has used U.S. presidents' inaugural speeches, such as Barack Obama's here in 2009, to discern their psychological motives.

Karen Ballard/ZUMAPRESS/Newscom

power motive, but the affiliation motive becomes dominant as peace draws near (Langner & Winter, 2001). When the German Archduke Franz Ferdinand was assassinated in 1914, communications between the British and German governments were at first friendly and high in affiliation motive. As the crisis deepened, both sides displayed a higher power motive, and World War I began. After the United States discovered that the USSR had nuclear missile sites in Cuba in 1962, the two governments' communications were high in power motive. During this tense time, known as the Cuban Missile Crisis, the world waited with bated breath as the two countries seemed to be on the brink of a nuclear war. As the crisis went on, however, government communications grew higher in affiliation motive, and the incident was resolved peacefully (Winter, 1993).

Self-Determination Theory

LO 7.4 **Name and describe self-determination theory's three universal human needs.**

Self-determination theory (SDT) argues that three needs—autonomy, competence, and relatedness—can explain much of human behavior (Deci, 1975; Deci & Ryan, 1991; Ryan & Connell, 1989) (Figure 7.5). These three needs overlap with Murray's three primary motives: power (autonomy), achievement (competence), and affiliation (relatedness) (Schüler et al., 2013) (see Figure 7.5). The two systems were developed at different times using different methods, but seem to identify the same three basic needs or motives. The biggest difference between them is that SDT focuses on explicit motives and Murray on implicit motives. SDT also considers these three needs as essential to human functioning (Reis et al., 2000), while most research on implicit motives focuses on variations among people. Take the questionnaire to get a better sense of how your psychological needs are balanced.

self-determination theory
argues that three needs—autonomy, competence, and relatedness—can explain much of human behavior

---

Figure 7.5 The Overlap between the Three Needs of Self-Determination Theory and Implicit Motives: Power (Autonomy); Achievement (Competence); and Affiliation (Relatedness)

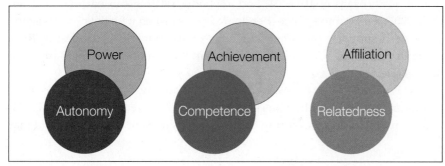

TAKE
the
Questionnaire
in **REVEL**

Questionnaire 7.3 BALANCED MEASURE OF PSYCHOLOGICAL NEEDS

Interactive

1. I was free to do things my own way.
- Strongly Agree
- Moderately Agree
- Neither Agree nor Disagree
- Moderately Disagree
- Strongly Disagree

2. I had a lot of pressures I could do without.
- Strongly Agree
- Moderately Agree
- Neither Agree nor Disagree
- Moderately Disagree
- Strongly Disagree

Previous   Next

---

autonomy

having control over your actions and life

Autonomy means having control over your actions and life. When autonomy is absent, you feel controlled by forces alien to the self, either external (such as someone else) or internal (such as uncontrollable desires or compulsions). For example, children often struggle to feel autonomous. Adults are always telling them what to do, and their emotions can overwhelm them. Adults usually have more autonomy, though some jobs have more autonomy than others. Working for a boss who "micromanages" by telling you what to do all the time would lead to low feelings of autonomy.

competence

being able to use your skills effectively and learn new ones

Competence means being able to use your skills effectively and learn new ones. For example, some jobs might offer the opportunity to continually learn new things, which fulfills the need for competence. But if you're instead stuck doing the same thing over and over, you would not satisfy the need for competence.

relatedness

feeling connected to others, both personally and in your community

Relatedness means feeling connected to others, both personally and in your community (Deci & Ryan, 2008). The need for relatedness could be met through spending time with family, helping a friend, caring for a child, or volunteering at a homeless shelter.

These needs are fundamental because people are mentally healthy and happy when the needs are satisfied and mentally unhealthy and unhappy when they are not (Reis et al., 2000). People whose needs are satisfied perform better in their jobs (Baard et al., 2004) and are better relationship partners (Patrick et al., 2007). For example, close friends are more satisfied with their relationships when each supports the other's feelings of autonomy by listening to their thoughts and ideas. It is especially important for friends to feel this support is mutual (Deci et al., 2006).

SDT maintains that these three needs of autonomy, competence, and relatedness are universal for humans across time and culture (Sheldon et al., 2001). Sure enough, a study measuring the three needs in eight countries found that they predicted meaning in life and personal growth about equally well in all eight cultures (Church et al., 2013). However, some cultures are better than others at satisfying these fundamental needs. For example, some cultures such as India have stronger family structures and tighter communities, features that promote a greater sense of relatedness (Vansteenkiste et al., 2004). Other cultures may not allow much autonomy. For example, people in Asian cultures, such as China, Japan, and Malaysia, report less autonomy and competence (Church et al., 2013). If a culture or its economic system does not do a good job satisfying one or more of the needs, the culture might undergo a change or even a revolution (Inghilleri, 1999). Much of the unrest in Middle Eastern countries such as Egypt stems from protests against dictatorships that restrict autonomy. Greece has experienced political change after the debt crisis put half of its young people out of work, depriving them of their need for competence.

The three needs can also be viewed as individual orientations—areas more or less important to certain people (Deci & Ryan, 1985). Similar to the implicit motives, some people focus more on autonomy and less on relatedness, and others are the opposite. These individual differences are correlated with certain outcomes. For example, people with a high autonomy orientation are self-aware and directive—they know what they want and go about trying to get it. As a result, they like their jobs more (Gagne & Deci, 2005) and are more successful at dieting (Williams et al., 1996). The Balanced Measure of Psychological Needs that you took should give you an idea of which areas are more and less important to you.

The three needs can help people meet the same goals in different ways. Take, for example, three students who all want to do well in school (a goal) but for different reasons (needs). Anna, who is high in autonomy motivation, wants to make good grades because she wants to chart her own destiny, and she knows school will help her make that happen by providing her with more career choices. Charles, who is high in competence motivation, wants to achieve academically as well, but because he wants to develop and refine his mental skills. Raul, who is high in relatedness motivation, strives to do well at school because that allows him to form strong relationships with his classmates in the honors programs and, eventually, to earn enough money to support his parents.

JOURNAL PROMPT: UNDERSTANDING YOURSELF

What are your motivations for wanting to do well in school? Think about your response as you read the next module on intrinsic versus extrinsic goals.

Extrinsic Versus Intrinsic Goals

LO 7.5 Describe intrinsic and extrinsic goals, and intrinsic and extrinsic motivation.

extrinsic goals
financial success, popularity or fame, and image or physical attractiveness

intrinsic goals
personal growth, affiliation, and community feeling

Emily knows what she wants out of life: to be rich, famous, and beautiful. Ian's goals are different: to understand himself, be close to family and friends, and make the world a better place. Clearly, Emily and Ian have very different life goals that motivate them and reflect their values. Emily's aspirations are **extrinsic goals**: financial success, popularity or fame, and image or physical attractiveness. Ian's aspirations are **intrinsic goals**: personal growth, affiliation, and community feeling (Grouzet et al., 2005; Kasser & Ryan, 1996; Schwartz, 1992). Take the Aspirations Index to get a better sense of the type of goals you value most.

TAKE the Questionnaire in **REVEL**

Questionnaire 7.4 ASPIRATIONS INDEX

Intrinsic goals are the things we know we "should" value, such as helping others. However, popular culture in the United States more often promotes extrinsic goals (Crompton & Kasser, 2009). Paparazzi usually don't follow people around for loving and being good to their families. You don't get on the cover of *Us Weekly* for volunteering at the homeless shelter. The world might be a better place if you did, but with plenty of beautiful and famous celebrities as well as an endless parade of scandals to cover, it's not going to happen anytime soon.

JOURNAL PROMPT: UNDERSTANDING YOURSELF

Which type of goal do you feel is most likely to motivate you? Extrinsic or intrinsic? Can you supply examples from your life that support your choice?

Which Goals Are More Likely to Make You Happy?

Despite modern Western culture's emphasis on extrinsic goals, people like Emily who focus on money, fame, and image are more likely to suffer from anxiety and depression and less likely to be happy (Kasser & Ryan, 1996; Kasser et al., 2014). They are also more likely to suffer from headaches and stomachaches (Dittmar et al., 2012). Becoming rich, famous, and beautiful is difficult, and even when these goals are met, people are left feeling empty. People who win the lottery are not any happier than anyone else, at least in the long term (Brickman et al., 1978). People like Ian, who instead value their relationships and try to make a difference, are happier—probably because these things are not as difficult to do and often provide a deep sense of satisfaction and meaning. In terms of SDT, these goals are more likely to satisfy the human needs of autonomy, competence, and relatedness.

The Science of Personality HOW TO DO AN EXPERIMENT

Interactive

	Extrinsic values
Facebook (Experimental)	7.10 (1.57) $n = 54$
Google Maps (Control)	6.05 (1.45) $n = 54$
t	3.61
p	$< .001$

Step 5: Enter and Compute the Data
- You'd enter the data for each of your participants, noting whether they were in the experimental or control group and then entering their extrinsic values score.
- Then you'd have statistical software compute the mean scores for extrinsic values for the experimental and control groups.
- Let's say the data looked like the table above:
  - Remember that p < .05 or less is considered statistically significant.
  - So which group scored higher on extrinsic values, and was the difference statistically significant?

6 of 9   Previous   Next

EXPLORE in **REVEL**

How Are Goals the Same and Different Across Cultures?

The same structure of goals and findings for their consequences emerges across 15 different cultures (Grouzet et al., 2005). Valuing intrinsic goals has benefits for the nation and the world as well. For example, Americans who were reminded of the nation's generosity, family values, and willingness to pull together in times of need were more likely to favor environmentally friendly measures such as smaller houses, more use of public transportation, and eating more locally grown food (Sheldon et al., 2011).

A culture's focus on these goals can also impact the well-being of its citizens. In cultures with more people focused on extrinsic goals, children's well-being is lower—for example, more children live in poverty (Kasser, 2011). Among wealthier countries, Sweden and the Netherlands score high in child well-being, while the United States and Britain score low.

How Do Goals Affect the Way You Think?

Just thinking about money, even in a brief or subtle way, seems to change people's mindsets. When people were reminded of money—by seeing Monopoly money or reading an essay about growing up rich—they were less willing to ask for help and less willing to give help to others (Vohs et al., 2006; see Figure 7.6).

Overall, focusing on one type of goal makes it more difficult to focus on a different type. In one study, students focused either on achievement words such as *ambitious, capable,* and *successful* or on helping words such as *forgiving, helpful,* and *honest*. Achievement-focused participants performed better at a word-search game but were less likely to volunteer their time. Helping-focused people performed more poorly on the game but were more likely to volunteer (Maio et al., 2009).

In other words, achievement-focused people might not be able to focus as much on caring for others. That has big implications for how we live our

Figure 7.6 Differences in Requesting Help Caused by Money Priming

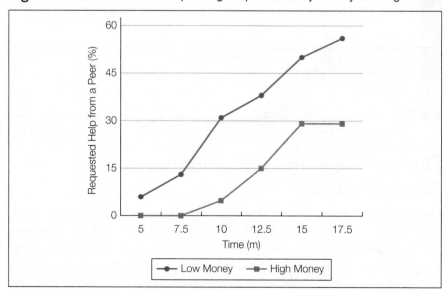

SOURCE: Vohs et al., 2006

lives—does that mean we can't "have it all"? It might—at least we might not be able to have it all at one time. If you're really focused on making good grades, it might be tough to spend as much time with your romantic partner. One thing is certain: The question of whether you can "have it all" is likely to inspire a lively debate whether you raise it in class, around the dinner table at home, or with your friends.

What Works Better: Extrinsic or Intrinsic Motivation?

Extrinsic goals are, by definition, those outside the self. Seeking money, fame, and image is similar to studying a lot because your parents promised they'd fund your spring break trip if you got a 4.0. You're not studying because you are inherently interested in learning—that's intrinsic motivation. Extrinsic rewards such as money and recognition sound good, but they can actually decrease intrinsic motivation to do well. In fact, the labels for intrinsic and extrinsic goals originally came from classic studies of motivation—or what motivates people to perform certain behaviors. As you might guess, **extrinsic motivation** comes from outside the self (such as money or praise from others), and **intrinsic motivation** comes from inside the self (such as taking joy in an activity).

extrinsic motivation
motivation outside the self, such as money or praise from others

intrinsic motivation
motivation inside the self, such as taking joy in an activity

Let's try a thought experiment: One day your professor says, "I will give you a great letter of recommendation if you read your psychology text." You do it and, as promised, your professor gives you the letter. Here is the question: After that, would you be more or less likely to want to read the psychology text in your free time?

Surprisingly, the answer is less likely. Extrinsic rewards can actually decrease intrinsic motivation. In one study, preschoolers who liked to draw were told they could earn a certificate with a large gold star and a red ribbon. Other children drew a picture but either didn't get an award or got one unexpectedly. A week later, the experimenter returned to observe what activities the children chose to engage in during free-play time. The children who got their expected award for drawing—those who were extrinsically motivated—spent only half as much time drawing as those who did not get an award or who received it unexpectedly (Lepper et al., 1973; see Figure 7.7). Doing something for an extrinsic reward killed their intrinsic motivation.

This classic study was widely reported in the popular press, one reason parents of the 1970s and 1980s like mine (J. M. T.) heard it was better not to pay children for grades (much to our disappointment). Since then, research has shown that paying children for academic achievement works only for some kids and only for a short time (Conley, 2012). Money and other extrinsic rewards can be motivating, but their effects disappear when they are removed. Overall, both kids and adults are more motivated in the long term

Figure 7.7 Extrinsic Rewards and Motivation

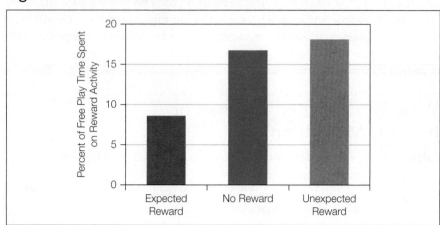

SOURCE: Lepper et al., 1973

when the drive comes from within. A job you do just for money is usually a miserable one.

Beliefs about ability can also have a big impact on motivation. In one experiment, adults praised children for good performance on difficult problems by saying, "You must be smart at these problems," instead saying, "You must have worked hard at these problems." The children who were praised for working hard later did better on an even more difficult task—presumably because

Children praised for working hard perform better than those praised for being smart.

working hard was under their control. If they were praised for being smart, however, they worried about failing on the next task—if they failed, maybe they wouldn't be smart anymore (Mueller & Dweck, 1998). Another study told college students they had failed at a task. They were then asked to continue working on that task or to work on a different one. American students spent more time working on a different task; Japanese students were more likely to spend time on the task on which they'd failed, perhaps thinking they could improve their performance (Heine et al., 2001). That may be one reason why Asians and Asian Americans perform better, on average, on academic tests. Overall, the belief that ability is malleable ("I can get better if I work hard") leads to greater motivation and better performance than the belief that ability is fixed ("I'm either smart or I'm not").

Mindfulness, Flow, and Meaning

LO 7.6 Explain the benefits of mindfulness, flow, and meaning in life.

So far you've gotten a view of how people think about their goals (approach and avoidance), humans' fundamental needs (Maslow and SDT), and individual differences in needs and motives (implicit motives and intrinsic and extrinsic motives). All of these topics tackle big questions about how humans survive, but also how humans can thrive. This emphasis on thriving has drawn humanistic psychologists concerned with the whole person as well as researchers focused on **positive psychology**, or research on what makes our lives better and what makes us happier. In this section we focus on three positive motivational experiences that can help you become more engaged in life: mindfulness, flow, and meaning. Before going any further in this section, take the questionnaire on mindfulness.

positive psychology
an area of psychology focused on what can make our lives better and what might make us happier.

Questionnaire 7.5 MINDFUL ATTENTION AWARENESS SCALE

TAKE the Questionnaire in **REVEL**

Mindfulness

mindfulness

being aware of your thoughts and perceptions without clinging to them or judging whether they are good or bad

Mindfulness is being aware of your thoughts and perceptions without clinging to them or judging whether they are good or bad (Brown & Ryan, 2003). The practice of mindfulness goes back to early Buddhist psychology. In the *Satipatthana Sutta* (2008), mindfulness is described as "the case where a monk remains focused on the body in and of itself—ardent, alert, and mindful—putting aside greed and distress with reference to the world." This same nonjudgmental focus is applied to thoughts and feelings as well. People can practice mindfulness in certain situations, such as when they are anxious or stressed. Mindfulness relates to personality because some people are more mindful than others across most situations. In Big Five terms, people who are low in neuroticism and high in conscientiousness tend to be better at practicing mindfulness (Giluk, 2009). The mindfulness questionnaire you took can help you figure out whether you are already mindful—or could become more so.

Mindfulness sounds easy, but it can be a very difficult practice. Just try a simple meditation exercise—close your eyes and try to focus on your breath. When your mind wanders, gently return your focus to your breath. You'll probably find that your mind takes off on all sorts of crazy directions. You think about work, then think about your boyfriend, then about the hot guy who plays the wolf in the *Twilight* movies, and then a full moon, and then how good a large pizza would taste for dinner, and then that you hate yourself for eating so much all the time, and then, OK, back to the breath. The mind is a mess.

Meditation increases mindfulness and decreases neuroticism, even without the cool magic blue lights.

Mindfulness practice not only slows the crazy nature of the mind but also makes you feel better and happier and can even help treat many psychological problems, such as anxiety disorders, binge eating, and pathological gambling (Baer, 2003; Broderick, 2005; Brown & Ryan, 2003; Lakey et al., 2007). It's not entirely clear why mindfulness improves mental health, but mindfulness might reduce neuroticism (Feltman et al., 2009), possibly through decreasing psychological reactions to negative events. So when bad things happen to you—say, your girlfriend picks a fight with you or you fail a test—mindfulness might help you stay calm and handle the issue appropriately (Barnes et al., 2007).

The most common way to practice mindfulness is with mindfulness meditation, which involves focusing on your sensations and thoughts without judgment (Kabat-Zinn, 1995). For people who get really distracted just sitting, however, other practices can help with mindfulness. Yoga, for example, links physical postures with breath and attention focus. One result is increased dispositional mindfulness, or the tendency to be more mindful across many situations (Shelov et al., 2009). I (W. K. C.) started doing yoga when I realized I, like many people over age 40, could no longer touch my toes. After doing yoga for a few years, I felt a bit more mindful and had more strength, flexibility, and balance. Plus, I can do cartwheels with my daughters, which not too long ago would have caused me to literally break into pieces.

Peak Experiences and Flow

Mindfulness can also lead to **peak experiences**—times when people transcend themselves and feel one with the world. This might happen when you are completely engaged in an activity, such as rock climbing, painting, playing or listening to music, or experiencing a flash of creativity. In sports it's called being "in the zone." I (W. K. C.) was snowboarding one morning when I noticed the fresh powder snow was lit up like diamonds. I heard a hippie-looking snowboarder say, "This is just like an acid trip," capturing the transcendent nature of the experience (and, best of all, snow has no flashbacks).

peak experiences
times when people can transcend themselves and feel one with the world

Peak experiences often result in a **flow state**: the mental experience of the smooth passage of time when you are completely immersed in an activity in the present moment (Csikszentmihalyi, 1996, 2000). Peak experiences are challenging, not easy, but they are rewarding because the intense focus required to produce flow quiets the usual chatter in our minds. Interestingly, people are more likely to have flow experiences at work than during leisure activities (Csikszentmihalyi & LeFevre, 1989). Flow has some overlap with mindfulness, as both involve focusing on the present moment. But flow is more likely to happen during activity and mindfulness during quiet meditation; flow has more energy to it.

flow state
the smooth passage of time that occurs during a peak experience, when you are completely immersed in an activity in the present moment

> **JOURNAL PROMPT: UNDERSTANDING YOURSELF**
>
> Think of a time when you experienced a flow state. What were you doing? How did it feel? Why do you think this activity induced such a state in you?

Csikszentmihalyi (1996) identified a "flow channel" between anxiety (when something is too difficult) and boredom (when something is too easy) (see Figure 7.8). Think about playing tennis with Rafael Nadal. What do you feel when he aims the first serve and the ball comes hurtling toward you at a hundred miles an hour? It wouldn't be flow—it would be anxiety bordering on terror. Now think about playing tennis with a 10-year-old beginner. It wouldn't be flow either—it

Figure 7.8 The Flow Channel

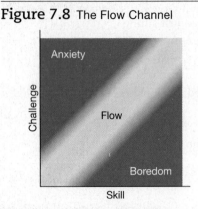

SOURCE: Csikszentmihalyi (1990, p. 74)

would be boring. But what about playing against someone at your level or slightly better? That would be engaging and the most likely to produce a flow state. Video games are so addictive because they are designed to keep you in a state of flow, with a constant stream of challenges that are difficult but not insurmountable.

If you stay in the flow channel, you will naturally get better at what you are doing. So, if you play tennis with a matched partner, your skills will naturally improve with practice. You will need a more and more challenging partner to maintain flow. It's the same with video games—if you just focus on flow, you will keep seeking greater challenges and higher levels to maintain that flow state.

Meaning and Purpose in Life

As the theater lights come up, an orange puppet in a sweater vest begins to sing. "What do you do," he asks, "with a BA in English?" Princeton, the main character in the Tony Award–winning musical *Avenue Q*, says he wants to make a difference in the world and find his "purpose"—something that will motivate him and give his life meaning. One of the other characters has already found his purpose, spending many hours on his computer. "The Internet," Trekkie Monster sings, "is for porn."

meaning in life
having a purpose and putting time and energy into attaining important goals

Most people are more like Princeton than like Trekkie (at least I hope they are)—they want to find **meaning in life** by having a purpose and putting time and energy into attaining important goals (Ryff & Singer, 1998). Meaning can also come from religion, personal relationships, behaving in a way consistent with your beliefs, or self-improvement (Allport, 1961; Baumeister, 1991; Ebersole, 1998). Both students and working adults agreed that people who felt their lives had meaning had "good" lives and that meaning was more important than being wealthy (King & Napa, 1998).

A frequent character in Hollywood movies is the ambitious, hard-charging, wealthy man who discovers there is more to life when a crisis occurs. The classic example is Scrooge in Dickens's *A Christmas Carol*, who reexamines his priorities when the Ghost of Christmas Future shows him his eventual loneliness and despair. Similarly, religious stories often punish blind ambition and meaningless achievement. As just one example, the Old Testament tells the story of a powerful king who marched into a church and began to burn incense at the altar, a privilege reserved only for priests. God struck him with leprosy, and he was exiled for the rest of his life. These cultural stories suggest that achieving your goals is not enough—you must also find meaning and integrity in them. That often means making sure your goals fit your personality. For example, people focused on affiliation were happiest when their goals were fun (McGregor & Little, 1998).

When your friend talks about pursuing her "passion," she probably means striving for goals that feel meaningful and true to her.

People who find their lives meaningful are happier, and happier people find more meaning in life. Feeling happy might be almost interchangeable with finding life meaningful (King et al., 2006). Many people cope with negative moods or events by focusing on the meaning they might gain from them (Janoff-Bulman & Berg, 1998). So finding a sense of meaning is important in both good times and bad. Graduating from college, getting married, having a child, and other happy events are important because they bring meaning and purpose to life. And failing a class, going through a breakup, and losing a loved one can create meaning through learning how to deal with adversity or learning more about yourself and your choices, though this process takes time (Davis et al., 1998).

Concluding Thoughts

Let's get back to our opening question: What gets you out of bed in the morning? What are your most cherished goals? People vary widely in their answers to these questions, due to both personality and situation. In times of poverty and war, people get up and go about their lives just to survive. In more privileged times and places, our lives are infused with meaning when we reach our goals—and which goals are most important can differ from one person to another. As SDT and Murray's needs both point out, those goals are most likely to include accomplishing something, feeling a sense of control, or spending quality time with friends and family. The research on approach–avoidance motivation adds another twist, suggesting that the way we see our goals—as success to be achieved versus failures to be avoided—also differs among people.

Theories of motives argue that some needs are universal, but also recognize that people differ in the strength of their needs and motives. Everyone needs to feel they belong in some way (relatedness in SDT), but this is a more central motivation for some than for others (affiliation in Murray's needs). Everyone wants to accomplish something in life (competence in SDT), but some people are more driven by challenge and big dreams than others (achievement in Murray's needs). Everyone wants to feel they have control of their lives (autonomy in SDT), but some people also want to control others (power in Murray's needs).

Those high-power-motive students are also the ones who, after reading this chapter, will wear their red shirt to the next exam.

Learning Objective Summaries

LO 7.1 Distinguish approach and avoidance motivation.

Approach motivation means anticipating rewards for success. Avoidance motivation means focusing on the negative consequences of failure.

LO 7.2 Name the needs in Maslow's hierarchy and describe the contributions of humanistic psychology.

Maslow theorized that basic needs must be satisfied before higher needs; the needs are physiological, safety and security, love and belonging, self-esteem, and self-actualization. Humanistic psychologists such as Maslow and Rogers believe that the whole person should be considered, and that therapists must show their clients unconditional positive regard.

LO 7.3 Describe the three major implicit motives, how they are measured, and how they affect behavior.

The three major implicit motives are power, achievement, and affiliation. They are usually measured with projective tests such as telling stories in response to pictures. Implicit motives predict some behaviors better than explicit motives. The implicit motives of U.S. presidents predict some aspects of their administrations.

LO 7.4 Name and describe self-determination theory's three universal human needs.

Self-determination theory posits that autonomy, competence, and relatedness are basic, universal human needs.

LO 7.5 Describe intrinsic and extrinsic goals and intrinsic and extrinsic motivation.

Intrinsic goals include personal growth, affiliation, and community feeling; extrinsic goals include money, fame, and image. Intrinsic goals are linked to greater happiness and extrinsic goals to more anxiety and depression. Generally, intrinsic motivation (found within the self) leads to better performance than extrinsic motivation (for something outside the self, such as a monetary reward).

LO 7.6 Explain the benefits of mindfulness, flow, and meaning in life.

Mindfulness, often increased through techniques such as meditation, can lower anxiety and improve mental health. Getting so involved in an activity that time seems to stop, called flow, is a highly positive experience. Finding meaning in life is also closely linked to happiness.

Key Terms

goals, p. 180
motives, p. 180
needs, p. 181
approach motivation, p. 182
avoidance motivation, p. 182
humanistic psychology, p. 187
self-actualization, p. 189

unconditional positive regard, p. 190
implicit motives, p. 192
projective measures, p. 192
power motive, p. 192
achievement motive, p. 192
affiliation motive, p. 192

explicit motives, p. 194
self-determination theory, p. 197
autonomy, p. 198
competence, p. 198
relatedness, p. 198
extrinsic goals, p. 200

intrinsic goals, p. 200

extrinsic motivation, p. 203

intrinsic motivation, p. 203

positive psychology, p. 205

mindfulness, p. 206

peak experiences, p. 207

flow state, p. 207

meaning in life, p. 208

Essay Questions

1. Define and explain the differences among a goal, a need, and a motive.

2. Discuss the difference between approach motivation and avoidance motivation.

3. What is Maslow's hierarchy of needs, and what according to Maslow is the ideal state of being?

4. Compare and contrast the three implicit motives discussed in this chapter with the three needs outlined by self-determination theory. In what ways do these needs and motives overlap? In what ways are they different?

5. Define intrinsic versus extrinsic goals, and explain how each is related to motivation.

6. How are mindfulness and flow related?

Chapter 8
How Learning Shapes Behavior

Learning Objectives

LO 8.1 Describe the types of reinforcement in operant conditioning.

LO 8.2 Explain how behavior modification works.

LO 8.3 Define internal and external locus of control and how they relate to expectancies.

LO 8.4 Explain how classical conditioning works.

Dan Freedman sat on the bench in the museum, so exhausted and sore after just 10 minutes of walking that his brother had to find him a wheelchair. Once vigorous and healthy, Dan had gained weight gradually over the years. That day in the museum, he weighed 230 pounds and, at age 50, had been diagnosed with diabetes and had the signs of early heart disease.

Today, Dan weighs 165 pounds—without surgery, pills, or extreme exercise. Instead, he follows a program that rewards good behavior. Every morning, he weighs himself on a special scale that sends the information via Twitter to other participants in his program. When he lost weight, they congratulated him, and he did the same when they lost weight. He used a computer program to count the calories of his meals and log how many minutes he'd walked that day, allowing him to see the progress he was making toward his goal (Freedman, 2012).

Why did this work? In brief, because people do what they are rewarded for and avoid doing what they are punished for. The weight-loss program that worked for Dan is based on the principles of **behaviorism**, a branch of psychology that focuses on (relatively) simple explanations for outward behavior and is unconcerned with the inner workings of the mind. It's a direct contrast to psychoanalytic theories, which put the unconscious mind at the center. Behaviorism documents how our personalities are built by the rewards and punishments we receive throughout our lives—how we learn to behave. It's also the basis for programs to improve child behavior, treat addiction, and help people sleep better.

Behavior is a key basis for personality (Buss & Craik, 1983). Extraverts like to talk; agreeable people like to help; neurotic people cry more; people high in openness to experience try new things; conscientious people work efficiently toward goals. Behaviorism explores how people learn to behave, and thus helps us understand how personality is shaped through the environment. From a behaviorist perspective, individual differences in personality are due to social learning that occurs in the environment (including culture, peers, and family). Well-known behaviorist B. F. Skinner (1971) believed that personality was the result of someone's learning experiences. For example, someone high in Big Five agreeableness might have been rewarded for helping others, and punished when she didn't. Through many of these experiences, she learned to behave like a highly agreeable person. By the way, we use agreeableness and conscientiousness frequently as examples throughout this chapter because they are influenced by family environment somewhat more than other traits.

Although strict behavioral approaches to personality are no longer central to mainstream personality science, these approaches are still very useful for understanding some mechanisms for how personality can be created or shaped. Learning shapes behavior, and patterns of behavior are a central aspect of what we call personality. For example, a child who is showered with praise and never disciplined—in other words, spoiled—is likely to develop narcissistic traits (Brummelman et al., 2015). So how exactly does learning shape behavior, and thus personality?

behaviorism
a branch of psychology that focuses on (relatively) simple explanations for outward behavior and is unconcerned with the inner workings of the mind

Weight-loss programs that focus on rewards are more likely to be effective, consistent with the principles of behaviorism.

Operant Conditioning: How to Get People (and Pets) to Do What You Want

LO 8.1 Describe the types of reinforcement in operant conditioning.

A woman in a green wetsuit rises out of the water, seemingly by magic. Then you see she's riding on the nose of a dolphin swimming swiftly through a huge tank, gliding by you until she hops off to the cheers of the crowd.

Why did the dolphin do this? How did they get him to swim with a trainer on his nose? Simple: dead, slimy fish in a bucket. Over many months, trainers worked with the dolphin to get him to perform tricks like these. When he behaved as the trainer wanted—or, at first, even came close to the correct behavior—he was rewarded with his favorite food.

Dolphins are highly intelligent; one science fiction writer imagined that dolphins would eventually build their own spaceship and depart Earth, leaving behind a note that said, "So long, and thanks for all the fish" (Adams, 1984). But dolphins don't just learn tricks because they are smart, and they are not the only animals that can be trained. Mice learn to press a lever to receive food. Horses are trained to race at top speed around a track. Dogs can learn tricks (though the first order of business is usually teaching them not to relieve themselves in the house). Many animals, in fact, can learn simple behaviors.

operant conditioning
shaping behavior through rewards and punishments

Dolphins learn to perform tricks through operant conditioning, which shapes their behavior through rewards.

The question most relevant to us, however, is how do people learn?

Let's say you want your child, roommate, boyfriend, girlfriend, spouse, or partner to behave in a certain way. Slimy fish aren't going to do it, so how can you motivate them? **Operant conditioning** is the general term for shaping behavior through rewards and punishments.

Four Ways of Modifying Behavior

Behavior can be modified in four major ways: Positive reinforcement, negative reinforcement, positive punishment, and negative punishment (see Table 8.1). We should say from the start that "positive" and "negative" don't mean "good" or "bad" as they usually do. Instead, positive means the addition of something, either good or bad: for example, a reward (a good thing, for reinforcement) or a spanking (a bad thing, for punishment). "Negative" means the removal of something: for example, an unwanted homework

Table 8.1 Four Ways to Shape Behavior

	Good thing	Bad (aversive) thing
Administering	Positive reinforcement (a reward: money, candy)	Positive punishment (spanking)
Taking away	Negative punishment (taking a toy away; time-out)	Negative reinforcement (turning off a shock)

assignment (taking away a bad thing, for reinforcement) or a recess period (taking away a good thing, for punishment). This can be confusing, so we'll go over this again in more detail for each modification type. But for now, just try to get good and bad out of your head every time you hear positive and negative! (Did you do it yet?)

POSITIVE REINFORCEMENT. **Positive reinforcement** for good behavior—also known as rewards or incentives—is often the most effective way to shape behavior. When our pet, kid, or significant other does something we like, we tend to give them something they like. For a dog or cat, that's usually food—any food. Kids like food, too, but are usually more picky (candy, yes; spinach, no). Boyfriends and girlfriends are more complex but often respond to praise, special meals, or compliments (try telling your guy he looks sexy when he vacuums).

B. F. Skinner's (1938) classic experiments with animals relied on positive reinforcement. Animals in "Skinner boxes" would learn to press a lever to receive food.

In more complex experiments, animals learned to play a toy piano or push a small shopping cart, usually by rewards given for behaviors progressively closer to the desired one. A pig might first be rewarded for getting close to the shopping cart, then for standing on his rear legs, then for standing and putting his legs on the handle, and finally for walking upright while pushing the cart. Similar techniques are used to train dolphins for theme park shows. This gradual process of reinforcement is called **shaping**.

After learning about operant conditioning, some psychology classes have supposedly decided to experiment with their professors. These stories are hard to verify, but most go something like this: The students get together and decide which behavior they'd like their professor to display—say, standing off to the

positive reinforcement
rewards or incentives for good behavior

shaping
gradual training that rewards behavior progressively closer to the desired one

To learn to push the cart, the dog was likely rewarded for behaviors closer and closer to the desired behavior, known as *shaping*. Next time, let's shape the dog to buy dog food instead of pineapples and eggs, though.

right side of the room instead of in the middle. When she lectures standing in the middle of the room, they look down at their feet, pretend to sleep, and generally don't pay attention. When she moves even a little to the right, they start to perk up and look interested. The further she moves to the right, the more attentive they get. Within a few weeks, she's lecturing from the doorway. When asked why she's standing there, she'll reply, "Oh, the light is so much better over here," or some other seemingly plausible reason. Giggling, the students then confess to their informal experiment.

The same process can work for rewarding more complex behaviors, such as helping others (part of agreeableness). Let's say Alberto helps his little sister climb the stairs. His mother praises him and gives him a hug. If she's consistent in rewarding Alberto's altruistic behavior, he might grow up to be higher in agreeableness. If Alberto's mother does not reward or even notice when he helps, Alberto might decide to stop being helpful.

B. F. Skinner argued that positive reinforcement is more effective than punishment, because positive reinforcement focuses on what the person or animal is doing well instead of what he is not doing well (Skinner, 1970). That's especially true for children, as it's easier to continue doing a desired behavior than to learn to behave differently (Van Duijvenvoorde et al., 2008). Even verbal praise is a reward, so it's a good idea to catch children being good and praise them for it. This is difficult, as people naturally seem to focus on negative things (Baumeister et al., 2001), but it's more positive and more effective. Children who receive attention only when they act badly soon learn to act badly more often. But children who receive attention for positive things are eager to show their parents how well they can behave.

Positive reinforcement is a great technique when used to reward good behavior, but it can also reinforce unhealthy behavior. Some people become addicted to alcohol, drugs, smoking, or sweets because these substances provide the positive reinforcement of pleasure. They drink and feel good, so they drink again. They eat dessert and love the taste, so they want to eat more. They get a rush from cocaine or methamphetamine, and they just have to feel that way again. Over time it takes more and more of the drug to produce the same feeling, which can result in an overdose. People high in conscientiousness and self-control are better at recognizing that it is usually preferable to resist short-term reinforcement (such as alcohol) to receive long-term reinforcement later on (not being hungover; Vuchinich & Simpson, 1998).

NEGATIVE REINFORCEMENT **Negative reinforcement** also rewards desired behavior—but instead of giving something good, you take away something bad. Let's say your child is at the dentist getting a filling—with all of the drilling and mouth-opening, it's no fun. "If you sit quietly, it will be over soon," you say. In other words, the better you behave, the sooner the unpleasant thing will be over (another example of self-control or high conscientiousness). Animals can learn to pull a lever to stop receiving a shock—one of the few things potentially more unpleasant than a dental filling. In one of the earliest behavioral experiments, Edward Thorndike confined cats to "puzzle boxes." When the cats pressed a lever or pulled a string, a door would open and the cats would escape and be rewarded with food—a combination of negative reinforcement (escaping the confinement of the box) and positive reinforcement (the food). The cats slowly learned what would help them escape and then repeated that behavior (Dewsbury, 1984; Thorndike, 1911).

> **negative reinforcement**
> rewards desired behavior by taking away something aversive

POSITIVE PUNISHMENT.   How do you deal with bad behavior? The best way is to reward good behavior so the bad behavior doesn't happen in the first place. But sometimes we don't behave as well as we should. That's when punishment can be used. Punishment comes in two forms. The first is **positive punishment**, or administering something aversive after misbehavior (it's "positive" not in the sense of being good but in the sense that the aversive thing is applied rather than a good thing being taken away). The classic example of positive punishment is physical pain. In my (J. M. T.) middle school outside of Dallas in the 1980s, everyone feared the vice principal because he had his own wooden paddle, carefully wrapped in white athletic tape (similar to the ones the high school seniors have in the movie *Dazed and Confused*). Getting a "paddling" was a common form of punishment. (Fortunately, I was too nerdy to ever be on the receiving end.) We now know that punishment, especially physical punishment such as spanking and paddling, is not the most effective discipline technique; it changes behavior only temporarily and can cause children to become more aggressive (Gershoff, 2002).

> **positive punishment**
> administering something aversive after misbehavior; what people usually mean when they refer to *punishment*

Even when it's not physical, punishment must follow very precise guidelines to be effective. First, punishment must immediately follow the bad behavior; an animal or a small child who is punished hours after knocking over the trash will have no idea why he's being punished. Second, punishment needs to be consistent. If punishment isn't applied consistently, every time the bad behavior occurs, the dog or the kid will often still play with the trash—he'll just try not to get caught. One way to use punishment less harshly is to give a verbal warning first: "Sit back in your chair by the time I count to five or . . . ." As long as the child knows you mean it—usually because you have followed through with punishment in the past—such a verbal warning can dramatically reduce the use of punishment.

More useful punishments are **natural consequences**. For example, if a 4-year-old purposely dumps her milk on the kitchen floor, she must help clean it up. If she touches a hot stove, she gets burned. Nature itself is an excellent forum for receiving natural consequences. Surfing, for example, is a process filled with the natural consequence of being held underwater after you make a mistake.

natural consequences
punishments enacted naturally as a consequence of the negative behavior

negative punishment
stopping bad behavior by taking away something good; also known as a time-out

NEGATIVE PUNISHMENT. The second form of punishment is **negative punishment** (also known as *time-out*), which means stopping bad behavior by taking away something good (it's "negative" not in the sense of being bad, but because something is taken away instead of something being applied, as in positive punishment). A parent who sends a child to bed without dinner has applied negative punishment by taking away food. For adults, an iPhone app called GymPact fines users $5 if they don't go to the gym as many times as they said they would—punishing laziness by taking away money (Freedman, 2012). Lifeguards who make misbehaving kids get out of the pool are using negative punishment—the mean kid dunking the others loses the pleasure of swimming in the pool. If your parents ever grounded you when you were a teenager, you've experienced a time-out; they took away time with your friends. Likewise, taking away a treasured object—such as a cell phone, toy, or computer—is another effective negative punishment technique.

For time-out to be effective, the child must be removed from social interaction with the rest of the family. Social interaction is a good thing, and time-out removes that.

For young children, negative punishment usually involves sitting in a (preferably boring) room for a few minutes, with no interaction with anyone else. Kids want to be with their parents and siblings, so time-out takes away the social interaction they crave. It doesn't sound like it would work, but it does—particularly if it's done correctly and the parent doesn't speak to the child while she's in time-out. When my (J. M. T.) daughter Kate had just learned to walk, she kept venturing to a section of our yard with large rocks. I didn't want her to fall and hurt herself, so I told her not to go there, but she kept doing it. The third or fourth time, I told her no again, and she laughed at me. That's when Kate got her very first time-out, spending a minute and a half in the laundry room. The next time we were in the yard, she said, "No rocks," and didn't go there. Time-out had worked.

As children grow and learn, they sometimes even give themselves a time-out, showing they are starting to internalize the rules—an early sign that conditioning might be having an effect on their personality. One day Kate said, "Grandma, go away." Grandma replied, "That's not nice." Kate picked up her stuffed monkey and sat down in the time-out room all on her own. "We in time-out," she told her monkey. "We not nice." As Kate has gotten older, she's wondered what happens to "bad guys" when the police catch them. We told her they go to jail. "Is that time-out for big people?" she asked. Basically, it is. Sending someone to prison takes away their freedom and many of life's pleasures, so it is a form of time-out or negative punishment.

Like the other techniques, negative punishments such as time-out might shape personality. Many parents automatically send a child to time-out if he hits someone else or is verbally aggressive (for example, yelling "I hate you!"). Basically, parents are punishing low agreeableness and low conscientiousness, hoping that the child will learn to control his aggression. At least in their less ambitious moments, parents hope that sending their kids to time-out now will prevent their kids from getting the ultimate time-out (prison) later.

Reinforcement Schedules

Reinforcement isn't just about giving a reward; it is also important to give out reinforcements at certain intervals. This is called a **reinforcement schedule** (Table 8.2). Let's say you want to reward someone for a good behavior—maybe you want your partner to take out the trash more often. At first, you'll want to use a **continuous reinforcement schedule**: Every time he takes out the trash, you give him a kiss. Eventually you can move to one of four **partial reinforcement schedules**: **fixed-ratio reinforcement** (giving him a kiss only after he's taken out the trash twice—so a certain number of good behaviors), **variable-ratio reinforcement** (a kiss after an unpredictable or random number of times—so a random number of good behaviors), **fixed-interval reinforcement** (a kiss every 3 days—a certain amount of time), or **variable-interval reinforcement** (kissing him randomly at intervals of 1 to 5 days—a random amount of time). As you can see, *fixed* versus *variable* refers to a set amount of time versus a random amount, and *ratio* versus *interval* refers to whether the reward is given after the behavior versus after a certain amount of time has passed.

Imagine sitting in front of a slot machine at a casino. You pull the lever, and most of the time, nothing happens except the screen changes and you lose the money you put in. But every once in a while, bells and whistles go off, the screen

reinforcement schedule
giving out rewards for good behavior at certain intervals

continuous reinforcement schedule
always giving out a reward for good behavior

partial reinforcement schedule
only sometimes giving out a reward for good behavior

fixed-ratio reinforcement
giving out a reward after a certain number of behaviors

variable-ratio reinforcement
giving out a reward after a random number of behaviors

fixed-interval reinforcement
giving out a reward after a certain amount of time has passed

variable-interval reinforcement
giving out a reward after a random amount of time has passed

Table 8.2 Four Reinforcement Schedules

	Fixed	Variable
Interval	Reward steadily given after a certain amount of time (e.g., every 3 days)	Reward at random amount of time (e.g., anywhere from 1 to 5 days)
Ratio	Reward after certain number of behaviors (e.g., taking out the trash 3 times)	Reward after random number of behaviors (e.g., taking out the trash anywhere from 1 to 5 times)

lights up, and money comes out of the machine. This is a variable-ratio schedule, and it's uniquely addictive; you keep repeating the behavior because you never know when you're going to get your payoff. You keep putting money into the slot machine even after it doesn't pay off because you think you're just on a bad streak and next time you just know you will hit it big. For this reason,

Gambling often works on a variable-ratio schedule, one reason it can be addictive.

variable-ratio schedules usually lead to the greatest increase in the desired behavior. Interestingly, this is the same reward system used for publishing in scientific journals. Papers are accepted in a highly variable pattern—most of the time, they are rejected, but occasionally they are accepted. It is very challenging to predict what happens. As a result, scientists just persist at submitting papers.

Of course, context matters, and sometimes the other schedules work better. Many jobs are paid on a fixed-interval schedule; you work and every 2 weeks you get a paycheck. This kind of schedule gets you to show up and do your job, but not much more.

Other jobs might pay you for specific behaviors. These fixed-ratio schedules are common in sales—for example, you might get a commission for each piece of clothing that you sell. That reinforcement schedule can really motivate behavior, but it can also lead someone to focus only on sales and throw other parts of the job aside. A salesperson also might find herself stretching the truth a bit to customers, telling a 48-year-old textbook author how good he looks in a V-neck cashmere sweater with no shirt underneath (I [W. K. C.] have no comment).

JOURNAL PROMPT: UNDERSTANDING YOURSELF

Put operant conditioning to the test. What schedule of reinforcement would you use to get your boy/girlfriend to do something that you wanted them to do?

Another disadvantage of commission jobs on a fixed-ratio schedule is that as soon as the fixed reinforcement is taken away (that is, the commission), the behavior stops (the increased effort to sell). A variable-ratio reinforcement schedule—as used in casinos—is better at maintaining a desired behavior for extended periods of time. When the ratio is variable, you never know when it will pay off, so you keep going. This schedule has a better chance of making the salesperson's motivation become more intrinsic—part of the self—instead of purely extrinsic (recall Chapter 7).

Watch BEHAVIOR MODIFICATION

WATCH the video in **REVEL**

Socialization

Visit a mall, an airport, a store, or a family restaurant and you'll see young children running away from their parents, yelling, throwing things, eating with their mouths open, and taking things from shelves (hopefully not all at once). The adults (at least most of them) are instead sitting quietly and talking without yelling or crying. They have learned to control their impulses through years of being rewarded for proper behavior and punished for negative behavior through operant conditioning. This process is known as **socialization** or enculturation: How children slowly learn how to become mature members of society and learn their culture's rules. Of course, cultures vary in what they consider acceptable behavior, one source of the cultural differences we discuss in Chapter 11. Different families might also have different standards for socialization. In some families, yelling and arguing might be considered relatively acceptable. Thus, children might not be punished for yelling and arguing, which might socialize them to be lower in agreeableness.

socialization
how children learn to become mature members of society; also known as *acculturation*

As another example, operant conditioning helps enforce culturally determined gender differences (the topic of Chapter 10), such as in crying. Male and female babies cry the same amount, but adult men cry much less often than women (Lombardo et al., 2001). Boys experience more disapproval for crying ("Stop crying right now! Boys don't cry") than girls do ("It's OK, honey—let me give you a hug"). Clothing provides an even starker example of gender role learning through operant conditioning: Any boy who doubts the power of conditioning for gender roles just has to go to school wearing a dress.

However, most boys don't need to be explicitly told not to wear dresses, or not to cry. They learn these behaviors by observing other males and their behaviors. They might also see someone else get rewarded or punished for behavior. This is called **social learning** (Bandura, 1986, 2006). Traditional operant conditioning involves shaping someone's behavior through rewards and punishments that they experience, but humans are also capable of learning by observing others. In a famous experiment, preschool children watched an adult woman repeatedly punch a Bobo doll (a large plastic toy that bounces back when hit), punctuating her smacks and kicks with instructive comments such as "Pow, right in the nose, boom, boom" and "Sockeroo—stay down." Some children saw the woman receive praise and candy for her actions; others saw her get hit with a rolled-up magazine and warned not to hit the doll again; a third group saw no consequences. In contrast to those who saw her get punished, the kids who saw the woman rewarded for her aggression and those who saw no consequences were more likely to copy her actions. They punched and kicked the Bobo doll, often using the woman's exact words "Pow! Sockeroo!" (Bandura, 1965).

social learning
observational learning that occurs when someone watches others get rewarded or punished for behavior

In other words, children (and sometimes adults) look to role models to see how to behave. Echoing the results of the Bobo doll experiment, children who watch violent TV and play violent video games are more aggressive—possibly because aggression on TV is rarely punished, and in video games it is even rewarded directly with points (Anderson et al., 2010; Huesmann et al., 1987). Some of these studies are correlational—meaning they find that aggressive kids play aggressive video games. In those cases, children who are more aggressive might be drawn to more violent media, or outside factors such as family background might lead to both violent media use and more aggression. But experimental laboratory studies, which randomly assign people to view violent versus nonviolent media, also find that violent media causes aggression. Games can also teach good behavior through reward: People who play video games rewarding prosocial behaviors such as helping are later more likely to help someone in real life (Gentile et al., 2009). In personality terms, video games are teaching low or high agreeableness. As Doug Gentile and Craig Anderson (2011) conclude, "Video games are excellent teachers."

Behavior Modification: Using Operant Conditioning in the Real World

LO 8.2 **Explain how behavior modification works.**

The practical applications of operant conditioning are endless. Using conditioning to improve behavior is called **behavior modification**. "Behavior mod" or "b-mod" is often instituted in challenging cases—kids who won't go to school, people who suffer from mental disorders, people addicted to drugs, or youth engaging in violence. One study found that among children with attention-deficit/hyperactivity disorder (ADHD), those who participated in a b-mod treatment were half as likely to later be arrested for a felony as those who did not receive treatment (Satterfield & Schell, 1997). However, b-mod techniques can be used with normal populations as well. If you're trying to modify someone's behavior (or even your own behavior) using operant conditioning, you're using b-mod. For example, if you'd like to become a more agreeable and conscientious person, b-mod techniques might help you do that.

behavior modification
using conditioning to improve behavior

How Behavior Modification Works

The idea behind b-mod is to reward only acceptable behavior. For example, some psychiatric hospitals have a **token economy**, in which good behavior is rewarded with tokens that can be exchanged for privileges such as walking around the grounds (Silverstein et al., 2006). Some schools and parents use a similar system with children. At my daughter Julia's preschool, kids who behave well can choose an item from the "treasure box" at the end of the week. One program called "triple P" (for "Positive Parenting Program") teaches parents to reward good behavior, use logical consequences for misbehavior, and employ time-out. At least

token economy
a program in which good behavior is rewarded with tokens that can be exchanged for privileges

If you're good, you can choose a prize from the treasure box! (Such prizes are more attractive when you are 4 years old.)

according to the parents, children were significantly better behaved after parents instituted b-mod techniques (De Graaf et al., 2008).

One of the best therapies for depression is called behavioral activation (Jacobson et al., 1996; Lejuez et al., 2011; Spates et al., 2006). Depressed people are encouraged to do specific things that will lead to rewards, based on values that are important to them. For example, if you want to get more education, you could ask a friend for advice about school and write out a plan for enrolling in school. This technique helps depressed people refocus on behaviors that will bring rewards, rescuing them from the lethargy and inaction that can lead to bad consequences.

For addictions (to drugs, alcohol, or cigarettes), behavior modification uses a variety of methods. For example, alcoholics can take a drug (disulfiram) that makes them nauseous when they drink alcohol. Instead of being rewarded with a buzz, they are punished with throwing up when they drink (Smith et al., 1997). (Of course, the problem is that they have to take the pills for this to work.) Drug users can also be rewarded for staying clean; in one study, even a group of hard-core cocaine addicts were twice as likely to stay away from drugs if they were paid progressively more each week for having clean drug tests (Silverman et al., 2001). Another technique centers on changing the usual cues that lead to use. Many rehabilitation programs require people to live at a facility, in an attempt to eliminate not just their access to drugs but also the situations that remind them of getting high. Slowly, they learn to gain pleasure from other things (Elsheikh, 2008).

B-mod sounds like common sense—of course, people will reward good behavior and punish (or at least ignore) bad behavior. But that's less common than you might think, partially due to a misguided sense of compassion. Consider the true story of Jasper the cat, who hides under the kitchen table and swipes at passersby with his claws. Isabella, Jasper's owner, will then pick him up and say soothingly, "Aww, poor Jasper—what's the matter?" Isabella has just rewarded Jasper's bad behavior, making it more likely Jasper will scratch people's ankles again in the future. Although it seems that Isabella is being compassionate toward Jasper, she's actually enabling his bad behavior, which is not good for the scratched humans or for the cat in the long run—if he continues to behave badly, they might not want him in the house anymore. Isabella should instead either ignore the swiping or use positive punishment (perhaps by using a water gun to spray a little water onto his fur—cats hate getting wet, so every time Jasper claws at someone's socks, he will suddenly feel wet and uncomfortable). She could also use positive reinforcement by rewarding Jasper with cuddles or treats for sitting under the table quietly without swiping at anyone.

Remembering b-mod techniques is even more important in raising children, who will eventually need to behave for someone other than you. Toddlers, for example, love to grab the candy in the grocery checkout aisle (cleverly put at their eye level by the store owners, who are not dumb). Most of the time, Mom will say, "No, Jaden," and put it back. Sometimes Jaden will start to cry and scream for the candy. Mom's reaction here is crucial—does she give in? If she does, she's just rewarded Jaden for his bad behavior. Jaden has learned that if he wants something, he should scream and cry. Mom's other alternative is to ignore Jaden's tantrum—more difficult to do in the short term but better in the long term because Jaden will learn that screaming gets him nowhere. Mom will have to tough it out, back a few feet away, and let him scream until he decides to give up. The authors of the parenting guide *Toddler 411*, who recommend behavior modification techniques, have been there. "Be prepared for well-meaning adults who think your child has been abandoned and needs to be comforted," they note. "Sometimes we wish we had portable orange safety cones we could set out by our child" (Fields & Brown, 2007, p. 30).

Providing incentives—economists' term for rewards—to illicit a desired behavior is also not as simple as it might seem. Consider a common problem at daycare centers and preschools: parents who pick up their children late. One daycare center in Israel decided to solve this problem by imposing a fine of $3 on late parents. But the fine backfired: More, not fewer, parents started picking up their kids after the closing time. Apparently $3 was enough to alleviate the guilt they had previously felt for a late pickup and not enough to be an economic disincentive (Gneezy & Rustichini, 2000). If the center instead imposed a $100 fine, that wouldn't work either—it's too big and would create resentment even if it did eliminate late pickups. So the daycare center needs to settle on the right amount between $3 and $100 that will produce the best behavior. This echoes a common problem in business: how to price a product so it's not too suspiciously cheap, not too egregiously expensive, and makes a profit while still staying competitive in the marketplace. The overall lesson: Incentives are more complicated than they first appear.

Using Behavior Modification on Yourself

You can also use behavior modification to change your own habits. Let's say you want to stop eating so much junk food. If you've met that goal for a week, reward yourself with something pleasurable that's not food related—say, something you've wanted to buy for awhile or a movie you've been wanting to see. Or follow a program like the one Dan Freedman did, keeping track of your progress and getting support from others when you succeed. The basic idea is to increase your self-control, one of the main aspects of Big Five conscientiousness.

If you're prone to self-criticism, try to redirect your inner voice to praise yourself when you're doing something well instead of focusing on negative things. This inner praise should be specific and real ("That's good—I stayed calm") not general or grandiose ("I'm the best!"); the first is self-compassion, which has many benefits (Neff et al., 2007); the second is narcissism, which does not.

JOURNAL PROMPT: UNDERSTANDING YOURSELF

Think of a bad habit you would like to change. How could you use behavior modification techniques to eliminate or reduce it?

Another way to change your behavior is to consider your habits. Almost half of what you do every day is not a choice in the moment but a habit. Let's say you want to break a bad habit, such as having dessert after every meal. First, you have to figure out what makes you have the urge to eat that cookie or piece of cake. In this case it's finishing a meal. Since you can't stop eating meals, you have to focus on changing what you do afterward when you've previously been raiding the cabinet for sugar. If you do something else after meals and are vigilant about not slipping up, you might be able to break your bad habit—but only if it truly is a habit (something you do often) and not just a temptation (something you do to make yourself feel good right now) (Quinn et al., 2010). After awhile, the automatic urge will go away and it will be much easier to stick with your healthier plan. When dessert is a temptation instead of a habit, you'll only *occasionally* feel the need to eat frosting out of the can. If you end up eating only 20% of the frosting you did before, that's still significant progress. Highly conscientious people don't just resist urges; they structure the situation so the temptation isn't as automatic (Baumeister & Tierney, 2011).

Get out of the habit of eating dessert after every meal and the automatic urge will go away.

Different strategies will be necessary for different habits. In one study of college students, the most common bad habit (at 23%) was staying up too late. The second most common (at 17%) was eating junk food; procrastinating came in third at 10% (Quinn et al., 2010). So if you stayed up late last night eating pizza and playing video games, fell asleep in class, and realized you still haven't studied for your exam tomorrow, you are not alone. But you might want to do some b-mod on yourself ASAP.

How Far Can Behavior Modification Go?

John Watson once wrote, "Give me a dozen healthy infants, well formed, and my own specified world to bring them up in. I'll guarantee to take any one at random and train him to become any type of specialist I might select—doctor, lawyer, artist, merchant, chief—and yes, beggarman and thief" (1924/1970, p. 104). In other words, Watson theorized that, regardless of genetics, he could use the environment to shape children into any type of person he chose. Similarly, B. F. Skinner wrote several books (*Walden Two, Beyond Freedom and Dignity*) suggesting that behavior modification could be used to create a utopian society in which no one is aggressive or violent.

As you read in Chapter 4, however, a good amount of personality is determined by genetics. Thus, Watson's and Skinner's visions of people shaped solely by their environment are probably not realistic. However, you might also recall that genetics explains only half the variance in personality. Thus, people are born with certain tendencies, but how they behave may still depend in large part on which of their behaviors were rewarded and which were punished, especially because that's often determined by culture and individual experience as well as family environment. So, as is often the case, the truth lies somewhere in the middle: We are born with certain tendencies, but our environment—including rewards and punishments—also shapes how we behave.

In addition, people often choose the environments they enter and then change them—called **reciprocal determinism** (Bandura, 1989). For example, when Sophia joins her high school swim team, she will be rewarded for swimming strokes correctly and keeping up with others during practice. Left alone, Sophia would probably just play in the pool instead of swimming laps. Yet she still had some degree of choice—she chose to join the swim team in the first place. Sophia will also change her environment by participating in it. If she wins a race, another swimmer will not. Her family interacts differently when she's there to help her younger brother with his homework, compared to when she stays late at swim practice.

reciprocal determinism
the idea that people choose the environments they enter and then change them

Thus, although early behaviorists such as Skinner rejected the notion of humans having free will, behaviorism does not necessarily rule out the idea that humans can make impactful choices. We explore this notion of free will further in the next section.

Expectancies and Locus of Control

LO 8.3 Define internal and external locus of control and how they relate to expectancies.

In its original form, behaviorism saw no need to consider what went on in people's (or animals') heads. Thinking was not necessary because organisms would automatically do what had worked in the past. But researchers such as Julian Rotter thought this view was overly simplistic. Although many behaviors require little thought, people do think and make decisions about their actions every day.

Let's say you're trying to decide if you will go to your friend's upcoming party. You'll think about whether you had a good time at parties in the past, whether your friend will throw the type of party you like, and whether you'll meet anyone interesting. Rotter et al. (1972) called these considerations **expectancies**. Our expectancies are based on our past experiences of what was rewarding, just as a behaviorist would predict, but they involve some thought and contemplation. Our expectancies can also be wrong: maybe you never have fun at parties but optimistically think that this party will be different because your friend is hosting it.

Our decisions are also based on the **reinforcement value** of the rewards in different situations. If you just went to a party the night before, the reinforcement value of a new party is less than if you haven't been to a party in awhile. If you are already in a relationship, the reinforcement value of meeting new people is less than if you are single and looking. Our personalities and motivations also influence what rewards we value the most. If you're high in achievement motivation, for example, you might decide not to go to the party if it's on a school night. If you're high in affiliation motive, you might decide to go because it will make your friend happy.

You also have to make decisions about situations you've never encountered before. Pure behaviorism would have no prediction about behavior in new situations, as you wouldn't know what would be rewarding versus not. In this case, you would use what Rotter called **generalized expectancies**—your belief about how often your actions usually lead to rewards versus punishment. Let's say you are trying to decide how much you're going to prepare for an upcoming job or graduate school interview. Some people have the generalized expectancy that preparing won't make much of a difference—who gets the job or gets into graduate school is more a matter of luck and the arbitrary decisions of powerful people. Rotter called this having an **external locus of control** (Rotter, 1966). On the other end of the spectrum are people who believe that their actions do have an effect, those with an **internal locus of control**. Internally controlled people are more likely to prepare for the interview. Thus, people differ in their locus of control, making it important for understanding personality. Take the questionnaire below to see whether your locus of control is internal or external, at least relative to the norm sample.

expectancies
what someone expects to happen, based on past experiences of what was rewarding

reinforcement value
how enticing a particular reward is

generalized expectancies
beliefs about how often actions lead to rewards versus punishment

external locus of control
believing that events are more a matter of luck and the arbitrary decisions of powerful people

internal locus of control
believing that your actions have an effect on events

TAKE the Questionnaire in **REVEL** →

Questionnaire 8.1 NOWICKI LOCUS OF CONTROL SCALE

Interactive

1. Do you believe that most problems will solve themselves if you just don't fool with them?
   ○ True
   ○ False

2. Do you believe that you can stop yourself from catching a cold?
   ○ True
   ○ False

3. Are some people just born lucky?
   ○ True
   ○ False

4. Most of the time, do you feel that getting good grades meant a great deal to you?
   ○ True
   ○ False

| Previous | Next |

Internal locus of control is a strong predictor of getting better grades (Cappella & Weinstein, 2001; Findley & Cooper, 1983; Kalechstein & Nowicki, 1997). Among racial minority children, internal locus of control was a better predictor of school achievement than any other variable (Coleman et al., 1966). Believing that studying matters leads to more studying, which leads to better grades.

People with an external locus of control, on the other hand, are more likely to be anxious and depressed (Benassi et al., 1988; Mirowsky & Ross, 1990) and have lower conscientiousness and self-control (Karabenick & Srull, 1978; Mischel et al., 1974).

External locus of control may be a response to negative life circumstances: People who have bad experiences may give up and decide they can't have an impact on their life outcomes. That makes them even more vulnerable to poor academic performance, anxiety, and depression, creating a vicious cycle.

JOURNAL PROMPT: UNDERSTANDING YOURSELF

Are you more internal or external in your locus of control? What are the advantages and disadvantages of that point of view?

During the early 1970s, Rotter observed more externality and feelings of alienation among young people, a trend that continued into the 2000s (Twenge et al., 2004). "Our society has so many critical problems that it desperately needs as many active, participating internal-minded members as possible," Rotter wrote, in a statement that may still hold true today, "If feelings of external control, alienation and powerlessness continue to grow, we may be heading for a society of dropouts—each person sitting back, watching the world go by" (1971, p. 59).

Especially if you scored as external, you might respond that cynicism is justified in modern life—just look at how big our problems are and how difficult it is for one person to have an influence. That's a good issue to debate with your classmates. But, especially given the links between external locus of control and failure, taking action in your own life is almost always better. Sure, bad luck might have cost you that last job, but that doesn't mean you shouldn't work hard to prepare for the next opportunity to come your way.

Classical Conditioning: How to Get People (and Pets) to Drool

LO 8.4 **Explain how classical conditioning works.**

Ivan Pavlov did not set out to change psychology. When he began his work with dogs in the 1890s, he was studying digestion. He wanted to find out how much they salivated when they were fed. This work won him the 1904 Nobel Prize in Medicine.

I hear the can opener again!

classical conditioning
associating two things not normally associated with each other

unconditioned stimulus
the stimulus normally produced by the unconditioned response (for example, food producing salivation)

unconditioned response
the response normally produced by the conditioned response (for example, salivation being produced by food)

conditioned stimulus
the stimulus that produces the conditioned response after classical conditioning (for example, a bell causing dogs to salivate)

But, as sometimes happens in science, the digestion experiments didn't go exactly as Pavlov expected. He thought that the dogs would salivate when they ate their food, but instead they started to drool *before* they ate—sometimes even before they saw the food. For example, they might start salivating when they saw the lab worker (let's call him Igor) who usually fed them. The dogs had learned to associate Igor with food, so they started to drool when they saw him. Sound worked as well; if Igor always rang a bell before the dogs were fed, they would soon salivate at the sound of the bell. If you have a dog or cat who eats canned food, you might have noticed that she will come running when you open a can—even if you've opened fruit cocktail in heavy syrup for yourself. This is known as **classical conditioning**, or associating two things not normally associated with each other.

In all of these examples, the animal's food is the **unconditioned stimulus** (UCS)—the thing that naturally produces the **unconditioned response** (UCR) of salivating. But then your pet begins to associate the sound of the can opener with food, so the can opener becomes the **conditioned stimulus** (CS) that produces the **conditioned response** (CR) of your pet, salivation (Figure 8.1). Salivation is the response in both cases, but when *unconditioned* it's merely the natural response to food and when *conditioned* it's the response to something not normally associated with food, such as Igor, a bell, or the sound of the can opener.

Classical Conditioning and Fear

Classical conditioning goes far beyond salivation. It can apply to any two things that become associated with each other. One of the most famous examples is John Watson and Rosalie Rayner's experiment with a baby they called Little Albert. At the beginning, Albert displayed no fear when he saw a white rat. But

Figure 8.1 The cat food is the unconditioned stimulus that produces the unconditioned response of the cat salivating. The sound of the can opener is the conditioned stimulus, which will eventually produce the conditioned response of the cat salivating.

Cat Food (UCS)

The Sound of Can Opener (CS)

Cat Salivating (USR and CR)

then Watson and Rayner would make a loud, unpleasant noise (clanging two metal things together) every time Albert saw the rat. Before long, Albert would cry when he saw the rat. Albert's fear also became **generalized**—meaning his conditioned response applied to other, similar things: He also began to fear white rabbits, white dogs, and even a white fur coat. His fear became generalized even though these things had not been paired with the loud noise (Watson & Rayner, 1920). One hopes his mother didn't put him on Santa's lap that year.

Unfortunately, Watson and Rayner did not decondition Albert—they did not reverse the conditioning to eliminate his fear, known as **deconditioning**. They could have begun with **discrimination**—making the fear less broad—by repeatedly showing Albert white things when he felt safe and relaxed, and without the loud noise. Then they could show him the white rat, again without the loud noise and while he was calm. Eventually this process would result in the **extinction** of Albert's

conditioned response
the response produced by the conditioned stimulus after classical conditioning (for example, salivation following the sound of the bell)

generalization
when a conditioned response is elicited in response to things similar to the conditioned stimulus

deconditioning

reversing conditioning to eliminate the conditioned response

association of the white rat with fear, so eventually he would not fear white objects anymore. Ethically, this is what they should have done. It's quite possible that Albert spent his entire life afraid of fuzzy white things. However, even if he had been deconditioned, any further pairing of a white rat with something frightening might have brought Albert's fear back. Having learned the association once, learning it again would happen more quickly, known as **spontaneous recovery**.

Personality's Past

The Scandal of John B. Watson

John Broadus Watson was at the pinnacle of his career in 1920. He had stunned the world with his classical conditioning studies of Little Albert and served as president of the American Psychological Association. He also received a large raise from his university, Johns Hopkins. But then, like many before him, he lost it all for love. Watson started a relationship with his graduate student, Rosalie Raynor. He left his wife and the divorce made the newspapers. The indiscretion and the bad press resulted in Watson being fired from Johns Hopkins (Chamberlin, 2012).

Watson ended up marrying Raynor, but could not find another academic job because he was tainted by the scandal. He then moved to New York City to work in advertising. Watson was a successful advertising executive and even purportedly came up with the term "coffee break" to market Maxwell House coffee (Chamberlin, 2012).

But the real scandal was how Watson's story was covered in psychology textbooks. Starting in the

1970s—50 years after Watson's firing from Johns Hopkins—some textbook authors began to embellish Watson's story. Some alleged that Watson engaged in secret sex research with Raynor and that is what led him to be fired. According to James Vernon McConnell (as cited in Chamberlin, 2012) and described in 200 psychology textbooks (Benjamin et al., 2007):

> John B. Watson was one of the first Americans to investigate the physiological aspects of the sexual response. . . . Watson wanted to know what kinds of biological changes occurred in humans during the stress of intercourse. Watson tackled the issue directly, by connecting his own body (and that of his female partner) to various scientific instruments while they made love.

According to a detailed review of the historical evidence, however, there is little support for this accusation. Watson was not a faithful husband, but the more colorful stories about his downfall are not accurate (Benjamin et al., 2007).

discrimination

narrowing the conditions that produce the conditioned response

extinction

eliminating the conditioned response

spontaneous recovery

relearning a conditioned response

Classical conditioning associations can occur in everyday life after traumatic or unpleasant experiences. Let's say you ate a salmon burger and a fruit smoothie and then, an hour later, found yourself barfing into the toilet. You'll probably find it very hard to eat salmon burgers and smoothies again. You might even cringe when you pass Jamba Juice or Smoothie King on your way to campus, especially if you can smell the smoothies (Garcia et al., 1966).

Associations are one of the main mechanisms behind posttraumatic stress disorder (PTSD). A combat veteran may experience fear after all loud noises, not just the gunfire and explosions that originally caused her fear. Reducing PTSD involves learning to stay calm in the face of these stressors. Some new treatments for PTSD put the veteran back into the stressful situation with virtual reality technology. For example, one program created a "virtual Iraq" so PTSD veterans could reexperience stressors in a controlled and safe environment. That way, veterans can gradually learn to associate the stressors with relaxation instead of fear (Rizzo et al., 2012).

We can also associate other people with unpleasantness. In one study, a woman with short hair and glasses was rude to a student who asked her a question. When the students later had to approach someone else, they were more likely to avoid a different woman with short hair and glasses and instead approach a woman with long hair and no glasses. Even though short-haired, glasses-wearing woman number 2 had nothing to do with the first woman's insult, the students automatically associated her appearance with something negative. When quizzed about it later, however, the students didn't even realize they had avoided the second woman due to her appearance (Lewicki, 1985). (Now you know why you avoid that friend, teacher, or coworker who looks like the mean girl from your high school days.)

Habituation

In the classic movie *The Blues Brothers*, an elevated train rumbles by on tracks just outside the window of Elwood's room, making a deafening noise. "How often does the train go by?" asks Jake. "So often that you won't even notice it," answers Elwood.

Elwood is talking about **habituation**—getting used to something in the environment and not responding as strongly anymore, a principle related to classical conditioning. Elwood probably didn't sleep the first night he spent in the room next to the train tracks, but over time he got used to it. People who live near airports or busy highways often have similar experiences. You can also habituate to sensations. For example, most of us don't notice the feeling of clothes against our skin. That's good, as we'd be distracted from more important things if we did.

habituation
getting used to something in the environment and not responding as strongly anymore

Over time, the occupants of these houses likely adjusted to the noise of the airplanes flying overhead through the process known as *habituation*.

That's probably why habituation evolved in the first place—to help us pay attention to the most important things. Something that happens over and over, or is always there, is probably not that important. But when that saber-tooth tiger charges out of the bushes, we needed to be ready. Perhaps as a result, habituation occurs even in animals such as worms with barely developed nervous systems (Wyers et al., 1973).

Habituation is very useful for studying infants. Babies will look at a novel stimulus—something new—longer than something familiar. For example, babies first became habituated to a toy sitting on a table, until they didn't look at it as long. But when the toy was moved, they looked at it again for a longer time (Kaufman & Needham, 1999). Because the object moved, they were dehabituated to it, and that told the researchers that the babies noticed that the toy moved.

Sleep Conditioning: How Did You Sleep Last Night?

Many people would like to sleep better—to fall asleep quickly, to stay asleep the whole night, and to wake up feeling rested. One of the secrets to sleeping well is simple classical conditioning: Make sure you associate your bed with relaxation and sleep. That's especially helpful for people who score high in neuroticism, who are more prone to insomnia.

Maria often studies while sitting on her bed, working on class readings and problem sets right up until bedtime. When she's not studying, she sits on her bed and talks to or texts her boyfriend. Sometimes they fight. Then when it's time to go to bed, she lies in the dark with her eyes wide open, too keyed up to sleep. It doesn't help that her cell phone is still on (just in case her boyfriend decides to text back an apology).

JOURNAL PROMPT: UNDERSTANDING YOURSELF

What do you usually do before you go to sleep at night? Are you classically conditioning your body for restful sleep, or not?

Maria has come to associate her sleep space with being awake and with tasks that require focus and sometimes involve anxiety and anger. She associates her bed with feeling tense and wired. After several weeks of sleeping poorly, Maria is starting to fall behind in her classes and is fighting with her boyfriend even more. She's just so tired.

Maria then decides to use classical conditioning to help with her sleep issues. She knows she needs to learn to associate her bed with sleep. So she studies at the kitchen table instead and stays out of the bedroom when she's calling or texting with her boyfriend. She also tries to relax for at least a half an hour before going to bed. At first, she still has a hard time sleeping. But after a few nights, she starts to feel tired as soon as she lies down in bed, and her sleep improves.

The associations formed by classical conditioning are also why you shouldn't toss and turn in bed for too long; you'll start to associate your bed with your restless

Using the principles of classical conditioning may help you sleep better.

insomnia. If you haven't fallen asleep after about half an hour, get up and do something relaxing somewhere else for about 15 minutes, and then try again to sleep.

Who knew that an idea based on dog drool would help you sleep better?

Phobias and Their Cure

Have you ever known someone who was afraid of flying, heights, or snakes? The technical name is a **phobia**, or an intense fear of a specific thing. (Not surprisingly, they are more common among people who score high in neuroticism.) Phobias have unpronounceable names, some for those fears you know (acrophobia is the fear of heights; claustrophobia is the fear of confined spaces) and many that you didn't (triskaidekaphobia is the fear of the number 13; novercaphobia is fear of your stepmother).

Fortunately, phobias are remarkably curable, usually using some form of classical conditioning and habituation. One technique is called **systematic desensitization**, which involves reducing fear in many small steps. As an example, let's try to treat Harry Potter's friend Ron Weasley for his arachnophobia (fear of spiders). First, Ron will learn how to make his body relax by closing his eyes and breathing deeply. Often called **progressive relaxation**, it's a very useful technique for calming down under stress. Even as your mind is freaking out, your body feels relaxed, so eventually your mind gets the message (Klipper & Benson, 2000). While relaxed, Ron imagines something that merely resembles a spider—maybe a black inkblot. That goes fine, so then he imagines a plastic spider ring like the kids wear on Halloween. Then he imagines a real spider—and then holding a real spider. Then he holds a piece of paper with the spidery inkblot, holds the toy spider, looks at a real spider from a distance, looks at it more closely, and finally touches a spider. Maybe he won't ever let a tarantula crawl up his arm, but he's not scared of spiders anymore.

phobia
an intense fear of a specific thing

systematic desensitization
a treatment for phobias that attempts to reduce fear in many small steps by associating the feared thing with calmness

progressive relaxation
learning how to systematically relax your body so your mind calms

If you have a phobia of talking on the phone, you might be able to use systematic desensitization to cure it. Just send this phone back to 1978 when you're done with it.

flooding
confronting your worst fear head-on, all at once

Another treatment for phobias is **flooding**—basically, the person confronts her worst fear head-on, all at once, and finds out that nothing bad happens (Rachman, 1990). If Heejung is scared of flying on an airplane, for example, she would force herself (or get someone to force her) onto a plane. When the flight goes fine and she arrives at her destination safely (let's hope), she'd realize that flying isn't so scary. Ron would get over his arachnophobia by going straight to touching a spider. Flooding is a more acutely upsetting treatment than desensitization, but it can also be completed much more quickly.

Watch THEORIES IN ACTION: BEHAVIORAL THERAPY

WATCH
the video in
REVEL

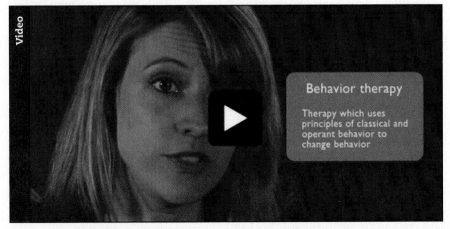

Video

Behavior therapy

Therapy which uses principles of classical and operant behavior to change behavior

Concluding Thoughts

Our experiences and what we learn from them have a great impact on our behavior and personalities. Operant conditioning observes that we do what we have been rewarded for and avoid what we have been punished for. Classical conditioning describes the process in which we learn to associate one thing with another. Behaviorism has led to practical solutions to common problems including better treatment for addictions and depression and more straightforward ways to influence the behavior of animals and people. It also provides a deeper context for understanding personality traits such as conscientiousness, which is, at base, the ability to focus on long-term rewards instead of short-term rewards. Behaviorism doesn't explain all personality or behavior, but understanding learning is a powerful tool for understanding ourselves and others. Using behaviorism can help you overcome bad habits, sleep better, become a better parent, and train your pet. Maybe your dog won't be able to do fancy tricks, but at least he won't pee on the floor.

Learning Objective Summaries

LO 8.1   Describe the types of reinforcement in operant conditioning.

Operant conditioning includes positive reinforcement (rewards after good behavior), negative reinforcement (removing adverse experiences after bad behavior), positive punishment (adverse experiences after bad behavior), and negative punishment (removing rewards after bad behavior).

LO 8.2   Explain how behavior modification works.

Behavior modification works by rewarding desired behaviors and punishing undesired behaviors. It can be used to influence children's behavior, break bad habits, and treat serious conditions such as drug or alcohol addiction.

LO 8.3   Define internal and external locus of control and how they relate to expectancies.

Internal and external locus of control capture generalized expectancies about how often behaviors lead to rewards or punishment. People with an internal locus of control believe that outcomes are under their control, and people with an external locus of control believe that outcomes are under the control of external forces such as luck or powerful others.

LO 8.4   Explain how classical conditioning works.

Classical conditioning occurs when an animal or person comes to associate two things not normally associated with each other, so that behavior follows from a stimulus that does not normally produce that behavior. For example, a dog might associate the ringing of a bell with food and will begin salivating. Or, if you work in bed, you might come to associate your bed with working instead of sleeping, and not sleep well. Phobias can often be treated using classical conditioning associations.

Key Terms

behaviorism, p. 213
operant conditioning, p. 214
positive reinforcement, p. 215
shaping, p. 215
negative reinforcement, p. 217
positive punishment, p. 217
natural consequences, p. 218
negative punishment, p. 218
reinforcement schedule, p. 219
continuous reinforcement
    schedule, p. 219
partial reinforcement schedule,
    p. 219
fixed-ratio reinforcement, p. 219
variable-ratio reinforcement,
    p. 219

fixed-interval reinforcement,
    p. 219
variable-interval reinforcement,
    p. 219
socialization, p. 222
social learning, p. 222
behavior modification, p. 223
token economy, p. 223
reciprocal determinism, p. 227
expectancies, p. 228
reinforcement value, p. 228
generalized expectancies, p. 228
external locus of control, p. 228
internal locus of control, p. 228
classical conditioning, p. 230
unconditioned stimulus, p. 230

unconditioned response, p. 230
conditioned stimulus, p. 230
conditioned response, p. 231
generalization, p. 231
deconditioning, p. 232
discrimination, p. 232
extinction, p. 232
spontaneous recovery, p. 232
habituation, p. 233
phobia, p. 235
systematic desensitization,
    p. 235
progressive relaxation, p. 235
flooding, p. 236

Essay Questions

1. List and describe the four different ways of modifying behavior.

2. What are the schedules of reinforcement? Provide examples of how to apply each to a real situation.

3. Describe the process of classical conditioning and how it applies to everyday life.

Part III

Applying Personality Psychology in the Real World

Despite the name, personality isn't just about what's inside the person. Personality also faces outward—it shapes how we interact with the real world. In this part, we examine how personality works across a variety of real-world domains, from development and gender, to culture and the workplace, and finally to emotional and mental health.

In Chapter 9, we focus on the changing nature of personality throughout the life course. Does personality stay the same as we grow older or does it change? In Chapters 10 and 11, we focus on differences in personality between genders and across cultures. What are the important similarities and differences in personality across these groups? Chapter 12 focuses on the workplace. What makes a person a good (or bad) employee, coworker, or leader? Chapter 13 looks at relationships. We discuss how personality emerges from early relationships and how personality influences adult relationships. And, of course, we discuss the new world of online relationships. Chapter 14 looks at the important role that personality plays in mental health. We examine the link between personality and mental disorders, such as depression and substance use. And we spend a good deal of time understanding personality disorders. We conclude with Chapter 15 on personality and physical health. Which personality traits predict living a long and healthy life? And which predict illness and disease? Throughout this section, you learn the important role that personality plays across many of the most important aspects of your life.

Chapter 9
Personality Across the Lifespan

LO 9.1 Name and define the two primary methods of studying age differences in personality.

LO 9.2 Describe how childhood temperament and adult personality are similar and different concepts, and explain how personality changes between childhood and adolescence.

LO 9.3 Explain how personality changes from young adulthood to old age and why.

LO 9.4 Describe how working at a job, having a stable romantic relationship, becoming a parent, or experiencing positive or negative life events changes personality.

LO 9.5 Explain how birth order influences personality.

LO 9.6 Understand how personality predicts life outcomes.

She was a troubled and moody teenager. At age 15, she and her boyfriend began experimenting with sadomasochism, including cutting each other with knives as part of their sexual foreplay. "You're young, you're drunk, you're in bed, you have knives; [stuff] happens," she commented later. For her first wedding at age 20, she wore a shirt with her husband's name scrawled in blood. During her second marriage, she and her husband wore vials around their necks containing each other's blood and got tattoos of each other's names.

Then, at 27, Angelina Jolie adopted a Cambodian baby boy she named Maddox. She and blood-vial-wearing husband Billy Bob Thornton divorced. Jolie started doing humanitarian work and visiting refugee camps; she was appointed a special ambassador to the United Nations. She began dating Brad Pitt and eventually became the mother of six children.

Jolie credits Maddox's adoption for her transformation from sadomasochistic teen to revered global humanitarian. "For me, becoming a parent changed everything," she said. "My priorities straightened out. My life is all different" (Tauber, 2003).

Yoshikazu Tsunoa/AFP/Getty Images/ Newscom

From blood-vial-wearing rebel to mother of six: Angelina Jolie's journey to maturity.

Angelina Jolie's story raises a number of intriguing questions about personality and change. How much does personality change with age and maturity? Can becoming a parent or having another life-altering experience change your personality for good? Does the personality you formed as a child and adolescent stay with you for your entire life?

Personality research on these questions has burgeoned in recent years, as researchers finally have the extensive datasets and computing tools necessary to find out how personality changes. In this chapter, we begin by exploring how personality develops over the lifespan. We also consider how experiences in childhood affect you, including how your birth order—whether you are an only child, a firstborn, a middle child, or the baby of the family—shaped your personality.

Methods for Measuring Personality over Time

LO 9.1 Name and define the two primary methods of studying age differences in personality.

longitudinal study
a study following a group of people as they age

Let's say you want to know if 20-year-olds are more or less neurotic on average than 60-year-olds. How would you design a study to answer that question? You would have two choices. The first possibility is a **longitudinal study**, which follows a group of people as they age. The advantage is you're comparing the *same people* at 20 and at 60. The disadvantage is it takes a very long time and is thus expensive and time-consuming. The longest-running longitudinal study started in 1921 when participants were 10 years old and continued until they died. The researcher who started the study died himself in 1956, and younger colleagues continued the project (Friedman & Martin, 2011). Other longitudinal studies are shorter; for example, some follow students during 4 years of college (Robins et al., 2001). But a longitudinal study that answers your main question (differences in neuroticism between 20-year-olds and 60-year-olds) would take 40 years to conduct.

cross-sectional study
data collected at one time that compares people of different ages

That's why researchers sometimes turn to the second choice, a **cross-sectional study**, which collects data at one time and compares people of different ages. The downside is the younger people are *different people* than the older ones, so the younger people might differ from the older people in ways other than age. For example, they represent different generations, so they had different experiences during their lifetimes (for example, growing up in the 1950s was quite different from growing up in the 2000s). They might also vary in other ways, such as education level or computer use. So if a cross-sectional study finds that older people are less neurotic, that could be due to age, but it could also be due to generation or some other difference. Longitudinal studies have issues as well: Changes found in a longitudinal study could also be due to time period (historical changes that affect people of all ages), but at least a longitudinal study looks at the same people of the same generation.

Do a quick cross-sectional analysis of your own. How do you think your perspective at this point in your life differs from that of your parents and your grandparents?

As much as possible, we rely on longitudinal studies when we describe age differences in personality (for example, how personality might be different at 60 than it was at 20). Because longitudinal studies are so difficult to conduct, in some cases we mention cross-sectional studies—those done at one time on different people—when longitudinal data are unavailable or incomplete. We start by exploring how personality changes in childhood and adolescence and then move on to how it changes between young adulthood and old age—the Angelina Jolie effect.

The Science of Personality HOW TO DESIGN A LONGITUDINAL STUDY

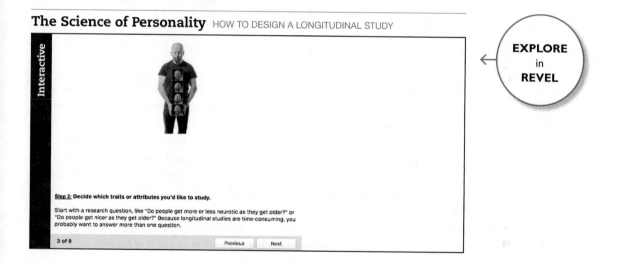

Interactive

Step 2: Decide which traits or attributes you'd like to study.

Start with a research question, like "Do people get more or less neurotic as they get older?" or "Do people get nicer as they get older?" Because longitudinal studies are time-consuming, you probably want to answer more than one question.

3 of 9   Previous   Next

EXPLORE
in
REVEL

Personality During Childhood and Adolescence

LO 9.2 **Describe how childhood temperament and adult personality are similar and different concepts, and explain how personality changes between childhood and adolescence.**

Let's now explore the typical course of personality changes from childhood to adolescence.

Child Temperament

Three-year-old Aiden is an energetic and happy child. He adapts well to new situations and is more cautious than many boys his age. He still cries sometimes, but usually calms down quickly when his parents tend to him.

temperament
genetically based
behavioral tenden-
cies seen in young
children

Could we describe Aiden's personality in terms of the Big Five—say, high in extraversion, low in neuroticism, and high in conscientiousness? Maybe, although personality in childhood is not as clear as it is in adulthood, partially because children Aiden's age are too young to answer questions about their own personalities. Historically, many researchers have instead focused on child **temperament**, or genetically based behavioral tendencies seen in young children, even babies. For example, some babies are more restless, some are easier to calm, and some adapt to a schedule more quickly (Rothbart & Bates, 1998). These behaviors are relatively easy for an outsider or a parent to observe, which is essential when gauging the personality of someone who can't yet talk.

JOURNAL PROMPT: UNDERSTANDING YOURSELF

How would your caregivers describe your temperament as a child? Does it seem to align with your personality today? Which of your life experiences might explain why your personality is the same or different? Explain.

As children grow older and their personalities form, temperament begins to solidify into personality (Shiner & Caspi, 2003). A newborn baby's temperament resembles a blob of clay that slowly becomes molded into shape as the baby grows from a tiny infant to a toddler and then from a preschooler into a "big kid." In many ways, the slow emergence of a child's personality resembles their physical development. Newborns come out red and squinty eyed. Babies get cuter at about 3 months, but well into toddlerhood their faces are still somewhat obscured by baby fat. As they grow older, the face they'll have as an adult slowly begins to take shape, just as their personality begins to emerge over the same ages. Get a sense of your temperament as a child by (if you can) having your parent or guardian take the questionnaire here, thinking of when you were about 8 years old. Otherwise, complete it for how you remember being at about that age.

TAKE
the
Questionnaire
in **REVEL**

Questionnaire 9.1 TEMPERAMENT ASSESSMENT BATTERY FOR CHILDREN, PARENT FORM

Interactive

1. My child can sit quietly through a family meal.
- Strongly Agree
- Moderately Agree
- Somewhat Agree
- Neither Agree nor Disagree
- Somewhat Disagree
- Moderately Disagree
- Strongly Disagree

2. When my child moves about in the house or outdoors, he/she runs rather than walks.
- Strongly Agree
- Moderately Agree
- Somewhat Agree
- Neither Agree nor Disagree
- Somewhat Disagree
- Moderately Disagree
- Strongly Disagree

Previous   Next

TEMPERAMENT AND THE BIG FIVE Many models of child temperament overlap with some of the Big Five personality traits. One describes children

Table 9.1 The Big Five and Corresponding Child Temperament Constructs

Child Temperament Constructs	Adult Personality Traits (the Big Five)
Positive affect	Extraversion
Affiliativeness	Agreeableness
Effortful control	Conscientiousness
Negative affect	Neuroticism
Orienting sensitivity	Openness

SOURCE: Hampson (2012).

in terms of extraversion/surgency, effortful control (similar to high conscientiousness), and negative affectivity (high neuroticism) (Rothbart et al., 2001). Agreeableness and openness are not as clearly seen among young children (Shiner & Caspi, 2003), but they can still be described (Hampson, 2012; see Table 9.1). By late childhood to adolescence, children's personality traits begin to more clearly resemble the Big Five structure common in adults (Allik et al., 2004; Lamb et al., 2002). One study found that the Big Five traits were only somewhat recognizable among 12-year-olds but became virtually identical to the adult Big Five structure by age 16 (Allik et al., 2004).

From newborn to baby to toddler to child: Just as their faces become more defined, so do their personalities.

DOES TEMPERAMENT PREDICT PERSONALITY? Temperament factors in childhood are reasonably good at predicting personality during early young adulthood. Among one group of children in Georgia, temperament at age 4½ predicted about a third of the variance in personality at age 18 in a longitudinal study (Deal et al., 2005). In another longitudinal study, New Zealand children who were "undercontrolled" at age 3—similar to low conscientiousness or impulsivity—scored high on danger seeking, aggression, and impulsivity as young adults (Caspi & Silva, 1995). Even in their early 30s, those who were undercontrolled as children were more likely to abuse alcohol and drugs and to have financial problems (Moffitt et al., 2011). In other words, the kids who thought jumping off a roof would be fun were more likely to grow up and think that getting high on cocaine might be fun. Another study found that 3-year-old children with the opposite tendencies—those who were overcontrolled—were more likely to have conservative political beliefs at age 23. So preschoolers who were inhibited, prone to guilt, and who preferred certainty were drawn to conservatism, one facet of low openness to experience (Block & Block, 2006). How does your temperament, described by your parent or guardian on the temperament questionnaire, compare with your Big Five scores from Chapter 3?

Overall, childhood temperament can predict adult personality—but far from perfectly. Undercontrolled preschoolers are more likely to become impulsive adults, but some will not be any more impulsive than the average adult.

Personality's Past

The Q-Sort: Building a Personality Scale for the Future

One of the biggest challenges in doing longitudinal research that is designed to span decades is finding the right personality measures. If a researcher uses measures that she is interested in today, how does she know if researchers in 30 or 40 years will also be interested in them? What good is 30 years of data on a measure nobody cares about? And what if there are new aspects of personality discovered in 30 years that you want to study in data collected today?

Personality psychologist Jack Block proposed a creative solution to this problem. Block and his wife Jeanne started a famous study of 100 children in Northern California and followed them for several decades. Block's (1961) solution was the California Q-sort.

The Q-sort works by having experts rate individuals on 100 personality items after getting to know the individuals' behavior through methods such as direct observation. These 100 items are written on cards and the raters put the cards into stacks that represent the most and least relevant to the person being rated. Here are a few sample items:

"Is critical, skeptical, not easily impressed."
"Behaves in a giving way toward others."
"Has a wide range of interests."

Raters cannot rate a person high or even average on all the traits. Instead, raters have to put the cards into a forced normal distribution. There are five cards at the low end, five at the high end, and 18 in the middle. The full distribution looks like this:

5, 8, 12, 16, 18, 16, 12, 8, 5

The Q-sort method is unusual because it is not a measure of any specific trait. Instead, it describes the full personality of a person. It is up to researchers to translate this description into a specific measure. So, if a researcher wanted to measure, say, curiosity, she would use the Q-sort cards to make a description of a curious person. Next, she would correlate the curiosity profile with the profile of each person in the study. The result would be a correlation for each person—very curious people would have a positive correlation, and less curious people would have a negative correlation. These correlations are her measure of curiosity for each person. This makes the Q-sort uniquely suited for longitudinal studies, since researchers can measure new traits and concepts unrecognized when the first wave of the study was done.

Changes in the Big Five Personality Traits During Childhood and Adolescence

How does personality change during childhood, on average (Figure 9.1)? Overall, children's personalities mature as they learn to better control their emotions and actions. As children grow from 18 months to 9 years, emotionality declines, shyness increases, and activity declines. Children also become more inhibited (roughly equivalent to high conscientiousness) with age, especially between the ages of 4 and 9 (Janson & Mathiesen, 2008; Lamb et al., 2002). Many parents notice that their kindergartener leaves his jacket at school if he's not reminded to bring it home, but by the time he's in third grade he keeps better track of his things. I (W. K. C.) communicated with my (then) 5-year-old's pre-K teacher by pinning notes to the back of my daughter's clothing. She tried to remember to hand notes to her teacher but often forgot.

The teen years bring many changes as children go through puberty and, physically at least, begin to resemble adults. Personality also changes, though not as much as you might think (Figure 9.2). Two longitudinal and two cross-sectional

Figure 9.1 Average Changes in the Big Five Traits During Childhood

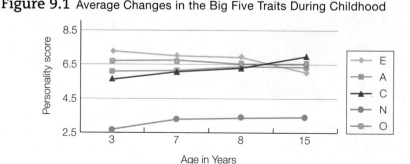

SOURCE: Based on Lamb et al. (2002)

Figure 9.2 Average Changes in the Big Five Traits During Adolescence

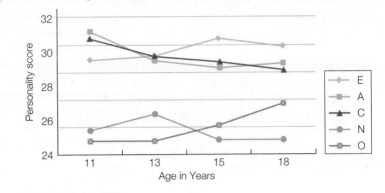

SOURCE: Based on Allik et al. (2004)

studies find that both boys' and girls' openness to experience increases between age 11 and age 18 (Allik et al., 2004; Branje et al., 2007; McCrae et al., 2002; Soto et al., 2011). Many teens begin to play around with intellectual ideas—to debate politics with their friends, explore ideas about religion, and grapple with philosophical questions. Adolescents' greater capacity for understanding abstract ideas shapes their personality to become more questioning and less rule bound. It's one reason why children often accept the rules, but teens question why the rule exists in the first place.

What about the other Big Five traits? Among Dutch teens, girls became more conscientious as they grew into late adolescence (Branje et al., 2007), and among American teens, girls increased in neuroticism (McCrae et al., 2002). However, the other Big Five traits didn't change very much.

After middle school, self-esteem increases among both boys and girls.

Changes in Self-Esteem During Childhood and Adolescence

When you were a child, you were probably fairly confident. Like most 6-year-olds, you liked to proclaim that your cartwheel (or drawing, or unrecognizable blob of clay) was "the best EVER!!" Then, when you were 11 or 12, weird things started happening. Your feet grew before the rest of your body, and other things started to grow too. You got pimples.

Figure 9.3 Stages of the Life Span

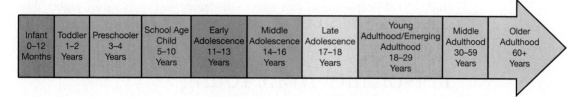

| Infant 0–12 Months | Toddler 1–2 Years | Preschooler 3–4 Years | School Age Child 5–10 Years | Early Adolescence 11–13 Years | Middle Adolescence 14–16 Years | Late Adolescence 17–18 Years | Young Adulthood/Emerging Adulthood 18–29 Years | Middle Adulthood 30–59 Years | Older Adulthood 60+ Years |

Kids a little older than you started holding hands in the school hallway. You still felt OK, but maybe not as much. Then your body caught up with your feet and you started to feel more grown-up. *You* held hands with someone in the hallway. You felt better about yourself, and that continued as you graduated from high school and went to college (see Figure 9.3 for the labels for these stages of the life span).

Most studies of changes in self-esteem square fairly well with this picture. Self-esteem is moderate during elementary school, dips during the early teen years, and then increases during high school and young adulthood (Erol & Orth, 2011; Twenge & Campbell, 2001; Wagner et al., 2013). This is consistent with popular conceptions of confident children who become awkward and self-conscious around age 11 or 12, with braces on their teeth and limbs out of proportion to the rest of their bodies. Within a few years, though, teens come into their own—their braces come off, their natural grace returns, and their confidence grows. And although there's a perception that girls' self-esteem plunges at adolescence (Pipher, 1994), the small decline in self-esteem during middle school is very similar for boys and girls. However, girls' self-esteem doesn't increase as fast as boys' does between middle school and high school, leading to a larger sex difference in self-esteem during those years (Twenge & Campbell, 2001; see Figure 9.4). From there,

Figure 9.4 Changes in Self-Esteem with Age Among Males and Females

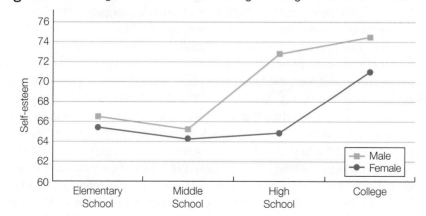

SOURCE: Based on Twenge and Campbell (2001, Table 1).

studies diverge: A large meta-analysis found that men score only a little higher in self-esteem during college (Twenge & Campbell, 2001), but a 20-year longitudinal study of 104 people found that men's self-esteem was significantly higher than women's at age 23 (Block & Robins, 1993).

Personality from Young Adulthood to Old Age

LO 9.3 **Explain how personality changes from young adulthood to old age and why.**

It makes sense that personality would change from babyhood to adolescence as personality is formed. But how much do people change once they are adults? In this module, we see how the Big Five traits and self-views change from young adulthood to old age; in other words, the systematic changes in personality over a long period of time.

Changes in the Big Five Personality Traits from Young Adulthood to Old Age

This is the question posed by Angelina Jolie's story: Do people's personalities mellow as they move into full adulthood? Most studies suggest they do: On average, people become less neurotic and more conscientious as they age from young adulthood to middle adulthood (Roberts et al., 2006; Wortman et al., 2012) (see Figure 9.5), with neuroticism continuing to decline into old age (Mroczek & Spiro, 2003). The increase in conscientiousness is especially striking: A cross-sectional study found that the typical 65-year-old is more self-disciplined than 85% of early adolescents, and more than half of that increase occurs after young adulthood (Soto et al., 2011). Some studies find smaller changes, concluding that much of the change in adult personality is complete by age 30 (McCrae & Costa, 1994)—though even that perspective allows for significant change during your 20s.

In other words, 40-year-olds—compared to 20-year-olds—are less likely to play with knives and more likely to make plans, restrain their impulses, and not get upset over minor things. Take Nicole "Snooki" Polizzi of *Jersey Shore* fame. Arrested for disorderly conduct after falling down drunk on the beach in 2010, she had her son, Lorenzo, in 2012. "I can't handle shots [of alcohol] anymore," she says. "I always think of the next day: If I'm hungover, how am I going to take care of Lorenzo? . . . I take everything more seriously. I'm organizing my closet. I've never done that in my life!" (Puliti, 2013). In other words, she became more conscientious.

The decline in neuroticism is primarily a good development—neurotic people are at risk for both mental and physical health problems (we explore this more in Chapters 14 and 15 on mental and physical health). But some adults look back on the moodiness of their teenage years with at least a little wistfulness. In the classic high school movie *The Breakfast Club*, one character says, "When you grow

Figure 9.5 Age-Related Changes in Conscientiousness, Agreeableness, and Emotional Stability (Low Neuroticism)

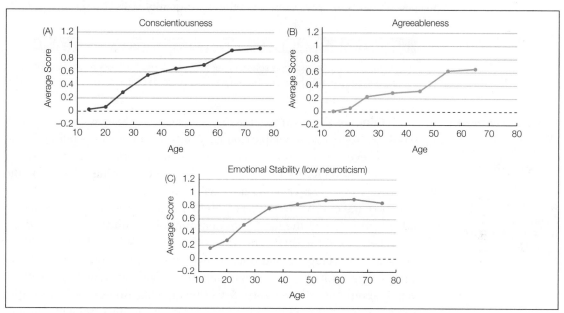

SOURCE: Roberts et al. (2006, Figure 2, p. 15).

up, your heart dies." Overly dramatic, perhaps, but it does capture how *everything* is a big deal when you're a teen, but not as much when you're an adult. What about other personality traits? Many people increase in assertiveness, a facet of extraversion, between their teen years and their 40s. Average levels of agreeableness increase a little between childhood and age 50 and then more between age 50 and 60 (see Figure 9.5; Roberts et al., 2006). Openness increases between ages 18 and 22—probably because many people are enrolled in college during these years, which may encourage them to be open to more ideas. From ages 60 to 70, openness declines (Roberts et al., 2006; Wortman et al., 2012).

Then there's the question of when personality changes the most. As you probably guessed, personality is developing and changing the most during childhood and becomes the most stable when people are in their 40s and 50s (Hampson & Goldberg, 2006; Roberts & DelVecchio, 2000). The most notable exception is agreeableness, which increases more after age 50 (Roberts et al., 2006; Srivastava et al., 2003).

How does personality change over a shorter span of time—say, in the time after high school? Two studies find that by their fourth year after high school (often the last year of college), people were higher in agreeableness, conscientiousness, and openness and lower in neuroticism; extraversion was unchanged (Ludtke et al., 2011; Robins et al., 2001). In another study, two out of three college students shifted significantly on at least one of the Big Five between their freshman and senior years. The highest number of students changed in neuroticism, with one out of four decreasing in neuroticism from their first year to their last year of college. But only 7% increased in openness, 13% in conscientiousness, and 14% in agreeableness, suggesting more stability in these personality traits (Robins et al., 2001).

mean-level changes
shifts in a population's average scores with age

rank-order consistency
comparing someone to the average person his or her age

Everything we discussed so far involves **mean-level changes**—shifts in average scores with age. But do people change relative to others their same age? Can a teen who is even moodier than most teens turn into a middle-aged adult who's calmer than most middle-aged adults? This idea of comparing someone to the average person her age is called **rank-order consistency**.

Let's say the overly moody teen is in the 95th percentile in neuroticism. Would she still rank in the top 5% in neuroticism in middle age, even if the average level of neuroticism declined? Most research suggests she would likely still score above average in neuroticism, even if she wasn't necessarily still in the top 5%. Personality has fairly high rank-order consistency, with correlations averaging about $r = .50$ (Hampson & Goldberg, 2006; Roberts & DelVecchio, 2000; Roberts et al., 2006; Robins et al., 2001). That means it's extremely unusual for someone to go from the top 5% to the bottom 5%, and that someone who scored above average in neuroticism as a teen will most likely still score above average as a 40-year-old. But some people who were at the 60th percentile (a little above average) as teens will be at the 40th percentile (a little below

If you are high in neuroticism compared to others when you are young, you are likely to be high in neuroticism compared to others when you are older.

average) as 40-year-olds. Some studies, especially those using informant reports, find even more stability in personality traits, especially after age 30 (Costa & McCrae, 1988), though in some studies personality stability declined during old age, when people's life experiences become more variable (Specht et al., 2014). Overall, people can and do change, but most of the time the change isn't radical.

Changes in Self-Esteem and Narcissism from Young Adulthood to Old Age

Do people grow more comfortable with themselves as they mature into adults? Most studies suggest they do, though not by much: Self-esteem increases slightly as people age from their 20s to their 60s (Orth et al., 2010, 2012). After that, self-esteem decreases, possibly due to retirement and declines in income. Families, relationships, and careers take a long time to build during adulthood, and self-esteem appears to suffer as these identities become less central during old age. Health issues also seem to suppress self-esteem in old age—it's tough to feel good about yourself when you don't feel well (Orth et al., 2010, 2012). Cross-sectional studies find a similar pattern, with increases from young adulthood to middle adulthood and small declines during old age (Robins, et al., 2002). Because none of these studies followed people for more than 12 years, however, it's also possible that older people had lower self-esteem because their generation was not exposed to the same cultural emphasis on self-esteem—something we explore further in Chapter 11.

No longitudinal study has yet measured levels of narcissism from young adulthood to middle adulthood, but some studies suggest declines with age. One study found that hypersensitive narcissism (meaning entitlement and resentment of criticism) declined significantly from age 38 to 58 (Cramer, 2011). Cross-sectional studies from the United States, New Zealand, and China suggest that narcissism declines with age: teens score the highest, followed by those in their 20s, and so on, with the oldest respondents usually reporting the least narcissism, though this could be due to generational differences (Cai et al., 2012; Foster et al., 2003; Wilson & Sibley, 2011). The age/generation difference found in these studies is about twice as large as the generational difference in narcissism (Twenge & Foster, 2010), suggesting that at least some of the difference these studies find in narcissism is due to age. But we need a longitudinal study to know for sure.

The benefits and costs of narcissism may also differ from one stage of life to another. Narcissism feels good and works well for a young person—relationships can be fleeting, everything is fun, and the consequences of self-centeredness have yet to catch up with him. But as he gets older, the narcissistic individual is likely to pay the price. More than likely, his relationships will fall apart, leading to anxiety and depression later in life (Hill & Roberts, 2012; Miller et al., 2007). A young narcissist can be dashing with his flashy car, carefully gelled hair, and name-brand duds, but a middle-aged narcissist rocking a comb-over and a sports car is just not as cool—and at some point, he knows it.

Significant Life Experiences and Social Investment Theory

LO 9.4 **Describe how working at a job, having a stable romantic relationship, becoming a parent, or experiencing positive or negative life events changes personality.**

In the previous section, we saw how personality changes over long periods of time. But what about changes over short periods of time, such as transformations due to life experiences? When I (J. M. T.) teach personality, one of the first questions my students usually ask is, "Can someone's personality change completely after he or she gets in a car accident/falls in love/has children/loses a limb/moves cross-country/becomes famous/wins a wet t-shirt contest?" I often suspect they're actually asking if their boyfriend or girlfriend will ever change, or would it be better to break up. (A little beyond my pay grade.) But even apart from relationship advice, it's an intriguing concept: Does personality change after certain life events?

Given the strong genetic basis for personality, it's unlikely that someone's personality would change very dramatically even after a traumatic or life-altering event. Researchers take this so much for granted that there's much more research on (say) whether people with certain personalities are more likely to get into car accidents than the effects of car accidents on personality (Taubman-Ben-Ari & Yehiel, 2012). Radical personality change—called **quantum change**—happens very infrequently, such as when a person with chronic alcoholism gets sober (C'de Baca & Wilbourne, 2004).

However, more common life experiences do affect personality in fascinating ways. According to psychologist Brent Roberts's **social investment theory**, young people's personalities mature as they enter important adult social roles such as establishing a career and starting a family (Lodi-Smith & Roberts, 2007). It's not simply getting older and biological aging that causes maturity; it's settling down into adult responsibilities and relationships. A study of 70,000 Facebook users' language use illustrates these age differences very clearly: High school students write about school; college students about studying, swearing, and drinking; 20-somethings about work; and adults over age 30 about family relationships (Schwartz et al., 2013; see Figure 9.6). As we see in Chapters 12 and 13 (on the workplace and on relationships), being callous rather than agreeable, impulsive rather than conscientious, and neurotic rather than emotionally stable makes keeping a job or a relationship much more difficult. Researchers have labeled the pattern of more conscientiousness, more agreeableness, and less neuroticism the **maturation of personality**, as these traits are consistent with being more mature and grown-up (Roberts et al., 2006). In other words, young people's personalities mature as they invest in their lives and the greater society through stable relationships and steady work (Roberts et al., 2005). Let's explore each of these life changes in turn.

quantum change
radical personality change

social investment theory
the idea that personalities mature as people enter important adult social roles such as establishing a career and starting a family

maturation of personality
growth in traits consistent with being more mature and grown-up, such as higher conscientiousness, higher agreeableness, and lower neuroticism

Figure 9.6 Age Differences in Language Use on Facebook

This study based on more than 70,000 people shows the changes in social roles that lead to the maturation of personality. Interests shift from studying and partying to work to family relationships as people move from adolescence to mature adulthood.

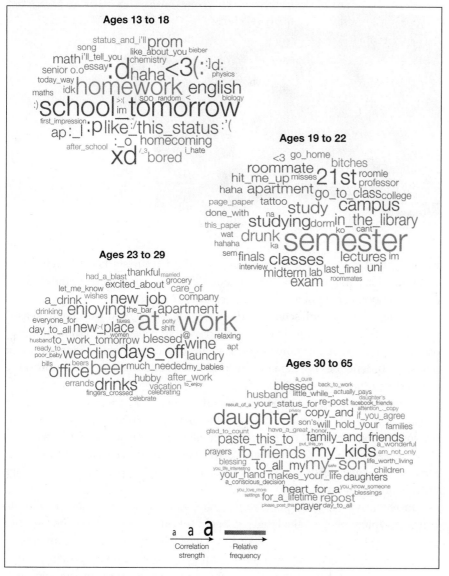

SOURCE: Schwartz et al. (2013).

Entering the Full-time Workforce

Graduating from high school is not just a rite of passage but a big decision point. Many people go to school with the same peers from age 5 to age 18—and then they scatter to the winds. Some go to college. Others go into a work

Starting a career often contributes to the maturation of personality, including higher conscientiousness.

training program or a trade apprenticeship. A third group starts work right away. You might keep in touch on Facebook, but it's not the same. How do these different postschooling experiences shape personality?

Among German high school graduates, those who started working increased in conscientiousness faster than those who went to college. Even though it may not always feel like it, the more loosely organized, occasionally keg-laden world of a college student does not demand sticking to a schedule as much as the working world does (Ludtke et al., 2011).

Even after young adulthood, men and women who are successful in their careers increase more in self-confidence, dominance, and norm-adherence (similar to conscientiousness) and decrease more in neuroticism (Clausen & Gilens, 1990; Roberts, 1997; Roberts & Chapman, 2000). Working, and especially progressing forward in a career, leads to positive personality change as people invest in things outside of themselves.

In recent years, these personality changes have occurred later in the life course as young people take longer to begin serious careers. Before the late 20th century, most young people settled down into jobs, marriage, and parenthood during their early 20s. Among more recent generations, however, many young people use their 20s to explore different career options and romantic partners, postponing the traditional markers of adulthood until later. Some believe there now is a new life stage between adolescence and adulthood, known as **emerging adulthood** (Arnett, 2000).

emerging adulthood
a new life stage between adolescence and adulthood

Consider the characters on the HBO series *Girls*: During the first season, 23-year-old Hannah's parents pay her rent as she tries to make a living from her

Watch IDENTITY

WATCH
the video in
REVEL

writing; Marnie wants a career in art curation but doesn't get very far; Jessa travels constantly and has numerous affairs; Charlie is hoping his band will make it big; Ray is 33 and still working at a coffee shop. If they had been born in the 1940s instead of the 1980s, they would probably be living very different lives—working at steady jobs, married, and parents to a child or two.

If the maturation of personality during young adulthood is caused by taking on adult roles, as social investment theory suggests, that maturation might be delayed for today's young people. Sure enough, personality maturation occurs at younger ages in countries (such as Pakistan or Mexico) where young people take on adult roles sooner, and at older ages in countries (such as the United States or the Netherlands) where working and having children are postponed until later (Bleidorn et al., 2013).

People who settle into a stable romantic relationship experience lowered neuroticism.

Being in a Serious Relationship or Getting Married

Being in love is fantastic. Everything seems brighter, and worries float away. Even after the initial honeymoon period has worn off, it's nice to know that you have someone to depend on.

Does falling in love and starting a serious romantic relationship change your personality? One study followed German young adults (between the ages of 18 and 30) for 4 years (Figure 9.7). Those who had settled down into a stable romantic relationship increased in conscientiousness and

Figure 9.7 Changes in Personality with Long-Term Romantic Relationships: Neuroticism (A) and Conscientiousness (B)

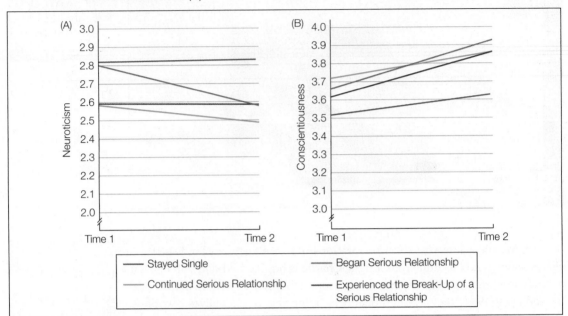

SOURCE: Adapted from Neyer and Asendorph (2001).

decreased in neuroticism. Those who stayed single did not change much (Neyer & Asendorpf, 2001). Another 4 years later, those who found a partner during that time also decreased in neuroticism (Neyer & Lehnart, 2007). The same pattern appeared among young adults in Michigan, with decreases in neuroticism after people entered their first long-term romantic relationship (Lehnart et al., 2010).

Entering a partnership tempers neuroticism even among older people. Middle-aged men who married or remarried declined in neuroticism faster than those who did not get married during a 12-year period (Mroczek & Spiro, 2003). Having a stable romantic partner seems to make people less neurotic, no matter what their age.

The idea of personality maturation is consistent with some classic theories such as Erik Erikson's life stages (Erikson, 1950; see Table 9.2). For example, Erikson posited that the central conflict of young adulthood is intimacy versus isolation. Settling into a relationship is one way of resolving the conflict in the direction of intimacy. According to Erikson, the next stage is generativity versus stagnation—having children, doing meaningful work, or otherwise guiding the next generation. Erikson's more theoretical view of life stages dovetails with the empirical research, suggesting that relationships have a positive influence on personality development.

Table 9.2 Erikson's Life Stages

Age	Central Conflict
Infancy (0 to 1½ years)	Trust vs. mistrust
Early childhood (1½ to 3 years)	Autonomy vs. shame
Preschool (3 to 5)	Initiative vs. guilt
School age (5 to 12)	Industry vs. inferiority
Adolescence (12 to 18)	Ego identity vs. role confusion
Young adulthood (18 to 40)	Intimacy vs. isolation
Middle adulthood (40 to 65)	Generativity vs. stagnation
Older adulthood (65+)	Ego integrity vs. despair

Becoming a Parent

"Being a parent," author Jill Smokler wrote, "is dirty and scary and beautiful and hard and miraculous and exhausting and thankless and joyful and frustrating all at once. It's everything." Smokler's bestselling book was titled *Confessions of a Scary Mommy* (2012).

Maybe she is a scary mommy, but she's right. Parenting can be extremely positive, extremely negative, or anything in between. But does it fundamentally change your personality?

Shockingly few studies have explored this question. One study that followed people as they became parents (or not) looked at changes across 9 years among

Finnish adults in sociability (similar to the gregariousness facet of extraversion) and emotionality (similar to neuroticism). Those who had two or more children increased in neuroticism. This was especially true for people already high in neuroticism (Jokela et al., 2009). So it's true—parents really do worry more (or, more precisely, worry-prone people worry even more when they became parents).

The effects for sociability were complex. They appeared only for men and seemed to reinforce existing tendencies: Those who were initially high in sociability increased in sociability, and those who were low decreased (Jokela et al., 2009). This makes some sense: If you're the type to go and make friends, having kids is a great excuse to talk to other dads at the playground. If you're the shy type, watching kids is a great excuse to stay at home or to not talk to anyone else.

Future research might address whether parenthood causes an increase in conscientiousness. Because most people become parents between the ages of 20 and 40, parenthood is a very likely explanation for the increases in conscientiousness during this time—after all, parenthood requires a lot of responsibility. Your boss might cut you some slack if you're late a few times, but if you're late with a baby's feeding, no slack is given (only crying—very, very loud crying—though that might describe a few bosses, too).

Experiencing Negative or Positive Life Events

Matt had always been a worrier. Then his sister got into a serious car accident and was in the hospital for weeks. Matt suddenly found himself with a lot more to worry about—would his sister be OK? Would she be able to work again? What if he got in a car accident himself?

Matt's experience raises the question of how much specific life events can affect personality traits. Not surprisingly, college students who had negative experiences—such as a friend dying, a family member getting sick, or having sexual problems—increased in neuroticism, just as Matt did. Those who had good experiences—such as starting a new relationship, getting promoted at work, or traveling to another country—decreased in neuroticism and increased in extraversion, agreeableness, and conscientiousness (Ludtke et al., 2011). However, the changes were relatively small, suggesting that different people respond to life events in different ways.

JOURNAL PROMPT: UNDERSTANDING YOURSELF

Think about an important life experience that you've had: working at a job, starting a serious romantic relationship, studying abroad, losing a loved one, or becoming a parent. Did those experiences change your personality? How?

The causation also went the other way: Personality traits predicted experiences. For example, highly neurotic people were more likely to have sexual problems or to quit a job. Extraverted people were more likely to experience positive events such as starting a new relationship or traveling to another country. Highly conscientious people were more likely to have won an academic award, gotten promoted at work, or successfully quit smoking. Those high in openness experienced both more negative and more positive events—apparently being open to experience did lead to more experiences, but those experiences could be good or bad (Ludtke et al., 2011).

Another study of people in their 40s and 50s found that negative experiences had a negligible effect on personality, though those who said their lives had changed significantly for the worse increased in neuroticism (Costa et al., 2000). That suggests that the effect of events partially depends on how you perceive them.

In a study of college students (Ludtke et al., 2011), personality traits were more likely to predict life events than events were to predict personality traits. This is another indicator of the basic stability and the innate nature of your personality and, at the same time, evidence for the existence of free will. Sometimes, of course, we're victims of events outside our control. But on many days, you choose what happens to you, what life events you have, and how you react to them.

Birth Order

LO 9.5 Explain how birth order influences personality.

"Hey, let's go someplace new tonight," Leah suggested. "How about that Italian restaurant down the street?"

"No—I don't like that place," Olivia said firmly. "Let's go get sushi like we usually do. Come on, I'll drive."

"You're so bossy—and you always want to do the same things," Leah said. "It's so easy to tell you're an oldest child!"

So is Leah right—is Olivia bossy and conventional because she is the oldest in her family?

Some childhood experiences resonate throughout life, and **birth order**— whether you are the oldest, middle, or youngest in your family, or an only child— seems likely to be one of them. How much does being an only, first, middle, or youngest child shape personality?

When we discuss birth order in class, my (J. M. T.) students are often convinced that their personality was determined—perhaps primarily so—by their birth order. Oldest children are presumed to be dominant and responsible, and youngest children to be coddled and creative, perhaps even rebellious (Herrera et al., 2003; Rohde et al., 2003; Sulloway, 1996). One early study—charmingly titled "A Study of Peculiar and Exceptional Children"—concluded that only children were misfits (Bohannon, 1896). Alfred Adler (1930) also wrote extensively on the topic, also arguing that only children were maladjusted (see Chapter 6).

So what do the data actually show? Birth order does affect personality, but not as much as most people would predict. Remember our conclusion (in Chapter 4) that genetics explains about 40–50% of differences among people in the Big Five personality traits? Birth order explains, at most, 4% of differences (Sulloway,

birth order
whether you are the oldest, middle, or youngest in your family or an only child

1995). Thus birth order effects are about one-tenth the size of genetic effects on personality. In addition, many effects have not been **replicated**, meaning some studies find differences and others do not.

replicated
when another study finds the same result

Still, some differences have been found across several studies. For example, younger siblings are higher in openness to experience (Sulloway, 1995). In *Born to Rebel*, Frank Sulloway (1996) argues that oldest children are more likely to perpetuate the beliefs of their parents and the society, and younger siblings more likely to challenge them. Sulloway points out that revolutionary thinkers such as Charles Darwin and Nicolaus Copernicus were the youngest or almost-youngest children in their families. Only a youngest child, Sulloway argues, would propose as Copernicus did that the entire structure of the universe was different from what his parents told him.

Studies generally find support for Sulloway's theory: Younger siblings do tend to be more reckless. Among brothers who both played Major League Baseball, the younger brother was more likely to take risks such as stealing bases or getting hit by a pitch. Overall, younger siblings were 50% more likely to participate in dangerous sports such as football, downhill skiing, and car racing (Sulloway & Zweigenhaft, 2010). Younger siblings are also more likely to have been arrested (Zweigenhaft & Von Ammon, 2000). Oldest children, the theory goes, have already established their position with their parents, but younger children must distinguish themselves by being more rebellious. However, even Sulloway acknowledges that the differences are small; only about half of studies find any differences in openness based on birth order (Jefferson et al., 1998; Sulloway, 1995).

Growing up the oldest, middle, or youngest child has only small effects on personality.

Firstborns also score a little higher in conscientiousness and neuroticism, and lastborns higher in agreeableness; this last result is one of the few that seems fairly consistent across studies (Jefferson et al., 1998; Michalski & Shackelford, 2002; Saroglou & Fiasse, 2003; Sulloway, 1995). So Leah might have had a point when she said Olivia was bossy because she was the oldest—especially if she was commenting on Olivia's lack of consideration for Leah's input. A laterborn child, used to deferring to older siblings, might be more agreeable.

Older children are also "bossy" in the sense of being dominant, one of the facets of extraversion (Beck et al., 2006). This may play a role in seeking leadership positions. Of the last nine U.S. presidents, six were oldest children (at least in their mother's family).

What about middleborns? If you're a middleborn, you're probably not surprised that we neglected you until now. Somewhat surprisingly, however, there's very little evidence that middleborns differ from their siblings (Hardman et al., 2007), suggesting parents might not treat them any differently. A few studies find that middleborns are not as close to their parents (Eckstein et al., 2010; Salmon & Daly, 1998; Ziv & Hermel, 2011), but others find no effects (Hardman et al., 2007). One study found that middleborns were lower in conscientiousness (Saroglou & Fiasse, 2003).

JOURNAL PROMPT: UNDERSTANDING YOURSELF

What birth order were you in your family? Does your personality profile fit your birth order, according to the research, or not?

Then there's the perennial questions around only children. Although many people believe that only children are selfish and poorly adjusted, research does not back this up (Falbo, 2012; Mottus et al., 2008; Polit & Falbo, 1987). A meta-analysis found no differences between only children and those with siblings on leadership, maturity, cooperativeness, autonomy, self-control, anxiety, popularity with peers, or extraversion (Polit & Falbo, 1987). This may be because only children have slightly better relationships with their parents, which may have compensated for the lack of siblings (Falbo, 2012). A study in China found that only children were more narcissistic, but that may have been due to other effects of that country's one-child policy (Cai et al., 2012). The biggest difference between only children and those with siblings is one that has little to do with personality: Their parents are more likely to be able to afford to send them to college, and they are more likely to inherit more money from their parents.

Life Outcomes

LO 9.6 Understand how personality predicts life outcomes.

Imagine two children: Emma, an "easy" child (who controlled her emotions and was nice to others), and Dylan, a more difficult one (who was messy and argumentative). Later on, this would mean that Emma was high in conscientiousness and agreeableness and Dylan was low. What impact would those personality types have on their lives?

One study followed people from ages 10 to 30 and found that children higher in conscientiousness and agreeableness (such as Emma) were more likely to graduate from college and to succeed at work. Children high in the extraversion facet of assertiveness or dominance were more likely to have satisfying friendships and romantic relationships (Shiner et al., 2003). Experiences also shaped personality: Children who did poorly in school or acted aggressively experienced more negative emotions (neuroticism) between the ages of 10 and 20 (Shiner et al., 2002).

As you might remember from Chapter 1, personality psychology was criticized in the 1960s for not predicting behavior enough to matter. In the ensuing decades, much has changed, partially due to longitudinal studies that examine whether personality traits in childhood predict outcomes in adulthood.

JOURNAL PROMPT: UNDERSTANDING YOURSELF

Reflect on the personalities of people you know. Do you see a correlation between their personalities and their life outcomes? Provide examples to explain your observations.

The challenge is that these studies are correlational; it's not possible to randomly assign people to personalities and then measure their outcomes as a true experiment would. So, as you may recall from Chapter 2, there are three possibilities: Personality causes life outcomes, life outcomes cause personality, or a third variable (such as socioeconomic status [SES] or family background) causes both. Longitudinal studies that measure personality traits in children and examine life outcomes in adulthood help rule out the possibility that life outcomes are causing personality because personality is measured before the life outcomes occur. Third variables can never be completely eliminated, but some—such as SES—can be entered into analyses as controls (meaning that their influence is removed statistically).

Studies that take these careful steps find that personality is a significant predictor of important life outcomes such as health, living a long life, having a successful marriage, and performing well at work and at school (Over & Benet-Martinez, 2006; Roberts et al., 2007). Among the Big Five traits, high conscientiousness is the best predictor of health, long life, and school and work performance (Bogg & Roberts, 2004). Low neuroticism and high agreeableness are the best predictors of staying married versus getting divorced (Kelly & Conley, 1987; Robins, Caspi, & Moffitt, 2002).

Even subtle and surprising correlates of personality, such as facial expressions, can predict life outcomes. Imagine you're flipping through your college yearbook looking at pictures of your friends. Some of them smile broadly, but others manage only a fake-looking or weak smile. Two studies found that students who smiled more broadly in their yearbook photograph were more likely—even three decades later—to have a happy marriage (Harker & Keltner, 2001; Hertenstein et al., 2009). Another study found that college students who smiled more broadly in their Facebook photos had better social relationships during their first semester at college (Seder & Oishi, 2012). So even a cheesy yearbook or Facebook photo can predict life outcomes—possibly because smiling is correlated with personality traits related to positive emotions such as extraversion and agreeableness.

Or consider this: What's most important for succeeding at work—the SES of your family, your IQ score, or your personality? If you guessed IQ, you'd be right, with a correlation of about $r = .27$. But personality is not far behind at $r = .18$ and far outpaces family SES, at $r = .09$. So having a "good" personality is more

How can smiling be correlated with better life outcomes?

important for being successful at work than coming from a well-off or educated family (Roberts et al., 2007).

But are these effects large enough to matter? Much of the time, the correlation between a personality trait (say, high conscientiousness) and an important outcome (say, living a long life, or longevity) is no more than $r = .25$. That means that only about 6% of the variation in how long people live is determined by conscientiousness. So 94% of what determines long life is *not* conscientiousness. Dylan the difficult child can breathe a sigh of relief.

But, of course, living even a few years longer—especially if they are years of good health—is a pretty big deal. And the size of many otherwise important effects is also surprisingly small. The correlation between secondhand smoke and lung cancer is about $r = .03$ (Taylor et al., 2007). Laws against smoking in public places prevent hundreds, and possibly thousands, of lung cancer deaths. The effect of conscientiousness is twice as big.

The even better news is that some aspects of conscientiousness can be learned; in Chapter 15, we reveal the best strategies for increasing conscientiousness. High neuroticism can also change. In one study of people treated for major depression, their neuroticism declined significantly after treatment with psychotherapy and antidepressant drugs. They also increased in agreeableness, conscientiousness, and openness (De Fruyt et al., 2006). So personality traits can be changed—at least somewhat—with the right steps, and that could, in turn, shape your destiny.

Concluding Thoughts

As you look back on your life, you can probably see both continuity and change in your personality. Some aspects of your personality have probably stayed the same, and others have changed significantly. Angelina Jolie settled down when she became a mother, but she retained her sense of adventure and openness to experience.

My brother Dan and I (J. M. T.) are good examples of change and continuity over the life span. From the beginning, we had different personalities and different interests. We grew up in a modest house in the suburbs of Dallas, in adjacent bedrooms. If one of us played music too loud, the other would bang on the shared wall. As a child, I was energetic and ran around; Dan sat quietly and played with socks. When we built Lego houses together, I wanted to keep our creation forever, and he wanted an imaginary but very destructive tornado to knock it down so we could start over. I spent my allowance on books; my brother saved his and watched his money grow. Appropriately enough, I now write books (and hope they will stay around), and Dan works in investment banking (where money is, by definition, fleeting).

Yet other aspects of our childhood personalities are surprising given our adult lives. I was terrified of public speaking in high school but now teach large lecture classes. Dan watched endless hours of TV and put off doing his one required chore—taking out the trash—until my father reminded him for the fifth time, usually while he was in front of the TV. The night before Dan left for college, I asked him what he wanted to major in—what did he like? "TV," he said. "You could major in media studies," I suggested. "No," he replied, "I don't want to study TV. I just want to watch it." Nevertheless, he now works long hours at his job and, for most of his adult life, didn't even have a TV in his apartment. I've always considered that the absolute proof that people really can change.

As you continue on your own life journey, keep this in mind: You will always be who you are, even though you can and will change. In the immortal words of B-movie hero Buckaroo Banzai, "No matter where you go, there you are."

Learning Objective Summaries

LO 9.1 Name and define the two primary methods of studying age differences in personality.

A longitudinal study follows a group of people as they age. A cross-sectional study collects data at one time on people of different ages.

LO 9.2 Describe how childhood temperament and adult personality are similar and different concepts, and explain how personality changes between childhood and adolescence.

Child temperament is considered more biologically based than adult personality, but many temperament traits overlap with the Big Five. Children tend to become more conscientious and less neurotic as they grow older, and adolescents become more open to experience. Self-esteem grows in childhood, decreases slightly during early adolescence, and increases from adolescence to young adulthood.

LO 9.3 Explain how personality changes from young adulthood to old age and why.

As people age from young adulthood to old age, they tend to become less neurotic and more conscientious. Self-esteem increases from young adulthood until about age 60 and then declines.

LO 9.4 Describe how working at a job, having a stable romantic relationship, becoming a parent, or experiencing positive or negative life events changes personality.

Social investment theory suggests that age differences in personality may be due to taking on adult roles, and studies show that people become more conscientious and less neurotic after they start working or establish a stable romantic relationship. Positive and negative life events are more often influenced by personality, rather than personality being influenced by them.

LO 9.5 Explain how birth order influences personality.

Younger siblings are higher in openness to experience and agreeableness, and older siblings in dominance and conscientiousness. However, the effects of birth order on personality are only about one-tenth the size of genetics. Only children show few differences from children with siblings.

LO 9.6 Understand how personality predicts life outcomes.

Personality is an important predictor of health, relationships, and work performance.

Key Terms

longitudinal study, p. 242
cross-sectional study, p. 242
temperament, p. 244
mean-level changes, p. 252

rank-order consistency, p. 252
quantum change, p. 254
social investment theory, p. 254
maturation of personality, p. 254

emerging adulthood, p. 256
birth order, p. 261
replicated, p. 262

Essay Questions

1. What are the two primary methods for studying personality over the lifespan? Describe the advantages and disadvantages of each.

2. Describe the general changes in personality over the lifespan, from childhood to old age.

3. Explain social investment theory and how life events can impact personality.

4. In what ways is personality a predictor of life outcomes? Name two personality traits and the outcomes they're associated with.

Chapter 10
Gender and Personality

⌄ Learning Objectives

LO 10.1 Explain how biology, culture, and their interaction shape sex differences.

LO 10.2 Describe sex differences in personality traits, leadership, masculinity and femininity, jobs and hobbies, nonverbal behaviors and appearance, self-esteem, sexual behaviors and attitudes, and cognitive abilities.

For a year in 2003, Norah Vincent became a man. She didn't have surgery; she just altered her appearance enough to "pass" as male with the help of a tight sports bra and some glued-on stubble. As a lesbian and a lifelong tomboy, Norah initially thought that being a man would come naturally. She had little trouble convincing others that she was male but never felt entirely comfortable as a man during her year-long experiment.

On one foray to a singles bar to pick up women with her "wingman" male friend, she recalled that he kept "kicking me under the table. . . . I still talked too much with my hands, and sometimes I still applied my Chapstick with a girlish lip smack" (Vincent, 2006, p. 93). She did pass for long enough to join an all-male bowling league and make some friends, but after a few months she decided to let them in on her secret. At first, they didn't even believe her. Finally, her friend Jim said, "I gotta say, that takes balls . . . or not, I guess. Wow, you're a [freaking] chick. No wonder you listen so good" (Vincent, 2006, p. 50).

Norah found being male exhausting: "It wasn't being found out as a woman that I was really worried about. It was being found out as less than a real man, and I suspect this is something a lot of men endure their whole lives. . . . Somebody is always evaluating your manhood" (Vincent, 2006, p. 276).

How relevant is being male or female in our modern era of (relative) gender equality? Here's a question I (J. M. T.) often ask my classes that cuts to the heart of the issue: "Suppose you could only have one child. Would you prefer that it be a boy or a girl?" The Gallup poll has asked this question of Americans 10 times since 1941. What would you say? And, more importantly, why? Responses to this question say a lot about views of gender.

When we discuss the "boy-versus-girl" question in class, students often mention playing sports as a reason to have a boy (though many point out that girls play sports too now). Women often say they want a girl so they can do "girl stuff"

Author Norah Vincent passed as a man for a year. Does gender still matter?

like shopping for clothes. Then, inevitably, a young man will say something like this: "I don't want a girl because I know what teenage boys are thinking about girls." I was surprised by this argument when I first began teaching, but it gave me some needed preparation when my husband and I found out that our first child was a girl. The first thing he said was, "Uh-oh—what if she's hot?"

Gender roles are considerably more flexible than they once were, especially in industrialized nations such as the United States, Canada, and Australia (Koenig et al., 2011; Twenge, 1997). Men diaper babies, women argue court cases, and it's no longer assumed that women can't play sports or men can't be nurses or flight attendants. Nevertheless, 40% of Americans in the Gallup poll in 2011 said they would prefer to have a boy—about the same percentage as in the 1940s (28% said girl, and 26% said it didn't matter). Gender still matters. The question we want to address in this chapter is, how does it matter for personality?

JOURNAL PROMPT: UNDERSTANDING YOURSELF

If you passed as the other sex as Norah Vincent did, what habits or behaviors would be most likely to give you away? How good do you think you would be at passing as the other sex?

---

sex
a biological division of males and females based on chromosomes, genitals, and secondary sexual characteristics

gender
roles and behaviors attributed to one gender or another such as cognitive abilities, sexual behavior, hair length, clothing, and preferences for jobs

Before we get into our discussion of gender and personality, let's define some terms. Though we often use the terms "sex" and "gender" synonymously, in the social sciences, the word **sex** usually refers to males and females as two biological categories based on chromosomes, genitals, and secondary sexual characteristics such as female breasts and more copious male facial hair; the word **gender** usually refers to roles and behaviors caused by biology, culture, or both, such as cognitive abilities, sexual behavior, hair length, clothing, and preferences for jobs (Lifton, 1985; Wood & Eagly, 2002). Gender refers to attributes and activities *associated* with each sex, such as shopping for women and watching sports on TV for men, while sex is simply one's biological category. Contrary to what comedians might contend, a man who enjoys

---

WATCH
the video in
REVEL
→

Watch SEX AND GENDER DIFFERENCES: GENDER SOCIALIZATION

shopping still has a penis. A woman may be physically female (sex) but can—like Norah Vincent did—dress and act like a man (gender). Even when she was not passing as male, Norah preferred to wear her hair short, behave assertively, and play sports, gender roles traditionally associated with men. But her sex was still female.

Here's a story that illustrates the difference between sex and gender. Gender researcher Sandra Bem taught her son and daughter to understand the physical differences between men and women (sex) while letting them explore whatever interested them regardless of the usual cultural expectations for boys versus girls (gender). Bem's son, Jeremy, decided to wear barrettes to preschool one day. When another boy told him that only girls wore barrettes, Jeremy informed his friend that he was still a boy because he had a penis. The other boy retorted, "That's not true. *Everybody* has a penis—only girls wear barrettes" (Bem, 2001).

Of course, Jeremy was right. Having a penis is sex. Wearing barrettes is gender.

This distinction between sex and gender is sometimes applied to the terms "sex differences" versus "gender differences," with the implication that sex differences are due to biology and gender differences are due to culture. However, most differences are likely caused by a complex interplay between biology and culture, so it doesn't make sense to decide which term to use on the basis of what caused the difference. So should we use the term "sex differences" or "gender differences"? In our view, **sex differences** is more accurate, as most studies compare males and females—the two biologically based categories. However, that does *not* mean the differences are due to biology alone; they can be due to biology, culture, or (most often) both. If men are more aggressive than women, that sex difference may have roots in biology (perhaps hormones such as testosterone), culture (perhaps girls are punished more for aggression, and boys rewarded), and their intersection (culture puts boys in competitive situations more often, which increases their testosterone). And it's likely even more complicated than that.

The ongoing arguments we still have about men and women often center on this nature-versus-nurture question. Not too long ago, for example, women were considered "naturally" inferior to men. We now know that's certainly not the case (if not the reverse—let's see a guy give birth). Nevertheless, biologically based sex differences do exist, and culture still has important influences on the different characteristics of men and women. What's important now is that we have an accurate perspective on the sex differences that do exist and how small or large they are.

sex differences
average differences between males and females

Boy or girl? In most cultures, gender is indicated via clothing, hair length, and other aspects of appearance. But anatomy is the only true indicator of the child's sex.

We begin this chapter by discussing where differences among men and women come from in the first place, and will then nail down what those differences actually are. To get us started thinking about how men and women differ, consider a study of the language of 70,000 Facebook users (see Figure 10.1). Words used more often by women included "shopping," "excited," and "love you"; words used more often by men included swear words, "xBox," and "world cup" (Schwartz et al., 2013). So why do these differences exist? Where do they come from?

Figure 10.1 Words with the Largest Sex Differences Among 70,000 Facebook Users

SOURCE: Schwartz et al. (2013)

Biology, Culture, and Their Interaction: Origins of Sex Differences

LO 10.1 Explain how biology, culture, and their interaction shape sex differences.

When identical twins Brian and Bruce were 8 months old, a doctor recommended they be circumcised. The procedure was botched, and Bruce's penis was damaged so badly it could not be repaired surgically. After consulting with psychologist John Money, the twins' parents decided to raise Bruce as a girl, renamed Brenda (Colapinto, 2006; Money, 1975). Money published several accounts of Brenda's success in becoming a girl, with all of the requisite personality traits and interest in appearance. He quoted her mother as saying, "She seems to be daintier. One thing that really amazes me is that she is so feminine" (Money, 1975, p. 68). No one, Money argued, would ever guess that the child was once a boy. For years, the case was used as an example of the purely cultural nature of gender.

Except it wasn't. Brenda was continually unhappy and didn't fit in with other girls. When she was 14 her parents finally told her about her sex reassignment, and everything suddenly made sense. She decided to begin living as a male again, using the name David. He underwent treatment with testosterone and surgery and in 1990 married a woman and became a stepfather to her three children (Colapinto, 2006; Diamond & Sigmundson, 1997). Unfortunately, David's story did not have a happy ending. On May 5, 2004, he committed suicide.

The lesson of this very sad story is clear: Sex and gender cannot be changed at will, and they are not purely cultural (Diamond & Sigmundson, 1997). Clearly, some sex differences have biological origins. The most basic of these is gender identity: feeling and knowing that one is male or female (Stoller, 1985). Most of the time, gender identity aligns with birth sex. Bruce never fully became Brenda. People whose gender identity and biological sex are congruent are called **cisgender** (*cis* means "same"). Some people find that their gender identity and their biological sex are different, known as **transgender** (or, sometimes, simply "trans"). A male who feels she should be female or a female who feels he should be male are transgender. Transgender people make a variety of choices about their bodies and whether they live as men or women. Some choose sex reassignment surgery (once known as a "sex change operation") and then live as the other sex. Some transgender people live as the other sex but do not surgically alter their bodies, or only partially alter them (Stoller, 1985). Thomas Beatie, the "pregnant man" who

cisgender
someone whose gender identity and biological sex are the same (when a biological male feels psychologically male, or a biological female feels psychologically female)

transgender
when a male feels psychologically that she should be female or a female feels psychologically he should be male

Raised as a girl, David Reimer eventually reverted to his birth sex of male.

Bruce Jenner was born male and won a gold medal in decathlon in the 1976 Olympics. For years, she felt like a woman in a man's body, experiencing the disconnect between birth sex and gender identity common in transgender individuals. In 2015, she chose the name Caitlyn Jenner and began living as a woman.

gained national attention in 2007, was born female. He later lived as a man but kept his female reproductive organs, using them to bear three children (Abbey, 2012).

The Origins of Gender Roles

What about gender roles, the more complex array of behaviors, personality traits, and interests? Determining the origin of sex differences in these areas is difficult. Are girls born being more dainty and liking dolls, or do they learn these behaviors? Are boys genetically predisposed to play with trucks and get dirty?

The usual method for separating genetics from environment is to study identical twins raised by different parents. That doesn't work for sex differences because identical twins are always the same sex. Even with children like Bruce/Brenda who are born one sex but raised another, their brains and bodies are shaped by sex hormones even before they are born. This makes it difficult to separate hormonal influences from purely genetic ones. As we learned in Chapter 4, genetic influences are different from biological influences. Genetics are the DNA living beings have at conception, but biological attributes (such as height or brain activity) can be due to a combination of genetics and environment, and/or an interaction between the two.

It's common for newspaper accounts of sex differences to use a genetic explanation—the idea of a "math gene," for example (Williams & King, 1980). However, no one gene determines math ability (or any psychological sex difference). Sex differences in actual genes are minimal, as males and females differ genetically in only one way: Females have two X chromosomes, and males have one X and one Y. Only one gene, known as testis-determining factor (TDF), determines sex. It does so by directing the early fetal development of testes, which subsequently begin producing male hormones such as testosterone (Berta et al., 1990). That begins the cascade that results in the biologically based differences between the sexes.

This differentiation begins in the womb, when a boy's brain is shaped by testosterone, and continues after birth as testosterone may fuel a greater tendency toward aggression and dominance, and toward an interest in things versus people (see, for example, Archer, 1991; Purifoy & Koopmans, 1979). Boys get another testosterone boost during puberty. However, the role of testosterone in causing aggression—at least directly—is controversial and unclear (Archer, 1991, 2006b; Archer et al., 2005). Most studies find that aggressive and violent men have higher testosterone levels (Book et al., 2001; Dabbs et al., 1991). But correlational studies cannot determine if testosterone causes more aggression or aggression causes more testosterone. Research often finds that testosterone is the *result* of experiences such as an angering encounter (Cohen et al., 1996), handling a weapon (Klinesmith et al., 2006), or a favored sports team or political candidate winning (Bernhardt et al., 1998; Stanton et al., 2009). So although higher testosterone may be one of the reasons men are more aggressive than women, situations and circumstances play a large role as well.

Another question is whether sex differences are inevitable, given biology and evolution, or are changeable from one society to another. Some gender roles are clearly cultural. For example, whether men wear skirts, grow their hair long, wear certain colors, or adorn themselves with jewelry varies from one culture to another and over time. For example, for centuries both boy and girl children wore white dresses until they were about 6 years old (Kidwell & Steele, 1989). Other differences, such as women being more likely to tend to children and men being more aggressive, are more universal across cultures (Buss, 2008; Eagly & Wood, 1999).

The Roles of Evolution and Culture

Evolutionary psychology argues that many sex differences in personality and sexuality occur due to fundamental differences in reproduction (Trivers, 1972).

Franklin Delano Roosevelt, the future president of the United States, as a child in 1884. At the time, it was common to dress young children in white dresses regardless of sex.

Having a child is a much bigger investment for women, who must be pregnant for 9 months and may breastfeed for a year or more. Thus, women should be more cautious about casual sex. Evolutionary psychologists argue that these tendencies are innate (Buss, 2008). Sex differences in personality traits may also be rooted in reproduction: Dominance and aggressiveness may have helped men compete for mates, and agreeableness and people orientation may have helped women care for children and appease more physically powerful men (Buss, 2008).

Watch EVOLUTION AND CULTURE

WATCH
the video in
REVEL
→

If sex differences appear across many cultures, it seems more likely that they are rooted in biology. If they appear in one culture but not another, it seems more likely that they are cultural (Lippa, 2010). However, the truth may be more complicated than that. Virtually all societies have men in positions of social power and assign different roles to men and women. As a consequence, similarities across cultures might represent male social power rather than evolved differences (Eagly & Wood, 1999; Wood & Eagly, 2000, 2002).

The social roles traditionally taken by men versus women are often rooted in biologically based differences but are not necessarily biological themselves. For example, women gathered food and men hunted in early societies in part because it was easier for women to combine gathering with pregnancy, breastfeeding, and childcare. These roles became ingrained into society and were culturally encouraged in children from a young age; for example, boys developed the skills they would need to hunt, and women the skills they would need to gather and to care for babies (Eagly, 1987; Wood & Eagly, 2002). Men's greater physical strength may have also led to patriarchy being the most common system. Thus, in most societies girls would play with dolls and be encouraged to be submissive, whereas boys would play with weapons and be encouraged to be dominant. Biology and culture interact.

Cultural Change and Cross-Cultural Variations in Sex Differences

As cultures change, sex differences should change as well—and this has indeed been the case. In 1960, only 35% of bachelor's degrees, 32% of master's degrees, and 11% of doctoral and professional degrees in the United States went to women. By 2012, women earned 57% of bachelor's degrees, 60% of master's degrees, and 52% of doctoral and professional degrees (Digest of Education Statistics, 2012). In the 1800s, many believed that women did not have the "constitution" to work as doctors or lawyers; in other words, people thought women's personalities were too soft and agreeable for such professions. However, these past restrictions on women's employment were clearly culturally rooted and not biologically based.

Men's gender roles have also shifted. For example, men have entered traditionally female professions such as nurse, airline flight attendant, and elementary school teacher. Family roles have also shifted considerably: The time fathers spend caring for children has tripled since the 1960s (Sayer et al., 2004). My (J. M. T.) uncle, born in the 1930s, had three children but bragged he had never changed a diaper—virtually unthinkable for a father today. We don't know yet what effect this has had on men's personalities, but it's clearly more acceptable now for men to freely express caring traits.

JOURNAL PROMPT: UNDERSTANDING YOURSELF

Consider behaviors or interests of yours that are typical for your sex. Can you remember learning them directly, or do you think you learned them indirectly? Or do you think they are instead rooted in biology?

Some cross-cultural studies also report lower or nonexistent sex differences in countries with more gender equality. For example, men are generally better than women at mentally rotating objects, known as **spatial ability**. However, in Indian villages with more female leaders, the sex difference in spatial ability was smaller or nonexistent (Else-Quest et al., 2010; Hoffman et al., 2011). Male-on-female domestic violence is lower in the United States than in more traditional societies such as Korea and Japan (Archer, 2006a).

spatial ability
the ability to mentally rotate objects

Modern, individualistic cultures do not always mean fewer sex differences, however. Three studies find larger sex differences in personality traits in more individualistic and industrialized nations (Costa et al., 2001; McCrae & Terracciano, 2005; Schmitt et al., 2008). Perhaps people in traditional cultures are comparing themselves only to those of the same sex, thus minimizing sex differences (Guimond et al., 2007). Schmitt and colleagues (2008) propose that in collectivistic cultures men are closer to the norm for women in industrialized nations—for example, higher in agreeableness—and this minimizes sex differences. They also argue that these findings are evidence against the idea that social roles influence sex differences in personality.

Where does this leave us? Some sex differences—such as men having a penis, having greater upper body strength, and being taller—are clearly biological in origin, primarily genetic. Some, such as clothing, some leisure interests, and perhaps math ability, are more rooted in culture. But most sex differences seem to be caused by a complex interaction of genetics, biology, social roles, and culture.

Comparing Men and Women

LO 10.2 **Describe sex differences in personality traits, leadership, masculinity and femininity, jobs and hobbies, nonverbal behaviors and appearance, self-esteem, sexual behaviors and attitudes, and cognitive abilities.**

stereotypes
commonly held beliefs about groups

We're all familiar with **stereotypes**—commonly held beliefs about groups, about how males and females differ—and sometimes these stereotypes reflect reality. Some stereotypes seem to be true but have yet to be studied extensively—for example, that women are more likely to go to the bathroom in pairs (maybe one of you will study this; I suggest titling the paper "Gender and Group Peeing in Dining Establishments: An Observational Analysis"). Other stereotypes have been verified; for example, women cry more often than men (Lombardo et al., 2001), and men are more aggressive (Archer, 2004; Hyde, 1984; Knight et al., 2002; for a history of the study of sex differences, see Figure 10.2).

Not all stereotypes are true, however. One large study found that *men* actually talk more than women overall. The largest difference appeared in "mean length of utterance"—in other words, when men talk, they talk for longer (Leaper & Ayres, 2007). Other studies have found that women talk more when collaborating with others, with no sex difference in unstructured situations (Mehl et al., 2007; Onnela et al., 2014). Women also talk more about emotional support, called affiliative speech. Interestingly, among dating partners, women talk more, but among spouses, men talk more (Leaper & Ayres, 2007). However it's sliced, the nonexistent or small sex difference in talking is a far cry from the common stereotype of the hypertalkative woman and the silent man.

And who's the better driver? Conventional gender stereotypes would say men. But if that's the case, why are men far more likely to get in serious accidents compared to women (Waldron et al., 2005)? It's hard to be "the best" driver if you can't get to your destination in one piece.

In this section, we consider the *real* differences among men and women—not just the stereotypes. Overall, gender plays a profound role in our lives from the moment we're born. Thus it's difficult to fully understand how it shapes our personalities as well as the choices we make (or don't make), the way we act (or don't act), and the feelings we express (or don't express). Personality is complicated. So is gender. Thus, we not only examine personality traits directly, but also

Figure 10.2 A Brief and Selected History of the Study of Sex Differences and Psychological Masculinity and Femininity

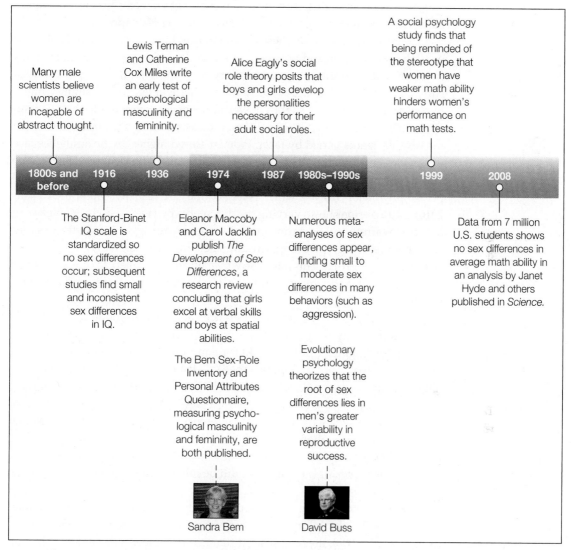

widen our lens to view other sex differences that interact with personality, such as interests, cognitive abilities, and sexuality.

Big Five Personality Traits

How do men and women differ in personality traits? Let's begin with the Big Five. Women score higher in neuroticism and agreeableness and slightly higher in extraversion (Costa et al., 2001; Feingold, 1994; Lippa, 2010; Schmitt et al., 2008;

Vianello et al., 2013). So, on average, women are warmer, more outgoing, more anxious, and more sympathetic than men. The difference in neuroticism also appears in neuroimaging studies, which find that women's brains, on average, react more strongly to negative emotions (Stevens & Hamann, 2012).

However, keep in mind these are differences in averages—there is plenty of overlap between men and women (see Figure 10.3). Sex differences in openness to experience and conscientiousness vary depending on the sample and measure. One large cross-cultural study found that women scored slightly higher in conscientiousness and slightly lower in openness compared to men (Schmitt et al., 2008). Two others, using a different measure of Big Five traits, found that the sex differences varied by facet. Women scored higher on the aesthetics facet of openness, and men on the ideas facet (Costa et al., 2001; McCrae & Terracciano, 2005); that would suggest more female art majors (aesthetics) and more male philosophy majors (ideas), which is indeed the case (U.S. Bureau of the Census, 2010). Extraversion shows varying sex differences by facet as well—women score higher in warmth and gregariousness, and men score higher in assertiveness and excitement-seeking, including sensation-seeking and risk taking (Costa et al., 2001; Cross et al., 2011). This might be why men are more likely to chase tornadoes or go skydiving, and why more boys than girls think that jumping off a roof is a fun idea.

Statistically speaking, these differences are small to moderate in size. To understand exactly what that means, you'll need to think back to your statistics class (or Chapter 2 in this book) for a minute or two. Remember standard deviations? In a "normal" (bell-shaped) distribution, about two-thirds of the data are within one standard deviation (SD) of the mean. Imagine two of these bell curves: one for men and one for women (see Figure 10.3). We'll first consider a characteristic with a large sex difference: height. Men are 1.41 SDs taller than women (this is often written $d = 1.41$; d is the difference in terms of SDs). Put in other terms, 92% of men are taller than the average woman—so in 92 of 100 random pairings, the man would be taller than the woman (McGraw & Wong, 1992).

Sex differences in the Big Five personality traits are considerably smaller than those in height. In one large study of women and men from 55 countries (Schmitt et al., 2008), the largest sex difference was in neuroticism ($d = .40$), with women scoring higher. So only about one-third (34%) of men score higher than

---

Figure 10.3 The Overlap Between Males and Females for Three Sex Differences

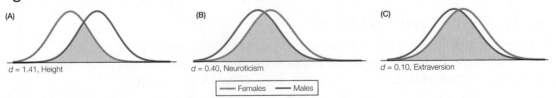

(A) $d = 1.41$, Height

(B) $d = 0.40$, Neuroticism

(C) $d = 0.10$, Extraversion

Females   Males

Figure 10.4 Sex Differences in Neuroticism

Although the sex difference in neuroticism is moderate on average, two to three times as many females have very high scores (two SDs above the mean), partially explaining women's two-fold risk for depression).

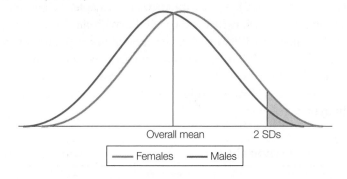

Overall mean   2 SDs

—— Females   —— Males

the average woman on neuroticism (if there were no sex difference in neuroticism, 50% of men would score higher than the average woman). The other Big Five facets had smaller sex differences: 46% of men score higher than the average woman on extraversion, 44% on agreeableness, 45% on conscientiousness, and 52% on openness.

The relatively small size of these differences have led some researchers to argue that instead of spending so much time on sex differences, psychology should focus on sex similarities (Hyde, 2005). Men and women are more similar than they are different on the vast majority of psychological traits. In a meta-compilation of 386 large comparisons of males and females on psychological traits, the average sex difference was $d = .21$ (Zell et al., 2015). Even a very large sex difference such as height still produces overlapping bell curves (see Figure 10.3).

So despite the popularity of the 1990s bestseller *Men Are from Mars, Women are from Venus*, men and women are both from planet Earth. For three out of five of the Big Five traits, it's more like men are from Minneapolis and women are from St. Paul (the Twin Cities of Minnesota— different, but right next to each other). For neuroticism and agreeableness, which show larger but still not interplanetary differences, men and women might be from New York versus New Jersey, or Arizona versus California. (So which states are female and which are male? Try debating that with your classmates.)

However, even small differences at the average can produce larger differences at the extremes (see Figure 10.4), so that at very low and high points the sex difference is larger.

Although the average sex difference in aggression is moderate in size, four times as many men as women are arrested for violent crimes.

For example, the moderate difference in neuroticism means that more than twice as many women as men will score very high in neuroticism. Neuroticism is a risk factor for developing anxiety disorders and depression, so it is not surprising that twice as many women as men are diagnosed with these mental health issues (McLean et al., 2011; Nolen-Hoeksema, 2002). As we explore more in Chapter 14, personality traits are a continuum, and at their extremes they overlap with clinical disorders.

Men and women also differ in physical aggression, $d = .60$ on average (Hyde, 1984; Knight et al., 2002). Yet four times as many men as women are arrested for violent crimes and nine times for murder (U. S. Bureau of the Census, 2012). So a moderate difference on average multiplies when we consider the most extreme forms of human aggression.

EXPLORE in REVEL

The Science of Personality DOING DATA ANALYSIS TO DISCOVER SEX DIFFERENCES

Interactive

You've just learned about the sex differences in the Big Five based on published research studies. How would you like to play researcher yourself, to see if these same differences appear in data you can analyze?

In this activity, you'll use a common statistical test (a *t*-test) to see if men and women score significantly different, on average, for Big Five Neuroticism. You'll then see how big this difference is in standard deviations (the *d*) and see what that *d* looks like with bell curves for men and women.

1 of 9   Previous   Next

Leadership

So, women are more agreeable, less impulsive, less aggressive, and less likely to take sexual advantage of someone else. Pretty much the only negatives are that women worry more than men (high neuroticism) and are less assertive. Thus, it's not surprising that the stereotype of women is, overall, more positive than that of men (Eagly & Mladinic, 1989; Rudman & Goodwin, 2004). Researchers call this the "women are wonderful" effect (Eagly & Mladinic, 1989).

Some researchers, however, suggest that it should instead be called the "women are wonderful when they are not in charge" effect (Rudman & Glick, 2010). Powerful women, or those with more dominant personality traits, are often judged more harshly than men with the same power and dominance (Richeson & Ambady, 2001; Rudman, 1998). "More so than men, ambitious women may have to choose between being respected but not liked (by displaying agentic qualities) or being liked but not respected (by displaying communal qualities)," write Rudman and Glick (2010, p. 163). This double bind places women at a disadvantage at every stage of work, from hiring to salary negotiations to promotions (Buttner &

McEnally, 1996; Heilman et al., 2004; Rudman & Glick, 2010). The association of leadership with men has declined in the last few decades, though it still remains (Koenig et al., 2011).

Watch PSYCHOLOGY OF GENDER: LEADER STEREOTYPES

WATCH
the video in
REVEL

Despite the traditional association of men with leadership, women perform slightly better as leaders in most areas, although the differences are relatively small (Eagly et al., 2003). The difference also depends on whom you ask: Men rate themselves as better leaders, but other people (peers, employees, bosses) rate women as better leaders. Cultural change has also had its effects; between the 1960s and the 2010s, the sex difference in leadership increasingly favored women (Paustian-Underdahl et al., 2014).

Nevertheless, women still have lower status, even in our modern culture. Although many more women have entered prestigious professions including medicine, academia, politics, journalism, and law, overall women still only make about 80 cents to a man's dollar (U.S. Bureau of the Census, 2012). Few large companies are headed by women. As of 2015, only 19% of U.S. senators and representatives were women (Center for American Women and Politics, 2015). And there has still not been a female president of the United States.

"Masculinity" and "Femininity"

Many children become curious about gender while watching their parents and interacting with their peers. Why does my dad mow the lawn instead of my mom? Why does my mom cook instead of my dad? Why do the girls play different games at recess than the boys do? In short, children wonder how men and women are different and how they got that way. Eventually they also notice that some moms mow the lawn, some dads cook, and some girls play

Figure 10.5 Gauging Masculinity and Femininity—The One-Variable (A) and Two-Variable (B) Models of Masculinity and Femininity

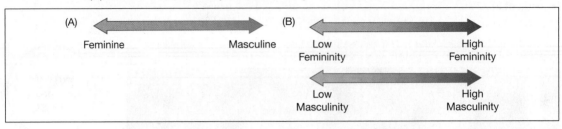

with the boys at recess. In other words, gender roles vary within the sexes as well as between them.

Lewis Terman and Catherine Cox Miles (1936) wrote one of the earliest assessments of psychological masculinity and femininity—scales attempting to capture the most striking differences among men and women. The test involved identifying ambiguous drawings (Is the rectangle with a twisted line coming out of the top a chimney, or is it a spool of thread?). Terman and Miles found that male college athletes and engineers scored the most "masculine" on their test. The most "feminine" women were domestic workers.

The Terman and Miles test and other measures of masculinity–femininity (Gough, 1957) had at least one major problem, however: They assumed that masculinity and femininity were on one scale, so it was not possible to score high on both (see Figure 10.5). The 1970s prompted several researchers to develop scales of psychological masculinity and femininity with separate scales for M and F such as the Personal Attributes Questionnaire (PAQ; Spence & Helmreich, 1978), which you can take right now below.

TAKE the Questionnaire in **REVEL** →

Questionnaire 10.1 PERSONAL ATTRIBUTES QUESTIONNAIRE

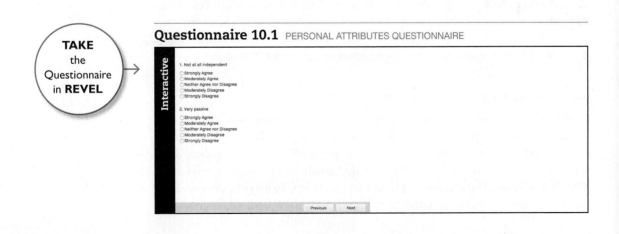

The PAQ focuses primarily on **stereotypically masculine personality traits** and **stereotypically feminine personality traits**—traits people believe to be typical of men versus women. The M scale measures instrumentality or agency, which is very similar to the assertiveness dimensions of extraversion. The F scale overlaps with agreeableness. More recent studies have found that people still associate the M scale traits with men, and the F scale traits with women (Spence & Buckner, 2000).

How can you understand your own PAQ scores? You've already compared your M and F scores to others' on the percentile score. You can also see which gender personality type you are. If you score above the overall mean (for both men and women) on the M scale, note that as high, and do the same with the F scale. Then see which of the four boxes you fit into (see Table 10.1). Someone who is high in both masculinity and femininity is called *androgynous*; someone who scores low on both is *undifferentiated*.

It's worth saying explicitly that the PAQ is *not* a measure of sexual orientation (being gay, lesbian, bisexual, or straight). Who you are attracted to sexually is a very different question from how assertive or caring you are. And although one might expect gay men to be more likely to score as feminine and lesbians to score as masculine, the data on this question are mixed. Some studies find that gay men are more likely to score as feminine or androgynous than straight men (Robinson et al., 1982), and lesbians score higher on masculinity but similar on femininity to straight women (Oldham et al., 1982). Other studies find no such relationship when examining gay, lesbian, and straight couples (Kurdek & Schmitt, 1986).

Women's scores on masculine traits have increased steadily since the test was created in the 1970s (Twenge, 1997). Women also reported considerably higher assertiveness between the 1960s and the 1990s (Andre et al., 2010; Twenge, 2001). This suggests that at least some of the sex difference in these traits is rooted in women's roles in the culture, which became considerably more focused on work over these decades.

stereotypically masculine personality traits traits believed to be typical of men; these primarily involve instrumentality or agency, similar to the assertiveness dimensions of extraversion

stereotypically feminine personality traits traits believed to be typical of women; these primarily involve expressiveness or caring traits, which overlap with the Big Five trait of agreeableness

Table 10.1 Category Labels for the PAQ Measure of Stereotypical Masculine and Feminine Personality Traits

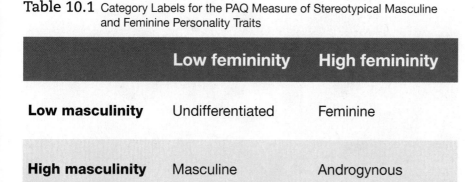

	Low femininity	High femininity
Low masculinity	Undifferentiated	Feminine
High masculinity	Masculine	Androgynous

Jobs and Hobbies

Measures of psychological masculinity and femininity developed in the 1970s, such as the PAQ, focused on personality traits rather than interests and hobbies. Researchers soon began to explore how men and women differed in their interests. Orlofsky (1981) developed a scale measuring gender-stereotyped recreational activities (football vs. knitting), vocational interests (plumber vs. nurse), social and dating behaviors (asking someone out vs. primping in front of a mirror), and marital behaviors (yard work vs. laundry), finding very large sex differences ($d = 5.06$). However, the items were specifically chosen to produce large sex differences.

A better-designed study examined sex differences in preferences for occupations in a large sample of men and women from 53 cultures, finding $d = 1.40$. This is the same as the gender difference in height, so only 8% of women score higher than the average man on the scale (Lippa, 2010). Hobbies also differ significantly. College men reported being much more interested in sports (both playing and watching) than women, $d = 2.49$, and college women reported more interest in shopping, dancing, and talking to friends, $d = 1.23$. Few sex differences appeared in activities such as playing cards, cooking, and going to parties (Twenge, 1999). The study on Facebook users earlier in the chapter showed the same trends toward more female interest in shopping and more male interest in sports (Schwartz et al., 2013).

On average, men are more interested in things and women in people (Lippa, 1998; Su et al., 2009). Many traditionally male professions such as car mechanic and engineer fit this profile of interest in things, and many traditionally female

As you'd probably guess, men are more interested in sports than women are, on average.

professions such as teacher and nurse are based on an interest in people. However, doctors and lawyers—two professions dominated by men until very recently—are also focused on people. Thus, the large increase in the number of women in these professions makes sense. In recent years, about 50% of law and medical school graduates have been women (U. S. Bureau of the Census, 2012).

Assuming the sex difference in people versus things endures, this suggests that women may eventually be the majority of doctors and lawyers but may always be the minority of engineers and car mechanics. This is not to say that women cannot succeed in these professions—many have—but that fewer women may be interested in them. However, context matters, as does whether a person feels welcome or not in a certain environment. When sitting in a room adorned with a *Star Trek* poster and comic books in one experiment, women expressed significantly less interest in computer science than men. When the room was instead adorned with an art poster and news magazines, women's interest in computer science was equal to men's (Cheryan et al., 2009). So sometimes sex differences in interests can be a self-fulfilling prophecy: If you think your gender isn't welcome, you won't be interested.

The sex difference in interests may begin early in childhood, and may be shaped by both biology and culture. Consider the reaction you might get if you asked people some questions about gender and children's toys. For example, "Is it OK for a girl to play with toy cars and trucks?" Most people will probably say yes. Then ask, "Is it OK for a boy to play with a baby doll?" Here there may be more discussion. Some people—perhaps especially older men—will be opposed to boys playing with dolls. Others will say it's OK as long as the boy's friends

Because medicine involves people, it may become a female-dominated profession in the future.

Boys who engage in "girl" activities are usually judged more harshly than girls who engage in "boy" activities.

don't know about it. Some might comment, "If I had a son who played with dolls I would worry he was gay." Others might then point out that this argument is somewhat ironic: Playing with dolls is practice for parenting, and it's more likely that a straight man will have a baby to help care for.

Sex differences in interests highlight a common theme in the gender roles of modern, individualistic societies: Both males and females can do male things, but only females are supposed to do female things (Davis, 1992; Kidwell & Steele, 1989). For example, Orlofsky's (1981) study found larger sex differences in female interests and activities than in male interests and activities. In most contexts in mainstream American culture, it's acceptable for girls to wear pants, play with "boy" toys such as cars and trucks, and aspire to male professions such as fire-fighter. But not so when a boy wears a dress, plays with "girl" toys such as dolls or (worse) Barbies, and wants to be a nurse when he grows up. Those preferences can be a quick trip to getting beaten up on the playground. Not surprisingly, toys marketed as being for "both boys and girls" were more similar in color to those aimed at boys than to toys aimed at girls (Auster & Mansbach, 2012). "Neutral" toys are often blue, green, or red, just like "boy" toys, but pink marks a toy as exclusively female.

Nonverbal Behaviors and Appearance

When Norah Vincent spent a year passing as a man, she had to learn how to walk differently, how to stop talking as much with her hands, and how to project male strength. She also learned how to smile less: On the cover of her book, she is smiling in her picture as a woman and virtually expressionless while dressed as a man (Vincent, 2006). In fact, women do smile more than men (d = .63); only 26% of men smile more than the average woman. Women are also much more likely to show their emotions through facial expressions (d = 1.01) (Hall, 1984; LaFrance et al., 2003). This sex difference is apparently learned in late childhood: American boys and girls smile just as often in their elementary school pictures, but by sixth grade, girls smile significantly more than boys (Wondergem & Friedmeier, 2012).

Girls and women also cry more often than boys and men (Jellesma & Vingerhoets, 2012; Lombardo et al., 2001). At least in terms of emotional expression, the stereotype that women are more emotional than men is true (Brebner, 2003). However, men and women experience the same emotions at the same intensity. Male and female babies do not differ in how much they cry (Feldman et al., 1980), and the increase in heart rate after seeing emotional content is similar between men and women (Vrana & Rollock, 2002). That suggests the difference is rooted not in biology but in culture: It is culturally acceptable for women to cry, but not as much for men.

Men take up more space than women even apart from their greater height and weight—they sprawl over chairs, stretch out their arms, and sit with their legs spaced widely apart (online, people call it "manspreading" and post pictures of egregious offenders). The sex difference in such **body expansiveness** (taking up more space with your body) is large (d = 1.04), so only 16% of women expand their bodies as much as the average man (Hall, 1984). Men and women also walk differently. In one study, people easily guessed the sex of others who were walking in a dark room with small points of light attached to their joints (Kozlowski & Cutting, 1977). Physical abilities such as throw velocity and grip strength also show large sex differences, with men outperforming women by considerable margins (d = 2.18 for throw velocity; Thomas & French, 1985).

body expansiveness
taking up more space with your body

And, of course, men and women dress differently. Once again, the story is that males must wear male clothes, but females have more latitude. Men wear suits with pants, but women can wear either pantsuits or suits with skirts, or a dress. Girls can go to school wearing a boys' soccer outfit and no one will look twice—my (J. M. T.) daughter does sometimes—but a boy who went to school in a dress would be teased mercilessly.

Men are higher in body expansiveness—they are more likely to sit or stand with their arms and legs extended.

Men and women differ not only in what they wear but in how much of it they own, how much they care about it, and how long they spend on their appearance. For example, college women own many more pairs of shoes than college men (16 vs. 6, d = 1.64) and spend much more time on their appearance in the morning (25 minutes vs. 15 minutes, d = .72; Twenge, 1999). Are you above or below average for your sex on these gendered appearance behaviors?

Do these jeans make my butt look big? Body-image issues are more pronounced among women.

Women are also more focused on how others view their physical appearance, a state known as self-objectification (Fredrickson & Roberts, 1997). On average, women focus on how their bodies look, and men on how their bodies perform (such as in sports). This body self-consciousness (McKinley & Hyde, 1996) may be partially responsible for some mental health issues that plague women more than men, such as eating disorders and higher rates of neuroticism and depressive symptoms (Fredrickson et al., 1998; Miner-Rubino et al., 2002). In fact, boys actually report slightly more depressive symptoms than girls as children, but girls report more depressive symptoms beginning around puberty (Twenge & Nolen-Hoeksema, 2002). This is most likely due to body-image issues for girls and the greater ambivalence surrounding their adolescent bodies and sexuality (Hankin & Abramson, 2001).

Self-Esteem

You may have heard that females, especially adolescent girls, have a major self-esteem problem. That's not really true. Girls and women do report lower general self-esteem than boys and men, but not by much, with the difference between $d = .14$ and $d = .21$ (Kling et al., 1999; Major et al., 1999). About 43% of females score higher than the average male in self-esteem. The sex difference is largest during the teenage years, but that's not because girls' self-esteem goes down.

It's because boys' self-esteem goes up more during high school. By the time they get to college, men and women's self-esteem is back to being fairly similar (Twenge & Campbell, 2001).

To get a clearer picture of how this relates to gender, it's helpful to break self-esteem down into different facets—such as academic self-esteem, appearance self-esteem, and so on. The sex difference in appearance self-esteem is larger than most ($d = .35$; Gentile et al., 2009). So 36% of females are higher in appearance self-esteem than males. Males also score higher in athletic self-esteem ($d = .41$). Girls and women score higher on two scales: behavioral conduct (basically, not going to the principal's office) and moral–ethical self-esteem (which has some overlap with agreeableness).

Given its correlation with general self-esteem, it is not surprising that men also score higher in narcissism (Grijalva et al., 2015). In addition, about 60% more men than women fit the diagnosis for narcissistic personality disorder (Stinson et al., 2008).

Sexual Behaviors and Attitudes

You're walking on campus one day when an attractive member of the other sex approaches you. "Hi, I've been noticing you around campus lately, and I find you very attractive. Would you have sex with me tonight?" What would you do? At Florida State University, 75% of men said they would, and none of the women (Clark & Hatfield, 1989). When asked instead if they would go on a date, about the same percentage of men and women said yes (Clark, 1990; Clark & Hatfield, 1989).

Perhaps women might be afraid of being physically harmed or robbed, although when asked why they declined, few women directly mentioned safety;

You're on campus one day when an attractive man or woman comes up to you and says, "Would you sleep with me tonight?" Your answer heavily depends on whether you are male or female.

instead, they said things such as "I don't know you well enough" or "I have a boyfriend" (Clark, 1990). Even when a friend said he or she knew and trusted the potential date, many more men (50%) than women (5%) agreed to have sex (Clark, 1990). In anonymous surveys as well, men are more likely than women to say they have had sex with someone they just met (Michael et al., 1994).

Studies consistently find that men have a stronger sex drive than women—men think about sex more and desire sex more often (Baumeister et al., 2001; Lippa, 2009). Men masturbate more than women ($d = .53$), so that only 30% of women masturbate more than the average man (Petersen & Hyde, 2010). Interestingly, the sex difference is only about half of what it was a few decades ago; for studies conducted in 1992 and before, the sex difference in masturbation was $d = .96$ (Oliver & Hyde, 1993). So women are masturbating more, or men are masturbating less, or both (what's your guess?).

Among 30 sexual attitudes and behaviors in a comprehensive meta-analysis, the largest sex difference was in consumption of pornography ($d = .63$), so that only 26% of women view more pornography than the average man (Petersen & Hyde, 2010). In one study of 18- to 26-year-olds, 87% of young men and 31% of young women reported using pornography (Carroll et al., 2008). This is apparently not solely due to the pornography industry catering to male desires; pornographic magazines aimed at heterosexual women (such as *Playgirl*) sell only a fraction of the copies of those marketed to men (such as *Playboy*) (Baumeister et al., 2001).

Men and women differ only slightly in some aspects of sexual attitudes, however. Attitudes toward premarital sex and reported frequency of sexual intercourse showed only small sex differences. In fact, most of the 30 sexual attitudes and behaviors examined in a large meta-analysis showed only small differences (Petersen & Hyde, 2010).

But not all. President Calvin Coolidge and his wife, Grace, once toured a chicken farm. The farmer showed Mrs. Coolidge through first, remarking that the rooster mated dozens of times a day. "Tell that to the President when he comes by," she said. When Mr. Coolidge learned this, he asked, "Same hen every time?" To which the farmer replied, "A different one every time." "Tell *that* to Mrs. Coolidge," said the president (Hatfield & Walster, 1978, p. 75).

Are men like roosters, wanting many different sex partners? It appears so: On average, men said they wanted at least 18 partners during their lives; women, about four or five. In a college student sample, women reported wanting three lifetime partners, and men a whopping 64 (Buss & Schmitt, 1993). However, that may have been due to outliers (extreme responses) because the average can be skewed upward by a minority of men who want hundreds of partners. In another study of college students, the most common number of sex partners desired over the next 30 years was one. Fifty-two percent of men and 66% of women wanted only one sex partner in the future. Ninety-nine percent of both men and women said they intended to settle down with one mutually exclusive sexual partner (Pedersen et al., 2002). Nevertheless, men report having more sexual partners than women ($d = .36$), so that only 36% of women had more partners than the average man (Petersen & Hyde, 2010). The average American man reports having 18 sexual partners as an adult, compared to six for women (Twenge et al., 2015). Men are also more likely to approve of casual sex, $d = .45$ (Lippa, 2009; Petersen & Hyde, 2010).

Cognitive Abilities

In 1992, toymaker Mattel got in a lot of trouble when they introduced a talking Barbie. She said such things as, "Want to go shopping? Okay, meet me at the mall!" She also said, "Math class is tough." This, some argued, encouraged the stereotype that women aren't good at math ("Company News," 1992). A few creative people soon got revenge: A few months later, the activist Barbie Liberation Organization altered some dolls by switching the voice boxes of the talking Barbie and a talking G. I. Joe so they would utter each other's phrases. This resulted in a Barbie that would yell, "Attack! Eat lead, Cobra!" and a G. I. Joe that said, "Let's plan our dream wedding!" (Firestone, 1993).

Was Barbie right about women finding math class tough? Many people seem to think so. The stereotype that women are not good at math is so strong that just checking a box for gender on a questionnaire before taking a math test is enough to decrease women's math performance (Spencer et al., 1998), a phenomenon known as *stereotype threat*.

Watch STEREOTYPE THREAT: WOMEN AND MATH

WATCH
the video in
REVEL

So are men actually better at math? Not as much as you might think. The math performance of males and females is virtually identical in recent studies (Kane & Mertz, 2012; Lindberg et al., 2010). Girls and women have always performed just as well or even better than boys and men at math computation and concepts (Hyde et al., 1990). The gender gap in general math ability has also narrowed considerably over time, even among the highest scorers. In 1970, 13

Figure 10.6 Sex Differences in Spatial Ability

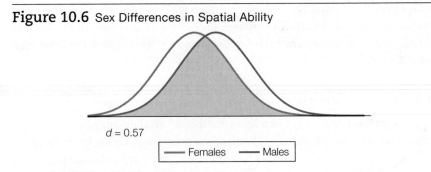

$d = 0.57$

——— Females   ——— Males

SOURCE: Based on Maeda & Yoon, 2013

times as many boys scored a 700 or above on the math SAT, but that has shrunk to three times more boys (Kane & Mertz, 2012). In some nations, there is no sex difference even among high scorers (Hyde & Mertz, 2009). This suggests that the sex difference in these cognitive abilities is partially, if not mostly, caused by culture.

The largest sex difference in abilities is in spatial ability (the mental rotation of objects), which is useful for advanced math and for mechanical tasks. The most recent analysis found the sex difference in spatial ability was $d = .57$, so about 28% of women have higher spatial ability than the average man (Maeda & Yoon, 2013; see Figure 10.6). This also means that about three times as many men as women will have very high spatial ability. However, the sex difference in spatial ability differs by culture and has shrunk over time (Cohen & Hegarty, 2012; Keith et al., 2011; Voyer et al., 1995), suggesting that this difference is at least partially cultural.

One practical application of spatial ability is finding your way while walking or driving, one reason why women often have a harder time driving (so women are safer drivers, but make wrong turns more often). Men and women also differ in *how* they find their way. Several studies have found that men are more likely to use vectors (such as north) in finding their way, and women more likely to use landmarks—for example, "Turn right after you pass the school" (Lawton & Kallai, 2002). When I (J. M. T.) was a teenager and learning my way around, my dad finally gave up on telling me to "go north on Story Road" because that meant nothing to me.

Most verbal abilities such as vocabulary and reading comprehension show few sex differences (Hyde & Linn, 1988), although girls and women perform better on some tests of spelling and language (Feingold, 1994). Women are better than men at decoding others' nonverbal behaviors, especially facial expressions ($d = .52$; Hall, 1984), although men and women are equally good at guessing what someone else is thinking (Ickes et al. 2000). The overall picture, then, is of moderate sex differences in spatial ability and nonverbal decoding, with only small sex differences in subjects such as language arts and math.

Concluding Thoughts

In the end, it's what we do with our knowledge of sex differences that matters. Given the substantial overlap between the sexes on many psychological traits, actively discriminating against someone on the basis of gender is clearly unwarranted. Virtually every social role, from political leader to nurse to murderer, could be filled by either a man or a woman. On the other hand, suggesting that males and females are exactly the same distorts the truth. Many psychological attributes demonstrate reliable sex differences, even across different cultures. The best approach is often a smart and empathic one: Don't necessarily assume that someone of the other gender will be like the average man or woman, but try to understand their perspective as someone who has had different life experiences than you have.

Maybe that's what women are secretly talking about when they go to the bathroom in pairs.

Learning Objective Summaries

LO 10.1 Explain how biology, culture, and their interaction shape sex differences.

Biological influences on sex differences begin in the womb and build through the different evolutionary pressures on males and females. Culture shapes sex differences as well, often through social structures. Most sex differences are produced through an interaction of biology and culture.

LO 10.2 Describe sex differences in personality traits, leadership, masculinity and femininity, jobs and hobbies, nonverbal behaviors and appearance, self-esteem, sexual behaviors and attitudes, and cognitive abilities.

Women score higher in neuroticism and men in self-esteem. Women make slightly better leaders but may be judged more harshly. When someone scores high in both femininity and masculinity, they are described as androgynous. Larger sex differences appear in preferences for jobs and hobbies, nonverbal behaviors and appearance, and sexual behaviors and attitudes. The largest sex difference in cognitive abilities is in spatial ability.

Key Terms

sex, p. 270
gender, p. 270
sex differences, p. 271
cisgender, p. 273
transgender, p. 273

spatial ability, p. 277
stereotypes, p. 278
stereotypically masculine
    personality traits, p. 285

stereotypically feminine
    personality traits, p. 285
body expansiveness, p. 289

Essay Questions

1. Distinguish between the terms *sex* and *gender*, and explain the complex interaction between nature and nurture that shape gender roles.

2. Choose two categories of sex differences discussed in the section "Comparing Men and Women" and summarize the data.

3. In general, it's more acceptable for girls to do "boy things" than for boys to do "girl things." Why is that, and how might it help explain the sex difference in self-esteem?

4. How do the cultural notions of "masculinity" and "femininity" inform what we know about gender and leadership?

Chapter 11
Culture and Personality

∨ Learning Objectives

LO 11.1 Describe some of the reasons why personality might vary by culture.

LO 11.2 Explain how individualistic and collectivistic cultures differ in self-views.

LO 11.3 Describe the cross-cultural and generational differences in the Big Five traits, and explain how researchers try to accurately assess these differences.

One day in the spring, you and your friends decide you should spend part of your summer vacation taking a trip to another country. To prepare, you decide to read a travel guide (Fisher, 2012). The section on restaurants is very specific in its advice:

— Don't sit down at the table of someone you don't know, even if there are empty chairs.
— Don't slurp or make loud noises when you eat.
— Be sure to tip your waiter at least 15%.
— If you are meeting friends, be on time.
— Don't kiss friends on the cheek.
— Don't smoke in the restaurant.

Wait, you might be thinking, doesn't everyone know these things?

Maybe, if you grew up in the United States. But this advice appears in a travel guide for people who are planning to visit the U.S. To someone who has never been to the U.S., this is new information. Europeans, for example, often greet each other with kisses on the cheek and often don't tip their waiters. In parts of Asia, it's common to smoke virtually everywhere, sit at tables with strangers in crowded restaurants, and burp to show appreciation for a good meal. Many other countries are not as strict about punctuality as we are here in the United States. In other words, different cultures have different **social norms**, rules for behavior within a society.

social norms
rules for behavior within a society

Everyone has a culture. You might take it for granted because it's all you've ever known, but to someone from another country, it's as foreign to them as their culture is to you. So what is this thing we all have whether we know it or not, what exactly is a "culture"?

Rules of behavior differ from one culture to another.

Culture is the customs, values, and behaviors characteristic of a nation, ethnic group, class, or time period. Culture influences nearly everything we do, so understanding culture is an essential part of understanding personality. The way we live, relate to others, and understand ourselves differ from one culture to another. As Mexican American author Sandra Cisneros writes, "When she thinks to herself in her father's language, she knows sons and daughters don't leave their parents' house until they marry. When she thinks in English, she knows she should've been on her own since eighteen" (Cisneros, 2009, p. xiii).

culture
the customs, values, and behaviors characteristic of a nation, an ethnic group, a class, or a time period

If you or your parents moved from one country to another, you've travelled a lot, or you're a member of a cultural minority, you're probably very aware of cultural differences. If not, you might not have thought very much about culture. Some of the white students in my (J. M. T.) classes are often confused when I ask them what culture they grew up in. Many will say "American," but they have trouble articulating exactly what that means. (And this is why culture is so impactful: We don't even know it's influencing us, just like a fish doesn't know it's in water.)

The truth is that white American culture has its own quirks, as humorously detailed in Christian Lander's book *Stuff White People Like* (which is really about stuff white people with higher incomes living in urban areas tend to like, such as "Organic Food," "Public Transportation That Is Not a Bus," "Snowboarding," "Public Radio," and "Asian Girls"). Under "Not Having a TV," Lander writes, "The number-one reason white people like not having a TV is so that they can tell you that they don't have a TV. . . . It is effective in making other white people feel bad, and making themselves feel good about their life and life choices. It is important that you *never* suggest they are making a mistake or that there is value to owning a TV. You should just try to steer the conversation to allow them to talk about how they are better than you" (Lander, 2008, pp. 34–35).

In an individualistic culture, it is common to specify one's preferences in an order for a coffee or a meal. In a collectivistic culture, such personalized requests are considered strange.

In this chapter, we explore how self-views and personality traits differ across cultures. We examine these differences based on four primary factors: geography, race/ethnicity, socioeconomic status, and generation.

Much of the research on cultural differences focuses on average variations based on country or world region. But cultural differences are much more complex than that; cultural difference doesn't merely begin or end at a nation's border. Regions within the same country may have important cultural variations—such as in the culture of honor particular to the southern United States (Cohen et al., 1996), or, as we discussed in Chapter 3, the variations in Big Five personality traits among the U.S. states (Rentfrow et al., 2008). Racial and ethnic groups often have their own distinct cultures—a culture within a culture such as Mexican Americans or Arab Americans.

socioeconomic status
social class, usually measured by income level, job prestige, and/or education level

birth cohort
everyone born in one year

generation
everyone born in a somewhat arbitrarily defined 20- to 30-year period

Cultural norms also differ based on social class, income level, and education level, often called **socioeconomic status**, or SES. Cultures change over time—what was normal in 1950 may not be normal now, and what was abnormal then may be normal now. In 1950, men usually wore suits and hats to baseball games, behavior that would be considered strange now. Cultural change leads to differences among generations, sometimes known as birth cohort differences. A **birth cohort** is everyone born in one year, and a **generation** is everyone born in a somewhat arbitrarily defined 20-year period (such as Millennials, born roughly between 1980 and 1994). We use *birth cohort* and *generation* interchangeably, as they both refer to being born at a certain time. Each of these types of cultural differences are discussed in relation to personality traits and attributes when there are research data available—unfortunately, this isn't always the case. Don't worry, though—we have more than enough data at this point to give a well-rounded picture of how culture influences not only the personalities of other people, but also your own.

How Cultures Shape People

LO 11.1 Describe some of the reasons why personality might vary by culture.

First, let's consider some theories about how culture works. Children learn the social norms of their culture through socialization—learning how to become mature members of their society (see Chapter 8). For example, American parents ask even small children lots of questions about their preferences, so children learn early on that they are expected to have opinions and express them. In many Asian countries, however, parents believe it is better that they decide on behalf of their children, so children do not learn to value personal preferences and self-expression as much (Iyengar & Lepper, 1999; Kim & Sherman, 2007).

cross-cultural differences
average variations based on country or world region

cultural products
the products of a culture such as song lyrics, TV shows, advertisements, and books useful for studying culture at a broad level

mutual constitution model
the idea that cultures and selves each cause the other

Some have theorized that **cross-cultural differences** arise from geography: terrain, climate, and other environmental characteristics. For example, UCLA geography professor Jared Diamond (1999) argued that the existence of large land mammals (such as cattle) in Europe set Europeans on a path toward agriculture as opposed to hunting and gathering, which led to advances in writing and mathematics. Similarly, Asian cultures may value hard work and collective action more because land in Asia is often used to grow rice, and cultivating rice paddies is labor intensive (Pomeranz, 2001; Talhelm et al., 2014). Another theory of cultural differences focuses on disease-causing pathogens, finding that regions more vulnerable to the spread of infectious disease are more likely to emphasize conformity to rules such as quarantines and mandatory vaccinations (Fincher et al., 2008; Varnum, 2012) .

Cultural differences are usually viewed in terms of people—do Canadians tend to have more positive views of themselves than the Chinese? Are Americans more extraverted than the British? But culture can also be seen in terms of what people produce—the artifacts of a culture. **Cultural products** such as song lyrics,

Cultural products such as magazines and newspapers capture cultural viewpoints.

TV shows, advertisements, and books convey cultural messages about proper behavior and beliefs. The sum of a culture's products can capture more distinct cultural differences than can be found in individuals, who vary from person to person based on genetics and individual personality traits (Morling & Lamoreaux, 2008).

Cultures and individuals constantly interact with each other. Culture shapes individuals, but individuals also shape culture. This is known as the **mutual constitution model** (Markus & Kitayama, 2010; see Figure 11.1). Cultural change may also happen through mutual constitution. For example, progressively more people in American culture might give individualistic advice ("Believe in yourself and anything is possible"), which in turn causes the next generation to be more individualistic (Twenge, 2014; Twenge et al., 2012c).

Of course, it's difficult to say whether the culture or the individuals changed first—it's the classic chicken-and-egg problem. More than likely, a few individuals began to spread new ideas, some new ideas caught on (especially in younger

Figure 11.1 The Mutual Constitution Model

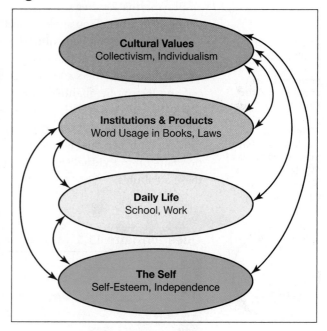

SOURCE: Based on Markus and Kitayama (2010).

people, who are more open to new ideas), generational change occurred, and the resulting culture was different. Gay and lesbian rights are one example of this process. A few people began to spread the idea that gays and lesbians should have equal rights, many people (especially the young) listened, and as time went on the average view shifted.

JOURNAL PROMPT: UNDERSTANDING YOURSELF

How has your life been different from your parents' and grandparents' generations? What influences do you think have shaped your generation the most?

Cultural Differences in Individualism and Collectivism

LO 11.2 Explain how individualistic and collectivistic cultures differ in self-views.

When a small Texas company wanted to increase productivity, managers suggested to employees that before coming to work in the morning, they should look in the mirror and repeat "I am beautiful" 100 times. At a Japanese company, employees instead begin the day by holding hands with their coworkers and telling each other, "You are beautiful" (Markus & Kitayama, 1991, p. 224).

individualism

a cultural system favoring the needs of the self over those of others and the society

The most researched cultural difference is the relationship between the self and others. One cultural system, called **individualism**, favors the needs of the self over those of others and the society. Individualism emphasizes the individual self and its unique qualities independent from others. In contrast, **collectivism** places the needs of others and the society first and promotes the idea that we need other people, and they need us (Markus & Kitayama, 1991). People can also differ in their personal levels of individualism and collectivism. Take the questionnaire on individualism and collectivism below to see how you compare on these attributes.

collectivism

a cultural system placing the needs of others and the society first

TAKE
the
Questionnaire
in **REVEL**

→

Questionnaire 11.1 INDIVIDUALISM–COLLECTIVISM SCALE

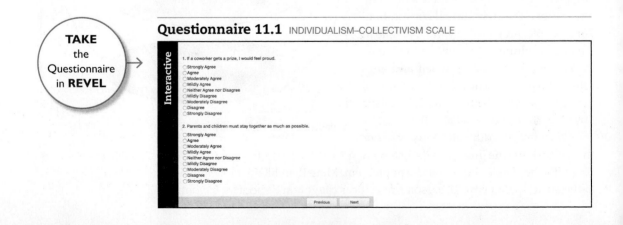

Figure 11.2 Diagrams of Self and Other

The independent (individualistic) view of the self (A), and the interdependent (collectivistic) view of the self (B).

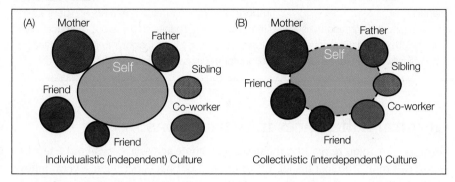

Individualistic (independent) Culture

Collectivistic (interdependent) Culture

SOURCE: Markus and Kitayama (1991, Figure 1).

The United States is an individualistic culture, and Japan a collectivistic one, one reason why the U.S. company told workers to praise themselves and the Japanese company asked them to praise each other. Sandra Cisneros's example of her Mexican American father wanting her to live at home echoes Latino Americans' interdependent and collectivistic subculture, and her view (at least when thinking in English) that she should be on her own reflects the independent and individualistic culture of Chicago, where she grew up (Cisneros, 2009). How did you score on individualism versus collectivism?

As you might remember from Chapter 5, people from individualistic cultures are more likely to mention personal attributes when they finish the sentence "I am . . . " ("I am tall," "I am ambitious"), and people from collectivistic cultures are more likely to mention group memberships and affiliations ("I am a daughter," "I am Puerto Rican") (Cousins, 1989). As Figure 11.2 illustrates, individualism separates the self from others, but collectivism unites the self and others.

Personality's Past

Harry Triandis and Individualism–Collectivism

Cultures differ in many ways, from governing structures to language and from childrearing to food. Psychologists have focused on many of these differences, but have found they needed a more comprehensive, broader way to describe cultural differences. The most common broad description of cultural difference is individualism–collectivism, popularized by Harry Triandis (1995).

Triandis made an explicit link between individualism–collectivism in culture and personality traits. He argued that the cultural context directly shaped the personality of individuals in each culture. People in more individualistic cultures would be more likely to have personality traits that were more idiocentric: *Idio-* is a Greek root meaning "personal or individual," so idiocentric people were centered on the individual self. People in collectivistic cultures would be more likely to have allocentric personality traits: *Allo* is a Greek root meaning "other," so allocentric people are centered on others (Triandis et al., 1985).

Triandis had a cross-cultural background himself. He was born in Greece in the 1920s and then moved to Canada after World War II, finally settling in the United States. He then spent his career studying individuals from areas like Greece, Puerto Rico, and the mainland United States. This allowed him to understand the importance of cultural differences in personality (Triandis, 2001). Thanks to the work of Triandis and others like him, we have insight into the importance of culture for understanding personality.

Cultural Differences in Attributions

One day when you're reading the news, you come across a story about a terrible murder: A man who lost his job returned to shoot his supervisor, several fellow workers, and then himself.

If you're reading a U.S. news site, the story is more likely to focus on the man himself—that he had "a psychological problem" or "had a short fuse." If you're reading a Chinese news site, however, it's more likely to mention the situation—"the gunman had been recently fired" or "the murder can be traced to the availability of guns" (Morris & Peng, 1994).

attributions
explanations for the reasons behind people's behavior

internal attribution
an explanation for behavior focusing on the individual and his or her choices and personality

external attribution
an explanation for behavior focusing on the surrounding situation

When explaining reasons behind people's behavior, known as **attributions**, individualistic cultural systems focus more on the individual and his choices and personality. Such an emphasis on the person is called an **internal attribution**. In contrast, collectivistic systems focus more on the surrounding situation, called an **external attribution**. When shown an underwater scene and later asked to describe it, Japanese remembered more of the background features (such as rocks and plants), and Americans were more likely to focus on a single object, such as the biggest fish (Chua et al., 2005; see Figure 11.3). Or imagine seeing a picture of a group of children and being asked to say how happy (vs. angry) one of the

WATCH
the video in
REVEL

Watch EXPLAINING ATTRIBUTION

Figure 11.3 What Grabs Your Attention?

American observers of this scene usually focus on the biggest fish, but Japanese observers describe the background and other features. (The arrows indicate the movements of the fish and frog.)

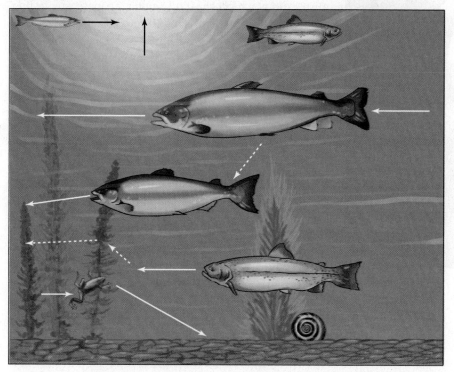

children was. American students looked at the expression on the individual child's face, but Japanese students' ratings differed depending on the expressions of the surrounding children (Masuda et al., 2008). In collectivistic cultural systems, context is emphasized; in individualistic ones, the lone person matters more.

If context is emphasized, people are also more likely to consider others' perspectives before they act. Try this: Recall a favorite memory. Do you literally see yourself in the memory, or do you see the memory through your own eyes, as you would have seen it then? East Asians are more likely than Westerners (those from Western Europe, the United States, Canada, and Australia) to see themselves in the memory, which means they take the perspective of the audience. They remember the event as it would have appeared through others' eyes (Cohen & Gunz, 2002). East Asians were also better at taking someone else's perspective in a game—for example, in a game in which players could see some objects and not others, they were less likely to look at objects their game partner couldn't see (Wu & Keysar, 2007). In another study, students took a test either with or without a mirror in front of them. The self-awareness and external perspective

Songs such as Justin Timberlake's "Sexy Back" reflect the individualism of modern culture.

of the mirror usually reduces cheating in Western populations; the mirror literally makes us "see" ourselves, so we become more conscious of doing something bad, as others would view such an act. However, the presence of the mirror did not affect cheating among Japanese, suggesting they already "saw themselves" through the perspective of others, even without the mirror (Heine et al., 2008).

Frames of reference also differ by generation. American college students in the 2000s scored lower on a measure of perspective taking than students in the 1980s (the questionnaire included items such as "Before criticizing somebody, I try to imagine how I would feel if I were in their place;" Konrath et al., 2011). This suggests that American culture has shifted toward a more individualistic and self-focused mindset and away from a more collectivistic mindset (Myers, 2000; Twenge, 2014). Cultural products such as music lyrics have also become more self-focused. Between 1980 and 2007, the song lyrics of the Billboard top hits were more likely to use first-person singular pronouns (such as "I" and "me") and less likely to mention positive social relationships (DeWall et al., 2011). Early 1980s songs used the word *love* a lot ("Crazy Little Thing Called Love," "Keep on Loving You"), but by the mid-2000s songs were more individualistic, from Carrie Underwood smashing her ex's windshield so he'll think twice "Before He Cheats" to Justin Timberlake singlehandedly bringing "Sexy Back."

Cultural Differences in Views of the Self

Individualistic and collectivistic cultures also encourage different self-views—both in how positively people view themselves, how they see themselves in relation to others, and how much they value uniqueness.

POSITIVE SELF-VIEWS   Think about how you would describe yourself versus how your friends would describe you. If you were raised in the United States or another individualistic country, you're more likely to describe yourself a little more positively than your friends would describe you. But if you were raised in Asia, your friends describe you more positively than you would describe yourself (Heine & Remshaw, 2002).

Individualistic and collectivistic cultures differ in how much they encourage **self-enhancement**—unrealistically positive views of the self and personal abilities. Westerners are much more likely than East Asians to focus on the more positive aspects of themselves, at least on most measures (Heine & Hamamura, 2007). For example, white Canadian students were more likely to self-enhance than Japanese students were. Asian Canadians' scores fell in the middle (Heine & Renshaw, 2002). This difference occurred even when the students were distracted,

self-enhancement
unrealistically positive views of the self and personal abilities

suggesting that the cultural difference was internalized and not just due to "knowing what to say" (Falk et al., 2009).

People from individualistic cultures such as the United States have higher self-esteem than those from collectivistic cultures such as Japan (Schmitt & Allik, 2005; Twenge & Crocker, 2002). In one large international study, the residents of Serbia, Chile, and Israel reported the highest self-esteem (the United States was 6th out of 53 nations). Residents of Japan scored the lowest, followed by Hong Kong, Bangladesh, and Taiwan (Schmitt & Allik, 2005).

Emigrating from one country to another can influence self-esteem scores, also showing the influence of culture. Among Japanese immigrants to Canada, those who had been in the country the longest had the highest self-esteem (Heine et al., 1999). Cultural influences also grow as children are socialized: Asian American children's self-esteem is about the same as white American children's, but by the time they reach high school Asian Americans report significantly lower self-esteem than whites (Twenge & Crocker, 2002).

Within the United States, African Americans have the highest self-esteem on average, followed by whites, Latinos, and finally Asian Americans, who have the lowest (Bachman et al., 2011; Twenge & Crocker, 2002) (Figure 11.4). The most likely explanation is the **subcultures** of these ethnicities: African American culture is more individualistic, whereas Asian American culture is more collectivistic (Oyserman et al., 2002). Another possibility is that African Americans encourage high self-esteem as protection against racial prejudice (Crocker & Major, 1989).

subcultures
a culture within a culture, based on ethnicity, class, region, or some other variable

Figure 11.4 Black, Hispanic, Asian, and American Indian Self-Esteem Scores Compared with Whites, U.S. Data

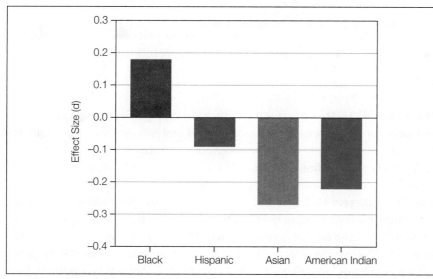

SOURCE: From Twenge and Crocker (2002).

**collective
self-esteem**

self-esteem based on
group membership

Of course, self-esteem is an inherently individualistic concept. What about self-esteem based on your group—the pride you feel in your ethnic group, nationality, religion, or gender? That's called **collective self-esteem**. Perhaps people from more collectivistic cultures, such as Asian Americans, might have higher collective self-esteem even if their individual self-esteem is lower. However, Asian Americans have slightly lower collective self-esteem than whites (Crocker et al., 1994). This suggests a more general disinterest in self-enhancement in collectivistic cultures rather than just a disinterest in individual self-esteem (Heine & Buchtel, 2009).

On average, people with lower SES—those with less income and education—are more collectivistic than those with higher SES. Consistent with this idea, lower-SES individuals report slightly lower self-esteem (Twenge & Campbell, 2002) and lower narcissism (Foster et al., 2003; Piff, 2013). Students from lower-SES backgrounds are better at judging others' emotions and show more compassion toward others (Kraus et al., 2010; Stellar et al., 2012).

The emphasis on positive self-views has also changed over time. Fifteen times more education articles in the 1990s (vs. the 1960s) mentioned self-esteem (Twenge & Campbell, 2001). Perhaps due to the cultural shift encouraging more positive self-views, more recent generations of young Americans score higher on self-esteem and narcissism than Baby Boomers (born between 1946 and 1964) did (Gentile et al., 2010; Stewart et al., 2010; Twenge & Foster, 2010). In China, people with more modern lifestyles (those who were younger, lived in a city, or were only children) scored higher on narcissism (Cai et al., 2012). Recent American college students are also more likely than their 1960s counterparts to describe themselves as above average in individualistic attributes, such as self-confidence and leadership ability, but no more likely to say they were exceptional in collectivistic traits such as understanding others (Twenge et al., 2012a).

JOURNAL PROMPT: UNDERSTANDING YOURSELF

Are you the product of self-esteem-enhancing culture, or not? Do you think attempts to bolster self-esteem are helpful? Why or why not?

SELF VERSUS OTHER Cultural products such as advertisements illustrate cross-cultural differences in views of the self and others (Morling & Lamoreaux, 2008). For example, online ads in Korea are more likely to show groups of people than U.S. online ads (An, 2006). Korean print advertisements emphasize fitting in and tradition: "Our ginseng drink is produced according to the methods of 500-year tradition" or "Seven out of 10 people are using this product." American ads are more likely to emphasize standing out—"Choose your own view" or (in an ad that gives away its 1990s vintage) "The Internet isn't for everybody. Then again, you are not everybody" (Kim & Markus, 1999). Japanese textbooks are more likely to feature themes of conformity, tradition, and interdependence, and American textbooks themes of self-direction, stimulation, and power (Imada, 2012).

Cultures and generations have also changed over time in views of the self. In Renaissance times in Western Europe (roughly the years 1300–1600), people made very few individual choices. Class systems were rigid, gender roles were inflexible, and everyone obeyed the landowners and the king. Marriages were arranged, and boys usually entered the profession of their fathers. The idea of an individual self was rarely recognized. Slowly, individuals gained more rights, democracy became more widespread, restrictions based on gender and class loosened somewhat, and marriage for love became more popular (Baumeister, 1987). By the 20th century in the West, discrimination based on race and gender began to fall out of fashion, with more emphasis placed on the talents and wishes of the individual rather than the rules of group membership. This shift toward more focus on the individual may have led to less focus on outside events. For example, in 1983, Finnish teens mentioned war and terrorism as their greatest fears, but by 2007, they were more likely to mention personal fears such as loneliness and work worries (Lindfors et al., 2012).

Both the cross-cultural and over-time differences in self-focus may be caused by differences in **relational mobility**—how easy it is to move in and out of relationships (Falk et al., 2009). In traditional, more collectivistic cultures, divorce is rare—as is dating, as many marriages are arranged. Family relationships are tightly enmeshed, with adult children—especially women—living with their parents until they marry. Such expectations prevailed in Western countries until the 20th century and persist today in collectivistic

relational mobility
how easy it is to move in and out of relationships

Relational mobility—and thus divorce and breakups—are more common in modern, individualistic cultures.

countries such as India. In this environment, focusing oneself has few benefits but several costs, especially if self-focus leads to less harmonious relationships and less compromise.

In more modern, individualistic cultures, relationships are more fluid—divorce is more common, unmarried partners date and break up, and adult children live on their own. This is the system in the United States and other Western countries today. In this environment, focusing on oneself may help people have the confidence to form new relationships—though not always the collectivism necessary to maintain them for decades.

NEED FOR UNIQUENESS Imagine you're expecting your first child and trying to decide what to name the baby. Do you want to give your child a common name, so he or she can fit in, or a more unique name, so he or she can stand out? People in more recently settled areas—the United States versus Europe and the West Coast versus the East Coast—are less likely to give their children common names (Varnum & Kitayama, 2011). These choices have also changed over time. Back in the 1950s, many parents chose common names: One-third of American boys received one of the ten most popular names, as did one-fourth of girls. By 2007, however, parents gave less than 10% of babies one of the ten most popular names. In other words, preferences shifted from fitting in to standing out (Twenge et al., 2010; see Figure 11.5). Celebrities have been on the leading edge of this trend, with Bear Blue (actress Alicia Silverstone's son), Apple (actress Gwyneth Paltrow's daughter), Pilot Inspektor (actor Jason Lee's son), and Moxie Crime-Fighter (magician Penn Jillette's daughter). Even pets now receive more unique names (Ogihara et al., 2015). This shows an increasing emphasis on the individual self standing out from others, another change consistent with individualism.

Figure 11.5 Percentage of U.S. Babies Receiving One of the Ten Most Popular Names, by Year of Birth, 1881–2007

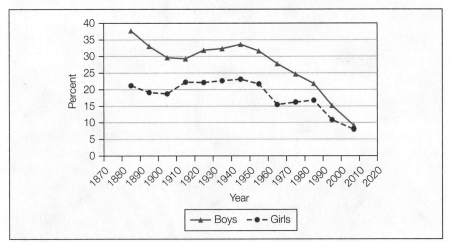

SOURCE: Twenge, Abebe, and Campbell (2010).

As you might expect, individualistic countries such as the United States value uniqueness more than collectivistic countries (Markus & Kitayama, 1991). In the United States, a common saying points out that "[t]he squeaky wheel gets the grease," while the Japanese observe that "[t]he nail that stands out gets pounded down."

In one clever study, participants in the United States and Korea were given the choice of which pen to take as a gift. They were shown a group of three green pens and one orange pen. The Americans were more likely to choose the orange pen—the one that stood out—and the Koreans were more likely to choose one of the green pens—the one that fit in (Kim & Markus, 1999). Another large study found that people from Asian countries were less likely to feel autonomous from others (Church et al., 2013).

The Science of Personality HOW TO STUDY TRENDS IN NAMES

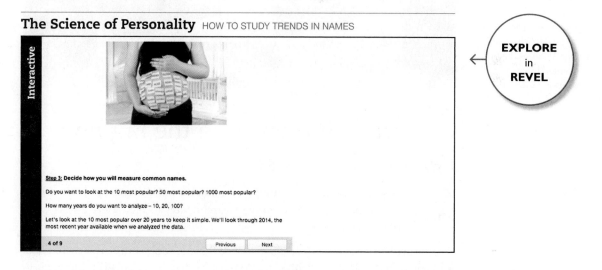

Interactive

Step 3: Decide how you will measure common names.

Do you want to look at the 10 most popular? 50 most popular? 1000 most popular?

How many years do you want to analyze – 10, 20, 100?

Let's look at the 10 most popular over 20 years to keep it simple. We'll look through 2014, the most recent year available when we analyzed the data.

4 of 9   Previous   Next

EXPLORE
in
REVEL

APPROACH VERSUS AVOIDANCE MOTIVATION   Imagine you come to a psychology lab and take an intelligence test. The experimenter tells you that you didn't do very well—your score was below the 45th percentile. You then either continue working on that test or do a different test. American and Canadian students were more likely to spend more time working at the new test, guessing that they might do better on it. But Japanese students spent more time on the task they'd done badly on; it was more important to them to improve than to feel good about themselves (Heine et al., 2001).

This may be related to cross-cultural differences in approach versus avoidance—how much someone focuses on attaining success versus avoiding failure (covered in Chapter 7). Compared to Westerners, East Asians are motivated more by avoidance: They are more likely to see losing as an opportunity (Lee et al., 2000) and are more likely to focus on negative role models—people who represent outcomes they would like to avoid (Lockwood et al., 2005). So, on average, if you'd like to motivate Asians, focus on what can go wrong and how to avoid it. To motivate Westerners, focus on winning and the good things that will happen from success.

North American students who did badly on a test wanted to do something else, but Asian students wanted to keep working to improve.

Cultural Differences in the Big Five Personality Traits

LO 11.3 Describe the cross-cultural and generational differences in the Big Five traits, and explain how researchers try to accurately assess these differences.

There's an old saying in Europe: "In Heaven, the mechanics are German, the chefs are French, the police are British, the lovers are Italian, and everything is organized by the Swiss. In Hell, the mechanics are French, the police are German, the chefs are British, the lovers are Swiss, and everything is organized by the Italians."

In personality terms, this saying implies—among other things—that the Swiss are highly conscientious but Italians are not, and that Germans are highly conscientious but not very agreeable.

Or consider how Americans are viewed by the rest of the world: as loud, gregarious people who talk a lot and are unafraid to interrupt others—in other words, as more extraverted.

Is there any truth to these ideas that, on average, the residents of different countries differ in their personality traits?

The answer to this question is more complicated than it first appears.

Cross-Cultural Research Methods

As you know, most personality questionnaires are self-report instruments that ask participants to rate themselves as high or low on a trait. However, there is no universal standard or comparison group. Most people compare themselves to other people they know. The problem is that almost everyone they know will also be a member of their own culture. This is known as the **reference-group effect** (Heine et al., 2002), and it can make cross-cultural comparisons of personality traits difficult.

Let's take two extreme examples. Grog lives in a cave with three other families in the Paleolithic era. With no running water, bathing is difficult, especially in the winter. But Grog does his best to keep clean; when he goes out hunting, he always stops at the stream to wash his face and hands, even when it's cold. He thinks he's pretty clean compared to his cavemates who rarely wash. Then there's Charlotte, a modern-day, well-off city dweller. She showers once every three days or so and washes her hands twice a day. Most people she knows shower every day and wash their hands five times a day, so Charlotte sees herself as not very clean. Yet, objectively, she is much cleaner than Grog on an average day. Grog's and Charlotte's comparison groups skew their perceptions of how clean they are.

This works at the levels of cultures and personality traits, too, because most people primarily compare themselves to others in their own culture. For example, Germans are usually viewed by other Europeans as neat and organized. But if Helga the German compares herself mostly to other Germans who are also neat and organized, Helga might rate herself as fairly low on neatness, even though she might be high by the standards of another country. Thus, the reference-group effect can sometimes make cross-cultural differences in personality traits difficult to determine.

We revisit these challenges as we go through the research on each of the Big Five traits, since the reference-group effect is stronger for some traits than others (Oishi & Roth, 2009). One way to get around the problem of reference groups is to ask people to describe the typical member of a culture, known as a **perception of national character**. This actually measures stereotypes, but, as we see later, it can sometimes be more accurate in describing the overall personality of a culture than self-reports (Heine et al., 2008). This seems strange at first, but it's because

reference-group effect
when people compare themselves to other people they know when completing personality questionnaires

perception of national character
asking people to describe the typical member of a culture

Someone who grew up in a cave is going to have a different perception of cleanliness than someone who grew up in a penthouse apartment.

these perceptions of national character are based on a wider view of many cultures, while self-reports of personality usually rely on comparisons to others within the same culture.

Then there's the question of which personality questionnaire to use. Most questionnaires, including those measuring the Big Five, were developed in the United States. Thus, it's fair to ask if the Big Five captures the personality traits most relevant to other cultures. As you might remember from Chapter 3, the Big Five personality structure appears across most cultures, with a few variations here and there (McCrae & Terracciano, 2005). For example, openness to experience does not appear in every culture, and some cultures add traits, such as interpersonal relatedness in China (Cheung et al., 2001). Questionnaires also need to be translated into different languages. Usually, one bilingual person will translate a questionnaire from (for example) English to Spanish, and then another bilingual person translates it back from Spanish to English. You can then see if the two English versions match. If they don't, the two bilingual research assistants might discuss the correct translation until they both agree.

People from individualistic cultures may also find the very idea of personality more useful and relevant than those from collectivistic countries, who are more likely to focus on the situation. When Korean students described their personality across different situations (for example, with their parents vs. a friend), their descriptions varied much more across situations than Americans' did (Suh, 2002). In other words, Koreans viewed their personalities as less consistent from one situation to another, whereas Americans were more likely to focus on having "one true self" (Kashima et al., 2004). These were more than just perceptions: Parents and friends also differed more in their descriptions of the students in Korea than in the United States, suggesting that the Korean students really were behaving differently with their parents versus their friends (Suh, 2002).

Even the immediate context matters: Japanese participants completed the "I am . . . " statements differently if they were alone, with one other person, or in a group; Americans' self-descriptions did not differ as much across these situations (Kanagawa et al., 2001). Overall, people from collectivistic cultures are more likely to believe that roles or duties describe people better than personality traits and that behavior will differ depending on the situation (Church et al., 2006). Personality is, nevertheless, still a useful concept in Eastern cultures, but not as much as in the West. Some subcultures, such as Latino Americans, are also less likely to explain behavior in terms of personality traits (Zarate et al., 2001).

Below we describe the differences in each of the Big Five across nations, generations, ethnic groups, and SES groups, where there's data available.

Cultural Differences in Extraversion

On a typical summer day in Paris, American tourists are easy to spot. For one thing, they wear t-shirts, shorts, and white tennis shoes. They also tend to speak loudly and boisterously. In other words, they are extraverted.

This stereotype of the extraverted American seems to hold true in actual cross-cultural comparisons, though the United States is bested in extraversion by a few other countries, some unexpected. In surveys of the residents of 36 countries, those high in extraversion include Norway, Switzerland, Austria, Canada, and the United States. Low-extraversion countries include Taiwan, Malaysia, and Zimbabwe (Allik & McCrae, 2004). In a different study of 56 countries, the residents of Croatia and Serbia were the most extraverted, and those from South Korea, Bangladesh, and France the least extraverted (Schmitt et al., 2007).

Extraversion is linked to cultural individualism—which makes sense, as extraversion includes individualistic traits such as dominance and assertiveness. Countries high in extraversion also tend to be lower in **power distance**, or formal hierarchies of power and status. If you call your boss by his first name, you're likely in a low power-distance culture; if you call him "Mr." and his last name, you're probably in a high power-distance culture. In a high power-distance culture, children are more likely to obey parents without question and employees display considerable respect for their bosses. High-extraversion countries are also more economically prosperous (Allik & McCrae, 2004) and have more liberal views of sexuality (Schmitt et al., 2007).

power distance
a cultural system emphasizing formality and greater difference in power among people

Within the United States, white Americans score slightly higher on extraversion than Hispanics and moderately higher than Native Americans and black Americans, especially on the sociability (or gregariousness) facet. Whites score higher than Asian Americans on the dominance facet of extraversion (related to being a leader). Black Americans score moderately higher than Asian Americans on both the dominance and sociability facets of extraversion (Foldes et al., 2008).

High power distance cultures have lower extraversion and more distinctions based on status and rank.

Extraversion—especially the subfacet of dominance—has increased over the generations in samples from Australia, the Netherlands, Sweden, and the United States (Andre et al., 2010; Gentile et al., 2015; Scollon & Diener, 2006; Smits et al., 2011; Twenge, 2001a, 2001b). In previous eras, more people lived in small towns and interacted with the same people much of the time. Now, most of us meet new people every day, making extraversion a useful trait.

Cultural Differences in Agreeableness

Canadians have a reputation for being nice. There's a running joke that Canadians will apologize for anything, even if it wasn't their fault. In Big Five terms, this means they are high in agreeableness. In fact, most people believe that Canadians are more agreeable than Americans (Terracciano et al., 2005). So what's the reality? Well, it's complicated.

If we go by just self-report measures, there basically is no difference. The average score on agreeableness is about the same in Canada and the United States. By this measure alone, Canadian niceness might be just an unfounded stereotype. But we need to take into account the reference-group effect we discussed at the start of the chapter. Canadians are probably comparing themselves with other Canadians when they rate their agreeableness. Similarly, Americans are comparing themselves with other Americans. A Canadian who rates herself as very nice (say 8 out of 10) compared to other Canadians probably is very nice. Likewise, an American who rates himself an 8 out of 10 on niceness compared to other Americans will also probably be very nice compared to other Americans. However, these same self-reports will do a poor job when used to compare Canadians to Americans. On self-report measures, people are comparing themselves to those in their own cultural groups. They're the fish that don't understand the effects of the water they're swimming in.

> The reference-group effect might prevent Canadians from seeing themselves as agreeable compared to their fellow citizens.

However, if we bring in an outsider perspective—that is, people who are neither Canadian nor American—to rate the perceived national character of the two groups, we get a different result. These raters are explicitly comparing across cultures, and then the difference appears: People think Canadians are more agreeable than Americans. Usually we'd see this kind of generalization as a bad thing (a stereotype), but in this case it allows an explicit

comparison across cultures that doesn't happen when people are describing themselves. Overall, we can safely infer that both the Canadian and the American are probably relatively nice people, but the Canadian overall is more likely to be nicer.

With that caution in mind, the residents of Greece, Congo, and Jordan self-report being highest in agreeableness, and Argentina, Ukraine, and Japan lowest in agreeableness among 56 countries (Schmitt et al., 2007). Alcohol consumption is higher in low-agreeableness countries—perhaps some countries have more angry drunks (Oishi & Roth, 2009).

Among U.S. ethnic groups, Asian Americans score higher on agreeableness than white Americans, although only a few studies are available. Black and Hispanic Americans score about the same as white Americans on agreeableness (Foldes et al., 2008). Agreeableness may also not come as naturally to those who grow up privileged: College students from affluent homes were less likely to help others (Piff et al., 2010; Stephens et al., 2007).

Some aspects of agreeableness have declined over generations in the United States. Compared to college students in the 1970s, those in the 2000s scored lower on a measure of empathy for others, closely related to agreeableness (Konrath et al., 2011). Recent generations are also more likely to believe that people get what they deserve ("People who meet with misfortune have often brought it on themselves"), another indicator of low agreeableness (Malahy et al., 2009). However, Dutch college students in 2007 scored higher in agreeableness than students did in 1982 (Smits et al., 2011).

Cultural Differences in Conscientiousness

Remember the saying that Heaven is organized by the Swiss and Hell by the Italians? Contrary to this perception of national character, people from more southern latitudes actually score higher in conscientiousness than those from more northern latitudes (Allik & McCrae, 2004; Schmitt et al., 2007). By self-report, high-conscientiousness countries include Ethiopia, Zimbabwe, and Tanzania. Low-conscientiousness countries include Japan, Germany, and South Korea (Schmitt et al., 2007).

If you think those results are strange, you're not alone—most people think of Japan, Germany, and South Korea as countries replete with organized, efficient people. And they are—when conscientiousness is measured using actual behavior. Researchers visited 25 countries and measured behavioral indicators of conscientiousness such as postal workers' speed, the accuracy of clocks in banks, and walking speed on public streets during business hours in downtowns (Levine & Norenzayan, 1999). For example, the postal workers in Germany were more efficient than the postal workers in Mexico. Bank clocks were very accurate in Switzerland but not in Indonesia or Greece. Citizens walked quickly in Ireland, the Netherlands, and Switzerland but not in Brazil, Romania, or Jordan.

Not surprisingly, these behavioral indicators of conscientiousness lined up very well with perceptions of national character by both natives and others;

Researchers used walking speed as a behavioral measure of conscientiousness.

countries perceived as highly conscientious had more accurate clocks, for example. However, these behavioral measures were not correlated with average self-reports of conscientiousness from each country, and in some cases were even negatively correlated (for example, countries with fast postal workers actually had lower average scores on conscientiousness; Heine et al., 2008). The reference group effect has struck again. Apparently, when Germans judge their own conscientiousness, they think they fall short compared to their fellow Germans who are also high in conscientiousness. But when someone compares the average German to the average person from Chile or Indonesia, Germans are rated as more conscientious. Overall, conscientiousness appears to be particularly influenced by reference-group effects, though no one is yet sure why (Oishi & Roth, 2009).

Low-conscientiousness cultures are often "event-time" cultures, relying more on spontaneity and less on planning (Levine & Norenzayan, 1999). In these cultures, it's considered relatively normal to be late. One of my (J. M. T.) college friends always joked that his parents and their friends, who were raised in India, were on "Indian time" because their gatherings usually started an hour or even 2 hours late. He switched back and forth between the two cultures, arriving on time for events organized by white American friends and late for those organized by Indians.

Within the United States, black, Hispanic, Native Americans, and Asian Americans all score slightly higher on conscientiousness than white Americans (Foldes et al., 2008). It is not clear if these comparisons have the same reference-group effect issues as the cross-cultural studies of conscientiousness.

Studies of change over time in conscientiousness are conflicting: U.S. college students do not show generational differences (Gentile et al., 2015), Dutch college

students are now higher in conscientiousness than they were in previous generations (Smits et al., 2011), and older Swedish women are now less conscientious
(Andre et al., 2010).

Cultural Differences in Neuroticism

Which country wins the prize for having the most nervous residents? Putting
together the results of two different surveys, it's Japan.

Other countries high in neuroticism include Russia, France, Spain, and
Belgium. Low-neuroticism countries include Sweden, Denmark, the Netherlands,
and Indonesia (Allik & McCrae, 2004). In another study, high-neuroticism countries were Argentina, Japan, and Spain, and low-neuroticism countries were the
Congo, Slovenia, and Ethiopia (Schmitt et al., 2007).

Countries high in neuroticism tend to have more formal systems of rules that
attempt to minimize cultural and situational ambiguity (Allik & McCrae, 2004).
This is called **uncertainty avoidance**. It isn't clear, though, if the rules are in place
because more people are neurotic, or if the greater number of rules leads people
to become more neurotic.

**uncertainty
avoidance**
a cultural system of
rules that minimizes
ambiguity

In contrast to the findings for conscientiousness, behavioral criteria do align
with self-reports of neuroticism. For example, countries with higher neuroticism
have more psychiatric ward beds per capita than those lower in neuroticism
(Oishi & Roth, 2009). Japan, which makes the high-neuroticism list in both
surveys, has a high suicide rate, twice that of the United States.

Asian Americans and Native Americans score higher than white Americans
on neuroticism. Hispanics score lower and black Americans higher than white

Suicide rates are
high in Japan, which
tops international
surveys in levels of
neuroticism.

Americans, though only a few studies are available. The largest racial difference appeared between blacks and Asian Americans, with Asians reporting higher neuroticism (Foldes et al., 2008). People in lower-SES groups tend to experience more mental health issues in general and score higher on neuroticism (Greene & Murdock, 2013; McCann, 2011).

Neuroticism is higher among more recent generations. Eighty percent of college students in the early 1990s scored higher in neuroticism than the average student in the 1950s (Twenge, 2000). Four times as many college students in the 2000s (vs. the 1930s) scored at a problematic level of anxiety on a common measure of mental health, and high school students' anxiety increased as well (Twenge et al., 2010). Chinese and Australian samples also show increases in neuroticism and anxiety (Scollon & Diener, 2006; Xin et al., 2010).

It seems that something about modern life is stressing us out. It doesn't seem to be the economy—anxiety was actually lower during the Great Depression than it was in the go-go early 2000s. It could be that we are more disconnected from each other—more likely to live alone, more likely to get divorced, and less likely to know our neighbors and participate in the community (Putnam, 2000; Twenge, 2000). Cultural values in the United States—and possibly other countries as well—have also shifted toward extrinsic values such as money, fame, and image, and people with those values are more likely to feel anxious and depressed (Kasser & Ryan, 1993).

Cultural Differences in Openness to Experience

At least by self-report, high-openness cultures include Chile, Belgium, and Bangladesh. Low-openness cultures include Ukraine and Japan (Schmitt et al., 2007). Within the United States, Asian Americans score slightly higher than whites and blacks slightly lower, with no differences between Hispanics and whites in openness to experience (Foldes et al., 2008). Higher-SES groups score higher on openness, mostly because education tends to lead to higher openness (Jonassaint et al., 2011; Rentfrow et al., 2008; Rottinghaus et al., 2002).

JOURNAL PROMPT: UNDERSTANDING YOURSELF

Think about the places you have traveled (either within your country or outside of it). Where were people the most and least extraverted, neurotic, conscientious, agreeable, and open to experience?

Openness to experience is lower in more recent generations. Scores on a standard test of creative thinking have declined (Kim, 2011). Recent college students also score lower on measures of Big Five openness than college students did in the past (Gentile et al., 2013). High school students are less likely to agree that "finding meaning and purpose in life" is important, and college students are less likely to say that "developing a meaningful philosophy of life" is important (Twenge et al., 2012b). Thus, although more recent generations seem to be more open to ethnic and cultural differences, they are less interested in abstract ideas than previous generations such as the Baby Boomers, who were known for exploring their inner worlds in the late 1960s and 1970s. It's not entirely clear why this happened; it seems to be part of a general shift toward extrinsic values (such as money, fame, and image) and away from intrinsic values (such as community feeling, affiliation, and self-acceptance).

Overall, cultural differences in the Big Five vary in their probable accuracy. Conscientiousness is apparently difficult to measure because of reference-group effects, and few studies have examined differences in openness to experience. In the future, research might explore cross-cultural differences using implicit measurement techniques, such as reaction-time studies or fMRI brain scans.

Concluding Thoughts

My (J. M. T.) neighborhood in northern San Diego has many Asian American residents, and our closest grocery store is an Asian market called Lucky Seafood. I first ventured there when the fish counter at our usual grocery store was closed due to a labor dispute. I was somewhat distressed to find that most of the fish at Lucky Seafood were whole, their dead eyes staring accusingly at me. These were, I realized, *not* the lucky seafood—they were the *un*lucky seafood who'd gotten caught. I bought the only fish that didn't look at me: the already cut salmon steaks.

A Chinese American friend later told me that Asian markets keep the fish whole because the eyes are the first to rot, and it's easier to tell that the fish is fresh. This made so much sense I wondered why my usual grocery store didn't do things this way. Then I realized I didn't care—I still didn't want the fish staring at me. I'd reached the crossroads of cultural differences: understanding a different way of doing things, seeing that both ways had advantages, and realizing I couldn't completely change my ingrained perspective as a white American raised in the middle of the country. I also realized I couldn't expect someone raised with a different perspective to change hers in an instant either.

Every baby is born with genetic predispositions to certain personality traits. But personality and self-views are also heavily determined by context—where, when, and into what family that baby is born. (Remember that the twin studies we discussed in Chapter 4 were done within one culture and one generation, so they leave out cultural differences entirely.) Those differences in context produce the

The Lucky Seafood grocery store in San Diego, where the fish are fresh, but have eyeballs.

cross-cultural, generational, ethnic, and class differences we learned about in this chapter. Of course, these are differences in averages, and people within a culture vary more than these averages. You cannot know someone's personality by knowing the culture they were raised in, so it's better not to assume you can.

But learning about the basis for cultural differences may help you better understand people who grew up in a different cultural context than you did. You might see your grandmother's perspective better if you realize the cultural context of her generation, and you might understand your friend from a different country or a different ethnicity better if you realize he might have been taught a different perspective. And in doing so, you'll understand your own culture and perspectives better, too. Culture is like that: Fish don't realize they are in water until someone takes them out—and they become the unlucky seafood.

For most people, feeling like a fish out of water is uncomfortable at first and enlightening later. Unlike the fish, we can learn to adapt to this new air even if it feels unfamiliar. Through understanding cultural differences, we gain needed perspective on our own lives as well as that of others. That makes us some very lucky seafood.

Learning Objective Summaries

LO 11.1 Describe some of the reasons why personality might vary by culture.

Cultural differences may arise from geography and other factors, and shape people through mechanisms such as cultural products (e.g., songs, TV, ads). Cultures shape people, and people shape cultures.

LO 11.2 Explain how individualistic and collectivistic cultures differ in self-views.

The cultural system of individualism favors the needs of the self over those of others and the society, whereas collectivism places the needs of others and the society first. Individualism attributes actions to the person, and collectivism to the situation. Individualism encourages more positive self-views, a view of the self as separate from others, and promotes uniqueness.

LO 11.3 Describe the cross-cultural and generational differences in the Big Five traits, and explain how researchers try to accurately assess these differences.

The reference-group effect can make cross-cultural comparisons of personality traits based on self-reports difficult. Researchers sometimes rely on perceptions of national character or behavioral measures to circumvent this. Extraversion tends to be higher in individualistic countries and those with less power distance, and neuroticism in countries with more uncertainty avoidance.

Key Terms

social norms, p. 298
culture, p. 299
socioeconomic status, p. 300
birth cohort, p. 300
generation, p. 300
cross-cultural differences,
    p. 300
cultural products, p. 300

mutual constitution model,
    p. 300
individualism, p. 302
collectivism, p. 302
attributions, p. 304
internal attribution, p. 304
external attribution, p. 304
self-enhancement, p. 306

subcultures, p. 307
collective self-esteem, p. 308
relational mobility, p. 309
reference-group effect, p. 313
perception of national
    character, p. 313
power distance, p. 315
uncertainty avoidance, p. 319

Essay Questions

1. Define culture, and discuss three factors that shape cultural norms and values.

2. Describe the mutual constitution model and how it attempts to explain the interaction of people and culture.

3. Define individualism and collectivism, and explain cultural differences between the two in terms of attribution and views of the self.

4. Choose two Big Five traits and compare and contrast the data on these traits across cultures.

Chapter 12
Personality in the Workplace

Learning Objectives

LO 12.1 Understand the careers that fit your personality.

LO 12.2 Name the traits that make people satisfied, high-performing, well compensated, and good leaders at work.

LO 12.3 Describe the traits that are used to select good employees.

LO 12.4 Evaluate the role of passion and motivation at work.

Everyone has a story about doing something dumb or silly at work. One day when I (W. K. C.) was in my early 20s and was working as a bellman at a resort hotel, we were given golf carts to drive around the property. The first thing I tried was driving the cart as fast as I could to "get air" off a hill. Unfortunately, I was outsmarted by the cart, which had a regulator on the engine that prevented it from going very fast. As soon as it hit 30 miles an hour, it stopped accelerating. No air was caught that day. Clearly, I was not the only one dumb enough to try this, which is probably why the carts had the regulator on them in the first place.

I wasn't alone in doing dumb things at work. One friend of mine worked at a Mexican fast-food restaurant. On his first day, he was supposed to cook the refried beans. He took the entire plastic container of beans and threw it in the cook pot—nobody had told him to take the beans out of the container. He quickly realized his mistake but decided just to let the plastic melt into the beans so he didn't get in trouble. He didn't, but dozens of customers ate plastic.

Plastic in food is bad enough—but what about putting stuff in food on purpose? Entire websites are filled with nasty things servers do to food, from spitting in it to—in the case of at least one group of pizza workers—allegedly doing far worse.

In each of these cases, personality is showing its face in the workplace. My desire to jump the cart was probably due to my high openness to experience. My friend's concern over getting in trouble—even if it meant feeding plastic to Mexican-food lovers—was evidence of neuroticism and avoidance motivation. The pizza workers must have been low in agreeableness—no matter what someone said to you, putting nasty things in their food just isn't nice.

As we explore in this chapter, personality matters in all aspects of work life, from choosing a career to job satisfaction. A quick word on language: The terms *workplace*, *organization*, and *company* all refer to places people work. We use them somewhat interchangeably, but they have slightly different meanings—for example, a school is an organization but not a company. However, the influences of personality are roughly the same at a nonprofit organization or a lucrative Fortune 500 company.

Let's begin with a question most every young person must face: What should I do with my life?

Vocational Fit

LO 12.1 Understand the careers that fit your personality.

What's the worst job you've ever had? One friend of ours had a great summer job: He had to wash vomit off the asphalt of an amusement park. It was especially bad under the roller coasters. At least the vomit came from his own species—a TV show called *Dirty Jobs* includes wonderful professions such as "owl vomit collector."

My (W. K. C.) worst job was working a graveyard shift taking inventory in a department store. I couldn't imagine anything more boring, but it wasn't all that difficult or gross—at least it didn't deal with stomach contents.

Some jobs can seem great—high-paying and interesting—but may not fit your personality. An introvert might find it difficult to do a service job (say, a cashier in an airport) that involves constant interaction with strangers. Individuals high in openness to experience find it challenging to work in jobs that offer little opportunity for creativity or growth. Individuals low in conscientiousness find it difficult to perform well in jobs requiring a lot of organization.

The issue often isn't whether a job is "good" or "bad"; if your personality doesn't fit the job, you are far less likely to be happy doing it. Imagine being an accountant if you didn't care about order or neatness (i.e., low conscientiousness) or being a trial lawyer if you liked pleasant relationships in which people were always happy and nice (i.e., high agreeableness). Either your personality would have to change to meet the job or you would be very unhappy and would quit and find another career.

If you're like most college students, you've probably spent a lot of time thinking about what you'd like to do for a living. You might have first considered your talents and skills—what are you good at? If you're a good listener, you might consider being a therapist. If you're good at math, you might consider engineering or the physical sciences. But your personality also plays a big role in your happiness in a profession. Perhaps you're good at listening but don't like talking to strangers, which would make being a therapist unpleasant. Perhaps you're good at math but aren't very conscientious, so engineering might not be a good choice.

It's also important to consider the full range of personality traits and not just a few. My (J. M. T.) husband once bought a book about personality and careers and completed the suggested personality questionnaire (which was based on the Myers–Briggs, the Jungian measure you learned about in Chapter 6). When we

Some jobs are not for everyone.

flipped to the back of the book with the suggested professions for his personality type, it listed things like pilot and ambulance driver. We both laughed out loud—he has to take anti-anxiety medication just to step on an airplane, so stepping into the cockpit would probably send him into a full-blown panic attack. The problem was that the Myers–Briggs doesn't measure neuroticism. With his N above average, the list of professions was way off.

Of course, taking neuroticism into account is just the beginning. People have

Watch CAREER CHOICE

WATCH
the video in
REVEL

different **vocational interests**—the type of professions that interest them. Some people think driving an ambulance sounds fun; others think it sounds terrifying. Vocational interests are one of the factors used to determine **vocational fit**—figuring out which personalities are best suited to which jobs. Everyone is happiest if people do jobs that suit their personalities. Vocation means *calling*; for example, priests in the Catholic Church are said to have a vocation because they must have a strong calling to give up so much for a career. Finding your vocation is really about finding a career path that brings you meaning—one that matches who you are.

One way to determine vocational fit is to take a vocational interest scale such as the Oregon Vocational Interest Scales (ORVIS), which you can take here. These scales don't directly measure personality, but most people probably have their personality traits in mind when they think about which jobs might suit them. Vocational interest scales can be surprisingly accurate. When I (J. M. T.) took one in high school, the guidance counselor looked over my results and said, "You'll probably end up teaching somewhere." "No way," I answered—my parents were former middle school teachers, and that sounded like no fun to me. But in the end the guidance counselor was right—I just teach adults instead of early adolescents.

vocational interests
the type of professions you are interested in

vocational fit
determining which profession fits your personality

JOURNAL PROMPT: UNDERSTANDING YOURSELF

What career paths are you interested in and why? After you take the ORVIS, see if the results align with your answers here.

TAKE
the
Questionnaire
in **REVEL**

Questionnaire 12.1 OREGON VOCATIONAL INTEREST SCALES (ORVIS)

Interactive

1. Be a professional athlete
○ Strongly Agree
○ Moderately Agree
○ Neither Agree nor Disagree
○ Moderately Disagree
○ Strongly Disagree

2. Engage in exciting adventures
○ Strongly Agree
○ Moderately Agree
○ Neither Agree nor Disagree
○ Moderately Disagree
○ Strongly Disagree

Previous   Next

leadership
on the Oregon Vocational Interest Scales, jobs involving leading and directing people

organization
on the Oregon Vocational Interest Scales, jobs involving organizing large amounts of data or materials

altruism
on the Oregon Vocational Interest Scales, jobs involving helping others

creativity
on the Oregon Vocational Interest Scales, jobs involving creating some sort of product

analysis
on the Oregon Vocational Interest Scales, jobs involving analyzing information

production
on the Oregon Vocational Interest Scales, jobs involving building or producing things

adventure
on the Oregon Vocational Interest Scales, jobs involving risky and engaging experiences

The ORVIS is designed to tell you which of eight career paths suits you best. These include:

- **Leadership**, or leading and directing people. Items include: "Be the chief executive of a large company." "Make important things happen."

- **Organization**, including organizing large amounts of data or materials. Items include: "Keep track of a company's inventory." "Plan budgets."

- **Altruism**, or helping others. Items include: "Care for sick people." "Counsel persons who need help."

- **Creativity**, including creating some sort of product. Items include: "Write short stories or novels." "Create works of art."

- **Analysis**, or analyzing information. Items include: "Solve complex puzzles." "Be a physicist."

- **Production**, including building or producing things. Items include: "Construct new buildings." "Repair cars or trucks."

- **Adventure**, having risky and engaging experiences. Items include: "Survive in the wilderness." "Be a bounty hunter."

- **Erudition**, or gaining knowledge on many topics. Items include: "Be a librarian." "Speak fluently on any subject."

The ORVIS suggests a range of careers that might fit your personality, not a specific job. That's partially because your specific career choice will also depend on your interests, skills, and education level. For example, many careers in varying fields involve adventure—say, bush pilot, ethnobotanist, special forces operator, or war correspondent. The adventure scale is based on the idea that if being a bounty hunter sounds pretty good to you, other adventure careers will too. It doesn't necessarily mean you should become an actual bounty hunter.

Most people do not fall into just one category on the ORVIS. A writer such as Ernest Hemingway might have scored high on both adventure and creativity.

A doctor such as Albert Schweitzer, who won the Nobel Prize for his humanitarian work, would score high on erudition, altruism, and leadership. A politician and scientist like Angela Merkel might score high on leadership and erudition.

Many of the ORVIS categories are correlated with the Big Five traits (see Table 12.1). So, if you are highly extraverted, a career that involves leadership might be a good idea, and a highly agreeable person might enter a helping profession such as social work or nursing.

Several other tests also measure career paths; the best known of these is Holland's **RIASEC** (1973), which measures six career types: *r*ealistic, *i*nvestigative, *a*rtistic, *s*ocial, *e*nterprising, and *c*onventional. These types overlap with the ORVIS for all but the last ORVIS category (see Table 12.1). The Holland scales and the ORVIS were written by different authors, so they differ in their categories and category labels. However, the two systems overlap more than they differ; they just use different names for the same types of careers (for example, "leadership" on the ORVIS equates to "enterprising" on the Holland).

Ernest Hemingway was both creative and an adventurer.

Table 12.1 The ORVIS Categories, Typical Careers, Big Five Personality Correlates, and Related Holland Scales

ORVIS Interest	Career Ideas	Big Five Correlates	Holland Scale
Leadership	Teacher, manager, doctor	Extraversion	Enterprising
Organization	Inventory manager, project manager, budget director	Conscientiousness	Conventional
Altruism	Nurse, social worker, therapist	Agreeableness	Social
Creativity	Artist, writer, graphic designer	Openness to experience	Artistic

Table 12.1 (Continued)

ORVIS Interest	Career Ideas	Big Five Correlates	Holland Scale
Analysis	Financial analyst, chemist, insurance actuary	Openness to experience	Investigative
Production	Contractor, master plumber, mechanic	None	Realistic
Adventure	Outdoor guide, bounty hunter, military contractor	None	Realistic
Erudition	Librarian, college professor, antiques dealer	Openness to experience	No equivalent

The Science of Personality CORRELATION TABLES: MATCHING PERSONALITIES AND CAREERS

EXPLORE in REVEL →

As you've learned, psychologists can help people choose careers by looking at how they respond to career preference measures such as the ORVIS, which you took. The ORVIS scales correlate with personality measures such as the Big Five.

Take your turn playing personality scientist to see if these correlations replicate in the norm sample. Studies sometimes find different results based on the sample or other factors; plus, we'll see how big the correlations really are. This will show us what types of personalities are best suited for certain jobs – something you might be thinking about as you finish college.

1 of 6   Previous   Next

erudition
on the Oregon Vocational Interest Scales, jobs involving gaining knowledge on many topics

RIASEC
the job types on the Strong–Campbell Interest Inventory: realistic, investigative, artistic, social, enterprising, and conventional

The Role of Personality in Getting the Job Done

LO 12.2 **Name the traits that make people satisfied, high-performing, well compensated, and good leaders at work.**

Imagine someone who is always early, does his work on time, and is always cheerful and happy while at work. This "perfect worker" probably doesn't exist, but thinking about the ideal personality for work illustrates that some personality traits make it easier to do a good job. Others make it more likely that you'll be happy at work or will be paid more. In this section we cover how personality predicts four job outcomes: job satisfaction, job performance, compensation (pay), and leadership.

Job Satisfaction: What Traits Make You Happy at Work?

Think about your last shift at work: Were you happy? In general, do you like your job? **Job satisfaction** means what it sounds like—how satisfied you are with your job (Judge & Kammeyer-Mueller, 2012). Job satisfaction has been studied extensively because researchers assume that satisfied employees are high-performing employees (Hoppock, 1935). However, research has shown the two are positively correlated, but more weakly than you'd expect (Judge et al., 2001). Job satisfaction is partially determined by the job itself. Most people would rather be a lifeguard on a Southern California beach than work construction during a hot, humid Georgia summer. This is also a matter of fit: Some people will like some jobs better than others.

job satisfaction
how satisfied you are with your job

To illustrate how the Big Five traits relate to job satisfaction, let's say you are working in a small office at a university library along with five other students with different personalities. Nick, who runs the book scanner, is highly neurotic. He is often anxious at work, sometimes sad, and occasionally becomes irritable, snapping at patrons and coworkers. Eduardo, who pushes the book trolley around, is highly extraverted. He is energetic and has no problem interacting with all the people he meets while moving the trolley through the library. Olivia, who does a lot of computer entry, is highly open to experience. She is intellectually curious and interested in art and fantasy. Andrew, who mans the front desk, is highly agreeable. He gets along well with most of the staff and patrons. Finally, Corrine, who also runs the book scanner, is highly conscientious. She works hard, is dutiful, and is careful in her work.

Being a lifeguard is hard work, but the office is nice.

Of these five, who do you think will be the most satisfied and who the least satisfied? On average, conscientious Corrine will be the most satisfied; she will find meaning just doing her job. Extraverted Eduardo and agreeable Andrew will also be above average in their job satisfaction because they get to interact with and help people in their jobs. Neurotic Nick, though, will probably be the least satisfied; he is not a happy or satisfied person in general, and that spreads to his work (Judge et al., 1998). Olivia's satisfaction will depend on the job and specific

work. If the computer entry she's doing is too routine and mundane, she might be less satisfied. If her job was instead highly creative, her openness might be more satisfied. These different situations average out when you consider all jobs, which is probably why openness to experience is not related to job satisfaction overall (Judge et al., 2002b).

Job Performance: What Traits Make for a Good Worker?

You've already learned what your personality says about what types of careers might be a good fit for you. But are some personality traits useful in most professions? In other words, are some personality traits a good fit for almost any job?

The short answer is yes: Conscientiousness is the best predictor of work performance. Someone who shows up on time and does the job responsibly is usually a great employee, and that's the essence of conscientiousness (Barrick et al., 2003). (If you scored low in conscientiousness and wonder about your future job prospects, go to the end of Chapter 15 for tips on how to increase your conscientiousness. Also recall from Chapter 9 that your conscientiousness will rise once you start a steady job.) Being low in neuroticism—not worrying too much or getting angry too easily—is also key. (Chapters 14 and 15 discuss ways to lower neuroticism.)

The other three Big Five traits—agreeableness, extraversion, and openness to experience—are not correlated with job performance overall but can be important in certain situations (Barrick et al., 2003; Judge et al., 2006). If it's important to speak your mind during meetings in a particular job, for example, extraversion would lead to better performance (LePine & VanDyne, 2001). Openness to experience is useful for jobs requiring creativity but could lead to dissatisfaction and poor performance in jobs that involve lots of routine. Being highly open to experience and running the fry machine at McDonald's is a recipe for dissatisfaction.

Extraversion is also useful for sales jobs—but not too much extraversion. In one study, call center workers who were moderately extraverted sold the most (Grant, 2013). Someone with too little extraversion doesn't push for the sale, but someone with too much extraversion comes on too strong. Overall, conscientiousness is more important than extraversion for success in sales (Furnham & Fudge, 2008; Stewart, 1996; Yang et al., 2011).

One basic requirement for good work performance is showing up when you should. Once again, conscientious people are less likely to miss work. Surprisingly, highly extraverted people are actually more likely to be absent, perhaps because staying up late and going to parties is not conducive to getting to work on time the next morning (Judge et al., 1997).

organizational citizenship behavior (OCB)
doing positive things for the organization beyond a defined job

Being a good colleague is also important. That often includes doing positive things for the organization beyond a defined job, such as organizing the holiday party or leading the company softball team. This is known as **organizational citizenship behavior (OCB)** (Bateman & Organ, 1983; Organ & Ryan, 1995).

People who engage in OCBs are more conscientious and agreeable. Agreeable people are nice, interpersonally kind, and caring, so organizational citizenship comes naturally to them (see, for example, Organ & Lingl, 1995). Somewhat surprisingly, openness to experience is also connected to OCB (Chiaburu et al., 2011). Highly open people may see areas that need change and improvement and then take the time to make those changes. Extraversion, however, is not related to OCBs on average (Chiaburu et al., 2013).

The opposite of OCB is **counterproductive workplace behavior (CWB)** (Dalal, 2005). These include things people shouldn't do at work but do anyway, such as stealing, bullying, harassment, aggression toward others, and abusing alcohol or drugs at work (Fox et al., 2001; Martinko et al., 2002). If you've ever seen a coworker come in drunk or high, heard someone spread unfounded rumors about a colleague, or witnessed a boss yelling at an employee, you've experienced CWB.

counterproductive workplace behavior (CWB)
unethical, illegal, or unwise workplace behaviors such as stealing and bullying

In the cult classic movie *Office Space*, a group of employees facing downsizing invent a convoluted plan to steal money from the company. They should have been caught, but they are spared when a perpetually disgruntled employee, Milton, commits the ultimate CWB: burning down the building. What type of personality is most likely to be like Milton, perpetually upset about his itinerant stapler and mumbling about workplace arson? People low in conscientiousness and low in agreeableness are the most likely to engage in CWB; in other words, people who behave badly at work are often irresponsible, lazy, careless, and emotionally callous (Salgado, 2002). Narcissism also predicts CWBs, especially when a narcissist thinks the organization is taking advantage of him (Michel & Bowling, 2012; Penney & Spector, 2002).

Milton from *Office Space*: counterproductive workplace behaviors in action.

Compensation: What Traits Predict High Pay?

Now let's get to the good stuff: Which personality types make more money? The answers might surprise you.

We start with the unsurprising results: High conscientiousness and low neuroticism predict higher pay. In other words, emotionally stable people who work hard are going to do well. Extraverts also make more money, probably because extraverted people are goal oriented and assert themselves (Spurk & Abele, 2011).

The real surprise is agreeableness: Agreeable people make *less* money (Spurk & Abele, 2011). So people who are callous, self-serving, and immodest get paid more than people who are kind, caring, and humble. This "nice guys finish last" phenomenon is truer for men than for women; across three large surveys low agreeable men make $9,772 a year more than high agreeable men (an 18.3% difference), but low agreeable women made "only" $1,828 more than high agreeable women, a 5.5% difference (Judge et al., 2012).

Then again, maybe this isn't such a surprise. Disagreeable people may find it easier to ask for a raise. They may also be drawn to high-paying, cutthroat professions such as trial lawyer or investment banker. Although many wealthy people are involved in philanthropy, the classic stereotype of the fat-cat rich guy doesn't usually include kindness and caring. The assumption is he had to step on a few other people on his way up the ladder.

George Washington was highly conscientious.

Leadership: What Personality Traits Make for a Good Leader?

If you listen to people talking about the workplace, you'll often hear statements such as "What we need is better leadership," "There's a real lack of leadership at that company," or "They've done well because they have great leadership."

Almost all organizations have leaders such as CEOs, military generals, principals, or university department heads. Leadership has been defined as the way a leader "influences a group of individuals to achieve a common goal" (Northouse, 2012, p. 6).

Let's start with leaders at the highest levels: U.S. presidents. One study asked presidential biographers to rate the president they wrote about on the Big Five (Rubenzer et al., 2000). As you'd expect, the average U.S. president scores high in conscientiousness—a full standard deviation higher than average. U.S. presidents are about average in neuroticism—they are not necessarily cool customers, but they are not particularly anxious or depressed, either.

Presidents are higher than average in extraversion, consistent with the glad-handing necessary for successful campaigning. But, just like the men who make a lot of money, presidents are lower in agreeableness. The average personality of a president is driven and socially outgoing but not so nice or straightforward.

Finally, U.S. presidents are low in openness to experience; on average, they are not curious or intellectual. But those who *were* high in openness were more likely to be considered great leaders (Rubenzer et al., 2000; see Figure 12.1). This pattern of high openness to experience appears in many fields among **transformational leaders**—those who change their organizations in large and fundamental ways rather than simply managing them (Judge & Bono, 2000; Judge & Piccolo, 2004). For example, Abraham Lincoln was rated high in openness (Rubenzer et al., 2000), and he transformed the United States with his leadership during the Civil War.

transformational leader

leaders who change their organizations in large and fundamental ways rather than simply managing the organization

Personality's Past

Consideration and Initiation in Leadership

Before the 1940s, the most common ideas about leadership focused on the person's traits: Great people make great leaders. Beginning in the 1940s, however, researchers then began to consider specific behaviors and how they related to leadership.

A focal point of this research was Ohio State University, where researchers like Ralph Stogdill (1950) studied a range of processes associated with leadership. This research focused on two important sets of leader behaviors. The first was consideration, or being more personal, empathic and approachable. The second, initiating structure, involved being more task-focused and directive. A considerate leader cares for people; a leader high in initiating structure focuses on getting the job done.

Decades later, research shows that both these approaches to leadership can lead to positive outcomes. Consideration leads to more employee satisfaction, and initiating structure leads to higher levels of organizational performance (Judge et al., 2004).

But what about personality traits? Does this research mean that they do not matter? No. Both of these aspects of leadership are linked to the Big Five traits of conscientiousness and extraversion. What sets them apart is agreeableness. Consideration is associated positively with leader agreeableness and initiating structure is not (Derue et al., 2011).

Overall, this line of research makes it clear that specific patterns of leader behavior together with leader personality predict leadership performance. The simple formula, great people make great leaders, is not correct.

Steve Jobs, whom we discussed in Chapter 1, was a quintessential transformational leader high in openness to experience. When he returned to Apple in the late 1990s, he radically changed Apple's product strategies, focusing on products that changed the landscape of technology, music, and retail. Jobs was also known for his creativity, his wide-ranging interests, and his interest in questioning established ideas—all harbingers of openness (Issacson, 2011).

Figure 12.1 Presidential Personality

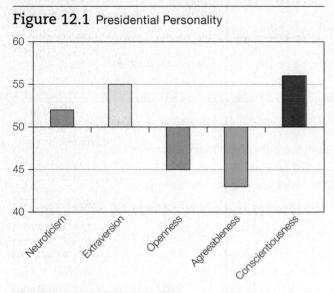

SOURCE: Based on Rubenzer et al. (2000).

NOTE: Scores above 50 are above average; scores below 50 are below average.

emergent leadership

the ability to rise as a leader in an organization

effective leadership

the ability to be a successful leader once in a management or leadership role

dominance

intimidating others to gain social status

prestige

rising to the top based on ability, talent, or moral force

In general, leadership involves two different skills: **emergent leadership**, or the ability to become a leader in an organization, and **effective leadership**, or the ability to be a successful leader once you have the job (Judge et al., 2002a). For example, Emmet does all the right things to get promoted: He stays late, flatters his boss, and is not shy about making his case for why he deserves a promotion. He clearly has the skills for becoming or emerging as a leader, but maybe not an effective leader. In contrast, Effie didn't promote herself much and was lucky to get a leadership position as a manager in her firm, but once she got the job, she did it well, building good relationships with her employees. She doesn't have good emergent leader skills, but has the skills needed to be an effective leader. Some people are skilled at both emergent and effective leadership, but others are good at one and not the other. Most people can think of someone who was very good at getting promoted (emergent leadership) but not very good at actually leading people (effective leadership).

Consistent with that observation, emergent leaders and effective leaders have some key personality similarities but also differences. Both emergent and effective leaders are high in extraversion, openness to experience, and conscientiousness and low on neuroticism (Judge et al., 2002a). As Figure 12.2 shows, the main difference is in agreeableness—emergent leaders are just average in agreeableness, but effective leaders are high. In other words, the sharp elbows that allow people to fight their way to the top may hinder their ability to perform there. For example, narcissists—who are low in agreeableness and high in extraversion—tend to emerge as leaders when researchers ask groups of students to work together in lab studies (Brunell et al., 2008). But after a group has met a few times, the rest of the group comes to dislike the narcissistic leader—mostly because the leader doesn't care about anyone except herself (Rosenthal & Pittinsky, 2006). In other words, narcissists are emergent leaders but not necessarily effective leaders. On the TV show *The Office*, Dwight is a skilled emergent leader; he becomes his boss's buddy and eventually gets to fulfill his dream of becoming a manager. But he is too obsessed with petty power struggles to become an effective leader.

Leadership emergence can take two different forms: **dominance** and **prestige**. Dominance involves intimidating others to gain social status.

Dominance can involve many different behaviors, including emotional bullying (such as the popular girls in the movie *Mean Girls*); ruthlessness, such as a mob boss who rules using the threat of violence; or personal force, like that exhibited by Donald Trump ("You're fired!"). Prestige, however, involves rising to the top based on ability, talent, or moral force. Martin Luther King, Jr. and Pope Francis are examples of prestigious leaders—they are admired but not feared. Overall, dominance is pushing your way to the top, and prestige is being lifted to the top (Cheng et al., 2010, 2013). Some leaders, such as Steve Jobs, exhibit both dominance and prestige—his anger and emotion led people to fear him, but he was also admired for his vision and talent.

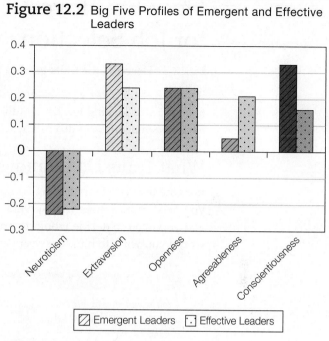

Figure 12.2 Big Five Profiles of Emergent and Effective Leaders

Emergent Leaders   Effective Leaders

SOURCE: Based on Judge et al. (2002).

Dominant and prestigious leaders differ primarily in agreeableness, with dominant leaders low in agreeableness and prestigious leaders high in agreeableness (Cheng et al., 2010). In the medieval-times HBO series *Game of Thrones*, Ned Stark, a prestigious leader, and Joffrey Baratheon, a dominant leader, jockeyed for power. Baratheon was willing to do whatever it took to gain power, including falsely accusing and then decapitating Stark. As this example shows, low agreeableness and dominant leadership are also linked to poor ethics.

JOURNAL PROMPT: UNDERSTANDING YOURSELF

What personality traits do you possess that might strengthen your leadership ability? Which of your personality traits might weaken your leadership ability?

In sum, personality plays an important role in leadership, but the story is not simple. Conscientiousness seems to be the most important trait. Extraversion is generally good. Agreeableness, however, can go either way. Agreeableness helps leaders be effective and admired. However, agreeableness can hinder people from emerging as leaders, especially if the situation favors dominance over prestige. It's a bad news/good news story: Some people get to be the boss because they're jerks, but the good bosses are the nicer ones.

How Employers Use Personality for Job Selection

LO 12.3 Describe the traits that are used to select good employees.

If you've applied for a job before, you've probably wondered what the hiring manager was looking for. Beyond the education and skills required for the job, what personal qualities do employers want?

What Traits Do Employers Look For?

Imagine that you're managing an upscale restaurant in a university town and you need to hire three new servers. More than 50 people applied for the job, and you need to decide whom to bring in for an interview. What information would you want to have to select your employees?

> **JOURNAL PROMPT: UNDERSTANDING YOURSELF**
>
> If you were hiring an applicant for an entry-level job, which Big Five trait would you place the most value in? Why?

If you are like many managers, the most important quality you want in an employee is someone who shows up on time, does the job responsibly, and tries not to screw up—in other words, someone high in conscientiousness. Sure enough, conscientiousness is the most important personality trait for selecting an employee (Barrick et al., 2001). Imagine trying to manage a slacker who shows up late to his shift, messes up orders, is sloppy with the food, and leaves early so he can catch a band playing downtown. This is a manager's nightmare.

Managers also have trouble with people who are irritable, moody, and depressed. Employees who break down in tears when a customer gets upset are problematic, as are those who lash out at other employees. Drama should occur on reality television, not at work. You would rather have employees who are, for the most part, emotionally calm and stable—in other words, low in neuroticism (Barrick et al., 2001).

Finally, you probably want a server who is nice, friendly, and kind—and thus high in agreeableness. Agreeableness is especially important for jobs that require face-to-face interactions with others such as restaurant server (Mount et al., 1998). Agreeableness might even pay off directly—diners leave bigger tips when waitresses draw a happy face on the check (now you know why they do that; Rind & Bordia, 1996). Extraversion and openness to experience are not as important in job selection (Barrick et al., 2001), mostly because they vary so much from one job to another.

To see a similar pattern from a completely different line of work, consider a recent study that analyzed the Big Five scores of U.S. astronauts since the 1980s

What if none of your employees were agreeable?

(Musson & Keeton, 2011; see Figure 12.3). Astronauts have very low levels of neuroticism, which is useful when your job involves being shot into outer space where all sorts of things can go wrong and nobody can fix it but you. (Just think about how someone high in neuroticism might react to being launched into space!) Astronauts are also high in conscientiousness. This is good when missing an item in the countdown might mean depressurization. They also have fairly high levels of agreeableness—nice to have when you're stuck in a small spacecraft with several other people. So from restaurant server to astronaut, being high in conscientiousness, low in neuroticism, and high in agreeableness is better.

The Use of Personality Tests

Many laws and regulations guide the use of personality testing in jobs. These vary from one place to another, but they have some general themes. For example, personality tests used should be designed for

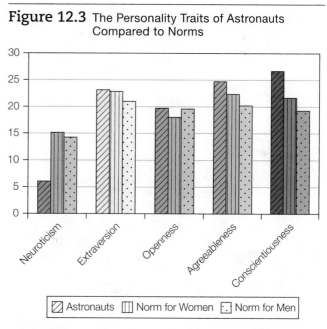

Figure 12.3 The Personality Traits of Astronauts Compared to Norms

Legend: ▨ Astronauts ▥ Norm for Women ⋮ Norm for Men

SOURCE: Based on Musson and Keeton (2011).

normal (not clinical) populations, the tests should not be inherently discriminatory, and they should be clearly related to the job outcomes (U.S. Department of Labor, 2006). Furthermore, in this text, we are focusing on broad factors of the Big Five, such as conscientiousness, to simplify our description. Most managers or human resource professionals would focus on more specific traits or subfacets, perhaps relying on personality measures designed to measure the traits needed for a specific job.

What About People Who Lie on Personality Tests?

slight image creation
a small amount of positive self-presentation during a job search

extensive image creation
a major amount of positive self-presentation during a job search

fake good
personality questionnaire responses putting the self in a positive light

So, you might be thinking, this is all well and good, but maybe job applicants will just lie on questionnaires and in interviews and make themselves look higher in conscientiousness than they actually are. And what if they lie on their résumé, too? This can make it a challenge to pick a good employee.

Résumés and job interviews suffer from a fair amount of creative embellishment. Knowing enough Spanish to get by on a beach trip to Mexico—*Donde podemos surfear?*—will appear on the résumé as "fluent in Spanish." In one recent study using college students, researchers found that people engage in a wide range of faking—everything from **slight image creation** (saying you have past server experience, even though you'd only served popcorn at a movie theater) to **extensive image creation** (saying you have experience with a new software program when you'd never heard of it before). A huge percentage of people report slight image creation (85–99%), and a surprisingly large number engage in extensive image creation (65–92%) (Levashina & Campion, 2007).

Given this willingness of potential employees to bend the truth—and sometimes even break it—on résumés and in interviews, perhaps job candidates will also **fake good** (see Chapter 2) on personality tests used in employee selection. Somewhat surprisingly, however, trying to fake a personality test doesn't have a major impact on its effectiveness for employee selection, at least for the Big Five (Ones et al., 2007). Applicants may not always realize what personality tests are measuring or which traits would be a good fit for the job. So even if they are trying to fake, they might not do a very good job of it.

Not everyone is honest on résumés.

Another danger is that some personality types come off well in interviews even though they often don't make good employees in the long run. For example, narcissists often appear knowledgeable and confident during interviews, making them more likely to get hired (Campbell et al., 2011; Paulhus et al., 2013). Yet, once

"Everything on your resume is true ... right?"

on the job, narcissistic people don't work well with others and don't take responsibility for their mistakes. Sometimes it's best not to go with your first impression about a job candidate and instead look at more objective data.

Finding Passion at Work

LO 12.4   Evaluate the role of passion and motivation at work.

Warren Buffett, one of the wealthiest men in America, says that he "tap dances to work." He has enough money to do anything he wants, yet he has no plans to stop working even though he's in his 80s. He tells young people to figure out what they would do if they didn't need the money, and then do that: "Find your passion. I was very, very lucky to find it when I was seven or eight years old. . . . And you can't guarantee you'll find it in your first job out. But I always tell college students . . . 'Take the job you would take if you were independently wealthy. You're going to do well at it.'" (Cripen, 2012). People who are passionate about their work will often say, "I have never worked a day in my life" or "I love getting up in the morning." And they can't imagine retiring.

Buffett is not alone in giving this advice. Students at Sarah Lawrence College often came to Joseph Campbell—a professor known for his work on mythology—for advice about the career they should pursue. He told them to do what brought them joy and what inspired them. It's difficult to know what the best ways to make money will be in 10 or 20 years, he argued, but you can more easily figure out what brings you joy. In other words, he says, follow your bliss (Campbell & Kudler, 2004).

Personality research lends support to the idea that finding joy in work can have positive outcomes for both individuals and their organizations. One important area of research has been on the experience of flow. As we discussed in Chapter 7, flow occurs when our challenges match our abilities and we become deeply engaged in what we are doing (Csikszentmihalyi, 1997). Flow is common in sports (being "in the zone"), but it is also found in work. For example, a heart surgeon might experience flow while deeply engaged in a surgery (Csikszentmihalyi, 1997).

Joseph Campbell's advice to his students.

In one study, researchers measured teachers' flow state experiences and what contributed to them. As you might expect, supportive work environments encouraged flow. In addition, teachers who experienced flow eventually created better work environments (Salanova et al., 2006).

That suggests that the joy people experience at work can create a better work environment for others.

Joy and bliss at work is also known as *intrinsic motivation* (Ryan & Deci, 2000). As we discussed in Chapter 7, intrinsic motivation is based on joy—think about the word en*joy*ment, for example. In contrast, *extrinsic motivation* is based on external motivators, such as money or fear of punishment (Gagné & Deci, 2005).

amotivation
a state of no
motivation

Sometimes people are not motivated by anything—that's called **amotivation**. Imagine a slacker who just doesn't care one way or the other about his job—fire him, reward him, he couldn't care less. For example, Peter, the main character in *Office Space*, is hypnotized to relax and never snaps out of it. He decides at that point to do nothing—pure amotivation. The joke is that he keeps getting promoted for being a relaxed slacker who wears flip-flops to work and guts fish on the desk in his cubicle.

Extrinsic motivation at work includes all of the motivators that don't involve true passion for the work, including reward and punishment (such as money or not getting fired). Somewhere in between fully extrinsic motivation (like the threat of getting fired) and pure intrinsic motivation are internalized motives such as maintaining self-esteem, meeting goals, and fulfilling core values. Pure intrinsic motivation involves true passion and joy in doing a job. For example, if a nurse in the cancer unit at a hospital was fully intrinsically motivated, she would say she does her job because she loves it. It is tough, and not always fun, but she wakes up every day ready to go to work and dig right in (Gagné & Deci, 2005). Intrinsic motivation is also the experience Warren Buffett was referring to when he talked about tap dancing to work. Key outcomes such as job satisfaction usually increase when people are intrinsically motivated instead of extrinsically motivated (Gagné & Deci, 2005).

JOURNAL PROMPT: UNDERSTANDING YOURSELF

What drives you to be your most productive at work—getting rewarded, fear of being punished, or simply enjoying what you're doing?

However, people are often motivated in multiple ways from day to day in their jobs. I (W. K. C.), for example, love my work and have a high level of intrinsic motivation. But sometimes I do things I don't want to do—like paperwork—simply because I don't want to get chided or punished (fully extrinsic). Sometimes I do things that don't bring me joy (say, serve on a committee to create a new program of study) because I think they are important (this is between extrinsic and intrinsic). And sometimes I sit back at my desk and fall asleep listening to the Van Morrison channel on Pandora (amotivation). Overall, a combination of different types of motivation, especially if they contain some intrinsic motivation, can be positive in the workplace (Moran et al., 2012).

The bottom line is that the more you can enjoy your work, and the more that your work aligns with who you are as a person, the more satisfied and productive you will be. To put it bluntly, some jobs always suck, and parts of all jobs suck. That's life. The goal is to keep increasing the joy and decreasing the negativity. Having passion for your work will help you to do that.

Concluding Thoughts

People often have to take any job they can get to support themselves and their families—even if that means installing asphalt roofing in the humid summer or collecting owl vomit. But if you are fortunate enough to be able to select a career, the science of personality has some useful insights.

First, your personality can tell you a lot about careers you're likely to enjoy. Use your scores on the Big Five and the ORVIS to consider the types of careers that might be a good fit for you. Second, ponder your level of conscientiousness because it's by far the best predictor of success at work. As we discuss in Chapters 14 and 15, it's possible to raise your level of conscientiousness if you're not happy with it. Just don't take it so far that you become a micromanager or perfectionist unable to make good decisions for fear of not making perfect decisions. Neuroticism can also cause problems at work, but again, it can be managed and even lowered (see Chapters 14 and 15).

Agreeableness is trickier. Being low in agreeableness might help you earn more money and become a leader, but it may not help you actually be a good leader. If you're lucky enough to find yourself in a leadership position, it's probably worth taking a step back and thinking about the feelings of others. Good leaders can take their employees' perspective and know what works for them. On the other hand, if you're high in agreeableness, put aside your desire to be nice and ask for a raise (don't be a total jerk about it, of course, but be assertive). And especially if you are kind by nature, fight for that leadership role because your personality will serve you—and the people who work for you—very well once you're there.

Perhaps most important, try to "follow your bliss." If you are passionate about your work, odds are you will be more successful than if you do something you dislike in the hopes you'll make a buck somewhere down the line. Of course, a lot of people are passionate about acting or sports—where very few people can make a living—and not as many are passionate about accounting or engineering, which often have many well-paying jobs. But if you think about what motivates you the most, and what you love, chances are you can get paid for doing it in one way or another. Getting up every day excited to get to work is one of life's most precious gifts.

Learning Objective Summaries

LO 12.1 Understand the careers that fit your personality.

Different people's personalities fit with different careers, known as vocational fit or vocational interest. This is often measured with scales such as the Oregon Vocational Interest Scales (ORVIS).

LO 12.2 Name the traits that make people satisfied, high-performing, well compensated, and good leaders at work.

High conscientiousness and low neuroticism are the Big Five traits most related to job performance and satisfaction. Agreeableness, extraversion, and openness to experience can be important in certain situations, such as extraversion to leadership and (low) agreeableness to achieving a higher salary.

LO 12.3 Describe the traits that are used to select good employees.

Job candidates are often selected on the Big Five traits of conscientiousness, (low) neuroticism, and agreeableness. Other traits are relevant in more specific contexts.

LO 12.4 Evaluate the role of passion and motivation at work.

Greater passion as well as more intrinsic motivation are predictors of workplace satisfaction and workplace performance.

Key Terms

vocational interests, p. 327
vocational fit, p. 327
leadership, p. 328
organization, p. 328
altruism, p. 328
creativity, p. 328
analysis, p. 328
production, p. 328
adventure, p. 328

erudition, p. 330
RIASEC, p. 330
job satisfaction, p. 331
organizational citizenship behavior (OCB), p. 332
counterproductive workplace behavior (CWB), p. 333
transformational leader, p. 335
emergent leadership, p. 336

effective leadership, p. 336
dominance, p. 336
prestige, p. 336
slight image creation, p. 340
extensive image creation, p. 340
fake good, p. 340
amotivation, p. 342

Essay Questions

1. Discuss ways you can better assess what careers might be best for you.
2. How are each of the Big Five traits related to work performance?
3. Name the types of motivation involved in workplace performance and satisfaction, and what outcomes tend to result from each.

Chapter 13
Personality and Relationships

Learning Objectives

LO 13.1 Name the three main types of attachment and explain how they impact adult relationships.

LO 13.2 Describe the effect of Big Five traits on long-term relationships.

LO 13.3 Describe how compassion, empathy, and self-control can improve relationships.

LO 13.4 Describe the dark triad and its effects on relationships.

LO 13.5 List the key benefits of online dating and describe how personality is expressed on social media.

Taylor Swift has made a career out of singing about her relationships—none of which seem to work out.

When Taylor Swift and Jake Gyllenhaal first started dating, everything seemed great. The two had a cozy Thanksgiving together in New York City, walking down the street with their arms around each other, bundled up against the chill. Taylor even introduced Jake to her parents at her house in Nashville. But it was not to be: A few months later, Taylor wrote a song titled "We Are Never Ever Getting Back Together."

What went wrong? We will likely never know the details, but clearly Taylor and Jake weren't compatible as romantic partners in the long term.

For most people, finding a compatible romantic partner and keeping that relationship going is a central life goal. You likely want someone who you're physically attracted to, who shares your beliefs and values, and who loves you back. Then there are the more elusive qualities: Someone you click with, who is fun to be around, who's reliable, and who's attached to you—but not too attached.

That's where personality comes in. Personalities are central to relationships. Your personality makes a difference in whom you are attracted to—and who is attracted to you. Your partner's personality can result in a relationship that ranges from satisfying and meaningful to so rocky and dramatic that it deserves its own country song. Your personality may also predict the type of person you like in a friend and how many friends you have on Facebook.

In this chapter, we explore all of these issues. Our primary focus is on romantic relationships, such as dating and marriage, but we will also explore relationships with parents (as those influence later romantic relationships) and relationships with friends. To do this, we draw on four models of personality: attachment style, the Big Five, and the contrast between self-control, empathy, and compassion and darker, more negative personality traits. These are not the only personality variables that matter in relationships, of course, but they provide a good overview of the current research in the area. We will also try to answer the age-old question of compatibility—Do opposites attract, or are you better off with someone similar? And we will also explore how new technologies such as dating websites and social networking sites are leading to cultural changes in how people see relationships.

Attachment: The Building Blocks of Relationships

LO 13.1 **Name the three main types of attachment and explain how they impact adult relationships.**

Most people's first relationships are with their parents. These early relationships set the stage for later relationships; what we learn about relationships as children carries into our adult relationships with friends, spouses, and our own children. Attachment theory (Bowlby, 1969) explores these early experiences and how they shape our personalities and adult relationships. Before we get started, take this questionnaire below on your experiences in close relationships.

Questionnaire 13.1 EXPERIENCES IN CLOSE RELATIONSHIPS SCALE

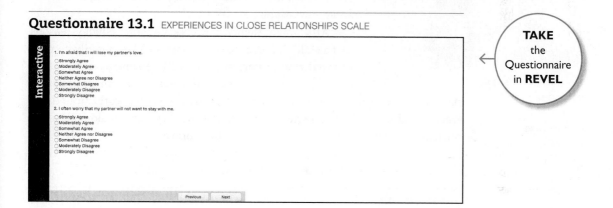

Interactive

1. I'm afraid that I will lose my partner's love.
   ○ Strongly Agree
   ○ Moderately Agree
   ○ Somewhat Agree
   ○ Neither Agree nor Disagree
   ○ Somewhat Disagree
   ○ Moderately Disagree
   ○ Strongly Disagree

2. I often worry that my partner will not want to stay with me.
   ○ Strongly Agree
   ○ Moderately Agree
   ○ Somewhat Agree
   ○ Neither Agree nor Disagree
   ○ Somewhat Disagree
   ○ Moderately Disagree
   ○ Strongly Disagree

Previous   Next

TAKE the Questionnaire in **REVEL**

Childhood Attachment

When they arrived at the playground, Liam's mother put him down and let go of his hand. He was nervous at first, only slowly wandering over to climb on the jungle gym. But after his first few times down the slide, he was off running around with the other kids. His mom stood at the edge of the playground watching, and occasionally Liam glanced back at her to see if she was still there. Suddenly, Liam trips and bumps his head into the side of the slide. He is scared and screams for his mother, who runs over to take care of him. He calms down, wipes away his tears, and then goes off to play with the other kids again.

This story, typical of interactions between young children and their parents, involves the core features of **attachment**, the link between a child and her primary **caregiver**, the person primarily responsible for the care of a child (Bowlby, 1969).

attachment
the link between a child and his or her primary caregiver

caregiver
the individual, often a parent, who cares for the child

Attachment starts at a young age.

secure base
the caregiver's role as a place of safety for the child

The caregiver is a **secure base** for the child, providing security and protection so she can go off and explore her world (Ainsworth & Bell, 1970). Think of the caregiver's secure base like a harbor and the child like a boat. The boat (child) will go out during the day to the open sea (exploration) but will return to the harbor (secure base) during a storm. The security of the port makes it possible for the boats to go out to sea.

In our example from the playground, Liam felt secure in his relationship with his mother, which allowed him to play and explore on his own at the playground. This same link between attachment and exploration carries through to adulthood (Elliot & Reis, 2003). In one study, students thought about someone who made them feel either secure or insecure. Those who thought of a secure relationship scored higher on the Exploration index (Green & Campbell, 2000). Take the Exploration Index yourself, below, to see how adventurous you are.

Attachment theory, developed by John Bowlby, reasons that a child's attachment experiences will eventually become **internalized**, or part of the child's personality as the child develops. If the caregiver is emotionally warm and reliable, the child will come to understand relationships, and therefore the world around her, as stable and secure; if the caregiver is cold and unsupportive, the child will have a much more negative view of relationships and the world around her (Bowbly, 1990).

TAKE
the
Questionnaire
in REVEL

→

Questionnaire 13.2 EXPLORATION INDEX

Interactive

1. If I had the time and money, I would love to travel overseas this summer.

○ Strongly Agree
○ Moderately Agree
○ Somewhat Agree
○ Neither Agree nor Disagree
○ Somewhat Disagree
○ Moderately Disagree
○ Strongly Disagree

2. I would take a class that is totally unrelated to my major just because it interests me.

○ Strongly Agree
○ Moderately Agree
○ Somewhat Agree
○ Neither Agree nor Disagree
○ Somewhat Disagree
○ Moderately Disagree
○ Strongly Disagree

Previous   Next

attachment theory
a theory specifying that a child's attachment experiences will eventually become a part of the child's personality

internalized
become a stable part of the personality

Bowlby believed that attachment applied not just to humans but to all mammals. Another researcher, Harry Harlow, demonstrated this rather dramatically using rhesus monkeys. In a famous set of experiments, monkeys were raised with "caregivers" who were just wire shells with faces. In some cases, these "mothers" were covered in a warm cloth; in others, they were just left as wire. The monkeys with wire mothers had significant social problems. When put in new situations, they would often act aggressively, or they would sit in the corner of the cage and rock back and forth. Those with cloth mothers were better adjusted because they derived a sense of security and warmth from the cloth (Harlow, 1959).

Humans are, fortunately, never raised by wire mothers. However, some children endure horrific upbringings, growing up with abusive parents or parents disabled by severe psychiatric disorders, alcoholism, or other problems. The infamous orphanages in Romania left babies alone for long periods of time, providing them with food but no comfort. Many of these children developed attachment disorders (Morison & Ellwood, 2000).

Even in the normal ranges of parenting, children learn to see the world differently depending on the relationship they develop with their parents. Bowlby labeled these learned tendencies **attachment styles**.

A baby monkey showing attachment to the cloth mother in Harlow's study.

Each attachment style suits a particular environment and helps the child survive. There are three primary attachment styles: secure, anxious, and avoidant. (Thus, both anxious and avoidant attachment are sometimes labeled "insecure" attachment). The attachment styles questionnaire you took had scales for anxious and avoidant attachment; someone who scores low on both has secure attachment. **Secure attachment** develops when a child's caregiver is a source of comfort and security; the child learns to trust others. When he feels scared, he knows the caregiver will provide help and comfort. Thus, the child feels ready to explore the environment. Most research shows that a secure attachment style is associated with the best psychological outcomes. That said, children develop the attachment style that is best for their particular situation. For example, being securely attached to a caregiver in a Romanian orphanage might be a bad choice for a child if the caregiver isn't consistently present or comforting. Problems arise when a child develops an attachment style in one environment and then uses the same style in a different environment. The child in the orphanage who survived by not becoming attached to anyone might have trouble if she is adopted into a home with loving parents.

The second attachment style is anxious-ambivalent attachment—though we will use the shorter label **anxious attachment**. Someone with anxious attachment is nervous that the other person won't love her back. When a caregiver is unreliable—for example, when he is depressed or abuses drugs—the child is likely to develop anxiety about relationships. The child might be difficult to comfort when she is scared. She might also become clingy, not wanting the caregiver to leave because she is afraid that he will not come back.

attachment style
the general way an individual attaches or relates to others

secure attachment
a trusting, open style of attachment

anxious attachment
an anxious, uncertain, and clingy style of attachment; in some models, includes a negative view of the self

avoidant attachment

a removed, isolated style of attachment; in some models, includes a negative view of others

Someone with **avoidant attachment** avoids closeness and may be uncomfortable with emotional intimacy. This attachment style develops when a caregiver is consistently unavailable or even abusive; children learn to distrust the caregiver and relationships more generally. The child often learns to get by on his own without seeking support from the caregiver (Bowlby, 1990). Those who grow up with this attachment style are less inclined to become close to others and may avoid intimacy altogether.

Strange Situation

a paradigm used to test attachment in young children that involves separation from a parent

Children's attachment styles were originally studied using a paradigm called the **Strange Situation**, in which 1-year-old children and their mothers would come to a lab and meet another adult. Then the mother would leave the room. Almost all babies cry or look upset when their mothers leave, but they differ in how they react when their mothers return. Securely attached babies smile and look happy to see their mothers. Anxious babies will keep crying after their mothers return and are difficult to comfort. Avoidant babies will look away from their mothers and refuse to acknowledge them (Ainsworth & Bell, 1970).

WATCH
the video in
REVEL →

Watch PARENT–CHILD ATTACHMENTS

Video

Attachment in Adult Relationships

Early attachment experiences with caregivers predict attachment later in life. For example, someone with a depressed mother or an absent father is more likely to be high in avoidant attachment. However, strong friendships can help lessen these effects; teens with good close friends are lower in avoidant attachment (Fraley et al., 2013). Childhood attachment styles can shape adult romantic relationships as well: How we relate to our parents influences how we relate to romantic partners as adults (Hazan & Shaver, 1987).

To illustrate these adult attachment styles, imagine you have three friends with different relationship styles. Sara seems secure in her relationships and trusts her current boyfriend. She was upset when her last relationship ended, but she didn't fall apart completely. Anna is more anxious. She falls in love quickly and spends all her time with her new boyfriend—although you do hear from her from time to time when the relationship hits a rough patch and she thinks it's the end of the world. When the relationship ends, she becomes distraught. She eats whole tubs of ice cream and listens to Taylor Swift songs for days. Finally, your friend Ava is more avoidant in her relationships. She dates but doesn't let herself get too close to anyone. Some of her boyfriends have wondered if she really cared about them, which has led to a few breakups. But Ava never seemed too bothered by the breakups.

JOURNAL PROMPT: UNDERSTANDING YOURSELF

Think about your relationship with your parents and other caregivers. How do you think those relationships have affected your adult romantic relationships?

One clever study measured attachment styles and then observed couples saying goodbye at the airport. Avoidant men were less likely to seek contact from their partners (such as hugging or holding hands), and anxious men and women were more likely to be upset—for example, crying openly (Fraley & Shaver, 1998). However, avoidant people may not truly dislike relationships. In one study, avoidantly attached people were even more pleased to be accepted by others than securely and anxiously attached people. The authors titled their paper "No Man is an Island" (Carvallo & Gabriel, 2006). Thus, avoidant people may want to be in a relationship but hold back from being emotionally connected to others because of the risk of getting hurt.

As you might expect, adult attachment styles are linked to the Big Five personality scores. Adults high in anxious attachment are more likely to score high on Big Five neuroticism and lower on conscientiousness. Links between personality traits and avoidant attachment are not as strong, but people high in avoidant attachment tend to score low on extraversion, agreeableness, and conscientiousness (Noftle & Shaver, 2006).

The Science of Personality ATTACHMENT STYLE AND THE BIG FIVE

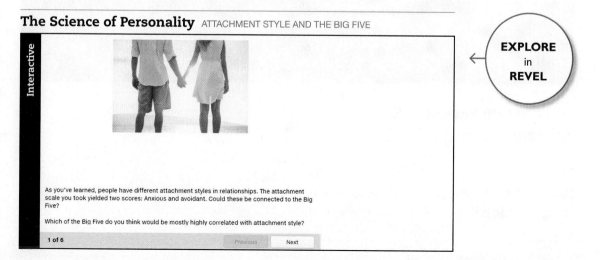

Interactive

As you've learned, people have different attachment styles in relationships. The attachment scale you took yielded two scores: Anxious and avoidant. Could these be connected to the Big Five?

Which of the Big Five do you think would be mostly highly correlated with attachment style?

1 of 6   Previous   Next

EXPLORE
in
REVEL

Can attachment styles change? Apparently they can. Being in a stable, positive relationship can increase attachment security. For example, one study found that anxiously attached people who were in a stable, trusting marriage became less anxious over time (Fuller & Fincham, 1995). Unfortunately, attachment style can also lead to issues when relationships end: Among couples who divorced, those with anxious or avoidant attachment suffered more (Birnbaum et al., 1997).

The Dimensional Approach to Attachment

In more recent years, some researchers have developed another approach to adult attachment, known as the *dimensional approach*. This system measures how people score on two dimensions: **anxiety**, nervousness about relationships along with a negative view of oneself, and **avoidance**, a desire not to be connected emotionally to relationship partners and a negative view of others (Fraley & Shaver, 2000).

This results in four types of attachment: secure attachment (low anxiety, low avoidance), **preoccupied attachment** (high anxiety, low avoidance), **dismissing attachment** (low anxiety, high avoidance), and **fearful attachment** (high anxiety, high avoidance) (see Table 13.1). Secure is the same as the secure style from the original attachment types, and preoccupied is the same as anxious attachment (Bartholomew & Horowitz, 1991). Dismissing and fearful are two subtypes of the original avoidant style. Both are uncertain of relationships, but for different reasons: Fearful people are afraid of getting hurt, and dismissing people just don't care about relationships that much.

To give a simple example of these two styles, imagine two individuals, one dismissing and one fearful. Dismissing Darnell avoids relationships because he doesn't want to get emotionally close to other people, but he doesn't feel anxious. Darnell is a bit of a loner and can cause lots of suffering to his significant others

anxiety
attachment dimension suggesting a negative view of oneself

avoidance
attachment dimension suggesting a negative view of others

preoccupied attachment
attachment style with high anxiety but low avoidance; a style of attachment with a positive view of the other but a negative view of the self

dismissing attachment
attachment style with low anxiety but high avoidance; a style of attachment with a positive view of the self and a negative view of the other

Table 13.1 The Dimensional Model of Attachment

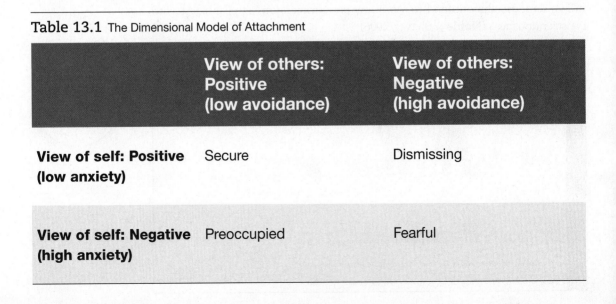

	View of others: Positive (low avoidance)	View of others: Negative (high avoidance)
View of self: Positive (low anxiety)	Secure	Dismissing
View of self: Negative (high anxiety)	Preoccupied	Fearful

when he is in relationships because he just won't commit fully to them. However, he is very confident and has a positive view of himself. On the other side, Fearful Fiona is anxious being in relationships and avoids them; she shows the exact opposite of secure attachment. She has a negative view of herself and a negative view of others. There is a catch, however: Fearfully attached individuals think others are difficult to trust, but do want to form relationships. Dismissive people are not as interested in forming relationships (Pietromonaco & Feldman Barrett, 1997). Interestingly, more college students in recent years (vs. the 1990s) scored as dismissing, suggesting that positive views of the self combined with negative views of others are now more common (Konrath et al., 2014).

fearful attachment
attachment style with high anxiety and high avoidance; a style of attachment with a negative view of both self and other

The Big Five: Basic Personality Traits and Relationships

LO 13.2   Describe the effect of Big Five traits on long-term relationships.

The link between the Big Five and relationships is large and complex. Here we focus on two basic questions, What do the Big Five traits predict in relationships? And do opposites attract, or are you better off with someone who's similar to you? For example, if you are a highly neurotic, conscientious person, should you be in a relationship with someone who's similarly neurotic and conscientious?

The Relationship Outcomes of Each of the Big Five Traits

Extraverts are good at forming relationships (Hills & Argyle, 2001; Selfhout et al., 2010), are more satisfied in relationships (White et al., 2004), and maintain a large number of relationships (Stokes, 1985). Extraverted people have no problem meeting friends and potential romantic partners. They also seem to know everyone there is to know and are socially connected. However, their relationships might also be more shallow and less involved (Schmitt & Shackelford, 2008).

Agreeable people have positive, satisfying relationships (Donnellan et al., 2004; White et al., 2004). People who are agreeable are nice, and being nice is one of the most important qualities for making a relationship work well. Agreeable people have close relationships that are generally positive (except for some occasions where they tolerate jerks). People with low levels of agreeableness often have difficulty in relationships because they can be argumentative and uncaring. Agreeableness is about the approach to relationships—from nice to nasty.

Neuroticism is linked to having troubled, unstable relationships. Neurotic people can find relationships challenging because they are anxious about how the relationship is going (Donnellan et al., 2004; White et al., 2004). Neurotic people also cause problems for their partners. For example, depressed people can spend so much time looking for social reassurance from others that they drive them away (Potthoff et al., 1995). Neurotic people have a tendency to be depressed and need you to constantly lift their spirits. This is OK sometimes, but often you don't have the energy to take the negativity, so you avoid them.

Conscientiousness can help relationships because conscientious individuals experience less conflict (see, for example, Jensen-Campbell & Malcolm, 2007), including violence (Bogg & Roberts, 2004). Conscientious people are more likely to catch themselves before they say something destructive during an argument. They are also more likely to be on time for dates and be more organized.

self-expansion
the desire to expand the self by including traits, qualities, and skills of another

High openness to experience is linked to **self-expansion**, the motivation to incorporate aspects of the partner's identity to expand the self (Aron et al., 1991). For example, if you date someone from another culture, you will learn about that culture from your partner. You might learn another language or about another religion. You might also form relationships with others from that culture, such as the friends and family of your partner. This self-expansion—basically, learning about the exotic—is part of what makes the "new guy" or the "foreign girl" so attractive. Open people are more likely to explore these types of new relationship experiences.

You can also expand in your relationships by trying new experiences with your partner. In one experiment, couples tried new things together, such as running in a three-legged race and climbing through a strange obstacle course. These couples felt more satisfied with their relationships after these new experiences (Reissman et al., 1993). This is something you can try in your own relationship. Just pick a new activity to try every week—even silly things like disco bowling. Go on vacation to a new place, or try a new restaurant. Theoretically, your satisfaction and closeness with each other should increase.

Self-expansion is a way of learning about people and cultivating stronger relationships.

Do your relationship outcomes line up with your Big Five personality traits, given the research discussed in the text?

Do Opposites Really Attract (and Stay Together)?

Are relationships better when couples are different ("opposites attract") or similar ("birds of a feather flock together")? Most of the original research in this area, which focused on attitudes and beliefs, found that similarity is best—strangers with similar attitudes and values were more attracted to each other, and relationships among people with similar beliefs and views lasted longer (see, for example, Botwin et al., 1997; Byrne, 1961; Byrne et al., 1970). Attitudes, however, are not the same as personality. It makes sense that people who have the same attitudes about politics, religion, gender roles, and how to raise a child will have smoother relationships—there will be much less to negotiate and argue about. But what about personality? Do, say, neurotic people do better with neurotic people?

Surprisingly, the answer seems to be no: Several recent studies have not found a similarity effect for personality traits such as those of the Big Five. One recent study of married couples, for example, found that couples with similar personalities were actually less satisfied with their marriages in the long run (Shiota & Levenson, 2007). Another major study found no relationship between personality matching and relationship satisfaction (Dyrenforth et al., 2010). And in one special case of personality—dominance—those of opposite types were actually more attracted to each other (Dryer & Horowitz, 1997; Tiedens & Fragale, 2003), probably because two dominant people in a relationship might have power struggles.

Why did the earlier studies on attitudes differ from the later ones on personality traits? As we noted, having a romantic partner with different attitudes might lead to more conflict, but sharing similar attitudes to less conflict. However, it's less clear how personality matching would help in relationships. An agreeable person would get along best with an agreeable partner—but a disagreeable person would also do better with an agreeable partner, not a similarly disagreeable one. Most people will be more satisfied with a partner who is nice rather than mean. Someone who is low in conscientiousness would probably do better with someone higher in conscientiousness, not someone else low in conscientiousness who will also forget to pay the rent on time. Sure, a conscientious partner might nag you to make the bed in the morning, but he will also be less likely to get drunk and fight with you, so overall conscientiousness is a good thing.

Sometimes it is tough to live with someone low in conscientiousness.

Next, we examine a little different level of traits—empathy, compassion, and self-control on one hand, and darker traits like narcissism on the other.

Empathy, Compassion, and Self-Control: Three Positive Forces in Relationships

LO 13.3 Describe how compassion, empathy, and self-control can improve relationships.

You're online one day when you see a video of impoverished children in a country far away. They are starving, their eyes vacant, and their mother is desperately trying to find them food. "How would I feel if I were that hungry?" you think. "Or if my children were starving?" You feel sick to your stomach and tears come to your eyes. You have never met these children or their mother, but you feel emotional just thinking about their plight.

empathy
a response to another individual's experiences that takes the other's perspective

perspective-taking
the ability to see the world from another's point of view

Psychologists refer to this as **empathy**, or the ability to understand and feel the experiences that another person is having (Davis, 1983). Empathy includes **perspective-taking**, or being able to put yourself in someone else's shoes. Perspective-taking is very important for relationships. Imagine you are dating Yin, who is high in empathy. You come home carrying a large bag of groceries. Yin sees you walking toward the door. Because she's able to take your perspective, Yin realizes that it will be a challenge for you to open the door to the apartment. She jumps out of her chair and opens the door for you. You walk in, put your groceries on the kitchen counter, and thank her.

JOURNAL PROMPT: UNDERSTANDING YOURSELF

Who is your ideal romantic partner? Does his or her Big Five personality match the description in the text? Which traits do you find especially attractive in a partner?

If Yin lacked empathy, however, she wouldn't have had the same reaction. Instead of noticing your suffering and opening the door for you, she would have remained oblivious. As you struggled through the door, Yin would have continued texting on her phone. You would be upset, and the relationship would suffer. Take the Interpersonal Reactivity Index to give you a general idea of how empathic you are compared to others.

Empathy is especially important for encouraging helping behaviors and diminishing hurting behaviors. Highly empathic people prefer situations where they can volunteer to help others (Davis et al., 2001) and are less aggressive after they are insulted (Richardson et al., 1998). People who can put themselves in another's shoes

Questionnaire 13.3 INTERPERSONAL REACTIVITY INDEX

Interactive

1. I often have tender, concerned feelings for people less fortunate than me.

- ○ Strongly Agree
- ○ Moderately Agree
- ○ Neither Agree nor Disagree
- ○ Moderately Disagree
- ○ Strongly Disagree

2. Sometimes I don't feel very sorry for other people when they are having problems.

- ○ Strongly Agree
- ○ Moderately Agree
- ○ Neither Agree nor Disagree
- ○ Moderately Disagree
- ○ Strongly Disagree

Previous   Next

TAKE the Questionnaire in **REVEL**

are less likely to get angry or aggressive. Empathy is also related to forgiveness, an especially important behavior in marriage (Fincham et al., 2002), especially for men (Toussaint & Webb, 2005). When you can at least try to understand why your spouse, partner, or friend did what he did, you are more likely to be able to preserve the relationship. So, imagine your wife told a secret of yours to a group of friends. You would probably be upset. But if you were able to see the situation through her eyes—she was having a deep conversation with friends, got caught up in it, and accidently let your secret slip—you will be more likely to forgive her.

People experience **compassion** when they see someone or something suffering and want to remove that suffering (Goetz et al., 2010). What is the difference between empathy and compassion? Empathy is a general feeling and concern for someone, whether they are doing well or badly. Compassion involves feeling empathy specifically toward people who are suffering. Compassion is linked to helping others in need, especially when someone is able to help, thinks the target deserves help, and experiences no emotional cost for helping (Goetz et al., 2010).

Self-control (an aspect of conscientiousness) is another important trait in relationships because it helps us to do the right thing for our partner—even when it is difficult. People are often torn between what they want to do and what they know is best for the relationship. If your girlfriend crashes her car into yours in the driveway, your knee-jerk response might be, "What were you thinking? Are you blind?" However, the response you know is best for the relationship is, "Don't worry about the car. Are you OK?" Moving from a selfish, knee-jerk response to a more

compassion
witnessing someone suffering and wanting to remove that suffering

Compassion includes caring for others in need.

Accommodation is better.

caring, relationship-centered response is called **accommodation**, or acting in a constructive way rather than a destructive way in response to a partner's behavior (Rusbult et al., 1991; Yovetich & Rusbult, 1994).

Accommodation is incredibly important for making relationships work. No matter how much you love someone, if you cannot stop yourself from saying destructive things, your relationship will suffer. And personality, especially self-control, plays a major role in accommodation. It takes self-control to stop yourself from saying mean things and instead say, "I can always get a new car, but I could never find anyone else like you."

People high in self-control are more accommodating (Finkel & Campbell, 2001) and are less likely to engage in negative relationship behaviors, ranging from infidelity to physical abuse (Finkel, 2014; Tangney et al., 2004). The higher your self-control, the better your relationships are likely to be.

Fortunately, self-control can be increased. First, take care of yourself by getting enough sleep, eating right, and not drinking too much alcohol, because your self-control suffers when you don't do these things (Baumeister et al., 1994; see also Chapter 5). That's why so many arguments occur when people are tired, hungry, or drunk. Second, you can increase your self-control by practicing mindfulness meditation (Tang et al., 2007; see also Chapter 7), as higher mindfulness predicts better functioning in relationships (Barnes et al., 2007). Either approach will save you a good deal of relationship drama and conflict.

accommodation
moving from the given to the transformed matrix by acting in a constructive way rather than a destructive way toward a partner

The Dark Triad: Three Negative Forces in Relationships

LO 13.4 Describe the dark triad and its effects on relationships.

Another group of traits represents a more negative force in relationships. Some people seem cold in their lack of empathy, are highly manipulative, or tend to put themselves first. These three types of individuals form the **dark triad**: psychopathy, Machiavellianism, and narcissism (Paulhus & Williams, 2002) (Figure 13.1). These traits are "dark" because they describe an uncaring or callous interpersonal style, including low levels of empathy and a willingness to use people in relationships. However, these are normal variations in personality traits, not a caricature

dark triad
a combination of three negative traits: psychopathy, Machiavellianism, and narcissism

of an evil villain. Everyone falls somewhere on the continuum of these dark triad traits; some will be low, some average, and some high.

Psychopathy includes a lack of empathy mixed with impulsivity; people with high levels of psychopathy tend not to be affected by the suffering of others. The most extreme examples of psychopathy are serial killers such as Ted Bundy or Jeffrey Dahmer. Eric Harris, one of the shooters at Columbine High School, was apparently a psychopath, plotting a mass murder to gain fame and managing to deceive everyone around him, including his ex-military father (Cullen, 2009).

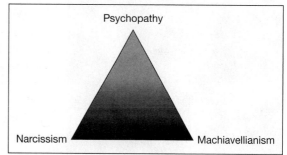

Figure 13.1 The Dark Triad

SOURCE: From Paulhus and Williams (2002).

However, normal people also vary in psychopathy, and some people high in psychopathy can be successful professionals because they are willing to make tough decisions that hurt some people but might help a business make money (Babiak & Hare, 2007).

psychopathy
a lack of empathy mixed with impulsivity

Machiavellianism includes a lack of empathy and a willingness to exploit others. The term *Machiavellianism* comes from *The Prince*, Niccolo Machiavelli's masterpiece on how to rule a country. People high in this trait can be manipulative and deceptive, willing to do whatever it takes to stay in power, win a game, or succeed. Machiavellian individuals are often unemotional and ignore conventional morality (Christie & Geis, 1970). Machiavellianism is prevalent in reality shows like *Survivor*, where the goal is to "play the game" to win even if it means lying to others. Another good example is Francis Underwood, the character played by Kevin Spacey in *House of Cards*.

Machiavellianism
a lack of empathy and a willingness to exploit others

Finally, **narcissism** includes a lack of empathy and a sense of grandiosity (for more on narcissism, look back at Chapter 5). Narcissistic people care only about themselves and preserving their positive self-image. All of these traits can have negative consequences for relationships.

narcissism
a lack of empathy and a sense of grandiosity

People high in dark triad traits are more likely to take a game-playing approach to relationships (Campbell et al., 2002; Jonason & Kavanaugh, 2006). When your friend calls you to complain that the guy she hooked up with didn't contact her for 3 days, you're witnessing a mild form of game-playing. When your friend says the guy came by with flowers, then secretly stole her credit card, maxed it out at a bar, and cheated on her with a server, that's a stronger form of game-playing. Dark triad individuals are willing to exploit others and can be "players," engaging in short-term relationships even when their partners desire a longer-term relationship. People high in these traits are also more likely to have a more pragmatic approach to relationships, thinking about what the other person can do for them (Jonason & Kavanaugh, 2006).

Those high in dark triad traits are also more likely to engage in **mate-poaching** by stealing someone else's partner. Interestingly, dark triad individuals are also more likely to report that people have taken their mates. Perhaps people who start

mate-poaching
stealing someone else's relationship partner

A statue of Niccolo Machiavelli in Florence, Italy.

relationships with others' partners are more likely to lose their partners the same way (Jonathon et al., 2010).

Why are people high in dark triad traits good at mate-poaching and game-playing? It might be because they are good-looking—sort of. Physical attractiveness is generally seen as a good thing in relationships. We want to date, marry, and even hire people who are attractive (Dipboye et al., 1977; Eagley et al., 1991; Hosoda et al., 2003). Dark triad individuals, however, tend to fake physical attractiveness: they enhance their appearance with makeup, strategic facial hair, attractive clothes, and accessories so they appear to be more attractive than they actually are. In one clever study, students were photographed as they entered the lab and then again after their facial enhancements were removed, including removing makeup and jewelry and even shaving facial hair. Strangers then rated these before-and-after photos. Those high in dark triad traits showed the biggest difference between their adorned and unadorned attractiveness. In other words, they made themselves appear more attractive than they really were (Holtzman & Strube, 2013).

Why do these dark traits exist among humans, and at such surprisingly high rates? (This is the academic way of asking, "Why are so many guys [or girls] jerks?") If dark triad traits are generally negative for relationships, shouldn't they vanish from the human personality profile and be replaced by more positive traits such as agreeableness? (Recall our discussion on evolved personality from Chapter 4.)

JOURNAL PROMPT: UNDERSTANDING YOURSELF

Think about a relationship you had that ended badly. Did your partner have any of the dark triad traits?

More than likely, these traits have persisted because they are useful for forming sexual relationships, which enabled them to be passed down through the generations. People high in dark triad traits look attractive, are confident, and can be charming, all traits useful for initiating sexual relationships. However, relationships with dark triad individuals tend to be short-term relationships filled with drama. If you want a spring break fling worthy of a reality show, fall for someone with dark traits; if you want a stable, long-term relationship, avoid the dark traits. In our evolutionary past, these short-term liaisons produced enough children to keep dark triad traits around to the present day (Jonason et al., 2009). Those high in dark triad traits employ a range of strategies to help them start short-term relationships and keep those relationships from becoming long term.

These strategies include the truly dark (becoming violent and abusive), the moderately dark (blaming alcohol for bad behavior), and the more straightforward and honest (just telling your partner that you are interested only in a short-term relationship; Jonason & Buss, 2012).

Another way to understand dark personality traits is with the **chocolate cake model**, a model of relationships that start off well and end poorly, originally developed to explain relationships with narcissists (Campbell, 2005). Imagine you have the choice of eating either chocolate cake or broccoli. You think for about half a second and then make a move for the chocolate cake. The cake tastes so good, and you get a big sugar rush that makes you feel like you are soaring with the eagles. Unfortunately, 20 minutes later the inevitable crash to earth occurs. You feel empty and lethargic—and you ask yourself why you ate the stupid chocolate cake in the first place.

The broccoli would have produced a different outcome: You wouldn't have had any rush, but 20 minutes later, you wouldn't have had a massive crash. Instead, you would feel healthy and think, "I eat right and take care of myself."

The challenge of eating healthy food—the seductive short-term choice versus the less glamorous long-term choice—mirrors the challenge of relationships. The person we are really attracted to at a party (say, the sexy-looking guy wearing the cool leather jacket) is not always the best person to have a long-term relationship with. (I [J. M. T.] have always thought this was the ultimate proof that life is not fair.)

Imagine you meet a guy—let's call him Kevin. Kevin is confident and charming. He speaks with big hand gestures and is the center of attention when he goes out. You fall for Kevin, and the relationship is very exciting at first. You feel special and important whenever you are out with him, and you can't believe that you have such a popular boyfriend.

Then things get a little rough. You want to form an emotional connection with Kevin—people in relationships should truly care about each other, right?—but he doesn't seem that interested in emotional intimacy. Instead, he's emotionally distant and even controlling when you are in private (although still the

chocolate cake model
the tendency of a relationship with a narcissist to start positively but end very negatively

Do you prefer chocolate cake or broccoli?

life of the party in public). You don't understand what is going on, so you try to figure out what you are doing wrong that might be driving Kevin away. He blames you for problems in the relationship and even says it is your fault that he flirts with other women. Eventually, you find out that Kevin cheated on you throughout most of the relationship. You leave, and he quickly starts dating someone else.

Compare this to dating a non-narcissistic guy—let's call him Michael. You meet Michael at a party. He is neither highly confident nor exciting, but he seems like a decent, nice person. He eventually asks you out on a date and you say yes. No fireworks occur, but you have a good time. You start a relationship and you find that, even though Michael lacks a lot of flash, he is a great relationship partner. The more you get to know Michael, the closer you grow and the more love you feel. Eventually, you and Michael break up—you have different life goals and the relationship just doesn't work. Still, you remain friends with Michael, and never wonder why you had the relationship. Even today, if either of you needed a favor, you would still support each other.

Narcissistic Kevin is chocolate cake—great for 20 minutes (or its relationship equivalent, 3 months) and then leaving you sick to your stomach—and humble Michael is the broccoli—not the most exciting meal, but one that leaves you healthier and happier in the long run.

So, combining all of the research in this chapter, what type of person will make the best long-term partner? Probably someone high in secure attachment, agreeableness, conscientiousness, empathy, compassion, and self-control; low in neuroticism and dark triad traits; and perhaps opposite from you in dominance. That said, successful relationships can and do occur between people of many personality types—and there is more to making a relationship work than a partner's personality, including attitudes, values, and the complexities of life like health and work.

Online Relationships: The Next Frontier

LO 13.5 List the key benefits of online dating and describe how personality is expressed on social media.

With the increasing popularity of the Internet, many relationships have moved online. Sometimes the relationship has an online and offline element (such as friending a roommate on Facebook), sometimes the relationship exists only online (correspondence with a potential dating partner on Match.com), and sometimes relationships start one way and end another (as with a childhood friend who moves away but keeps in touch online). We start by discussing one of the fastest-growing areas of online relationships: online dating.

Online Dating

When you're a traditional-age college student, it isn't terribly difficult to find potential dates or relationship partners—you're surrounded by people your age. (Finding a great partner is another issue, of course.) When you graduate, however, the dating world gets much more difficult. I (W. K. C.) often tell my class to imagine they are working in a typical corporate "cube farm"—a large room filled with work cubicles. The other workers are different ages, and many are married or otherwise coupled. The highlight of the week's social activity at the office might be a bowling night or heading to happy hour at T.G.I. Fridays. It's not an ideal situation to find a mate.

A popular solution is to join one of the many online dating sites, which offer access to huge numbers of potential partners. One site, Plenty of Fish, even asks users to hit a "go fishing" button to look at potential mates. This brings up a long list of photos and brief self-descriptions of partners. This site, like many others, allows users to communicate with these potential partners. Indeed, these two qualities of online dating sites, access and communication, make online dating different from traditional face-to-face dating contexts (Finkel et al., 2012).

The third quality of online dating is **personality matching** (Finkel et al., 2012). On several dating sites, such as eHarmony, Match.com, and Chemistry.com, individuals are matched in part on their self-reported personalities. Some sites match people based on how similar they are; others on how complementary (different) they are. However, as you just learned, the jury is still out on whether similar people actually do have more successful relationships—that seems to be true for beliefs and values but not necessarily for personality traits. Most studies have found that couples similar in personality traits are not necessarily any more satisfied with their relationships (Dyrenforth et al., 2010).

personality matching
the use of personality testing to match potential mates based on personality

---

Personality's Past

The Minnesota Computer Dance Study

There is a booming interest in using computer algorithms and social networking to match romantic partners. Sites like eHarmony, Match, and OKcupid use these tools to bring people together who are likely to form a romantic bond.

The first use of computer matching in a psychology study occurred 50 years ago. Elaine Walster and her colleagues conducted what it is often called the computer dance study in 1966 (Walster et al., 1966).

This study took place during the University of Minnesota's "welcome week" for freshmen. Psychologists set up a Friday night dance for students. But it wasn't just any dance—it was a computer match where students were told that they would be matched on psychological traits with a partner.

Sophomore research assistants rated the 664 dance participants on physical attractiveness, secretly observing them as they completed questionnaires on self-esteem, nervousness, and mental health.

But here was the catch. All students were randomly assigned to dates (with the exception that men were always taller than the women they were matched with).

There was no actual computer matching. The researchers were interested in how attractiveness and personality would predict how much someone liked his or her date.

The dance started at 8:00 P.M. All students had a slip of paper with their participant ID on it. When the intermission started at 10:30, the men and women were separated and everyone was asked to privately rate his or her date on likability and related variables.

The results? Physical attractiveness mattered—a lot. The attractive dates were far and away the most well-liked. There were a few correlations with personality—people who were more sociable, had higher self-esteem and were more extraverted were liked more. These effects, however, were much smaller than the attractiveness effects.

At least in the context of a dance, looks mattered much more than personality. Thus, this study can be

seen as a major blow to the importance of personality in dating. Later research has confirmed this crucial role for physical attractiveness, especially in situations of brief acquaintance.

The short duration of the interaction—only 2 hours—likely minimized the impact of personality traits. Second, the dance created a very scripted interaction. Everyone showed up to the same event and did similar things. There wasn't a lot of opportunity for personality to emerge. Consistent with this, in some very recent research, it has been found that the importance of looks compared to personality decreases the longer you know someone (Hunt et al., in press). Overall, looks matter for first impressions, but who you are may be more important in the long run.

So here is the billion-dollar question: Do dating sites based on personality matching actually work? They definitely allow people to see and communicate with a wide range of potential partners—much wider than anyone with a full-time job could ever hope to meet in "real life." So in that sense, these sites are very effective.

But the effectiveness of personality matching for forming good relationships is still unknown. As Finkel and colleagues put it in their large review of the issue,

> In sum, online dating sites frequently claim that people will achieve better romantic outcomes when seeking partners through their site than through conventional offline dating (or through other dating sites). . . . Our investigation suggests, however, that dating sites have failed to provide any compelling evidence for these claims. As such, the claims simply cannot be accepted as valid. (2012, p. 28)

In other words, online dating definitely allows you to access a large pool of potential partners, but it's not clear if the matching some sites employ actually works or not.

JOURNAL PROMPT: UNDERSTANDING YOURSELF

Do you think online dating sites allow people to present their personalities in an authentic way? Why or why not?

What does work? One classic study explored which factors really matter in dating. The researchers measured the personality and physical attractiveness of a large group of students and then told them a computer program would match them with the best partner. Instead, the students were matched randomly to partners and met them at a dance.

So what characteristic best predicted how much the students liked their partners and whether they wanted to date him or her again? Physical attractiveness. Personality had very little to do with it (Walster et al., 1966). More recent studies have found this effect as well: On average, established romantic partners are about equal in attractiveness (Carmalt et al., 2008; McKillip & Redel, 1983). In online dating, users were more likely to receive replies if they contacted someone who was similar in physical attractiveness (Taylor et al., 2011).

So if physical appearance is so important, how can people fall for someone online when they haven't physically met? It's often because they see a picture and believe their online love really looks that way—or believe it emotionally even if intellectually they know she might not actually look that way. It's no coincidence that "catfish" schemes, in which people get someone to fall for a fake online persona, usually use photos of physically attractive women (or men).

Another more recent solution is to have people see each other online and then if there is mutual interest to communicate and meet that same day. Apps like Tinder are growing in popularity because they bridge the online and "real" world in this way. These products are too new to be the subject of much research, but some psychologists have argued that they might be a good strategy for meeting compatible strangers (Finkel, 2015).

Personality and Social Networking Websites

Social networking sites such as Facebook have become one of the most common ways to maintain interpersonal relationships. Facebook reports having 1 billion users, making the population of Facebook roughly three times the population of the United States.

Do people present only one side of themselves on Facebook? Apparently not: Most studies find that people's personality on Facebook looks a lot like their personality in the rest of their lives (Back et al., 2010; Gosling et al., 2007; Wilson et al., 2012). This is even true for first impressions—initial liking based on Facebook profiles is very similar to initial liking after meeting in real life (Weisbuch et al., 2009).

People who self-enhance offline, such as narcissists, also self-enhance on Facebook. Offline, Nick the narcissist likes to be the center of attention, dresses provocatively, and has shallow relationships. Sure enough, Nick will do the same thing on his Facebook page—he will have many "friends," post a provocative main photo, and describe himself in self-enhancing ways (Buffardi & Campbell, 2008; Vazire et al., 2008), all in an attempt to look good in his profile (Kapidzic, 2013).

Third and finally, social networks activate certain personality traits. For example, Facebook users get a boost to self-esteem (Gentile et al., 2012). Several studies find that narcissists have more friends on Facebook, suggesting that social networks reward narcissistic behavior (Buffardi & Campbell, 2008; Rosen et al., 2013), but there is no evidence that Facebook use directly causes narcissism

Do you try to self-enhance online?

(Horton et al., 2014). Much more research needs to be done in this area, however. Facebook, like all media, can have a range of positive and negative effects on personality.

Concluding Thoughts

Starting from the very beginning of our lives, our personality and our relationships are fully entwined: Our relationships shape our personalities and our personalities shape our relationships. The personality of our relationship partners also matters. We know we want caring, emotionally stable, and dependable romantic partners, but we can be fooled by people with dark personalities. These individuals have some positive traits—such as social confidence and charm—that can initially hide their negative traits. Potential partners will not announce, "I'm a self-absorbed swine. Date me and I promise to massively mess up your life, cheat on you, and then have a love child with your best friend—all while blaming you for it." Most people don't see this coming, one reason why these relationships can be so distressing.

Online dating and social networking technologies are rapidly changing the ways that people relate to each other. Personality research is trying to get a handle on these technologies, but much more research will eventually emerge. In an era where we live more and more of our lives online, personality is increasingly digital—and so are our relationships. Meanwhile, people will continue to meet, fall in love, have children, and care for those children, starting the cycle of personality and relationships all over again.

Learning Objectives Summaries

LO 13.1 Name the three main types of attachment and explain how they impact adult relationships.

The three main types of attachment are secure, anxious, and avoidant. These attachment styles form in childhood and affect adult relationships. In general, secure attachment is positive for relationships, whereas anxious and avoidant attachment predict relationship problems.

LO 13.2 Describe the effect of Big Five traits on long-term relationships.

In general, extraversion predicts relationship formation, and neuroticism predicts relationship problems. Similar personalities do not always attract, nor do opposites, with the exception of dominance.

LO 13.3 Describe how compassion, empathy, and self-control can improve relationships.

Empathy, compassion, and self-control predict greater helping behavior in relationships and less harmful behavior. For example, individuals with high self-control are less likely to get into fights with their partners.

LO 13.4 Describe the dark triad and its effects on relationships.

The dark triad traits of psychopathy, Machiavellianism, and narcissism generally predict short-term relationship behaviors such as game-playing and infidelity. These traits are usually problematic in long-term relationships.

LO 13.5 List the key benefits of online dating and describe how personality is expressed on social media.

Online dating offers three key benefits: access to a large pool of potential mates, the ability to communicate with them, and personality matching. In general, personality on social media is similar to personality in "real life."

Key Terms

attachment, p. 347
caregiver, p. 347
secure base, p. 348
attachment theory, p. 348
internalized, p. 348
attachment style, p. 349
secure attachment, p. 349
anxious attachment, p. 349
avoidant attachment, p. 350

Strange Situation, p. 350
anxiety, p. 352
avoidance, p. 352
preoccupied attachment, p. 352
dismissing attachment, p. 352
fearful attachment, p. 353
self-expansion, p. 354
empathy, p. 356
perspective-taking, p. 356

compassion, p. 357
accommodation, p. 358
dark triad, p. 358
psychopathy, p. 359
Machiavellianism, p. 359
narcissism, p. 359
mate-poaching, p. 359
chocolate cake model, p. 361
personality matching, p. 363

Essay Questions

1. Why is attachment important in childhood and how might it influence one's relationships in adulthood?

2. Summarize the relationship outcomes for each of the Big Five personality traits.

3. Which three traits discussed in the chapter lead to positive relationship outcomes, and why is this so?

4. Which three traits discussed in this chapter lead to negative relationship outcomes, and why is this so?

Chapter 14
Personality and Mental Health

 Learning Objectives

LO 14.1 Understand how mental disorders are diagnosed, name the personality disorders, and explain how they relate to the Big Five traits.

LO 14.2 Explain how personality and the Big Five traits are related to other mental disorders, such as depression, anxiety disorder, schizophrenia, and eating and addiction disorders.

LO 14.3 Describe strategies for becoming a happier, nicer, and more conscientious person.

Daniel Smith stood, frozen with anxiety, in front of the fixin's bar at a Roy Rogers restaurant off the New Jersey Turnpike, trying to decide what to put on his roast beef sandwich. He added "a single slice of whitish-pink tomato and absolutely no lettuce" without incident, "and yet the condiments," he wrote later, "caused me immediate trouble." Quickly ruling out mustard and mayonnaise, he was paralyzed deciding between ketchup and barbeque sauce. "I deliberated for a long time. I scrutinized the tubs of sauce with their white nasal spouts as if I were consulting the oracle at Delphi. [I realized that] even piddling actions can wind up having big consequences." Smith calls this crippling indecision over small things "The Roy Rogers Problem—or, if you prefer, the Vinaigrette–Blue Cheese Dilemma, or the Haagen-Dazs–Ben & Jerry's Conundrum."

Smith had everything most of us want: a great job, a nice place to live, a good relationship. "Yet," he wrote, "every day was torture. I slept fitfully, with recurring nightmares—tsunamis, feral animals, the violent deaths of loved ones. I had intestinal cramps and nausea and headaches. A sense of impending catastrophe colored every waking moment. Worse, I had the distinct sense that catastrophe had already occurred. I had made the wrong decisions, gone down the wrong path, screwed up in a ruinous, irrevocable, epoch-making way" (Smith, 2012).

Is Smith high in neuroticism? It sure seems that way. But is that all he's experiencing? Definitely not. Although Smith doesn't identify his problem as such, his anxiety has crossed over from being a personality trait to being a **mental disorder**—a pattern of mental symptoms causing significant problems in his life. Mental disorders—sometimes referred to as mental illness or **psychopathology**—are disorders because they cause people distress beyond what is normal, typical, or culturally appropriate. Mental disorders include everything from phobias (irrational fears) to sleep disorders (such as insomnia) to kleptomania (compulsive stealing).

At first, mental disorders and personality may seem unrelated. However, researchers are increasingly recognizing that personality traits and mental disorders are often on a continuum (Hopwood et al., 2012; Krueger et al., 2012). For example, someone like Smith, who has an anxiety disorder, is also high in neuroticism. Anxiety is a continuum—some people have only a little, most people have a moderate amount, and a few have so much it causes problems in their lives serious enough that their anxiety could be classified as an anxiety disorder. Narcissism also runs on a continuum. When someone's narcissism becomes so high it causes significant problems in her life, she might be diagnosed with narcissistic personality disorder.

mental disorder
a pattern of mental symptoms causing significant problems in life

psychopathology
an alternate term for mental disorder

Daniel Smith, whose memoir of anxiety is titled *Monkey Mind*.

The relationships between personality and mental disorders are complex. Personality in childhood, for example, could lead to mental disorders in adulthood, adult mental disorders could alter personality, or a single biological cause might influence both personality and mental disorders. Other causes and components of mental disorders do not involve personality at all. That said, mental disorders often co-occur with a certain personality profile.

An enormous amount of research explores mental disorders, so we want to be upfront about the limited goals for this chapter. Overall, a broad range of mental disorders are related to personality in remarkably similar ways. For example, neuroticism, a single factor of the Big Five, is related to a significant number of mental disorders (Lahey, 2009). The line between normal and abnormal is often in quantity, not quality. In other words, abnormal personality can be described using terms associated with normal personality traits (Widiger & Samuel, 2005).

And, finally, a word of warning: When students learn about mental disorders, they often start seeing those disorders everywhere, including in themselves. When I (W. K. C.) took a psychology course as a college student, I became convinced I suffered from depression, generalized anxiety disorder, and several personality disorders and was on the brink of experiencing a full schizophrenic break. It turned out I was just experiencing the normal ups and downs of being 19 years old.

This overdiagnosis was first noticed in medical students, who sometimes think they have a large number of rare diseases. The experience is called medical student syndrome (Howes & Salkovskis, 1998). The same thing can happen when students learn about mental disorders (Hardy & Calhoun, 1997)—especially if you happen to be high in neuroticism (Deo & Lymburner, 2011).

Most people feel depressed or anxious from time to time. We all have strange thoughts. These experiences are different than suffering from a mental disorder. For that reason, the questionnaires in this chapter are specifically designed for normal populations; they gauge symptoms but—and this is important—*do not diagnose mental disorders*. If you are truly concerned that you or someone close to you is suffering from a mental illness, please seek the counsel of a trained clinical psychologist or a physician who is qualified to make psychological diagnoses.

And with that, let's begin.

Personality Disorders

LO 14.1 Understand how mental disorders are diagnosed, name the personality disorders, and explain how they relate to the Big Five traits.

Rachel is upset when she calls her husband Tim at work. "I hate this house," she says. "The kids are napping, but I just don't feel like cleaning it." Tim, trying to be kind, replies, "Then don't clean it. I can help you clean when I get home." But, he explains, he won't be home until after six because he has some late meetings.

Rachel starts to cry. "I'm such an idiot. . . . I must make you sick," she says.

"You don't make me sick. . . . But I've got to go," says Tim. Rachel then starts crying and screaming, off on a rant that makes little sense and includes plenty of unprintable words.

"Is that all you care about, what the neighbors think?" she yells. "Let this [expletive] house rot; let the [expletive] kids starve. I don't give a [expletive]. And I don't need your [expletive]" (Reiland, 2004, pp. 11–12).

And this was a relatively good day. Rachel eventually ended up in a psychiatric hospital, where she hit herself against the walls so hard she became covered with bruises.

When someone's entire personality leads to significant problems in how she feels, acts, or relates to other people, she may have a **personality disorder**. (Psychologists use the shorthand term "PD.") For example, Rachel was eventually diagnosed with borderline PD, characterized by cycles of affection and anger, fear of abandonment, anxiety and depression, and even physical self-harm and suicide. Rachel's book on her diagnosis and recovery is called *Get Me Out of Here*; another book on borderline PD is titled *I Hate You—Don't Leave Me*.

personality disorders
extreme and inflexible personality configurations that lead to significant impairment

Glenn Close played a woman with borderline personality features in the movie *Fatal Attraction*.

Diagnosing Personality Disorders

Before diving into this section, an important caution:

Warning: Personality disorders are extreme manifestations of personality. Only professionals should diagnose personality disorders, which is why we do not include any diagnostic scales in this book. Confusion arises because many personality disorders are derived from—and share the same name with—personality traits. For example, describing a friend as narcissistic is reasonable because narcissism is a personality trait. However, describing a friend as suffering from narcissistic personality disorder should be avoided (unless they have a professional diagnosis).

Personality disorders and personality traits are similar but also different in important ways. Someone who is self-centered, eccentric, overly dramatic, odd, or generally socially isolated, but who can work effectively and doesn't harm himself or others, does not have a personality disorder. He just has a personality (even though it might be a bit weird or annoying). Also, culture matters. If someone is behaving according to his cultural traditions or expectations—even if that behavior seems strange to us—he should not be seen as having a personality disorder.

To be diagnosed with a personality disorder, a person must fit six specific requirements: experiencing problems in most aspects of life, such as relationships and thinking (Criterion A); being inflexible in his behavior, such as not acting differently even when she should (Criterion B); experiencing major life problems (Criterion C); and showing signs of the personality disorder since adolescence (Criterion D). In addition, the problematic behaviors cannot be due to another mental disorder (Criterion E) or to a physical disorder, such as a brain tumor or a reaction to drugs (Criterion F). Overall, these requirements mean that a personality disorder must cause problems, be pervasive, and not be caused by something else.

Once a clinician has determined someone has a personality disorder, the next step is to determine which PD (or PDs—people can have more than one) he or she has. A good place to start is the *Diagnostic and Statistical Manual of Mental Disorders* (*DSM*)—the "official" manual for diagnosis published by the American Psychiatric Association (APA), now in its fifth edition, the *DSM-5* (2013). The *DSM* personality disorders are arranged into three clusters, labeled A, B, and C. **Cluster A** is odd-eccentric, **Cluster B** dramatic-emotional, and **Cluster C** anxious-fearful (APA, 2013). Sometimes students refer to Clusters A, B, and C as "weird, wild, and worried," respectively (see Table 14.1 and Figure 14.1). Others call them "mad, bad, and sad" (it's "mad" as in cognitively odd and "bad" as in misbehavior).

The other option is to say that a person has a personality disorder that is "not otherwise specified," or PDNOS. In fact, PDNOS is one of the most common personality disorder diagnoses; about 1 in 4 people with a personality disorder are diagnosed as PDNOS (Verheul & Widiger, 2004). Altogether, about 1 in 10 people has some form of personality disorder (Lenzenweger, 2008).

Cluster A
odd or eccentric personality disorders; "weird" or "mad"

Cluster B
dramatic or emotional personality disorders; "wild" or "bad"

Cluster C
anxious or fearful personality disorders; "worried" or "sad"

Table 14.1 The Ten Personality Disorders

Cluster A: odd-eccentric ("weird" or "mad")	Brief Description	Possible Behaviors	Big Five Correlates
Paranoid personality disorder	Paranoid and suspicious	• Has trouble trusting friends • Thinks benign remarks made by others are actually hostile • Carries grudges for long periods	High N Low A
Schizoid personality disorder	Detachment from close relationships and overall lack of pleasure in life	• Shows no interest in forming friendships, spending time with family, or having a romantic partner • Appears to not enjoy any aspect of life	Low E
Schizotypal personality disorder	Problematic social relationships and odd or eccentric thinking	• Has *ideas of reference*, the belief that certain aspects of the external world—like the shape of a tree or an odd coincidence—might have special meaning • Has unusual beliefs in psychic powers or *body illusions*, thinking that aspects of his or her body are not under his or her control, or has an out-of-body experience	High N Low E Low A
Cluster B: dramatic-emotional ("wild" or "bad")			
Antisocial personality disorder	Unwillingness to follow social norms and obey authority	• Displays law-breaking, fighting, risky behavior, irresponsibility, and a lack of remorse for harming others • Dishonorably discharged from the military for not following orders • Steals and abuses drugs and alcohol	Low A Low C
Borderline personality disorder	Unstable emotions, fluctuating self-esteem, and turbulent relationships with others	• Sees relationships as very positive and then, suddenly, as very negative (for example, loves someone and then despises him or her—and then loves him or her again) • Thinks about suicide • Cuts him- or herself on purpose (known as *cutting*) • Feels empty inside, and then binges on food, sex, or drugs to feel better	High N Low A Low C
Histrionic personality disorder	Dramatic and attention-seeking	• Seems like a "diva"; very dramatic • Is inappropriately sexual	High E
Narcissistic personality disorder	An inflated, grandiose view of the self, a desire for attention, lack of warmth, empathetic relationships with others	• Brags, shows off, or otherwise tries to draw attention to him- or herself • Is arrogant • Considers him- or herself to be special • Wants to associate only with popular, high-status people	High E Low A
Cluster C: anxious-fearful ("worried" or "sad")			
Avoidant personality disorder	Socially anxious and withdrawn	• Has trouble starting relationships due to fear of rejection • Worries about being criticized so much that close relationships are difficult	High N Low E
Dependent personality disorder	A need to be cared for or dependent upon another individual	• Unable to make decisions without the approval of someone else • Needs a tremendous amount of reassurance; unable to act effectively without it	High N
Obsessive–compulsive personality disorder	Overly concerned with being perfect or orderly	• Has trouble working with other people because he or she has to control every aspect of a situation • Has trouble adapting to new situations because of her need for control	High C

Note: Description based on APA (2013); Big Five correlations (−.2 < *r* > .2) based on Saulsman and Page (2004).

Figure 14.1 The Three Clusters of Personality Disorders

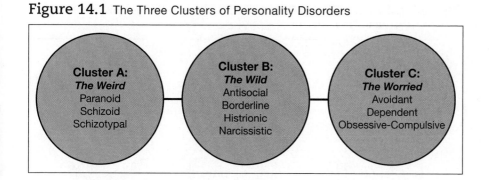

Watch   JANNA: BORDERLINE PERSONALITY DISORDER

WATCH
the video in
REVEL

Personality Disorders and the Big Five

People with personality disorders—any PD—are usually high in neuroticism and low in agreeableness (see Figure 14.2 and Table 14.1). They are more anxious, depressive, hostile, callous, grandiose, and manipulative than the average person. Only those with dependent PD—those who want to please their partners—score a little above average in agreeableness.

In contrast, personality disorders vary widely in extraversion. People with histrionic PD and narcissistic PD are high in extraversion, and those with avoidant PD, schizoid PD, and schizotypal PD are low. Openness to experience is generally unrelated to the personality disorders (Lynam & Widiger, 2001; Saulsman & Page, 2004).

Let's look at examples from a few PDs to give you an idea of how this works. Rachel, who had borderline PD, was described at the beginning of this section. Her low agreeableness is obvious; she screamed at her husband when he said he'd be an hour or two late. She's also high in neuroticism, experiencing lots of ups and downs in her mood. Low conscientiousness is also evident, as she lacks the

Figure 14.2 Correlations of Personality Disorders with Agreeableness and Neuroticism

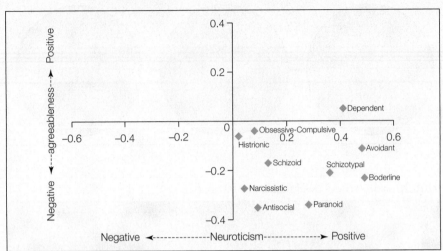

SOURCE: From Saulsman and Page (2004).

Figure 14.3 Borderline PD and the Big Five

How the average person with borderline personality disorder scores on each of the Big Five compared to the mentally healthy (difference in standard deviations).

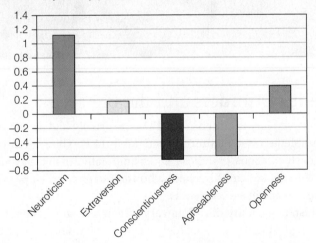

SOURCE: From Lynam and Widiger (2001).

self-control to rein in her anger. This pattern is very consistent with the average personality profile of borderline PD (see Figure 14.3).

Sam has schizoid personality disorder. He's just as low in agreeableness as Rachel, but expresses it in a less dramatic way because he's lower in neuroticism and doesn't interact much with other people. He's also much more introverted, preferring to spend more time alone. Overall, he's withdrawn and socially isolated (see Figure 14.4).

DeLisa, who has dependent personality disorder, seems like the opposite of Sam. She feels a deep need to be loved and cared for by someone else, and perhaps for this reason is above average in agreeableness and extraversion. But she's also high in neuroticism, worrying constantly about whether she's making the right decisions and depending on her partner to help her (see Figure 14.5).

Developing Personality Disorders

How do personality disorders develop—why do some people have a PD while others don't? As with personality in general, genetic factors explain around 50% of the variation in PDs—sometimes higher and sometimes lower. Identical twins are more likely to suffer from the same PD compared to fraternal twins (Coolidge et al., 2001; Jang et al., 1996; Torgersen et al., 2000).

Parenting also seems to play a role. More people with PDs had parents who were emotionally cold and distant. Their parents were more likely to have extreme parenting styles (either too harsh or too inconsistent), use guilt or shame to control children, and/or not express affection (Johnson et al., 2006). The more negative experiences children have, the more likely they are to develop a PD as an adult (see Figure 14.6).

Personality disorders also differ by gender and culture. Men are more likely than women to suffer from narcissistic PD, obsessive–compulsive PD, schizotypal PD, and antisocial PD (Golomb et al., 1995; Grilo et al., 1996; Johnson et al., 2003). Men are more than twice as likely to have any personality disorder

Figure 14.4 Schizoid PD and the Big Five

How the average person with schizoid personality disorder scores on each of the Big Five compared to the mentally healthy (difference in standard deviations).

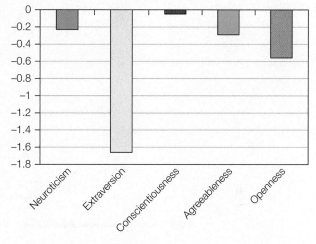

SOURCE: From Lynam and Widiger (2001).

Figure 14.5 Dependent PD and the Big Five

How the average person with dependent personality disorder scores on each of the Big Five compared to the mentally healthy (difference in standard deviations).

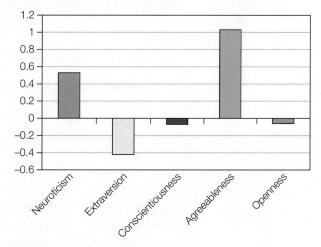

SOURCE: From Lynam and Widiger (2001).

Figure 14.6 Childhood Problems and Adult Personality Disorders

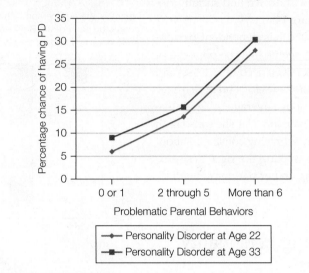

SOURCE: From Johnson et al., 2006.

as women and five times as likely to have a personality disorder in Cluster A—paranoid, schizoid, or schizotypal (Huang et al., 2009). Although borderline PD is often stereotyped as a female disorder, just as many men suffer from it as women (Grant et al., 2008).

JOURNAL PROMPT: UNDERSTANDING YOURSELF

Why do you think there's a sex difference in personality disorders? Do you think it's based more on a biological difference between men and women, or is it a socialized difference that shapes how men and women behave, as well as how we assess that behavior?

Little research has examined variations in personality disorders across cultures. One study found low rates of personality disorders in Western Europe and Nigeria (about 2% of the population) and higher rates in the United States (about 8% of the population; Huang et al., 2009). As yet, it's not clear why these cross-cultural differences exist.

Most of the time, personality disorder symptoms lessen as people mature, peaking during early adolescence and then declining (Cohen et al., 2005; Lenzenweger et al., 2004). Some of this decline is a normal part of growing up. As we discussed in Chapter 9, most people become more conscientious and less neurotic as they mature. Because personality disorders are linked to high neuroticism and low conscientiousness, personality disorders and their severity decline with age and maturity.

Can personality disorders be treated effectively? They can, but it is often difficult. People with narcissistic personality disorder, for example, are notorious for not

negative affectivity
extreme neuroticism

detachment
extreme introversion

staying in therapy because they don't think there's anything wrong with them (after all, they're great!). Historically, therapists used psychodynamic approaches—those focused on issues from childhood—to treat PDs. These days, personality disorders are often treated with cognitive-behavioral therapy (CBT) or even with medications. Therapists also try to target treatments to specific people. For example, psychodynamic treatments are most effective among people who are motivated and insightful (Sperry, 2012).

The PID-5 Diagnostic Model

Personality disorders clearly have a certain personality profile on the Big Five. Yet the Big Five isn't designed to capture the more extreme and pathological behaviors characteristic of personality disorders.

For this reason, researchers recently developed a Big Five of pathological personality to measure these more extreme aspects. The questionnaire based on this model is called the Personality Inventory for *DSM-5* (PID-5; Krueger et al., 2012; Hopwood et al., 2012). The PID-5 is basically an extreme, negative version of the Big Five.

The PID-5 consists of five main traits: **negative affectivity**, **detachment**, **antagonism**, **disinhibition**, and **psychoticism** (Krueger et al., 2012). These can be abbreviated NDAIP, with *I* standing for disinhibition so we don't have two Ds (disinhibition basically means impulsivity, making the *I* fit even better). Rearranged, these letters spell PAIND—spell it PAINeD and it's an easy way to remember it measures pathology. Each trait captures a negative aspect of personality, and each has facets just as the Big Five for normal personality does (see Table 14.2; De Fruyt et al., 2013).

Researchers have debated whether psychology should use normal personality traits like the Big Five to understand mental disorders or, alternatively, rely on more extreme measures of personality like the PAINeD traits. It might be best to take the middle ground on this issue (Markon et al., 2005). Using normal personality traits demonstrates the similarities between normal and

antagonism
extreme low agreeableness

disinhibition
extreme low conscientiousness

psychoticism
extreme openness to experience

Table 14.2 The PID-5 (PAINeD) Traits and Facets

Negative affectivity (extreme neuroticism)
Submissiveness
Restricted affectivity
Separation insecurity
Anxiousness
Emotional instability
Hostility
Perseveration
Detachment (extreme introversion)
Suspiciousness
Depressivity
Withdrawal
Intimacy avoidance
Anhedonia
Antagonism (extreme low agreeableness)
Manipulativeness
Deceitfulness
Callousness
Attention-seeking
Grandiosity
Disinhibition (extreme low conscientiousness)
Irresponsibility
Impulsivity
Distractibility
Rigid perfectionism
Risk taking
Psychoticism (extreme openness to experience)
Eccentricity
Perceptual dysregulation
Unusual beliefs and experiences

abnormal personality and helps predict who will be at risk for mental disorders. Thus, this approach might enable clinicians to help people before they begin to suffer from a disorder. For example, reducing neuroticism in the normal population might lower the number of people who will develop mental disorders (Lahey, 2009).

In contrast, using an extreme model of personality like the PID-5 might capture the nuances and complexities of mental disorders more completely. That approach might allow researchers to better understand the similarities and differences between disorders.

Personality's Past

The MMPI

One of the great breakthroughs in the use of personality tests for diagnosing mental illness was the *Minnesota Multiphasic Personality Inventory*, or MMPI. The MMPI was developed in the 1930s at the University of Minnesota for use in psychiatric settings (Hathaway & McKinley, 1940).

Two aspects of the MMPI set it apart from other questionnaires. First, it was a highly complex measure designed to assess a range of mental disturbances such as depression, schizophrenia, and hypomania. Second, the items were grouped into scales using not theory, but the responses of participants. This became known as the empirical method.

The developers of the scale, Stark Hathaway and John McKinley, selected 1,000 items based on

descriptions in psychiatric papers, other scales, and so on. They then had two types of people complete the items: those with a psychiatric diagnosis, and the presumably mentally healthy. The researchers kept the 540 items that were answered differently by the two groups. This empirical approach means that the scale is based solely on whether or not the items discriminate between types of people, and not whether they make rational sense to researchers. As a result, there are some strange items on the MMPI such as "My feet and hands are often cold," "I have no difficulty having a bowel movement," and "I prefer baths to showers." (The exact items cannot be reprinted, so these are paraphrases.)

The popularity of the MMPI peaked in the mid to late 1960s, and in 1982 the MMPI was fully updated to create the MMPI-2 (Butcher, 1989). The MMPI-2 is still used widely today.

Other Mental Disorders Associated with Personality

mood disorders
disorders characterized by significant problems with mood and emotion

major depressive disorder
a mood disorder featuring major depressive episodes (episodes of depressed mood or loss of pleasure in life that lasts at least 2 weeks)

LO 14.2 Explain how personality and the Big Five traits are related to other mental disorders, such as depression, anxiety disorder, schizophrenia, and eating and addiction disorders.

It makes sense that personality disorders are linked to personality traits. But what about other mental disorders? We focus here on a small but important selection of these disorders, beginning with depression. A caveat: Mental disorders are not necessarily caused by personality and cannot be described solely using personality terms. Nevertheless, emerging research has examined the personality profile typically found in people who suffer from mental disorders. These correlations are far from the whole picture, but they do provide a key part of the puzzle.

Major Depressive Disorder

The product of a brooding New England childhood, Spalding Gray grew up fascinated by the dark side of the human condition. That dark side grew even more dark after his mother committed suicide when he was 26.

Gray went on to become an actor, writer, and monologist. His monologue on the making of the movie *The Killing Fields* was made into the cult classic movie *Swimming to Cambodia*, and he penned a memoir about his childhood titled *Sex and Death to the Age 14*.

Gray struggled with depression his entire life. He sought numerous treatments for his depression and was hospitalized several times, hitting a low point in 2001 when he was seriously injured in a car accident. Then, in January 2004, he disappeared after taking his children to the movies. Nobody knows for sure what happened next, but it's thought he committed suicide by stepping off the Staten Island ferry in New York. His body was found in the East River nearly 2 months after he disappeared.

Spalding Gray

Fortunately, most cases of depression are not as severe as Gray's. Yet even when depression and **mood disorders** don't lead to thoughts of suicide, these afflictions can cause significant suffering. **Major depressive disorder** is diagnosed when someone has one or more **major depressive episodes**— depressed mood or loss of pleasure in life that lasts at least 2 weeks. Other symptoms include problems sleeping, low energy, low self-esteem, trouble thinking and focusing, thoughts of suicide, and unintended changes in weight—either losing or gaining (APA, 2013). Take a moment here to complete the questionnaire below.

major depressive episodes episodes of depressed mood or loss of pleasure in life that lasts at least 2 weeks

Questionnaire 14.1 CENTERS FOR EPIDEMIOLOGICAL STUDIES DEPRESSION SCALE

Interactive

1. I was bothered by things that usually don't bother me.
   - Strongly Agree
   - Agree
   - Disagree
   - Strongly Disagree

2. I did not feel like eating; my appetite was poor.
   - Strongly Agree
   - Agree
   - Disagree
   - Strongly Disagree

3. I felt that I could not shake off the blues even with help from my family or friends.
   - Strongly Agree
   - Agree
   - Disagree
   - Strongly Disagree

4. I felt that I was just as good as other people.
   - Strongly Agree
   - Agree
   - Disagree

Previous   Next

TAKE the Questionnaire in **REVEL**

The scale you took, the Center for Epidemiological Studies Depression Scale (CES-D; Radloff, 1977), is designed to measure symptoms of depression in normal populations, not to diagnose major depression. Still, it demonstrates what depression measures are like.

People high in neuroticism, low in extraversion, and low in conscientiousness are the most likely to suffer from depression (Kotov et al., 2010). The correlation is especially strong for neuroticism, as anxiety and depression are closely linked (Bjelland et al., 2002; Brady & Kendall, 1992). In brief, anxiety is the anticipation of negative events, and depression is what settles in after the negative events occur (or are perceived to occur). Extraversion is linked with positive emotions and happiness, so it tends to protect against depression (Costa & McCrae, 1995).

It is worth noting again that personality is not destiny. Plenty of people high in neuroticism never experience major depression, and some people high in extraversion do. But neuroticism is a risk factor for experiencing depression, and extraversion is a protective factor. Nicole, who is typically anxious and easily upset, is more likely than Emily, who's typically calm and resilient, to slip into clinical depression.

Drug companies often advertise antidepressant medications by noting that depression is a "chemical imbalance" in the brain. For example, taking the most common type of antidepressant, **selective serotonin reuptake inhibitors** (SSRIs), increases levels of serotonin in the brain. So, you might be thinking, if depression is a chemical imbalance, and thus is a physiological disorder, what does that have to do with a more elusive thing like personality?

selective serotonin reuptake inhibitors
a common form of antidepressant medication

This is a great question. As you might remember from Chapter 4, researchers are beginning to investigate how personality is related to neurotransmitters. Sure enough, taking SSRIs decreases neuroticism and increases extraversion. These changes in personality are, in turn, linked to decreases in depression (Tang et al., 2009). Peter Kramer, the author of *Listening to Prozac* (1993), foresaw such a

WATCH the video in **REVEL**

Watch INDIVIDUAL DIFFERENCES IN EMOTION, MOOD, OR PERSONALITY ON THE RISK FOR DEPRESSION

conclusion when he noticed that his patients became more outgoing and laid-back after they began taking antidepressants. Kramer found himself torn: He was happy that his patients were better, but wondered if the drugs changed who they were as people and thus their personalities. In the future, we might find that one of the major keys to treating mental disorders like depression is changing personality. Whether or not that's a good thing will no doubt continue to be debated.

Anxiety Disorders

Anxiety disorders, as the name implies, are a cluster of mental disorders involving excessive anxiety. Four anxiety disorders are linked to personality, and we briefly review each one here.

Guss is always anxious. He wakes up on edge, feels nervous at school, and has trouble sleeping because he stays awake worrying. Guss has **generalized anxiety disorder**, with high levels of anxiety over a period of 6 months or more. This anxiety is not linked to a specific situation or context. The person might "feel on edge," have trouble sleeping, or be irritable and tense (APA, 2013). Daniel Smith, the writer mentioned earlier who couldn't decide what condiment to put on his sandwich, may suffer from generalized anxiety disorder.

anxiety disorders
a cluster of mental disorders involving excessive anxiety

generalized anxiety disorder
a disorder characterized by high levels of anxiety over a period of 6 months or more

Watch PHILIP: ANXIETY DISORDER

WATCH
the video in
REVEL

Paula feels fine most of the time but is sometimes suddenly hit with intense anxiety. The first time it happened she thought she was having a heart attack—it was that scary—and went to the emergency room, but there was nothing wrong with her heart. Paula experiences **panic disorder**; her episodes are called **panic attacks**—intense, short bursts of intense fear and anxiety. Panic attacks are often accompanied by physical symptoms such as heart palpitations, sweating, chest pain, a fear of going crazy or dying, and chills, numbness, or hot flashes (APA, 2013). Especially with their first panic attack, many people think they are having a heart attack.

panic disorder
a mood disorder involving panic attacks (intense, short bursts of intense fear and anxiety)

panic attacks
intense, short bursts of intense fear and anxiety

Agoraphobia can trap
people in their homes.

agoraphobia
a fear or phobia of
public places

social phobia
an intense fear of
social situations

bipolar disorder
a mood disorder
featuring manic epi-
sodes followed by
depressive episodes

manic episodes
periods of elevated
and expansive mood

April also had anxiety attacks, so she started avoiding the places that triggered them. She eventually spent most of her time in her apartment. She suffers from **agoraphobia**. *Agora* is the ancient Greek term for a public gathering place. People with agoraphobia become fearful of public places and start to avoid them. At the extremes of agoraphobia, people stay isolated in their homes and are afraid to go outside (APA, 2013). In the movie *Nim's Island*, agoraphobic adventure writer Alexandra Rover is, ironically, too anxious to leave her San Francisco apartment. When she gets a message from a girl on a remote island who needs her help, Alexandra has to overcome her anxiety step by step to travel to the island and help the girl.

Sebastian is anxious only in social situations, especially speaking in front of strangers. He gets anxious just thinking about public speaking. Sebastian has **social phobia**, an intense fear of social situations, especially those that involve performing in front of others or being with strangers (APA, 2013). Social phobia is fairly common—about 1 out of 8 people will experience it in their lifetimes (Magee et al., 1996).

Although these four anxiety disorders present themselves very differently, their personality profiles are remarkably consistent. Anxiety disorders, like depression, are linked to high neuroticism, low extraversion, and low conscientiousness (Kotov et al., 2010; see Figure 14.7).

Bipolar Disorder

When I (W. K. C.) was in graduate school, I lived in the apartment above that of an artist—let's call him Vincent—and his girlfriend. One week, Vincent stopped sleeping and stayed awake for days making art. Everything turned into art. He painted his furniture with strange designs and went to the beach to paint elaborate graffiti. Then he disappeared from the apartment complex. His girlfriend later told me Vincent was in the hospital—he had **bipolar disorder**, characterized by **manic episodes** of high energy followed by a crash into depression (which is why the disorder was once called manic depression).

Vincent's manic episode was typical for bipolar disorder, with an elevated, expansive mood, high self-esteem, little need for sleep, impulsive decisions, and a mind that races through ideas. Kay Redfield Jamison suffered from bipolar disorder and later became a psychiatrist. She wrote that during her adolescent manic episodes she felt she could do anything and saw the beauty of a massive web of connections in the universe. Although she tried to live with the dark sides of bipolar disorder to keep the positive sides, she eventually took medications to control her disorder (Jamison, 1996).

Figure 14.7 Anxiety Disorders and the Big Five

How the average person with each type of anxiety disorder scores on each of the Big Five compared to the mentally healthy (difference in standard deviations).

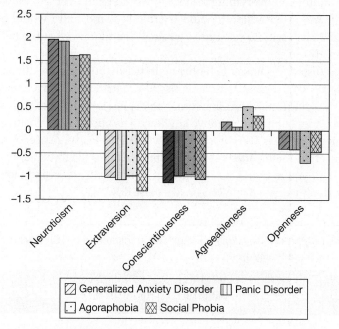

Generalized Anxiety Disorder   Panic Disorder

Agoraphobia   Social Phobia

SOURCE: Based on Kotov et al. (2010).

In her book *Touched with Fire* (1996), Jamison describes the manic episodes of famous writers and poets. Poet Theodore Roethke wrote: "For no reason I started to feel very good. One day I was passing by a diner and all of a sudden knew what it felt like to be a lion. I went into the diner and said to the counter-man, 'Bring me a steak. Don't cook it. Just bring it.' So he brought me this raw steak and I started eating it. The other customers made like they were revolted, watching me. And I began to see that maybe it was a little strange" (p. 28).

Mania might sound like it could be fun, but it can be very destructive. In 2012, actor and writer Carrie Fisher (Princess Leia in the *Star Wars* movies) made headlines when she performed a show

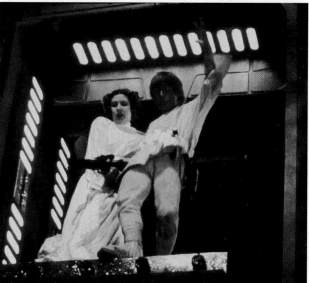

Carrie Fisher in her famous role as Princess Leia in *Star Wars*.

on a cruise ship while apparently drunk. Fisher later revealed she was actually experiencing a manic state caused by her bipolar disorder. "I don't really remember what I did. . . . I was just trying to survive," she said later. "I wasn't sleeping. I was writing on everything. I literally would bend over and be writing on the ground and [my assistant] would try to talk to me, and I would be unable to respond. I can't wait to see what I wrote. I don't know what the hell it says" (Leonard, 2013).

Bipolar disorder is linked to higher neuroticism, but the correlation is smaller than for depression. Bipolar disorder is also linked to higher extraversion, which is the opposite of the low extraversion seen with depression (Quilty et al., 2009). These are the two poles of bipolar: negative emotion (neuroticism) and positive emotion (extraversion). Mania is also correlated with openness to experience, perhaps why it is seen so often among artists and other creative types (Bagby et al., 1996; Quilty et al., 2009). (If you're trying to keep track of all of the disorders and their Big Five correlates, don't worry—Table 14.3 breaks these down.)

Table 14.3 Mental Disorders and Their Relationships to the Big Five Personality Traits

Mental disorder	Primary Big Five correlates
Depression	High N, low E, low C
Anxiety disorders	High N, low E, low C
Bipolar disorder	High N, high E, high O
Schizophrenia	High N, low E, low C, low A
Eating disorders	High N, low E, low C, low A (overcontrolled type has high C)
Addictive disorders	High N, low C, low A

Schizophrenia

John Nash was sure he was saving the world. A brilliant mathematician, he used his code-breaking skills to help CIA agents work against the Soviets during the Cold War. Night after night, he poured over newspapers to find the secret messages the Soviet agents were sending to each other.

John Nash, who suffered from mental illness, won a Nobel Prize in economics.

As exciting as this secret life was, there was a catch: The papers he obsessively read were just ordinary newspapers, and the espionage existed only in Nash's head. He didn't actually work with the government; these thoughts were part of his struggles with **schizophrenia**, a mental disorder characterized by delusions. Nash's life, from the lows of his schizophrenic delusions to the high of winning a Nobel Prize for his work on game theory, are chronicled in the book and movie *A Beautiful Mind*.

People with schizophrenia can experience **hallucinations**, or hearing or seeing things that are not there; Nash believed he was interacting with government agents who did not exist. The movie also shows Nash imagining a college roommate who didn't exist, but there's no evidence he did this. Most of the time, schizophrenic hallucinations involve hearing things, not seeing things (APA, 2013). Schizophrenia can also entail **delusions**, such as someone believing an elaborate plot will trap or humiliate him (APA, 2013).

To be formally diagnosed with schizophrenia, someone must have experienced symptoms for at least a month. Other classic features of schizophrenia include "disorganized speech" (e.g., rambling or odd speech or newly created words—sometimes called "word salad"), disorganized or catatonic behavior (i.e., an inability to move), and flat affect (i.e., not feeling any emotions; APA, 2013). It's important to know that schizophrenia has nothing to do with multiple or "split" personalities, contrary to some portrayals.

The personality profile associated with schizophrenia is low levels of extraversion, conscientiousness, and agreeableness (Malouff et al., 2005; see Figure 14.8). This pattern is even evident in the initial stages of schizophrenia, suggesting that this personality profile is not simply a consequence of schizophrenia (Beauchamp et al., 2011). On the recent cable TV series *Perception*, schizophrenic psychology professor Daniel Pierce isolates himself, argues with people, and needs an assistant to help him get organized enough to teach his classes—behaviors typical of someone low in extraversion, conscientiousness, and agreeableness.

schizophrenia

a mental disorder characterized by disordered thinking, perceptions, and delusions

hallucinations

hearing or seeing things that are not there

delusions

odd and false belief systems

Figure 14.8 Schizophrenia and the Big Five

How the average person with schizophrenia scores on each of the Big Five compared to the mentally healthy (difference in standard deviations).

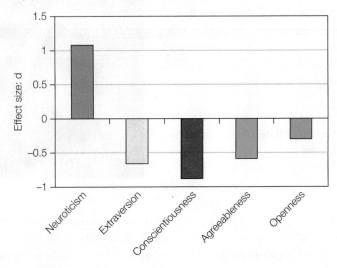

SOURCE: Based on Malouff et al. (2005).

Eating Disorders

Portia de Rossi was starving. It wasn't for lack of money. She was a successful actress who had just been hired to play a lawyer on the hit show *Ally McBeal*. Already very thin, de Rossi became convinced she needed to lose even more weight. She started eating only 300 calories a day (a little more than a cup of white rice). She knew from past experience that she would lose one pound a day for 3 days, nothing for the next 2 days, three pounds the following day, and one pound on the seventh day.

In 2001, de Rossi collapsed with near organ failure and was hospitalized, weighing only 82 pounds. Eventually, she began the process of recovery and made her way back to health. Now married to Ellen DeGeneres, de Rossi related her struggles with eating in her book *Unbearable Lightness* (2010).

eating disorders
psychological problems surrounding eating

Eating disorders are psychological problems surrounding eating. **Anorexia nervosa**, often simply called anorexia, is the desire to maintain a very low body weight—not just thin, but skeletal. People with anorexia have a severe fear of getting fat; their body weight is so important that it becomes central to how they see themselves (APA, 2013). They sometimes become so thin they develop kidney or heart failure. Some literally starve themselves to death.

anorexia nervosa
the pathological desire to maintain a very low body weight

bulimia nervosa
an eating disorder including binging and purging

Bulimia nervosa, often simply called bulimia, includes binging and purging. People with bulimia eat a lot of food all at once, even though they know they shouldn't. They then throw up, use laxatives, fast, or exercise intensely to rid themselves of the calories (APA, 2013).

Figure 14.9 Eating Disorders and the Big Five

How the average person with an eating disorder scores on each of the Big Five compared to the mentally healthy (difference in standard deviations).

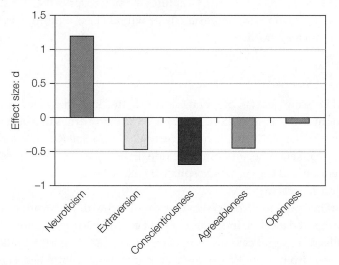

SOURCE: Based on Malouff et al. (2005).

Anorexia and bulimia are not as distinct as they sound. Many people with anorexia also binge and purge, and some people switch back and forth between anorexia and bulimia (APA, 2013; Eddy et al., 2008).

The typical personality profile for someone suffering from an eating disorder is the familiar one of high neuroticism and low extraversion, with some evidence of low conscientiousness and low agreeableness (Malouff et al., 2005; see Figure 14.9). This eating disorder personality profile is not found among people who are simply trying to lose weight in a program such as Weight Watchers (Podar et al., 1999).

People with eating disorders fall into three distinct personality types. The "resilient/high-functioning" group's personality profile is no different from that of a normal population. They are average people who develop eating disorders but continue to function reasonably well (Claes et al., 2006).

"Undercontrolled/emotionally dysregulated" people often become emotional and do impulsive things. They have high neuroticism (the emotional dysregulation) coupled with low conscientiousness and low agreeableness (the undercontrolled part—similar to impulsivity). This group is more likely to binge and purge (Bollen & Wojciechowski, 2004; Slane et al., 2013; Wonderlich et al., 2005).

JOURNAL PROMPT: UNDERSTANDING YOURSELF

Eating disorders are common among young people today. Does the personality profile associated with eating disorders match what you have observed about people who may have eating disorders?

Last, an "overcontrolled/constricted group" has high neuroticism, high conscientiousness, and low openness to experience. These last two traits indicate overcontrol—someone becomes so controlled that she cannot experience new things (Claes et al., 2006). This group captures the stereotype of the high-achieving, perfectionistic person with anorexia whose willpower is a positive trait until it leads her to starve herself.

Addictive Disorders

substance-related disorders
disorders involving problems with intoxicating substances such as drugs and alcohol

On the MTV show *Jackass*, Stephen Glover (better known as Steve-O) became famous for his risky, painful stunts. He abused so many drugs that he began hearing voices (Greene, 2013). In the movie *Steve-O: Demise and Rise*, Glover is shown doing cocaine, ketamine, and nitrous oxide. Eventually, the *Jackass* crew staged an intervention and Glover was hospitalized. He sobered up and has apparently managed to stay clean.

gambling disorder
gambling to an extent that it harms one's life

Substance-related disorders involve problems with intoxicating substances such as drugs and alcohol. Individuals might continue to ingest a substance even though it leads to significant problems in their lives, such as losing relationships or being fired from a job. People are considered dependent when they need to take more and more to get the same effect (known as *tolerance*) or experience withdrawal symptoms after quitting. One beer used to be enough to get your friend Sid buzzed; now it takes six beers. Then Sid's drinking starts to cause problems in his life. He's falling behind in school and his girlfriend is fed up with his drinking. He tried to quit, but couldn't. That's when his drinking fits the definition of a substance-related disorder (APA, 2013).

Addiction can be a destructive psychological disorder.

Substance use disorders have the same familiar profile of high neuroticism and low extraversion (Kotov et al., 2010; see Figure 14.10). People who abuse substances also tend to be low on conscientiousness and agreeableness (Bogg & Roberts, 2004; Kotov et al., 2010). Stopping at a few drinks, or not starting in the first place, requires self-control and dutifulness, both aspects of conscientiousness (Costa & McCrae, 1995). Substance abuse also often means hurting other people, which explains the low agreeableness.

Pathological gambling is also an addictive disorder. The phrase **gambling disorder** conjures up images of a disheveled man down on his luck in an off-the-strip casino

Figure 14.10 Drugs and the Big Five

How the average person with addiction disorder scores on each of the Big Five compared to the mentally healthy (difference in standard deviations).

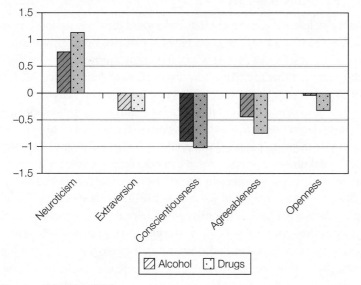

SOURCE: Based on Kotov et al. (2010).

in Vegas or a sorry loser who can't keep away from the horse track. With the emergence of online gambling sites and state lotteries, however, gambling disorder has become both more widespread and less overtly noticeable (Griffiths et al., 2010).

To be diagnosed as a disorder, gambling must have resulted in major life problems. The *DSM-5* uses nine specific criteria to diagnose pathological gambling (APA, 2013), some of which overlap with substance abuse disorders. For example, pathological gamblers constantly think about gambling and need to wager more and more money to get the same rush, very similar to tolerance to drugs and alcohol. Other symptoms include "chasing losses" (betting more and more to make up lost money), lying to friends and family about gambling, and manipulating others to get additional money for gambling.

The personality profile of pathological gamblers has the typical high neuroticism. In other words, most pathological gamblers do not have the suave, confident, and unflappable personality of George Clooney's character in the *Oceans* movies. Pathological gamblers also tend to have low conscientiousness—pathological gambling, at its base, is a breakdown in self-control (Bagby et al., 2007; Miller et al., 2012; Myrseth et al., 2009).

So, given this brief tour of personality and mental disorders, is there anything that can be done?

Types of Therapy

LO 14.3 **Describe strategies for becoming a happier, nicer, and more conscientious person.**

Now that we've learned about mental disorders and their connection to personality traits, we turn to treatment. The good news is that psychotherapy works. Across hundreds of studies, 75% of people who get therapy improve more (or faster) than those who don't get therapy (American Psychological Association, 2013; Smith & Glass, 1977). Interestingly, the type of therapy (say, psychoanalytic vs. cognitive-behavioral) or who administers it (whether a psychiatrist or someone with a master's in social work) doesn't seem to matter on average—the key seems to be targeting the right therapy to the right people (Wampold et al., 1997). Therapy does not always eliminate mental illness, of course, but it can help many people feel better.

Even self-help books—especially those based on well-researched techniques—can be effective. The fancy term for this is **bibliotherapy** (Marrs, 1995). Many self-help books teach a form of **cognitive-behavioral therapy**, which emphasizes changing your thoughts and behaviors. For example, someone who is anxious or depressed may think that one bad decision will cause the rest of his life to fall apart—say, that failing one exam means his whole life has been a failure. CBT teaches clients to question these beliefs, deciding instead that one exam doesn't mean much and it's better to focus on doing better next time. CBT is effective for treating a wide range of mental disorders (Butler et al., 2006).

Antidepressant drugs such as SSRIs are also effective for treating a wide array of mood, anxiety, and depressive disorders, especially when they are moderate to severe—they do not work as well for mild depression (Kirsch et al., 2008). Antidepressants seem to work about as well as psychotherapy (although this is still a debated issue: Pinquart et al., 2006). Antidepressants can also lower neuroticism (Tang et al., 2009). In the next chapter, we discuss additional, more natural strategies for combating neuroticism and depression.

What if you're not overly anxious or depressed, but just think you could be happier? You're in luck because some research suggests that you can make yourself happier (Lyubomirsky et al., 2005). Everyone has a "set point" for happiness: Some people are happier than others to start with. As you learned in Chapter 4, we're all born with certain tendencies and predispositions. However, happiness can be increased with practice (Sin & Lyubomirsky, 2009).

bibliotherapy
treating oneself with self-help books

cognitive-behavioral therapy
psychotherapy that emphasizes changing thoughts and behaviors

Gratitude in many languages.

Figure 14.11 Do Happiness Strategies Work?

The effect of practicing happiness strategies (vs. a control group) on changes in well-being based on degree of effort (low, average, and high).

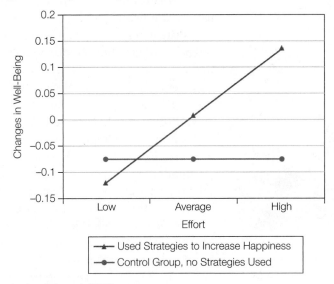

SOURCE: From Lyubomirsky et al. (2011).

In one study, researchers asked people to practice happiness strategies such as trying to be optimistic and showing gratitude (for example, focusing on the good things about where you are living, rather than thinking about the mansion you would have if only you were a billionaire). The control group simply listed what they did the past week. After 8 months, those who used the strategies were happier—and those who practiced the strategies the most diligently were the happiest (Lyubomirsky et al., 2011; see Figure 14.11).

Watch BREAKING A HABITUAL MINDSET

WATCH
the video in
REVEL

Yoga is a form of moving meditation.

Social confidence can also be increased. For example, people can put themselves in social situations even if they are uncomfortable, knowing that their anxiety will dissipate in time. Another technique is to challenge negative thoughts about social situations. In addition, relaxation training teaches people to breathe deeply and relax during scary social situations—it's also a great way to lower anxiety in general. Finally, social skills training can teach people to introduce themselves and make small talk (Heimberg, 2002).

Kindness—or high agreeableness—comes with practice too. One study examined the effect of emotional competence training on social relationships and agreeableness. People who underwent three 6-hour sessions in emotional competence had higher levels of agreeableness 6 months later (Nelis et al., 2011). Another simple but effective approach to increasing kindness—as well as happiness—is to count your acts of kindness, keeping track of the kind things you do for a week or two (Otake et al., 2006). You should feel a shift toward greater happiness and perhaps find yourself becoming a nicer person even in this short period of time.

Finally, low self-control, low conscientiousness, and impulsivity—doing unsafe or unwise things without thinking—is the source of many behavioral problems. Again, though, it can be changed with practice. One of the best ways to increase self-control is through meditation, especially mindfulness meditation (see Chapter 6). People who undergo even a week of meditation training improve their self-control (Tang et al., 2007). Meditation can even help you regain control when your self-control is starting to become depleted. For example, people often get mentally depleted when they have to repress their emotional responses (such as smiling at rude people when working at a restaurant). Meditation counteracts mental depletion and increases self-control (Friese et al., 2012). Perhaps best of all, people who practice mindfulness meditation are less likely to fight with their romantic partners (Barnes et al., 2007). In the next chapter, we reveal even more ways to increase your conscientiousness and self-control.

JOURNAL PROMPT: UNDERSTANDING YOURSELF

Have you ever practiced a happiness strategy? If so, which one did you do and how effective was it? If not, which one would you be most apt to choose, and why?

Concluding Thoughts

Reading about mental health disorders can be depressing—and anxiety inducing. Mental health problems cause so much human suffering, and it's difficult to read about people who are in pain. As entertaining as it might be to watch someone with a personality disorder implode on reality TV, they are real people causing real harm to themselves and others. You might also worry that you or someone you know might develop a mental disorder. Some of you have already experienced the pain of these disorders, either in yourself or in someone close to you.

The good news is that mental health disorders can be treated, and current treatments are much better than those available in the past. There's also a surprising amount you can do on your own to improve your mental health. Changing your thinking and adopting healthy habits can lower anxiety, help prevent depression, and increase happiness (Ilardi, 2010; Lyubomirsky, 2008). These techniques are not a magic bullet, but they can make the difference between being happy and being unhappy and between feeling sad and being clinically depressed. With that said, don't let this tempt you to blame the victim when someone else suffers from a mental disorder. Some people are more prone to mental illness than others, and not all mental illness can be prevented. Instead, let this knowledge inspire you to improve your own life where you can.

That's especially true if you understand mental health disorders through the lens of normal personality. In particular, high levels of neuroticism and low levels of extraversion, conscientiousness, and agreeableness are linked to many mental disorders. This suggests that reducing levels of neuroticism and increasing extraversion, conscientiousness, and agreeableness might reduce or minimize mental illness. This will be an important area of research as scientists continue to uncover the links between personality and mental disorders.

Learning Objective Summaries

LO 14.1 Understand how mental disorders are diagnosed, name the personality disorders, and explain how they relate to the Big Five traits.

Personality disorders are diagnosed using specific criteria, arranged into Cluster A (i.e., paranoid, schizoid, and schizotypal), Cluster B (i.e., antisocial, borderline, histrionic, and narcissistic) and Cluster C: (i.e., avoidant, dependent, and

obsessive–compulsive). Each disorder has a specific pattern of relationships with the Big Five, with many linked to low agreeableness and high neuroticism.

LO 14.2 Explain how personality and the Big Five traits are related to other mental disorders, such as depression, anxiety disorder, schizophrenia, and eating and addiction disorders.

Depressive disorders and anxiety disorders are correlated with high neuroticism, bipolar disorder with high neuroticism and high extraversion, and schizophrenia with low extraversion, conscientiousness, and agreeableness. Eating disorders are linked to high neuroticism and low extraversion, and addiction disorders to high neuroticism, low conscientiousness, and low agreeableness.

LO 14.3 Describe strategies for becoming a happier, nicer, and more conscientious person.

Both psychotherapy and pharmaceutical therapies can be effective for mental health issues. A range of practices can help increase general happiness and self-control, including practicing kindness, gratitude, and mindfulness meditation.

Key Terms

mental disorder, p. 370
psychopathology, p. 370
personality disorders, p. 372
Cluster A, p. 373
Cluster B, p. 373
Cluster C, p. 373
negative affectivity, p. 378
detachment, p. 378
antagonism, p. 379
disinhibition, p. 379
psychoticism, p. 379
mood disorders, p. 380
major depressive disorder, p. 380

major depressive episodes, p. 381
selective serotonin reuptake inhibitors, p. 382
anxiety disorders, p. 383
generalized anxiety disorder, p. 383
panic disorder, p. 383
panic attacks, p. 383
agoraphobia, p. 384
social phobia, p. 384
bipolar disorder, p. 384
manic episodes, p. 384
schizophrenia, p. 387

hallucinations, p. 387
delusions, p. 387
eating disorders, p. 388
anorexia nervosa, p. 388
bulimia nervosa, p. 388
substance-related disorders, p. 390
gambling disorder, p. 390
bibliotherapy, p. 392
cognitive-behavioral therapy, p. 392

Essay Questions

1. What criteria do psychologists use to decide if someone is suffering from a mental disorder?

2. Summarize three personality disorders in relation to the Big Five traits.

3. Aside from personality disorders, choose two other mental health disorders and explain their associations with personality.

4. What are some ways to become a nicer, more conscientious person?

Chapter 15
Personality and Physical Health

 Learning Objectives

LO 15.1 Explain the influence of the Big Five and the types (A, D, and T) on physical health.

LO 15.2 Explain the influence of psychological motives and explanatory style on physical health.

The number 4 sounds similar to the word for death in some Asian languages and is thus sometimes omitted in floor numbers.

In both Chinese and Japanese, the word for the number 4 is pronounced almost exactly like the word for death. Hospitals in these countries routinely skip 4 when numbering rooms and floors (just as some buildings in the United States and Europe skip 13), and Chinese and Japanese restaurants in the United States avoid having a 4 in their phone numbers. This superstition is purely psychological, of course, based on nothing more than a coincidence of pronunciation. But can the psychological have a physical effect—can being afraid of something actually kill you?

Apparently, it can. Among 48 million Americans who died of heart disease, Chinese Americans and Japanese Americans—but not white Americans—were significantly more likely to die on the fourth day of the month (Phillips et al., 2001). Other dates can also be dangerous: People are about 20% more likely to die of a heart attack on their birthdays compared to other days (Ajdacic-Gross et al., 2012; Pena et al., 2015). If psychological stress based solely on a number or a birthday can cause chronic heart disease to become fatal, psychosomatic symptoms are clearly not "all in your head"—they have real effects on the body.

How we think and what we think clearly matters. And how and what we think are dictated largely by our personalities. In this chapter, we cover the links between personality and physical ailments, finding out how your personality might be making you sick—or, if you're lucky, protecting you from disease.

As we've done in other chapters, we use the Big Five to explore the impact of personality—this time on physical health. We also highlight research on **types**, personality profiles linked to certain diseases (such as "Type A" or "Type D"). Much of the original research on personality and physical health focused on types, but most types overlap quite a bit with the Big Five. Finally, we look at how our motives and perception affects our health.

types

personality profiles linked to certain diseases (such as "Type A" or "Type D")

The Big Five and Physical Health

LO 15.1 **Explain the influence of the Big Five and the types (A, D, and T) on physical health.**

Just as personality traits influence your career choices, your relationships, and your mental health, they can also impact your physical health. Let's explore how each of the Big Five is related to different physical health conditions.

Conscientiousness

One day in September 1921, 11-year-olds Patricia and John were summoned out of class to meet Stanford University psychologist Lewis Terman. Terman was beginning a study of highly intelligent children, and Patricia and John had been identified as possible participants for the study. Terman collected extensive data on Patricia, John, and 1,500 other California children, asking their parents and teachers long lists of questions about their habits, personalities, and behaviors. Terman surveyed them every few years, asking about their personalities and documenting their lives as they grew into adults. After Terman's death in 1956, other researchers continued the project until it became the longest-running longitudinal study ever conducted (Friedman & Martin, 2011; Terman & Oden, 1947).

Most of Terman's participants—whimsically called "Termites"—were born from 1910 to 1913, so most of them have since died. That makes the Termites a great dataset for studying why some people live long lives and others do not.

Jess Oppenheimer (right), the creator of the 1950s TV show *I Love Lucy*, was one of the "Termites" followed in the longitudinal study.

So, out of all of the Termites' personality traits, which one was by far the best predictor of who lived the longest?

The answer is conscientiousness. The personality trait that best predicted longevity was what some people consider boring: Someone who is dutiful, makes lists, keeps plans, and is cautious about taking risks (Friedman & Martin, 2007; Friedman et al., 2014). Another larger and more recent longitudinal study of American adults found the same: Among the Big Five, conscientiousness was the best predictor of who lived and who died over a 14-year period (Turiano et al., 2015).

Conscientious people are not inherently robust, but they do keep their doctors' appointments and take their medication. Highly conscientious college students are more likely to wear a seat belt, exercise, get enough sleep, and eat more fruits and vegetables and are less likely to smoke or to drink alcohol (Raynor & Levine, 2009). Across almost 200 studies, conscientious people were less likely to get drunk, use drugs, smoke, be obese, or get into car accidents (Bogg & Roberts, 2004; Kotov et al., 2010; Turiano et al., 2015). They were also less likely to engage in risky sex, defined as having more sexual partners and using condoms less often, and less likely to contemplate suicide. They were less likely to get into fights, commit vandalism, or be sexually aggressive. They didn't exercise more, but they also weren't as likely to do dangerous things like risky sports or unwise things like eating an entire box of donuts (Bogg & Roberts, 2004). Overall, highly conscientious people are more likely to eat healthy diets, including eating more vegetables (Mottus et al., 2013), and have a smaller waist circumference—an important predictor of health (Turiano et al., 2015). Conscientious Carla is more likely to live a long life than low-self-control Lucinda.

Conscientiousness overlaps with self-control or willpower—the ability to control impulses, make good choices, and think before you act. It's also called *self-regulation*, as if the self is a chariot-master controlling the unruly impulses of the mind, which have an unfortunate tendency to run off like skittish horses. Self-control means being able to override both inner responses (say, distracting thoughts about potato chips) and outer behaviors (eating the entire bag of potato chips). College students high in self-control make better grades, have better interpersonal skills, and are less likely to binge-eat or abuse alcohol (Tangney et al., 2004). The opposite of self-control is impulsivity, or acting without thinking.

Impulsivity is linked to obesity. Highly impulsive people weigh 24 pounds (11 kg) more than those very low in impulsivity (Sutin et al., 2011). This makes some sense: Few people have a sudden impulse to eat broccoli or chicken. But it's all too common to crave fattening food such as pizza, pastries, and desserts, and often difficult to limit yourself to two cookies instead of the whole box—or, my personal (J. M. T.) favorite, a few spoonfuls of frosting from the can instead of the whole thing. (Though, admittedly, eating *any* frosting straight out of the can smacks of low self-control.)

So, you might be thinking, if conscientiousness is the best predictor of health and I'm a disorganized mess, am I just doomed? Not at all. In fact, it's possible to increase your self-control and thus, with luck, your health.

People high in conscientiousness are more likely to eat healthy diets, exercise, keep doctor's appointments, and have other habits linked to longer and healthier lives.

In one experiment, college students learned a program of study skills based on planning and self-control, such as dividing tasks into smaller, concrete goals; creating a study schedule; and keeping a diary of their study time. Compared to those in a control group, the students who learned the study skills studied for more hours. That's to be expected. What's remarkable, though, is that the students were also less likely to smoke or drink alcohol, less likely to leave dirty dishes or laundry around, and more likely to eat healthier food. When the students practiced self-control in one area, they improved their self-control overall (Oaten & Cheng, 2006a).

In follow-up studies, students who exercised regularly or carefully monitored their spending also performed better on seemingly unrelated self-control tasks such as eating better and controlling their emotions (Oaten & Cheng, 2006b, 2007). Apparently, self-control operates like a muscle: It gets stronger with repeated use (Muraven et al., 1999).

What exactly did these students do to increase their self-control and conscientiousness—and how can you try it too? Students tried to resist smoking, alcohol, caffeine, and junk food. They also tried to study instead of watching TV, avoided spending too much money, and stopped leaving dishes in the sink. They created a study schedule and gave themselves earlier deadlines to curb procrastination (Oaten & Cheng, 2006a, 2006b). So if you think you're a hot mess, start with one of these areas, like studying or eating better, and over a few months you should develop better self-control overall. If that sounds like too much, begin with just keeping dirty dishes out of the sink and used beer cans off the floor. Then you can move on to getting rid of the beer entirely—or drinking only when you're out.

One big caution: Do not try to change your entire life at once because your self-control muscle will get tired quickly and you'll be more likely to give up. For example, many people make a New Year's resolution to lose weight. They give up dessert and pizza and start going to the gym every day. But this is really hard to do—in lab studies, people who exerted self-control on one task (say, eating radishes instead of cookies) were more likely to fail at another task that required self-control (such as working hard to solve difficult puzzles; Baumeister et al., 1998). To use the analogy of a muscle again, self-control can get tired if used too much during a short period (Muraven et al., 1999).

The key is to plan ahead and set up routines so your self-control doesn't get depleted too much at once. One study found that people with high self-control spent less time resisting their desires—not because they didn't have them but because

Self-control operates like a muscle: It gets stronger with repeated use but can get tired if you use it too much in a short period of time.

they avoided procrastination and developed healthy routines (De Ridder et al., 2012). Perhaps due to forward-thinking choices like these, people high in self-control also report feeling less stress (Crescioni et al., 2011).

Neuroticism

Remember the word cluster for people high in neuroticism, based on the large study of Facebook users? Neurotic people used words like *depressed* and *lonely* more often. But they also used swear words, *hate*, and *sick of* more often, showing a tendency toward hostility and anger (Kern et al., 2014). Overall, high neuroticism people experience more negative emotions whether they are turned inward (anxiety and depression) or outward (anger). Research on the link between neuroticism and physical health explores both types of negative emotions and the personality types that go with them.

ANXIETY AND TYPE D.   People who score high on neuroticism are already prone to worry about their health—after all, they tend to worry about everything. Not surprisingly, neurotic people often have physical symptoms associated with worry, such as headaches and stomach problems (Hazlett-Stevens et al., 2003). Neuroticism is also linked to other health problems such as heart disease, high blood pressure, and obesity (Mommersteeg & Pouwer, 2012; Sutin et al., 2011; Terracciano et al., 2008; Turiano et al., 2012a). For example, in a large longitudinal study, women high in anxiety were more than seven times more likely to have a heart attack (Eaker et al., 1992). The negative emotion typical of high neuroticism may even directly accelerate the aging process; people high in neuroticism have shorter chromosomes, indicative of more biological aging (Brydon et al., 2012; Epel et al., 2004). Perhaps as a result, neurotic people don't live as long (Shipley et al., 2007; Wilson et al., 2003).

Neuroticism also increases the likelihood of becoming depressed, and depression is, in turn, linked to many physical ailments (Booth-Kewley & Friedman, 1987). Neurotic people are also more likely to abuse alcohol and drugs and to smoke cigarettes, probably because they are self-medicating to cope with anxiety and depression (Kotov et al., 2010; Mroczek et al., 2009). Of course, substance abuse can lead to more health problems.

social inhibition

not expressing emotions that risk others' disapproval; overlaps with introversion

Another trait linked to health issues is **social inhibition**, a reluctance to express emotions that risk others' disapproval. People high in social inhibition agree with statements such as "I find it hard to start a conversation" and "I often feel inhibited in social interactions." Social inhibition is linked to low extraversion (Bunevicius et al., 2013). The combination of high neuroticism and high social inhibition has been called **Type D (distressed) personality**.

Type D (distressed) personality

a personality type high in negative emotions (very similar to neuroticism) and high in social inhibition

Type Ds are four times more likely to have had psychotherapy in the past month than non–Type Ds—7% versus 1.5% (Beutel et al., 2012). In one study of young, healthy adults, Type D people's blood pressure went up more after stress (Habra et al., 2003). Type D teenagers were also four times more likely to have trouble sleeping (Conden et al., 2013). If a Type D develops heart disease, he is two to seven times as likely to have a heart attack, develop cancer, or die from any cause as a non–Type D person (Denollet, 2005; Grande et al., 2012).

Does this mean that if you're high in neuroticism, you're doomed for an early death? Not necessarily, for a number of reasons. Most of these studies are correlational, and, as you might remember from Chapter 2, correlational studies cannot prove causation. Health problems can cause people to worry, so the causation might be reversed—perhaps poor health causes neuroticism instead of the other way around. Confounding variables could also cause both neuroticism and illness. For example, some people just complain more, about everything: If physical health is self-reported, the same people who report negative feelings might also report negative health problems, just because they are the type of people who like to complain (MacLeod et al., 2002). That explanation doesn't work for the studies looking at death, though—people can't complain that they're dead.

Neuroticism is correlated with physical health issues.

Most studies control for possible confounding variables such as income, but it's still possible that people who have challenging lives (due to child abuse, parental alcoholism, or other reasons) are both more neurotic and more likely to get sick. It's also possible that neuroticism does not directly lead to health problems, but instead that neuroticism leads to poor health choices such as eating unhealthy foods or drinking too much alcohol. Or the link between neuroticism and earlier death could be solely due to suicide and accidents, as one study found (Keehn et al., 1974). Thus, the deaths could be directly caused by negative emotion or depression, rather than by deficits in physical health.

Let's assume that neuroticism does mean a higher risk for developing health issues. The good news is that being aware of your neuroticism can be very helpful if it means you take steps to combat health issues such as depression before they start. That's not only good for physical health but good in general—worrying all the time is no way to live.

Fortunately, diet and lifestyle changes can combat depression even among people resistant to antidepressant drugs. In his book *The Depression Cure*, clinical psychologist Steve Ilardi (2010) describes a program that combines mental and physical strategies, including social interaction, exercise, omega-3 fatty-acid supplements, sleep, and exposure to sunlight, based on research showing that these factors can lower depression (Golden et al., 2005; Hibbeln et al., 1998; McNamera & Carlson, 2006; Penedo & Dahn, 2005; Thase, 2005). Depression is also linked to **rumination**, the common practice of letting stressful thoughts run through your mind, over and over (Nolen-Hoeksema & Morrow, 1993). Thus, strategies

rumination
the common practice of letting stressful thoughts run through your mind, over and over

designed to reduce rumination (such as meditation) can help guard against depression as well. These lifestyle changes are not a cure-all by any means, but they have been shown to reduce depressive symptoms.

Cognitive–behavioral therapy, considered the most effective psychological therapy (recall Chapter 14), can also help stop rumination. When you start to think negative thoughts, you think, "Stop!" and try to think about something else (Gillham et al., 2007). You can also try focusing on things you're grateful for. Gratitude is linked with increased happiness. Women who wrote letters expressing their gratitude reported greater happiness and fewer depressive symptoms (Toepfer et al., 2012).

Another strategy is to write in a journal. In one study, students wrote either about a traumatic event or about an innocuous topic. Those who journaled about their trauma were less likely to get sick. And it wasn't just all in their heads—they produced more white blood cells, meaning their disease-fighting **immune system** was functioning better and they were less likely to get sick with a cold or the flu (Pennebaker, 1997). Even people who threw away what they wrote experienced health benefits. And it does not have to take much time; even writing for 2 minutes can result in better health (Burton & King, 2008), though the benefits appear to be stronger if the writing is done over a period of weeks or months (Smyth, 1998).

Why is journal writing different from rumination, which has negative consequences instead? Apparently putting things on paper—or speaking to someone who just listens, such as in psychotherapy—allows people to express their negative emotions so they can stop thinking about them so much. Talking to a friend sometimes doesn't work, as he or she will do more than listen—usually, because she's a friend, she will agree with you or say she's gone through something similar. Or she'll try to help you solve the problem, which might get you thinking even

immune system
the body's system for fighting disease

Studies have shown that writing in a journal can improve physical health.

more. This can turn into collective rumination, which can make things worse. That's why a journal, a voice recorder, or a therapist might be better options.

If these activities lower your neuroticism, it's possible they might even help you live longer. Some studies show that people whose neuroticism declines subsequently live longer than those whose neuroticism stays the same or increases. Among men high in neuroticism, those whose neuroticism decreased were 50% less likely to die over the next 18 years than those whose neuroticism increased (Mroczek & Spiro, 2007). It's encouraging news that changes in personality—not just inborn levels of traits—can impact physical health and even how long you live.

HOSTILITY AND TYPE A.   Antonio is always busy. He keeps a detailed daily calendar so he can balance his schoolwork, his part-time job, and his family responsibilities. Any time he gets delayed or has to wait, he gets impatient and a little hostile, even angry. One day, Antonio's friend Bruce invites him to a spur-of-the-moment party. "I can't—I have too much work," Antonio says. "Oh, come on," Bruce says. "Live a little! Yolo, dude! You're so Type A. You're going to give yourself a heart attack someday!"

Is Bruce right? Antonio does seem to have a **Type A personality**, meaning he's hardworking, scheduled, and impatient. Bruce seems to have a **Type B personality**, laid-back and less interested in planning. As Bruce guessed, Type A personalities are more likely to have heart attacks (Friedman & Rosenman, 1974). Take the questionnaire below to get a sense of whether you have a Type A or Type B personality.

> **Type A personality**
> a personality type that is hardworking, scheduled, and impatient
>
> **Type B personality**
> a personality type that is laid back and less scheduled

Questionnaire 15.1 JENKINS ACTIVITY SURVEY

Interactive

1. Your everyday life is filled mostly by:
   - problems needing solution.
   - challenges needing to be met.
   - a rather predictable routine of events.
   - not enough things to keep me interested or busy.

2. When you are under pressure or stress, you usually:
   - do something about it immediately.
   - plan carefully before taking any action.

Previous   Next

> **TAKE**
> the
> Questionnaire
> in **REVEL**

The idea that heart disease might be linked to personality originated with two cardiologists whose office waiting-room chairs needed repair. When an upholstery repairman arrived, he found that only the front part of the chairs was worn out. The doctors' patients, almost all men with heart conditions, were apparently sitting on the edges of their seats—literally (Friedman & Rosenman, 1974). It certainly brings to mind a certain personality type: someone who's always checking

The impatient hostility aspect of Type A is most closely linked to heart disease.

his watch, tapping his foot, and getting angry that it's taking so long.

Type A personality predicts heart disease risk best when it's measured by observing people's behavior during an interview (Booth-Kewley & Friedman, 1987; Friedman & Rosenman, 1974). For example, how did they react when the interviewer spoke very slowly? Type A people are more likely to interrupt and finish sentences for the interviewer, often becoming visibly agitated. When measured this way, Type A personality is a better predictor of heart disease than smoking history or cholesterol level (Jenkins et al., 1976). In a comprehensive meta-analysis, the correlation between Type A (measured by interview) and having a heart attack was .18 (Booth-Kewley & Friedman, 1987). Thus (using a statistical conversion), a Type A person was 43% more likely to have a heart attack than a Type B person.

Once when my Type A friend, Aaron, picked me (J. M. T.) up from the airport, we had to wait in a line of cars to pay for parking. He looked at his watch and realized he'd been parked almost 30 minutes, which would mean paying $5 instead of $2. As each minute passed in the line, Aaron became more and more upset and impatient, hitting the steering wheel and saying, "Come on! Let's go!" Telling him to calm down just made it worse. The more upset he got, the more I wondered if he was going to have a heart attack right there over the possibility of losing $3. I can't remember if we made it through the line in time, but I do remember how red his face got. Might you have had the same reaction as my friend Aaron? Take the questionnaire below to get a better sense of how you deal with stress and express anger.

TAKE the Questionnaire in **REVEL**

Questionnaire 15.2 MULTIDIMENSIONAL ANGER INVENTORY

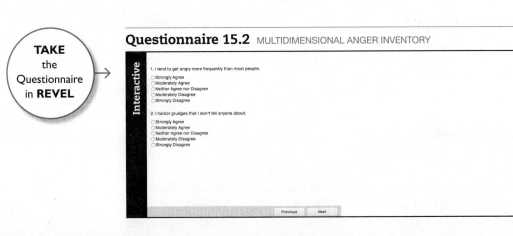

Why are Type A people like Aaron more prone to heart attacks? Does planning things and working hard lead to stress and bad health? Apparently not: Hardworking, successful people actually live longer (Kern et al., 2009). The unhealthy element of the Type A personality isn't hard work, it's impatient **hostility** or a distrustful, overly time-conscious, and angry attitude like what Aaron displayed in the parking line. Hostility alone, even outside of Type A, correlates .19 with having a heart attack (Booth-Kewley & Friedman, 1987; see also Dembroski & Costa, 1987; Wiebe & Smith, 1997). In another study, people high in hostility were 56% more likely to have a heart attack (Barefoot et al., 1995). Thus, the true personality culprit for heart attacks is hostility or anger, a facet of neuroticism (Mommersteeg & Pouwer, 2012; Smith et al., 2004; Suls & Bunde, 2005).

hostility
feelings of anger and frustration.

Hostility may lead to heart attacks because hostile people have elevated white blood cell counts, an indication of **inflammation**, when bodily tissues swell in response to a perceived or real threat (Surtees et al., 2003). Inflammation is increasingly believed to cause a long list of diseases including heart disease, arthritis, and asthma. In heart disease, the elevated blood pressure caused by hostility damages and inflames the arteries, making it easier for fat and cholesterol deposits to collect at these injured places and block the arteries. When an artery becomes completely or mostly blocked and blood can no longer pass, a heart attack occurs. So hostility doesn't cause a heart attack all at once; it causes a series of events that eventually lead to heart disease and heart attack. Hostile people are also more likely to smoke, drink alcohol, and have a poor diet, which may also contribute to heart disease (Mommersteeg & Pouwer, 2012).

inflammation
when bodily tissues swell in response to a perceived or real threat

The Science of Personality CORRELATION IN THE LAB: THE CASE OF TYPE A

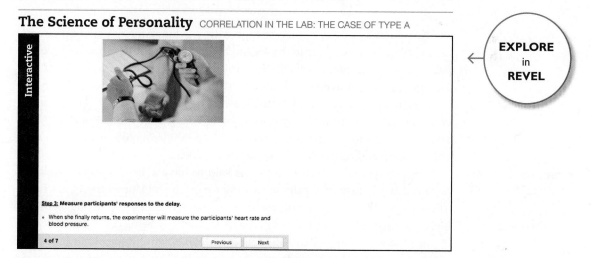

Interactive

Step 3: Measure participants' responses to the delay.

• When she finally returns, the experimenter will measure the participants' heart rate and blood pressure.

4 of 7   Previous   Next

EXPLORE in REVEL

It's important to know that the link between hostility and heart disease is not absolute. Although hostile people are more likely to get heart disease, not all hostile people actually will. Just as smoking is linked to lung cancer, not everyone who smokes will get it. This same caution goes for all of the studies in this chapter: none have a "perfect" correlation of 1.0, so the personality type never guarantees an outcome, just suggests it is more likely. So if you or someone you know has one of these personality types, realize that these studies can make risk assessments but cannot predict perfectly what physical health problems someone will suffer. Same thing if the questionnaire you took identified you as Type A—it doesn't mean you're going to have a heart attack. So don't let the result freak you out; instead, have it guide you to a better understanding of your natural tendencies.

Extraversion (and Type T)

Have you ever wanted to go skydiving, chase a tornado, or drive way over the speed limit? Then you might be high in sensation-seeking. Take the questionnaire below to get a better sense of how you score on sensation-seeking.

TAKE
the
Questionnaire
in **REVEL**

Questionnaire 15.3 BRIEF SENSATION-SEEKING SCALE

Interactive

1. I would like to explore strange places.
   ○ Strongly Agree
   ○ Moderately Agree
   ○ Neither Agree nor Disagree
   ○ Moderately Disagree
   ○ Strongly Disagree

2. I get restless when I spend too much time at home.
   ○ Strongly Agree
   ○ Moderately Agree
   ○ Neither Agree nor Disagree
   ○ Moderately Disagree
   ○ Strongly Disagree

Previous   Next

Sensation-seeking is linked to high extraversion. Among college students, extraverts were more likely to smoke and binge-drink. They also had more sexual partners, a risk factor for sexually transmitted diseases (Raynor & Levine, 2009). College student extraverts are more likely to have been caught violating conduct rules such as underage alcohol possession (Thalmayer et al., 2011). The effect of extraversion on health may also differ by age: Positive emotions may lead younger people to take risks and get hurt but might help older people deal with heart disease and cancer (Pressman & Cohen, 2005).

Type T (thrill-seeking) personality
a personality type that seeks out exciting experiences

An extraverted sensation-seeker is said to have a **Type T (thrill-seeking) personality** because they pursue exciting experiences (Morehouse et al., 1990). Most of the time their explorations don't kill them, but their risk taking leads to a higher chance of being killed or injured in accidents or being convicted of speeding or reckless driving (Furnham & Saipe, 1993). Olympic snowboarder Shaun White, known for doing quadruple flips on the halfpipe over frozen ground, is probably Type T. And although White has so far escaped serious injury, his fellow competitive snowboarder Kevin Pearce fell and struck his head during a run in late 2009 and was in the hospital for 5 months.

Type T overlaps considerably with sensation-seeking and high impulsivity (which you might remember from Chapter 4). Sensation-seekers want thrills and excitement, enjoy unpredictability, and like change and novelty

(Zuckerman, 2002). Sensation-seekers are more likely to get into accidents and to use drugs and alcohol as adolescents (Sargent et al., 2010). They are especially attracted to drugs that are illegal and thus less socially acceptable (Crawford et al., 2003; Donohew et al., 1999). They are also more likely to start having sex earlier in adolescence (Khurana et al., 2012) and to drive cars before they get a driver's license (Begg et al., 2012). Basically, sensation-seekers like to break the rules, partially because the forbidden activity is exciting, but mostly because breaking the rules is exciting.

People high in thrill-seeking and sensation-seeking want exciting experiences.

   Although sensation-seeking and impulsivity are related, impulsivity is the better predictor of risk-taking behaviors relevant for health. Impulsivity usually involves acting without thinking, which can lead to risky actions. Those high in sensation-seeking but not in impulsivity are able to exert more control. For example, they might try drugs but then decide not to use them regularly (Magid et al., 2007).

Agreeableness

Amy has lots of friends and doesn't like to argue—the classic agreeable type. Does her agreeable nature mean she will live longer and be healthier? Based on the available research, it's hard to say. Some studies find agreeable people live longer, some find they die sooner, and some find no connection (Jackson et al., 2015; Turiano et al., 2015; Weiss & Costa, 2005). Peer ratings of women's agreeableness do predict longer life, suggesting that it's how agreeable you actually are to others—and not how agreeable you think you are—that matters (Jackson et al., 2015). People high in agreeableness are slightly less likely to be diagnosed with diabetes or have a stroke (Weston et al., 2015), and are less likely to smoke (Hampson et al., 2007).

   Agreeableness is also correlated with **social support**—fulfilling relationships with friends and family that provide both emotional and practical support (Heaven et al., 2013). People with high levels of social support tend to be healthier and live longer (House et al., 1988; Shor et al., 2013). Thus, the benefits of agreeableness might not come from the personality trait itself but from the network of friends and family that follows from it.

social support
fulfilling relationships with friends and family that provide both emotional and practical support

Openness to Experience

Openness to experience is often the odd one out among the Big Five, and links to physical health are no different. In a large longitudinal study, the only Big Five

trait not related to self-reported health or living longer was openness to experience (Turiano et al., 2012a, 2015). However, openness to experience is linked to
some health benefits. Older men who described themselves as more creative (one
of the facets of openness to experience) were 12% less likely to die over 18 years
than those who were uncreative (Turiano et al., 2012b). Creative people might be
more willing to try different approaches to reducing their stress or managing their
health care (Jonassaint et al., 2007).

Trying to keep track? Table 15.1 is a quick summary of how the Big Five traits
relate to health outcomes.

Table 15.1 The Big Five and How They Relate to Physical Health

Personality Type	Description	Health Outcomes
High conscientiousness	Dutiful, organized, high in self-control	Eat healthier food, less likely to smoke or use drugs, live longer
High neuroticism, Type D, and Type A	Anxious, hostile, high in negative emotion, at risk for depression	Headaches, stomach problems, heart disease
High extraversion and Type T	Thrill-seeking	Smoking, drug use, binge drinking, more likely to die in accidents
High agreeableness	Pleasant and friendly to other people	Mixed results; peer-rated linked to longer life for women
High openness	Creative, interested in ideas	Mixed results; creativity linked to living longer

Which of your personality traits and motives might increase your risk for physical health problems, and which might decrease your risk?

Motives and Explanatory Style

LO 15.2   Explain the influence of psychological motives and explanatory style on physical health.

The Big Five goes a long way toward capturing the links between personality and physical health, but of course it can't explain everything. What about our motivations? How do they impact our health? And does it make a difference how we interpret what happens to us?

Psychological Motives

Paula is high in power motive, which means she has a strong desire to control her own actions and those of others (recall Chapter 7). She purposefully entered a job that gave her influence and control over others by working as a high school teacher. She'd always had the freedom to design her own lesson plans and has a sign at the front of her classroom that says, "I dismiss this class." But now a new principal has started to micromanage all of the teachers, setting universal lesson plans and mandating that students be released as soon as the bell rings.

Paula soon becomes frustrated by the situation, and it begins to cause her a great deal of stress. But is it likely to affect her physical health as well?

Some research suggests it will. People high in power motive don't usually suffer from heart disease any more than those low in power motive. But when a high-power person feels controlled by others, they often become distressed (McClelland, 1989; McClelland et al., 1982). Paula won't suffer ill-effects to her health just from being high in power motive. But when the situation with the principal causes her stress, Paula might eventually find herself in the waiting room of the local cardiologist—or at home with the flu.

How does this happen? A "blocked" or thwarted need for power leads to stress, which leads to chronic high blood pressure, which can then lead to immune system problems (Jemmott et al., 1990). For example, male prisoners high in the need for power had compromised immune system function and suffered from more illnesses than prisoners low in power motive. Obviously, their need for power was constantly thwarted in prison (McClelland et al., 1982).

Personality's Past

Shock the "Executive" Monkey

One of the first and most well-known experiments on psychological processes and physical health was conducted on monkeys. The study was designed to understand the stress experienced by human business executives. Instead of humans facing the stress of the workplace, four "executive" monkeys had to make decisions and faced electric shocks to their feet (Brady, 1958).

In the executive monkey study, pairs of monkeys were placed in contraptions that limited their movement. Both monkeys also had electric wires attached to their feet that created shocks. One monkey, the executive, was trained to pull a lever that could stop the shocks. So, for example, if a shock was to come in a 20-second timeframe, the executive monkey could pull the lever and stop it. The other monkey had no control; it was just shocked whenever the executive was.

This cruel experiment went on for almost a month, with 6-hour intervals of shock followed by rest periods. As a result, several executive monkeys died from ulcers caused by the stress. The other monkeys seemed to fare better from the shocks. The researchers concluded that the control and stress experienced by the executives played a role in their demise.

Despite its conclusions that control leads to negative coping with stress, this experiment had several key flaws: the sample size (a total of eight monkeys) was tiny, monkeys were not randomly assigned to conditions, and the outcome variable was death with stress inferred from autopsies.

The research in this area since then has led to a very different conclusion about control and health. Across multiple studies and outcomes, a sense of control actually helps protect individuals from stress—even if the control is only perceived and is not real (Geer et al., 1970).

The importance of perceived control is especially relevant in the workplace. Unlike executive monkeys, humans who experience control at work report less depression, burnout, and stress (Glass & McKnight, 1996; Spector, 1986).

Other challenges to identity can also lead to immune system problems. People who think about how they fall short of their ideal selves have lower levels of natural killer cells that fight off disease. In other words, their immune system wasn't working as well as it should have (Strauman et al., 1993). Similar to the health effects of thwarted power motive, not being able to achieve your desired personality leads to stress, which can then lead to immune system issues and physical illness.

Another psychological motive, however, might protect against immune system problems. People high in affiliation motive—those who focus on relationships—have better immune system function (Jemmott et al., 1990; McClelland et al., 1985). During times of stress, such as during final exams, high-affiliation students are more likely to stay healthy than those low in affiliation (McClelland, 1989).

This might happen due to hormonal changes. Students who watched a high-affiliation movie (the romance *The Bridges of Madison County* or a film showing Mother Teresa's compassion toward the poor) experienced increased levels of **progesterone**, a hormone associated with feelings of closeness to others (McClelland & Kirshnit, 1988; Schultheiss et al., 2004). Progesterone also increased after women had an intimate conversation with someone, compared

progesterone
a hormone associated with feelings of closeness to others

to a neutral conversation (Brown et al., 2009). Progesterone may promote a "tend and befriend" response to stress—seeking social support from others (Taylor et al., 2000)—instead of the fight-or-flight response to stress more common among those high in power motive. In the long run, the tend-and-befriend response (found more often among women) might be healthier for the immune system and possibly for heart health as well. It might be one reason why women are less likely to have heart attacks than men.

Before we move on to the next section on explanatory style, take the questionnaire below.

Questionnaire 15.4 ATTRIBUTION STYLE QUESTIONNAIRE

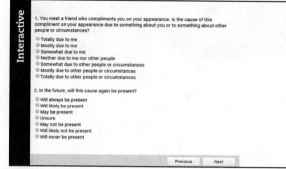

TAKE the Questionnaire in **REVEL**

Pessimistic Versus Optimistic Explanatory Style

Childhood favorite Pooh Bear has two friends with completely opposite personalities: Eeyore the donkey, the classic sad pessimist, and Tigger, the bouncy tiger optimist. Let's ask a question we won't share with Pooh's innocent preschool-age friends: Who is likely to die first? And, even more interesting, why?

As you might have guessed, optimist Tigger is likely to live longer than pessimist Eeyore. Optimistic people have better immune system functioning and recover more quickly from heart attacks and surgery (Carver et al., 1993; Tindle et al., 2012). In one study, people agreed to be exposed to a cold virus (through a nasal spray). Those who described themselves as happy, cheerful, and lively were three times less likely to get the cold (Cohen et al., 2003). Probably due to better immune system functioning, cheerful people really are less likely to get sick (Pressman & Cohen, 2005).

How can we define optimism and pessimism? Pessimists and optimists perceive negative events differently. Someone with an **optimistic explanatory style** sees bad events as transient (won't happen again), specific (only affecting one aspect of life), and external (caused by something outside the self). Someone with a **pessimistic explanatory style**, though, sees bad events as stable (likely

optimistic explanatory style
believing negative events are temporary and specific

pessimistic explanatory style
seeing bad events as all-encompassing

to keep happening), global (affecting many aspects of life), and internal (caused by the self) (Forgeard & Seligman, 2012). Pessimistic people believe that bad events will happen again and cause more bad events—kind of like the Lemony Snicket book, *A Series of Unfortunate Events*. It's sometimes called "Chicken Littling"—believing that "the sky is falling" all the time, or **catastrophizing**, thinking that even small negative events are catastrophes (Peterson et al., 1998). These beliefs are reversed for good events: Optimists believe good events are stable, global, and internal, and pessimists believe good events are transient, specific, and external (see Table 15.2). The questionnaire you took should give

catastrophizing
believing that bad events are all-encompassing

Table 15.2 Explanations for Good and Bad Events by People High in Optimistic Versus Pessimistic Explanatory Style

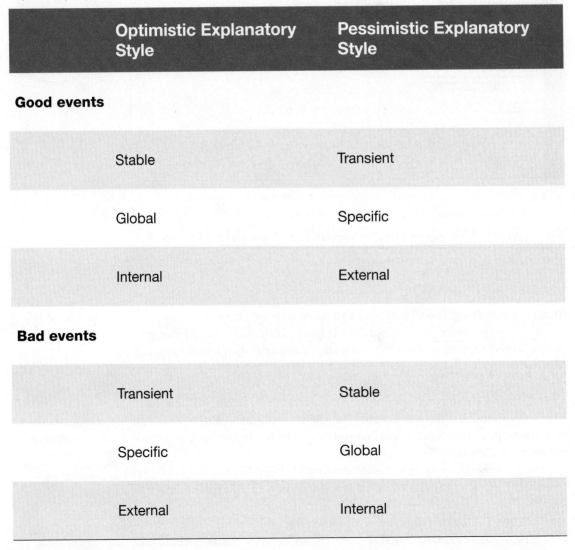

	Optimistic Explanatory Style	Pessimistic Explanatory Style
Good events		
	Stable	Transient
	Global	Specific
	Internal	External
Bad events		
	Transient	Stable
	Specific	Global
	External	Internal

you a good idea of whether you have an optimistic or pessimistic explanatory style, or some of both.

A pessimistic explanatory style is different from the defensive pessimism you read about in Chapter 6; defensive pessimists are not convinced that the worst will continue to happen but try to prepare in case it does. Both types of pessimists are different from optimists, who instead see the bright side of everything. For example, Pooh is almost as optimistic as Tigger. "What day is it?" he asks. "It's today," Piglet answers. "My favorite day," says Pooh.

One large study headed by Chris Peterson followed more than 1,000 men for 50 years and saw whether optimism predicted a longer life. It did, but not for the reasons Peterson originally thought. Pessimists were not any more likely to die of cancer or heart disease. But they were more likely to die from accidents or violence (Peterson et al., 1998; see Figure 15.1). In a follow-up study, Peterson found that college students with a pessimistic explanatory style were more likely to say they had experienced at least one accident, assault, injury, or poisoning during the past 24 months. Pessimists were drawn to hazardous situations (Peterson & Bossio, 2001).

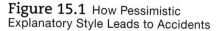

Figure 15.1 How Pessimistic Explanatory Style Leads to Accidents

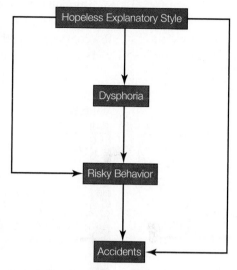

SOURCE: Based on Peterson et al. (1998).

You might wonder how both extraverted sensation-seekers (usually associated with positive emotion) and pessimistic depressives could both be drawn to dangerous activities. It could be that accident-prone people are two different groups—the pessimists, who do dangerous things because they're trying to use the rush to feel better or just don't care, and the extraverts, who want to stay at a high level of stimulation. Pessimistic explanatory style is like Type T or sensation-seeking's dark cousin—not the calculated risk taking of a snowboarder, but risk taking because they felt like they didn't have anything to lose.

JOURNAL PROMPT: UNDERSTANDING YOURSELF

What is your explanatory style? Why do you think this is so? Is it reflective of your overall personality, such as your scores on the Big Five?

Optimism—the opposite of pessimism—also has benefits for mental health, which can then lead to better physical health and recovery. People with positive illusions adjust better to difficult circumstances (Taylor & Armor, 1996). Although you'd expect depressed people to be pessimists, on average they're actually realists. People who report being less depressed are, on average, more optimistic than they should be (Taylor & Brown, 1988). Apparently it's necessary to be a little too optimistic to keep from being depressed.

This suggests that people might benefit from optimism training. Such training would focus on teaching people a more optimistic explanatory style, leading them to see negative events as unlikely to occur again (Gillham et al., 2007; Jaycox et al., 1994). For example, a program based on cognitive-behavioral therapy trained pessimistic college students to question their automatic negative thoughts and keep on task using time management and anti-procrastination techniques. Compared to a control group, the trained students developed a more optimistic explanatory style and were less likely to feel depressed (Seligman et al., 1999).

Watch PSYCHOLOGICAL RESILIENCE

WATCH the video in REVEL →

Video

Concluding Thoughts

The links between personality traits and physical health mean you might be able to improve your health using some psychological techniques. Here are a handful of ideas:

- Learn to relax. Reduce anger, arousal, and frustration by practicing deep breathing or mindfulness meditation.

- Be happy and optimistic as much as possible. This doesn't mean denying reality, but instead, leaning toward the positive. The glass isn't overflowing—but it is half full rather than half empty.

- Take care of yourself by being conscientious about your health. If something is out of whack, get it checked out. Eat healthy food—real stuff, not junk in a package. If you're the risk-taking type, plan beforehand (say, by wearing a helmet). The rush will still be there.

- Develop your self-control muscle, remembering that just as building physical muscle takes time, your self-control muscle needs a steady workout to get stronger. A single resolution on New Year's Eve won't magically make you healthy—it will take weeks and months of effort. But you can make a choice to do it.

With its emphasis on innate dispositions, genetic influences, and mind–body links, personality psychology can sometimes seem like one big body blow to the idea of free will. Yet, as you've seen throughout this book, it's possible to harness the findings of personality psychology to live a better life. The link between conscientiousness and a long life is a perfect example. This is what personality psychology should do: Help us understand ourselves, but also help us see how we can be better and do more.

Learning Objective Summaries

LO 15.1 Explain the influence of the Big Five and the types (A, D, and T) on physical health.

Conscientiousness is strongly linked to better physical health and to living longer. Neuroticism, Type A, and Type D are linked to inflammation and heart disease. Extraversion and Type T are linked to drug and alcohol abuse and having accidents.

LO 15.2 Explain the influence of psychological motives and explanatory style on physical health.

Poor physical health can result when psychological motives are thwarted. People with a pessimistic (vs. optimistic) explanatory style have compromised immune systems and are more likely to have accidents.

Key Terms

types, p. 398
social inhibition, p. 402
Type D (distressed) personality, p. 402
rumination, p. 403
immune system, p. 404
Type A personality, p. 405

Type B personality, p. 405
hostility, p. 407
inflammation, p. 407
Type T (thrill-seeking) personality, p. 408
social support, p. 409
progesterone, p. 412

optimistic explanatory style, p. 413
pessimistic explanatory style, p. 413
catastrophizing, p. 414

Essay Questions

1. Summarize physical health in relation to each of the Big Five.

2. What are some possible third variables that might explain the correlation between neuroticism and poor health?

3. Explain the connection between psychological motives and physical health.

4. Define the two types of explanatory styles and their relationship to physical health.

References

Abbey, J. (2012). "Pregnant man" Thomas Beatie separates from wife. *ABCNews.com*. Retrieved April 20, 2012, from http://abcnews.go.com/blogs/health/2012/04/20/pregnant-man-thomas-beatie-separates-from-wife/.

Abrahamson, A. C., Baker, L. A., & Caspi, A. (2002). Rebellious teens?: Genetic and environmental influences on the social attitudes of adolescents. *Journal of Personality and Social Psychology, 83*, 1392–1408.

Ackerman, P. L., & Heggestad, E. D. (1997). Intelligence, personality, and interests: Evidence for overlapping traits. *Psychological Bulletin, 121*, 219–245.

Adams, D. (1984). *So long and thanks for all the fish*. New York: Del Ray.

Adams, H. E., Wright, L. W., & Lohr, B. A. (1996). Is homophobia associated with homosexual arousal? *Journal of Abnormal Psychology, 105*, 440–445.

Adelstein, J. S., Shehzad, Z., Mennes, M., DeYoung, C. G., Zuo, X., Kelly, C., et al. (2011). Personality is reflected in the brain's intrinsic functional architecture. *PLoS One, 6*(11), e27633.

Adler, A. (1917). *Study of organ inferiority and its psychical compensation: A contribution to clinical medicine* (No. 24). New York: Nervous and Mental Disease Publishing Company.

Adler, A. (1928). Characteristics of the first, second and third child. *Children, 3*, 14–52.

Adler, A. (1930). *Problems of neurosis*. New York: Cosmopolitan Book Corporation.

Adler, A. (1970). *Superiority and social interest: A collection of later writings*. Chicago: Northwestern University Press.

Ainsworth, M. D. S., & Bell, S. M. (1970). Attachment, exploration, and separation: Illustrated by the behavior of one-year-olds in a strange situation. *Child Development, 41*, 49–67.

Ajdacic-Gross, V., Knopfli, D., Landolt, K., Gostynski, M., Engelter, S. T., Lyrer, P. A., et al. (2012). Death has a preference for birthdays: An analysis of death time series. *Annals of Epidemiology, 22*, 603–606.

Allik, J., Laidr, K., Realo, A., & Pullmann, H. (2004). Personality development from 12 to 18 years of age: Changes in mean levels and structure of traits. *European Journal of Personality, 18*, 445–462.

Allik, J., & McCrae, R. R. (2004). Toward a geography of personality traits: Patterns of profiles across 36 cultures. *Journal of Cross-Cultural Psychology, 35*, 13–28.

Allport, G. (1937). *Personality: A psychological interpretation*. New York: Holt, Rinehart & Winston.

Allport, G. W. (1961). *Pattern and growth in personality*. New York: Holt, Rinehart, & Winston.

Allport, G. W., & Odbert, H. S. (1936). Trait-names: A psycho-lexical study. *Psychological Monographs, 47*(1, Whole no. 211).

American Psychiatric Association. (2013). *Diagnostic and statistical manual of mental disorders* (5th ed.). Arlington, VA: Author.

Amichai-Hamburger, Y., & Vinitzky, G. (2010). Social network use and personality. *Computers in Human Behavior, 26*, 1289–1295.

Amin, Z., Constable, R. T., & Canli, T. (2004). Attentional bias for valenced stimuli as a function of personality in the dot-probe task. *Journal of Research in Personality, 38*, 15–23.

Amodio, D. M., Jost, J. T., Master, S. L., & Yee, C. M. (2007). Neuro-cognitive correlates of liberalism and conservativism. *Nature Neuroscience, 10*, 1246–1247.

An, D. (2006). A content analysis of multinational advertisers' localization strategy in Web advertising. *International Journal of Marketing and Advertising, 3*, 120–141.

Andersen, P., & Nordvik, H. (2002). Possible Barnum effect in the Five Factor model: Do respondents accept random NEO Personality Inventory–Revised scores as their actual trait profile? *Psychological Reports, 90*, 539–545.

Anderson, C. A., Shibuya, A., Ihori, N., Swing, E. L., Bushman, B. J., Sakamoto, A., et al. (2010). Violent video game effects on aggression, empathy, and prosocial behavior in Eastern and Western countries: A meta-analytic review. *Psychological Bulletin, 136,* 151–173.

Andre, M., Lissner, L., Bengtsson, C., Hallstrom, T., Sundh, V., & Bjorkelund, C. (2010). Cohort differences in personality in middle-aged women during a 36-year period. *Scandinavian Journal of Public Health, 38,* 457–464.

Antonucci, A. S., Gansler, D. A., Tan, S., Bhadelia, R., Patz, S., & Fulwiler, C. (2006). Orbitofrontal correlates of aggression and impulsivity in psychiatric patients. *Psychiatry Research, 147,* 213–220.

Archer, J. (1991). The influence of testosterone on human aggression. *British Journal of Psychology, 82,* 1–28.

Archer, J. (2004). Sex differences in aggression in real-world settings: A meta-analytic review. *Review of General Psychology, 8,* 291–322.

Archer, J. (2006a). Cross-cultural differences in physical aggression between partners: A social-role analysis. *Personality and Social Psychology Review, 10,* 113–133.

Archer, J. (2006b). Testosterone and human aggression: An evaluation of the challenge hypothesis. *Neuroscience and Biobehavioral Reviews, 30,* 319–345.

Archer, J., Graham-Kevan, N., & Davies, M. (2005). Testosterone and aggression: A re-analysis of Book, Starzyk, and Quinsey's (2001) study. *Aggression and Violent Behavior, 10,* 241–261.

Arglye, M., & Lu, L. (1990). Happiness and social skills. *Personality and Individual Differences, 11,* 1255–1261.

Arnett, J. J. (2000). Emerging adulthood: A theory of development from the late teens through the twenties. *American Psychologist, 55,* 469–480.

Aron, A., Aron, E. N., Tudor, M., & Nelson, G. (1991). Close relationships as including other in the self. *Journal of Personality and Social Psychology, 60,* 241–253.

Ashton, M. C., & Lee, K. (2010). On the cross-language replicability of personality factors. *Journal of Research in Personality, 44,* 436–441.

Associated Press. (2008). Formula for Ig Nobel fame: Strippers and coke. Retrieved October 2, 2008, from www.msnbc.msn.com/id/26996167/ns/technology_and_science-science/t/formula-ig-nobel-fame-strippers-coke/\#.UKaHUY7VmQc.

Atherton, O. E., Robins, R. W., Rentfrow, P. J., & Lamb, M. E. (2014). Personality correlates of risky health outcomes: Findings from a large Internet study. *Journal of Research in Personality, 50,* 56–60.

Atkinson, J. W., Heyns, R. W., & Veroff, J. (1958). The effect of experimental arousal of the affiliation motive on thematic apperception. In J. W. Atkinson (Ed.), *Motives in fantasy, action, and society: A method of assessment and study* (pp. 95–104). Princeton, NJ: Van Nostrand.

Attrill, M. J., Gresty, K. A., Hill, R. A., & Barton, R. A. (2008). Red shirt colour is associated with long-term team success in English football. *Journal of Sports Sciences, 26,* 577–582.

Auster, C. J., & Mansbach, C. S. (2012). The gender marketing of toys: An analysis of color and type of toy on the Disney store website. *Sex Roles, 67*(7), 375–388.

Austin, E. J., Manning, J. T., McInroy, K., & Mathews, E. (2002). A preliminary investigation of the associations between personality, cognitive ability and digit ratio. *Personality and Individual Differences, 33,* 1115–1124.

Baard, P. P., Deci, E. L., & Ryan, R. M. (2004). Intrinsic need satisfaction: A motivational basis of performance and well-being in two work settings. *Journal of Applied Social Psychology, 34,* 2045–2068.

Babiak, P., & Hare, R. D. (2007). *Snakes in suits: When psychopaths go to work.* New York: HarperBusiness.

Bachman, J. G., O'Malley, P. M., Freedman-Doan, P., Trzesniewski, K. H., & Donnellan, M. B. (2011). Adolescent self-esteem: Differences by race/ethnicity, gender, and age. *Self and Identity, 10,* 445–473.

Back, M. D., Stopfer, J. M., Vazire, S., Gaddis, S., Schmukle, S. C., Egloff, B., et al. (2010). Facebook profiles reflect actual personality, not self-idealization. *Psychological Science, 21,* 372–374.

Baer, R. A. (2003). Mindfulness training as a clinical intervention: A conceptual and empirical review. *Clinical Psychology: Science and Practice, 10,* 125–143.

Bagby, R. M., Bindseil, K. D., Schuller, D. R., Rector, N. A., Young, L. T., Cooke, R. G., et al. (1997). Relationship between the Five-Factor Model of personality and unipolar, bipolar and schizophrenic patients. *Psychiatry Research, 70*(2), 83–94.

Bagby, R. M., Vachon, D. D., Bulmash, E. L., Toneatto, T., Quilty, L. C., & Costa, P. T. (2007). Pathological gambling and the Five-Factor Model of personality. *Personality and Individual Differences, 43,* 873–880.

Baldwin, M. W. (1992). Relational schemas and the processing of social information. *Psychological Bulletin, 112*(3), 461–484

Balint, M. (1991). *The basic fault: Therapeutic aspects of regression.* Chicago: Northwestern University Press.

Bandura, A. (1965). Influences of models' reinforcement contingencies on the acquisition of imitative responses. *Journal of Personality and Social Psychology, 1,* 589–595.

Bandura, A. (1977). Self-efficacy: Toward a unifying theory of behavioral change. *Psychological Review, 84,* 191–215.

Bandura, A. (1986). *Social foundations of thought and action: A social cognitive theory.* Englewood Cliffs, NJ: Prentice-Hall.

Bandura, A. (1989). Human agency in social cognitive theory. *American Psychologist, 44,* 1175–1184.

Bandura, A. (2006). Human agency in social cognitive theory. *American Psychologist, 44,* 1175–1184.

Barefoot, J. C., Larsen, S., Lieth, L., & Schroll, M. (1995). Hostility, incidence of acute myocardial infarction and mortality in a sample of older men and women. *American Journal of Epidemiology, 142,* 477–484.

Barnes, S., Brown, K. W., Krusemark, E., Campbell, W. K., & Rogge, R. D. (2007). The role of mindfulness in romantic relationship satisfaction and responses to relationship stress. *Journal of Marital and Family Therapy, 33,* 482–500.

Barr, L., & Barr, N. (1989). *The leadership equation: Leadership, management, and the Myers-Briggs.* Woodway, TX: Eakin Press.

Barrick, M. R., & Mount, M. K. (1991). The Big Five personality dimensions and job performance: A meta-analysis. *Personnel Psychology, 44,* 1–26.

Barrick, M. R., Mount, M. K., & Judge, T. A. (2001). Personality and performance at the beginning of the new millennium: What do we know and where do we go next. *International Journal of Selection and Assessment, 9,* 9–29.

Bartholomew, K., & Horowitz, L. M. (1991). Attachment styles among young adults: A test of a four-category model. *Journal of Personality and Social Psychology, 61,* 226–244.

Bateman, T. S., & Organ, D. W. (1983). Job satisfaction and the good soldier: The relationship between affect and employee citizenship. *Academy of Management Journal, 26,* 587–595.

Baumeister, R. F. (1987). How the self became a problem. *Journal of Personality and Social Psychology, 52,* 163–176.

Baumeister, R. F. (1991). *Meanings of life.* New York: Guilford Press.

Baumeister, R. F., Bratslavsky, E., Finkenauer, C., & Vohs, K. D. (2001). Bad is stronger than good. *Review of General Psychology, 5,* 323–370.

Baumeister, R. F., Bratslavsky, E., Muraven, M., & Tice, D. M. (1998). Ego depletion: Is the active self a limited resource? *Journal of Personality and Social Psychology, 74,* 1252–1265.

Baumeister, R. F., Campbell, J. D., Krueger, J. I., & Vohs, K. D. (2003). Does high self-esteem cause better performance, interpersonal success, happiness, or healthier lifestyles? *Psychological Science in the Public Interest, 4,* 1–44.

Baumeister, R. F., Catanese, K. R., & Vohs, K. D. (2001). Is there a gender difference in strength of sex drive?: Theoretical views, conceptual distinctions, and a review of relevant evidence. *Personality and Social Psychology Review, 5,* 242–273.

Baumeister, R. F., Dale, K., & Sommer, K. L. (1998). Freudian defense mechanisms and empirical findings in modern social psychology: Reaction formation, projection, displacement, undoing, isolation, sublimation, and denial. *Journal of Personality, 66,* 1081–1124.

Baumeister, R. F., Heatherton, T., & Tice, D. M. (1994). *Losing control: How and why people fail at self-regulation.* New York: Academic Press.

Baumeister, R. F., & Leary, M. R. (1995). The need to belong: Desire for interpersonal attachments as a fundamental human motivation. *Psychological Bulletin, 117,* 497–529.

Baumeister, R. F., Smart, L., & Boden, J. M. (1996). Relation of threatened egotism to violence and aggression: The dark side of high self-esteem. *Psychological Review, 103,* 5–33.

Baumeister, R. F., & Tierney, J. (2011). *Willpower: Rediscovering the greatest human strength.* New York: Penguin.

Beaton, E. A., Schmidt, L. A., Schulkin, J., & Hall, G. B. (2010). Neural correlates of implicit processing of facial emotions in shy adults. *Personality and Individual Differences, 49,* 755–761.

Beauchamp, M. C., Lecomte, T., Lecomte, C., Leclerc, C., & Corbière, M. (2011). Personality traits in early psychosis: Relationship with symptom and coping treatment outcomes. *Early Intervention in Psychiatry, 5,* 33–40.

Beck, E., Burnet, K. L., & Vosper, J. (2006). Birth-order effects on facets of extraversion. *Personality and Individual Differences, 40,* 953–959.

Beer, J. S., & Lombardo, M. V. (2007). Insights into emotion regulation from neuropsychology. In J. J. Gross (Ed.), *Handbook of emotion regulation* (pp. 69–86). New York: Guilford Press.

Begg, D., Sullman, M., & Samaranayaka, A. (2012). The characteristics of young pre-licensed drivers: Evidence from the New Zealand drivers study. *Accident Analysis and Prevention, 45,* 539–546.

Bem, S. L. (1974). The measurement of psychological androgyny. *Journal of Consulting and Clinical Psychology, 42,* 155–162.

Bem, S. L. (2001). *An unconventional family.* New Haven, CT: Yale University Press.

Benassi, V. A., Sweeney, P. D., & Dufour, C. L. (1988). Is there a relation between locus of control orientation and depression? *Journal of Abnormal Psychology, 97,* 357–367.

Benderlioglu, Z., & Nelson, R. J. (2004). Digit length ratios predict reactive aggression in women, but not in men. *Hormones and Behavior, 46,* 558–564.

Benet, V., & Waller, N. G. (1995). The "Big Seven" model of personality description: Evidence for its cross-cultural generality in a Spanish sample. *Journal of Personality and Social Psychology, 69,* 701–718.

Bergeman, C. S., Chipuer, H. M., Plomin, R., Pedersen, N. L., McClearn, G. E., Nesselroade, J. R., et al. (1993). Genetic and environmental effects on openness to experience, agreeableness, and conscientiousness: An adoption/twin study. *Journal of Personality, 61,* 159–179.

Bernhardt, P. C., Dabbs, J. M., Jr., Fielden, J. A., & Lutter, C. D. (1998). Testosterone changes during vicarious experiences of winning and losing among fans at sporting events. *Physiology and Behavior, 65,* 59–62.

Bernstein, D. M., & Roberts, B. (1995). Assessing dreams through self-report questionnaires: Relations with past research and personality. *Dreaming, 5,* 13–27.

Berta, P., Hawkins, J. R., Sinclair, A. H., Taylor, A., Griffiths, B. L., Goodfellow, P. N., et al. (1990). Genetic evidence equating SRY and the testis-determining factor. *Nature, 348,* 448–450.

Bettina Hannover, B., & Kühnen, U. (2002). "The clothing makes the self" via knowledge activation. *Journal of Applied Social Psychology, 32,* 2513–2525.

Beutel, M. E., Wiltink, J., Till, Y., Wild, P. S., Münzel, T., Ojeda, F. M., et al. (2012). Type D personality as a cardiovascular risk marker in the general population: Results from the Gutenberg Health Study. *Psychotherapy and Psychosomatics, 81,* 108–117.

Bezdjian, S., Baker, L. A., & Tuvblad, C. (2010). Genetic and environmental influences on impulsivity: A meta-analysis of twin, family and adoption studies. *Clinical Psychology Review, 31,* 1209–1223.

Biernat, M. (1989). Motives and values to achieve: Different constructs with different effects. *Journal of Personality, 57,* 69–95.

Birnbaum, G. E., Orr, I., Mikulincer, M., & Florian, V. (1997). When marriage breaks up: Does attachment style contribute to coping and mental health? *Journal of Social and Personal Relationships, 14,* 643–654.

Bjelland, I., Dahl, A. A., Haug, T. T., & Neckelmann, D. (2002). The validity of the Hospital Anxiety and Depression Scale: An updated literature review. *Journal of Psychosomatic Research, 52,* 69–77.

Blass, T. (1991). Understanding behavior in the Milgram obedience experiment: The role of personality, situations, and their interactions. *Journal of Personality and Social Psychology, 60,* 398–413.

Bleidorn, W., Klimstra, T., Denissen, J., Rentfrow, P., Potter, J., & Gosling, S. (2013). Personality maturation around the world: A cross-cultural examination of social investment theory. *Psychological Science, 24*(12), 2530–2540.

Bleske-Rechek, A., Remiker, M. W., & Baker, J. P. (2008). Narcissistic men and women think they are so hot—but they are not. *Personality and Individual Differences, 45*, 420–424.

Block, J., & Block, J. H. (2006). Nursery school personality and political orientation two decades later. *Journal of Research in Personality, 40*, 734–749.

Block, J., & Robins, R. W. (1993). A longitudinal study of consistency and change in self-esteem from early adolescence to early adulthood. *Child Development, 94*, 909–923.

Blohowiak, B. B., Cohoon, J., de-Wit, L., Eich, E., Farach, F. J., Hasselman, F., et al. (2014). Badges to acknowledge open practices. Open Science Framework. Available at https://osf.io/tvyxz/.

Boden, J. M., Fergusson, D. M., & Horwood, L. J. (2007). Self-esteem and violence: Testing links between adolescent self-esteem and later hostility and violent behavior. *Social Psychiatry and Psychiatric Epidemiology, 42*, 881–891.

Boden, J. M., Fergusson, D. M., & Horwood, L. J. (2008). Does adolescent self-esteem predict later life outcomes?: A test of the causal role of self-esteem. *Development and Psychopathology, 20*, 319–339.

Bogg, T., & Roberts, B. W. (2004). Conscientiousness and health-related behaviors: A meta-analysis of the leading behavioral contributors to mortality. *Psychological Bulletin, 130*, 887–919.

Bohannon, E. W. (1896). A study of peculiar and exceptional children. *Pedagogical Seminary, 4*, 3–60.

Bollen, E., & Wojciechowski, F. L. (2004). Anorexia nervosa subtypes and the Big Five personality factors. *European Eating Disorders Review, 12*, 117–121.

Bono, J. E., & Judge, T. A. (2004). Personality and transformational and transactional leadership: A meta-analysis. *Journal of Applied Psychology, 89*, 901–910.

Book, A. S., Starzyk, K. B., & Quinsey, V. L. (2001). The relationships between testosterone and aggression: A meta-analysis. *Aggression and Violent Behavior, 6*, 579–599.

Booth-Kewley, S., & Friedman, H. S. (1987). Psychological predictors of heart disease: A quantitative review. *Psychological Bulletin, 101*, 343–362.

Borkenau, P., & Liebler, A. (1992). Trait inferences: Sources of validity at zero acquaintance. *Journal of Personality and Social Psychology, 62*, 645–657.

Borkenau, P., & Liebler, A. (1995). Observable attributes as cues and manifestations of personality and intelligence. *Journal of Personality, 63*, 1–25.

Borkenau, P. R., Riemann, R., Angleitner, A., & Spinath, F. M. (2001). Genetic and environmental influences on observed personality: Evidence from the German Observational Study of Adult Twins. *Journal of Personality and Social Psychology, 80*, 655–668.

Bosson, J. K., Lakey, C. E., Campbell, W. K., Zeigler-Hill, V., Jordan, C. H., & Kernis, M. H. (2008). Untangling the links between narcissism and self-esteem: A theoretical and empirical review. *Social and Personality Psychology Compass, 2*, 1415–1439.

Bosson, J. K., Swann, W. B., & Pennebaker, J. W. (2000). Stalking the perfect measure of implicit self-esteem: The blind men and the elephant revisited? *Journal of Personality and Social Psychology, 79*, 631–643.

Botwin, M. D., Buss, D. M., & Shackelford, T. K. (1997). Personality and mate preferences: Five factors in mate selection and marital satisfaction. *Journal of Personality, 65*, 107–136.

Bouchard, T. J., & McGue, M. (2003). Genetic and environmental influences on human psychological differences. *Journal of Neurobiology, 54*, 4–45.

Bowlby, J. (1969). *Attachment and loss: Vol. I. Attachment.* London: Hogarth Press.

Bowlby, J. (1990). *A secure base: Parent–child attachment and healthy human development.* New York: Basic Books.

Boyce, T. E., & Geller, E. S. (2002). Using the Barnum effect to teach psychological research methods. *Teaching of Psychology, 29*, 316–318.

Brady, E. U., & Kendall, P. C. (1992). Comorbidity of anxiety and depression in children and adolescents. *Psychological Bulletin, 111*, 244–255.

Branje, S. J. T., Van Lieshout, C. F. M., & Gerris, J. R. M. (2007). Big Five personality development in adolescence and adulthood. *European Journal of Personality, 21*, 45–62.

Brebner, J. (2003). Gender and emotions. *Personality and Individual Differences, 34*, 387–394.

Brennan, K. A., & Morns, K. A. (1997). Attachment styles, self-esteem, and patterns of seeking feedback from romantic partners. *Personality and Social Psychology Bulletin, 23*, 23–31.

Brickman, P., Coates, D., & Janoff-Bulman, R. (1978). Lottery winners and accident victims: Is happiness relative? *Journal of Personality and Social Psychology, 36*, 917–927.

Briggs, M. I., McCaulley, M. H., Quenk, N. L., Hammer, A. L., & Mitchell, W. D. (2009). *MBTI step III manual: Exploring personality development using the Myers-Briggs type indicator instrument.* Palo Alto, CA: Consulting Psychologists Press.

Broderick, P. C. (2005). Mindfulness and coping with dysphoric mood: Contrasts with rumination and distraction. *Cognitive Therapy and Research, 29*, 501–510.

Brown, K. W., & Ryan, R. M. (2003). The benefits of being present: Mindfulness and its role in psychological well-being. *Journal of Personality and Social Psychology, 84*, 822–848.

Brown, M. A., & Olshansky, E. F. (1997). From limbo to legitimacy: A theoretical model of the transition to the primary care nurse practitioner role. *Nursing Research, 46*, 46–51.

Brown, S. L., Fredrickson, B. L., Wirth, M. M., Poulin, M. J., Meier, E. A., Heaphy, E. D., et al. (2009). Social closeness increases salivary progesterone in humans. *Hormones and Behavior, 56*, 108–111.

Brown, S., & Taylor, K. (2014). Household finances and the "Big Five" personality traits. *Journal of Economic Psychology, 45*, 197–212.

Brück, C., Kreifelts, B., Kaza, E., Lotze, M., & Wildgruber, D. (2011). Impact of personality on the cerebral processing of emotional prosody. *NeuroImage, 58*, 259–268.

Brummelman, E., Thomaes, S., Nelemans, S. A., de Castro, B. O., Overbeek, G., & Bushman, B. J. (2015). Origins of narcissism in children. *Proceedings of the National Academy of Sciences, 112*, 3659–3662.

Brunell, A. B., Gentry, W. A., Campbell, W. K., Hoffman, B. J., Kuhnert, K. W., & Demarree, K. G. (2008). Leader emergence: The case of the narcissistic leader. *Personality and Social Psychology Bulletin, 34*, 1663–1676.

Bryant, G. A., & Haselton, M. G. (2009). Vocal cues of ovulation in human females. *Biology Letters, 5*, 12–15.

Brydon, L., Lin, J., Butcher, L., Hamer, M., Erusalimsky, J. D., & Blackburn, E. H. (2012). Hostility and cellular aging in men from the Whitehall II cohort. *Biological Psychiatry, 71*, 767–773.

Buffardi, L. E., & Campbell, W. K. (2008). Narcissism and social networking websites. *Personality and Social Psychology Bulletin, 34*, 1303–1314.

Bullock, W. A., & Gilliland, K. (1993). Eysenck's arousal theory of introversion–extraversion: A converging measures investigation. *Journal of Personality and Social Psychology, 64*, 113–123.

Bunevicius, A., Staniute, M., Brozaitiene, J., Stropute, D., & Bunevicius, R. (2013). Type D (distressed) personality and its assessment with the DS14 in Lithuanian patients with coronary artery disease. *Journal of Health Psychology, 18*, 1242–1251.

Burke, S. M., van de Glessen, E., de Win, M., Schilt, T., van Herk, M., van den Brink, W., et al. (2011). Serotonin and dopamine transporters in relation to neuropsychological functioning, personality traits, and mood in young adult healthy subjects. *Psychological Medicine, 41*, 419–429.

Burnstein, E., Crandall, C., & Kitayama, S. (1994). Some neo-Darwinian decision rules for altruism: Weighing cures for inclusive fitness as a function of the biological importance of the decision. *Journal of Personality and Social Psychology, 67*, 773–789.

Burton, C. M., & King, L. A. (2008). Effects of (very) brief writing on health: The two-minute miracle. *British Journal of Health Psychology, 13*, 9–14.

Bushman, B. J. (2002). Does venting anger feed or extinguish the flame?: Catharsis, rumination, distraction, anger, and aggressive responding. *Personality and Social Psychology Bulletin, 28*, 724–731.

Bushman, B. J., Moeller, S. J., & Crocker, J. (2011). Sweets, sex, or self-esteem?: Comparing the value of self-esteem boosts with other pleasant rewards. *Journal of Personality, 79*, 993–1012.

Buss, A. R. (1979). The trait-situation controversy and the concept of interaction. *Personality and Social Psychology Bulletin, 5*, 191–195.

Buss, D. M. (1989). Sex differences in human mate preferences: Evolutionary hypotheses tested in 37 cultures. *Behavioral and Brain Sciences, 12*, 1–49.

Buss, D. M. (1991). Evolutionary personality psychology. In *Annual review of psychology*, 459–492. Palo Alto, CA: Annual Reviews.

Buss, D. M. (2003). *The evolution of desire: Strategies of human mating* (2nd ed.). Boston: Allyn & Bacon.

Buss, D. M. (2008). Human nature and individual differences: Evolution of human personality. In O. P. John, R. W. Robins, & L. A. Pervin (Eds.), *Handbook of personality: Theory and research*, 29–60. New York: Guilford Press.

Buss, D. M., & Barnes, M. L. (1986). Preferences in human mate selection. *Journal of Personality and Social Psychology, 50*, 559–570.

Buss, D. M., & Craik, K. H. (1983). The act frequency approach to personality. *Psychological Review, 90*, 105–126.

Buss, D. M., & Schmitt, D. P. (1993). Sexual strategies theory: An evolutionary perspective on human mating. *Psychological Review, 100*, 204–232.

Butler, A. C., Chapman, J. E., Forman, E. M., & Beck, A. T. (2006). The empirical status of cognitive-behavioral therapy: a review of meta-analyses. *Clinical Psychology Review, 26*, 17–31.

Buttner, E. H., & McEnally, M. (1996). The interactive effect of influence tactic, applicant gender, and type of job on hiring recommendations. *Sex Roles, 34*, 581–591.

Byrne, D. (1961). Interpersonal attraction and attitude similarity. *Journal of Abnormal and Social Psychology, 62*, 713–715.

Byrne, D., Ervin, C. R., & Lamberth, J. (1970). Continuity between the experimental study of attraction and real-life computer dating. *Journal of Personality and Social Psychology, 16*, 157–165.

Byrne, K. A., Silasi-Mansat, C. D., & Worthy, D. A. (2015). Who chokes under pressure?: The Big Five personality traits and decision-making under pressure. *Personality and Individual Differences, 74*, 22–28.

Cai, H., Kwan, V. S. Y., & Sedikides, C. (2012). A sociocultural approach to narcissism: The case of modern China. *European Journal of Personality, 26*, 529–535.

Cain, N. M., Pincus, A. L., & Ansell, E. B. (2008). Narcissism at the crossroads: Phenotypic description of pathological narcissism across clinical theory, social/personality psychology, and psychiatric diagnosis. *Clinical Psychology Review, 28*, 638–656.

Cain, S. (2012). *Quiet: The power of introverts in a world that can't stop talking*. New York: Crown.

Campbell, J. (1949). *The hero with a thousand faces*. New York: Pantheon.

Campbell, J. B. (1983). Differential relationships of extraversion, impulsivity, and sociability to study habits. *Journal of Research in Personality, 17*, 308–314.

Campbell, J., & Kudler, D. (2004). *Pathways to bliss: Mythology and personal transformation*. Novato, CA: New World Library.

Campbell, W. K. (2005). *When you love a man who loves himself*. Chicago: Sourcebooks Casablanca.

Campbell, W. K., Bonacci, A. M., Shelton, J., Exline, J. J., & Bushman, B. J. (2004). Psychological entitlement: Interpersonal consequences and validation of a self-report measure. *Journal of Personality Assessment, 83*, 29–45.

Campbell, W. K., Bosson, J. K., Goheen, T. W., Lakey, C. E., & Kernis, M. H. (2007). Do narcissists dislike themselves "deep down inside"? *Psychological Science, 18*, 227–229.

Campbell, W. K., & Campbell, S. M. (2009). On the self-regulatory dynamics created by the peculiar benefits and costs of narcissism: A contextual reinforcement model and examination of leadership. *Self and Identity, 8*, 214–232.

Campbell, W. K., & Foster, C. A. (2002). Narcissism and commitment in romantic relationships: An Investment Model analysis. *Personality and Social Psychology Bulletin, 28*, 484–495.

Campbell, W. K., Foster, C. A., & Finkel, E. J. (2002). Does self-love lead to love for others?: A story of narcissistic game playing. *Journal of Personality and Social Psychology, 83*, 340–354.

Campbell, W. K., Goodie, A. S., & Foster, J. D. (2004). Narcissism, confidence, and risk attitude. *Journal of Behavioral Decision Making, 17*, 297–311.

Campbell, W. K., Hoffman, B. J., Campbell, S. M., & Marchisio, G. (2011). Narcissism in organizational contexts. *Human Resource Management Review, 21*, 268–284.

Campbell, W. K., Reeder, G. D., Sedikides, C., & Elliot, A. J. (2000). Narcissism and comparative self-enhancement strategies. *Journal of Research in Personality, 34,* 329–347.

Campbell, W. K., & Sedikides, C. (1999). Self-threat magnifies the self-serving bias: A meta-analytic integration. *Review of General Psychology, 31,* 23–43.

Canli, T., Haas, B., Amin, Z., & Constable, R. T. (2003). An fMRI study of personality traits during performance of the emotional Stroop task. *Society for Neuroscience Abstracts, 33,* 725–727.

Canli, T., Zhao, Z., Desmond, J. E., Kang, E., Gross, J., & Gabrieli, J. D. E. (2001). An fMRI student of personality influences on brain reactivity to emotional stimuli. *Behavioral Neuroscience, 115,* 33–42.

Caplan, B. (2011). *Selfish reasons to have more kids: Why being a great parent is more fun and less work than you think.* New York: Basic Books.

Cappella, E., & Weinstein, R. S. (2001). Turning around reading achievement: Predictors of high school students' academic resilience. *Journal of Educational Psychology, 93,* 758–771.

Carhart-Harris, R. (2007). Waves of the unconscious: the neurophysiology of dreamlike phenomena and its implications for the psychodynamic model of the mind. *Neuropsychoanalysis, 9,* 183–211.

Carmalt, J. H., Cawley, J., Joyner, K., & Sobal, J. (2008). Body weight and matching with a physically attractive romantic partner. *Journal of Marriage and the Family, 70,* 1287–1296.

Carroll, J. S., Padilla-Walker, L. M., Nelson, L. J., Olson, C. D., Barry, C. M., & Madsen, S. D. (2008). Generation XXX: Pornography acceptance and use among emerging adults. *Journal of Adolescent Research, 23,* 6–30.

Carvallo, M., & Gabriel, S. (2006). No man is an island: The need to belong and dismissing avoidance attachment style. *Personality and Social Psychology Bulletin, 32,* 697–709.

Carver, C. S., Pozo, C., Harris, S. D., Noriega, V., Scheier, M. F., Robinson, D. S., et al. (1993). How coping mediates the effect of optimism on distress: A study of women with early stage breast cancer. *Journal of Personality and Social Psychology, 65,* 375–390.

Carver, C. S., & White, T. L. (1994). Behavioral inhibition, behavioral activation, and affective responses to impending reward and punishment: The BIS/BAS scales. *Journal of Personality and Social Psychology, 67,* 319–333.

Cassidy, A. (2012). Eric Cartman. Retrieved August 31, 2012, from http://psyc2301.wikispaces.com/Eric+Cartman.

Caspi, A., Roberts, B. W., & Shiner, R. L. (2005). Personality development: Stability and change. *Annual Review of Psychology, 56,* 453–484.

Caspi, A., & Silva, P. A. (1995). Temperamental qualities at age three predict personality traits in young adulthood: Longitudinal evidence from a birth cohort. *Child Development, 66,* 486–498.

Cattell, R. B. (1943). The description of personality: Basic traits resolved into clusters. *Journal of Abnormal and Social Psychology, 38,* 476–506.

Cattell, R. B., Eber, H. W., & Tatsuoka, M. M. (1970). *Handbook for the Sixteen Personality Factor Questionnaire (16PF).* Champaign, IL: Institute for Personality and Ability Testing.

Cavallera, G. M., & Giudici, S. (2008). Morningness and eveningness personality: A survey in literature from 1995 up till 2006. *Personality and Individual Differences, 44,* 3–21.

C'de Baca, J., & Wilbourne, P. (2004). Quantum change: Ten years later. *Journal of Clinical Psychology, 60*(5), 531–541.

Center for American Women and Politics. (2015). Women in the U.S. Congress 2015. Retrieved March 13, 2015, from www.cawp.rutgers.edu/fast_facts/levels_of_office/documents/cong.pdf.

Cheng, J. T., Tracy, J. L., Foulsham, T., Kingstone, A., & Henrich, J. (2013). Two ways to the top: Evidence that dominance and prestige are distinct yet viable avenues to social rank and influence. *Journal of Personality and Social Psychology, 104,* 103–125.

Cheng, J. T., Tracy, J. L., & Henrich, J. (2010). Pride, personality, and the evolutionary foundations of human social status. *Evolution and Human Behavior, 31,* 334–347.

Cherek, D. R., & Lane, S. D. (2001). Acute effects of D-fenfluramine on simultaneous measures of aggressive escape and implusive responses of adult males with and without a history of conduct disorder. *Psychopharmacology, 157,* 221–227.

Cheryan, S., Plaut, V. C., Davies, P. G., & Steele, C. M. (2009). Ambient belonging: How stereotypical cues impact gender participation in computer science. *Journal of Personality and Social Psychology, 97,* 1045–1060.

Cheung, F. M., Kwok, L., Zhang, J., Sun, H., Gan, Y., Song, W., et al. (2001). Indigenous Chinese personality constructs: Is the Five-Factor Model complete? *Journal of Cross-Cultural Psychology, 32*, 407–433.

Cheung, F. M., Leung, K., Zhang, J., Sun, H., Song, W., & Xie, D. (2001). Indigenous Chinese personality constructs: Is the Five-Factor Model complete? *Journal of Cross-Cultural Psychology, 32*, 407–433.

Chiaburu, D. S., Lorinkova, N. M., & Van Dyne, L. (2013). Employees' social context and change-oriented citizenship: A meta-analysis of leader, coworker, and organizational influences. *Group and Organization Management, 38*, 291–333.

Chiaburu, D. S., Oh, I. S., Berry, C. M., Li, N., & Gardner, R. G. (2011). The Five-Factor Model of personality traits and organizational citizenship behaviors: A meta-analysis. *Journal of Applied Psychology, 96*, 1140–1166.

Christie, R., & Geis, F. (1970). *Studies in Machiavellianism.* New York: Academic Press.

Chua, H. F., Boland, J. E., & Nisbett, R. E. (2005). Cultural variation in eye movements during scene perception. *Proceedings of the National Academy of Sciences, 102*, 12629–12633.

Church, A. T., Katigbak, M. S., Del Prado, A. M., Ortiz, F. A., & Mastor, K. A. (2006). Implicit theories and self-perceptions of traitedness across cultures: Toward integration of cultural and trait psychology perspectives. *Journal of Cross-Cultural Psychology, 37*, 694–716.

Church, A. T., Katigbak, M. S., Locke, K. D., Zhang, H., Shen, J., Vargas-Flores, J., et al. (2013). Need satisfaction and well-being: Testing self-determination theory in eight cultures. *Journal of Cross-Cultural Psychology, 44*, 507–534.

Cisneros, S. (1991). *The house on Mango Street.* New York: Random House.

Claes, L., Vandereycken, W., Luyten, P., Soenens, B., Pieters, G., & Vertommen, H. (2006). Personality prototypes in eating disorders based on the Big Five model. *Journal of Personality Disorders, 20*, 401–416.

Clark, R. D. (1990). The impact of AIDS on gender differences in willingness to engage in casual sex. *Journal of Applied Social Psychology, 20*, 771–782.

Clark, R. D., & Hatfield, E. (1989). Gender differences in receptivity to sexual offers. *Journal of Psychology and Human Sexuality, 2*, 39–55.

Clausen, J. A., & Gilens, M. (1990). Personality and labor force participation across the life course: A longitudinal study of women's careers. *Sociological Forum, 5*, 595–618.

Claxton, A., O'Rourke, N., Smith, J. Z., & DeLongis, A. (2012). Personality traits and marital satisfaction within enduring relationships: An intra-couple discrepancy approach. *Journal of Social and Personal Relationships, 29*, 375–396.

Cloninger, C. R. (1987). A systematic method for clinical description and classification of personality variants: A proposal. *Archives of General Psychiatry, 44*, 573–588.

Cohen, C. A., & Hegarty, M. (2012). Inferring cross sections of 3D objects: A new spatial thinking test. *Learning and Individual Differences, 22*(6), 868–874.

Cohen, D., & Gunz, A. (2002). As seen by the other . . . : Perspective on the self in the memories and emotional perceptions of Easterners and Westerners. *Psychological Science, 13*, 55–59.

Cohen, D., Nisbett, R. E., Bowdle, B. F., & Schwarz, N. (1996). Insult, aggression, and the Southern culture of honor: An experimental ethnography. *Journal of Personality and Social Psychology, 70*, 945–960.

Cohen, J. (1988). *Statistical power in the behavioral sciences* (2nd ed.). Hillsdale, NJ: Erlbaum.

Cohen, P., Crawford, T. N., Johnson, J. G., & Kasen, S. (2005). The children in the community study of developmental course of personality disorder. *Journal of Personality Disorders, 19*, 466–486.

Cohen, S., Doyle, W. J., Turner, R. B., Alper, C. M., & Skoner, D. P. (2003). Emotional style and susceptibility to the common cold. *Psychosomatic Medicine, 65*, 652–657.

Cohen, S., & Wills, T. A. (1985). Stress, social support, and the buffering hypothesis. *Psychological Bulletin, 98*, 310–357.

Colapinto, J. (2006). *As nature made him: The boy who was raised as a girl.* New York: HarperPerennial.

Coleman, J. S., Campbell, E. Q., Hobson, C. J., McPartland, J., Mood, A. M., Weinfeld, F. D., et al. (1966). *Equality of educational opportunity. Report from the office of education.* Washington, DC: U. S. Government Printing Office.

Company news: Mattel says it erred; Teen Talk Barbie turns silent on math. (1992, October 21). *New York Times*, Business Day section.

Conden, E., Ekselius, L., & Aslund, C. (2013). Type D personality is associated with sleep problems in adolescents: Results from a population-based cohort study of Swedish adolescents. *Journal of Psychosomatic Research, 74*, 290–295.

Confer, J., Easton, J. A., Fleischman, D. S., Goetz, C. D., Lewis, D. M. G., Perilloux, C., et al. (2010). Evolutionary psychology: Controversies, questions, prospects, and limitations. *American Psychologist, 65*, 110–126.

Conley, A. M. (2012). Patterns of motivation beliefs: Combining achievement goal and expectancy-value perspectives. *Journal of Educational Psychology, 104*, 32–47.

Coolidge, F. L., Thede, L. L., & Jang, K. L. (2001). Heritability of personality disorders in childhood: A preliminary investigation. *Journal of Personality Disorders, 15*, 33–40.

Costa, P. T., Herbst, J. H., McCrae, R. R., & Siegler, I. C. (2000). Personality at midlife: Stability, intrinsic maturation, and response to life events. *Assessment, 7*, 365–378.

Costa, P. T., & McCrae, R. R. (1980). Influence of extraversion and neuroticism on subjective well-being: Happy and unhappy people. *Journal of Personality and Social Psychology, 38*, 668–678.

Costa, P. T., & McCrae, R. R. (1988). Personality in adulthood: A six-year longitudinal study of self-reports and spouse ratings on the NEO Personality Inventory. *Journal of Personality and Social Psychology, 54*, 853–863.

Costa, P. T., & McCrae, R. R. (1992a). Normal personality assessment in clinical practice: The NEO Personality Inventory. *Psychological Assessment, 4*, 5–13.

Costa, P. T., & McCrae, R. R. (1992b). *Revised NEO Personality Inventory (NEO PI-R) and the NEO Five-Factor Inventory (NEO-FFI) professional manual*. Odessa, FL: PAR.

Costa, P. T., & McCrae, R. R. (1995). Domains and facets: Hierarchical personality assessment using the Revised NEO Personality Inventory. *Journal of Personality Assessment, 64*, 21–50.

Costa, P. T., Terracciano, A., & McCrae, R. R. (2001). Gender differences in personality traits across cultures: Robust and surprising findings. *Journal of Personality and Social Psychology, 81*, 322–331.

Cousins, S. D. (1989). Culture and self-perception in Japan and the United States. *Journal of Personality and Social Psychology, 56*, 124–131.

Cramer, P. (2011). Narcissism through the ages: What happens when narcissists grow older? *Journal of Research in Personality, 45*, 479–492.

Crawford, A. M., Pentz, M. A., Chou, C.-P., & Dwyer, J. H. (2003). Parallel developmental trajectories of sensation seeking and regular substance use in adolescents. *Psychology of Addictive Behaviors, 17*, 179–192.

Crescioni, W. A., Ehrlinger, J., Alquist, J. L., Conlon, K. E., Baumeister, R. F., Schatschneider, C., et al. (2011). High trait self-control predicts positive health behaviors and success in weight loss. *Journal of Health Psychology, 16*, 750–759.

Cripen, A. (2013, November 21). Warren Buffett shares his secret: How you can "tap dance to work." *CNBC*. Retrieved June 17, 2014, from www.cnbc.com/id/49918773.

Crocker, J., Luhtanen, R., Blaine, B., & Broadnax, S. (1994). Collective self-esteem and psychological well-being among white, black, and Asian college students. *Personality and Social Psychology Bulletin, 20*, 503–513.

Crocker, J., & Major, B. (1989). Social stigma and self-esteem: The self-protective properties of stigma. *Psychological Review, 96*, 608–630.

Crompton, T., & Kasser, T. (2009). *Meeting environmental challenges: The role of human identity*. Surrey, UK: World Wildlife Fund UK.

Cross, C. P., Copping, L. T., & Campbell, A. (2011). Sex differences in impulsivity: A meta-analysis. *Psychological Bulletin, 137*, 97–130.

Crowne, D. P., & Marlowe, D. (1960). A new scale of social desirability independent of psychopathology. *Journal of Consulting Psychology, 24*, 349–354.

Crowne, D. P., & Marlowe, D. (1964). *The approval motive*. New York: Wiley.

Csikszentmihalyi, M. (1990). *Flow: The psychology of optimal experience*. New York: Harper & Row.

Csikszentmihalyi, M. (1996). *Creativity: Flow and the psychology of discovery and invention*. New York: HarperCollins.

Csikszentmihalyi, M. (1997). *Finding flow: The psychology of engagement with everyday life*. New York: Basic Books.

Csikszentmihalyi, M., & LeFevre, J. (1989). Optimal experience in work and leisure. *Journal of Personality and Social Psychology, 56*, 815–822.

Csikszentmihalyi, M. (2000). The contribution of flow to positive psychology. In J. E. Gillham (Ed.), *The science of optimism and hope: Research essays in honor of Martin E. P. Seligman*, 387–395. West Conschohocken, PA: Templeton Foundation Press.

Cuijpers, P., Smith, F., Penninx, B. J. H., de Graaf, R. T., Have, M., & Beeksman, A. T. F. (2010). Economic costs of neuroticism. *Archives of General Psychiatry, 67*, 1086–1093.

Cullen, D. (2009). *Columbine*. New York: Twelve.

Cumming, G. (2014). The new statistics: Why and how. *Psychological Science, 25*(1), 7–29.

Curtin, N., Stewart, A. J., & Duncan, L. E. (2010). What makes the political personal?: Openness, personal political salience, and activism. *Journal of Personality, 78*, 943–968.

Curtis, R. G., Windsor, T. D., Soubelet, A. (2015). The relationship between Big-5 personality traits and cognitive ability in older adults: A review. *Aging, Neuropsychology, and Cognition, 22*, 42–71.

Dabbs, J. M., Jr., Carr, T. S., Frady, R. L., & Riad, J. K. (1991). Testosterone, crime, and misbehavior among 692 prison inmates. *Personality and Individual Differences, 18*, 627–633.

Dabbs, J. M., Frady, R. L., Carr, T. S., & Besch, N. F. (1987). Saliva testosterone and criminal violence in young adult prison inmates. *Psychosomatic Medicine, 49*, 174–182.

Dalal, R. S. (2005). A meta-analysis of the relationship between organizational citizenship behavior and counterproductive work behavior. *Journal of Applied Psychology, 90*, 1241–1255.

Dalley, J. W., & Roiser, J. P. (2012). Dopamine, serotonin, and impulsivity. *Neuroscience, 215*, 42–58.

Davis, C. G., Nolen-Hoeksema, S., & Larson, J. (1998). Making sense of loss and benefitting from the experience: Two construals of meaning. *Journal of Personality and Social Psychology, 75*, 561–574.

Davis, F. (1992). *Fashion, culture, and identity*. Chicago: University of Chicago Press.

Davis, M. H. (1983). Measuring individual differences in empathy: Evidence for a multidimensional approach. *Journal of Personality and Social Psychology, 44*, 113–126.

Davis, M. H., Mitchell, K. V., Hall, J. A., Lothert, J., Snapp, T., & Meyer, M. (2001). Empathy, expectations, and situational preferences: Personality influences on the decision to participate in volunteer helping behaviors. *Journal of Personality, 67*, 469–503.

Dawkins, R. (1976). *The selfish gene*. Oxford, UK: Oxford University Press.

De Fruyt, F., De Clercq, B., De Bolle, M., Wille, B., Markon, K., & Krueger, R. F. (2013). General and maladaptive traits in a Five-Factor framework for DSM-5 in a university student sample. *Assessment, 20*, 295–307.

De Fruyt, F., Van Leeuwen, K., Bagby, R. M., Rolland, J. P., & Rouillon, F. (2006). Assessing and interpreting personality change and continuity in patients treated for major depression. *Psychological Assessment, 18*, 71–80.

De Moor, M. H. M., Costa, P. T., Terracciano, A., Krueger, R. F., de Geus, E. J., Toshiko, T., et al. (2012). Meta-analysis of genome-wide association studies for personality. *Molecular Psychiatry, 17*, 337–349.

De Ridder, D. T. D., Lensvelt-Mulders, G., Finkenauer, C., Stok, F. M., & Baumeister, R. F. (2012). Taking stock of self-control: A meta-analysis of how trait self-control relates to a wide range of behaviors. *Personality and Social Psychology Review, 16*, 76–99.

de Rossi, P. (2010). *Unbearable lightness*. New York: Atria.

Deal, J. E., Halverson, C. F., Havill, V., & Martin, R. P. (2005). Temperament factors as longitudinal predictors of young adult personality. *Merrill-Palmer Quarterly, 51*, 315–334.

deCharms, R., & Moeller, G. H. (1962). Values expressed in American children's readers, 1800–1950. *Journal of Abnormal and Social Psychology, 64*, 136–142.

Deci, E. L. (1975). *Intrinsic motivation*. New York: Plenum Press.

Deci, E. L., LaGuardia, J. G., Moller, A. C., Scheiner, M. J., & Ryan, R. M. (2006). On the benefits of giving as well as receiving autonomy support: Mutuality in close friendships. *Personality and Social Psychology Bulletin, 32*, 313–327.

Deci, E. L., & Ryan, R. M. (1985). The General Causality Orientations Scale: Self-determination in personality. *Journal of Research in Personality, 19,* 109–134.

Deci, E. L., & Ryan, R. M. (1991). Motivational approach to self: Integration in personality. In R. A. Dienstbier (Ed.), *Nebraska Symposium on Motivation, 1990,* 237–288. Lincoln: University of Nebraska Press.

Decuyper, M., De Pauw, S., De Fruyt, F., De Bolle, M., & De Clercq, B. J. (2009). A meta-analysis of psychopathy-, antisocial PD- and FFM associations. *European Journal of Personality, 23,* 531–565.

deGraaf, I., Speetjens, P., Smit, F., de Wolff, M., & Tavecchio, L. (2008). Effectiveness of the Triple P Positive Parenting Program on behavioral problems in children: A meta-analysis. *Behavioral Modification, 32,* 714–735.

Dembroski, T. M., & Costa, P. T. (1987). Coronary prone behavior: Components of the Type A pattern and hostility. *Journal of Personality, 55,* 211–235.

Denollet, J. (2005). DS14: Standard assessment of negative affectivity, social inhibition, and Type D personality. *Psychosomatic Medicine, 67,* 89–97.

Deo, M. S., & Lymburner, J. A. (2011). Personality traits and psychological health concerns the search for psychology student syndrome. *Teaching of Psychology, 38,* 155–157.

Depue, R. A., & Collins, P. F. (1999). Neurobiology of the structure of personality: Dopamine, facilitation of incentive motivation, and extraversion. *Behavioral and Brain Sciences, 22,* 491–569.

DeRaad B., Barelds, D. P. H., Levert, E., Ostendorf, F., Mlacic, B., Di Blas, L., et al. (2010). Only three factors of personality description are fully replicable across languages: A comparison of 14 trait taxonomies. *Journal of Personality and Social Psychology, 98,* 160–173.

deRooij, S. R., Veenendaal, M. V. E., Raikkonen, K., & Rosebloom, T. J. (2012). Personality and stress appraisal in adults prenatally exposed to the Dutch famine. *Early Human Development, 88,* 321–325.

DeWall, C. N., MacDonald, G., Webster, G. D., Masten, C., Baumeister, R. F., Powell, C., et al. (2010). Acetaminophen reduces social pain: Behavioral and neural evidence. *Psychological Science, 21,* 931–937.

DeWall, C. N., Pond, R. S., Campbell, W. K., & Twenge, J. M. (2011). Tuning in to psychological change: Linguistic markers of psychological traits and emotions over time in popular U.S. song lyrics. *Psychology of Aesthetics, Creativity, and the Arts, 5,* 200–207.

DeWall, C. N., Twenge, J. M., Gitter, S. A., & Baumeister, R. F. (2009). It's the thought that counts: The role of hostile cognition in shaping aggressive responses to social exclusion. *Journal of Personality and Social Psychology, 96,* 45–59.

Dewsbury, D. A. (1984). *Comparative psychology in the twentieth century.* Stroudsburg, PA: Hutchinson Ross.

DeYoung, C. G., Cicchetti, D., Rogosch, F. A., Gary, J. R., Eastman, M., & Grigorenko, E. L. (2011). Sources of cognitive exploration: Genetic variation in the prefrontal dopamine system predicts openness/intellect. *Journal of Research in Personality, 45,* 364–371.

DeYoung, C. G., Peterson, J. B., & Higgins, D. M. (2005). Sources of openness/intellect: Cognitive and neuropsychological correlates of the fifth factor of personality. *Journal of Personality, 73,* 825–858.

DeYoung, C. G., Shamosh, N. A., Green, A. E., Braver, T. S., & Gray, J. R. (2009). Intellect as distinct from openness: Differences revealed by fMRI of working memory. *Journal of Personality and Social Psychology, 97,* 883–892.

Diamond, J. (1999). *Guns, germs, and steel.* New York: Norton.

Diamond, M., & Sigmundson, H. K. (1997). Sex reassignment at birth: Long-term review and clinical implications. *Archives of Pediatrics and Adolescent Medicine, 151,* 298–304.

Digest of Education Statistics. (2012). Degrees conferred by degree-granting institutions, by level of degree and sex of student (Table 283). Retrieved from http://nces.ed.gov/programs/digest/d11/tables/dt11_283.asp.

Dingemanse, N. J., Botha, C., Drenta, P. J., van Oersa, K., & van Noordwijka, A. J. (2002). Repeatability and heritability of exploratory behavior in great tits from the wild. *Animal Behavior, 64,* 929–938.

Dipboye, R. L., Arvey, R. D., & Terpstra, D. E. (1977). Sex and physical attractiveness of raters and applicants as determinants of resumé evaluations. *Journal of Applied Psychology, 62,* 288–294.

Dittmar, H., Bond, R., Hurst, M., & Kasser, T. (2012). *A meta-analysis of the materialism literature.* Unpublished manuscript, Brighton, UK: University of Sussex.

Donnellan, M. B., Conger, R. D., & Bryant, C. M. (2004). The Big Five and enduring marriages. *Journal of Research in Personality, 38,* 481–504.

Donohew, R. L., Hoyle, R. H., Clayton, R. R., Skinner, W. F., Colon, S. E., & Rice, R. E. (1999). Sensation seeking and drug use by adolescents and their friends: Models for marijuana and alcohol. *Journal of Studies on Alcohol, 60,* 622–631.

Dougherty, D. M., Marsh, D. M., Mathias, C. W., Dawes, M. A., Bradley, D. M., Morgan, C. J., et al. (2007). The effects of alcohol on laboratory-measured impulsivity after L-tryptophan depletion or loading. *Psychopharmacology, 193,* 137–150.

Dryer, D. C., & Horowitz, L. M. (1997). When do opposites attract?: Interpersonal complementarity versus similarity. *Journal of Personality and Social Psychology, 72,* 592–603.

Dugatkin, L. A. (1992). Tendency to inspect predators predicts mortality risk in the guppy, *Poecilia reticulata. Behavioral Ecology, 3,* 124–127.

Dundes, A. (1978). Into the endzone for touchdown: Psychoanalytic consideration of American football. *Western Folklore, 37,* 75–88.

Durante, K. M., Li, N. P., & Haselton, M. G. (2008). Changes in women's choice of dress across the ovulatory cycle: Naturalistic and laboratory task-based evidence. *Personality and Social Psychology Bulletin, 34,* 1451–1460.

Dyrenforth, P. S., Kashy, D. A., Donnellan, M. B., & Lucas, R. E. (2010). Predicting relationship and life satisfaction from personality in nationally representative samples from three countries: The relative importance of actor, partner, and similarity effects. *Journal of Personality and Social Psychology, 99,* 690–702.

Eagly, A. H. (1987). *Sex differences in social behavior: A social-role interpretation.* Hillsdale, NJ: Erlbaum.

Eagly, A. H., Ashmore, R. D., Makhijani, M. G., & Longo, L. C. (1991). What is beautiful is good, but . . . : A meta-analytic review of research on the physical attractiveness stereotype. *Psychological Bulletin, 110,* 109–128.

Eagly, A. H., Johannesen-Schmidt, M. C., & van Engen, M. (2003). Transformational, transactional, and laissez-faire leadership styles: A meta-analysis comparing women and men. *Psychological Bulletin, 95,* 569–591.

Eagly, A. H., & Mladinic, A. (1989). Gender stereotypes and attitudes toward women and men. *Personality and Social Psychology Bulletin, 15,* 543–558.

Eagly, A. H., & Wood, W. (1999). The origins of sex differences in human behavior: Evolved dispositions versus social roles. *American Psychologist, 54,* 408–423.

Eaker, E. D., Pinsky, J., & Castelli, W. P. (1992). Myocardial infarction and coronary death among women: Psychosocial predictors from a 20-year follow-up of women in the Framingham study. *American Journal of Epidemiology, 135,* 854–864.

Ebersole, P. (1998). Types and depth of written life meanings. In P. T. P. Wong & S. P. Fry (Eds.), *The human quest for meaning: A handbook of psychological research and clinical applications* (pp. 179–191). Mahwah, NJ: Erlbaum.

Eckstein, D., Aycock, K. J., Sperber, M. A., McDonald, J., Van Wiesner, V., Watts, R. E., et al. (2010). A review of 200 birth-order studies: Lifestyle characteristics. *Journal of Individual Psychology, 6,* 408–434.

Eddy, K., Dorer, D., Franko, D., Tahilani, K., Thompson-Brenner, H., & Herzog, D. (2008). Diagnostic crossover in anorexia nervosa and bulimia nervosa: Implications for DSM-V. *American Journal of Psychiatry, 165,* 245–250.

Edelstein, R. S., Chopik, W. J., & Kean, E. L. (2011). Sociosexuality moderates the association between testosterone and relationship status in men and women. *Hormones and Behavior, 60,* 248–255.

Eisenberger, N. I., Lieberman, M. D., & Satpute, A. B. (2005). Personality from a controlled processing perspective: An fMRI study of neuroticism, extraversion, and self-consciousness. *Cognitive, Affective and Behavioral Neuroscience, 5,* 169–181.

Eisenberger, N. I., Lieberman, M. D., & Williams, K. D. (2003). Does rejection hurt?: An fMRI study of social exclusion. *Science, 302,* 290–292.

Elliot, A. J., Maier, M. A., Moller, A. C., Friedman, R., & Meinhardt, J. (2007). Color and psychological functioning: The effect of red on performance attainment. *Journal of Experimental Psychology: General, 136,* 154–168.

Elliot, A. J., & Niesta, D. (2008). Romantic red: Red enhances men's attraction to women. *Journal of Personality and Social Psychology, 95,* 1150–1164.

Elliot, A. J., Niesta Kayser, D., Greitemeyer, T., Lichtenfeld, S., Gramzow, R. H., Maier, M. A., et al. (2010). Red, rank, and romance in women viewing men. *Journal of Experimental Psychology: General, 139*, 399–417.

Elliot, A. J., & Reis, H. T. (2003). Attachment and exploration in adulthood. *Journal of Personality and Social Psychology, 85*, 317–331.

Elliot, A. J., & Sheldon, K. M. (1998). Avoidance personal goals and the personality-illness relationship. *Journal of Personality and Social Psychology, 75*, 1282–1299.

Elliot, A. J., & Thrash, T. M. (2002). Approach–avoidance motivation in personality: Approach and avoidance temperaments and goals. *Journal of Personality and Social Psychology, 82*, 804–818.

Elliot, A. J., & Thrash, T. M. (2010). Approach and avoidance temperament as basic dimensions of personality. *Journal of Personality, 78*, 865–906.

Elliot, A. J., Thrash, T., M., & Murayama, K. (2011). A longitudinal analysis of self-regulation and well-being: Avoidance personal goals, avoidance coping, stress generation, and subjective well-being. *Journal of Personality, 79*, 643–674.

Elliot, A. J., Tracy, J. L., Pazda, A. D., & Beall, A. T. (2013). Red enhances women's attractiveness to men: First evidence suggesting universality. *Journal of Experimental Social Psychology, 49*, 165–168.

Ellis, B. J., Simpson, J. A., & Campbell, L. (2002). Trait-specific dependence in romantic relationships. *Journal of Personality, 70*, 611–660.

Ellison, P. T. (2001). *On fertile ground: A natural history of reproduction.* Cambridge, MA: Harvard University Press.

Else-Quest, N. M., Hyde, J. S., & Linn, M. C. (2010). Cross-national patterns of gender differences in mathematics: A meta-analysis. *Psychological Bulletin, 136*, 103–127.

Elsheikh, S. E. (2008). Factors affecting long-term abstinence from substances use. *International Journal of Mental Health Addiction, 6*, 306–315.

Epel, E. S., Blackburn, E. H., Lin, J., Dhabhar, F. S., Adler, N. E., Morrow, J. D., et al. (2004). Accelerated telomere shortening in response to life stress. *Proceedings of the National Academy of Sciences, 49*, 17312–17315.

Epstein, S. (1979). The stability of behavior: I. On prediction most of the people much of the time. *Journal of Personality and Social Psychology, 37*, 1266–1282.

Erikson, E. H. (1950). *Childhood and society* (2nd ed.). New York: Norton.

Erol, R. Y., & Orth, U. (2011). Self-esteem development from age 14 to 30 years: A longitudinal study. *Journal of Personality and Social Psychology, 101*, 607–619.

Erwin, E. (2002). *The Freud encyclopedia: Theory, therapy, and culture.* New York: Taylor & Francis.

Eysenck, H. J., & Eysenck, S. B. G. (1967). On the unitary nature of extraversion. *Acta Psychologica, 26*, 383–390.

Eysenck, H. J., & Eysenck, S. B. G. (1975). *Manual of the Eysenck Personality Questionnaire.* San Diego, CA: EdITS.

Fairbairn, W. R. D. (1949). Steps in the development of an object-relations theory of the personality. *British Journal of Medical Psychology, 22*(1–2), 26–31.

Fakra, E., Hyde, L. W., Gorka, A., Fisher, P. M., & Munoz, K. E. (2009). Effects of HTR1A C(-1019)G on amygdala reactivity and trait anxiety. *Archives of General Psychiatry, 66*, 33–40.

Falbo, T. (2012). Only children: An updated review. *Journal of Individual Psychology, 68*, 38–49.

Falk, C. F., Heine, S. J., Yuki, M., & Takemura, K. (2009). Why do Westerners self-enhance more than East Asians? *European Journal of Personality, 23*, 183–203.

Feinberg, M. E., & Heatherington, E. M. (2000). Sibling differentiation in adolescence: Implications for behavioral genetic theory. *Child Development, 71*, 1512–1524.

Feingold, A. (1994). Gender differences in personality: A meta-analysis. *Psychological Bulletin, 116*, 429–456.

Feist, G. J. (1998). A meta-analysis of personality in scientific and artistic creativity. *Personality and Social Psychology Review, 2*, 290–309.

Feldman, J. F., Brody, N., & Miller, S. A. (1980). Sex differences in non-elicited neonatal behaviors. *Merrill-Palmer Quarterly, 26*, 63–73.

Feltman, R., Robinson, M. D., & Ode, S. (2009). Mindfulness as a moderator of neuroticism–outcome relations: A self-regulation perspective. *Journal of Research in Personality, 43*, 953–961.

Fichten, C. S., & Sunerton, B. (1983). Popular horoscopes and the "Barnum effect." *Journal of Psychology, 114*, 123–134.

Fields, D., & Brown, A. (2007). *Toddler 411*. Boulder, CO: Windsor Peak Press.

Fincham, F. D., Paleari, F., & Regalia, C. (2002). Forgiveness in marriage: The role of relationship quality, attributions, and empathy. *Personal Relationships, 9*, 27–37.

Fincher, C. L., Thornhill, R., Murray, D. R., & Schaller, M. (2008). Pathogen prevalence predicts human cross-cultural variability in individualism/collectivism. *Proceedings of the Royal Society B, 275*, 1279–1285.

Findley, M. J., & Cooper, H. M. (1983). Locus of control and academic achievement: A literature review. *Journal of Personality and Social Psychology, 44*, 419–427.

Finkel, E. J. (2014). The I^3 Model: Metatheory, theory, and evidence. In J. M. Olson & M. P. Zanna (Eds.), *Advances in experimental social psychology* (Vol. 49, pp. 1–104). San Diego, CA: Academic Press.

Finkel, E. J. (2015, February). In defense of Tinder. *New York Times*. Retrieved February 6, 2015, from www.nytimes.com/2015/02/08/opinion/sunday/in-defense-of-tinder.html?_r=0.

Finkel, E. J., & Campbell, W. K. (2001). Self-control and accommodation in close relationships: An interdependence analysis. *Journal of Personality and Social Psychology, 81*, 263–277.

Finkel, E. J., Eastwick, P. W., Karney, B. R., Reis, H. T., & Sprecher, S. (2012). Online dating: A critical analysis from the perspective of psychological science. *Psychological Science in the Public Interest, 13*, 3–66.

Firestone, D. (1993, December 31). While Barbie talks tough, G.I. Joe goes shopping. *New York Times*, http://www.nytimes.com/1993/12/31/us/while-barbie-talks-tough-g-i-joe-goes-shopping.html.

Fishbein, M., & Ajzen, I. (1974). Attitudes toward objects as predictors of single and multiple behavioral criteria. *Psychological Review, 81*, 59–74.

Fisher, M. (2012, June 1). Welcome to America, please be on time: What guide books tell foreign visitors to the U.S. *The Atlantic*. Retrieved from www.theatlantic.com/international/archive/2012/06/welcome-to-America-please-be-on-time-what-guide-books-tell-foreign-visitors-to-the-us/257993/.

Fleeson, W. (2001). Toward a structure- and process-integrated view of personality: Traits as density distributions of states. *Journal of Personality and Social Psychology, 80*, 1011–1027.

Fleeson, W. (2004). Moving personality beyond the person-situation debate. *Current Directions in Psychological Science, 13*, 83–87.

Flowe, H. D., Swords, E., & Rockey, J. C. (2012). Women's behavioural engagement with a masculine male heightens during the fertile window: Evidence for the cycle shift hypothesis. *Evolution and Human Behavior, 33*, 285–290.

Fodor, E. M. (1985). The power motive, group conflict, and physiological arousal. *Journal of Personality and Social Psychology, 49*, 1408–1415.

Foldes, H. J., Duehr, E. E., & Ones, D. S. (2008). Group differences in personality: Meta-analyses comparing five U.S. racial groups. *Personnel Psychology, 61*, 579–616.

Forer, B. R. (1949). The fallacy of personal validation: A classroom demonstration of gullibility. *Journal of Abnormal and Social Psychology, 44*, 118–123.

Forester, J., Friedman, R. S., Ozelsel, A., & Denzler, M. (2006). The influence of approach and avoidance cues on the scope of perceptual and conceptual attention. *Journal of Experimental Social Psychology, 42*, 133–146.

Forgeard, M., & Seligman, M. P. (2012). Seeing the glass half full: A review of the causes and consequences of optimism. *Pratiques Psychologiques, 18*, 107–120.

Forkman, B., Furuaug, I. L., & Jensen, P. (1995). Personality, coping patterns, and aggression in piglets. *Applied Animal Behaviour Science, 45*, 31–42.

Forsyth, D. R., Lawrence, N. K., Burnette, J. L., & Baumeister, R. F. (2007). Attempting to improve the academic performance of struggling college students by bolstering their self-esteem: An intervention that backfired. *Journal of Social and Clinical Psychology, 26*, 447–459.

Foster, J. D., & Campbell, W. K. (2007). Are there such things as "narcissists" in social psychology?: A taxometric analysis of the Narcissistic Personality Inventory. *Personality and Individual Differences, 43*, 1321–1332.

Foster, J. D., Campbell, W. K., & Twenge, J. M. (2003). Individual differences in narcissism: Inflated self-views across the lifespan and around the world. *Journal of Research in Personality, 37,* 469–486.

Foster, J. D., Shrira, I., & Campbell, W. K. (2006). Theoretical models of narcissism, sexuality, and relationship commitment. *Journal of Social and Personal Relationships, 23,* 367–386.

Fox, S., Spector, P. E., & Miles, D. (2001). Counterproductive work behavior (CWB) in response to job stressors and organizational justice: Some mediator and moderator tests for autonomy and emotions. *Journal of Vocational Behavior, 59,* 291–309.

Fraley, R. C., Roisman, G. I., Booth-LaForce, C., Owen, M. T., & Holland, A. S. (2013). Interpersonal and genetic origins of adult attachment styles: A longitudinal study from infancy to early adulthood. *Journal of Personality and Social Psychology, 104,* 817–838.

Fraley, R. C., & Shaver, P. R. (1998). Airport separations: A naturalistic study of adult attachment dynamics in separating couples. *Journal of Personality and Social Psychology, 75,* 1198–1212.

Fraley, R. C., & Shaver, P. R. (2000). Adult romantic attachment: Theoretical developments, emerging controversies, and unanswered questions. *Review of General Psychology, 4,* 132–154.

Franklin, B. (2014). *The autobiography of Benjamin Franklin.* New York: Space and Time. (Original work published 1906)

Franklin, T. B., Linder, N., Russig, H., Thony, B., & Mansuy, I. M. (2011). Influence of early stress on social abilities and serotonergic functions across generations in mice. *PLoS One, 6,* e21842.

Fredrickson, B. L., & Roberts, T. (1997). Objectification theory: Toward understanding women's lived experiences and mental health risks. *Psychology of Women Quarterly, 21,* 173–206.

Fredrickson, B. L., Roberts, T., Noles, S., Quinn, D. M., & Twenge, J. M. (1998). That swimsuit becomes you: Objectification theory, mathematical performance, and disordered eating. *Journal of Personality and Social Psychology, 75,* 269–284.

Freedman, D. H. (2012). The perfected self. *The Atlantic.* Retrieved June, 2012, from www.theatlantic.com/magazine/archive/2012/06/the-perfected-self/308970/.

Freud, S. (1913). *The interpretation of dreams.* New York: Macmillan. (Original work published 1900)

Freud, S. (1947). *Leonardo da Vinci: A case study in psychosexuality* (A. A. Brill, Trans.). New York: Random House.

Freud, S. (1962a). *The ego and the id.* New York: Norton. (Original work published 1923)

Freud, S. (1962b). *Three essays of the theory of sexuality* (J. Strachey, Trans.). New York: Basic Books. (Original work published 1905)

Freud, S. (1989a). *Civilization and its discontents.* New York: Norton. (Original work published 1930)

Freud, S. (1989b). *Jokes and their relation to the unconscious.* New York: Norton. (Original work published 1905)

Freud, A. (1992). *The ego and the mechanisms of defence.* Sterling, VA: Stylus Publishing. (Original work published 1936)

Fried-Buchalter, S. (1992). Fear of success, fear of failure, and the imposter phenomenon: A factor analytic approach to convergent and discriminant validity. *Journal of Personality Assessment, 58,* 368–379.

Friedan, B. (1963). *The feminine mystique.* New York: Norton.

Friedman, H. S., Kern, M. L., Hampson, S. E., & Duckworth, A. L. (2014). A new lifespan approach to conscientiousness and health: Combining the pieces of the causal puzzle. *Developmental Psychology, 50,* 1377–1389.

Friedman, H. S., & Martin, L. R. (2011). *The longevity project: Surprising discoveries for health and long life from the landmark eight-decade study.* New York: Hudson Street Press.

Friedman, M. (2011, January 13). Horoscope hang-up: Earth rotation changes zodiac signs. Retrieved December 9, 2011, from http://newsfeed.time.com/2011/01/13/horoscope-hang-up-earth-rotation-changes-zodiac-signs.

Friedman, M., & Rosenman, R. H. (1974). *Type A behavior and your heart.* New York: Knopf.

Friedman, R. S., & Forester, J. (2010). Implicit affective cues and attentional tuning: An integrative review. *Psychological Bulletin, 136,* 875–893.

Friese, M., Messner, C., & Schaffner, Y. (2012). Mindfulness meditation counteracts self-control depletion. *Consciousness and Cognition, 21,* 1016–1022.

Fuller, T. L., & Fincham, F. D. (1995). Attachment style in married couples: Relation to current marital functioning, stability over time, and method of assessment. *Personal Relationships, 2,* 17–34.

Funder, D. C. (2008). Persons, situations, and person-situation interactions. In O. P. John, R. W. Robins, & L. A. Pervin (Eds.), *Handbook of personality: Theory and research* (3rd ed.), 568–580. New York: Guilford Press.

Funder, D. C., Levine, J. M., Mackie, D. M., Morf, C. C., Sansone, C., Vazire, S., et al. (2014). Improving the dependability of research in personality and social psychology: Recommendations for research and educational practice. *Personality and Social Psychology Review, 18,* 3–12.

Funder, D. C., & Ozer, D. J. (1983). Behavior as a function of the situation. *Journal of Personality and Social Psychology, 44,* 107–112.

Furnham, A. (1996). The Big Five versus the Big Four: The relationship between the Myers-Briggs Type Indicator (MBTI) and NEO-PI Five Factor Model of personality. *Personality and Individual Differences, 21,* 303–307.

Furnham, A., & Bradley, A. (1997). Music while you work: The differential distraction of background music on the cognitive test performance of introverts and extroverts. *Applied Cognitive Psychology, 11,* 445–455.

Furnham, A., & Fudge, C. (2008). The Five Factor Model of personality and sales performance. *Journal of Individual Differences, 29,* 11–16.

Furnham, A., & Saipe, J. (1993). Personality correlates of convicted drivers. *Personality and Individual Differences, 14,* 329–336.

Furr, R. M., & Funder, D. C. (2004). Situational similarity and behavioral consistency: Subjective, objective, variable-centered, and person-centered approaches. *Journal of Research in Personality, 38,* 421–447.

Gagne, M., & Deci, E. L. (2005). Self-determination theory and work motivation. *Journal of Organizational Behavior, 26,* 331–362.

Gallup, G. G., Burch, R. L., & Platek, S. M. (2002). Does semen have antidepressant properties? *Archives of Sexual Behavior, 31,* 289–293.

Gangstead, S. W., & Simpson, J. A. (1990). Toward an evolutionary history of female sociosexual variation. *Journal of Personality, 58,* 69–96.

Garcia, J., Ervin, F. R., & Koelling, R. A. (1966). Learning with prolonged delay of reinforcement. *Psychonomic Science, 5*(3), 121–122.

García, O., & García, L. F. (2002). A comparative study of Zuckerman's three structural models for personality through the NEO PI-R, ZKPQ-III-R, EPQ-RS, and Goldberg's 50-bipolar adjectives. *Personality and Individual Differences, 33,* 713–726.

Gazzola, V., & Keysers, C. (2009). The observation and execution of actions share motor and somatosensory voxels in all tested subjects: Single-subject analyses of unsmoothed fMRI data. *Cerebral Cortex, 19,* 1239–1255.

Geen, R. G. (1984). Preferred stimulation levels in introverts and extraverts: Effects on arousal and performance. *Journal of Personality and Social Psychology, 46,* 1303–1312.

Gentile, B., Grabe, S., Dolan-Pascoe, B., Twenge, J. M., Wells, B. E., & Maitino, A. (2009). Gender differences in domain-specific self-esteem: A meta-analysis. *Review of General Psychology, 13,* 34–45.

Gentile, B., Twenge, J. M., & Campbell, W. K. (2010). Birth cohort differences in self-esteem, 1988–2008: A cross-temporal meta-analysis. *Review of General Psychology, 14,* 261–268.

Gentile, B., Twenge, J. M., & Campbell, W. K. (2015). *Birth cohort differences in the Big Five traits, 1985–2012.* Unpublished manuscript.

Gentile, B., Twenge, J. M., Freeman, E. C., & Campbell, W. K. (2012). The effect of social networking websites on positive self-views: An experimental investigation. *Computers in Human Behavior, 28,* 1929–1933.

Gentile, D. A., & Anderson, C. A. (2011, June 30). Don't read more into the Supreme Court's ruling on the California video game law [Press release]. Retrieved from www.psychology.iastate.edu/faculty/caa/Multimedia/VGV-SC-OpEdDDAGCAA.pdf.

Gentile, D. A., Anderson, C. A., Yukawa, S., Ihori, N., Slaeem, M., Ming, L. K., et al. (2009). The effects of prosocial video games on prosocial behaviors: International evidence from correlational, longitudinal, and experimental studies. *Personality and Social Psychology Bulletin, 35,* 752–763.

Gershoff, E. T. (2002). Corporal punishment by parents and associated child behaviors and experiences: A meta-analytic and theoretical review. *Psychological Bulletin, 128,* 539–579.

Gildersleeve, K. A., Haselton, M. G., Larson, C. M., & Pillsworth, E. G. (2012). Body odor attractiveness as a cue of impending ovulation in women: Evidence from a study using hormone-confirmed ovulation. *Hormones and Behavior, 61,* 157–166.

Gillham, J. E., Reivich, K. J., Freres, D. R., Chaplin, T. M., Shatté, A. J., Samuels, B., et al. (2007). School-based prevention of depressive symptoms: A randomized controlled study of the effectiveness and specificity of the Penn Resiliency Program. *Journal of Consulting and Clinical Psychology, 75,* 9–19.

Giluk, T. L. (2009). Mindfulness, Big Five personality, and affect: A meta-analysis. *Personality and Individual Differences, 47,* 805–811.

Gneezy, U., & Rustichini, A. (2000). A fine is a price. *Journal of Legal Studies, 29*(1), 1–17.

Goetz, J. L., Keltner, D., & Simon-Thomas, E. (2010). Compassion: An evolutionary analysis and empirical review. *Psychological Bulletin, 136,* 351–374.

Golden, R. N., Gaynes, B. N., Ekstrom, R. D., Hamer, R. M., Jacobsen, F. M., Suppes, T., et al. (2005). The efficacy of light therapy in the treatment of mood disorders: A review and meta-analysis of the evidence. *American Journal of Psychiatry, 162,* 656–662.

Golomb, M., Fava, M., Abraham, M., & Rosenbaum, J. F. (1995). Gender differences in personality disorders. *American Journal of Psychiatry, 152,* 579–582.

Gosling, S. D. (2008). *Snoop: What your stuff says about you.* New York: Basic Books.

Gosling, S. D., Augustine, A. A., Vazire, S., Holtzman, N., & Gaddis, S. (2011). Manifestations of personality in online social networks: Self-reported Facebook-related behaviors and observable profile information. *Cyberpsychology, Behavior, and Social Networking, 14,* 483–488.

Gosling, S. D., Gaddis, S., & Vazire, S. (2007, March). Personality impressions based on Facebook profiles. In *Proceedings of the International Conference on Weblogs and Social Media* (pp. 26–28). Boulder, CO: AAAI.

Gosling, S. D., & John, O. P. (1998, May). *Personality dimensions in dogs, cats, and hyenas.* Paper presented at the annual meeting of the American Psychological Society, Washington, DC.

Gosling, S. D., & John, O. P. (1999). Personality dimensions in nonhuman animals: A cross-species review. *Current Directions in Psychological Science, 8,* 69–75.

Gosling, S. D., Ko, S. J., Mannarelli, T., & Morris, M. E. (2002). A room with a cue: Personality judgments based on offices and bedrooms. *Journal of Personality and Social Psychology, 82,* 379–398.

Gosling, S. D., Sandy, C. J., & Potter, J. (2010). Personalities of self-identified "dog people" and "cat people." *Anthrozoos, 23,* 213–222.

Gough, H. (1956). *California Psychological Inventory.* Palo Alto, CA: Consulting Psychologists Press.

Gough, H. G. (1957). *Manual for the California Psychological Inventory.* Palo Alto, CA: Consulting Psychologists Press.

Grande, G., Romppel, M., & Barth, J. (2012). Association between type D personality and prognosis in patients with cardiovascular diseases: A systematic review and meta-analysis. *Annals of Behavioral Medicine, 43,* 299–310.

Grant, A. M. (2013). Rethinking the extraverted sales ideal: The Ambivert advantage. *Psychological Science, 24,* 1024–1030.

Grant, B. F., Chou, S. P., Goldstein, R. B., Huang, B., Stinson, F. S., Saha, T. D., et al. (2008). Prevalence, correlates, disability, and comorbidity of DSM-IV borderline personality disorder: Results from the Wave 2 National Epidemiologic Survey on alcohol and related conditions. *Journal of Clinical Psychiatry, 69,* 533–545.

Grant, B. S. (2004). Allelic melanism in American and British peppered moths. *Journal of Heredity, 95,* 97–102.

Grant, I. E., Eriksen, H. R., Marquis, P., Orre, I. J., Palinkas, L. A., Suefeld, P., et al. (2007). Psychological selection of Antarctic personnel: The "SOAP" instrument. *Aviation, Space, and Environmental Medicine, 78,* 793–800.

Gray, J. A. (1982). *The neuropsychology of anxiety.* New York: McGraw-Hill.

Green, J. D., & Campbell, W. K. (2000). Attachment and exploration in adults: Chronic and contextual accessibility. *Personality and Social Psychology Bulletin, 26,* 452–461.

Greenberg, J., Solomon, S., & Pyszczynski, T. (1997). Terror management theory of self-esteem and social behavior: Empirical assessments and conceptual refinements. In M. P. Zanna (Ed.), *Advances in experimental social psychology* (Vol. 29, pp. 61–139). New York: Academic Press.

Greene, A. (2013, February 1). Q&A: Steve-O talks "Jackass," veganism and quitting drugs. *Rolling Stone.* Retrieved June 17, 2014, from www.rollingstone.com/culture/news/q-a-steve-o-talks-jackass-veganism-and-quitting-drugs-20130201.

Greene, C. A., & Murdock, K. K. (2013). Multidimensional control beliefs, socioeconomic status, and health. *American Journal of Health Behavior, 37,* 227–237.

Greenwald, A. G., & Farnham, S. D. (2000). Using the implicit association test to measure self-esteem and self-concept. *Journal of Personality and Social Psychology, 79,* 1022–1038.

Greenwald, A. G., McGhee, D. E., & Schwartz, J. L. (1998). Measuring individual differences in implicit cognition: The Implicit Association Test. *Journal of Personality and Social Psychology, 74,* 1464–1480.

Greiling, H., & Buss, D. M. (2000). Women's sexual strategies: The hidden dimension of extra-pair mating. *Personality and Individual Differences, 28,* 929–963.

Griffiths, M., Parke, J., Wood, R., & Rigbye, J. (2010). Online poker gambling in university students: Further findings from an online survey. *International Journal of Mental Health and Addiction, 8,* 82–89.

Grijalva, E., Newman, D. A., Tay, L., Donnellan, M. B., Harms, P. D., Robins, R. W., et al. (2015). Gender differences in narcissism: A meta-analytic review. *Psychological Bulletin, 141*(2), 261–310.

Grilo, C. M., Becker, D. F., Walker, M. L., Edell, W. S., & McGlashan, T. H. (1996). Gender differences in personality disorders in psychiatrically hospitalized young adults. *Journal of Nervous and Mental Disease, 184,* 754–757.

Grossman, M., & Wood, W. (1993). Sex differences in intensity of emotional experience: A social role interpretation. *Journal of Personality and Social Psychology, 65,* 1010–1022.

Grotevant, H. D. (1978). Sibling constellations and sex typing of interests in adolescence. *Child Development, 49,* 540–542.

Grouzet, F. M. E., Kasser, T., Ahuvia, A., Dols, J. M. F., Kim, Y., Lau, S., et al. (2005). The structure of goal contents across 15 cultures. *Journal of Personality and Social Psychology, 89,* 800–816.

Guimond, S., Branscombe, N. R., Runot, S., Buunk, A. P., Chatard, A., Desert, M., et al. (2007). Culture, gender, and the self: Variations and impact of social comparison processes. *Journal of Personality and Social Psychology, 92,* 1118–1134.

Haas, B. W., Omura, K., Amin, Z., Constable, R. T., & Canli, T. (2006). Functional connectivity with the anterior cingulated is associated with extraversion during the emotional Stroop task. *Social Neuroscience, 1,* 16–24.

Haas, B. W., Omura, K., Constable, R. T., & Canli, T. (2007). Is automatic emotion regulation associated with agreeableness? *Psychological Science, 18,* 130–131.

Habra, M. E., Linden, W., Anderson, J. C., & Weinberg, J. (2003). Type D personality is related to cardiovascular and neuroendocrine reactivity to acute stress. *Journal of Psychosomatic Research, 55,* 235–245.

Hagerty, M. R. (1999). Testing Maslow's hierarchy of needs: National quality-of-life across time. *Social Indicators Research, 46,* 249–271.

Hall, J. A. (1984). *Nonverbal sex differences: Communication accuracy and expressive style.* Baltimore: Johns Hopkins University Press.

Hampson, S. E. (2012). Personality processes: Mechanisms by which personality traits "get outside the skin." *Annual Review of Psychology, 63,* 315–339.

Hampson, S. E., & Goldberg, L. R. (2006). A first large cohort study of personality trait stability over the 40 years between elementary school and midlife. *Journal of Personality and Social Psychology, 91,* 763–779.

Hampson, S. E., Goldberg, L. R., Vogt, T. M., & Dubanoski, J. P. (2007). Mechanisms by which childhood personality traits influence adult health status: Educational attainment and healthy behaviors. *Health Psychology, 26,* 121–125.

Hankin, B. L., & Abramson, L. Y. (2001). Development of gender differences in depression: An elaborated cognitive vulnerability-transactional stress theory. *Psychological Bulletin, 127,* 773–796.

Hardman, D., Villiers, C., & Roby, S. (2007). Another look at birth order and familial sentiment: Are middleborns really different? *Journal of Evolutionary Psychology, 5,* 197–211.

Hardy, M. S., & Calhoun, L. G. (1997). Psychological distress and the "medical student syndrome" in abnormal psychology students. *Teaching of Psychology, 24,* 192–193.

Harker, L., & Keltner, D. (2001). Expressions of positive emotion in women's college yearbook pictures and their relationship to personality and life outcomes across adulthood. *Journal of Personality and Social Psychology, 80,* 112–124.

Harlow, H. F. (1959). *Love in infant monkeys.* San Francisco: Freeman.

Hatfield, E. H., & Walster, G. W. W. (1978). *A new look at love.* Reading, MA: Addison-Wesley.

Hazan, C., & Shaver, P. (1987). Romantic love conceptualized as an attachment process. *Journal of Personality and Social Psychology, 52,* 511–524.

Hazlett-Stevens, H., Craske, M. G., Mayer, E. A., Chang, L., & Naliboff, B. D. (2003). Prevalence of irritable bowel syndrome among university students: The role of worry, neuroticism, anxiety sensitivity, and visceral anxiety. *Journal of Psychosomatic Research, 55,* 501–505.

Heaven, P. L., Ciarrochi, J., Leeson, P., & Barkus, E. (2013). Agreeableness, conscientiousness, and psychoticism: Distinctive influences of three personality dimensions in adolescence. *British Journal of Psychology, 104,* 481–494.

Heider, F. (1958). *The psychology of interpersonal relations.* Hoboken, NJ: Wiley.

Heilman, M. E., Wallen, A. S., Fuchs, D., & Tamkins, M. M. (2004). Penalties for success: Reactions to women who succeed at male gender-typed tasks. *Journal of Applied Psychology, 89,* 416–427.

Heimberg, R. G. (2002). Cognitive-behavioral therapy for social anxiety disorder: Current status and future directions. *Biological Psychiatry, 51,* 101–108.

Heine, S. J., & Buchtel, E. E. (2009). Personality: The universal and the culturally specific. *Annual Review of Psychology, 60,* 369–394.

Heine, S. J., Buchtel, E. E., & Norenzayan, A. (2008). What do cross-national comparisons of personality traits tell us?: The case of conscientiousness. *Psychological Science, 19,* 309–313.

Heine S. J., & Hamamura T. (2007). In search of East Asian self-enhancement. *Personality and Social Psychology Review, 11,* 4–27.

Heine, S.J., Lehman, D. R., Ide, E., Leung, C., Kitayama, S., Takata, T., et al. (2001). Divergent consequences of success and failure in Japan and North America: An investigation of self-improving motivations and malleable selves. *Journal of Personality and Social Psychology, 81,* 599–615.

Heine, S. J., Lehman, D. R., Markus, H. R., & Kitayama, S. (1999). Is there a universal need for positive self-regard? *Psychological Review, 106,* 766–794.

Heine, S. J., Lehman, D. R., Peng, K., & Greenholtz, J. (2002). What's wrong with cross-cultural comparisons of subjective Likert scales?: The reference-group effect. *Journal of Personality and Social Psychology, 82,* 903–918.

Heine, S. J., & Renshaw, K. (2002). Interjudge agreement, self-enhancement, and liking: Cross-cultural divergences. *Personality and Social Psychology Bulletin, 28,* 578–587.

Herrera, N. C., Zajonc, R. B., Wieczorkowska, G., & Cichomski, B. (2003). Beliefs about birth rank and their reflection in reality. *Journal of Personality and Social Psychology, 85,* 142–150.

Hertenstein, M. J., Hansel, C. A., Butts, A. M., & Hile, S. N. (2009). Smile intensity in photographs predicts divorce later in life. *Motivation and Emotion, 33,* 91–105.

Hibbeln, J. R., Linnolla, M., Umhau, J. C., Rawlings, R., George, D. T., & Salem, N. (1998). Essential fatty acids predict metabolites of serotonin and dopamine in cerebrospinal fluid among healthy control subjects, and early- and late-onset alcoholics. *Biological Psychiatry, 44,* 235–242.

Higgins, E. T. (1987). Self-discrepancy: A theory relating self and affect. *Psychological Review, 94,* 319–340.

Hill, P. L., & Roberts, B. W. (2012). Narcissism, well-being, and observer-rated personality across the lifespan. *Social Psychological and Personality Science, 3,* 216–223.

Hill, R., A., & Barton, R. A. (2005). Red enhances human performance in contests. *Nature, 435,* 7040.

Hills, P., & Argyle, M. (2001). Happiness, introversion-extraversion and happy introverts. *Personality and Individual Differences, 30,* 595–608.

Hofer, J., Busch, H., Chasiotis, A., & Kiessling, F. (2006). Motive congruence and interpersonal identity status. *Journal of Personality, 74,* 511–542.

Hoffman, M., Gneezy, U., & List, J. A. (2011). Nurture affects gender differences in spatial abilities. *Proceedings of the National Academy of Sciences of the United States of America, 108,* 14786–14788.

Hogan, M. J., Staff, R. T., Bunting, B. P., Deary, I. J., & Whalley, L. J. (2012). Openness to experience and activity engagement facilitate the maintenance of verbal ability in older adults. *Psychology and Aging, 27,* 849–854.

Hogan, R., & Hogan, J. (2001). Assessing leadership: A view from the dark side. *International Journal of Selection and Assessment, 9*(1–2), 40–51.

Holland, J. L. (1973). *Making vocational choices: A theory of careers* (Vol. 37). Englewood Cliffs, NJ: Prentice-Hall.

Holtzman, N. J., & Strube, M. J. (2010). Narcissism and attractiveness. *Journal of Research in Personality, 44,* 133–136.

Holtzman, N. S., & Strube, M. J. (2013). People with dark personalities tend to create a physically attractive veneer. *Social Psychological and Personality Science, 4,* 461–467.

Honekopp, J., & Schuster, M. (2010). A meta-analysis on 2D:4D and athletic prowess: Substantial relationships but neither hand out-predicts the other. *Personality and Individual Differences, 48,* 4–10.

Honekopp, J., & Watson, S. (2011). Meta-analysis of the relationship between digit-ratio 2D:4D and aggression. *Personality and Individual Differences, 51,* 381–386.

Hoppock, R. (1935). *Job satisfaction.* New York: Harper.

Hopwood, C. J., Thomas, K. M., Markon, K. E., Wright, A. G., & Krueger, R. F. (2012). DSM-5 personality traits and DSM-IV personality disorders. *Journal of Abnormal Psychology, 121,* 424–432.

Horney, K. (1924). On the genesis of the castration complex in women. *International Journal of Psychoanalysis, 5,* 50–65.

Horney, K. (1967). *Feminine psychology.* New York: Nova York.

Horney, K. (2013). *Our inner conflicts: A constructive theory of neurosis.* Oxon, UK: Routledge. (Original work published 1946)

Horton, R. S., Reid, C. A., Barber, J. M., Miracle, J., & Green, J. D. (2014). An experimental investigation of the influence of agentic and communal Facebook use on grandiose narcissism. *Computers in Human Behavior, 35,* 93–98.

Hosoda, M., Stone-Romero, E. F., & Coats, G. (2003). The effects of physical attractiveness on job related outcomes: A meta-analysis of experimental studies. *Personnel Psychology, 56,* 431–462.

House, J. S., Landis, K. R., & Umberson, D. (1988). Social relationships and health. *Science, 241,* 540–545.

Howes, O. D., & Salkovskis, P. M. (1998). Health anxiety in medical students. *Lancet, 351,* 1332.

Hoyle, R. H., Fejfar, M. C., & Miller, J. D. (2000). Personality and sexual risk taking: A quantitative review. *Journal of Personality, 68,* 1203–1231.

Huang, Y., Kotov, R., de Girolamo, G., Preti, A., Angermeyer, M., Benjet, C., et al. (2009). DSM-IV personality disorders in the WHO World Mental Health Surveys. *British Journal of Psychiatry, 195,* 46–53.

Huesmann, L. R., Eron, L. D., Dubow, E. F., & Seebauer, E. (1987). Television viewing habits in children and adult aggression. *Child Development, 58,* 357–367.

Hutchinson, J. C., Sherman, T., Martinovic, N., & Tenenbaum, G. (2008). The effect of manipulated self-efficacy on perceived and sustained effort. *Journal of Applied Sport Psychology, 20,* 457–472.

Hyde, J. S. (1984). How large are gender differences in aggression?: A developmental meta-analysis. *Developmental Psychology, 20,* 722–736.

Hyde, J. S. (2005). The gender similarities hypothesis. *American Psychologist, 60,* 581–592.

Hyde, J. S., Fennema, E., & Lamon, S. J. (1990). Gender differences in mathematics performance: A meta-analysis. *Psychological Bulletin, 107,* 139–155.

Hyde, J. S., & Linn, M. C. (1988). Gender differences in verbal ability: A meta-analysis. *Psychological Bulletin, 104,* 53–69.

Hyde, J. S., & Mertz, J. E. (2009). Gender, culture, and mathematics performance. *Proceedings of the National Academy of Sciences, 106,* 8801–8807.

Ickes, W., Gesn, P. R., & Graham, T. (2000). Gender differences in empathic accuracy: Differential ability or differential motivation? *Personal Relationships, 7,* 95–109.

Ilardi, S. S. (2010). *The depression cure: The six-step program to beat depression without drugs.* Cambridge, MA: Da Capo Press.

Imada, T. (2012). Cultural narratives of individualism and collectivism: A content analysis of textbook stories in the United States and Japan. *Journal of Cross-Cultural Psychology, 43,* 576–591.

Inghilleri, P. (1999). *From subjective experience to cultural change.* New York: Cambridge University Press.

Ioannidis, J. P. A. (2005). Why most published research findings are false. *Plos Med, 2*(8), e124.

Ioannidis, J. A., Munafò, M. R., Fusar-Poli, P., Nosek, B. A., & David, S. P. (2014). Publication and other reporting biases in cognitive sciences: Detection, prevalence, and prevention. *Trends in Cognitive Sciences, 18*(5), 235–241.

Isaacson, W. (1997, January). In search of the real Bill Gates. *Time,* http://content.time.com/time/magazine/article/0,9171,1120657,00.html.

Issacson, W. (2011). *Steve Jobs.* New York: Simon & Schuster.

Ivcevic, Z., & Ambady, N. (2012). Personality impressions from identity claims on Facebook. *Psychology of Popular Media Culture, 1,* 38–45.

Iyengar, S. S., & Lepper, M. R. (1999). Rethinking the value of choice: A cultural perspective on intrinsic motivation. *Journal of Personality and Social Psychology, 76,* 349–366.

Jackson, J. J., Connolly, J. J., Garrison, S. M., Leveille, M. M., & Connolly, S. L. (2015). Your friends know how long you will live: A 75-year study of peer-rated personality traits. *Psychological Science, 26,* 335–340.

Jacobson, N., Dobson, K., Truax, P., Addis, M., Koerner, K., Gollan, J. K., et al. (1996). A component analysis of cognitive-behavioral treatment for depression. *Journal of Consulting and Clinical Psychology, 64,* 295–304.

Jackson, J. J., Hill, P. L., Payne, B. R., Roberts, B. W., & Stine-Morrow, E. A. L. (2012). Can an old dog learn (and want to experience) new tricks?: Cognitive training increases openness to experience in older adults. *Psychology and Aging, 27,* 286–292.

Jaffe, S. R., Caspi, A., Moffitt, T., Polo-Thomas, M., Price, T. S., & Taylor, A. (2004). The limits of child effects: Evidence for genetically mediated child effects on corporal punishment but not on physical maltreatment. *Developmental Psychology, 40,* 1047–1058.

James, W. (1891). *The principles of psychology* (Vol. 1). London: Macmillan.

James, W. (1950). *The principles of psychology.* New York: Dover. (Original work published 1890)

Jamison, K. R. (1996). *Touched with fire: Manic-depressive illness and the artistic temperament.* New York: Free Press.

Jang, K. L., Dick, D. M., Wolf, H., Livesley, W. J., & Paris, J. (2005). Psychosocial adversity and emotional instability: An application of gene-environment interaction models. *European Journal of Personality, 19,* 359–372.

Jang, K. L., Livesley, W. J., & Vernon, P. A. (1996). Heritability of the Big Five personality dimensions and their facets: A twin study. *Journal of Personality, 64,* 577–591.

Jang, K. L., Livesley, W. J., Vernon, P. A., & Jackson, D. N. (1996). Heritability of personality disorder traits: A twin study. *Acta Psychiatrica Scandinavica, 94,* 438–444.

Janoff-Bulman, R., & Berg, M. (1998). Disillusionment and the creation of value: From traumatic losses to existential gains. In J. Harvey (Ed.), *Perspectives on loss: A sourcebook* (pp. 35–47). Philadelphia: Brunner/Mazel.

Janson, H., & Mathiesen, K. S. (2008). Temperament profiles from infancy to middle childhood: Development and associations with behavior problems. *Journal of Personality and Social Psychology, 96,* 218–230.

Javaris, K. N., Schaefer, S. M., van Reekum, C. M., Lapate, R. C., Greischar, L. L., Bachhuber, D. R., et al. (2012). Conscientiousness predicts greater recovery from negative emotion. *Emotion, 12,* 875–881.

Jaycox, L. H., Reivich, K. J., Gillham, J., & Seligman, M. E. P. (1994). Prevention of depressive symptoms in school children. *Behavior Research and Therapy, 32,* 801–816.

Jefferson, T., Herbst, J. H., & McCrae, R. R. (1998). Associations between birth order and personality traits: Evidence from self-reports and observer ratings. *Journal of Research in Personality, 32,* 498–509.

Jellesma, F. C., & Vingerhoets, A. J. (2012). Crying in middle childhood: A report on gender differences. *Sex Roles, 67*(7–8), 412–421.

Jemmott, J. B., Hellman, C., McClelland, D. C., Locke, S. E., Kraus, L., Williams, R. M., et al. (1990). Motivational syndromes associated with natural killer cell activity. *Journal of Behavioral Medicine, 13,* 53–73.

Jenkins, C. D. (1976). Recent evidence supporting psychologic and social risk factors for coronary disease. *New England Journal of Medicine, 294,* 987–994.

Jensen-Campbell, L., Adams, R., Perry, D. G., Workman, K. A., Furdella, J. Q., & Egan, S. K. (2002). Agreeableness, extraversion, and peer relations in early adolescence: Winning friends and deflecting aggression. *Journal of Research in Personality, 36,* 224–251.

Jensen-Campbell, L., & Graziano, W. (2001). Agreeableness as a moderator of interpersonal conflict. *Journal of Personality, 69,* 323–362.

Jensen-Campbell, L. A., & Malcolm, K. T. (2007). The importance of conscientiousness in adolescent interpersonal relationships. *Personality and Social Psychology Bulletin, 33,* 368–383.

John, O. P., Naumann, L. P., & Soto, C. J. (2008). Paradigm shift to the integrative Big Five trait taxonomy: History, measurement, and conceptual issues. In O. P. John, R. W. Robins, & L. A. Pervin (Eds.), *Handbook of personality: Theory and research* (3rd ed., pp. 114–158). New York: Guilford Press.

John, O. P., & Robins, R. W. (1994). Accuracy and bias in self-perception: Individual differences in self-enhancement and the role of narcissism. *Journal of Personality and Social Psychology, 66,* 206–219.

Johnson, D. M., Shea, M. T., Yen, S., Battle, C. L., Zlotnick, C., Sanislow, C. A., et al. (2003). Gender differences in borderline personality disorder: Findings from the Collaborative Longitudinal Personality Disorders Study. *Comprehensive Psychiatry, 44,* 284–292.

Johnson, J. G., Cohen, P., Chen, H., Kasem, S., & Brook, J. S. (2006). Parenting behaviors associated with risk for offspring personality disorder during adulthood. *Archives of General Psychiatry, 63,* 579–587.

Johnson, W., & Krueger, R. F. (2004). Genetic and environmental structure of adjectives describing the domains of the Big Five model of personality: A nationwide US twin study. *Journal of Research in Personality, 38,* 448–472.

Jokela, M., Kivimäki, M., Elovainio, M., & Keltikangas-Järvinen, L. (2009). Personality and having children: A two-way relationship. *Developmental Psychology, 44,* 1314–1328.

Jonason, P. K., & Buss, D. M. (2012). Avoiding entangling commitments: Tactics for implementing a short-term mating strategy. *Personality and Individual Differences, 52,* 606–610.

Jonason, P. K., & Kavanagh, P. (2010). The dark side of love: Love styles and the Dark Triad. *Personality and Individual Differences, 49,* 606–610.

Jonason, P. K., Li, N. P., Webster, G. W., & Schmitt, D. P. (2009). The dark triad: Facilitating short-term mating in men. *European Journal of Personality, 23,* 5–18.

Jonassaint, C. R., Boyle, S. H., Williams, R. B., Mark, D. B., Siegler, I. C., & Barefoot, J. C. (2007). Facets of openness predict mortality in patients with cardiac disease. *Psychosomatic Medicine, 69,* 319–322.

Jonassaint, C. R., Siegler, I. C., Barefoot, J. C., Edwards, C. L., & Williams, R. B. (2011). Low life course socioeconomic status (SES) is associated with negative NEP PI-R personality patterns. *International Journal of Behavioral Medicine, 18,* 13–21.

Jones, A., & Crandall, R. (1986). Validation of a short index of self-actualization. *Personality and Social Psychology Bulletin, 12,* 63–73.

Jones, S. E., Miller, J. D., & Lynam, D. R. (2011). Personality, antisocial behavior, and aggression: A meta-analytic review. *Journal of Criminal Justice, 39,* 329–337.

Joseph, J. (2001). Separated twins and the genetics of personality differences: A critique. *American Journal of Psychology, 114,* 1–30.

Judge, T. A. (2009). Core self-evaluations and work success. *Current Directions in Psychological Science, 18,* 58–62.

Judge, T. A., & Bono, J. E. (2000). Five-factor model of personality and transformational leadership. *Journal of Applied Psychology, 85,* 751–765.

Judge, T. A., & Bono, J. E. (2001). Relationship of core self-evaluations traits—self-esteem, generalized self-efficacy, locus of control, and emotional stability—with job satisfaction and job performance: A meta-analysis. *Journal of Applied Psychology, 86,* 80–92.

Judge, T. A., Bono, J. E., Ilies, R., & Gerhardt, M. W. (2002a). Personality and leadership: A qualitative and quantitative review. *Journal of Applied Psychology, 87,* 765–780.

Judge, T. A., Heller, D., & Mount, M. K. (2002b). Five-Factor Model of personality and job satisfaction: A meta-analysis. *Journal of Applied Psychology, 87,* 530–541.

Judge, T. A., Higgins, C. A., Thoresen, C. J., & Barrick, M. R. (2006). The Big Five personality traits, general mental ability, and career success across the life span. *Personnel Psychology, 52,* 621–652.

Judge, T. A., & Kammeyer-Mueller, J. D. (2012). Job attitudes. *Annual Review of Psychology, 63,* 341–367.

Judge, T. A., Livingston, B. A., & Hurst, C. (2012). Do nice guys—and gals—really finish last?: The joint effects of sex and agreeableness on income. *Journal of Personality and Social Psychology, 102,* 390–407.

Judge, T. A., Locke, E. A., Durham, C. C., & Kluger, A. N. (1998). Dispositional effects on job and life satisfaction: The role of core evaluations. *Journal of Applied Psychology, 83,* 17–34.

Judge, T. A., Martocchio, J. J., & Thoresen, C. J. (1997). Five-Factor Model of personality and employee absence. *Journal of Applied Psychology, 82,* 745–755.

Judge, T. A., & Piccolo, R. F. (2004). Transformational and transactional leadership: A meta-analytic test of their relative validity. *Journal of Applied Psychology, 89,* 755–768.

Judge, T. A., Thoresen, C. J., Bono, J. E., & Patton, G. K. (2001). The job satisfaction–job performance relationship: A qualitative and quantitative review. *Psychological Bulletin, 127*(3), 376–405.

Jung, C. G. (1915). *The theory of psychoanalysis.* New York: Journal of Nervous and Mental Disease Publishing Company.

Jung, C. G. (1959). *Archetypes and the collective unconscious.* Princeton, NJ: Princeton University Press.

Jung, C. G. (1962). *Psychological types: Or, the psychology of individuation.* New York: Pantheon Books.

Jung, C. G. (1968). *Man and his symbols.* New York: Random House.

Jung, C. G. (1993). *Synchronicity: An acausal connecting principle.* Bollingen, Switzerland: Bollingen Foundation. (Original work published 1952)

Kabat-Zinn, J. (1990). *Full catastrophe living: Using the wisdom of your body and mind to face stress, pain and illness.* New York: Delacorte.

Kabat-Zinn, J. (1995). *Wherever you go, there you are: Mindfulness meditation in everyday life.* New York: Hyperion.

Kalechstein, A. D., & Nowicki, S. (1997). A meta-analytic examination of the relationship between control expectancies and academic achievement: An 11-yr follow-up to Findley and Cooper. *Genetic, Social, and General Psychology Monographs, 123,* 27–56.

Kalivas, P. W., & Volkow, N. D. (2005). The neural basis of addiction: A pathology of motivation and choice. *American Journal of Psychiatry, 162,* 1403–1413.

Kanagawa, C., Cross, S. E., & Markus, H. R. (2001). "Who am I?": The cultural psychology of the conceptual self. *Personality and Social Psychology Bulletin, 27,* 90–103.

Kane, J. M., & Mertz, J. E. (2012). Debunking myths about gender and mathematics performance. *Notices of the American Mathematics Society, 59,* 10–21.

Kapidzic, S. (2013). Narcissism as a predictor of motivations behind Facebook profile picture selection. *Cyberpsychology, Behavior, and Social Networking, 16,* 14–19.

Karabenick, S. A., & Srull, T. K. (1978). Effects of personality and situational variation in locus of control on cheating: Determinants of the "congruence effect." *Journal of Personality, 46,* 72–95.

Kashima, Y., Kashima, E., Farsides, T., Kim, U., Strack, F., Werth, L., et al. (2004). Culture and context-sensitive self: The amount and meaning of context-sensitivity of phenomenal self differ across cultures. *Self and Identity, 3,* 125–141.

Kasser, T. (2011). *Values and human well-being.* Commissioned paper, the Bellagio Initiative.

Kasser, T., Rosenblum, K. L., Sameroff, A. J., Deci, E. L., Niemiec, C. P., Ryan, R. M., et al. (2014). Changes in materialism, changes in psychological well-being: Evidence from three longitudinal studies and an intervention experiment. *Motivation and Emotion, 38,* 1–22.

Kasser, T., & Ryan, R. M. (1993). A dark side of the American dream: Correlates of financial success as a central life aspiration. *Journal of Personality and Social Psychology, 65,* 410–422.

Kasser, T., & Ryan, R. M. (1996). Further examining the American dream: Differential correlates of intrinsic and extrinsic goals. *Personality and Social Psychology Bulletin, 22,* 80–87.

Kaufman, J., & Needham, A. (1999). Objective spatial coding by 6.5-month-old infants in a visual dishabituation task. *Developmental Science, 2,* 432–441.

Keehn, R. J., Goldberg, I. D., & Beebe, G. W. (1974). Twenty-four year mortality follow-up of army veterans with disability separations for psychoneurosis in 1944. *Psychosomatic Medicine, 36,* 27–46.

Keirsey, D. (1998). *Please understand me II.* New York: Prometheus Nemesis.

Keith, T. Z., Reynolds, M. R., Roberts, L. G., Winter, A. L., & Austin, C. A. (2011). Sex differences in latent cognitive abilities ages 5 to 17: Evidence from the Differential Ability Scales—Second Edition. *Intelligence, 39,* 389–404.

Keller, C., & Siegrist, M. (2015). Does personality influence eating styles and food choices?: Direct and indirect effects. *Appetite, 84,* 128–138.

Kelly, E. L., & Conley, J. J. (1987). Personality and compatibility: A prospective analysis of marital stability and marital satisfaction. *Journal of Personality and Social Psychology, 52,* 27–40.

Kelly, I. W. (1979). Astrology and science: A critical examination. *Psychological Reports, 44*(3, Pt. 2), 1231–1240.

Kern, M. L., Eichstaedt, J. C., Schwartz, H. A., Dziurzynski, L., Ungar, L. H., Stillwell, D. J., et al. (2014). The online social self: An open vocabulary approach to personality. *Assessment, 21,* 158–169.

Kern, M. L., Eichstaedt, J. C., Schwartz, H. A., Dziurzynski, L., Ungar, L. H., Stillwell, D. J., et al. (2014). The online social self: An open vocabulary approach to personality. *Assessment, 21,* 158–169.

Kern, M. L., & Friedman, H. S. (2008). Do conscientious individuals live longer?: A quantitative review. *Health Psychology, 27,* 505–512.

Kern, M. L., Friedman, H. S., Martin, L. R., Reynolds, C. A., & Luong, G. (2009). Conscientiousness, career success, and longevity: A lifespan analysis. *Annals of Behavioral Medicine, 37,* 154–163.

Kernis, M. H., & Goldman, B. M. (2006). A multicomponent conceptualization of authenticity: Theory and research. *Advances in Experimental Social Psychology, 38,* 283–357.

Khurana, A., Romer, D., Betancourt, L. M., Brodsky, N. L., Giannetta, J. M., & Hurt, H. (2012). Early adolescent sexual debut: The mediating role of working memory ability, sensation seeking, and impulsivity. *Developmental Psychology, 48,* 1416–1428.

Kidwell, C., & Steele, V. (1989). *Men and women: Dressing the part.* London: Booth-Clibborn Editions.

Kim, H., & Markus, H. R. (1999). Deviance or uniqueness, harmony or conformity?: A cultural analysis. *Journal of Personality and Social Psychology, 77,* 785–800.

Kim, H. S., & Sherman, D. K. (2007). "Express yourself": Culture and the effect of self-expression on choices. *Journal of Personality and Social Psychology, 92,* 1–11.

Kim, K. H. (2011). The creativity crisis: The decrease in creative thinking scores on the Torrance Tests of Creative Thinking. *Creativity Research Journal, 23,* 285–295.

King, A. C., Taylor, C. B., Albright, C. A., & Haskall, W. L. (1990). The relationship between repressive and defensive coping styles and blood pressure responses in healthy, middle-aged men and women. *Journal of Psychosomatic Research, 34,* 461–471.

King, L. A. (1995). Wishes, motives, goals, and personal memories: Relations of measures of human motivation. *Journal of Personality, 63,* 985–1007.

King, L. A., Hicks, J. A., Krull, J. L., & Del Gaiso, A. K. (2006). Positive affect and the experience of meaning in life. *Journal of Personality and Social Psychology, 90,* 179–196.

King, L. A., & Napa, C. K. (1998). What makes a life good? *Journal of Personality and Social Psychology, 75,* 156–165.

Kirsch, I., Deacon, B. J., Huedo-Medina, T. B., Scoboria, A., Moore, T. J., & Johnson, B. T. (2008). Initial severity and antidepressant benefits: A meta-analysis of data submitted to the Food and Drug Administration. *PLoS Medicine, 5*(2), e45.

Klein, M., & Mitchell, J. (1986). *Selected Melanie Klein* (J. Mitchell, Ed.). New York: Free Press.

Klein, R. A., Ratliff, K. A., Vianello, M., Adams, R. J., Bahník, Š., Bernstein, M. J., et al. (2014). Investigating variation in replicability: A "many labs" replication project. *Social Psychology, 45*(3), 142–152.

Klinesmith, J., Kasser, T., & McAndrew, F. T. (2006). Guns, testosterone, and aggression: An experimental test of a mediational hypothesis. *Psychological Science, 17,* 568–571.

Kling, K. C., Hyde, J. S., Showers, C. J., & Buswell, B. N. (1999). Gender differences in self-esteem: A meta-analysis. *Psychological Bulletin, 125,* 470–500.

Klipper, M. Z., & Benson, H. (2000). *The relaxation response.* New York: William Morrow.

Knight, G. P., Guthrie, I. K., Page, M. C., & Fabes, R. A. (2002). Emotional arousal and gender differences in aggression: A meta-analysis. *Aggressive Behavior, 28,* 366–393.

Koenig, A. M., Eagly, A. H., Mitchell, A. A., & Ristikari, T. (2011). Are leader stereotypes masculine?: A meta-analysis of three research paradigms. *Psychological Bulletin, 137*, 616–642.

Koestner, R., & McClelland, D. C. (1990). Perspectives on competence motivation. In L. A. Pervin (Ed.), *Handbook of personality: Theory and research* (pp. 527–548). New York: Guilford Press.

Konrath, S. H., Chopik, W., Hsing, C., & O'Brien, E. H. (2014). Changes in adult attachment styles in American college students over time: A meta-analysis. *Personality and Social Psychology Review, 18*(4), 326–348.

Konrath, S. H., O'Brien, E. H., & Hsing, C. (2011). Changes in dispositional empathy in American college students over time: A meta-analysis. *Personality and Social Psychology Review, 15*, 180–198.

Kotov, R., Gamez, W., Schmidt, F., & Watson, D. (2010). Linking "big" personality traits to anxiety, depressive, and substance use disorders: A meta-analysis. *Psychological Bulletin, 136*, 768–821.

Kozlowski, L. T., & Cutting, J. E. (1977). Guessing the sex of a walker from a dynamic point-light display. *Attention, Perception, and Psychophysics, 21*, 575–580.

Kraus, M. W., Cote, S., & Keltner, D. (2010). Social class, contextualism, and empathic accuracy. *Psychological Science, 21*, 1716–1723.

Krueger, R. F., Derringer, J., Markon, K. E., Watson, D., & Skodol, A. E. (2012). Constructing a personality inventory for DSM-5. *Psychological Medicine, 42*, 1879–1890.

Kuhn, M. H. (1960). Self-attitudes by age, sex and professional training. *Sociological Quarterly, 1*, 39–56.

Kuhn, M. H., & McPartland, T. S. (1954). An empirical investigation of self attitudes. *American Sociological Review, 19*, 68–76.

Kurdek, L. A., & Schmitt, J. P. (1986). Interaction of sex role self-concept with relationship and relationship beliefs in married, heterosexual cohabitating, gay, and lesbian couples. *Journal of Personality and Social Psychology, 51*, 365–370.

Kuzawa, C. W., Gettler, L. T., Huang, Y., & McDade, T. W. (2010). Mothers have lower testosterone than non-mothers: Evidence from the Philippines. *Hormones and Behavior, 57*, 441–447.

LaFrance, M., Hecht, M., & Paluck, E. (2003). The contingent smile: A meta-analysis of sex differences in smiling. *Psychological Bulletin, 129*, 305–334.

Lahey, B. B. (2009). Public health significance of neuroticism. *American Psychologist, 64*, 241–256.

Lakey, C. E., Campbell, W. K., Brown, K. W., & Goodie, A. S. (2007). Dispositional mindfulness as predictor of severity of gambling outcomes. *Personality and Individual Differences, 43*, 1698–1710.

Lamb, M. E., Chuang, S. S., Wessels, H., Broberg, A. G., & Hwang, C. P. (2002). Emergence and construct validation of the Big Five factors in early childhood: A longitudinal analysis of their ontogeny in Sweden. *Child Development, 73*, 1517–1524.

Lander, C. (2008). *Stuff white people like*. New York: Random House.

Langner, C. A., & Winter, D. G. (2001). The motivational basis of concessions and compromise: Archival and laboratory studies. *Journal of Personality and Social Psychology, 81*, 711–727.

Lawton, C. A., & Kallai, J. (2002). Gender differences in wayfinding strategies and anxiety about wayfindings. *Sex Roles, 47*, 389–401.

Leaper, C., & Ayres, M. M. (2007). A meta-analytic review of gender variations in adults' language use: Talkativeness, affiliative speech, and assertive speech. *Personality and Social Psychology Review, 11*, 328–363.

Leary, M. R. (1990). Responses to social exclusion: Social anxiety, jealousy, loneliness, depression, and low self-esteem. *Journal of Social and Clinical Psychology, 9*, 221–229.

Leary, M. R., Tambor, E. S., Terdal, S. K., & Downs, D. L. (1995). Self-esteem as an interpersonal monitor: The sociometer hypothesis. *Journal of Personality and Social Psychology, 68*, 518–530.

Lee, A. Y., Aaker, J. L., & Gardner, W. L. (2000). The pleasures and pains of distinct self-construals: The role of interdependence in regulatory focus. *Journal of Personality and Social Psychology, 78*, 1122–1134.

Lee, K., & Ashton, M. C. (2004). Psychometric properties of the HEXACO Personality Inventory. *Multivariate Behavioral Research, 39*, 329–358.

Lee, K., & Ashton, M. C. (2012). Getting mad and getting even: Agreeableness and honesty-humility as predictors of revenge intentions. *Personality and Individual Differences, 52*, 596–600.

Legassie, J., Zibrowski, E. M., & Goldszmidt, M. A. (2008). Measuring resident well-being: Impostorism and burnout syndrome in residency. *Journal of General Internal Medicine, 23,* 1090–1094.

Lehnart, J., Neyer, F. J., & Eccles, J. (2010). Long-term effects of social investment: The case of partnering in young adulthood. *Journal of Personality, 78,* 639–670.

Lejuez, C. W., Hopko, D. R., Acierno, R., Daughters, S. B., & Pagoto, S. L. (2011). Ten year revision of the brief behavioral activation treatment for depression: Revised treatment manual. *Behavior Modification, 35,* 111–161.

Lenzenweger, M. F. (2008). Epidemiology of personality disorders. *Psychiatric Clinics of North America, 31,* 395–403.

Lenzenweger, M. F., Johnson, M. D., & Willett, J. B. (2004). Individual growth curve analysis illuminates stability and change in personality disorder features: The longitudinal study of personality disorders. *Archives of General Psychiatry, 61,* 1015–1024.

Leonard, E. (2013, March 25). Carrie Fisher's bipolar crisis: "I was trying to survive." *People.* Retrieved June 17, 2014, from www.people.com/people/archive/article/0,,20684545,00.html.

LePine, J. A., & Van Dyne, L. (2001). Voice and cooperative behavior as contrasting forms of contextual performance: Evidence of differential relationships with Big Five personality characteristics and cognitive ability. *Journal of Applied Psychology, 86,* 326–336.

Lepper, M. R., Greene, D., & Nisbett, R. E. (1973). Undermining children's intrinsic interest with extrinsic reward: A test of the "overjustification" hypothesis. *Journal of Personality and Social Psychology, 28,* 129–137.

Levashina, J., & Campion, M. A. (2007). Measuring faking in the employment interview: Development and validation of an interview faking behavior scale. *Journal of Applied Psychology, 92,* 1638–1656.

Levine, R. V., & Norenzayan, A. (1999). The pace of life in 31 countries. *Journal of Cross-Cultural Psychology, 30,* 178–205.

Lewicki, P. (1985). Nonconscious biasing effects of single instances on subsequent judgments. *Journal of Personality and Social Psychology, 48,* 563–574.

Li, J. Y., Ma, H. A., Zhou, H. X., Huang, Y. L., Wu, L. J., Li, J., et al. (2011). Association between DARPP-32 gene polymorphism and personality traits in healthy Chinese-Han subjects. *Journal of Molecular Neuroscience, 44,* 48–52.

Lichtenfeld, S., Maier, M. A., Elliot, A. J., & Pekrun, R. (2009). The semantic red effect: Processing the word red undermines intellectual performance. *Journal of Experimental Social Psychology, 45,* 1273–1276.

Liebermann, D., Pillsworth, E. G., & Haselton, M. G. (2011). Kin affiliation across the ovulatory cycle: Females avoid fathers when fertile. *Psychological Science, 22,* 13–18.

Lifton, P. D. (1985). Individual differences in moral development: The relation of sex, gender, and personality to morality. *Journal of Personality, 53,* 306–334.

Lilienfeld, S. O., Waldman, I. D., Landfield, K., Watts, A. L., Rubenzer, S., & Faschingbauer, T. R. (2012). Fearless dominance and the US presidency: implications of psychopathic personality traits for successful and unsuccessful political leadership. *Journal of Personality and Social Psychology, 103,* 489–505.

Lindberg, S. M., Hyde, J. S., Petersen, J. L., & Linn, M. C. (2010). New trends in gender and mathematics performance: A meta-analysis. *Psychological Bulletin, 136,* 1123–1135.

Lindfors, P., Solantaus, T., & Rimpela, A. (2012). Fears for the future among Finnish adolescents in 1983–2007: From global concerns to ill health and loneliness. *Journal of Adolescence, 35,* 991–999.

Lippa, R. (1998). Gender-related individual differences and the structure of vocational interests: The importance of the people–things dimension. *Journal of Personality and Social Psychology, 74,* 996–1009.

Lippa, R. A. (2009). Sex differences in sex drive, sociosexuality, and height across 53 nations: Testing evolutionary and social structural theories. *Archives of Sexual Behavior, 38,* 631–651.

Lippa, R. A. (2010). Sex differences in personality traits and gender-related occupational preferences across 53 nations: Testing evolutionary and social-environmental theories. *Archives of Sexual Behavior, 39,* 619–636.

Locatelli, S. M., Kluwe, K., & Bryant, F. B. (2012). Facebook use and the tendency to ruminate among college students: Testing mediational hypotheses. *Journal of Educational Computing Research, 46,* 377–394.

Lockwood, P., Marshall, T. C., & Sadler, P. (2005). Promoting success or preventing failure: Cultural differences in motivation by positive and negative role models. *Personality and Social Psychology Bulletin, 31,* 379–392.

Lodi-Smith, J. J., Jackson, J., Bogg, T., Walton, K., Wood, D., Harms, P., et al. (2010). Mechanisms of health: Education and health-related behaviours partially mediate the relationship between conscientiousness and self-reported physical health. *Psychology and Health, 25,* 305–319.

Lodi-Smith, J., & Roberts, B. W. (2007). Social investment and personality: A meta-analysis of the relationship of personality traits to investment in work, family, religion, and volunteerism. *Personality and Social Psychology Review, 11,* 68–86.

Loehlin, J. C. (1992). *Genes and environment in personality development.* Newbury Park, CA: Sage.

Loehlin, J. C., McCrae, R. R., Costa, P. T., & John, O. P. (1998). Heritabilities of common and measure-specific components of the Big Five personality factors. *Journal of Research in Personality, 32,* 431–453.

Lombardo, W. K., Crester, G. A., & Roesch, S. C. (2001). For crying out loud—The differences persist into the '90s. *Sex Roles, 45,* 529–547.

Lowenstein, L. F. (2002). Ability and personality changes after brain injuries. *Criminal Lawyer, 120,* 5–8.

Lucas, R. E., Le, K., & Dyrenforth, P. S. (2008). Explaining the extraversion/positive affect relation: Sociability cannot account for extraverts' greater happiness. *Journal of Personality, 76,* 385–414.

Luciano, M., Houlihan, L. M., Harris, S. E., Gow, A. J., Hayward, C., Starr, J. M., et al. (2010). Association of existing and new candidate genes for anxiety, depression, and personality traits in older people. *Behavioral Genetics, 40,* 518–532.

Ludtke, O., Roberts, B. W., Trautwein, U., & Nagy, G. (2011). A random walk down University Avenue: Life paths, life events, and personality trait change at the transition to university life. *Journal of Personality and Social Psychology, 101,* 620–637.

Luxen, M. F., & Buunk, B. P. (2005). Second-to-fourth digit ratio related to verbal and numerical intelligence and the Big Five. *Personality and Individual Differences, 39,* 959–966.

Lynam, D. R., & Widiger, T. A. (2001). Using the Five-Factor Model to represent the DSM-IV personality disorders: An expert consensus approach. *Journal of Abnormal Psychology, 110,* 401–412.

Lyubomirsky, S. (2008). *The how of happiness: A scientific approach to getting the life you want.* New York: Penguin Press.

Lyubomirsky, S., Dickerhoof, R., Boehm, J. K., & Sheldon, K. M. (2011). Becoming happier takes both a will and a proper way: An experimental longitudinal intervention to boost well-being. *Emotion, 11,* 391–402.

Lyubomirsky, S., Sheldon, K. M., & Schkade, D. (2005). Pursuing happiness: The architecture of sustainable change. *Review of General Psychology, 9,* 111–131.

MacKinnon, D. P., Lockwood, C. M., Hoffman, J. M., West, S. G., & Sheets, V. (2002). A comparison of methods to test mediation and other intervening variable effects. *Psychological Methods, 7,* 83–104.

MacLaren, V. V., Fugelsang, J. A., Harrigan, K. A., & Dixon, M. J. (2011). The personality of pathological gamblers: A meta-analysis. *Clinical Psychology Review, 31,* 1057–1067.

MacLean, K. A., Johnson, M. W., & Griffiths, R. (2011). Mystical experiences occasioned by the hallucinogen psilocybin lead to increases in the personality domain of openness. *Journal of Psychopharmacology, 25,* 1453–1461.

MacLeod, J., Davey Smith, G., Heslop, P., Metcalfe, C., Carroll, D., & Hart, C. (2002). Psychological stress and cardiovascular disease: Empirical demonstration of bias in a prospective observational study of Scottish men. *British Medical Journal, 324,* 1247–1251.

Macmillan, M. B. (2000). Restoring Phineas Gage: A 150th anniversary retrospective. *Journal of the History of the Neurosciences, 9,* 42–62.

Maeda, Y., & Yoon, S. (2013). A meta-analysis on gender differences in mental rotation ability measured by the Purdue Spatial Visualization Tests: Visualization of Rotations (PSVT:R). *Educational Psychology Review, 25,* 69–94.

Magee, W. J., Eaton, W. W., Wittchen, H. U., McGonagle, K. A., & Kessler, R. C. (1996). Agoraphobia, simple phobia, and social phobia in the National Comorbidity Survey. *Archives of General Psychiatry, 53,* 159–168.

Magid, V., MacLean, M. G., & Colder, C. R. (2007). Differentiating between sensation seeking and impulsivity through their mediated relations with alcohol use and problems. *Addictive Behaviors, 32,* 2046–2061.

Maguire, E. A., Gadian, D. G., Johnsrude, I. S., Good, C. D., Ashburner, J., Frackowiak, R. S. J., et al. (2000). Navigation-related structural change in the hippocampi of taxi drivers. *Proceedings of the National Academy of Sciences, 97,* 4398–4403.

Maio, G. R., Pakizeh, A., Cheung, W.-Y., & Rees, K. J. (2009). Changing, priming, and acting on values: Effects via motivational relations in a circular model. *Journal of Personality and Social Psychology, 97,* 699–715.

Major, B., Barr, L., Zubek, J., & Baby, S. H. (1999). Gender and self-esteem: A meta-analysis. In W. B. Swann, J. H. Langlois, & L. A. Gilbert (Eds.), *Sexism and stereotypes in modern society,* 223–253. Washington, DC: American Psychological Association.

Malahy, L. W., Rubinlicht, M. A., & Kaiser, C. R. (2009). Justifying inequality: A cross-temporal investigation of U.S. income disparities and just-world beliefs from 1973 to 2006. *Social Justice Research, 22,* 369–383.

Malouff, J. M., Thorsteinsson, E. B., & Schutte, N. S. (2005). The relationship between the Five-Factor Model of personality and symptoms of clinical disorders: A meta-analysis. *Journal of Psychopathology and Behavioral Assessment, 27,* 101–114.

Manning, J. T., & Fink, B. (2011). Digit ratio (2D:4D) and aggregate personality scores across nations: Data from the BBC internet study. *Personality and Individual Differences, 51,* 387–391.

Manning, J. T., Scutt, D., Wilson, J., & Lewis-Jones, D. I. (1998). The ration of 2nd to 4th digit length: A predictor of sperm numbers and concentrations of testosterone, luteinizing hormone and estrogen. *Human Reproduction, 13,* 3000–3004.

Maples, J. L., Guan, A., Carter, N., & Miller, J. D. (2014). A test of the International Personality Item Pool representation of the Revised NEO Personality Inventory and development of a 120-item IPIP-based measure of the Five-Factor Model. *Psychological Assessment, 26,* 1070–1084.

Markon, K. E., Krueger, R. F., & Watson, D. (2005). Delineating the structure of normal and abnormal personality: An integrative hierarchical approach. *Journal of Personality and Social Psychology, 88,* 139–157.

Markus, H. R., & Kitayama, S. (1991). Culture and the self: Implications for cognition, emotion, and motivation. *Psychological Review, 98,* 224–253.

Markus, H. R., & Kitayama, S. (2010). Cultures and selves: A cycle of mutual constitution. *Perspectives on Psychological Science, 5,* 420–430.

Markus, H., & Nurius, P. (1986). Possible selves. *American Psychologist, 41,* 954–969.

Marrs, R. W. (1995). A meta-analysis of bibliotherapy studies. *American Journal of Community Psychology, 23,* 843–870.

Martin, L. R., Friedman, H. S., & Schwartz, J. E. (2007). Personality and mortality risk across the lifespan: The importance of conscientiousness as a biopsychosocial attribute. *Health Psychology, 26,* 428–436.

Martin, R. A., Puhlik-Doris, P., Larsen, J. G., Gray, J., & Weir, K. (2003). Individual differences in uses of humor and their relation to psychological well-being: Development of the Humor Styles Questionnaire. *Journal of Research in Personality, 37,* 48–75.

Martinko, M. J., Gundlach, M. J., & Douglas, S. C. (2002). Toward an integrative theory of counterproductive workplace behavior: A causal reasoning perspective. *International Journal of Selection and Assessment, 10,* 36–50.

Maslow, A. H. (1970). *Motivation and personality* (2nd ed.). New York: Harper & Row.

Masuda, T., Gonzalez, R., Kwan, L., & Nisbett, R. E. (2008). Culture and aesthetic preference: Comparing the attention to context of East Asians and Americans. *Personality and Social Psychology Bulletin, 34,* 1260–1275.

Mazur, A., & Booth, A. (1998). Testosterone and dominance in men. *Behavioral and Brain Sciences, 21,* 353–397.

Mazur, A., & Michalek, J. (1998). Marriage, divorce, and male testosterone. *Social Forces,* 325–330.

McAbee, S. T., & Oswald, F. L. (2013). The criterion-related validity of personality measures for predicting GPA: A meta-analytic validity competition. *Psychological Assessment, 25,* 532–544.

McAdams, D. (2006). *The redemptive self: Stories Americans live by.* New York: Oxford University Press.

McAdams, D. P., & Vaillant, G. E. (1982). Intimacy motivation and psychosocial adjustment: A longitudinal study. *Journal of Personality Assessment, 46,* 586–593.

McCann, S. J. H. (2011). Emotional health and the Big Five personality factors at the American state level. *Journal of Happiness Studies, 12,* 547–560.

McClelland, D. C. (1951). *Personality.* New York: Holt, Rinehart & Winston.

McClelland, D. C. (1961). *The achieving society*. New York: Van Nostrand.

McClelland, D. C. (1979). Inhibited power motivation and high blood pressure in men. *Journal of Abnormal Psychology, 88*, 182–190.

McClelland, D. C. (1987). *Human motivation*. New York: Cambridge University Press.

McClelland, D. C. (1989). Motivational factors in health and disease. *American Psychologist, 44*, 675–683.

McClelland, D. C., Alexander, C., & Marks, E. (1982). The need for power, stress, immune function, and illness among male prisoners. *Journal of Abnormal Psychology, 91*, 61–70.

McClelland, D. C., & Kirshnit, C. (1988). The effect of motivational arousal through films on salivary immunoglobulin A. *Psychology and Health, 2*, 31–52.

McClelland, D. C., Koestner, R., & Weinburger, J. (1989). How do self-attributed and implicit motives differ? *Psychological Review, 96*, 690–702.

McClelland, D. C., & Pilon, D. A. (1983). Sources of adult motives in patterns of parent behavior in early childhood. *Journal of Personality and Social Psychology, 44*, 564–574.

McClelland, D. C., Ross, G., & Patel, V. (1985). The effect of an academic examination on salivary norepinephrine and immunoglobulin levels. *Journal of Human Stress, 11*, 52–59.

McCrae, R. R. (1996). Social consequences of experiential openness. *Psychological Bulletin, 120*, 323–337.

McCrae, R. R., & Costa, P. T. (1985). Comparison of EPI and psychoticism scales with measures of the Five-Factor Model of personality. *Personality and Individual Differences, 6*, 587–597.

McCrae, R. R., & Costa, P. (1994). The stability of personality: Observations and evaluations. *Current Directions in Psychological Science, 3*, 173–175.

McCrae, R. R., Costa, P. T., Jr., Terracciano, A., Parker, W. D., Mills, C. J., De Fruyt, F., et al. (2002). Personality trait development from age 12 to age 18: Longitudinal, cross-sectional and cross-cultural analyses. *Journal of Personality and Social Psychology, 83*, 1456–1468.

McCrae, R. R., & Terracciano, A. (2005a). Personality profiles of cultures: Aggregate personality traits. *Journal of Personality and Social Psychology, 89*, 407–425.

McCrae, R. R., & Terracciano, A. (2005b). Universal features of personality traits from the observer's perspective: Data from 50 cultures. *Journal of Personality and Social Psychology, 88*, 547–561.

McGraw, K. O., & Wong, S. P. (1992). A common language effect size statistic. *Psychological Bulletin, 111*, 361–365.

McGregor, I., & Little, B. R. (1998). Personal projects, happiness, and meaning: On doing well and being yourself. *Journal of Personality and Social Psychology, 74*, 494–512.

McGuire, W. J., McGuire, C. V., Child, P., & Fujioka, T. (1978). Salience of ethnicity in the spontaneous self-concept as a function of one's ethnic distinctiveness in the social environment. *Journal of Personality and Social Psychology, 36*, 511–520.

McKillip, J., & Redel, S. L. (1983). External validity of matching on physical attractiveness for same and opposite sex couples. *Journal of Applied Social Psychology, 13*, 328–337.

McKinley, J. C., & Hathaway, S. R. (1940). A multiphasic personality schedule (Minnesota): II. A differential study of hypochondriasis. *Journal of Psychology, 10*, 255–268.

McKinley, N. M., & Hyde, J. S. (1996). The objectified body consciousness scale. *Psychology of Women Quarterly, 20*, 181–215.

McLean, C. P., Asnaani, A., Litz, B. T., & Hofmann, S. G. (2011). Gender differences in anxiety disorders: Prevalence, course of illness, comorbidity and burden of illness. *Journal of Psychiatric Research, 45*, 1027–1035.

McNamera, R. K., & Carlson, S. E. (2006). Role of omega-3 fatty acids in brain development and function: Potential implications for the pathogenesis and prevention of psychopathology. *Prostaglandins, Leukocites, and Essential Fatty Acids, 75*, 329–349.

Mehl, M. R., Vazire, S., Ramírez-Esparza, N., Slatcher, R. B., & Pennebaker, J. W. (2007). Are women really more talkative than men? *Science, 317*, 82.

Meier, B., Robinson, M., & Wilkowski, B. (2006). Turning the other cheek: Agreeableness and the regulation of aggression-related primes. *Psychological Science, 17*, 136–142.

Michael, R. T., Gagnon, J. H., Laumann, E. O., & Kolata, G. (1994). *Sex in America: A definitive survey*. New York: Little, Brown.

Michalski, R. L., & Shackelford, T. K. (2002). An attempted replication of the relationships between birth order and personality. *Journal of Research in Personality, 36,* 182–188.

Michel, J. S., & Bowling, N. A. (2012). Does dispositional aggression feed the narcissistic response?: The role of narcissism and aggression in the prediction of job attitudes and counterproductive work behaviors. *Journal of Business and Psychology, 28,* 1–13.

Milgram, S. (1963). Behavioral study of obedience. *Journal of Abnormal Social Psychology, 67,* 371–378.

Milgram, S. (1974). *Obedience to authority.* New York: Harper & Row.

Miller, G., Tybur, J., & Jordan, B. D. (2007). Ovulatory cycle effects on tip earnings by lap dancers. *Evolution and Human Behavior, 28,* 375–381.

Miller, J. D., & Campbell, W. K. (2010). The case for using research on trait narcissism as a building block for understanding Narcissistic Personality Disorder. *Personality Disorders: Theory, Research, and Treatment, 1,* 180–191.

Miller, J. D., Campbell, W. K., & Pilkonis, P. A. (2007). Narcissistic personality disorder: Relations with distress and functional impairment. *Comprehensive Psychiatry, 48,* 170–177.

Miller, J. D., Dir, A., Gentile, B., Wilson, L., Pryor, L. R., & Campbell, W. K. (2010). Searching for a vulnerable dark triad: Comparing factor 2 psychopathy, vulnerable narcissism, and borderline personality disorder. *Journal of Personality, 78,* 1529–1564.

Miller, J. D., Hoffman, B. J., Gaughan, E. T., Gentile, B., Maples, J., & Campbell, W. K. (2011). Grandiose and vulnerable narcissism: A nomological network analysis. *Journal of Personality, 79,* 1013–1032.

Miller, J. D., & Lynam, D. R. (2001). Structural models of personality and their relation to antisocial behavior: A meta-analysis. *Criminology, 39,* 765–798.

Miller, J. D., Lynam, D. R., & Jones, S. E. (2008). Externalizing behavior through the lens of the Five Factor Model: A focus on agreeableness and conscientiousness. *Journal of Personality Assessment, 90,* 158–164.

Miller, J. D., Lynam, D. R., Widiger, T. A., & Leukefeld, C. (2001). Personality disorders as an extreme variant of common personality dimensions: Can the Five-Factor Model represent psychopathy. *Journal of Personality, 69,* 253–276.

Miller, J. D., Lynam, D. R., Zimmerman, R., Logan, T., Leukefeld, C., & Clayton, R. (2004). The utility of the Five-Factor Model in understanding risky sexual behavior. *Personality and Individual Differences, 36,* 1611–1626.

Miller, J. D., MacKillop, J., Fortune, E. E., Maples, J., Lance, C. E., Campbell, W. K., et al. (2012). Personality correlates of pathological gambling derived from Big Three and Big Five personality models. *Psychiatry Research, 206,* 50–55.

Mineka, S., & Öhman, A. (2002). Phobias and preparedness: The selective, automatic, and encapsulated nature of fear. *Society of Biological Psychiatry, 52,* 927–937.

Miner-Rubino, K. N., Twenge, J. M., & Fredrickson, B. L. (2002). Trait self-objectification in women: Affective and personality correlates. *Journal of Research in Personality, 36,* 147–172.

Mirowsky, J., & Ross, C. E. (1990). Control or defense?: Depression and the sense of control over good and bad outcomes. *Journal of Health and Social Behavior, 31,* 71–86.

Mischel, W. (1968). *Personality and Assessment.* New York: Wiley.

Mischel, W. (1990). Personality dispositions revisited and revised: A view after three decades. In L. A. Pervin (Ed.), *Handbook of personality: Theory and research* (pp. 111–134). New York: Guilford Press.

Mischel, W., Zeiss, R., & Zeiss, A. (1974). An internal-external control test for young children. *Journal of Personality and Social Psychology, 29,* 265–278.

Moffitt, T. E., Arseneault, L., Belsky, D., Dickson, N., Hancox, R. J., Harrington, H., et al. (2011). A gradient of childhood self-control predicts health, wealth, and public safety. *Proceedings of the National Academy of Sciences, 108*(7), 2693–2698.

Mommersteeg, P. M. C., & Pouwer, F. (2012). Personality as a risk factor for the metabolic syndrome: A systematic review. *Journal of Psychosomatic Research, 73,* 326–333.

Money, J. (1975). Ablatio penis: Normal male infant sex-reassigned as a girl. *Archives of Sexual Behavior, 4,* 65–71.

Monk, T. H., & Leng, V. C. (1986). Interactions between inter-individual and inter-task differences in the diurnal variation of human performance. *Chronobiology International, 3,* 171–177.

Moran, C. M., Diefendorff, J. M., Kim, T. Y., & Liu, Z. Q. (2012). A profile approach to self-determination theory motivations at work. *Journal of Vocational Behavior, 81,* 354–362.

Morehouse, R. E., Farley, F. H., & Youngquist, J. V. (1990). Type T personality and the Jungian classification system. *Journal of Personality Assessment, 54,* 231–235.

Morf, C. C., & Rhodewalt, F. (2001). Unraveling the paradoxes of narcissism: A dynamic self-regulatory processing model. *Psychological Inquiry, 12,* 177–196.

Morison, S. J., & Ellwood, A. L. (2000). Resiliency in the aftermath of deprivation: A second look at the development of Romanian orphanage children. *Merrill-Palmer Quarterly, 46,* 717–737.

Morling, B., & Lamoreaux, M. (2008). Measuring culture outside the head: A meta-analysis of individualism-collectivism in cultural products. *Personality and Social Psychology Review, 12,* 199–221.

Morris, M. W., & Peng, K. (1994). Culture and cause: American and Chinese attributions for social and physical events. *Journal of Personality and Social Psychology, 67,* 949–971.

Mottus, R., Indus, K., & Allik, J. (2008). Accuracy of the only children stereotype. *Journal of Research in Personality, 42,* 1047–1052.

Mottus, R., McNeill, G., Jia, X., Craig, L. C. A., Starr, J. M., & Deary, I. J. (2013). The associations between personality, diet and body mass index in older people. *Health Psychology, 32,* 353–360.

Mount, M. K., Barrick, M. R., & Stewart, G. L. (1998). Five-Factor Model of personality and performance in jobs involving interpersonal interactions. *Human Performance, 11,* 145–165.

Mroczek, D. K., & Spiro, A. (2003). Modeling intraindividual change in personality traits: Findings from the normative aging study. *Journal of Gerontology: Psychological Sciences, 58B,* P153–P165.

Mroczek, D. K., & Spiro, A. (2007). Personality change influences mortality in older men. *Psychological Science, 18,* 371–376.

Mroczek, D. K., Spiro, A., & Turiano, N. A. (2009). Do health behaviors explain the effect of neuroticism on mortality?: Longitudinal findings from the VA Normative Aging Study. *Journal of Research in Personality, 43,* 653–659.

Mueller, C. M., & Dweck, C. S. (1998). Praise for intelligence can undermine children's motivation and performance. *Journal of Personality and Social Psychology, 75,* 33–52.

Multon, K. D., Brown, S. D., & Lent, R. W. (1991). Relation of self-efficacy beliefs to academic outcomes: A meta-analytic investigation. *Journal of Counseling Psychology, 38,* 30–38.

Muraven, M., Baumeister, R. F., & Tice, D. M. (1999). Longitudinal improvement of self-regulation through practice: Building self-control strength through repeated exercise. *Journal of Social Psychology, 139,* 446–457.

Murray, H. A. (1937). Techniques for a systematic investigation of fantasy. *Journal of Psychology, 3,* 115–143.

Musek, J. (2007). A general factor of personality: Evidence for the Big One in the Five-Factor Model. *Journal of Research in Personality, 41,* 1213–1233.

Musson, D., & Keeton, K. E. (2011). *Investigating the relationship between personality traits and astronaut career performance: Retrospective analysis of personality data collected 1989–1995.* Hanover, MD: National Aeronautics and Space Administration.

Myers, D. G. (2000). *The American paradox: Spiritual hunger in an age of plenty.* New Haven, CT: Yale University Press.

Myrseth, H., Pallesen, S., Molde, H., Johnsen, B. H., & Lorvik, I. M. (2009). Personality factors as predictors of pathological gambling. *Personality and Individual Differences, 47,* 933–937.

Naugle, W. (2015). Meet U.S. representative Elise Stefanik, the youngest woman to ever break into the Old Boys' Club of Congress. *Glamour.* Retrieved from www.glamour.com/inspired/2015/01/us-representative-elise-stefanik-youngest-woman-to-join-congress.

Naumova, O. Y., Lee, M., Koposov, R., Szyf, M., Dozier, M., & Grigorenko, E. L. (2012). Differential patterns of whole-genome DNA methylation in institutionalized children and children raised by their biological parents. *Development and Psychopathology, 24,* 143–155.

Neff, K. D. (2003). The development and validation of a scale to measure self-compassion. *Self and Identity, 2,* 223–250.

Neff, K. D., Rude, S. S., & Kirkpatrick, K. L. (2007). An examination of self-compassion in relation to positive psychological functioning and personality traits. *Journal of Research in Personality, 41*, 908–916.

Nelis, D., Kotsou, I., Quidbach, J., Hansenne, M., Weytens, F., Dupuis, P., et al. (2011). Increasing emotional competence improves psychological and physical well-being, social relationships, and employability. *Emotion, 11*, 354–366.

Nettle, D. (2006). The evolution of personality variation in humans and other animals. *American Psychologist, 61*, 622–631.

Nevid, J. S., & Pastva, A. (2014). "I'm a Mac" versus "I'm a PC": Personality differences between Mac and PC users in a college sample. *Psychology and Marketing, 31*, 31–37.

Neyer, F. J., & Asendorpf, J. B. (2001). Personality-relationship transaction in young adulthood. *Journal of Personality and Social Psychology, 81*, 1190–1204.

Neyer, F. J., & Lehnart, J. (2007). Relationships matter in personality development. Evidence from an 8-year longitudinal study across young adulthood. *Journal of Personality, 75*, 535–568.

Noftle, E. E., & Shaver, P. R. (2006). Attachment dimensions and the Big Five personality traits: Associations and comparative ability to predict relationship quality. *Journal of Research in Personality, 40*, 179–208.

Nolen-Hoeksema, S. (2002). Gender differences in depression. In C. L. Hammen & I. H. Gotlib (Eds.), *Handbook of depression* (pp. 492–509). New York: Guilford Press.

Nolen-Hoeksema, S., & Morrow, J. (1993). Effects of rumination on naturally occurring depressed mood. *Cognition and Emotion, 7*, 561–570.

Norem, J. K. (2002). *The positive power of negative thinking*. New York: Basic Books.

Norem, J. K., & Cantor, N. (1986). Defensive pessimism: Harnessing anxiety as motivation. *Journal of Personality and Social Psychology, 51*, 1208–1217.

Norman, W. T. (1963). Toward an adequate taxonomy of personality attributes: Replicated factor structure in peer nomination personality ratings. *Journal of Abnormal and Social Psychology, 66*, 574–583.

Northouse, P. G. (2012). *Leadership: Theory and practice*. Thousand Oaks, CA: Sage.

Oaten, M. & Cheng, K. (2006a). Improved self-control: The benefits of a regular program of academic study. *Basic and Applied Social Psychology, 28*, 1–16.

Oaten, M., & Cheng, K. (2006b). Longitudinal gains in self-regulation from regular physical exercise. *British Journal of Health Psychology, 11*, 717–733.

Oaten, M., & Cheng, K. (2007). Improvements in self-control from financial monitoring. *Journal of Economic Psychology, 28*, 487–501.

Ode, S., & Robinson, M. (2009). Can agreeableness turn gray skies blue?: A role for agreeableness in moderating neuroticism-linked dysphoria. *Journal of Social and Clinical Psychology, 28*, 436–462.

Ogihara, Y., Fujita, H., Tominaga, H., Ishigaki, S., Kashimoto, T., Takahashi, A., et al. (2015, February). *Are unique names increasing?: Rise in uniqueness and individualism in Japan*. Paper presented at the Society for Personality and Social Psychology Preconference "Advances in Cultural Psychology," Long Beach, CA.

Oishi, S., & Roth, D. P. (2009). The role of self-reports in culture and personality research: It is too early to give up on self-reports. *Journal of Research in Personality, 43*, 107–109.

Oldhamn, S., Farnill, D., & Ball, I. (1982). Sex-role identity of female homosexuals. *Journal of Homosexuality, 8*, 41–46.

Oliver, M. B., & Hyde, J. S. (1993). Gender differences in sexuality: A meta-analysis. *Psychological Bulletin, 114*, 29–51.

Ones, D. S., Dilchert, S., Viswesvaran, C., & Judge, T. A. (2007). In support of personality assessment in organizational settings. *Personnel Psychology, 60*, 995–1027.

Onnela, J-P., Waber, B. N., Pentland, A., Schnorf, S., & Lazer, D. (2014). Using sociometers to quantify social interaction patterns. *Scientific Reports, 4*, Article No. 5604.

Organ, D. W., & Lingl, A. (1995). Personality, satisfaction, and organizational citizenship behavior. *Journal of Social Psychology, 135*, 339–350.

Organ, D. W., & Ryan, K. (1995). A meta-analytic review of attitudinal and dispositional predictors of organizational citizenship behavior. *Personnel Psychology, 48*, 775–802.

Orlofsky, J. L. (1981). Relationship between sex role attitudes and personality traits and the sex role behavior scale: A new measure of masculine and feminine role behavioral and interests. *Journal of Personality and Social Psychology, 40,* 927–940.

Orth, U., & Robins, R. W. (2013). Understanding the link between low self-esteem and depression. *Current Directions in Psychological Science, 22,* 455–460.

Orth, U., Robins, R. W., & Widaman, K. F. (2012). Life-span development of self-esteem and its effects on important life outcomes. *Journal of Personality and Social Psychology, 102,* 1271–1288.

Orth, U., Trzesniewski, K. H., & Robins, R. W. (2010). Self-esteem development from young adulthood to old age: A cohort-sequential longitudinal study. *Journal of Personality and Social Psychology, 98,* 645–658.

O'Steen, S., Cullum, A. J., & Bennett, A. F. (2002). Rapid evolution of escape ability in Trinidadian guppies (*Poecilia reticulata*). *Evolution, 56,* 776–784.

O'Sullivan, S. S., Evans, A. H., & Lees, A. J. (2009). Dopamine dysregulation syndrome: An overview of its epidemiology, mechanisms, and management. *CNS Drugs, 23,* 157–170.

Otake, K., Shimai, S., Tanaka-Matsumi, J., Otsui, K., & Fredrickson, B. L. (2006). Happy people become happier through kindness: A counting kindnesses intervention. *Journal of Happiness Studies, 7,* 361–375.

Oyserman, D., Coon, H. M., & Kemmelmeier, M. (2002). Rethinking individualism and collectivism: Evaluation of theoretical assumptions and meta-analysis. *Psychological Bulletin, 128,* 3–72.

Ozer, D. J., & Benet-Martinez, V. (2006). Personality and the prediction of consequential outcomes. *Annual Review of Psychology, 57,* 401–421.

Pang, J. S., & Schultheiss, O. C. (2005). Assessing implicit motives in U.S. college students: Effects of picture type and position, gender and ethnicity, and cross-cultural comparisons. *Journal of Personality Assessment, 85,* 280–294.

Park, G., Schwartz, H. A., Eichstaedt, J. C., Kern, M. L., Kosinski, M., Stillwell, D. J., et al. (2015). Automatic personality assessment through social media language. *Journal of Personality and Social Psychology, 108*(6), 934–952.

Patrick, H., Knee, C. R., Canevello, A., & Lonsbary, C. (2007). The role of need fulfillment in relationship functioning and well-being: A self-determination theory perspective. *Journal of Personality and Social Psychology, 92,* 434–457.

Paul, A. M. (2010). *Origins: How the nine months before birth shape the rest of our lives.* New York: Free Press.

Paulhus, D. L. (1991). Measurement and control of response bias. In J. P. Robinson, P. R. Shaver, & L. S. Wrightsman (Eds.), *Measures of personality and social psychological attitudes* (pp. 17–59). New York: Academic Press.

Paulhus, D. L. (1998). Interpersonal and intrapsychic adaptiveness of trait self-enhancement: A mixed blessing? *Journal of Personality and Social Psychology, 74,* 1197–1208.

Paulhus, D. L. (2001). Normal narcissism: Two minimalist accounts. *Psychological Inquiry, 12,* 228–130.

Paulhus, D. L., Westlake, B. G., Calvez, S., & Harms, P. D. (2013). Self-presentation style in job interviews: The role of personality and culture. *Journal of Applied Social Psychology, 43,* 2042–2059.

Paulhus, D. L., & Williams, K. M. (2002). The dark triad of personality: Narcissism, Machiavellianism, and psychopathy. *Journal of Research in Personality, 36,* 556–563.

Paustian-Underdahl, S. C., Walker, L. S., & Woehr, D. J. (2014). Gender and perceptions of leadership effectiveness: A meta-analysis of contextual moderators. *Journal of Applied Psychology, 99,* 1129–1145.

Pavot, W., Diener, E., & Fujita, F. (1990). Extraversion and happiness. *Personality and Individual Differences, 11,* 1299–1306.

Pedersen, W. C., Miller, L. C., Putcha-Bhagavatula, A. D., & Yang, Y. (2002). Evolved sex differences in the number of partners desired?: The long and the short of it. *Psychological Science, 13,* 157–161.

Pena, P. A. (2015). A not so happy day after all: Excess death rates on birthdays in the U.S. *Social Science and Medicine, 126,* 59–66.

Penedo, F. J., & Dahn, J. R. (2005). Exercise and well-being: A review of mental and physical health benefits associated with physical activity. *Current Opinion in Psychiatry, 18,* 189–193.

Penke, L., & Asendorpf, J. (2008). Beyond global sociosexual orientations: A more differentiated look at sociosexuality and its effects on courtship and romantic relationships. *Journal of Personality and Social Psychology, 95,* 1113–1135.

Pennebaker, J. W. (1997). Writing about emotional experiences as a therapeutic process. *Psychological Science, 8,* 162–166.

Penney, L. M., & Spector, P. E. (2002). Narcissism and counterproductive work behavior: Do bigger egos mean bigger problems? *International Journal of Selection and Assessment, 10,* 126–134.

Peplau, L. A., & Perlman, D. (1979). Blueprint for a social psychological theory of loneliness. In M. Cook & G. Wilson (Eds.), *Love and attraction* (pp. 101–110). Oxford, UK: Pergamon.

Petersen, J. L., & Hyde, J. S. (2010). A meta-analytic review of research on gender differences in sexuality, 1993–2007. *Psychological Bulletin, 136,* 21–38.

Peterson, C., & Bossio, L. M. (2001). Optimism and physical well-being. In E. C. Chang (Ed.), *Optimism and pessimism: Implications for theory, research, and practice* (pp. 127–145). Washington, DC: American Psychological Association.

Peterson, C., Seligman, M. E. P., Yurko, K. H., Martin, L. R., & Friedman, H. S. (1998). Catastrophizing and untimely death. *Psychological Science, 9,* 49–52.

The Pew Center. (2012). Changing attitude on gay marriage. Retrieved November 13, 2012, from http://features.pewforum.org/same-sex-marriage-attitudes/slide2.php.

Phillips, D. P., Liu, G. C., Kwok, K., Jarvinen, J. R., Zhang, W., & Abramson, I. S. (2001). The Hound of the Baskervilles effect: Natural experiment on the influence of psychological stress on timing of death. *British Medical Journal, 323,* 1443–1446.

Pierce, T., & Lydon, J. (1998). Priming relational schemas: effects of contextually activated and chronically accessible interpersonal expectations on responses to a stressful event. *Journal of Personality and Social Psychology, 75*(6), 1441–1448.

Pietromonaco, P. R., & Barrett, L. F. (1997). Working models of attachment and daily social interactions. *Journal of Personality and Social Psychology, 73,* 1409–1423.

Piff, P. K. (2013). Wealth and the inflated self: Class, entitlement, and narcissism. *Personality and Social Psychology Bulletin, 40*(1), 34–43.

Piff, P. K., Kraus, M. W., Cote, S., Cheng, B. H., & Keltner, D. (2010). Having less, giving more: The influence of social class on prosocial behavior. *Journal of Personality and Social Psychology, 99,* 771–784.

Pincus, A. L., Ansell, E. B., Pimentel, C. A., Cain, N. M., Wright, A. G., & Levy, K. N. (2009). Initial construction and validation of the Pathological Narcissism Inventory. *Psychological Assessment, 21,* 365–379.

Pinquart, M., Duberstein, P., & Lyness, J. (2006). Treatments for later-life depressive conditions: A meta-analytic comparison of pharmacotherapy and psychotherapy. *American Journal of Psychiatry, 163,* 1493–1501.

Pipher, M (1994). *Reviving Ophelia: Saving the selves of adolescent girls.* New York: Ballantine.

Pipitone, R. N., & Gallup, G. G., Jr. (2008). Women's voice attractiveness varies across the menstrual cycle. *Evolution and Human Behavior, 29,* 268–274.

Plomin, R., & Daniels, D. (1987). Why are children in the same family so different from one another? *Behavioral and Brain Sciences, 10,* 1–60.

Podar, I., Hannus, A., & Allik, J. (1999). Personality and affectivity characteristics associated with eating disorders: A comparison of eating disordered, weight-preoccupied, and normal samples. *Journal of Personality Assessment, 73,* 133–147.

Polit, D., & Falbo, T. (1988). The intellectual achievement of only children. *Journal of Biosocial Science, 20,* 275–285.

Pomeranz, K. (2001). *The great divergence: China, Europe, and the making of the modern world economy.* Princeton, NJ: Princeton University Press.

Potthoff, J. G., Holahan, C. J., & Joiner, T. E. (1995). Reassurance seeking, stress generation, and depressive symptoms: An integrative model. *Journal of Personality and Social Psychology, 68,* 664–670.

Pratt, A. C. (2004). Retail therapy. *Geoforum, 35,* 519–521.

Pressman, S. D., & Cohen, S. (2005). Does positive affect influence health? *Psychological Bulletin, 131,* 925–971.

Puliti, A. (2013, March 18). Snooki's extreme makeover. *Us Weekly,* pp. 52–56.

Purifoy, F. E., & Koopmans, L. H. (1979). Androstenedione, testosterone, and free testosterone concentration in women of various occupations. *Biodemography and Social Biology, 26,* 179–188.

Putnam, R. D. (2000). *Bowling alone: The collapse and revival of American community*. New York: Simon & Schuster.

Quilty, L. C., Sellbom, M., Tackett, J. L., & Bagby, R. M. (2009). Personality trait predictors of bipolar disorder symptoms. *Psychiatry Research, 169*, 159–163.

Quinn, J. M., Pascoe, A., Wood, W., & Neal, D. T. (2010). Can't control yourself?: Monitor those bad habits. *Personality and Social Psychology Bulletin, 36*, 499–511.

Rachman, S. (1990). The determinants and treatment of simple phobias. *Advances in Behaviour Research and Therapy, 12*, 1–30.

Radloff, L. S. (1977). The CES-D scale: A self-report depression scale for research in the general population. *Applied Psychological Measurement, 1*, 385–401.

Randler, C. (2008). Differences in sleep and circadian preference between Eastern and Western German adolescents. *Chronobiology International, 25*, 565–575.

Raskin, R., & Terry, H. (1988). A principal-components analysis of the Narcissistic Personality Inventory and further evidence of its construct validity. *Journal of Personality and Social Psychology, 54*, 890–902.

Rawson, R. (1979, May 7). Two Ohio strangers find they're twins at 39—and a dream to psychologists. *People, 11*(18). Retrieved from www.people.com/people/archive/article/0,,20073583,00.html.

Raynor, D. A., & Levine, H. (2009). Associations between the Five-Factor Model of personality and health behaviors among college students. *Journal of American College Health, 58*, 73–81.

Reiland, R. (2004). *Get me out of here: My recovery from borderline personality disorder*. Center City, MN: Hazelden.

Reis, H. T., Sheldon, K. M., Gable, S. L., Roscoe, J., & Ryan, R. M. (2000). Daily well-being: The role of autonomy, competence, and relatedness. *Personality and Social Psychology Bulletin, 26*, 419–435.

Reissman, C., Aron, A., & Bergen, M. R. (1993). Shared activities and marital satisfaction: Causal direction and self-expansion versus boredom. *Journal of Social and Personal Relationships, 10*, 243–254.

Reisz, Z., Boudreaux, M. J., & Ozer, D. J. (2013). Personality traits and the prediction of personal goals. *Personality and Individual Differences, 55*, 699–704.

Rentfrow, P. J., Gosling, S. D., & Potter, J. (2008). A theory of the emergence, persistence, and expression of geographic variation in psychological characteristics. *Perspectives on Psychological Science, 3*, 339–369.

Richard, F. D., Bond, C. F., Jr., & Stokes-Zoota, J. J. (2003). One hundred years of social psychology quantitatively described. *Review of General Psychology, 7*, 331–363.

Richards, M. H., & Larson, R. (1993). Pubertal development and the daily subjective states of young adolescents. *Journal of Research on Adolescence, 3*, 145–169.

Richardson, D. R., Green, L. R., & Lago, T. (1998). The relationship between perspective-taking and nonaggressive responding in the face of an attack. *Journal of Personality, 66*, 235–256.

Richeson, J. A., & Ambady, N. (2001). Who's in charge?: Effects of situational roles on automatic gender bias. *Sex Roles, 44*, 493–512.

Rind, B., & Bordia, P. (1996). Effect on restaurant tipping of male and female servers drawing a happy, smiling face on the backs of customers' checks. *Journal of Applied Social Psychology, 26*, 218–225.

Rizzo, A., Reger, G., Gahm, G., Difede, J., & Rothbaum, B. O. (2012). Virtual reality exposure therapy for combat related PTSD. In P. Shiromani, T. Keane, & J. LeDoux (Eds.), *The neurobiology of PTSD* (pp. 375–399). Totawa, NJ: Humana Press.

Roberts, B. W. (1997). Plaster or plasticity: Are work experiences associated with personality change in women? *Journal of Personality, 65*, 205–232.

Roberts, B. W., & Chapman, C. (2000). Change in dispositional well-being and its relation to role quality: A 30-year longitudinal study. *Journal of Research in Personality, 34*, 26–41.

Roberts, B. W., & DelVecchio, W. F. (2000). The rank-order consistency of personality traits from childhood to old age: A quantitative review of longitudinal studies. *Psychological Bulletin, 126*, 3–25.

Roberts, B. W., Kuncel, N. R., Shiner, R., Caspi, A., & Goldberg, L. R. (2007). The power of personality: The comparative validity of personality traits, socio-economic status, and cognitive ability for predicting important life outcomes. *Perspectives on Psychological Science, 2*, 313–345.

Roberts, B. W., Walton, K. E., & Bogg, T. (2005). Conscientiousness and health across the life course. *Review of General Psychology, 9,* 156–168.

Roberts, B. W., Walton, K. E., & Viechtbauer, W. (2006). Patterns of mean-level change in personality traits across the life course: A meta-analysis of longitudinal studies. *Psychological Bulletin, 132,* 1–25.

Roberts, B. W., Wood, D., & Smith, J. L. (2005). Evaluating Five Factor theory and social investment perspectives on personality trait development. *Journal of Research in Personality, 39,* 166–184.

Robins, R. W., & Beer, J. S. (2001). Positive illusions about the self: Short-term benefits and long-term costs. *Journal of Personality and Social Psychology, 80,* 340–352.

Robins, R. W., Caspi, A., & Moffitt, T. E. (2002). It's not just who you're with, it's who you are: Personality and relationship experiences across multiple relationships. *Journal of Personality, 70,* 925–964.

Robins, R. W., Fraley, R. C., Roberts, B. W., & Trzesniewski, K. H. (2001). A longitudinal study of personality change in young adulthood. *Journal of Personality, 69,* 617–640.

Robins, R. W., & John, O. P. (1997). Effects of visual perspective and narcissism on self-perception: Is seeing believing? *Psychological Science, 8,* 37–42.

Robins, R. W., Trzesniewski, K. H., Tracy, J. L., Gosling, S. D., & Potter, J. (2002). Global self-esteem across the life span. *Psychology and Aging, 17,* 423–434.

Robinson, B. E., Skeen, P., & Flake-Hobson, C. (1982). Sex role endorsement among homosexual men across the life span. *Archives of Sexual Behavior, 11,* 355–359.

Rogers, C. R. (1959). A theory of therapy, personality and interpersonal relationships, as developed in the client-centered framework. in S. Koch (Ed.) *Psychology: A study of a science: Study 1, Vol. 3. Formulations of the person and the social context* (pp. 184–256). New York: McGraw-Hill.

Rogers, C. R. (1961). *On becoming a person: A therapist's view of psychotherapy.* London: Constable.

Rohde, P. A., Atzwanger, K., Butovskaya, M., Lampert, A., Mysterud, I., Sanchez-Andres, A., et al. (2003). Perceived parental favoritism, closeness to kin, and the rebel of the family: The effects of birth order and sex. *Evolution and Human Behavior, 24,* 261–276.

Rose, R. M., Holaday, J. W., & Bernstein, I. S. (1971). Plasma testosterone, dominance rank and aggressive behaviour in male rhesus monkeys. *Nature, 231,* 366–368.

Rosen, L. D., Whaling, K., Rab, S., Carrier, L. M., & Cheever, N. A. (2013). Is Facebook creating "iDisorders"?: The link between clinical symptoms of psychiatric disorders and technology use, attitudes and anxiety. *Computers in Human Behavior, 29,* 1243–1254.

Rosenberg, M. (1989). *Society and the adolescent self-image* (rev. ed.). Middletown, CT: Wesleyan University Press.

Rosenthal, S. A., & Pittinsky, T. L. (2006). Narcissistic leadership. *Leadership Quarterly, 17*(6), 617–633.

Ross, L., Greene, D., & House, P. (1977). The "false consensus effect": An egocentric bias in social perception and attribution processes. *Journal of Experimental Social Psychology, 13,* 279–301.

Ross, S. R., Stewart, J., Mugge, M., & Fultz, B. (2001). The imposter phenomenon, achievement dispositions, and the Five Factor Model. *Personality and Individual Differences, 31,* 1347–1355.

Rothbart, M. K., Ahadi, S. A., Hersey, K. L., & Fisher, P. (2001). Investigations of temperament at three to seven years: The Children's Behavior Questionnaire. *Child Development, 72,* 1394–1408.

Rothbart, M. K. & Bates, J. E. (1998). Temperament. In W. Damon & N. Eisenberg (Ed.), *Handbook of child psychology: Vol 3. Social, emotional and personality development* (5th ed.), 99–166. Hoboken, NJ: Wiley.

Rotter, J. B. (1966). Generalized expectancies for internal versus external control of reinforcement. *Psychological Monographs, 80*(Whole No. 609), 1–28.

Rotter, J. B. (1971). External control and internal control. *Psychology Today, 5,* 37–59.

Rotter, J. B., Chance, J. E., & Phares, E. J. (Eds.). (1972). *Applications of a social learning theory of personality.* New York: Holt, Rinehart, & Winston.

Rottinghaus, P. J., Lindley, L. D., Green, M. A., & Borgen, F. H. (2002). Educational aspirations: The contribution of personality, self-efficacy, and interests. *Journal of Vocational Behavior, 61,* 1–19.

Rubenzer, S. J., Faschingbauer, T. R., & Ones, D. S. (2000). Assessing the U.S. presidents using the

Revised NEO Personality Inventory. *Assessment, 7,* 403–419.

Rudman, L. A. (1998). Self-promotion as a risk factor for women: The costs and benefits of counterstereo-typical impression management. *Journal of Personality and Social Psychology, 74,* 629–645.

Rudman, L. A., & Glick, P. (2010). *The social psychology of gender: How power and intimacy shape gender relations.* New York: Guilford Press.

Rudman, L. A., & Goodwin, S. A. (2004). Gender differences in automatic in-group bias: Why do women like women more than men like men? *Journal of Personality and Social Psychology, 87,* 494–509.

Ruiz, J. M., Matthews, K. A., Scheier, M. F., & Schulz, R. (2006). Does who you marry matter for your health?: Influence of patients' and spouses' personality on their partners' psychological well-being following coronary artery bypass surgery. *Journal of Personality and Social Psychology, 91,* 255–267.

Rusbult, C. E., Verette, J., Whitney, G. A., Slovik, L. F., & Lipkus, I. (1991). Accommodation processes in close relationships: Theory and preliminary empirical evidence. *Journal of Personality and Social Psychology, 60,* 53–78.

Russell, D. W. (1996). UCLA Loneliness Scale (Version 3): Reliability, validity, and factor structure. *Journal of Personality Assessment, 66,* 20–40.

Ryan, R. M., & Connell, J. P. (1989). Perceived locus of causality and internalization: Examining reasons for acting in two domains. *Journal of Personality and Social Psychology, 57,* 749–761.

Ryan, R. M., & Deci, E. L. (2000). Self-determination theory and the facilitation of intrinsic motivation, social development, and well-being. *American Psychologist, 55,* 68–78.

Ryan, R. M., & Deci, E. L. (2008). Self-determination theory and the role of basic psychological needs in personality and the organization of behavior. In O. P. John, R. W. Robins, & L. A. Pervin (Eds.), *Handbook of personality: Theory and research,* 654–678. New York: Guilford Press.

Ryff, C. D., & Singer, B. (1998). The contours of positive human health. *Psychological Inquiry, 9,* 1–28.

Sagie, A., & Elizur, D. (1999). Achievement motive and entrepreneurial orientation: A structural analysis. *Journal of Organizational Behavior, 20,* 375–387.

Saklofske, D. H., Kelly, I. W., & McKerracher, D. W. (1982). An empirical study of personality and astrological factors. *Journal of Psychology: Interdisciplinary and Applied, 110*(2), 275–280.

Salanova, M., Bakker, A. B., & Llorens, S. (2006). Flow at work: Evidence for an upward spiral of personal and organizational resources. *Journal of Happiness Studies, 7,* 1–22.

Salgado, J. F. (2002). The Big Five personality dimensions and counterproductive behaviors. *International Journal of Selection and Assessment, 10,* 117–125.

Salmon, C. A., & Daly, M. (1998). Birth order and familial sentiment: Middleborns are different. *Evolution and Human Behavior, 19,* 299–312.

Samuel, D. B., & Widiger, T. A. (2008). A meta-analytic review of the relationships between the Five-Factor Model and DSM-IV-TR personality disorders: A facet level analysis. *Clinical Psychology Review, 28,* 1326–1342.

Sargent, J. D., Tanski, S., Stoolmiller, M., & Hanewinkel, R. (2010). Using sensation seeking to target adolescents for substance use interventions. *Addiction, 105,* 506–514.

Saroglou, V., & Fiasse, L. (2003). Birth order, personality, and religion: A study among young adults from a three-sibling family. *Personality and Individual Differences, 35,* 19–29.

Satipatthana Sutta. (2008). Frames of reference (T. Bhikkhu, Trans.). *Access to Insight.* Retrieved from www .accesstoinsight.org/tipitaka/mn/mn.010.than.html.

Satterfield, J. H., & Schell, A. (1997). A prospective study of hyperactive boys with conduct problems and normal boys: Adolescent and adult criminality. *Journal of the American Academy of Child and Adolescent Psychiatry, 36,* 1726–1735.

Saulsman, L. M., & Page, A. C. (2004). The Five-Factor Model and personality disorder empirical literature: A meta-analytic review. *Clinical Psychology Review, 23,* 1055–1085.

Sayer, L. C., Bianchi, S. M., & Robinson, J. P. (2004). Are parents investing less in children?: Trends in mothers' and fathers' time with children. *American Journal of Sociology, 110,* 1–43.

Scarr, S., Webber, P. L., Weinberg, R. A., & Wittig, M. A. (1981). Personality resemblance among adolescents and their parents in biologically related and adoptive families. *Journal of Personality and Social Psychology, 40*, 885–898.

Schindehette, S. (2006). My life as a sperm donor. *People*. Retrieved June 5, 2006, from www.people.com/people/archive/article/0,,20060497,00.html.

Schlinger, H. (1996). What's wrong with evolutionary explanations of human behavior. *Behavior and Social Issues, 6*, 35–54.

Schmitt, D. P., & Allik, J. (2005). Simultaneous administration of the Rosenberg self-esteem scale in 53 nations: Exploring the universal and culture-specific features of global self-esteem. *Journal of Personality and Social Psychology, 89*, 623–642.

Schmitt, D. P., Allik, J., McCrae, R. R., & Benet-Martinez, V. (2007). The geographic distribution of Big Five personality traits: Patterns and profiles of human self-description across 56 nations. *Journal of Cross-Cultural Psychology, 38*, 173–212.

Schmitt, D. P., Realo, A., Voracek, M., & Allik, J. (2008). Why can't a man be more like a woman?: Sex differences in Big Five personality traits across 55 cultures. *Journal of Personality and Social Psychology, 94*, 168–182.

Schmitt, D. P., & Shackelford, T. K. (2008). Big Five traits related to short-term mating: From personality to promiscuity across 46 nations. *Evolutionary Psychology, 6*, 246–282.

Schorn, D. (2006, March 19). Sperm donor siblings find family ties. In *60 Minutes* [TV series]. Retrieved from www.cbsnews.com/8301-18560_162-1414965.html.

Schredl, M. (2003). Effects of state and trait factors on nightmare frequency. *European archives of psychiatry and clinical neuroscience, 253*(5), 241–247.

Schredl, M. (2007). Personality correlates of flying dreams. *Imagination, Cognition and Personality, 27*(2), 129–137.

Schredl, M., Ciric, P., Götz, S., & Wittmann, L. (2003). Dream recall frequency, attitude towards dreams and openness to experience. *Dreaming, 13*(3), 145–153.

Schüler, J., Brandstätter, V., & Sheldon, K. M. (2013). Do implicit motives and basic psychological needs interact to predict well-being and flow?: Testing a universal hypothesis and a matching hypothesis. *Motivation and Emotion, 37*, 480–495.

Schultheiss, O. C. (2008). Implicit motives. In O. P. John, R. W. Robins, & L. A. Pervin (Eds.), *Handbook of personality: Theory and research*. New York: Guilford Press.

Schultheiss, O. C., & Brunstein, J. C. (1999). Goal imagery: Bridging the gap between implicit motives and explicit goals. *Journal of Personality, 67*, 1–38.

Schultheiss, O. C., & Brunstein, J. C. (2002). Inhibited power motivation and persuasive communication: A lens model analysis. *Journal of Personality, 70*, 553–582.

Schultheiss, O. C., Liening, S. H., & Schad, D. (2008). The reliability of a Picture Story Exercise measure of implicit motives: Estimates of internal consistency, retest reliability, and ipsative stability. *Journal of Research in Personality, 42*, 1560–1571.

Schultheiss, O. C., Pang, J. S., Torges, C. M., Wirth, M. M., & Treynor, W. (2005). Perceived facial expressions of emotion as motivational incentives: Evidence from a differential implicit learning paradigm. *Emotion, 5*, 41–54.

Schultheiss, O. C., Wirth, M. M., & Stanton, S. J. (2004). Effects of affiliation and power motivation arousal on salivary progesterone and testosterone. *Hormones and Behavior, 46*, 592–599.

Schultheiss, O. C., Wirth, M. M., Torges, C. M., Pang, J. S., Villacorta, M. A., & Welsh, K. M. (2005). Effects of implicit power motivation on men's and women's implicit learning and testosterone changes after social victory or defeat. *Journal of Personality and Social Psychology, 88*, 174–188.

Schwartz, H. A., Eichstaedt, J. C., Kern, M. L., Dziurzynski, L., Ramones, S. M., Agarwal, M., et al. (2013). Personality, gender, and age in the language of social media: The open-vocabulary approach. *Plos One, 8*(9): e73791.

Schwartz, S. H. (1992). Universals in the content and structure of values: Theory and empirical tests in 20 countries. In M. P. Zanna (Ed.), *Advances in experimental social psychology* (Vol. 25), 1–65. New York: Academic Press.

Scollon, C. N., & Diener, E. (2006). Love, work, and changes in extraversion and neuroticism over time. *Journal of Personality and Social Psychology, 91*, 1152–1165.

Seder, J. P., & Oishi, S. (2012). Intensity of smiling in Facebook photos predicts future life satisfaction. *Social Psychological and Personality Science, 3*, 407–413.

Sehlmeyer, C., Dannlowski, E., Schoning, S., Kugel, H., Pyka, M., Pfleiderer, B., et al. (2011). Neural correlates of trait anxiety in fear extinction. *Psychological Medicine, 41*, 789–798.

Seidman, G. (2013). Self-presentation and belonging on Facebook: How personality influences social media use and motivations. *Personality and Individual Differences, 54*, 402–407.

Selfhout, M., Burk, W., Branje, S., Denissen, J., Van Aken, M., & Meeus, W. (2010). Emerging late adolescent friendship networks and Big Five personality traits: A social network approach. *Journal of Personality, 78*, 509–538.

Seligman, M. E. P., Schulman, P., DeRubeis, R. J., & Hollon, S. D. (1999). The prevention of depression and anxiety. *Prevention and Treatment, 2*(1), Article 8.

Sheldon, K. M., Elliot, A. J., Kim, Y., & Kasser, T. (2001). What is satisfying about satisfying events?: Testing 10 candidate psychological needs. *Journal of Personality and Social Psychology, 80*, 325–339.

Sheldon, K. M., & Gunz, A. (2009). Psychological needs as basic motives, not just experiential requirements. *Journal of Personality, 77*, 1467–1492.

Sheldon, K. M., Nichols, C. P., & Kasser, T. (2011). Americans recommend smaller ecological footprints when reminded of intrinsic American values of self-expression, family, and generosity. *Ecopsychology, 3*, 97–104.

Shelov, D. V., Suchday, S., & Friedberg, J. P. (2009). A pilot study measuring the impact of yoga on the trait of mindfulness. *Behavioural and Cognitive Psychotherapy, 37*, 595–598.

Shiner, R. L., & Caspi, A. (2003). Personality differences in childhood and adolescence: Measurement, development, and consequences. *Journal of Child Psychology and Psychiatry, 44*, 2–32.

Shiner, R. L., Masten, A. S., & Roberts, J. M. (2003). Childhood personality foreshadows adult personality and life outcomes two decades later. *Journal of Personality, 71*, 1145–1170.

Shiner, R. L., Masten, A. S., & Tellegen, A. (2002). A developmental perspective on personality in emerging adulthood: Childhood antecedents and concurrent adaptation. *Journal of Personality and Social Psychology, 83*, 1165–1177.

Shiota, M. N., & Levenson, R. W. (2007). Birds of a feather don't always fly farthest: Similarity in Big Five personality predicts more negative marital satisfaction trajectories in long-term marriages. *Psychology and Aging, 22*, 666–675.

Shipley, B. A., Weiss, A., Der, G., Taylor, M. D., & Deary, I. J. (2007). Neuroticism, extraversion, and mortality in the UK Health and Lifestyle Survey: A 21-year prospective cohort study. *Psychosomatic Medicine, 69*, 923–931.

Shor, E., Roelfs, D. J., & Yogev, T. (2013). The strength of family ties: A meta-analysis and meta-regression of self-reported social support and mortality. *Social Networks, 35*, 626–638.

Shostrom, E. L. (1964). An inventory for the measurement of self-actualization. *Educational and Psychological Measurement, 24*, 207–218.

Sibley, C. G., & Bulbulia, J. A. (2014). How do religious identities and basic value orientations affect each other over time? *International Journal for the Psychology of Religion, 24*, 64–76.

Sibley, C. G., Osborne, D., & Duckitt, J. (2012). Personality and political orientation: Meta-analysis and test of a threat-constraint model. *Journal of Research in Personality, 46*, 664–677.

Silverman, K., Svikes, D., Robles, E., Stitzer, M. L., & Bigelow, G. E. (2001). A reinforcement-based therapeutic workplace for the treatment of drug abuse: Six-month abstinence outcomes. *Experimental and Clinical Psychopharmacology, 9*, 14–23.

Silverstein, S. M., Hatashita-Wong, M., Wilkniss, S., Bloch, A., Smith, T., Savitz, A., et al. (2006). Behavioral rehabilitation of the "treatment-refractory" schizophrenia patient: Conceptual foundations, interventions, and outcome data. *Psychological Services, 3*, 145–169.

Sin, N. L., & Lyubomirsky, S. (2009). Enhancing well-being and alleviating depressive symptoms with positive psychology interventions: A practice-friendly meta-analysis. *Journal of Clinical Psychology, 65*, 467–487.

Skinner, B. F. (1938). *The behavior of organisms: An experimental analysis.* New York: Appleton-Century-Crofts.

Skinner, B. F. (1970). *Walden Two.* New York: Macmillian.

Skinner, B. F. (1971). *Beyond freedom and dignity*. New York: Knopf.

Slane, J. D., Klump, K. L., Donnellan, M. B., McGue, M., & Iacono, W. G. (2013). The dysregulated cluster in personality profiling research: Longitudinal stability and associations with bulimic behaviors and correlates. *Journal of Personality Disorders, 27*, 1–22.

Sluming, V. A., & Manning, J. T. (2000). Second to fourth digit ratio in elite musicians: Evidence for musical ability as an honest signal of male fitness. *Evolution and Human Behavior, 21*, 1–9.

Smillie, L. D., Cooper, A. J., Wilt, J., & Revelle, W. (2012). Do extraverts get more bang for the buck?: Refining the affective-reactivity hypothesis of extraversion. *Journal of Personality and Social Psychology, 103*, 306–326.

Smith, C. P. (1992). *Motivation and personality: Handbook of thematic content analysis*. New York: Cambridge University Press.

Smith, D. (2012). *Monkey mind: A memoir of anxiety*. New York: Simon & Schuster.

Smith, J. W., Frawley, P. J., & Polisssar, N. L. (1997). Six- and twelve-month abstinence rates in inpatient alcoholics treated with either faradic aversion or chemical aversion compared with matched inpatients from a treatment registry. *Journal of Addictive Diseases, 16*, 5–24.

Smith, M. L., & Glass, G. V. (1977). Meta-analysis of psychotherapy outcome studies. *American Psychologist, 32*, 752–760.

Smith, T. W., Glazer, K., Ruiz, J. M., & Gallo, L. C. (2004). Hostility, anger, aggressiveness, and coronary heart disease: An interpersonal perspective on personality, emotion, and health. *Journal of Personality, 72*, 1217–1270.

Smits, I. A. M., Dolan, C. V., Vorst, H. C. M., Wicherts, J. M., & Timmerman, M. E. (2011). Cohort differences in Big Five personality factors over a period of 25 years. *Journal of Personality and Social Psychology, 100*, 1124–1138.

Smokler, J. (2012). *Confessions of a scary mommy*. New York: Gallery Books.

Smyth, J. M. (1998). Written emotional expression: Effect sizes, outcome types, and moderating variables. *Journal of Consulting and Clinical Psychology, 66*, 174–184.

Snyder, M. (1974). Self-monitoring of expressive behavior. *Journal of Personality and Social Psychology, 30*, 526–537.

Soto, C. J., John, O. P., Gosling, S. D., & Potter, J. (2011). Age differences in personality traits from 10 to 65: Big Five domains and facets in a large cross-sectional sample. *Journal of Personality and Social Psychology, 100*, 330–348.

Spangler, W. D. (1992). Validity of questionnaire and TAT measures of need for achievement: Two meta-analyses. *Psychological Bulletin, 112*, 140–154.

Spates, R. C., Pagoto, S., & Kalata, A. (2006). A qualitative and quantitative review of behavioral activation treatment of major depressive disorder. *Behavior Analyst Today, 7*, 508–517.

Specht, J., Luhmann, M., & Geiser, C. (2014). On the consistency of personality types across adulthood: Latent profile analyses in two large-scale panel studies. *Journal of Personality and Social Psychology, 107*, 540–556.

Spence, J. T., & Buckner, C. (2000). Instrumental and expressive traits, trait stereotypes, and sexist attitudes: What do they signify? *Psychology of Women Quarterly, 24*, 44–62.

Spence, J. T., & Helmreich, R. L. (1978). *Masculinity and femininity*. Austin: University of Texas Press.

Spence, J. T., & Helmreich, R. L. (1980). Masculine instrumentality and feminine expressiveness: Their relationships with sex role attitudes and behaviors. *Psychology of Women Quarterly, 5*, 147–163.

Spencer, S. J., Steele, C. M., & Quinn, D. M. (1998). Stereotype threat and women's math performance. *Journal of Experimental Social Psychology, 35*, 4–28.

Sperry, L. (2012). *Handbook of diagnosis and treatment of DSM-IV personality disorders*. New York: Routledge.

Spielberger, C. D. (1983). *Manual for the State–Trait Anxiety Inventory (Form Y)*. Menlo Park, CA: Mind Garden.

Spurk, D., & Abele, A. E. (2011). Who earns more and why?: A multiple mediation model from personality to salary. *Journal of Business and Psychology, 26*, 87–103.

Srivastava, S., Guglielmo, S., & Beer, J. S. (2010). Perceiving others' personalities: Examining the dimensionality, assumed similarity to the self, and stability of perceiver effects. *Journal of Personality and Social Psychology, 98,* 520–534.

Srivastava, S., John, O. P., Gosling, S. D., & Potter, J. (2003). Development of personality in early and middle adulthood: Set like plaster or persistent change? *Journal of Personality and Social Psychology, 84,* 1041–1053.

Stajkovic, A. D., & Luthans, F. (1998). Self-efficacy and work-related performance: A meta-analysis. *Psychological Bulletin, 124,* 240–261.

Stanton, S. J., Beehner, J. C., Saini, E. K., Kuhn, C. M., & LaBar, K. S. (2009). Dominance, politics, and physiology: Voters' testosterone changes on the night of the 2008 United States presidential election. *PLoS One, 4*(10), e7543.

Stanton, S. J., & Schultheiss, O. C. (2007). Basal and dynamic relationships between implicit power motivation and estradiol in women. *Hormones and Behavior, 52,* 571–580.

Stellar, J. E., Marzo, V. M., Kraus, M. W., & Keltner, D. (2012). Class and compassion: Socioeconomic factors predict responses to suffering. *Emotion, 12,* 449–459.

Stenstrom, E., Saad, G., Nepomuceno, M. V., & Mendenhall, Z. (2011). Testosterone and domain-specific risk: Digit ratios (2D:4D and rel2) as predictors of recreational, financial, and social risk-taking behaviors. *Personality and Individual Differences, 51,* 412–416.

Stephens, N. M., Markus, H. R., & Townsend, S. M. (2007). Choice as an act of meaning: The case of social class. *Journal of Personality and Social Psychology, 93,* 814–830.

Stevens, J. S., & Hamann, S. (2012). Sex differences in brain activation to emotional stimuli: A meta-analysis of neuroimaging studies. *Neuropsychologia, 50,* 1578–1593.

Stewart, G. L. (1996). Reward structure as a moderator of the relationship between extraversion and sales performance. *Journal of Applied Psychology, 81,* 619–627.

Stewart, K. D., & Bernhardt, P. C. (2010). Comparing millennials to pre-1987 students and with one another. *North American Journal of Psychology, 12,* 579–602.

Stinson, F. S., Dawson, D. A., Goldstein, R. B., Chou, S. P., Huang, B., Smith, S. M., et al. (2008). Prevalence, correlates, disability, and comorbidity of DSM-IV Narcissistic Personality Disorder: Results from the Wave 2 National Epidemiologic Survey on Alcohol and Related Conditions. *Journal of Clinical Psychiatry, 69,* 1033–1045.

Stokes, J. P. (1985). The relation of social network and individual difference variables to loneliness. *Journal of Personality and Social Psychology, 48,* 981–990.

Stoller, R. J. (1985). *Presentations of gender.* New Haven, CT: Yale University Press.

Stoolmiller, M. (1999). Implications of the restricted range of family environments for estimates of heritability and nonshared environment in behavior-genetic adoption studies. *Psychological Bulletin, 125,* 392–409.

Strain, J., Didehbani, N., Munro, C. C., Mansinghani, S., Conover, H., Kraut, M. A., et al. (2013). Depressive symptoms and white matter dysfunction in retired NFL players with concussion history. *Neurology, 81,* 25–32.

Strauman, T. J., Lemieux, A. M., & Coe, C. L. (1993). Self-discrepancy and natural killer cell activity: Immunological consequences of negative self-evaluation. *Journal of Personality and Social Psychology, 64,* 1042–1052.

Strelan, P. (2007). Who forgives others, themselves, and situations?: The roles of narcissism, guilt, self-esteem, and agreeableness. *Personality and Individual Differences, 42,* 259–269.

Su, R., Rounds, J., & Armstrong, P. I. (2009). Men and things, women and people: A meta-analysis of sex differences in interests. *Psychological Bulletin, 135,* 859–884.

Suh, E. M. (2002). Culture, identity consistency, and subjective well-being. *Journal of Personality and Social Psychology, 83,* 1378–1391.

Sulloway, F. J. (1995). Birth order and evolutionary psychology: A meta-analytic overview. *Psychological Inquiry, 6,* 75–80.

Sulloway, F. J. (1996). *Born to rebel: Birth order, family dynamics, and creative lives.* New York: Pantheon Books.

Sulloway, F. J., & Zweigenhaft, R. L. (2010). Birth order and risk taking in athletics: A meta-analysis and study of major league baseball. *Personality and Social Psychology Review, 14,* 402–416.

Suls, J., & Bunde, J. (2005). Anger, anxiety, and depression as risk factors for cardiovascular disease: The problems and implications of overlapping affective dispositions. *Psychological Bulletin, 131,* 260–300.

Surtees, P., Wainwright, N., Day, N., Brayne, C., Luben, R., & Khaw, K.-T. (2003). Adverse experience in childhood as a developmental risk factor for altered immune status in adulthood. *International Journal of Behavioral Medicine, 10,* 251–268.

Sutin, A. R., Ferrucci, L., Zonderman, A. B., & Terracciano, A. (2011). Personality and obesity across the adult lifespan. *Journal of Personality and Social Psychology, 101,* 579–592.

Sverko, B., & Fabulic, L. (1985). Stability of morningness-eveningness: Retest changes after seven years. *Revija za Psihologiju, 15,* 71–78.

Sykes, C. J. (1995). *Dumbing down our kids.* New York: St Martin's Griffin.

Szasz, T. S. (1990). *Anti-Freud: Karl Kraus's criticism of psychoanalysis and psychiatry.* Syracuse, NY: Syracuse University Press.

Talhelm, T., Zhang, X., Oishi, S., Shimin, C., Duan, D., Lan, X., et al. (2014). Large-scale psychological differences within China explained by rice versus wheat agriculture. *Science, 344,* 603–608.

Tang, T. Z., DeRubeis, R. J., Hollon, S. D., Amsterdam, J., Shelton, R., & Schalet, B. (2009). Personality change during depression treatment: A placebo-controlled trial. *Archives of General Psychiatry, 66,* 1322–1330.

Tang, Y. Y., Ma, Y., Wang, J., Fan, Y., Feng, S., Lu, Q., et al. (2007). Short-term meditation training improves attention and self-regulation. *Proceedings of the National Academy of Sciences, 104,* 17152–17156.

Tangney, J. P., Baumeister, R. F., & Boone, A. L. (2004). High self-control predicts good adjustment, less pathology, better grades, and interpersonal success. *Journal of Personality, 72,* 271–324.

Tauber, M. (2003, August 4). And baby makes two. *People,* http://www.people.com/people/article/0,,628272,00.html.

Taubman-Ben-Ari, O., & Yehiel, D. (2012). Driving styles and their associations with personality and motivation. *Accident Analysis and Prevention, 45,* 416–422.

Taylor, L. S., Fiore, A. T., Mendelsohn, G. A., & Cheshire, C. (2011). "Out of my league": A real-world test of the matching hypothesis. *Personality and Social Psychology Bulletin, 37,* 942–954.

Taylor, R., Najafi, F., & Dobson, A. (2007). Meta-analysis of studies of passive smoking and lung cancer: Effect of study type and continent. *International Journal of Epidemiology, 36,* 1048–1059.

Taylor, S. E., & Armor, D. A. (1996). Positive illusions and coping with adversity. *Journal of Personality, 64,* 873–898.

Taylor, S. E., & Brown, J. D. (1988). Illusion and well-being: A social psychological perspective on mental health. *Psychological Bulletin, 103,* 193–210.

Taylor, S. E., Klein, L. C., Lewis, B. P., Gruenewald, T. L., Gurung, R. A., & Updegraff, K. A. (2000). Biobehavioral responses to stress in females: Tend-and-befriend, not fight-or-flight. *Psychological Review, 107,* 411–429.

Taylor, S. P. (1967). Aggressive behavior and physiological arousal as a function of provocation and the tendency to inhibit aggression. *Journal of Personality, 35,* 297–310.

Tellegen, A., Lykken, D. T., Bouchard, T. J., Wilcox, K. M., Segal, N. L., & Rich, S. (1988). Personality similarity in twins reared apart and together. *Journal of Personality and Social Psychology, 54,* 1031–1039.

Tellegen, A., & Waller, N. G. (2008). Exploring personality through test construction: Development of the Multidimensional Personality Questionnaire. In G. J. Boyle, G. Matthews, & D. H. Saklofske (Eds.), *The Sage handbook of personality theory and assessment: Vol. II. Personality measurement and assessment* (pp. 261–292). London: Sage.

Terman, L. M., & Miles, C. C. (1936). *Sex and personality: Studies in masculinity and femininity.* New York: McGraw-Hill.

Terman, L. M., & Oden, M. H. (1947). *The gifted child grows up: Twenty-five years' follow-up of a superior group.* Palo Alto, CA: Stanford University Press.

Terracciano, A., Abdel-Khalek, A. M., Adám, N., Adamovová, L., Ahn, C. K., & Ahn, H. N., et al. (2005). National character does not reflect mean personality trait levels in 49 cultures. *Science, 310,* 96–100.

Terracciano, A., Lockenhoff, C. E., Zonderman, A. B., Ferrucci, L., & Costa, P. T. (2008). Personality predictors of longevity: Activity, emotional stability, and conscientiousness. *Psychosomatic Medicine, 70,* 621–627.

Terry, M. L., Leary, M. R., & Mehta, S. (2012). Self-compassion as a buffer against homesickness, depression, and dissatisfaction in the transition to college. *Self and Identity, 12,* 1–13.

Thalmayer, A. G., Saucier, G., & Eigenhuis, A. (2011). Comparative validity of brief to medium-length Big Five and Big Six personality questionnaires. *Psychological Assessment, 23,* 995–1009.

Thase, M. E. (2005). Pharmacologic strategies for treatment-resistant depression: An update on the state of the evidence. *Psychiatric Annals, 35,* 970–978.

Thomas, J. R., & French, K. E. (1985). Gender differences across age in motor performance: A meta-analysis. *Psychological Bulletin, 98,* 260–282.

Thorndike, E. L. (1911). *Animal intelligence.* New York: Macmillian.

Thrash, T. M., & Elliot, A. J. (2002). Implicit and self-attributed achievement motives: Concordance and predictive validity. *Journal of Personality, 70,* 729–755.

Thrash, T. M., Elliot, A. J., & Schultheiss, O. C. (2007). Methodological and dispositional predictors of congruence between implicit and explicit need for achievement. *Personality and Social Psychology Bulletin, 33,* 961–974.

Tiedens, L. Z., & Fragale, A. R. (2003). Power moves: Complementarity in dominant and submissive nonverbal behavior. *Journal of Personality and Social Psychology, 84,* 558–568.

Timberlake, D. S., Rhee, S. H., Haberstick, B. C., Hopfer, C., Ehringer, M., Lessem, J. M., et al. (2006). The moderating effects of religiosity on the genetic and environmental determinants of smoking initiation. *Nicotine and Tobacco Research, 8,* 123–133.

Timmer, R. (2010). *Into the storm: Violent tornadoes, killer hurricanes, and death-defying adventures in extreme weather.* New York: New American Library.

Tindle, H., Belnap, B. H., Houck, P. R., Mazumadar, S., Scheier, M. F., Matthews, K. A., et al. (2012). Optimism, response to treatment of depression, and rehospitalization after coronary artery bypass graft surgery. *Psychosomatic Medicine, 74,* 200–207.

Tobin, R. M., Graziano, W. G., Vanman, E. J., & Tassinary, L. G. (2000). Personality, emotional experience,

and efforts to control emotions. *Journal of Personality and Social Psychology, 79,* 656–669.

Toepfer, S. M., Cichy, K., & Peters, P. (2012). Letters of gratitude: Further evidence for author benefits. *Journal of Happiness Studies, 13,* 187–201.

Torgersen, S., Lygren, S., Øien, P. A., Skre, I., Onstad, S., Edvardsen, J., et al. (2000). A twin study of personality disorders. *Comprehensive Psychiatry, 41,* 416–425.

Toussaint, L., & Webb, J. R. (2005). Gender differences in the relationship between empathy and forgiveness. *Journal of Social Psychology, 145,* 673–685.

Trivers, R. L. (1972). Parental investment and sexual selection. In B. Campbell (Ed.), *Sexual selection and the descent of man: 1871–1971* (pp. 136–179). Chicago: Aldine.

Tsaousis, I. (2010). Ciracdian preferences and personality traits: A meta-analysis. *European Journal of Personality, 24,* 356–373.

Tucker, J. S., Kressin, N. R., Spiro, A., & Ruscio, J. (1998). Intrapersonal characteristics and the timing of divorce: A prospective investigation. *Journal of Social and Personal Relationships, 15,* 211–225.

Tupes, E. C., & Christal, R. C. (1961). *Recurrent personality factors based on trait ratings* [Technical report]. Lackland Air Force Base, TX: U.S. Air Force.

Turiano, N. A., Chapman, B. P., Gruenewald, T. L., & Mroczek, D. K. (2015). Personality and the leading behavioral contributors of mortality. *Health Psychology, 34,* 51–60.

Turiano, N. A., Pitzer, L., Armour, C., Karlamangla, A., Ryff, C. D., & Mroczek, D. K. (2012a). Personality trait level and change as predictors of health outcomes: Findings from a national study of Americans (MIDUS). *Journals of Gerontology: Series B: Psychological Sciences and Social Sciences, 67B,* 4–12.

Turiano, N. A., Spiro, A., & Mroczek, D. K. (2012). Openness to experience and mortality in men: Analysis of trait and facets. *Journal of Aging and Health, 24,* 654–672.

Turkheimer, E., & Waldron, M. (2000). Nonshared environment: A theoretical, methodological, and quantitative review. *Psychological Bulletin, 126,* 78–108.

Twenge, J. M. (1997). Changes in masculine and feminine traits over time: A meta-analysis. *Sex Roles, 36,* 305–325.

Twenge, J. M. (1999). Mapping gender: The multi-factorial approach and the organization of gender-related attributes. *Psychology of Women Quarterly, 23,* 485–502.

Twenge, J. M. (2001a). Birth cohort changes in extraversion: A cross-temporal meta-analysis, 1966–1993. *Personality and Individual Differences, 30,* 735–748.

Twenge, J. M. (2001b). Changes in women's assertiveness in response to status and roles: A cross-temporal meta-analysis, 1931–1993. *Journal of Personality and Social Psychology, 81,* 133–145.

Twenge, J. M. (2014). *Generation me: Why today's young Americans are more confident, assertive, entitled—and more miserable than ever before* (2nd ed.). New York: Atria Books.

Twenge, J. M. (2015). Time period and birth cohort differences in depressive symptoms in the U.S., 1982–2013. *Social Indicators Research, 121*(2), 437–454.

Twenge, J. M., Abebe, E. M., & Campbell, W. K. (2010). Fitting in or standing out: Trends in American parents' choices for children's names, 1880–2007. *Social Psychological and Personality Science, 1,* 19–25.

Twenge, J. M., Baumeister, R. F., DeWall, C. N., Ciarocco, N. J., & Bartels, J. M. (2007). Social exclusion decreases prosocial behavior. *Journal of Personality and Social Psychology, 92,* 56–66.

Twenge, J. M., Baumeister, R. F., Tice, D. M., & Stucke, T. S. (2001). If you can't join them, beat them: Effects of social exclusion on aggressive behavior. *Journal of Personality and Social Psychology, 81,* 1058–1069.

Twenge, J. M., & Campbell, W. K. (2001). Age and birth cohort differences in self-esteem: A cross-temporal meta-analysis. *Personality and Social Psychology Review, 5,* 321–344.

Twenge, J. M., & Campbell, W. K. (2002). Self-esteem and socioeconomic status: A meta-analytic review. *Personality and Social Psychology Review, 6,* 59–71.

Twenge, J. M., Campbell, W. K., & Freeman, E. C. (2012a). Generational differences in young adults' life goals, concern for others, and civic orientation, 1966–2009. *Journal of Personality and Social Psychology, 102,* 1045–1062.

Twenge, J. M., Campbell, W. K., & Gentile, B. (2012b). Increases in individualistic words and phrases in American books, 1960–2008. *PLoS ONE, 7,* e40181.

Twenge, J. M., Campbell, W. K., & Gentile, B. (2012c). Male and female pronoun use in U.S. books reflects women's status, 1900–2008. *Sex Roles, 67,* 488–493.

Twenge, J. M., Catanese, K. R., & Baumeister, R. F. (2002). Social exclusion causes self-defeating behavior. *Journal of Personality and Social Psychology, 83,* 606–615.

Twenge, J. M., & Crocker, J. (2002). Race and self-esteem: meta-analyses comparing whites, blacks, Hispanics, Asians, and American Indians and comment on Gray-Little and Hafdahl (2000). *Psychological Bulletin, 128,* 371–408.

Twenge, J. M., & Foster, J. D. (2010). Birth cohort increases in narcissistic personality traits among American college students, 1982–2009. *Social Psychological and Personality Science, 1,* 99–106.

Twenge, J. M., Gentile, B., DeWall, C. N., Ma, D. S., Lacefield, K., & Schurtz, D. R. (2010). Birth cohort increases in psychopathology among young Americans, 1938–2007: A cross-temporal meta-analysis of the MMPI. *Clinical Psychology Review, 30,* 145–154.

Twenge, J. M., & Im, C. (2007). Changes in the need for social approval, 1958–2001. *Journal of Research in Personality, 41,* 171–189.

Twenge, J. M., & Nolen-Hoeksema, S. (2002). Age, gender, race, socioeconomic status, and birth cohort difference on the children's depression inventory: A meta-analysis. *Journal of Abnormal Psychology, 111,* 578–588.

Twenge, J. M., Sherman, R. A., & Wells, B. E. (in press). Changes in American adults' sexual behavior and attitudes, 1972–2012. *Archives of Sexual Behavior.*

Twenge, J. M., Zhang, L., & Im, C. (2004). It's beyond my control: A cross-temporal meta-analysis of increasing externality in locus of control, 1960–2002. *Personality and Social Psychology Review, 8,* 308–319.

Turner, R. H., & Schutte, J. (1981). The true self method for studying the self-conception. *Symbolic Interaction, 4,* 1–20.

Ulrich, R. S. (1993). Biophilia, biophobia, and natural landscapes. In S. R. Kellert & E. O. Wilson (Eds.), *The biophilia hypothesis* (pp. 73–137). Washington, DC: Island Press.

U. S. Bureau of the Census. (2010). *Statistical Abstract of the United States.* Washington, DC: U.S. Government Printing Office.

U. S. Bureau of the Census. (2012). *Statistical Abstract of the United States*. Washington, DC: U.S. Government Printing Office.

U.S. Department of Labor. (2006). Testing and assessment: A guide to good practices for workforce investment professionals. Employment and Training Administration. Retrieved from www.onetcenter .org/dl_files/proTestAsse.pdf.

Valenstein, E. S. (1986). *Great and desperate cure: The rise and decline of psychosurgery and other radical treatments for mental illness*. New York: Basic Books.

Van Anders, S. M., & Siciliano, K. L. (2010). Testosterone and partnering are linked via relationship status for women and "relationship orientation" for men. *Hormones and Behavior, 58*, 820–826.

Van Beest, I., & Williams, K. D. (2006). When inclusion costs and ostracism pays, ostracism still hurts. *Journal of Personality and Social Psychology, 91*, 918–928.

van der Linden, D., Scholte, R. H. J., Cillessen, A. H. N., Nijenhuis, J. T., & Segers, E. (2010). Classroom ratings of likeability and popularity are related to the Big Five and the general factor of personality. *Journal of Research in Personality, 44*, 669–672.

Van Dijk, D., Seger-Guttmann, T., & Heller, D. (2013). Life-threatening event reduces subjective well-being through activating avoidance motivation: A longitudinal study. *Emotion, 13*(2), 216–225.

Van Duijvenvoorde, A. C. K., Zanolie, K., Rombouts, S. A., Raijmakers, M. E. J., & Crone, E. A. (2008). Evaluating the negative or valuing the positive?: Neural mechanisms supporting feedback-based learning across development. *Journal of Neuroscience, 28*, 9495–9503.

Van Honk, J., Tuiten, A., Hermans, E., Putman, P., Koppeschaar, H., Thijssen, J., et al. (2001). A single administration of testosterone induces cardiac accelerative responses to angry faces in healthy young women. *Behavioral Neuroscience, 115*, 238–242.

Vancouver, J. B., Thompson, C. M., Tischner, E. C., & Putka, D. J. (2002). Two studies examining the negative effect of self-efficacy on performance. *Journal of Applied Psychology, 87*, 506–516.

Vansteenkiste, M., Simons, J., Lens, W., Sheldon, K. M., & Deci, E. L. (2004). Motivating learning, performance, and persistence: The synergistic effects of intrinsic goal contents and autonomy-supportive contexts. *Journal of Personality and Social Psychology, 87*, 246–260.

Varnum, M. E. W. (2012). Frontiers, germs, and nonconformist voting. *Journal of Cross-Cultural Psychology, 44*, 832–837.

Varnum, M. E. W., & Kitayama, S. (2011). What's in a name?: Popular names are less common on frontiers. *Psychological Science, 22*, 176–183.

Vazire, S. A., & Gosling, S. D. (2004). E-Perceptions: Personality impressions based on personal Web sites. *Journal of Personality and Social Psychology, 87*, 123–132.

Vazire, S. A., Naumann, L. P., Rentfrow, P. J., & Gosling, S. D. (2008). Portrait of a narcissist: Manifestations of narcissism in physical appearance. *Journal of Research in Personality, 42*, 1439–1447.

Vedel, A. (2014). The Big Five and tertiary academic performance: A systematic review and meta-analysis. *Personality and Individual Differences, 71*, 66–76.

Verheul, R., & Widiger, T. A. (2004). A meta-analysis of the prevalence and usage of the personality disorder not otherwise specified (PDNOS) diagnosis. *Journal of Personality Disorders, 18*, 309–319.

Vianello, M., Schnabel, K., Sriram, N., & Nosek, B. (2013). Gender differences in implicit and explicit personality traits. *Personality and Individual Differences, 55*(8), 994–999.

Vincent, N. (2006). *Self-made man: One woman's year disguised as a man*. New York: Penguin.

Vohs, K. D., Mead, N. L., & Goode, M. R. (2006). The psychological consequences of money. *Science, 314*, 1154–1156.

Voyer, D., Voyer, S., & Bryden, M. P. (1995). Magnitude of sex differences in spatial abilities: A meta-analysis and consideration of critical variables. *Psychological Bulletin, 117*, 250–270.

Vrana, S. R., & Rollock, D. (2002). The role of ethnicity, gender, emotional content, and contextual differences in physiological, expressive, and self-reported emotional responses to imagery. *Cognition and Emotion, 16*, 165–192.

Vuchinich, R. E., & Simpson, C. A. (1998). Hyperbolic temporal discounting in social drinkers and problem drinkers. *Experimental and Clinical Psychopharmacology, 6*, 292–305.

Wacker, J., Chavanon, M. L., & Stemmler, G. (2006). Investigating the dopaminergic basis of extraversion in humans: A multilevel approach. *Journal of Personality and Social Psychology, 91,* 171–187.

Wagner, J., Lüdtke, O., & Jonkmann, K. (2013). Cherish yourself: Longitudinal patterns and conditions of self-esteem change in the transition to young adulthood. *Journal of Personality and Social Psychology, 104,* 148–163.

Waldron, I., McCloskey, C., & Earle, I. (2005). Trends in gender differences in accident mortality: Relationships to changing gender roles and other societal trends. *Demographic Research, 13,* 415–454.

Walster, E., Aronson, V., Abrahams, D., & Rottman, L. (1966). Importance of physical attractiveness in dating behavior. *Journal of Personality and Social Psychology, 4,* 508–516.

Wampold, B. E., Mondin, G. W., Moody, M., Stich, F., Benson, K., & Ahn, H. N. (1997). A meta-analysis of outcome studies comparing bona fide psychotherapies: Empiricially, "all must have prizes." *Psychological Bulletin, 122,* 203–215.

Watson, D., Clark, L. A., & Chmielewski, M. (2008). Structures of personality and their relevance to psychopathology: II. Further articulation of a comprehensive unified trait structure. *Journal of Personality, 76,* 1485–1522.

Watson, J. B. (1970). *Behaviorism.* New York: Norton. (Original work published 1924)

Watson, J. B., & Rayner, R. (1920). Conditioned emotional reactions. *Journal of Experimental Psychology, 3,* 1–14.

Watts, B. L. (1982). Individual differences in circadian activity rhythms and their effects on roommate relationships. *Journal of Personality, 50,* 374–384.

Weinberger, D. A., Schwartz, G. E., & Davidson, R. J. (1979). Low-anxious, high-anxious and repressive coping styles: Psychometric patterns and behavioral responses to stress. *Journal of Abnormal Psychology, 4,* 369–380.

Weinstein, S. M., Mermelstein, R. J., Hankin, B. L., Hedeker, D., & Flay, B. R. (2007). Longitudinal patterns of daily affect and global mood during adolescence. *Journal of Research on Adolescence, 17,* 587–600.

Weisbuch, M., Ivcevic, Z., & Ambady, N. (2009). On being liked on the Web and in the "real world": Consistency in first impressions across personal web-pages and spontaneous behavior. *Journal of Experimental Social Psychology, 45,* 573–576.

Weiss, A., & Costa, Jr., P. T. (2005). Domain and facet personality predictors of all-cause mortality among Medicare patients aged 65 to 100. *Psychosomatic Medicine, 67,* 724 –733.

Weston, S. J., Hill, P. L., & Jackson, J. J. (2015). Personality traits predict the onset of disease. *Social Psychological and Personality Science, 6,* 309–317.

White, J. K., Hendrick, S. S., & Hendrick, C. (2004). Big five personality variables and relationship constructs. *Personality and Individual Differences, 37,* 1519–1530.

Widiger, T. A., & Samuel, D. B. (2005). Diagnostic categories or dimensions?: A question for the Diagnostic and Statistical Manual of Mental Disorders. *Journal of Abnormal Psychology, 114,* 494–504.

Wilson, R. E., Gosling, S. D., & Graham, L. T. (2012). A review of Facebook research in the social sciences. *Perspectives on Psychological Science, 7,* 203–220.

Wilson, R. S., Bienas, J. L., Mendes de Leon, C. F., Evans, D. A., & Bennett, D. A. (2003). Negative affect and mortality in older persons. *American Journal of Epidemiology, 158,* 827–835.

Wicker, F. W., Brown, G., Wiehe, J. A., Hagen, A. S., & Reed, J. L. (1993). On reconsidering Maslow: An examination of the deprivation/dominance proposition. *Journal of Research in Personality, 27,* 118–133.

Widiger, T. A. (2011). The DSM-5 dimensional model of personality disorder: Rationale and empirical support. *Journal of Personality Disorders, 25,* 222–223.

Wiebe, D. J., & Smith, T. W. (1997). Personality and health: Progress and problems in psychosomatics. In R. Hogan, J. A. Johnson, & S. R. Briggs (Eds.), *Handbook of personality psychology* (pp. 891–918). San Diego, CA: Academic Press.

Williams, D. A., & King, P. (1980, December 15). Do males have a math gene? *Newsweek,* p. 73.

Williams, G. C., Grow, V. M., Freedman, Z., Ryan, R. M., & Deci, E. L. (1996). Motivational predictors of weight loss and weight-loss maintenance. *Journal of Personality and Social Psychology, 70,* 115–126.

Wilson, M. S., & Sibley, C. G. (2011). "Narcissism creep?": Evidence for age-related differences in narcissism in the New Zealand general population. *New Zealand Journal of Psychology, 40,* 89–95.

Winter, D. G. (1973). *The power motive*. New York: Free Press.

Winter, D. G. (1987). Leader appeal, leader performance, and the motive profiles of leaders and followers: A study of American presidents and elections. *Journal of Personality and Social Psychology, 52,* 196–202.

Winter, D. G. (1991). Measuring personality at a distance: Development of an integrated system for scoring motives in running text. In D. J. Ozer, J. M. Healy, & A. J. Stewart (Eds.), *Perspectives on personality* (Vol. 3, pp. 59–89). London: Kingsley.

Winter, D. G. (1993). Power, affiliation, and war: Three tests of a motivational model. *Journal of Personality and Social Psychology, 65,* 532–545.

Winter, D. G. (1996). *Personality: Analysis and interpretation of lives*. New York: McGraw-Hill.

Winter, D. G. (2002). Motivational dimensions of leadership: Power, achievement, and affiliation. In R. E. Riggio, S. E. Murphy, & F. J., Pirozzolo (Eds.), *Multiple intelligences and leadership,* 119–138. Mahwah, NJ: Erlbaum.

Winter, D. G. (2005). Things I've learned about personality from studying political leaders at a distance. *Journal of Personality, 73,* 557–584.

Winter, D. G. (2009). Predicting the Obama presidency. *International Society of Political Psychology, 20*(1), 6–8.

Winter, D. G. (2010). Why achievement motivation predicts success in business but failure in politics: The importance of personal control. *Journal of Personality, 78,* 1637–1667.

Wirth, M. M., Welsh, K. M., & Schultheiss, O. C. (2006). Salivary cortisol changes in humans after winning or losing a dominance contest depend on implicit power motivation. *Hormones and Behavior, 49,* 346–352.

Wohn, D. Y., & Wash, R. (2013). A virtual "room" with a cue: Detecting personality through spatial customization in a city simulation game. *Computers in Human Behavior, 29,* 155–159.

Wolf, R. (2011). *The paleo solution: The original human diet*. Auberry, CA: Victory Belt Publishing.

Wondergem, T. R., & Friedmeier, M. (2012). Gender and ethnic differences in smiling: A yearbook photographs analysis from kindergarten through 12th grade. *Sex Roles, 67,* 403–411.

Wonderlich, S. A., Crosby, R. D., Joiner, T., Peterson, C. B., Bardone-Cone, A., Klein, M., et al. (2005). Personality subtyping and bulimia nervosa: Psychopathological and genetic correlates. *Psychological Medicine, 35,* 649–657.

Wood, W., & Eagly, A. H. (2000). Once again, the origins of sex differences. *American Psychologist, 55,* 1062–1063.

Wood, W., & Eagly, A. H. (2002). A cross-cultural analysis of the behavior of women and men: Implications for the origins of sex differences. *Psychological Bulletin, 128,* 699–727.

Wood, J. M., Garb, H. N., Nezworski, M. T., Lilienfeld, S. O., & Duke, M. C. (2015). A second look at the validity of widely used Rorschach indices: Comment on Mihura, Meyer, Dumitrascu, and Bombel (2013). *Psychological Bulletin, 141,* 236–249.

Wood, W., & Eagly, A. H. (2002). A cross-cultural analysis of the behavior of women and men: Implications for the origins of sex differences. *Psychological Bulletin, 128,* 699–727.

Wortman, J., Lucas, R. E., & Donnellan, M. B. (2012). Stability and change in the Big Five personality domains: Evidence from a longitudinal study of Australians. *Psychology and Aging, 27,* 867–874.

Wu, S., & Keysar, B. (2007). The effect of culture on perspective taking. *Psychological Science, 18,* 600–606.

Wyers, E. J., Peeke, H. V. S., & Herz, M. J. (1973). Behavioral habituation in invertebrates. In H. V. S. Peeke & M. J. Herz (Eds.), *Habituation: Vol. 1. Behavioral studies* (pp. 1–57). New York: Academic Press.

Xin, Z., Zhang, L., & Liu, D. (2010). Birth cohort changes of Chinese adolescents' anxiety: A cross-temporal meta-analysis, 1992–2005. *Personality and Individual Differences, 48,* 208–212.

Yang, B., Kim, Y., & McFarland, R. G. (2011). Individual differences and sales performance: A distal-proximal mediation model of self-efficacy, conscientiousness, and extraversion. *Journal of Personal Selling and Sales Management, 31,* 371–382.

Young, S. M., & Pinsky, D. (2006). Narcissism and celebrity. *Journal of Research in Personality, 40,* 463–471.

Yovetich, N. A., & Rusbult, C. E. (1994). Accommodative behavior in close relationships: Exploring transformation of motivation. *Journal of Experimental Social Psychology, 30,* 138–164.

Zarate, M. A., Uleman, J. S., & Voils C. I. (2001). Effects of culture and processing goals on the activation and binding of trait concepts. *Social Cognition, 19*, 295–323.

Zelaniewicz, A. M., & Pawlowski, B. (2011). Female breast size attractiveness for men as a function of sociosexual orientation (restricted vs. unrestricted). *Archives of Sexual Behavior, 40*, 129–1135.

Zell, E., Krizan, Z., & Teeter, S. R. (2015). Evaluating gender similarities and differences using metasynthesis. *American Psychologist, 70*, 10–20.

Ziv, I., & Hermel, O. (2011). Birth order effects on the separation process in young adults: An evolutionary and dynamic approach. *American Journal of Psychology, 124*, 261–273.

Zuckerman, M. (2002). Zuckerman-Kuhlman Personality Questionnaire (ZKPQ): An alternative Five-Factorial model. In B. De Raad & M. Perungini (Eds.), *Big five assessment* (pp. 377–396). Seattle, WA: Hogrefe & Huber.

Zweigenhaft, R. L., & Von Ammon, J. (2000). Birth order and civil disobedience: A test of Sulloway's 'born to rebel' hypothesis. *Journal of Social Psychology, 140*, 624–627.

Glossary

2D:4D ratio   The length of someone's index finger divided by the length of their ring (third) finger; a low ratio is linked to a high testosterone level.

Accommodation   Moving from the given to the transformed matrix by acting in a constructive way rather than a destructive way toward a partner.

Achievement motive   Wanting to accomplish things, usually on one's own and without help.

Acquiescence response set   The tendency of some respondents to agree with many items on a questionnaire.

Adventure   A risky and engaging experience.

Affiliation motive   Being motivated by one's relationships with others.

Affiliative humor style   Humor that makes others laugh and brings people together.

Aggressive humor style   Humor used to mock or tease others.

Agoraphobia   A fear or phobia of public places.

Agreeableness   How caring a person is for others and how the person gets along with other people; part of the Big Five personality traits.

Altruism   Helping others.

Amotivation   A state of no motivation.

Amygdala   The part of the brain responsible for processing reactions to fear.

Anal expulsive   Gaining pleasure from releasing the bowels.

Anal retentive   Gaining pleasure from retaining the bowels.

Anal stage   The attachment of libido to the anus.

Analysis   The study of information.

Analytical psychology   The study of the personal and collective unconscious developed by Carl Jung.

Anima/animus   The soul; the archetype of the opposite sex of the individual.

Anorexia nervosa   The pathological desire to maintain a very low body weight.

Antagonism   Extreme low agreeableness.

Anxiety   Attachment dimension suggesting a negative view of oneself.

Anxiety disorders   A cluster of mental disorders involving excessive anxiety.

Anxious attachment   An anxious, uncertain, and clingy style of attachment; in some models, includes a negative view of the self.

Approach motivation   Anticipating rewards for success.

Archetypes   Unconscious psychic structures shared by all people.

Attachment   The link between a child and his or her primary caregiver.

Attachment style   The general way an individual attaches or relates to others.

Attachment theory   A theory specifying that a child's attachment experiences will eventually become a part of the child's personality.

Attributions   Explanations for the reasons behind people's behavior.

Authentic relationships   A relationship in which someone can be who they really are; part of authenticity.

Authenticity   The extent to which a person feels aligned to his or her true self.

Autonomy   Having control over your actions and life.

Avoidance   Attachment dimension suggesting a negative view of others.

Avoidance motivation   Worrying about the negative consequences of failure.

Avoidant attachment   A removed, isolated style of attachment; in some models, includes a negative view of others.

Awareness   Your motives, strengths, and weaknesses; part of authenticity.

Barnum effect   The tendency for people to believe vague, positive statements about themselves.

Basic fault   A lack of connection between the child and mother that can later impact adult relationships.

Behavior   Acting in a way that reflects the true self; part of authenticity.

Behavior modification   Using conditioning to improve behavior.

Behaviorism   A branch of psychology that focuses on (relatively) simple explanations for outward behavior and is unconcerned with the inner workings of the mind.

Bibliotherapy Treating oneself with self-help books.

Big Five Five comprehensive personality domains: extraversion, agreeableness, conscientiousness, neuroticism, and openness to experience.

Biology Everything that appears in the body and brain, whatever its origin.

Bipolar disorder A mood disorder featuring manic episodes followed by depressive episodes.

Birth cohort Everyone born in one year.

Birth order The order in which siblings are born, an important concept in Alfred Adler's psychology.

Body expansiveness Taking up more space with your body.

Bulimia nervosa An eating disorder including binging and purging.

Caregiver The individual, often a parent, who cares for the child.

Castration anxiety The male child's fear of being castrated by the father.

Catastrophizing Believing that bad events are all-encompassing.

Cathexis The attachment of libido to thoughts, objects, or parts of the body.

Censorship The process of keeping the unconscious from entering consciousness.

Chocolate cake model The tendency of a relationship with a narcissist to start positively but end very negatively.

Classical conditioning Associating two things not normally associated with each other.

Cluster A Odd or eccentric personality disorders; "weird" or "mad."

Cluster B Dramatic or emotional personality disorders; "wild" or "bad."

Cluster C Anxious or fearful personality disorders; "worried" or "sad."

Cognitive-behavioral therapy Psychotherapy that emphasizes changing thoughts and behaviors.

Collective self-esteem Self-esteem based on group membership.

Collective unconscious Carl Jung's term for the unconscious archetypes shared by all humans.

Collectivism A cultural system that values the needs of the group more than those of the individual self.

Common humanity The awareness that all humans make mistakes.

Compassion Witnessing someone suffering and wanting to remove that suffering.

Compensate To react against perceived inferiority by asserting power.

Competence Being able to use your skills effectively and learn new ones.

Conditioned response The response produced by the conditioned stimulus after classical conditioning (e.g., salivation following the sound of the bell).

Conditioned stimulus The stimulus that produces the conditioned response after classical conditioning (e.g., a bell causing dogs to salivate).

Confounding variables In a correlational study, an outside variable related to the primary variables; also known as *third variables*.

Conscientiousness How neat, organized, and achievement oriented a person is; part of the Big Five personality traits.

Conscious The part of the mind within our usual awareness.

Continuous reinforcement schedule Always giving out a reward for good behavior.

Convergent validity When a scale correlates with other scales measuring the same construct.

Correlational Studies that examine the relationship between two or more characteristics of people.

Correlations The statistical relationship between two variables.

Counterproductive workplace behavior (CWB) Unethical, illegal, or unwise workplace behaviors such as stealing and bullying.

Creativity The ability to make something.

Cronbach's alpha A statistical measure of internal reliability.

Cross-cultural differences Average variations based on country or world region.

Cross-sectional study Data collected at one time that compares people of different ages.

Cultural products The products of a culture such as song lyrics, TV shows, advertisements, and books useful for studying culture at a broad level.

Culture The customs, values, and behaviors characteristic of a nation, an ethnic group, a class, or a time period.

Dark triad A combination of three negative traits: psychopathy, Machiavellianism, and narcissism.

Day residue Experiences from the day incorporated into a dream's manifest content.

Deconditioning   Reversing conditioning to eliminate the conditioned response.

Defense mechanisms   Strategies used to keep unconscious thoughts from the conscious mind.

Defensive pessimism   Thinking negative thoughts to prepare for negative outcomes.

Delusions   Odd and false belief systems.

Denial   Not acknowledging unconscious content.

Dependent variable   The outcome the researcher is interested in measuring.

Descriptive statistics   Numbers such as the mean, median, and mode.

Detachment   Extreme introversion.

Developmental stages   The stages children go through as the libido moves through the body.

Discrepancy   The difference between where you are (your actual self) and where you want to be (e.g., your ideal or ought self).

Discrepancy detection   Noticing something that is different in the environment.

Discriminant validity   When a scale does not correlate with unrelated scales.

Discrimination   Narrowing the conditions that produce the conditioned response.

Disinhibition   Extreme low conscientiousness.

Dismissing attachment   Attachment style with low anxiety but high avoidance.

Displacement   Moving a troubling impulse onto a different, less threatening object.

Dominance   Intimidating others to gain social status.

Dream interpretation   The therapeutic technique of uncovering the hidden meaning of dreams.

Eating disorders   Psychological problems surrounding eating.

Effective leadership   The ability to be a successful leader once in a management or leadership role.

Ego   The conscious part of the mind that navigates between the ego and the super-ego.

Ego depletion   A state of exhausted self-control.

Ego functions   The ways the individual interprets the world.

Electra complex   The daughter's love for the father and wish for the mother's death; attributed to Carl Jung.

Emergent leadership   The ability to rise as a leader in an organization.

Emerging adulthood   A new life stage between adolescence and adulthood.

Empathy   A response to another individual's experiences that takes the other's perspective.

Epigenetics   The idea that some environments can influence how much genetics will matter.

Erudition   Gaining knowledge on many topics.

Evolutionary psychology   The field of research exploring how evolution shaped human psychology.

Expectancies   What someone expects to happen, based on past experiences of what was rewarding.

Experiment   A study in which people are randomly assigned to condition.

Explicit motives   Conscious motivations, usually measured by self-report.

Explicit self-esteem   Self-esteem you are aware of having.

Extensive image creation   A major amount of positive self-presentation during a job search.

External attribution   An explanation for behavior focusing on the surrounding situation.

External locus of control   Believing that events are more a matter of luck and the arbitrary decisions of powerful people.

Extinction   Eliminating the conditioned response.

Extraversion   How outgoing, assertive, and talkative a person is; part of the Big Five personality traits.

Extraversion versus introversion   Getting energy from social situations versus being alone, in Jungian theory.

Extrinsic goals   Financial success, popularity or fame, and image or physical attractiveness.

Extrinsic motivation   Motivation outside the self, such as money or praise from others.

Face validity   When scale items appear, at face value, to measure what they are supposed to measure.

Facets   More specific components of the Big Five; subcategories of Big Five traits.

Factor analysis   Analyzing correlations among items to see which form related clusters.

Fake good   Personality questionnaire responses putting the self in a positive light.

False consensus effect   The belief that others share your opinions.

Fearful attachment   Attachment style with high anxiety and high avoidance.

Fixed-interval reinforcement   Giving out a reward after a certain amount of time has passed.

Fixed-ratio reinforcement   Giving out a reward after a certain number of behaviors.

Flooding   Confronting your worst fear head-on, all at once.

Flow state   The smooth passage of time that occurs during a peak experience, when you are completely immersed in an activity in the present moment.

fMRI   Functional magnetic resonance imaging, a type of brain scanning.

Free association   A psychoanalytic technique involving saying whatever comes into your head.

Freudian slip   When what you really think deep down comes out as a slip of the tongue.

Frontal lobe   The front part of the brain, which makes plans and considers decisions.

Functional deformity   Functional physical problems like illnesses that can lead to a sense of inferiority in Alfred Adler's psychology.

Gambling disorder   Gambling to an extent that it harms one's life.

Gender   Roles and behaviors attributed to one gender or another such as cognitive abilities, sexual behavior, hair length, clothing, and job preferences.

Gene–environment interaction   When genetics and environment work together to shape personality.

Gene expression   How much a gene influences traits or outcomes.

Generalization   When a conditioned response is elicited in response to things similar to the conditioned stimulus.

Generalized anxiety disorder   A disorder characterized by high levels of anxiety over a period of 6 months or more.

Generalized expectancies   Beliefs about how often actions lead to rewards versus punishment.

Generation   Everyone born in a somewhat arbitrarily defined 20- to 30-year period.

Genetics   The DNA from one's biological mother and biological father.

Genital stage   When the child begins adult sexual development in puberty.

Goals   Specific outcomes people desire.

Grandiose narcissism   Narcissism including high extraversion and dominance but low neuroticism.

Habituation   Getting used to something in the environment and not responding as strongly anymore.

Hallucinations   Hearing or seeing things that are not there.

Hero's journey   Joseph Campbell's model of individuation, including a descent and a return.

Hostile attribution bias   The tendency to see others as hostile and aggressive.

Hostility   Feelings of anger and frustration.

Humanistic psychology   A branch of psychology focused on the "whole person," including free will, creativity, and human potential.

Hysteria   A psychological disorder characterized by unexplained physical symptoms such as blindness, fainting, or paralysis.

Id   The unconscious mind, motivated for pleasure and wish fulfillment.

Ideal self   The person you want to be.

Immune system   The body's system for fighting disease.

Implicit motives   Unconscious motivations, usually measured with projective tests.

Implicit self-esteem   Self-esteem you are not necessarily aware of having.

Imposter phenomenon   The experience of feeling like a phony, a fraud, or a fake.

Impulsivity   The tendency to take risks, not plan, and be high in sensation-seeking, roughly equivalent to low conscientiousness.

Independent variable   The experimental or control conditions in an experiment.

Individualism   A cultural system that values the needs of the individual self more than those of the group.

Individuation   Carl Jung's term for the process of psychological development.

Inferiority complex   The belief that one is of lower status or weaker than others.

Inflammation   When bodily tissues swell in response to a perceived or real threat.

Informant reports   When the people close to someone (e.g., roommates, family, friends) report on his or her personality.

Intercoder reliability   Occurs when people coding stories or written material agree, using a set of rules, that it meets certain criteria.

Internal attribution   An explanation for behavior focusing on the individual and his or her choices and personality.

Internal locus of control   Believing that your actions have an effect on events.

Internal reliability   When all of the items on a questionnaire measure the same thing.

Internalizing   Becoming a stable part of the personality.

Intrinsic goals   Personal growth, affiliation, and community feeling.

Intrinsic motivation   Motivation inside the self, such as taking joy in an activity.

Introversion   How shy and reserved a person is.

Intuition versus sensation   The irrational functions in Jungian theory.

Job satisfaction   How satisfied you are with your job.

Judging versus perceiving   Functions added to Carl Jung's types by Myers and Briggs; being planful versus more spontaneous.

Latent content   The unconscious meaning of a dream.

Latent stage   The quieting of the libido from age 6 until puberty.

Leadership   Leading and directing people.

Lexical hypothesis   Traits important for survival and reproduction are embedded in our language, with the most important traits represented by the largest number of words.

Libido   Sigmund Freud's term for sexual psychic energy.

Likert scale   A range of numbers that correspond to how much someone agrees or disagrees with an item.

Longitudinal study   A study that collects data on the same people at more than one time.

Machiavellianism   A lack of empathy and a willingness to exploit others.

Major depressive disorder   A mood disorder featuring major depressive episodes (episodes of depressed mood or loss of pleasure in life that lasts at least 2 weeks).

Major depressive episodes   Episodes of depressed mood or loss of pleasure in life that lasts at least 2 weeks.

Mandala   A squared circle; a classic representation of the Self in Jungian theory.

Manic episodes   Periods of elevated and expansive mood.

Manifest content   The outward content of a dream.

Many labs approach   When different groups of researchers do the exact same study at the same time.

Mate-poaching   Stealing someone else's relationship partner.

Material self   The extension of the self into the body, clothes, and possessions.

Maturation of personality   Growth in traits consistent with being more mature and grown-up, such as higher conscientiousness, higher agreeableness, and lower neuroticism.

Mean   The average score on a scale, calculated by adding everyone's scores and dividing by the number of scores.

Mean-level changes   Shifts in a population's average scores with age.

Meaning in life   Having a purpose and putting time and energy into attaining important goals.

Median   The score that falls in the middle of all the scores on the test; also called the *50th percentile*.

Mental disorder   A pattern of mental symptoms causing significant problems in life.

Meta-analysis   A study that statistically analyzes the results of many studies on the same topic.

Mindfulness   Being aware of your thoughts and feelings without becoming attached to them.

Mirror neurons   Neurons activated when you see someone else performing an action.

Mode   The most frequent score.

Monozygotic twins   Identical twins sharing the same genetic profile.

Mood disorders   Disorders characterized by significant problems with mood and emotion.

Morningness–eveningness   Whether you are a morning person (a lark) or a night person (an owl).

Morphological inferiority   Structural physical problems that can lead to a sense of inferiority in Alfred Adler's psychology.

Motives   The psychological entities that drive us to behave in ways that will help us meet our goals.

Moving against   Gaining control in a competitive world through exploitativeness and aggressiveness.

Moving away   Trying to find peace by avoiding others and escaping conflict.

Moving toward   Connecting with others as a way of dealing with anxiety.

Mutual constitution model   The idea that cultures and selves each cause the other.

Narcissism   A personality trait that includes a very positive, grandiose view of the self.

Natural consequences Punishments enacted naturally as a consequence of the negative behavior.

Nature–nurture debate The view that genetics causes personality traits versus the view that the environment causes personality traits.

Needs Something that is necessary to survive or thrive.

Negative affectivity Extreme neuroticism.

Negative correlation When one variable is high, the other variable tends to be low.

Negative punishment Stopping bad behavior by taking away something good; also known as a *time-out*.

Negative reinforcement Rewards desired behavior by taking away something aversive.

Neo-analytic theorists The psychodynamic theorists who came after Sigmund Freud and took his ideas in new and interesting directions.

Neuroticism How worried and angry a person is; part of the Big Five personality traits.

Neurotransmitters Chemicals that carry signals over the gap between synapses in the brain.

Nonshared environment Experiences not shared by siblings, such as certain friends, personal injuries, or participating in different activities.

Normal distribution A distribution of scores in which most people score in the middle and fewer score at the extremes; also known as a "bell curve."

Null correlation When two variables are not related to each other.

Object integration The level of unification of an internalized relationship.

Object relations theory A model for understanding individuals by examining how they think about other people.

Oedipus complex The male child's love for the mother and wish for the father's death during the phallic stage.

Open practices Scientific practices that result in a high level of transparency, such as making data or research materials available to other researchers.

Openness to experience How interested a person is in trying new activities and playing with new ideas, beliefs, and value systems; part of the Big Five personality traits.

Operant conditioning Shaping behavior through rewards and punishments.

Optimistic explanatory style Believing negative events are temporary and specific.

Oral fixation Having libido attached to the mouth.

Oral stage The attachment of libido to the mouth.

Organization Putting in order large amounts of data or materials.

Organizational citizenship behavior (OCB) Doing positive things for the organization beyond a defined job.

Ought self The person you think you should be.

Panic attacks Intense, short bursts of intense fear and anxiety.

Panic disorder A mood disorder involving panic attacks (intense, short bursts of intense fear and anxiety).

Partial reinforcement schedule Only sometimes giving out a reward for good behavior.

Peak experiences Times when people can transcend themselves and feel one with the world.

Penis envy The idea that girls desire to have penises.

Percentage of variance Explained by genetics or environment; this number refers to the variation among a group of people and not within one individual.

Percentile score The percentage of people someone scores higher than on a scale or test; a score at the 90th percentile means someone scores higher than 90% of the people who took the scale.

Perception of national character Asking people to describe the typical member of a culture.

Person–situation debate The view that stable personality traits predict behavior versus the view that personality doesn't really exist and the situation is much more important.

Person–situation interaction When a person and a situation work together in many different ways to determine behavior.

Personal unconscious Carl Jung's term for the unconscious of the individual.

Personality A person's usual pattern of behavior, feelings, and thoughts across time or across situations.

Personality assessment The way we measure and capture personality, using a variety of methods.

Personality disorders Extreme and inflexible personality configurations that lead to significant impairment.

Personality matching The use of personality testing to match potential mates based on personality.

Perspective-taking The ability to see the world from another's point of view.

Pessimistic explanatory style Seeing bad events as all-encompassing.

Phallic stage The attachment of libido to the genitals.

Phobia   An intense fear of a specific thing.

Physiological measures   Measurements assessing physical reactions such as heart rate or sweating.

Pleasure principle   The driving force of the unconscious that wants whatever brings pleasure.

Positive correlation   When one variable is high, the other variable tends to be high as well.

Positive psychology   An area of psychology focused on what can make our lives better and what might make us happier.

Positive punishment   Administering something aversive after misbehavior; what people usually mean when they refer to *punishment*.

Positive reinforcement   Rewards or incentives for good behavior.

Possible selves   The selves you imagine you could be, whether ideal or feared.

Power distance   A cultural system emphasizing formality and greater difference in power among people.

Power motive   Wanting to have an impact on others.

Preconscious mind   The barely conscious part of our minds that keeps the unconscious out of conscious awareness.

Predictive validity   When a scale is related to a concrete outcome or behavior.

Preoccupied attachment   Attachment style with high anxiety but low avoidance.

Prestige   Rising to the top based on ability, talent, or moral force.

Production   Building or producing things.

Progesterone   A hormone associated with feelings of closeness to others.

Progressive relaxation   Learning how to systematically relax your body so your mind calms.

Projection   Seeing one's own unconscious content in others rather than oneself.

Projective measures   Indirect measures.

Psychoanalysis   The study of the dynamics of the mind developed by Sigmund Freud.

Psychopathology   An alternate term for mental disorder.

Psychopathy   A lack of empathy mixed with impulsivity.

Psychoticism   Extreme openness to experience.

Quantum change   Radical personality change.

Random assignment   Participants are equally likely to experience the experimental or control condition.

Rank-order consistency   Comparing someone to the average person his or her age.

Reaction formation   Disguising unconscious content by turning it into its opposite.

Reality principle   The goals of the conscious mind, which finds what works in reality.

Reciprocal determinism   The idea that people choose the environments they enter and then change them.

Reference-group effect   When people compare themselves to other people they know when completing personality questionnaires.

Reinforcement schedule   Giving out rewards for good behavior at certain intervals.

Reinforcement value   How enticing a particular reward is.

Relatedness   Feeling connected to others, both personally and in your community.

Relational mobility   How easy it is to move in and out of relationships.

Reliability   Consistency, either within a scale or over time.

Replicate   When the same or a very similar study is conducted again, the results are similar.

Repression   Keeping the unconscious from consciousness by pushing it away.

Repressive coping   Not allowing your anxiety to become fully conscious.

Reverse-scored items   Items scored in the opposite direction from the responses.

RIASEC   The job types on the Strong–Campbell Interest Inventory: *r*ealistic, *i*nvestigative, *a*rtistic, *s*ocial, *e*nterprising, and *c*onventional.

Rumination   The common practice of letting stressful thoughts run through your mind, over and over.

Schizophrenia   A mental disorder characterized by disordered thinking, perceptions, and delusions.

Secure attachment   A trusting, open style of attachment.

Secure base   The caregiver's role as a place of safety for the child.

Selective serotonin reuptake inhibitors   A common form of antidepressant medication.

Self   The archetype at the center of the collective unconscious.

Self-actualization   The need to actualize or "make actual" your unique talents and abilities.

Self-compassion   Being kind to yourself; treating yourself with the same sense of compassion that you would treat others.

Self-concept   A person's image of him- or herself.

Self-control   Willpower; the ability to control one's own behavior.

Self-defeating humor style   Humor used to mock oneself.

Self-determination theory   Argues that three needs—autonomy, competence, and relatedness—can explain much of human behavior.

Self-discrepancy theory   A model linking the distance between the actual self and the ought and ideal selves to emotion.

Self-efficacy   The belief that one will be effective and successfully work toward goals.

Self-enhancement   The desire to maintain and increase the positivity of the self-concept.

Self-enhancing humor style   Humor used to help someone look and feel better.

Self-esteem   A person's attitude toward him- or herself.

Self-esteem regulation   The actions involved in maintaining high self-esteem.

Self-expansion   The desire to expand the self by including traits, qualities, and skills of another.

Self-kindness   Being kind to yourself.

Self-monitoring   The tendency to adapt behavior to fit the demands of the situation.

Self-regulation   The process of guiding and directing yourself to a desired state.

Self-report measure   Questionnaires asking people to report on their own personalities, usually through rating themselves on a list of adjectives or statements.

Self-serving bias   The tendency to take credit for success but deny responsibility for failure.

Sex   A biological division of males and females based on chromosomes, genitals, and secondary sexual characteristics.

Sex differences   Average differences between males and females.

Shadow   The archetype of the same sex as the individual.

Shaping   Gradual training that rewards behavior progressively closer to the desired one.

Shared environment   The effects of growing up with the same parents; also known as *family environment*.

Situation   The other people and the physical environment surrounding a person.

Slight image creation   A small amount of positive self-presentation during a job search.

Social inhibition   Not expressing emotions that risk others' disapproval; overlaps with introversion.

Social investment theory   The idea that personalities mature as people enter important adult social roles such as establishing a career and starting a family.

Social learning   Observational learning that occurs when someone watches others get rewarded or punished for behavior.

Social norms   Rules for behavior within a society.

Social phobia   An intense fear of social situations.

Social self   The part of the self related to group membership.

Social support   Fulfilling relationships with friends and family that provide both emotional and practical support.

Socialization   How children learn to become mature members of society; also known as *acculturation*.

Socially desirable responding   The tendency of people to make themselves look better than they actually are.

Socioeconomic status   Social class, usually measured by income level, job prestige, and/or education level.

Sociometer theory   A theory linking level of self-esteem with level of belongingness.

Sociosexuality   Individual differences in attitudes toward sex without commitment.

Spatial ability   The ability to mentally rotate objects.

Spiritual self   A person's moral center.

Split-object image   Thinking about a single person in extreme positive and negative ways.

Spontaneous recovery   Relearning a conditioned response.

Standard deviation (SD)   A measure of spread around the mean. In a normal distribution, two-thirds of the data will lie within one standard deviation of the mean.

Statistically significant   Having a probability of less than 5% that the results are due to random chance.

Stereotypes   Commonly held beliefs about groups.

Stereotypically feminine personality traits   Traits believed to be typical of women; these primarily involve expressiveness or caring traits, which overlap with the Big Five trait of agreeableness.

Stereotypically masculine personality traits   Traits believed to be typical of men; these primarily involve instrumentality or agency, similar to the assertiveness dimensions of extraversion.

Strange Situation   A paradigm used to test attachment in young children that involves separation from a parent.

Structural model   Sigmund Freud's model of the mind with three parts: the id (or "it"), the ego (or "I"), and the super-ego (or "above I").

Subculture   A culture within a culture, based on ethnicity, class, region, or some other variable.

Sublimation   Channeling unconscious impulses into work.

Substance-related disorders   Disorders involving problems with intoxicating substances such as drugs and alcohol.

Sufficiently large samples   Having enough observations or people in a study to reliably detect an effect.

Super-ego   The strict and demanding part of the mind.

Synchronicity   An acausal connecting principle in which things go together but are not causally linked.

Systematic desensitization   A treatment for phobias that attempts to reduce fear in many small steps by associating the feared thing with calmness.

Talking cure   Sigmund Freud's term for the treatment of hysteria by talking in therapy sessions.

Temperament   Genetically based behavioral tendencies seen in young children.

Test–retest reliability   When taking a test at two different times produces roughly the same result.

Testosterone   A hormone that is much higher in men than in women.

Thinking versus feeling   The rational functions in Jungian theory.

Token economy   A program in which good behavior is rewarded with tokens that can be exchanged for privileges.

Topographical model   Sigmund Freud's model of the mind that highlights the conflict between the pleasure principle and the reality principle.

Traits   Relatively stable tendencies of individuals.

Transference   The way the client perceives the therapist.

Transformational leader   Leaders who change their organizations in large and fundamental ways rather than simply managing the organization.

Transgendered   When a male feels psychologically that she should be female or a female feels psychologically he should be male.

Triangulation   Using different research methods to answer the same question, in order to be more certain of the answer.

True self   The person you really are.

Twin study   A study examining twins raised apart and together, usually to explore whether characteristics are caused by genetics or environment.

Type A personality   A personality type that is hardworking, scheduled, and impatient.

Type B personality   A personality type that is laid back and less scheduled.

Type D (distressed) personality   A personality type high in negative emotions (very similar to neuroticism) and high in social inhibition.

Type T (thrill-seeking) personality   A personality type that seeks out exciting experiences.

Types   Personality profiles linked to certain diseases (such as "Type A" or "Type D").

Unbiased processing   The ability to see the good and the bad in the world and make decisions based on this information; part of authenticity.

Uncertainty avoidance   A cultural system of rules that minimizes ambiguity.

Unconditional positive regard   Acceptance and love of someone's whole self without conditions attached.

Unconditioned response   The response normally produced by the conditioned response (e.g., salivation being produced by food).

Unconditioned stimulus   The stimulus normally produced by the unconditioned response (e.g., food producing salivation).

Unconscious   The part of the mind outside of conscious awareness.

Validity   When a scale measures what it's supposed to measure.

Variable-interval reinforcement   Giving out a reward after a random amount of time has passed.

Variable-ratio reinforcement   Giving out a reward after a random number of behaviors.

Vocational fit   Determining which profession fits your personality.

Vocational interests   The type of professions you are interested in.

Vulnerable narcissism   Narcissism including low extraversion and dominance but high neuroticism.

Wish fulfillment   The unconscious desire to have one's fantasies realized.

Photo Credits

Images; **page 313, left:** Paul Williams/Despite Straight Lines/Moment Open/Getty Images; **right:** Evirgen/E+/Getty Images; **page 315:** ArtFamily/Fotolia; **page 316:** Roz Chast/The New Yorker/Conde Nast Collection; **page 318:** Christian Mueller/Shutterstock; **page 319:** http://Kokoro-images.com/Moment/Getty Images; **page 321:** Posh/Fotolia.

Chapter 12   page 324: Tom Merton/OJO Images/Getty Images; **page 326:** Igor Mojzes/Fotolia; **page 329:** ITAR-TASS Photo Agency/Alamy; **page 331:** holbox/Shutterstock; **page 333:** AF archive/Alamy; **page 334:** Claudio Divizia/Fotolia; **page 339:** Creatista/Shutterstock; **page 340:** andrewgenn/Fotolia; **page 341:** Marekuliasz/Shutterstock.

Chapter 13   page 345: MNStudio/Shutterstock; **page 346:** George Pimentel/Lp5/Getty Images; **page 348:** Lena S./Fotolia; **page 349:** Science Source; **page 354:** Maridav/Getty Images; **page 355:** Jamie Grill/JGI/Blend Images/Getty Images; **page 357:** Barabas Attila/Fotolia; **page 358:** Arto/Fotolia; **page 360:** wjarek/Shutterstock; **page 361, left:** Iosif Szasz-Fabian/Fotolia; **right:** Sommai/Fotolia; **page 366:** Leonardo Patrizi/E+/Getty Images.

Chapter 14   page 369: Mystique/Fotolia; **page 370:** Courtesy of Daniel Smith; **page 372:** Everett Collection/Glow Images; **page 381:** ZUMA Press, Inc./Alamy; **page 384:** Ron Sumners/123RF; **page 385:** ZUMA Archive/ZUMA PRESS/Newscom; **page 387:** Joao Relvas/EPA/Newscom; **page 390:** Nomad_Soul/Fotolia; **page 392:** Daw666/Fotolia; **page 394:** YinYang/ iStock/Getty Images Plus/Getty Images.

Chapter 15   page 397: Mimadeo/Shutterstock; **page 398:** Zhu difeng/Fotolia; **page 399:** CBS Photo Archive/Getty Images; **page 400:** Rido/Fotolia; **page 401:** Andresr/Shutterstock; **page 403:** Antonio Guillem/Shutterstock; **page 404:** Aspen Photo/Shutterstock; **page 406:** TheSupe87/Fotolia; **page 409:** Dell/Fotolia.

Text Credits

Chapter 1   page 3: Isaacson, Walter. (2011). Steve Jobs. Simon & Schuster; **page 3:** Steve Jobs; **page 4:** Isaacson, W. (1997, January). In search of the real Bill Gates. Time; **page 5:** Malcolm X. The Autobiography of Malcolm X. Grove Press. 1965; **page 10, Fig. 1.2:** Park, G., Schwartz, H. A., Eichstaedt, J. C., Kern, M. L., Kosinski, M., Stillwell, D. J., Ungar, L.H., & Seligman, M. E. P. (2015). Automatic personality assessment through social media language. Journal of Personality and Social Psychology; **page 9:** John Steinbeck, Travels With Charley (Penguin); **page 10:** Gosling, S. D. (2008). Snoop: What your stuff says about you. New York: Basic Books; **page 12:** Fleeson, W. (2004). Moving personality beyond the person-situation debate. Current Directions in Psychological Science, 13, 83–87; **page 13:** Funder, D. C. (2008). Persons, situations, and person-situation interactions. In John, O. P., Robins, R. W., & Pervin, L. A. (Eds.), Handbook of Personality: Theory and Research, 3rd Edition. New York: Guilford Press, p. 568; **page 19:** James, W. (1890/1950). The principles of psychology. New York: Dover. (Original work published 1890), p. 121.

Chapter 2   page 34: Crowne, D. P., & Marlowe, D. (1964). The approval motive. New York: Wiley.

Chapter 3   page 53: Reed Timmer, Into The Storm: Violent Tornadoes, Killer Hurricanes, and Death-Defying Adventures in Extreme Weather (Penguin); **page 53:** Timmer, R. (2010). Into the storm: Violent tornadoes, killer hurricanes, and death-defying adventures in extreme weather. New York: New American Library (Penguin); **page 56, Fig. 3.1:** © Pearson Education, Inc.; **page 60:** On the Beach With Dave Chappelle. Sunday, May 15, 2005. TIME; **page 63, Fig. 3.3:** Data from Rentfrow, P. J., Gosling, S. D., & Potter, J. (2008). A theory of the emergence, persistence, and expression of geographic variation in psychological characteristics. Perspectives on Psychological Science, 3, 339–369; **page 64, Fig. 3.4:** Data from Kern, M. L., Eichstaedt, J. C., Schwartz, H. A., Dziurzynski, L., Ungar, L. H., Stillwell, D. J., & . . . Seligman, M. P. (2014). The online social self: An open vocabulary approach to personality. Assessment, 21, 158–169; **page 66, Fig. 3.5:** Courtesy of Robb Wolf (http://robbwolf.com); **page 66, Fig. 3.5:** Data from Rentfrow, P. J., Gosling, S. D., & Potter, J. (2008). A theory of the emergence, persistence, and expression of geographic variation in psychological characteristics. Perspectives on Psychological Science, 3, 339–369; **page 67, Fig. 3.6:** Data from Kern, M. L., Eichstaedt, J. C., Schwartz, H. A., Dziurzynski, L., Ungar, L. H., Stillwell, D. J., & . . . Seligman, M. P. (2014). The online social self: An open vocabulary approach to personality. Assessment, 21, 158–169; **page 70, Fig. 3.8:** Data from Kern, M. L., Eichstaedt, J. C., Schwartz, H. A., Dziurzynski, L., Ungar, L. H., Stillwell, D. J., & . . . Seligman, M. P. (2014). The online social self: An open vocabulary approach to personality. Assessment, 21, 158–169; **page 72:** McCrae, R. R. (1996). Social consequences of experiential openness. Psychological Bulletin, 120, 323–337; **page 72, Fig. 3.10:** Data from Rentfrow, P. J., Gosling, S. D., & Potter, J. (2008). A theory of the emergence,

persistence, and expression of geographic variation in psychological characteristics. Perspectives on Psychological Science, 3, 339–369; **page 76:** Galton, F. (1884). Measurement of character. Fortnightly Review, 36, 179–185., p. 179; **page 76:** Galton, F. (1884). Measurement of character. Fortnightly Review, 36, 179–185., p.183.

Chapter 4   page 83: Schindehette, S. (2006). My life as a sperm donor. People. Retrieved June 5, 2006, from http://www.people.com/people/archive/article/0,,20060497,00.html; Schorn, D. (2006). Sperm donor siblings find family ties. 60 Minutes. Broadcast March 19, 2006. Retrieved from http://www.cbsnews.com/8301-18560_162-1414965.html; **page 85:** Galton, F. (1883). Inquiries into human faculty and its development. London: Macmillan; **page 86:** Caplan, B. (2011). Selfish Reasons to Have More Kids: Why Being a Great Parent is More Fun and Less Work Than You Think. New York: Basic Books; **page 95:** Harlow, J. M. (1868). Recovery from the passage of an iron bar through the head. Publications of the Massachusetts Medical Society, 2, 327–347; **page 96, Fig 4.1:** Data from Adelstein JS, Shehzad Z, Mennes M, DeYoung CG, Zuo X-N, et al. (2011) Personality Is Reflected in the Brain's Intrinsic Functional Architecture. PLoS ONE 6(11): e27633; **page 99, Questionnaire 4.1:** Courtesy of J.A. Horne and O. Ostberg; **page 103, Questionnaire 4.2:** Penke, L., & Asendorpf, J. B. (2008). Beyond global sociosexual orientations: A more differentiated look at sociosexuality and its effects on courtship and romantic relationships. Journal of Personality and Social Psychology, 95, 1113–1135. DOI: 10.1037/0022-3514.95.5.1113; **page 107:** Associated Press. (2008). Formula for Ig Nobel fame: Strippers and Coke. October 2, 2008. http://www.msnbc.msn.com/id/26996167/ns/technology_and_science-science/t/formula-ig-nobel-fame-strippers-coke/#.UKaHUY7VmQc.

Chapter 5   page 117: Markus, H. R., & Kitayama, S. (1991). Culture and the self: Implications for cognition, emotion, and motivation. Psychological review, 98, 224–253; **page 119:** James, 1898, p. 292; **page 120:** James, W. (1918). The Principles of Psychology, Volume 1. New York: H. Holt and Company; **page 120:** Baldwin, J. M. (1930). Autobiography of James Mark Baldwin. In C. Murchison (Ed.), History of Psychology in Autobiography (Vol. 1, pp. 1–30). Worcester, MA: Clark University Press."; **page 120:** Ralph Waldo Emerson, Astræa; **page 121:** George Herbert Mead (1913); **page 122, Questionnaire 5.1:** Snyder, M. (1974). The self-monitoring of expressive behavior. Journal of Personality and Social Psychology, 30, 526–537; **page 123:** James, 1898, p. 296; **page 125, Questionnaire 5.2:** Courtesy of Morris Rosenberg. The Rosenberg SES may be used without explicit permission. **page 127:** Forsyth, D. R., Lawrence, N. K., Burnette, J. L., & Baumeister, R. F. (2007). Attempting to Improve the Academic Performance of Struggling College Students by Bolstering Their Self–esteem: An Intervention that Backfired. Journal of Social and Clinical Psychology, 26, 447–459; **page 132, Questionnaire 5.3:** Courtesy of Robert

Raskin; **page 136, Fig. 5.3:** Young, S. M., & Pinsky, D. (2006). Narcissism and celebrity. Journal of Research in Personality, 40, 463–471; **page 139, Fig. 5.4:** Based on Baumeister, R. F., Bratslavsky, E., Muraven, M., & Tice, D. M. (1998). Ego depletion: Is the active self a limited resource? Journal of Personality and Social Psychology, 74, 1252–1265.

Chapter 6 page 152: Cassidy, A. (2012). Eric Cartman. Retrieved from http://psyc2301.wikispaces.com/ Eric+Cartman, August 31, 2012; **page 154:** Freud, S. (1913). The interpretation of dreams. New York: MacMillan; **page 158, Fig. 6.3:** Adams & others (1996); **page 160, Fig. 6.4:** Weinberger, D.A., Schwartz, G.E., & Davidson, R.J. (1979). Low-anxious, high-anxious and repressive coping styles: Psychometric patterns and behavioral responses to stress. Journal of Abnormal Psychology, 4, 369–380; **page 161:** Dundes, A. (2012). Into the endzone for touchdown?: Psychoanalytic consideration of American football. Western Folklore, 37, 75–88; **page 161, Questionnaire 6.1:** Martin, Rod A., Patricia Puhlik-Doris, Gwen Larsen, Jeanette Gray, and Kelly Weir. Individual differences in uses of humor and their relation to psychological well-being: Development of the Humor Styles Questionnaire. Journal of Research in Personality 37 (2003) 48–75; **page 162, Questionnaire 6.2:** Courtesy of Julie Norem; page 169, Questionnaire 6.3: Courtesy of Personality Testing; **page 163:** Norem, J. K. (2002). The positive power of negative thinking. Basic Books: New York; **page 164:** Freud, S. (1900/1913). The interpretation of dreams. New York: MacMillan, p.185; **page 165–166:** Jung, C. G. (1965). Memories, Dreams, Reflections. New York: Knopf Publishing Group; **page 168, Fig. 6.5:** Data from Jung, C. G., & von Franz, M. L. (Eds.). (1968). Man and his symbols (Vol. 5183). Random House LLC; pages 174–175: Horney, K. (2013). Our inner conflicts: A constructive theory of neurosis. Oxon, UK: Routledge. First published 1946, p. 89; **page 169, Questionnaire 6.3:** Courtesy of Personality Testing; **page 174–175:** Horney, K. (2013). Our inner conflicts: A constructive theory of neurosis. Oxon, UK: Routledge. First published 1946, p. 89.

Chapter 7   page 183, Questionnaire 7.1: Elliot, A. J., & Thrash, T. M. (2010). Approach and avoidance temperament as basic personality dimensions. Journal of Personality, 78, 865–906; **page 189:** Maslow, A. H. (1970). Motivation and personality (2nd Ed.) New York: Harper & Row; **page 189, Questionnaire 7.2:** LeClerc, G., et al. (1999). Criterion validity of a new measure of self-actualization. Psychological Reports, 85, 1167–1176; **page195, Box,** 'Personality's Past': McClelland, D. C. (1967). The Achieving Society. New York: Simon and Schuster; **page 198, Questionnaire 7.3:** Sheldon, K. M. & Hilpert, J. C. (2012). The balanced measure of psychological needs (BMPN) scale: An alternative domain general measure of need satisfaction. Motivation and Emotion, 36, 439–451; **page 200, Questionnaire 7.4:** Courtesy of Tim Kasser; page 204, Fig. 7.7: Lepper, M. R., Greene, D., & Nisbett, R. E. (1973). Undermining children's intrinsic interest with extrinsic reward: A test of the "overjustification" hypothesis. Journal of Personality and Social Psychology, 28, 129–137; **page 205, Questionnaire 7.5:** Brown, K.W. & Ryan, R.M. (2003). The benefits of being present: Mindfulness and its role in psychological well being. Journal of Personality and Social Psychology, 84, 822 848; **page 206:** SatipatthanaSutta: Frames of Reference" (MN 10), translated from the Pali by ThanissaroBhikkhu. Access to Insight (Legacy Edition), 30 November 2013, http://www.accesstoinsight.org/ tipitaka/mn/mn.010.than.html; **page 208, Fig. 7.8:** Based on

Csikszentmihalyi, M. (1990). Flow: The psychology of optimal experience. New York: Harper & Row. (p. 74).

Chapter 8   page 214: Adams, D. (1984). So long and thanks for all the fish. New York: Del Ray; **page 223:** Gentile, D. A., & Anderson, C. A. (2011, June 30). Don't read more into the Supreme Court's ruling on the California video game law. Iowa State University press release. Retrieved from http:// www.psychology.iastate.edu/faculty/caa/Multimedia/ VGV-SC-OpEdDDAGCAA.pdf; **page 225:** Fields, Denise, & Brown, Ari. (2007). Toddler 411. Boulder, CO: Windsor Peak Press. p. 30; **page 226:** Watson, J. B. (1970). Behaviorism. Transaction Publishers; **page 226:** Watson, J. B. (1970). Behaviorism. Transaction Publishers; **page 228, Questionnaire 8.1:** Courtesy of Stephen Nowicki; **page 229:** Rotter, J. B. (1971). External control and internal control. Psychology Today, 5, 37–59; **page 232:** Chamberlin, J. (2012). Notes on a scandal: How a racy rumor about the father of behaviorism made its way into 200 psychology textbooks. American Psychologist, 43, 20.

Chapter 9   page 241: Tauber, Michelle. (2003). And Baby Makes Two. People, July 24, 2003; **page 244, Questionnaire 9.1:** Presley, R., & Martin R. P. (1994). Toward a structure of preschool temperament: Factor structure of the temperament assessment battery for children. Journal of Personality, 62, 445–448; **page 245, Table 9.1:** Hampson, S. E. (2012). Personality processes: Mechanisms by which personality traits "get outside the skin." Annual Review of Psychology, 63, 315–339; **page 247, Fig. 9.1:** Based on Lamb et al (2002); **page 248, Fig. 9.2:** Based on Allik et al (2004); **page 249, Fig. 9.4:** Based on Twenge, J. M., & Campbell, W. K. (2001). Age and birth cohort differences in self-esteem: A cross-temporal meta-analysis. Personality and Social Psychology Review, 5, 321–344; **page 250:** Puliti, A. (2013). Snooki's extreme makeover. Us Weekly, March 18, 2013. P. 52–56; **page 251, Fig. 9.5:** Roberts, B. W., Walton, K. E., & Viechtbauer, W. (2006). Patterns of mean-level change in personality traits across the life course: A meta-analysis of longitudinal studies. Psychological Bulletin, 132, 1–25; **page 255, Fig. 9.6:** Schwartz et al. (2013); **page 258, Fig. 9.7:** Neyer, F. J., & Asendorpf, J. B. (2001). Personality-relationship transaction in young adulthood. Journal of Personality and Social Psychology, 81, 1190–1204; **page 259:** Jill Smokler, Confessions of a Scary Mommy (Simon & Schuster).

Chapter 10   page 269: Vincent, N. (2006). Self-made man: One woman's year disguised as a man. New York: Penguin6, p. 93; **page 269:** Vincent, N. (2006). Self-made man: One woman's year disguised as a man. New York: Penguin, p. 50; **page 50:** Vincent, Norah. (2006). Self-Made Man: One woman's year disguised as a man. New York: Penguin Books; **page 271:** Bem, Sandra Lipsitz. (2001). An unconventional family. New Haven: Yale University Press; **page 272, Fig. 10.1:** According to the link http://journals.plos.org/plosone/ article?id=10.1371/ journal.pone.0073791, "© 2013 Schwartz et al. This is an open-access article distributed under the terms of the Creative Commons Attribution License, which permits unrestricted use, distribution, and reproduction in any medium, provided the original author and source are credited."; **page 273:** Money, J. (1975). Ablatio penis: Normal male infant sex-reassigned as a girl. Archives of Sexual Behavior, 4, 65–71; **page 282:** Rudman, L. A., & Glick. P. (2010). The social psychology of gender: How power and intimacy shape gender relations. New York: Guilford Press; **page 284: Questionnaire 10.1:** Courtesy of Janet Spence; **page 292:** Clark, R. D. (1990). The impact of AIDS on gender differences in willingness to engage in casual sex. Journal of Applied Social Psychology, 20, 771–782; **page 292:** Hatfield, E. H., & Walster, G. W. W. (1978). A new look at love. Reading, MA: Addison-Wesley, p. 75; **page 293:** Firestone, D. (1993, December 31). While Barbie talks tough, G. I. Joe goes shopping. New York Times; **page 294, Fig. 10.6:** based on Maeda, Y., & Yoon, S. (2013). A meta-analysis on gender differences in mental rotation ability measured by the Purdue Spatial Visualization Tests: Visualization of rotations (PSVT:R). Educational Psychology Review, 25, 69–94; **page 294:** Lawton, C. A., & Kallai, J. (2002). Gender differences in wayfinding strategies and anxiety about wayfindings. Sex Roles, 47, 389–401.

Chapter 11   page 299: Cisneros, Sandra. (1984). The House on Mango Street. Houston, TX: Arte Público Press; **page 299:** Christian Lander, Stuff White People Like (Random House); **page 301, Fig. 11.1:** Based on Markus, H. R., & Kitayama, S. (2010). Cultures and selves: A cycle of mutual constitution. Perspectives on Psychological Science, 5, 420–430; **page 302, Questionnaire 11.1:** Chen, Fang Fang (2003). Toward measuring individualism and collectivism in two cultures. PhD dissertation, Arizona State University; **page 303, Fig. 11.2:** Markus, H. R., & Kitayama, S. (1991). Culture and the self: Implications for cognition, emotion, and motivation. Psychological Review, 98, 224–253; **page 306:** Konrath, S. H., O'Brien, E. H., & Hsing, C. (2011). Changes in dispositional empathy in American college students over time: A meta-analysis. Personality and Social Psychology Review, 15, 180–198; **page 307, Fig. 11.4:** from Twenge, J. M., & Crocker, J. (2002). Race and self-esteem: Meta-analyses comparing Whites, Blacks, Hispanics, Asians, and American Indians and comment on Gray-Little and Hafdahl (2000). Psychological Bulletin, 128, 371–408; **page 310, Fig. 11.5:** from Twenge, J. M., Abebe, E. M., & Campbell, W. K. (2010). Fitting in or standing out: Trends in American parents' choices for children's names, 1880–2007. Social Psychological and Personality Science, 1, 19–25.

Chapter 12   page 328, Questionnaire 12.1: Courtesy of Julie Pozzebon; **page 334:** Northouse, P. G. (2012). Leadership: Theory and practice. SAGE Publications, Incorporated; **page 336, Fig. 12.1:** Data from Rubenzer, S. J., Faschingbauer, T. R., & Ones, D. S. (2000). Assessing the US presidents using the revised NEO Personality Inventory. Assessment, 7(4), 403–419; **page 337. Fig. 12.2:** Based on Judge, T. A., Bono, J. E., Ilies, R., & Gerhardt, M. (2002). Personality and leadership: A qualitative and quantitative review. Journal of Applied Psychology, 87, 765–780; **page 339, Fig. 12.3:** Musson, D., & Keeton, K. E. (2011). Investigating the relationship between personality traits and astronaut career performance: Retrospective analysis of personality data collected 1989–1995. Hanover, MD: National Aeronautics and Space Administration; **page 341:** Based on Crippen, Alex. Warren Buffett Shares His Secret: How You Can 'Tap Dance to Work'. CNBC. November 21, 2012.

Chapter 13   page 347, Questionnaire 13.1: Fraley, R. C., Waller, N. G., & Brennan, K. A. (2000). An item response theory analysis of self-report measures of adult attachment. Journal of Personality and Social Psychology, 78, 350–365; **page 348, Fig. 13.2:** Courtesy of Keith Campbell; **page 357, Questionnaire 13.3:** Courtesy of Mark Davis; **page 359, Fig 13.1:** Paulhus, D. L., & Williams, K. M. (2002). The dark triad of personality: Narcissism, Machiavellianism, and psychopathy. Journal of research in personality, 36(6), 556–563; **page 364:** Finkel, E. J., Eastwick, P. W., Karney, B. R., Reis, H. T., & Sprecher, S. (2012). Online dating: A critical

analysis from the perspective of psychological science. Psychological Science in the Public Interest, 13, 3–66.

Chapter 14   page 370: Daniel Smith, Monkey Mind (Simon & Schuster); **page 372:** Rachel Reiland, Get Me Out Of Here: My Recovery from Borderline Personality Disorder 2004; pp. 11–12; **page 374, Table 14.1:** based on APA (2013); Big Five correlations based on Saulsman & Page (2004); **page 376, Fig. 14.2:** Saulsman, L. M., & Page, A. C. (2004). The five-factor model and personality disorder empirical literature: A meta-analytic review. Clinical Psychology Review, 23, 1055–1085; **page 376, Fig. 14.3:** Lynam, D. R., & Widiger, T. A. (2001). Using the five-factor model to represent the DSM-IV personality disorders: An expert consensus approach. Journal of Abnormal Psychology, 110, 401–412; **page 377, Fig. 14.4:** Lynam, D. R., & Widiger, T. A. (2001). Using the five-factor model to represent the DSM-IV personality disorders: An expert consensus approach. Journal of Abnormal Psychology, 110, 401–412; **page 377, Fig. 14.5:** Lynam, D. R., & Widiger, T. A. (2001). Using the five-factor model to represent the DSM-IV personality disorders: An expert consensus approach. Journal of Abnormal Psychology, 110, 401–412; **page 381, Questionnaire 14.1:** The Center for Epidemiologic Studies Depression Scale Revised; **page 385, Fig. 14.7:** Kotov, R., Gamez, W., Schmidt, F., & Watson, D. (2010). Linking "big" personality traits to anxiety, depressive, and substance use disorders: A meta-analysis. Psychological Bulletin, 136, 768–821; page 385: Jamison, K. R. (1994). Touched with fire: Manic-depressive illness and the artistic temperament. New York: Free Press; **page 386:** Leonard, Elizabeth. Carrie Fisher's Bipolar Crisis: 'I Was Trying to Survive' People. March 25, 2013 Vol. 79 No. 12; **page 388. Fig. 14.8:** Based on Malouff, J. M., Thorsteinsson, E. B., & Schutte, N. S. (2005). The relationship between the five-factor model of personality and symptoms of clinical disorders: A meta-analysis. Journal of Psychopathology and Behavioral Assessment, 27(2), 101–114; **page 389, Fig. 14.9:** Based on Malouff, J. M., Thorsteinsson, E. B., & Schutte, N. S. (2005). The relationship between the five-factor model of personality and symptoms of clinical disorders: A meta-analysis. Journal of Psychopathology and Behavioral Assessment,27(2), 101–114; **page 391, Fig 14.10:** Kotov, R., Gamez, W., Schmidt, F., & Watson, D. (2010). Linking "big" personality traits to anxiety, depressive, and substance use disorders: A meta-analysis. Psychological Bulletin, 136, 768–821; **page 393, Fig. 14.11:** Lyubomirsky, S., Dickerhoof, R., Boehm, J. K., & Sheldon, D. M. (2011). Becoming happier takes both a will and a proper way: An experimental longitudinal intervention to boost well-being. Emotion, 11, 391–402.

Chapter 15   page 405, Questionnaire 15.1: C. David Jenkins, Ray H. Roseman, and Stephen J. Zyzanski. Coronary-Prone Behavior Patterns. JAMA. 1974;229(10): 1284; **page 406, Questionnaire 15.2:** Copyright © 1986 by the American Psychological Association. Reproduced with permission. The official citation that should be used in referencing this material is Siegel, J. M. (1986). The Multidimensional Anger Inventory. Journal of Personality and Social Psychology, 51, 191–200. No further reproduction or distribution is permitted without written permission from the American Psychological Association; **page 408, Questionnaire 15.3:** Courtesy of Rick Hoyle; **page 413, Questionnaire 15.4:** Scheier, M. F., & Carver, C. S. (1985). Optimism, coping, and health: Assessment and implications of generalized outcome expectancies. Health Psychology, 4, 219–247; **page 415, Fig.15.1:** Peterson, C., Bishop, M. P., et al. (2001). Explanatory style as a risk factor for traumatic mishaps. Cognitive Therapy and Research, 25, 633–649.

Name Index

A

Abbey, J., 274
Abebe, E. M., 310
Abele, A. E., 334
Abrahamson, A. C., 88
Abramson, L. Y., 290
Ackerman, P. L., 74
Adams, D., 214
Adams, H. E., 157, 158
Adelstein, J. S., 95
Adler, A., 143, 145, 165, 168, 172–174, 261
Ainsworth, M. D. S., 348, 350
Ajdacic-Gross, V., 398
Ajzen, I., 14
Allik, J., 62, 245, 248, 307, 315, 317, 319
Allport, G., 75, 99, 208
Aluja, A., 79
Ambady, N., 9, 282
American Psychiatric Association (APA), 373, 374, 381, 383, 384, 387, 388, 389, 390, 391, 392
Amichai-Hamburger, Y., 11
Amin, Z., 97
Amodio, D. M., 98
An, D., 308
Andersen, P., 34
Anderson, C. A., 223
Andre, M., 285, 316, 319
Antonucci, A. S., 98
Archer, J., 108, 275, 277, 278
Argyle, M., 61, 353
Armor, D. A., 415
Arnett, J. J., 256
Aro, A., 354
Asendorpf, J., 104
Asendorpf, J. B., 258
Ashton, M. C., 65, 79
Associated Press, 107
Atherton, O. E., 69
Atkinson, J. W., 192
Attrill, M. J., 186
Auster, C. J., 288
Austin, E. J., 110
Ayres, M. M., 278

B

Baard, P. P., 198
Babiak, P., 359
Bachman, J. G., 307
Back, M. D., 9, 365
Baer, R. A., 206
Bagby, R. M., 386, 391
Baldwin, J. M., 120–121
Baldwin, M. W., 176
Balint, M., 145, 175, 176
Bandura, A., 131, 222, 227
Barefoot, J. C., 407
Barnes, M. L., 103
Barnes, S., 206, 358, 395
Barnum, P. T., 33
Barr, L., 169
Barr, N., 169
Barrett, L. F., 353
Barrick, M. R., 61, 69, 332, 338
Bartholomew. K., 352
Barton, R. A., 186
Bateman, T. S., 332
Bates, J. E., 244
Baumeister, R. F., 44, 104, 125, 126, 139, 140, 163, 173, 188, 208, 216, 226, 292, 309, 358, 401
Beaton, E. A., 97
Beauchamp, M. C., 387
Beck, E., 262
Beer, J. S., 95, 135
Begg, D., 409
Bell, S. M., 348, 350
Bem, S., 271, 279
Benassi, V. A., 229
Benderlioglu, Z., 111
Benet, V., 79
Benet-Martinez, V., 4, 264
Benjamin, L., 232
Benson, H., 235
Berg, M., 209
Bergeman, C. S., 85, 86
Bernhardt, D. M., 109, 275
Bernreuter, R. G., 26
Berta, P., 275
Beutel, M. E., 402
Biernat, M., 195
Bin Laden, O., 64
Birnbaum, G. E., 352
Bjelland, I., 382
Blass, T., 12
Bleidorn, W., 257
Bleske-Rechek, A., 135
Block, J., 246–247, 250

Block, J. H., 246–247
Blohowiak, B. B., 46
Boden, J. M., 126
Bogg, T., 68, 264, 354, 390, 399
Bollen, E., 389
Bono, J. E., 61, 132, 335
Book, A. S., 108, 275
Booth, A., 109
Booth-Kewley, S., 402, 406, 407
Borkenau, P., 10, 87
Boss, M., 145
Bossio, L. M., 415
Bosson, J. K., 128, 133
Botwin, M. D., 355
Bouchard, T. J., 86, 88
Bourdain, A., 72
Bowlby, J., 347, 348, 349, 350
Bowling, N. A., 333
Boyce, T. E., 34
Bradley, A., 94
Brady, E. U., 382
Brady, J. V., 412
Brand, R., 60
Branje, S. J. T., 248
Brebner, J., 289
Brennan, K. A., 129
Breuer, J., 146
Brickman, P., 201
Briggs, M. I., 169, 170–171
Broderick, P. C., 206
Brown, A., 225
Brown, J. D., 415
Brown, K. W., 130, 206
Brown, M. A., 124
Brown, S., 62
Brown, S. L., 413
Brück, C., 41
Brummelman, E., 213
Brunell, A. B., 135, 336
Brunstein, J. C., 40, 193, 195
Bryant, G. A., 108
Brydon, L., 402
Buchtel, E. E., 308
Buckner, C., 285
Buffardi, L. E., 40, 136, 365
Buffett, W., 341
Bulbulia, J. A., 72
Bullock, W. A., 94
Bunde, J., 407

Bundy, T., 359
Bunevicius, A., 402
Burke, S. M., 98
Burnstein, E., 103
Burton, C. M., 404
Bush, G. H. W., 196
Bush, G. W., 196
Bushman, B. J., 39, 129
Buss, A. R., 16
Buss, D. M., 14, 101, 103, 104, 105, 107, 213, 245, 275, 276, 279, 292, 361, 409
Butcher, J. N., 380
Butler, A. C., 19, 392
Buttner, E. H., 282–283
Buunk, B. P., 110, 111
Byrne, D., 355
Byrne, K. A., 70

C

Cai, H., 253, 263, 308
Cain, N. M., 133
Cain, S., 60
Calhoun, L. G., 371
Campbell, J., 171, 341
Campbell, J. B., 94
Campbell, S. M., 133, 135
Campbell, W. K., 30, 31, 40, 129, 133, 134, 135, 136, 249, 250, 291, 308, 310, 340, 348, 358, 359, 361, 365
Campion, M. A., 340
Canli, T., 95, 97
Cantor, N., 163
Caplan, B., 86–87
Cappella, E., 229
Carhart-Harris, R., 145
Carlson, S. E., 403
Carmalt, J. H., 365
Carroll, J. S., 292
Carter, J., 196
Carvallo, M., 188, 351
Carver, C. S., 183, 413
Carver, G. W., 190
Caspi, A., 91, 244, 245, 246, 264
Cassidy, A., 152
Cattell, R. B., 54, 75
Cavallera, G. M., 101
C'de Baca, J., 254

Center for American
    Women and Politics, 283
Chamberlin, J., 232
Chapman, C., 256
Chappelle, D., 60
Cheng, J. T., 337
Cheng, K., 19, 139, 401
Cherek, D. R., 98
Cheryan, S., 287
Cheung, F. M., 79, 314
Chiaburu, D. S., 333
Christal, R. C., 75
Christie, R., 359
Chua, H. F., 304
Church, A. T., 199, 311, 314
Cisneros, S., 299, 303
Claes, L., 389, 390
Clark, R. D., 291, 292
Clausen, J. A., 256
Claxton, A., 69
Clinton, B., 60, 196
Cloninger, C. R., 183
Clooney, G., 391
Cohen, C. A., 294
Cohen, D., 110, 275,
    299, 305
Cohen, J., 26
Cohen, P., 378
Cohen, S., 188, 408, 413
Colapinto, J., 272
Coleman, J. S., 229
Collins, P. F., 61
Conden, E., 402
Confer, J., 101
Conley, A. M., 203
Conley, J. J., 264
Connell, J. P., 197
Cooley, C. H., 120
Coolidge, C., 292
Coolidge, F. L., 377
Coolidge, G., 292
Cooper, H. M., 229
Copernicus, N., 262
Costa, P. T., 57, 58, 79, 97,
    183, 250, 253, 261, 277,
    279, 280, 382, 390, 407
Costa, P. T., Jr., 409
Cousins, S. D., 117, 303
Craik, K. H., 14, 213
Cramer, P., 253
Crandall, R., 191
Crawford, A. M., 409
Crescioni, W. A., 402
Cripen, A., 341
Crocker, J., 126, 307, 308
Crompton, T., 200
Crowne, D. P., 34
Csikszentmihalyi, M., 181,
    207, 208, 341
Cuijpers, P., 71

Cullen,D., 359
Cumming, G., 46
Curtin, N., 73
Curtis, R. G., 74
Cutting, J. E., 289
Cyrus, M., 60

D

Dabbs, J. M., 108, 275
Dahmer, J., 359
Dahn, J. R., 403
Dalal, R. S., 333
Dalley, J. W., 98
Daly, M., 263
Daniels, D., 84
Darwin, C., 60, 99, 262
Davis, C. G., 209
Davis, F., 288
Davis, M. H., 356
Deal, J. E., 246
deCharms, R., 196
Deci, E. L., 181, 197, 198,
    199, 342
Decuyper, M., 68
De Fruyt, F., 265
De Fruyt et al., 2013, 379
DeGeneres, E., 388
deGraaf, I., 224
DelVecchio, W. F., 251, 252
Dembroski, T. M., 407
De Moor, M. H. M., 88
Denollet, J., 403
Deo, M. S., 371
Depue, R. A., 61
DeRaad B., 73, 79
De Ridder, D. T. D., 402
deRooij, S. R., 91
de Rossi, P., 388
Derue, D. S., 335
DeWall, C. N, 105, 306
DeWall, C. N., 104
Dewsbury, D. A., 217
DeYoung, C. G., 74, 98
Diamond, J., 300
Diamond, M., 273
Diana, Princess, 63–64
Dickens, C., 208
Diener, E., 316, 320
Digest of Education
    Statistics, 277
Dingemanse, N. J., 106
Dipboye, R. L., 360
Dittmar, H., 201
Donnellan, M. B., 353
Donohew, R. L., 409
Dougherty, D. M., 98
Dryer, D. C., 355
Dugatkin, L. A., 106
Dundes, A., 160–161
Dunham, L., 67

Durante, K. M., 108
Dweck, C. S., 205
Dyrenforth, P. S., 355, 363

E

Eagly, A. H., 107, 270, 275,
    276, 279, 282, 283, 360
Eaker, E. D., 402
Ebersole, P., 208
Eckstein, D., 263
Eddy, K., 389
Edelstein, R. S., 110
Einstein, A., 60
Eisenberger, N. I., 41,
    95, 105
Elizur, D., 192
Elliot, A. J., 182, 183, 184,
    185, 186, 194, 348
Ellis, B. J., 75, 105
Ellison, P. T., 110
Ellwood, A. L., 349
Else-Quest, N. M., 277
Elsheikh, S. E., 224
Emerson, R. W., 120
Epel, E. S., 402
Epstein, S., 14
Erikson, E., 145, 258–259
Erol, R. Y., 249
Erwin, E., 153
Eysenck, H. J., 37, 54, 61,
    77, 78, 93, 99
Eysenck, S. B. G., 37, 54,
    77, 78, 93

F

Fabulic, L., 101
Fairbairn, R., 175
Fakra, E., 97
Falbo, T., 263
Falk, C. F., 307, 309
Fallon, J., 60
Farnham, S. D., 128
Feinberg, M. E., 89
Feingold, A., 279, 294
Feist, G. J., 73
Feldman, J. F., 289
Feltman, R., 206
Ferdinand, F., 197
Fiasse, L., 262, 263
Fichten, C. S., 32
Fields, D., 225
Fincham, F. D., 352, 357
Fincher, C. L., 300
Findley, M. J., 229
Fink, B., 110
Finkel, E. J., 315, 358,
    363, 364
Firestone, D., 293
Fishbein, M., 14
Fisher, C., 385–386

Fisher, M., 298
Fleeson, W., 12, 14
Flowe, H. D., 108
Fodor, E. M., 193
Foldes, H. J., 315, 317,
    318, 320
Forer, B. R., 34
Forester, J., 184, 185
Forgeard, M., 414
Forkman, B., 80
Forsyth, D. R., 127, 128
Foster, C. A., 135
Foster, J. D., 133, 134,
    253, 308
Fox, S., 333
Fragale, A. R., 355
Fraley, R. C., 46–47, 351, 352
Fraley, R. C., 350
Francis, Pope, 337
Franklin, T. B., 93
Fredrickson, B. L., 290
Freedman, D. H., 213,
    218, 225
French, K. E., 289
Freud, A., 145, 156, 157, 159
Freud, Anna, 145, 156
Freud, S., 41, 51, 116,
    143, 144, 145, 146–164,
    165–166, 168, 169, 171,
    172, 174, 177, 181
Friedan, B., 153
Fried-Buchalter, S., 124
Friedman, H. S., 33, 68, 242,
    399, 402, 406, 407
Friedman, M., 405, 406
Friedman, R. S., 185
Friedmeier, M., 289
Friese, M., 394
Fudge, C., 332
Fuller, T. L., 352
Funder, D. C., 13, 16, 46
Furnham, A., 94, 171,
    332, 408

G

Gabriel, S., 188, 351
Gage, P., 94–95
Gagne, M., 199, 342
Gallup, G. G., 44
Gallup, G. G., Jr., 108
Galton, F., 76, 85, 99
Gandhi, M., 60, 190
Gangstead, S. W., 104
Garcia, J., 232
Garrett, H. E., 26
Gates, B., 3–4, 8
Gates, M., 3
Geen, R. G., 62, 94
Geer, J., 412
Geis, F., 359

Geller, E. S., 34
Gentile, B., 125, 291, 308, 316, 318, 320, 365
Gershoff, E. T., 217
Gibby, R. E., 26
Gildersleeve, K. A., 108
Gilens, M., 256
Gillham, J. E., 404, 416
Gilliland, K., 94
Giluk, T. L., 206
Giudici, S., 101
Glass, D. C., 412
Glass, G. V., 392
Glick, P., 282, 283
Glover, S. (Steve-O), 390
Gneezy, U., 225
Goetz, J. L., 357
Goldberg, L. R., 76, 251, 252
Golden, R. N., 403
Goldman, B. M., 123
Golomb, M., 377
Goodwin, S. A., 282
Gosling, R., 167
Gosling, S. D., 9, 10, 11, 40, 80, 365
Gough, H., 79
Gough, H. G., 284
Grande, G., 403
Grant, A. M., 332
Grant, B. F., 378
Grant, B. S., 106
Grant, I. E., 79
Gray, J. A., 95, 99, 183
Gray, S., 381
Graziano, W., 65
Green, J. D., 348
Greenberg, J., 157
Greene, A., 390
Greene, C. A., 320
Greenwald, A. G., 128
Greiling, H., 104
Griffiths, M., 391
Grijalva, E., 291
Grilo, C. M., 377
Grotevant, H. D., 89
Grouzet, F. M. E., 200, 201
Guimond, S., 277
Gunz, A., 181, 305
Gyllenhaal, G., 346

H
Haas, B. W., 95, 97
Habra, M. E., 402
Hagerty, M. R., 189
Hall, J. A., 289, 294
Hamamura T., 306
Hamann, S., 280
Hampson, S. E., 245, 251, 252, 409
Hankin, B. L., 290

Hannover, B., 119
Hardman, D., 263
Hardy, M. S., 371
Hare, R. D., 359
Hariri, A. R., 97
Harker, L., 264
Harlow, H. F., 349
Harlow, J. M., 95, 99
Harris, E., 359
Harris, J. R., 86
Hartmann, H., 181
Haselton, M. G., 108
Hatfield, E., 291
Hatfield, E. H., 292
Hathaway, S., 380
Hawking, S., 72
Hazan, C., 350
Hazlett-Stevens, H., 71, 402
Heatherington, E. M., 89
Heaven, P. L., 409
Hegarty, M., 294
Heggestad, E. D., 74
Heider, F., 129
Heilman, M. E., 283
Heimberg, R. G., 394
Heine, S. J., 205, 306, 307, 308, 311, 313, 318
Helmreich, R. L., 284
Hemingway, E., 329
Hermel, O., 263
Herrera, N. C., 261
Hertenstein, M. J., 264
Hibbeln, J. R., 403
Higgins, E. T., 137
Hill, P. L., 253
Hill, R., A., 186
Hills, P., 353
Hofer, J., 194
Hoffman, M., 277
Hogan, J., 175
Hogan, M. J., 74
Hogan, R., 175
Holtzman, N. S., 135, 360
Honekopp, J., 111
Hoppock, R., 331
Hopwood, C. J., 370, 379
Horney, K., 143, 145, 165, 174–175
Horowitz, L. M., 352, 355
Horton, R. S., 365–366
Hosoda, M., 360
House, J. S., 409
Howes, O. D., 371
Hoyle, R. H., 65, 68
Huang, Y., 378
Huesmann, L. R., 223
Hutchinson, J. C., 132
Hyde, J. S., 278, 279, 281, 282, 290, 292, 293, 294

I
Ickes, W., 294
Ilardi, S. S., 395, 403
Im, C., 37
Imada, T., 309
Inghilleri, P., 199
Ioannidis, J. P. A., 45, 46
Issacson, W., 3, 4, 335
Ivcevic, Z., 9
Iyengar, S. S., 300

J
Jacklin, C., 279
Jackson, J. J., 74, 409
Jacobson, N. S., 224
Jaffee, S. R., 91
James, H., 118
James, W., 19, 115, 116, 118–119, 120, 121, 123
Jamison, K. R., 384–385
Jang, K. L., 86, 92, 377
Janoff-Bulman, R., 209
Janson, H., 247
Javaris, K. N., 69
Jaycox, L. H., 416
Jefferson, T., 73, 262
Jellesma, F. C., 289
Jemmott, J. B., 411, 412
Jenner, B., 274
Jenner, C., 274
Jensen-Campbell, L., 65
Jensen-Campbell, L. A., 354
Jillette, P., 310
Jobs, S., 3–4, 5, 8, 9, 72, 335, 337
John, O. P., 54, 80, 134
Johnson, D. M., 377, 378
Johnson, W., 86, 87
Jokelam, M., 260
Jolie, A., 241–242
Jonason, P. K., 359, 360, 361
Jonassaint, C. R., 320, 410
Jones, A., 191
Jones, S. E., 65
Joseph, J., 90, 91
Judge, T. A., 11–12, 61, 65, 132, 331, 332, 334, 335, 336
Jung, C., 99, 143, 145, 153, 165–172

K
Kabat-Zinn, J., 131, 207
Kalechstein, A. D., 229
Kalivas, P. W., 98
Kallai, J., 294
Kammeyer-Mueller, J. D., 331

Kanagawa, C., 314
Kane, J. M., 293, 294
Kapidzic, S., 365
Karabenick, S. A., 229
Kardashian, K., 60
Kashima, Y., 314
Kasser, T., 200, 201, 202, 320
Kaufman, J., 234
Kavanagh, P., 359
Keehn, R. J., 403
Keeton, K. E., 339
Keillor, G., 60
Keirsey, D., 169
Keith, T. Z., 294
Keller, C., 69
Kelly, E. L., 264
Kelly, I. W., 33
Keltner, D., 264
Kendall, P. C., 382
Kennedy, J. F., 196
Kern, M. L., 60, 64, 67, 68, 69, 70, 72, 407
Kernis, M. H., 123
Keysar, B., 305
Khurana, A., 409
Kidwell, C., 275, 288
Kim, H., 308, 311
Kim, H. S., 300
Kim, K. H., 320
King, A. C., 41
King, L. A., 194, 208, 209, 404
King, M. L., Jr., 337
King, P., 274
Kirsch, I., 392
Kirshnit, C., 412
Kitayama, S., 117, 301, 302, 303, 310, 311
Klein, M., 145, 175, 176
Klein, R. A., 46
Klinesmith, J., 275
Kling, K. C., 290
Klipper, M. Z., 235
Knight, G. P., 278, 282
Koenig, A. M., 270, 283
Koestner, R., 192
Konrath, S. H., 306, 317, 353
Koopmans, L. H., 275
Kotov, R., 61, 65, 68, 70, 73, 382, 384, 385, 390, 391, 399, 402
Kozlowski, L. T., 289
Kramer, P., 382–383
Kraus, M. W., 308
Krueger, R. F., 86, 87, 370, 379
Kudler, D., 341
Kuhn, M. H., 116

Kühnen, U., 119
Kurdek, L. A., 285
Kuzawa, C. W., 110

L

LaFrance, M., 289
Lahey, B. B., 70, 371, 380
Lakey, C. E., 206
Lamb, M. E., 245, 247
Lamoreaux, M., 301, 308
Lander, C., 299
Lane, S. D., 98
Langner, C. A., 192, 197
Larson, R., 39
Lavin, C., 124
Lawton, C. A., 294
Leaper, C., 278
Leary, M. R., 104, 129, 188
Lee, A. Y., 311
Lee, J., 310
Lee, K., 65, 79
LeFevre, J., 207
Legassie, J., 124
Lehnart, J., 258
Lejuez, C. W., 224
Leng, V. C., 100
Lenzenweger, M. F., 373, 378
Leonard, E., 386
LePine, J. A., 332
Lepper, M. R., 74, 203, 204, 300
Levashina, J., 340
Levenson, R. W., 355
Levine, H., 399, 408
Levine, R. V., 317, 318
Lewicki, P., 233
Li, J. Y., 88
Lichtenfeld, S., 185
Liebermann, D., 108
Liebler, A., 10
Lifton, P. D., 270
Lilienfeld, S. O., 173
Lincoln, A., 73, 335
Lindberg, S. M., 293
Lindfors, P., 309
Lingl, A., 333
Linn, M. C., 294
Lippa, R., 286
Lippa, R. A., 107, 276, 279, 286, 292
Little, B. R., 208
Locatelli, S. M., 11
Lockwood, P., 311
Lodi-Smith, J., 69, 254
Loehlin, J. C., 86
Lombardo, M. V., 95
Lombardo, W. K., 222, 278, 289
Lowenstein, L. F., 95

Lu, L., 61
Lucas, R. E., 61
Luciano, M., 88
Ludtke, O., 251, 256, 260, 261
Luthans, F., 132
Luxen, M. F., 110, 111
Lydon, J., 176
Lymburner, J. A., 371
Lynam, D. R., 65, 68, 375, 376, 377
Lyubomirsky, S., 19, 392, 393, 395

M

Maccoby, E., 279
Machiavelli, N., 359, 360
MacKinnon, D. P., 184
MacLaren, V. V., 65, 68
MacLean, K. A., 74
MacLeod, J., 403
Macmillan, M. B., 95
Maeda, Y., 294
Magee, W. J., 384
Magid, V., 409
Maguire, E. A., 84
Maio, G. R., 202
Major, B., 290, 307
Malahy, L. W., 317
Malcolm, K. T., 354
Malcolm X, 5
Malouff, J. M., 387, 388, 389
Manning, J. T., 110, 111
Mansbach, C. S., 288
Maples, J. L., 57
Markon, K. E., 379
Markus, H., 136
Markus, H. R., 117, 301, 302, 303, 308, 311
Marlowe, D., 34
Marrs, R. W., 392
Martin, L. R., 12, 242, 399
Martin, R. A., 162
Martinko, M. J., 333
Maslow, A., 181, 187–191, 192, 205
Masuda, T., 305
Mathiesen, K. S., 247
Mazur, A., 109, 110
McAbee, S. T., 69
McAdams, D. P., 192
McCann, S. J. H., 320
McClelland, D. C., 192, 193, 194, 195, 196, 411, 412
McConaughey, M., 60
McConnell, J. V., 232
McCrae, R. R., 57, 58, 62, 72, 73, 79, 97, 183, 248, 250, 253, 277, 280, 314, 315, 317, 319, 382, 390

McEnally, M., 282–283
McGraw, K. O., 280
McGregor, I., 208
McGue, M., 86, 88
McGuire, W. J., 117
McKillip, J., 365
McKinley, J., 380
McKinley, N. M., 290
McKnight, J. D., 412
McLachlan, S., 83
McLean, C. P., 282
McNamera, R. K., 403
McPartland, T. S., 116
Mead, G. H., 121
Mehl, M. R., 278
Meier, B., 65
Mertz, J. E., 293, 294
Michael, R. T., 292
Michalek, J., 110
Michalski, R. L., 262
Michel, J. S., 333
Miles, C. C., 279, 284
Milgram, S., 12, 13
Miller, G., 107
Miller, J. D., 65, 68, 77, 133, 134, 135, 253, 391
Mineka, S., 102
Miner-Rubino, K. N., 290
Mirowsky, J., 229
Mischel, W., 12, 15, 229
Mitchell, J., 176
Mladinic, A., 282
Moeller, G. H., 196
Moffitt, T. E., 246, 264
Mommersteeg, P. M. C., 402, 407
Money, J., 272
Monk, T. H., 100
Moran, C. M., 342
Morehouse, R. E., 408
Morison, S. J., 349
Morling, B., 301, 308
Morns, K. A., 129
Morris, M. W., 304
Morrow, J., 403
Mother Teresa, 412
Mottus, R., 263, 400
Mount, M. K., 61, 338
Mroczek, D. K., 250, 258, 402, 405
Mueller, C. M., 205
Multon, K. D., 131
Muraven, M., 401
Murdock, K. K., 320
Murray, H., 181, 192
Musek, J., 79
Musson, D., 339
Myers, D. G., 306
Myhrvold, N., 4
Myrseth, H., 391

N

Napa, C. K., 208
Nash, J., 387
Naugle, W., 180
Naumova, O. Y., 92
Needham, A., 234
Neff, K. D., 130, 226
Nelis, D., 19, 394
Nelson, R. J., 111
Nettle, D., 76
Nevid, J. S., 9
Neyer, F. J., 258
Niedner, M., 83
Niesta, D., 186
Nixon, R., 64, 196
Noftle, E. E., 351
Nolen-Hoeksema, S., 282, 290, 403
Nordvik, H., 34
Norem, J., 163
Norem, J. K., 163
Norenzayan, A., 317, 318
Norman, W. T., 75
Northouse, P. G., 334
Nowicki, S., 229
Nurius, P., 136

O

Oaten, M., 139, 401
Oaten. M., 19
Obama, B., 196
Odbert, H. S., 75
Ode, S., 65
Oden, M. H., 399
Ogihara, Y., 310
Öhman, A., 102
Oishi, S., 264, 313, 317, 318, 319
Oldham, S., 285
Oliver, M. B., 292
Olshansky, E. F., 124
Ones, D. S., 340
Onnela, J-P., 278
Oppenheimer, J., 399
Organ, D. W., 332, 333
Orlofsky, J. L., 286, 288
Orth, U., 126, 249, 253
O'Steen, S., 106
O'Sullivan, S. S., 98
Oswald, F. L., 69
Otake, K., 394
Oyserman, D., 307
Ozer, D. J., 13, 264
Ozer. D. J., 4

P

Page, A. C., 374, 375, 376
Paltrow, G., 310
Pang, J. S., 194
Papurt, M. J., 26

Par, G., 39
Park, G., 9, 10
Pastva, A., 9
Patrick, H., 198
Paul, A. M., 91
Paulhus, D. L., 37, 133, 134, 135, 340, 358, 359
Paustian-Underdahl, S. C., 283
Pavlov, I., 229–230
Pavot, W., 61
Pawlowski, B., 104
Pearce, K., 408
Pedersen, W. C., 292
Pena, P. A., 398
Penedo, F. J., 403
Peng, K., 304
Penke, L., 104
Pennebaker, J. W., 404
Penney, L. M., 333
Peplau, L. A., 129
Perlman, D., 129
Perry, K., 60
Petersen, J. L., 292, 293
Peterson, C., 414, 415
Pew Center, The, 157
Phillips, D. P., 398
Piccolo, R. F., 335
Pierce, T., 176
Pietromonaco, P. R., 353
Piff, P. K., 308, 317
Pilon, D. A., 195
Pincus, A. L., 133
Pinquart, M., 392
Pinsky, D., 136
Pinsky, D. ("Dr. Drew"), 136
Pipher, M., 249
Pipitone, R. N., 108
Pitt, B., 241
Pittinsky, T. L., 336
Plomin, R., 84
Podar, I., 389
Polit, D., 263
Pomeranz, K., 300
Potthoff, J. G., 353–354
Pouwer, F., 402, 407
Pratt, A. C., 119
Pressman, S. D., 408, 413
Prior, T., 72
Puliti, A., 250
Purifoy, F. E., 275
Putnam, R. D., 320

Q

Quilty, L. C., 386
Quinn, J. M., 226

R

Rachman, S., 236
Radloff, L. S., 382

Randler, C., 101
Raskin, R., 133
Rawson, R., 88
Rayner, R., 230–231, 232
Raynor, D. A., 399, 408
Redel, S. L., 365
Reiland, R., 372
Reimer, B., 272
Reimer, D., 272
Reis, H. T., 197, 198, 348
Reissman, C., 354
Reisz, Z., 72
Renshaw, K., 306
Rentfrow, P. J., 63, 64, 65, 69, 71, 73, 299, 320
Rhodewalt, F., 133
Richard, F. D., 13
Richards, M. H., 39
Richardson, D. R., 356
Richeson, J. A., 282
Rizzo, A., 233
Roberts, B. W., 4, 12, 61, 68, 249, 250, 251, 252, 253, 254, 256, 264, 265, 354, 390, 399
Roberts, T., 290
Robins, R. W., 126, 134, 135, 242, 250, 251, 252, 253, 264
Robinson, B. E., 285
Robinson, M., 65
Roethke, T., 385
Rogers, C., 116, 190–191
Rohde, P. A., 261
Roiser, J. P., 98
Rollock, D., 289
Roosevelt, E., 190
Roosevelt, F. D., 65, 275
Roosevelt, T., 65
Rose, R. M., 108
Rosen, L. D., 365
Rosenberg, M., 125
Rosenman, R. H., 405, 406
Rosenthal, S. A., 336
Ross, C. E., 229
Ross, L., 163
Ross, S. R., 124
Roth, D. P., 313, 317, 318, 319
Rothbart, M. K., 244, 245
Rotter, J. B., 228, 229
Rottinghaus, P. J., 320
Rowling, J. K., 60
Rubenzer, S. J., 65, 73, 334, 335, 336
Rudman, L. A., 282, 283
Ruiz, J. M., 71
Rusbult, C. E., 358
Russell, D. W., 129
Rustichini, A., 225
Ryan, K., 332

Ryan, R. M., 130, 181, 197, 198, 199, 200, 201, 206, 320, 342
Ryff, C. D., 208

S

Sagie, A., 192
Saipe, J., 408
Saklofske, D. H., 33
Salanova, M., 341
Salgado, J. F., 333
Salkovskis, P. M., 371
Salmon, C. A., 263
Samuel, D. B., 61, 68, 70, 371
Sargent, J. D., 409
Saroglou, V., 262, 263
Satterfield, J. H., 223
Saulsman, L. M., 374, 375, 376
Sayer, L. C., 277
Scarr, S., 86
Schell, A., 223
Schindehette, S., 83
Schlinger, H., 107
Schmitt, D. P., 79, 277, 279, 280, 292, 307, 315, 317, 319, 320, 353
Schmitt, J. P., 285
Schneck, M. R., 26
Schorn, D., 83
Schredl, M., 156
Schüler, J., 197
Schultheiss, O. C., 40, 109, 192, 193, 194, 195, 200, 412
Schuster, M., 111
Schutte, J., 123
Schwartz, H. A., 254, 255, 272, 286
Schwartz, S. H., 200
Schweitzer, A., 329
Scollon, C. N., 316, 320
Sculley, J., 3
Seder, J. P., 264
Sedikides, C., 129
Sehlmeyer, C., 95
Seidman, G., 11
Seinfeld, J., 67
Selfhout, M., 353
Seligman, M. E. P., 414, 416
Shackelford, T. K., 262, 353
Shaver, P., 350
Shaver, P. R., 351, 352
Sheldon, K. M., 181, 183, 198, 201
Shelov, D. V., 207
Sherman, D. K., 300
Shiner, R. L., 244, 245, 263
Shiota, M. N., 355
Shipley, B. A., 71, 402

Shor, E., 409
Shostrom, E. L., 191
Sibley, C. G., 72, 73, 253
Siciliano, K. L., 110
Siegrist, M., 69
Sigmundson, H. K., 272
Silva, P. A., 246
Silverman, K., 224
Silverstein, S. M., 223
Silverstone, A., 310
Simpson, C. A., 217
Simpson, J. A., 104
Sin, N. L., 392
Singer, B., 208
Skinner, B. F., 213, 214, 215, 216, 227
Slane, J. D., 389
Sluming, V. A., 111
Smillie, L. D., 61
Smith, C. P., 192
Smith, D., 370, 383
Smith, J. W., 224
Smith, M. L., 392
Smith, T. W., 407
Smits, I. A. M., 316, 317, 319
Smokler, J., 259
Smyth, J. M., 404
Snicket, L., 414
Snyder, M., 122
Soto, C. J., 248, 250
Spacey, K., 359
Spangler, W. D., 40, 192, 194
Spates, R. C., 224
Specht, J., 253
Spector, P. E., 333
Spence, J. T., 284, 285
Spencer, S. J., 293
Sperry, L., 379
Spielberger, C. D., 77, 78
Spiro, A., 250, 258, 405
Spurk, D., 334
Srivastava, S., 65, 251
Srull, T. K., 229
Stajkovic, A. D., 132
Stanton, S. J., 109, 275
Steele, V., 275, 288
Stefanik, E., 180–182
Steinbeck, J., 9
Stellar, J. E., 308
Stenstrom, E., 110
Stephens, N. M., 317
Stevens, J. S., 280
Stewart, G. L., 332
Stewart, K. D., 308
Stinson, F. S., 291
Stogdill, R., 335
Stokes, J. P., 353
Stoller, R. J., 272
Stoolmiller, M., 90
Strain, J., 95
Strauman, T. J., 412

Strelan, P., 65
Strube, M. J., 135, 360
Su, R., 286
Suh, E. M., 314
Sulloway, F., 261–262
Suls, J., 407
Sunerton, B., 32
Surtees, P., 407
Sutin, A. R., 70, 400, 402
Sverko, B., 101
Swift, T., 346, 351
Sykes, C. J., 126
Szasz, T. S., 164

T

Talhelm, T., 300
Tang, T. Z., 382, 392
Tang, Y. Y., 358, 394
Tangney, J. P., 137, 358, 400
Tauber, M., 241
Taubman-Ben-Ari, O., 254
Taylor, K., 62
Taylor, L. S., 365
Taylor, R., 265
Taylor, S. E., 413, 415
Taylor, S. P., 39
Tellegen, A., 54, 86
Terman, L. M., 279, 284, 399
Terracciano, A., 62, 70, 277, 280, 314, 316, 402
Terry, H., 133
Terry, M. L., 131
Thalmayer, A. G., 9, 40, 408
Thase, M. E., 403
Thomas, J. R., 289
Thorndike, E. L., 217
Thornton, B. B., 241
Thrash, T. M., 182, 183, 184, 194
Tiedens, L. Z., 355
Tierney, J., 226
Timberlake, D. S., 92
Timberlake, J., 306
Timmer, R., 53, 61

Tindle, H., 413
Tobin, R. M., 95
Toepfer, S. M., 404
Torgersen, S., 377
Toussaint, L., 357
Triandis, H., 303–304
Trivers, R. L., 103, 275
Truman, H., 196
Trump, D., 60, 337
Tsaousis, I., 100
Tucker, J. S., 69
Tupes, E. C., 75
Turiano, N. A., 74, 399, 400, 402, 409, 410
Turkheimer, E., 90
Turner, R., 123
Twenge, J. M., 37, 104, 126, 188, 229, 249, 250, 253, 270, 285, 286, 289, 290, 291, 293, 301, 306, 307, 308, 310, 316, 320

U

Ulrich, R. S., 102
Underwood, C., 120, 306
U.S. Bureau of the Census, 280, 282, 283, 287
U.S. Department of Labor, 340

V

Vaillant, G. E., 192
Valenstein, E. S., 95
Van Anders, S. M., 110
Van Beest, I., 188
Vancouver, J. B., 132
van der Linden, D., 61
Van Duijvenvoorde, A. C. K., 216
Van Dyne, L., 332
Van Honk, J., 108
Vansteenkiste, M., 199
Varnum, M. E. W., 300, 310
Vazire, S. A., 9, 10, 46–47, 365

Vedel, A., 69
Verheul, R., 373
Vianello, M., 280
Vincent, N., 268–269, 271, 288–289
Vingerhoets, A. J., 289
Vinitzky, G., 11
Vohs, K. D., 202
Volkow, N. D., 98
Von Ammon, J., 262
von Franz, M.-L., 145
Voyer, D., 294
Vrana, S. R., 289
Vuchinich, R. E., 217

W

Wacker, J., 61
Wagner, J., 249
Waldron, I., 278
Waldron, M., 90
Waller, N. G., 54, 79
Walster, E., 363, 365
Walster, G. W. W., 292
Wampold, B. E., 392
Wash, R., 9
Washington, G., 334
Watson, D., 73
Watson, J. B., 226–227, 230–232
Watson, S., 111
Watts, B. L., 101
Webb, J. R., 357
Weinberger, D. A., 159, 160
Weinstein, R. S., 229
Weinstein, S. M., 39
Weisbuch, M., 365
Weiss, A., 409
Weston, S., 409
White, J. K., 353
White, R. W., 181
White, S., 408
White, T. L., 183
Wicker, F. W., 188
Widiger, T. A., 61, 68, 70, 73, 371, 373, 375, 376, 377

Wiebe, D. J., 407
Wilbourne, P., 254
Williams, D. A., 274
Williams, G. C., 199
Williams, K. D., 188
Williams, K. M., 358, 359
Wills, T. A., 188
Wilson, M. S., 253, 365
Winnicott, D., 145, 175
Winter, D. G., 192, 193, 196, 197
Wirth, M. M., 109
Wohn, D. Y., 9
Wojciechowski, F. L., 389
Wolf, R., 66
Wondergem, T. R., 289
Wonderlich, S. A., 389
Wong, S. P., 280
Wood, J. M., 40
Wood, W., 107, 270, 275, 276
Woodworth, R. S., 25–26
Wortman, J., 250, 251
Wu, S., 305
Wyers, E. J., 234

X

Xin, Z., 320

Y

Yang, B., 332
Yehiel, D., 254
Yoon, S., 294
Young, M., 136
Young, S. M., 136
Yovetich, N. A., 358

Z

Zarate, M. A., 314
Zelaniewicz, A. M., 104
Zell, E., 281
Zickar, M. J., 26
Zimmer, A., 72
Ziv, I., 263
Zuckerman, M., 408–409
Zweigenhaft, R. L., 262

Subject Index

A

Accommodation, 358
Acculturation. *See* Socialization
Achievement motive, 192–194, 195, 196
Achieving Society, The (McClelland), 195
Acquiescence response set, 24
Addictive disorders, 390–391
    behavior modification for, 224
    gambling disorder, 390–391
    substance-related disorders, 390
Adler's theories, 172–174
Adolescence, personality in. *See*
        Childhood and adolescence,
        personality in
Adventure, 328, 330
Affiliation motive, 192–194, 196–197
Affiliative humor style, 162
Affiliative speech, 278
Aggression
    genetics and, 88
    self-view and, 173
    sex differences in, 271, 275, 282
    social learning and, 222–223
    temperament and, 246
    testosterone and, 108–109, 275
    2D:4D ratio and, 111
    in workplace, 333
Aggressive humor style, 162
Agoraphobia, 384, 385
Agreeableness
    in addictive disorders, 386, 390, 391
    in anxiety disorders, 384, 385, 386
    behaviors, attitudes, and
        characteristics of, 63–66
    birth order and, 262
    in borderline PD, 375–376
    brain and, 95, 96
    changes in, during young
        adulthood to old age, 251, 252
    circadian rhythm and, 100
    as continuum, 58
    cultural differences in, 316–317
    defined, 56
    in dependent PD, 377
    in eating disorders, 386, 389
    facets of, 57–58
    life outcomes and, 263, 264, 265
    in maturation of personality, 254
    in personality and relationships, 353
    in personality in workplace, 325,
        326, 329, 331–339
    physical health and, 409, 410
    in schizoid PD, 376–377
    in schizophrenia, 386, 387, 388
    sex differences in, 276, 277, 279,
        281, 282, 285, 291
    survival ability and, 77
    in trait self-ratings, 55
    in United States, 65–66
    word clouds for, 64
Ally McBeal, 388
Altruism, 328, 329
Ambitions, in TST, 116
American Idol, 157
America's Got Talent, 157
Amotivation, 342
Amygdala, 95, 97
Anal expulsive, 152
Anal retentive, 151
Anal stage, 150, 151, 152
Analysis, 328, 330
Analytical psychology, 143
Androgynous, 285
Anima/animus archetype, 167–168
Animals
    Big Five personality traits in, 80
    classical conditioning and, 229–232
    operant conditioning and, 214, 215
Annals of Improbable Research
        (Associated Press), 107
Anorexia nervosa, 388–389
Antagonism, 63, 379
Antidepressant drugs, 382–383, 392
Antisocial personality disorder, 374,
        375, 376, 377
Anxiety
    defined, 352
    dimensional approach to, 352–353
    self-report measures of, 40–41,
        42, 44
    Type D personality and, 402–405
Anxiety disorders, 383–384
    agoraphobia, 384, 385
    Big Five in, 384, 385, 386
    generalized anxiety disorder, 383
    panic disorder, 383
    social phobia, 384, 385
Anxious attachment, 349
Appearance, in men *vs.* women, 289–290
Apple, 3–4
Approach motivation, 182–187, 311
Archetypes, 165–169
    anima/animus, 167–168
    defined, 165

Self, 168–169
    shadow, 166–167
Archival records, 40
Aspirations Index, 200
Assertiveness, 57, 61, 79, 251, 263
Attachment, 347–353
    in adult relationships, 350–352
    childhood, 347–350
    defined, 347
    dimensional approach to, 352–353
    dismissing, 352
    fearful, 352, 353
    preoccupied, 352
Attachment style, 349
Attachment theory, 348
Attention-deficit/hyperactivity
        disorder (ADHD), 223
Attitudes
    of ego, 169–171
    extraversion *vs.* introversion, 169, 170
Attributions, 304–306
*Austin Powers: The Spy Who Shagged
    Me*, 162
Authenticity, 123–124
    authentic relationships as part
        of, 124
    awareness as part of, 123–124
    behavior as part of, 124
    unbiased processing as part of, 124
Authentic relationships (as part of
        authenticity), 124
Autonomy
    defined, 198
    in self-determination theory,
        198–199
    vs. shame, in Erikson's life stages,
        259
Avenue Q, 208
Avoidance, 352–353
Avoidance motivation, 182–187, 311
Avoidant attachment, 350
Avoidant personality disorder, 374,
        375, 376
Awareness (as part of authenticity),
        123–124

B

Baby Boomers, 308, 321
Balanced Inventory of Desirable
        Responding, 37
Balanced Measure of Psychological
        Needs, 199

Barbie Liberation Organization, 293
Barnum effect, 33–34
Basic fault, 145, 176
Beautiful Mind, A, 387
"Before He Cheats" (Underwood), 120
Behavior
    affected by implicit/explicit motives, 194–195
    hormones and, 107–111
    measuring, 39
    nonverbal, in men *vs.* women, 288–289
    as part of authenticity, 124
    predicted by personality, 11–16
    sexual, in men *vs.* women, 291–293
    shaped by learning (*See* Learning, behavior shaped by)
Behavioral activation, 224
Behaviorism, 213
Behavior modification, 223–227
    for addictions, 224
    for ADHD, 223
    to change habits, 225–226
    children and, 223–225
    defined, 223
    for depression, 224
    extent of, 226–227
    overview of, 223–225
    reciprocal determinism in, 227
Bell curve, 35
Belonging, need for, 104–105
    in Maslow's hierarchy of needs, 187, 188
Bem Sex-Role Inventory, 279
Bernreuter Personality Inventory, 78
Beyond Freedom and Dignity (Skinner), 227
Bibliotherapy, 392
Big Five, 54–80
    in addictive disorders, 386, 390, 391
    agreeableness (*See* Agreeableness)
    in animals, 80
    in anxiety disorders, 384, 385, 386
    bipolar disorder and, 386
    in borderline PD, 375–376
    changes in, during childhood and adolescence, 247–248
    changes in, during young adulthood to old age, 250–253
    in comparing men and women, 279–282
    conscientiousness (*See* Conscientiousness)
    cultural differences in, 312–321
    defined, 54
    in dependent PD, 377
    depression and, 386
    development of, 75–76
    in eating disorders, 386, 389

extraversion (*See* Extraversion)
    facets of, 57–58
    in men *vs.* women, 279–282
    neuroticism (*See* Neuroticism)
    openness to experience (*See* Openness to experience)
    of pathological personality, 379–380
    in personality and relationships, 353–355
    personality types and, 402–409, 410
    physical health and, 398–411
    in schizoid PD, 376–377
    in schizophrenia, 386, 387, 388
    statements used instead adjectives, 79
    temperament and, 244–245
    translating across other cultures, 79–80
    translating to other personality research, 77–79
    usefulness of, 76–77
Biology
    defined, 84
    models of personality, history of, 99
    sex differences and, 273–278
Biology of personality, 93–101
    Big Five and brain, 95–98
    circadian rhythm in, 98–101
    neurotransmitters in, 98
Bipolar disorder, 384–386
Birth cohort, 90, 300
Birth order, 174, 261–263
    firstborns, 262
    genetics and, 261–262
    lastborns, 262
    middleborns, 262–263
    only children, 263
    personality and, 89
Blues Brothers, The, 233
Bobo doll experiment, 222
Body expansiveness, 289
Borderline personality disorder, 372, 374, 375–376, 378
Born to Rebel (Sulloway), 262
Brain, Big Five and, 95–98
Brain scans, 41–42, 95, 99
Breakfast Club, The, 250–251
Breaking Dawn, 168
Bridges of Madison County, The, 412
Bulimia nervosa, 388–389

C

California Psychological Inventory, 78, 79
Caregiver, 347
Castration anxiety, 152
Catastrophizing, 414
Cathexis, 150

Causation, determining, 44–45
Celebrities
    as extraverts, 60
    as introverts, 60
    as narcissists, 136
Censorship, 147
Center for Epidemiological Studies Depression Scale (CES-D), 381–382
Chemistry.com, 363
"Chicken Littling," 414
Childhood and adolescence, personality in, 243–250
    changes in Big Five during, 247–248
    changes in self-esteem during, 248–250
    temperament, 243–247
Children
    behavior modification and, 223–225
    classical conditioning and, 230–232
    operant conditioning and, 215–219
    sex differences in, 287–288
    socialization and, 222–223
Children's books, achievement motivation in, 195
Chocolate cake model, 361–362
Christmas Carol, A (Dickens), 208
Circadian rhythm, 98–101
Cisgender, 273
Classical conditioning, 229–236
    associations, 232–235
    defined, 230
    fear and, 230–233
    habituation and, 233–234
    overview of, 229–230
    phobias and, 235–237
    sleep conditioning and, 234–235
Classifications, in TST, 116
Clinical interviews, 39
Clinical psychology, 6
Cluster A, 373–375
Cluster B, 373–375
Cluster C, 373–375
Cognitive abilities, in men *vs.* women, 293–294
Cognitive-behavioral therapy (CBT), 379, 392, 404
Collective self-esteem, 308
Collective unconscious, 165
Collectivism, 117, 302–311
Common humanity, 130
Compassion, 357
Compensate, 173
Competence, 198–199
Compulsive stealing, 370
Computer dance study, 363–364
Conditioned response, 230, 231
Conditioned stimulus, 230, 231

Confessions of a Scary Mommy (Smokler), 259
Confounding variables, 44
Conscientiousness
  in addictive disorders, 386, 390, 391
  in anxiety disorders, 384, 385, 386
  behaviors, attitudes, and characteristics of, 66–69
  birth order and, 262
  in borderline PD, 375–376
  brain and, 96, 97–98
  changes in, during childhood and adolescence, 248
  changes in, during young adulthood to old age, 250, 252
  circadian rhythm and, 100
  as continuum, 58
  cultural differences in, 317–319
  defined, 14, 56
  in dependent PD, 377
  in eating disorders, 386, 389
  facets of, 57–58
  life outcomes and, 263, 264, 265
  in maturation of personality, 254
  neurotransmitters linked to, 98
  in personality and relationships, 354
  in personality in workplace, 326, 329, 331–340
  physical health and, 399–402, 410
  in schizoid PD, 376–377
  in schizophrenia, 386, 387, 388
  sex differences in, 280, 281
  survival ability and, 77
  in trait self-ratings, 55
  in United States, 68, 69
  word clouds for, 67
Conscious, 144
Continuous reinforcement schedule, 219–221
Contrast effect, 88–89
Convergent validity, 30–31
Correlation, 26–28
Correlational studies, 43–45
Counselor, The, 168
Counterproductive workplace behavior (CWB), 333
Creativity, 328, 329
Cronbach's alpha, 28
Cross-cultural differences, 297–323
  in attributions, 304–306
  in Big Five, 312–321
  in cultural norms, 300
  defined, 300
  individualistic *vs.* collectivistic, 302–311
  in personality, 300–302
  personality disorders and, 378–379
  socioeconomic status and, 300
  in views of self, 306–312

Cross-sectional study, 242–243
Cuban Missile Crisis, 197
Cultural products, 300–301
Culture
  defined, 299
  differences in (*See* Cross-cultural differences)
  goals across, 201–202
  mutual constitution model and, 301
  overview of, 298
  sex differences across, 275–278
  translating Big Five across, 79–80

D
Dark triad, 358–362
  chocolate cake model and, 361–362
  defined, 358
  Machiavellianism in, 359
  mate-poaching and, 359–361
  narcissism in, 359
  psychopathy in, 359
Dating, online, 363–365
Day residue, 154
Dazed and Confused, 217
Deconditioning, 231–232
Defense mechanisms, 156–164
  defensive pessimism, 162–163
  defined, 156
  denial, 157
  displacement, 159–160
  empirical evidence for, 163–164
  humor, 161–162
  projection, 158–159
  reaction formation, 157–158
  repression, 159
  sublimation, 160–161
Defensive pessimism, 162–163
Delusions, 387
Denial, 157
Dependent personality disorder, 374, 375, 376, 377
Dependent variable, 45
Depression
  antidepressant drugs for, 382–383, 392
  behavior modification for, 224
  major depressive disorder, 381–383
  major depressive episodes, 381
  Type D personality and, 403–404
Depression Cure, The (Ilardi), 403
Descriptive statistics, 34
Despicable Me, 193
Detachment, 378
Developmental psychology, 6
Developmental stages, 150–153
  anal stage, 150, 151, 152
  genital stage, 150, 151
  latent stage, 150, 151
  oral stage, 150, 151–152
  phallic stage, 150, 151, 152

Development of Sex Differences, The (Maccoby and Jacklin), 279
Diagnostic and Statistical Manual of Mental Disorders (DSM), 373. *See also* DSM-5
Dimensional model of attachment, 352–353
  anxiety in, 352–353
  avoidance in, 352–353
Dirty Jobs, 325
Disagreeableness, 63, 65–66
Discrepancy, 137
Discrepancy detection, 95
Discriminant validity, 31
Discrimination, 231–232
Disinhibition, 379
Dismissing attachment, 352
Displacement, 159–160
Distressed (Type D) personality, 402–405, 409, 410
Divergent, 64, 167
Dominance, 61, 336–337
Dopamine, 98
Dream interpretation, 153–156
Drive, 167
DSM-5, 373, 379–380, 391
Dunham, L., 67

E
Eating disorders, 388–390
Effective leadership, 336
Ego, 147–149
Ego depletion, 139
Ego functions, 169–171
  in action, 171
  defined, 169
  intuition *vs.* sensation, 169, 170
  thinking *vs.* feeling, 169, 170
Ego identity *vs.* role confusion, in Erikson's life stages, 259
Ego integrity *vs.* despair, in Erikson's life stages, 259
EHarmony, 363
Electra complex, 153
Electroencephalography (EEG), 99
Emergent leadership, 336
Emerging adulthood, 256–257
Emotional competence training, 394
Empathy, 356–357
Environment
  gene-environment interaction and, 91–93
  percentage of variance and, 86–88
Epigenetics, 92–93
Erikson's life stages, 258–259
Erudition, 328, 330
Evolutionary psychology, 101–107
  challenges to, 107
  defined, 101
  mating strategies and, 104
  need to belong in, 104–105

Evolutionary psychology (*Continued*)
  reproduction and, 103–104
  sex differences and, 275–276
  sociosexuality and, 104
  survival and, 102–103
  trait differences and, 105–106
Executive monkey study, 412
Expectancies, 228–229
Experiment, 45
Explanatory style, 413–416
Explicit motives
  behavior affected by, 194–195
  defined, 194
Explicit self-esteem, 128
Extensive image creation, 340
External attribution, 304
External locus of control, 228–229
Extinction, 231–232
Extraversion, 8, 9, 10, 13–14, 16
  in addictive disorders, 386, 390, 391
  in anxiety disorders, 384, 385, 386
  behaviors, attitudes, and
    characteristics of, 60–63
  birth order and, 262
  in borderline PD, 375–376
  brain and, 96, 97
  changes in, during young
    adulthood to old age, 251
  circadian rhythm and, 100
  as continuum, 58
  cultural differences in, 314–316
  defined, 56
  in dependent PD, 377
  in eating disorders, 386, 389
  facets of, 57–58
  vs. introversion, 169, 170
  life outcomes and, 263
  in personality and relationships, 353
  in personality in workplace, 329,
    331–339
  physical health and, 408–409, 410
  in schizoid PD, 376–377
  in schizophrenia, 386, 387, 388
  sex differences in, 279–281, 285
  survival ability and, 76–77
  in trait self-ratings, 55
  Type T personality and, 408–409, 410
  in United States, 62–63
  well-known extraverts, 60
  word clouds for high and low,
    9, 10–11
Extrinsic goals, 200–205
Extrinsic motivation, 203–205, 342
Eysenck Personality Inventory, 54, 78
Eysenck Personality Questionnaire,
  37, 54

F
Facebook
  interpersonal relationships and,
    365–366

language use on, 254, 255
  words used more frequently by
    introverts and extraverts, 9,
    10–11
  words with largest sex differences
    on, 272
Facets, 57–58
Face validity, 30
Facial expressions, life outcomes
  and, 264
Factor analysis, 75
Fake good, 340
False consensus effect, 163–164
Family environment. *See* Shared
  environment
Fear, classical conditioning and, 230–233
Fearful attachment, 352, 353
Femininity, masculinity *vs.*, 283–285
50th percentile, 34
Fight-or-flight response, 183–184, 413
Firstborns, 262
Five-Factor Model, 54. *See also* Big Five
Fixed-interval reinforcement, 219
Fixed-ratio reinforcement, 219–221
Flashcard function, 18
Flooding, 236
Flow state, 207–208
FMRI, 41–42
Free association, 146
Freudian slip, 148
Freud's theories, 146–164
  applied to modern psychology, 164
  challenges to, 164
  defense mechanisms, 156–164
  dream interpretation, 153–156
  of psychosexual development,
    150–153
  structural model of personality,
    147–149
  topographical model of
    personality, 146–147
Frontal lobe, 95, 97
Full-time workforce, entering, 255–257
Functional MRI (fMRI), 99

G
Galvanic skin response, 99
Gambling disorder, 390–391
Game of Thrones, 173, 337
Game theory, 387
Gender. *See also* Sex differences
  defined, 270
  personality and, 268–296
  roles, origins of, 274–275
  sex and, distinction between,
    270–271
Gene-environment interaction, 91–93
Gene expression, 92–93
Generalization, 231
Generalized anxiety disorder, 383
Generalized expectancies, 228

Generalized other, 115, 121
Generation, 300
Generativity *vs.* stagnation, in
  Erikson's life stages, 258, 259
Genetics
  birth order and, 261–262
  defined, 83
  gene-environment interaction and,
    91–93
  percentage of variance and, 86–88
  sex differences and, 274–275
  siblings and, 90
Genital stage, 150, 151
Genotype, 92
Get Me Out of Here (Reiland), 372
Girls, 256, 257
Glee, 192
Goals
  across cultures, 201–202
  defined, 180
  extrinsic motivation and, 203–205
  extrinsic *vs.* intrinsic, 200–205
  happiness and, 201
  intrinsic motivation and, 203–205
  thinking affected by, 202–203
Gone Girl, 168
"Good Thing He Can't Read My
  Mind" (Lavin), 124
Grandiose narcissism, 133–136

H
Habits, behavior modification to
  change, 225–226
Habituation, 233–234
Hallucinations, 387
Hamlet, 153
Hangover, The, 166, 167
Happiness strategies, 392–393
Harry Potter, 60, 64, 67, 72, 115, 144,
  168, 171, 172
Heart disease and personality type,
  398, 405–408
Hereditary Genius (Galton), 99
Heritability of personality, 85–91. *See
  also* Twin studies
Hero's journey, 171–172
Hierarchy of needs. *See* Maslow's
  hierarchy of needs
High impulsivity. *See* Low
  conscientiousness
Histrionic personality disorder, 374,
  375, 376
Hobbies, of men *vs.* women, 286–288
Holland scales, 329
Hormones, behavior and, 107–111
  high-fertility days, 107–108
  progesterone and, 412–413
  testosterone and, 108–111
Horney's theories, 174–175
Horoscopes as personality measures,
  32–34

Hostile attribution bias, 65
Hostility
    defined, 407
    Type A personality and, 405–408
"House dream," Jung's, 165–166
House of Cards, 359
Humanistic psychology
    defined, 187
    self-actualization and, 187, 189–191
Humor, 161–162
Humor Styles Questionnaire, 162
Hunger Games, The, 144, 168, 172
Hysteria, 146

I

"I am . . . " statements, 116–117
Id, 147–149
Ideal self, 137
Ideological beliefs, in TST, 116
I Hate You—Don't Leave Me (Kreisman and Strauss), 372
"I" in self-concept, 118
I Love Lucy, 399
Immune system, 404
Implicit Association Test (IAT), 128
Implicit motives, 191–197
    achievement, 192–194
    affiliation, 192–194
    behavior affected by, 194–195
    defined, 192
    power, 192–194
    of prtesidents and eras, 196–197
Implicit self-esteem, 128
Imposter phenomenon, 124
Impulsivity, 87–88, 97–98, 400
Independent variable, 45
Individualism, 117, 302–311
Individuation, 171–172
Industrial-organizational psychology, 6
Industry *vs.* inferiority, in Erikson's life stages, 259
Inferiority complex, 173
Inflammation, 407
Informant reports, 38
Initiative *vs.* guilt, in Erikson's life stages, 259
Insomnia, 370
Insults, testosterone and, 109–110
Intercoder reliability, 40
Interests, in TST, 116
Internal attribution, 304
Internalized, 348
Internal locus of control, 228–229
Internal reliability, 28
Interpersonal Reactivity Index, 356, 357
Interpretation of Dreams, The (Freud), 153
Intimacy *vs.* isolation, in Erikson's life stages, 258, 259
Intrinsic goals, 200–205
Intrinsic motivation, 203–205, 342

Introversion
    defined, 8
    extraversion *vs.*, 169, 170
    famous introverts, 60
    reactivity linked to, 94
Intuition *vs.* sensation, 169, 170
IQ, 31, 74, 264, 279

J

Jackass, 390
Jersey Shore, 250
Job performance, 332–333
Jobs, of men *vs.* women, 286–288
Job satisfaction, 331–332
Job selection, 338–341
    personality tests in, 339–341
    traits employers look for, 338–339
Journal writing, 404–405
Judging *vs.* perceiving, 169, 170–171
Jung's theories, 165–172
    archetypes, 165–169
    attitudes, 169–171
    ego functions, 169–171
    "house dream," 165–166
    individuation, 171–172
    judging *vs.* perceiving, 169, 170–171
Jung Type Indicator Questionnaire, 169

K

Keirsey Temperament Sorter, 169
Killing Fields, The, 381
Kindness, 394
Kleptomania, 370

L

Lastborns, 262
Latent content, 153
Latent stage, 150, 151
Law & Order: SVU, 192
Leadership
    in men *vs.* women, 282–283
    in ORVIS, 328, 329
    in personality in workplace, 334–337
Learning, behavior shaped by, 212–238
    behavior modification and, 223–227
    classical conditioning and, 229–236
    expectancies and, 228–229
    locus of control and, 228–229
    operant conditioning and, 214–223
Lexical hypothesis, 75, 76, 79
Libido, 150, 151
Lie scales, 31, 36, 37
Life outcomes, 263–265
Life outcomes data, 40
Life stages, Erikson's, 258–259
Likert scale, 24
Listening to Prozac (Kramer), 382–383
Little Albert, 230–232
Locus of control, 228–229
Loneliness, 129
Longitudinal study, 44, 242, 243

Looking-glass self, 115, 120
Lord of the Rings, 172
Love, in Maslow's hierarchy of needs, 187, 188
Loveline, 136
Low conscientiousness, 97–98
"Lunatics Have Taken Over the Asylum, The," 124

M

Machiavellianism, 359
Magnetic resonance imaging (MRI), 99
Major depressive disorder, 381–383
Major depressive episodes, 381
Man and His Symbols (Jung), 168
Mandala, 169
Manic episodes, 384–386
Manifest content, 153
Manspreading. *See* Body expansiveness
Many labs approach, 46
Marlowe-Crowne Social Desirability Scale, 28, 31, 34–38, 40–41, 159
Marriage, 257–258
Masculinity *vs.* femininity, 283–285
Maslow's hierarchy of needs, 187–191
    love and belonging, 187, 188
    physiological needs, 187–188
    safety and security, 187, 188
    self-actualization, 187, 189–191
    self-esteem, 187, 188
Match.com, 363
Mate-poaching, 359–361
Material self, 119–120
Math ability, in men *vs.* women, 274, 278, 279, 293–294
Mating strategies, 104
Maturation of personality, 254–261. *See also* Significant life experiences
Mean, 34
Mean Girls, 337
Meaning in life, 208–209
Mean-level changes, 252
Median, 34–35
Medical student syndrome, 371
Medications for mental disorders, 379, 382–383, 392
Meditation, 394–395
"Me" in self-concept, 118
Memories, Dreams, Reflections (Jung), 165
Men and women, comparing, 278–294
    appearance, 289–290
    Big Five, 279–282
    cognitive abilities, 293–294
    hobbies, 286–288
    jobs, 286–288
    leadership, 282–283
    masculinity/femininity, 283–285
    math ability, 274, 278, 279, 293–294
    nonverbal behaviors, 288–289

Men and women, comparing
(*Continued*)
self-esteem, 290–291
sexual behaviors/attitudes, 291–293
stereotypes, 278, 279
stereotypically feminine, 285
stereotypically masculine, 285
Men Are from Mars, Women are from Venus (Gray), 281
Mental disorders, 369–396
addictive disorders, 390–391
anxiety disorders, 383–384
bipolar disorder, 384–386
defined, 370
diagnosing, 373
eating disorders, 388–390
major depressive disorder, 381–383
overview of, 370–371
personality and, 371, 380–391 (*See also* Personality disorders)
schizophrenia, 387–388
therapy for (*See* Therapy for mental disorders)
Mental health. *See* Mental disorders
Meta-analysis, 46, 47
Microsoft, 3–4
Middleborns, 262–263
Millennials, 300
Mindfulness, 130–131, 206–207
Mindfulness meditation, 131, 394–395
Minnesota Multiphasic Personality Inventory (MMPI), 380
Mode, 34
Models of personality
biology, 99
Freud's, 146–149
Horney's, 174
traits, 78
Mona Lisa, 159, 160
Monkey Mind (Smith), 370
Monozygotic twins, 85, 86
Mood disorders, 381
Morningness-eveningness, 98–101
Motivation, 179–211
approach, 182–187, 311
avoidance, 182–187, 311
extrinsic, 342
extrinsic *vs.* intrinsic, 203–205
flow state and, 207–208
goals and, 180, 200–205
intrinsic, 342
Maslow's hierarchy of needs and, 187–191
meaning in life and, 208–209
mindfulness and, 206–207
motives and (*See* Motives)
needs and, 181–182
overview of theory and research on, 180–182
peak experiences and, 207–208
self-determination theory and, 197–199

Motives, 180–182. *See also* Motivation
based on needs, 181–182
defined, 180
explicit, 194–195
implicit, 191–197
physical health and, 411–413
Moving against, 174
Moving away, 174–175
Moving toward, 174
Multidimensional Personality Questionnaire, 54
Multifactor personality scale, 26
Mutual constitution model, 301
Myers-Briggs Type Indicator, 169, 326

N
Narcissism, 132–136
among celebrities, 136
changes in, during young adulthood to old age, 253
in dark triad, 359
defined, 133
grandiose, 133–136
positives and negatives of, 135–136
self-esteem and, 133–135
vulnerable, 133
Narcissistic personality disorder (NPD), 133, 371, 373–379
Narcissistic Personality Inventory (NPI), 132, 133, 135
Natural consequences, 218
Nature-nurture debate, 13
Need for social approval, 34
Needs
to belong, 104–105, 187, 188
defined, 181
in Maslow's hierarchy of needs, 187–191
motives based on, 181–182
in self-determination theory, 197–199
for uniqueness, 310–311
Negative affectivity, 378
Negative correlations, 26–27
Negative life experiences, 260–261
Negative punishment, 214, 215, 218–219
Negative reinforcement, 214, 215, 217
Neo-analytic theorists, 143
NEO (Neuroticism, Extraversion, and Openness) measure, 78
Neuroscience, 6
Neuroticism
in addictive disorders, 386, 390, 391
in anxiety disorders, 384, 385, 386
behaviors, attitudes, and characteristics of, 69–71
birth order and, 262
brain and, 95, 96
changes in, during childhood and adolescence, 248

changes in, during young adulthood to old age, 250–252
circadian rhythm and, 100
as continuum, 58
cultural differences in, 319–320
defined, 56
in dependent PD, 377
discrepancy detection and, 95
in eating disorders, 386, 389
facets of, 57–58
life outcomes and, 264
in maturation of personality, 254
in personality and relationships, 353–354
in personality in workplace, 325, 326–327, 331–332, 334, 336–339
physical health and, 402–408, 410
in schizoid PD, 376–377
in schizophrenia, 386, 387, 388
sex differences in, 279–282, 290
survival ability and, 77
in trait self-ratings, 55
Type A personality and, 405–408, 410
Type D personality and, 402–405, 410
in United States, 71
word clouds for, 69, 70
Neurotransmitters, 98
Nim's Island, 384
Nonshared environment, 84
Nonverbal behaviors, in men *vs.* women, 288–289
Normal distribution, 35
Norm sample, 34
Null correlation, 27–28

O
Obesity, impulsivity linked to, 400
Object integration, 175
Object relations theory, 145, 175–176
Obsessive-compulsive personality disorder, 374, 375, 376, 377
Oceans movies, 391
Ockham's razor, 164
Oedipus complex, 152–153
Oedipus Rex, 152–153
Office, The, 193
Office Space, 333, 342
OKcupid, 363
Old age, personality in. *See* Young adulthood to old age, personality in
Online dating, 363–365
Online relationships, 362–366
online dating, 363–365
personality matching, 363–365
social networking sites, 365–366
Only children, 263
On the Origin of the Species (Darwin), 99
Openness to experience
in addictive disorders, 386, 390, 391
in anxiety disorders, 384, 385, 386

behaviors, attitudes, and
characteristics of, 72–75
birth order and, 262
in borderline PD, 375–376
brain and, 98
changes in, during childhood and
adolescence, 248
changes in, during young
adulthood to old age, 251, 252
circadian rhythm and, 98
as continuum, 58
cultural differences in, 320–321
defined, 56
in dependent PD, 377
in eating disorders, 386, 389
facets of, 57–58
life outcomes and, 265
neurotransmitters linked to, 98
in personality and relationships, 354
in personality in workplace, 325,
326, 329–330, 332–333, 335–339
physical health and, 409–410
in schizoid PD, 376–377
in schizophrenia, 386, 387, 388
sex differences in, 280, 281
survival ability and, 77
in trait self-ratings, 55
in United States, 73, 74
word clouds for, 72
Open practices, 46
Operant conditioning, 214–223. See
also Behavior modification
defined, 214
punishment in, 214, 215, 217–219
reinforcement in, 214, 215–217
reinforcement schedules in,
219–221
socialization in, 222–223
Opposites, attraction to, 355–356
Optimistic explanatory style, 413–416
Oral fixation, 151–152
Oral stage, 150, 151–152
Oregon Vocational Interest Scales
(ORVIS), 327–330
Organization, 328, 329
Organizational citizenship behavior
(OCB), 332–333
Ought self, 137

P

Paleo Solution, The (Wolf), 66
Panic attacks, 383
Panic disorder, 383
Paranoid personality disorder, 374,
375, 376, 378
Paranormal Activity 10, 159
Parent, becoming, 259–260
Partial reinforcement schedule,
219–221
Passion in workplace, finding,
341–343
Pathological gambling, 390–391

Peak experiences, 207–208
Penile plethysmography, 158
Penis envy, 153, 174
Percentage of variance, 86–88
Percentile score, 35–36
Perception, 387
Perception of national character,
313–314
Personal Attributes Questionnaire
(PAQ), 279, 284–285, 286
Personality, 4–8
appearance of, 8–11
behavior predicted by, 11–16
biology of, 93–101
culture and, variations in, 300–302
defined, 4–8
disorders, 369–396 (*See also*
Mental disorders; Personality
disorders)
evolution and (*See* Evolutionary
psychology)
gender and, 268–296 (*See also* Sex
differences)
gene-environment interactions
and epigenetics, 91–93
heritability of, 85–91 (*See also* Twin
studies)
person and situation in, 11–16
physical health and (*See* Physical
health)
relationships and (*See*
Relationships, personality and)
research, questions answered by,
16–17
in workplace (*See* Workplace,
personality in)
Personality across lifespan, 240–267
birth order and, 261–263
childhood and adolescence,
243–250
emerging adulthood, 256–257
life outcomes, 263–265
maturation of personality, 254–261
(*See also* Significant life
experiences)
studying, methods of, 242–243
young adulthood to old age,
250–253
Personality assessment, 21–49. See also
Personality measures
best practices for scientific
research, 45–47
correlational *vs.* experimental
studies, 43–45
defined, 22
Personality disorder not otherwise
specified (PDNOS), 373
Personality disorders, 369–396. See
also Mental disorders
antisocial, 374, 375, 376, 377
avoidant, 374, 375, 376
Big Five and, 375–380

borderline, 372, 374, 375–376, 378
clusters of, 373–375
cross-cultural differences in,
378–379
defined, 372
dependent, 374, 375, 376, 377
developing, 377–379
diagnosing, 373
histrionic, 374, 375, 376
narcissistic, 133, 371, 373–379
obsessive-compulsive, 374, 375,
376, 377
paranoid, 374, 375, 376, 378
PID-5 and, 379–380
schizoid, 374, 375–377, 378
schizotypal, 374, 375, 376,
377, 378
sex differences in, 377–378
treating, 378–379 (*See also* Therapy
for mental disorders)
Personality hub, 6–7
Personality Inventory for *DSM-5*
(PID-5), 379–380
Personality matching, 363–365
Personality measures, 5, 7–8, 11–12,
13–15, 16. See also Personality
scales; Self-report measures
archival or life outcomes data, 40
of behavior, 39
clinical interviews, 39
correlational, 43–45
experimental, 45
informant reports, 38
longitudinal study, 44
physiological measures, 40–42
projective tests, 40
triangulation, 42
Personality psychology
major topics in, 6, 16–18
in personality hub, 6, 7
purpose of, 5, 6
Personality questionnaires. See Self-
report questionnaires
Personality scales
acquiescence response set and, 24
birth of, 25–26
Cat Person Scale example,
23–31, 43
correlations and, 26–28
evaluating, 28–34
goal of, 24
Likert scale, 24
multifactor, 26
reliability of, 28–29, 32
reverse-scored items in, 24
scoring, 24, 34–38
of social desirability (*See* Social
desirability scales)
validity of, 30–32
Woodworth Personal Data Sheet,
25–26
Personality's Past, 18

Personality tests, 339–341
Personality traits. *See also* Big Five;
    Traits
    conscientiousness, 14
    as continuum *vs.* distinct
        categories, 58–59
    cross-cultural comparisons of,
        312–314
    defined, 53
    differences in, evolutionary
        psychology and, 105–106
    extraversion, 8, 9, 10, 13–14, 16
    introversion, 8
    measures of, questionnaires for, 54
    in men *vs.* women (*See* Men and
        women, comparing)
    models, history of, 78
    self-ratings, 54–56
Personal unconscious, 165
Person-situation debate, 12–13
Person-situation interaction, 15–16
Perspective-taking, 356
Pessimistic explanatory style, 413–416
Phallic stage, 150, 151, 152
Phenotype, 92
Phobia, 235–237
    agoraphobia, 384, 385
    defined, 235
    flooding for, 236
    as mental disorder, 370
    progressive relaxation for, 235
    social, 384, 385
    systematic desensitization for, 235
Physical health, 397–417
    Big Five and, 398–411
    explanatory style and, 413–416
    motives and, 411–413
    personality profiles linked to
        certain diseases (*See* Types)
Physiological measures, 40–42
Picture Story Exercise (PSE), 192, 194, 196
Pleasure principle, 147
Plenty of Fish, 363
Positive correlations, 26–27
Positive life experiences, 260–261
Positive power of negative thinking, 163
Positive psychology, 205
Positive punishment, 214, 215, 217–218
Positive reinforcement, 214, 215–217
Positive self-views, 306–308
Possible selves, 136–137
Posttraumatic stress disorder (PTSD),
    25–26, 232–233
Power distance, 315
Power motive, 109, 192–194
Prairie Home Companion, A, 60
Preconscious mind, 147
Predictive validity, 30
Preoccupied attachment, 352
Pressey XO test, 78
Prestige, 336–337

Prince, The (Machiavelli), 359
Principles of Psychology, The (James),
    115, 116
Production, 328, 330
Progesterone, 412–413
Progressive relaxation, 235
Projection, 158–159
Projective measures, 192
Projective tests, 40
Psychoanalysis, 143
Psychodynamic approaches,
    142–178, 379
    Adler's, 172–174
    Freud's, 146–164
    Horney's, 174–175
    Jung's, 165–172
    object relations, 145, 175–176
    overview of theorists, 144–145
Psychopathology, 370. *See also* Mental
    disorders
Psychopathy, 359
Psychosexual development, Freudian
    theory of, 150–153
    developmental stages, 150–153
    libido, 150, 151
Psychoticism, 379
PsycInfo, 17
Punishment, in operant conditioning,
    214, 215, 217–219
    negative, 214, 215, 218–219
    positive, 214, 215, 217–218

Q
Q-sort, 246–247
Quantum change, 254
Questionnaires. *See* Self-report
    questionnaires
*Quiet: The Power of Introverts in a World
    That Can't Stop Talking* (Cain), 60

R
Random assignment, 45
Rank-order consistency, 252
Reaction formation, 157–158
Reactivity
    in brain, 97
    linked to introversion, 94
Reality principle, 147
Reciprocal determinism, 227
Reference-group effect, 313, 316, 321
Reinforcement, in operant
    conditioning, 214, 215–217
    fixed-interval, 219
    fixed-ratio, 219–221
    negative, 214, 215, 217
    positive, 214, 215–217
    variable-interval, 219–221
    variable-ratio, 219–221
Reinforcement schedules, 219–221
Reinforcement value, 228
Relatedness, 198–199

Relational mobility, 309
Relationships, personality and,
    345–368
    accommodation in, 358
    attachment in, 347–353
    attraction to opposites, 355–356
    Big Five in, 353–355
    compassion, 357
    dark triad in, 358–362
    empathy in, 356–357
    online relationships, 362–366
    overview of, 346
    perspective-taking in, 356
    self-control in, 357–358
Reliability, 28–29, 32
Replicate, 46
Replicated, 262
Repression, 41, 159
Repressive copers, 40–41
Repressive coping, 159
Reproduction, evolutionary
    psychology and, 103–104
"Restriction of range" problem, 90
Revel, 12, 18
Reverse-scored items, 24
RIASEC, 329
Roid rage, 108
Rorschach inkblots, 40, 144
Rosenberg Self-Esteem Scale, 115,
    125, 133
Rumination, 403–405

S
Safety and security, in Maslow's
    hierarchy of needs, 187, 188
Satipatthana Sutta, 206
Schizoid personality disorder, 374,
    375–377, 378
Schizophrenia, 387–388
Schizotypal personality disorder, 374,
    375, 376, 377, 378
Science of Personality features, 18
Scientific research, best practices for,
    45–47
Secure attachment, 349
Secure base, 348
Selective serotonin reuptake
    inhibitors (SSRIs), 382–383, 392
Self
    evaluating, 125–129 (*See also*
        Self-esteem)
    "I am . . . " statements and,
        116–117
    material, 119–120
    research on, 115–116
    social, 120–123
    spiritual, 123
    true, 123–124
    views, cultural differences in (*See*
        Self-views)
Self-actualization, 187, 189–191

Self archetype, 168–168
Self-compassion, 130–131
Self-concept, 118–124
    defined, 118
    "I" and "me" in, 118
    material self and, 119–120
    social self and, 120–123
    spiritual self and, 123
    true self and, 123–124
Self-control, 137–140
    building, 139–140
    defined, 137–138
    loss of, 138–139
    as mental muscle, 137–140
    physical health and, 400
    in relationships, 357–358
    therapy to increase, 394–395
Self-defeating humor style, 162
Self-determination theory (SDT),
        197–199
    autonomy in, 198–199
    competence in, 198–199
    defined, 197
    relatedness in, 198–199
Self-discrepancy theory, 137
Self-efficacy, 131–132
Self-enhancement, 129, 306
Self-enhancing humor style, 162
Self-esteem, 125–129
    changes in, during childhood and
        adolescence, 248–250
    changes in, during young
        adulthood to old age, 253
    defined, 125
    explicit *vs.* implicit, 128
    maintaining, 128–129
    in Maslow's hierarchy of needs,
        187, 188
    in men *vs.* women, 290–291
    narcissism and, 133–135
    pros and cons of, 125–128
    regulation, 129
Self-evaluations, in TST, 116
Self-expansion, 354
Self-kindness, 130
Self-monitoring, 122
Self-objectification, 290
Self-regulation, 136–140. *See also*
        Conscientiousness
    defined, 136
    possible selves and, 136–137
    self-control and, 137–140
Self-report measures, 22–28
    alternatives to, 38–42
    of anxiety, 40–41, 42, 44
    defined, 22
    horoscopes as, 32–34
    limits of, 23
    of shyness, 31
    of socially desirable responding,
        22–23, 31, 36–38, 43

Self-report questionnaires, 7–8, 16, 18.
        See also Personality scales; Self-
        report measures
    alternatives to, 38–42
    to assess personality, 22–28
    for measuring traits, 54
    reliability of, 28–29, 32
    statistical side of, 34–38
    validity of, 30–32
Self-serving bias, 129
Self-views, 306–312
    approach *vs.* avoidance
        motivation, 311
    need for uniqueness, 310–311
    positive self-views, 306–308
    self *vs.* other, 308–310
Sensation-seeking, 408–409
Series of Unfortunate Events, A
        (Snicket), 414
Serious relationships, 257–258
Serotonin, 98
Sex
    behaviors/attitudes, in men *vs.*
        women, 291–293
    defined, 270
    gender and, distinction between,
        270–271
    testosterone and sexual behavior,
        110
Sex and Death to the Age 14, 381
Sex differences, 271–294
    biology and, 273–278
    comparing men and women (See
        Men and women, comparing)
    culture and, 275–278
    defined, 271–272
    personality disorders and,
        377–378
Sex reassignment surgery, 273
Shadow archetype, 166–167
Shaping, 215
Shared environment, 83–84
Sherlock, 168
Siddhartha (Hesse), 144
Significant life experiences, 254–261
    becoming a parent, 259–260
    entering full-time workforce,
        255–257
    Erikson's life stages and, 258–259
    negative, 260–261
    positive, 260–261
    serious relationships or marriage,
        257–258
Situation
    behavior predicted by, 11–16
    defined, 12
    nature-nurture debate, 13
    person-situation debate, 12–13
    person-situation interaction, 15–16
Sixteen Personality Factor (16PF)
        measure, 54, 78

60 Minutes, 83
Skin conductance studies, 99
Skinner boxes, 215
Sleep conditioning, 234–235
Sleep disorders, 370
Slight image creation, 340
Snowball sampling, 85
Social confidence, therapy to
        increase, 394
Social desirability bias, 23, 38
Social desirability scales, 23
    Marlowe-Crowne scale, 28, 31,
        34–38, 40–41
    purpose of, 37
    repressive copers and, 40–41
    scores on, 37–38
Social groups, in TST, 116
Social inhibition, 402
Social investment theory, 254–261.
        See also Significant life
        experiences
Socialization, 222–223
Social learning, 222
Socially desirable responding,
        22–23
Social networking sites, 365–366
Social norms, 298
Social phobia, 384, 385
Social self, 120–123
Social support, 409
Society and the Adolescent Self-Image
        (Rosenberg), 115
Socioeconomic status (SES), 264–265,
        300, 308, 314, 320
Sociometer theory, 129
Sociosexuality, 104
Socius, 120
Soul, The (Blake), 168
South Park, 152
Spatial ability, 277
Spiritual self, 123
Split-object image, 176
Spontaneous recovery, 232
Standard deviation (SD), 35, 280
Stanford-Binet IQ scale, 279
Star Trek, 144, 171
Star Wars, 144, 150, 153, 168, 172, 385
State-Trait Anxiety Inventory, 77
Statistically significant, 27–28
Stereotypes, 278, 279
Stereotype threat, 293
Stereotypically feminine personality
        traits, 285
Stereotypically masculine personality
        traits, 285
Steroids, 108
Steve Jobs (Issacson), 3
Steve-O: Demise and Rise, 390
*Strange Case of Dr. Jekyll and Mr. Hyde,
        The*, 166, 167
Strange Situation, 350

Structural model of personality, 147–149
"Study of Peculiar and Exceptional Children, A," 261
Stuff White People Like (Landers), 299
Subcultures, 307
Sublimation, 160–161
Substance-related disorders, 390
Sufficiently large samples, 46
Super-ego, 147–149
Survival ability
  Big Five and, 76–77
  evolutionary psychology and, 102–103
Survivor, 359
Swimming to Cambodia, 381
"Switched at Birth" experiment, 86–87
Synchronicity, 172
Systematic desensitization, 235

T

Talking cure, 155
Target treatments, 379
Temperament, 243–247
  Big Five and, 244–245
  defined, 244
  personality predicted by, 246–247
Terman and Miles test, 284
Termites, 399
Terror management, 157
Test Bank, 16
Testis-determining factor (TDF), 275
Testosterone, 108–111
  aggression caused by, 108–109, 275
  insults and, 109–110
  power motive and, 109
  sex differences and, 275
  sexual behavior and, 110
  steroids and, 108
  2D:4D ratio and, 110–111
Test-retest reliability, 29
Thematic Apperception Test (TAT), 40, 191, 192, 196
Therapy for mental disorders, 392–395
  antidepressant drugs, 382–383, 392
  behavior modification, 224
  bibliotherapy, 392
  cognitive-behavioral therapy, 379, 392, 404
  emotional competence training, 394
  happiness strategies, 392–393
  to increase self-control, 394–395
  to increase social confidence, 394
  psychodynamic approaches, 379
  target treatments, 379
Thinking *vs.* feeling, 169, 170

Thrill-seeking (Type T) personality, 408–409, 410, 415
Time-out. *See* Negative punishment
Toddler 411 (Fields and Brown), 225
Token economy, 223–224
Tolerance, 390
Topographical model of personality, 146–147
Totalitarian ego, 115
Touched with Fire (Jamison), 385
Traits. *See also* Big Five; Personality traits
  as continuum *vs.* distinct categories, 58–59
  defined, 53
  measures of, questionnaires for, 54
  self-ratings, 54–56
Transference, 144
Transformational leader, 335
Transgender, 273–274
Triangulation, 42
True self, 123–124
Trust *vs.* mistrust, in Erikson's life stages, 259
21 & Over, 166, 167
Twenty Statements Test (TST), 116–117
Twilight, 168, 192, 206
Twin studies, 85–91
  beginning of, 85
  contrast effect and, 88–89
  limitations of, 90–91
  of nonshared environmental effects, 88–90
  percentage of variance in, 86–88
  usefulness of, 85
2D:4D ratio, 110–111
Type A personality, 405–408, 410
Type B personality, 405, 406
Type D (distressed) personality, 402–405, 409, 410
Types
  defined, 398
  Type A, 405–408, 410
  Type B, 405, 406
  Type D, 402–405, 409, 410
  Type T, 408–409, 410, 415
Type T (thrill-seeking) personality, 408–409, 410, 415

U

Unbearable Lightness (de Rossi), 388
Unbiased processing (as part of authenticity), 124
Uncertainty avoidance, 319
Unconditional positive regard, 190–191
Unconditioned response, 230, 231

Unconditioned stimulus, 230, 231
Unconscious, 143
Undifferentiated, 285
Unpleasantness, associating other people with, 233

V

Validity, 30–32
Variable-interval reinforcement, 219–221
Variable-ratio reinforcement, 219–221
Variables
  confounding, 44
  correlated, 26–27, 43–45
  dependent, 45
  independent, 45
  nonpersonality, 40
Ventral striatum, 97
Vocational fit, 325–330
  defined, 327
  determining, 327–330
Vocational interests, 327
Vulnerable narcissism, 133

W

Walden Two (Skinner), 227
Willpower, 115, 137–140. *See also* Self-regulation
Wish fulfillment, 153
Women, men compared to. *See* Men and women, comparing
Woodworth Personal Data Sheet, 25–26
Word clouds
  for agreeableness, 64
  for conscientiousness, 67
  for high and low extraversion, 9, 10–11
  for neuroticism, 69, 70
  for openness to experience, 72
Workplace, personality in, 324–344
  compensation and, 334
  job performance and, 332–333
  job satisfaction and, 331–332
  job selection and, 338–341
  leadership and, 334–337
  passion and, 341–343
  vocational fit and, 325–330
  vocational interests and, 327

Y

Yoga, 394
Young adulthood to old age, personality in, 250–253
  changes in Big Five during, 250–253
  changes in narcissism during, 253
  changes in self-esteem during, 253